# XML IN A NUTSHELL

*A Desktop Quick Reference*

# XML IN A NUTSHELL

*A Desktop Quick Reference*

*Elliotte Rusty Harold & W. Scott Means*

O'REILLY®

*Beijing • Cambridge • Farnham • Köln • Paris • Sebastopol • Taipei • Tokyo*

**XML in a Nutshell**

by Elliotte Rusty Harold and W. Scott Means





101 Morris Street, Sebastopol, CA 95472.

**Cover Designer:** Ellie Volckhausen

**Printing History:**

January 2001: First Edition.

Nutshell Handbook, the Nutshell Handbook logo, and the O'Reilly logo are registered trademarks of O'Reilly & Associates, Inc. The association of the image of a peafowl and the topic of XML is a trademark of O'Reilly & Associates, Inc.

Many of the designations used by manufacturers and sellers to distinguish their products are claimed as trademarks. Where those designations appear in this book, and O'Reilly & Associates, Inc. was aware of a trademark claim, the designations have been printed in caps or initial caps.

While every precaution has been taken in the preparation of this book, the publisher assumes no responsibility for errors or omissions, or for damages resulting from the use of the information contained herein.

*Library of Congress Cataloging-in-Publication Data can be found at: http://www.oreilly.com/catalog/xmlnut.*

ISBN: 0-596-00058-8
[M] [8/01]

# Table of Contents

## *Part IV: Reference*

# *Preface*

XML is one of the most important developments in document syntax in the history of computing. In the last few years it has been adopted in fields as diverse as law, aeronautics, finance, insurance, robotics, multimedia, hospitality, travel, art, construction, telecommunications, software design, agriculture, physics, journalism, theology, retail, and medieval literature. XML has become the syntax of choice for newly designed document formats across almost all computer applications. It's used on Linux, Windows, Macintosh, and many other computer platforms. Mainframes on Wall Street trade stocks with one another by exchanging XML documents. Children playing games on their home PCs save their documents in XML. Sports fans receive real-time game scores on their cell phones in XML. XML is simply the most robust, reliable, and flexible document syntax ever invented.

*XML in a Nutshell* is a comprehensive guide to the rapidly growing world of XML. It covers all aspects of XML, from the most basic syntax rules, to the details of DTD creation, to the APIs you can use to read and write XML documents in a variety of programming languages.

## *What This Book Covers*

There are hundreds of formally established XML applications from the W3C and other standards bodies, such as OASIS and the Object Management Group. There are even more informal, unstandardized applications from individuals and corporations, such as Microsoft's Channel Definition Format and John Guajardo's Mind Reading Markup Language. This book cannot cover them all, any more than a book on Java could discuss every program that has ever been or might ever be written in Java. This book focuses primarily on XML itself. It covers the fundamental rules that all XML documents and authors must adhere to, whether a web designer uses SMIL to add animations to web pages or a C++ programmer uses SOAP to serialize objects into a remote database.

This book also covers generic supporting technologies that have been layered on top of XML and are used across a wide range of XML applications. These technologies include:

*XLinks*
: An attribute-based syntax for hyperlinks between XML and non-XML documents that provide the simple, one-directional links familiar from HTML, multidirectional links between many documents, and links between documents you don't have write access to.

*XSLT*
: An XML application that describes transformations from one document to another, in either the same or different XML vocabularies.

*XPointers*
: A syntax for identifying particular parts of an XML document referred to by a URI; often used in conjunction with an XLink.

*XPath*
: A non-XML syntax used by both XPointers and XSLT for identifying particular pieces of XML documents. For example, an XPath can locate the third `address` element in the document, or all elements with an `email` attribute whose value is `elharo@metalab.unc.edu`.

*Namespaces*
: A means of distinguishing between elements and attributes from different XML vocabularies that have the same name; for instance, the title of a book and the title of a web page in a web page about books.

*SAX*
: The Simple API for XML, an event-based Java application programming interface implemented by many XML parsers.

*DOM*
: The Document Object Model, a tree-oriented API that treats an XML document as a set of nested objects with various properties.

All these technologies, whether defined in XML (XLinks, XSLT, and Namespaces) or in another syntax (XPointers, XPath, SAX, and DOM), are used in many different XML applications.

This book does not specifically cover XML applications that are relevant to only some users of XML. These include:

*SVG*
: Scalable Vector Graphics is a W3C-endorsed standard used for encoding line drawings in XML.

*MathML*
: The Mathematical Markup Language is a W3C-endorsed standard XML application used for embedding equations in web pages and other documents.

*CML*

The Chemical Markup Language was one of the first XML applications. It describes chemistry, solid-state physics, molecular biology, and the other molecular sciences.

*RDF*

The Resource Description Framework is a W3C-standard XML application used for describing resources, with a particular focus on the sort of metadata one might find in a library card catalog.

*CDF*

The Channel Definition Framework is a nonstandard, Microsoft-defined XML application used to publish web sites to Internet Explorer for offline browsing.

Occasionally we use one or more of these applications in an example, but we do not cover all aspects of the relevant vocabulary in depth. While interesting and important, these applications (and hundreds more like them) are intended primarily for use with special software that knows their format intimately. For instance, graphic designers do not work directly with SVG. Instead, they use their customary tools, such as Adobe Illustrator, to create SVG documents. They may not even know they're using XML.

This book focuses on standards that are relevant to almost all developers working with XML. We investigate XML technologies that span a wide range of XML applications, not those that are relevant only within a few restricted domains.

## Organization of the Book

Part I, *XML Concepts*, introduces you to the fundamental standards that form the essential core that all XML applications and software must adhere to. It teaches you about well-formed XML, DTDs, namespaces, and Unicode as quickly as possible.

Part II, *Narrative-Centric Documents*, explores technologies that are used mostly for narrative XML documents, such as web pages, books, articles, diaries, and plays. You'll learn about XSLT, CSS, XSL-FO, XLinks, XPointers, and XPath.

One of the most unexpected developments in XML was its enthusiastic adoption of data-heavy structured documents such as spreadsheets, financial statistics, mathematical tables, and software file formats. Part III, *Data-Centric XML*, explores the use of XML for such data-intensive documents. This part focuses on the tools and APIs needed to write software that process XML, including SAX, the Simple API for XML, and the W3C's Document Object Model.

Finally, Part IV, *Reference*, is a series of quick-reference chapters that form the core of any Nutshell handbook. These chapters give you detailed syntax rules for the core XML technologies, including XML, DTDs, XPath, XSLT, SAX, and DOM. Turn to this section when you need to quickly find out the precise syntax for something you know you can do but don't remember exactly how to do.

## *Conventions Used in This Book*

Body text, like the text you're reading now, is written in Garamond.

`Constant width` is used for:

- Code examples and fragments.
- Anything that might appear in an XML document, including element names, tags, attribute values, entity references, and processing instructions.
- Anything that might appear in a program, including keywords, operators, method names, class names, and literals.

**`Constant-width bold`**

- User input.
- Signifies emphasis should be deleted.

*`Constant-width italic`* is used for:

- Replaceable elements in code statements.

*Italic* is used for:

- New terms where they are defined.
- Pathnames, filenames, and program names. (However, if the program name is also the name of a Java class, it is written in constant-width font, like other class names.)
- Host and domain names (*www.xml.com*).
- URLs (*http://ibiblio.org/xml/*).

Significant code fragments, complete programs, and documents are generally placed into a separate paragraph like this:

```
<?xml version="1.0"?>
<?xml-stylesheet href="person.css" type="text/css"?>
<person>
  Alan Turing
</person>
```

XML is case sensitive. The `PERSON` element is not the same thing as the `person` or `Person` element. Case-sensitive languages do not always allow authors to adhere to standard English grammar. It is usually possible to rewrite the sentence so the two do not conflict, and when possible we have endeavored to do so. However, on rare occasions when there is simply no way around the problem, we let standard English come up the loser.

Finally, although most of the examples used here are toy examples unlikely to be reused, a few have real value. Please feel free to reuse them or any parts of them in your own code. No special permission is required. As far as we are concerned, they are in the public domain (though the same is definitely not true of the explanatory text).

## *Request for Comments*

We enjoy hearing from readers with general comments about how this book could be better, specific corrections, or topics you would like to see covered. You can reach the authors by sending email to *elharo@metalab.unc.edu* and *smeans@enterprisewebmachines.com*. Please realize, however, that we each receive several hundred pieces of email a day and cannot respond to every one personally. For the best chances of getting a personal response, please identify yourself as a reader of this book. And please send the message from the account you want us to reply to and make sure that your Reply-to address is properly set. There's nothing quite so frustrating as spending an hour or more carefully researching the answer to an interesting question and composing a detailed response, only to have it bounce because the correspondent sent the message from a public terminal and neglected to set the browser preferences to include their actual email address.

The information in this book has been tested and verified, but you may find that features have changed (or you may even find mistakes). We believe the old saying, "If you like this book, tell your friends. If you don't like it, tell us." We're especially interested in hearing about mistakes. As hard as the authors and editors worked on this book, inevitably there are a few mistakes and typographical errors that slipped by us. If you find a mistake or a typo, please let us know so we can correct it. You can send any errors you find, as well as suggestions for future editions, to:

O'Reilly & Associates, Inc.
101 Morris Street
Sebastopol, CA 95472
1-800-998-9938 (in the United States or Canada)
1-707-829-0515 (international/local)
1-707-829-0104 (fax)

We have a web site for the book, where we list errata, examples, and any additional information. You can access this site at:

*http://www.oreilly.com/catalog/xmlnut*

Before reporting errors, please check this web site to see if we already posted a fix. To ask technical questions or comment on the book, send email to:

*bookquestions@oreilly.com*

For more information about our books, conferences, software, Resource Centers, and the O'Reilly Network, see our web site at:

*http://www.oreilly.com*

## *Acknowledgments*

Many people were involved in the production of this book. The original editor, John Posner, got this book rolling and provided many helpful comments that substantially improved the book. When John moved on, Laurie Petrycki shepherded this book to its completion. Stephen Spainhour deserves special thanks for his work on the reference section. His efforts in organizing and reviewing material helped create a better book. We'd like to thank Matt Sergeant and Didier P. H. Martin for their thorough technical review of the manuscript and thoughtful suggestions.

We'd also like to thank everyone who has worked so hard to make XML such a success over the last few years and thereby give us something to write about. There are so many of these people that we can only list a few. In alphabetical order we'd like to thank Tim Berners-Lee, Jon Bosak, Tim Bray, James Clark, Charles Goldfarb, Jason Hunter, Michael Kay, Brett McLaughlin, David Megginson, David Orchard, Walter E. Perry, Simon St. Laurent, C. M. Sperberg-McQueen, James Tauber, B. Tommie Usdin, and Mark Wutka. Our apologies to everyone we unintentionally omitted.

Elliotte would like to thank his agent, David Rogelberg, who convinced him that it was possible to make a living writing books like this rather than working in an office. The entire Sunsite crew (now *ibiblio.org*) has also helped him to communicate better with his readers in a variety of ways over the last several years. All these people deserve much thanks and credit. Finally, as always, he offers his largest thanks to his wife, Beth, without whose love and support this book would never have happened.

Scott would most like to thank his lovely wife, Celia, who has already spent way too much time as a "computer widow." He would also like to thank his daughter Selene for understanding why Daddy can't play with her when he's "working," and Skyler for just being himself. Also, he'd like to thank the team at Enterprise Web Machines for helping him make time to write. Finally, he would like to thank John Posner for getting him into this and Laurie Petrycki for working with him when things got tough.

Elliotte Rusty Harold
*elharo@metalab.unc.edu*

W. Scott Means
*smeans@enterprisewebmachines.com*

# PART I

# *XML Concepts*

CHAPTER 1

# *Introducing XML*

XML, the Extensible Markup Language, is a W3C-endorsed standard for document markup. It defines a generic syntax used to mark up data with simple, human-readable tags. It provides a standard format for computer documents. This format is flexible enough to be customized for domains as diverse as web sites, electronic data interchange, vector graphics, genealogy, real estate listings, object serialization, remote procedure calls, and voice mail systems.

You can write your own programs that interact with, massage, and manipulate data in XML documents. If you do, you'll have access to a wide range of free libraries in a variety of languages that can read and write XML so that you can focus on the unique needs of your program. Or you can use off-the-shelf software like web browsers and text editors to work with XML documents. Some tools are able to work with any XML document. Others are customized to support a particular XML application in a particular domain like vector graphics and may not be of much use outside that domain. But in all cases, the same underlying syntax is used, even if it's deliberately hidden by more user-friendly tools or restricted to a single application.

## *What XML Offers*

XML is a meta-markup language for text documents. Data is included in XML documents as strings of text, and the data is surrounded by text markup that describes the data. A particular unit of data and markup is called an *element*. The XML specification defines the exact syntax this markup must follow: how elements are delimited by tags, what a tag looks like, what names are acceptable for elements, where attributes are placed, and so forth. Superficially, the markup in an XML document looks much like that in an HTML document, but some crucial differences exist.

Most importantly, XML is a *meta-markup language*. That means it doesn't have a fixed set of tags and elements that are always supposed to work for everyone in all areas of interest. Attempts to create a finite set of such tags are doomed to failure. Instead, XML allows developers and writers to define the elements they need as they need them. Chemists can use tags that describe elements, atoms, bonds, reactions, and other items encountered in chemistry. Real estate agents can use elements that describe apartments, rents, commissions, locations, and other items needed in real estate. Musicians can use elements that describe quarter notes, half notes, G clefs, lyrics, and other objects common in music. The *X* in XML stands for *Extensible*. Extensible means that the language can be extended and adapted to meet many different needs.

Although XML is flexible in the elements it allows to be defined, it is strict in many other respects. It provides a grammar for XML documents that regulates placement of tags, where tags appear, which element names are legal, how attributes are attached to elements, and so forth. This grammar is specific enough to allow development of XML parsers that can read and understand any XML document. Documents that satisfy this grammar are said to be *well-formed*. Documents that are not well-formed are not allowed any more than a C program containing a syntax error would be. XML processors reject documents that contain well-formedness errors.

To enhance interoperability, individuals or organizations may agree to use only certain tags. These tag sets are called *XML applications*. An XML application is not a software application that uses XML, like Mozilla or Microsoft Word. Rather, it's an application of XML to a particular domain, such as vector graphics or cooking.

The markup in an XML document describes the document's structure. It lets you see which elements are associated with which other elements. In a well-designed XML document, the markup also describes the document's semantics. For instance, the markup can indicate that an element is a date, a person, or a bar code. In well-designed XML applications, the markup says nothing about how the document should be displayed. That is, it does not say that an element is bold, italicized, or a list item. XML is a structural and semantic markup language, not a presentation language.*

The markup permitted in a particular XML application can be documented in a document type definition (DTD). The DTD lists all legal markup and specifies where and how the markup may be included in a document. Particular document instances can be compared to the DTD. Documents that match the DTD are said to be *valid*. Documents that do not match are *invalid*. Validity depends on the DTD; whether a document is valid or invalid depends on which DTD you compare it to.

Not all documents need to be valid. For many purposes, a well-formed document is enough. DTDs are optional in XML. On the other hand, DTDs may not always be sufficient. The DTD syntax is limited and does not allow you to make many

* A few XML applications, like XSL Formatting Objects, are designed to describe text presentation. However, these are exceptions that prove the rule. Although XSL-FO describes presentation, you'd never write an XSL-FO document directly. Instead, you'd write a more semantically marked-up XML document, then use an XSL Transformations stylesheet to change the semantic-oriented XML into presentation-oriented XML.

useful statements such as, "This element contains a number" or "This string of text is a date between 1974 and 2032." If you're writing programs to read XML documents, you may want to add code to verify statements like these, just as you would if you were writing code to read a tab-delimited text file. The difference is that XML parsers present you with the data in a much more convenient format to work with and do more of the work for you before you have to resort to your own custom code.



## *What XML Is Not*

XML is a markup language, and only a markup language. It's important to remember this fact. The XML hype has become so extreme that some people expect XML to do everything up to, and including, washing the family dog.

First of all, XML is not a programming language. There's no such thing as an XML compiler that reads XML files and produces executable code. You might define a scripting language that uses a native XML format and is interpreted by a binary program, but even this application would be unusual.* XML can be used as an instruction format for programs that make things happen. A traditional program, for example, may read a text config file and take different actions, depending on what it sees in the file. There's no reason why a config file can't be written in XML instead of unstructured text. Indeed, some recent programs are beginning to use XML config files. But in all cases the program, not the XML document, takes action. An XML document simply *is*. It does not *do* anything.

Furthermore, XML is not a network-transport protocol. XML, like HTML, won't send data across the network. However, data sent across the network using HTTP, FTP, NFS, or some other protocol might be in an XML format. XML can be the format for data sent across the network, but again, software outside the XML document must actually do the sending.

Finally, to mention the example in which the hype most often obscures reality, XML is not a database. You won't replace an Oracle or MySQL server with XML. A database can contain XML data as a VARCHAR, a BLOB, or a custom XML datatype; but the database itself is not an XML document. You can store XML data in a database or on a server or retrieve data from a database in an XML format, but to do so you need to run software written in a real programming language like C or Java. To store XML in a database, software on the client side sends the XML data to the server using an established network protocol like TCP/IP. Software on the server side receives the XML data, parses it, and stores it in the database. To retrieve an XML document from a database, you generally pass through a middleware product like Enhydra that makes SQL queries against the database and formats the result set as XML before returning it to the client. Indeed, some databases may integrate this software code into their core server or provide plug-ins, such as the Oracle XSQL servlet, to do it. XML serves very well as a ubiquitous, platform-independent transport format in these scenarios. However, XML is not the database and shouldn't be used as one.

* At least one XML application, XSL Transformations, has been proven to be Turing complete.

## *Portable Data*

XML offers the tantalizing possibility of truly cross-platform, long-term data formats. It's long been the case that a document written by one piece of software on one platform is not necessarily readable on a different platform, by a different program on the same platform, or even by a future or past version of the same software on the same platform. When the document can be read, all the information may not necessarily come across. Much of the data from the original moon landings in the late 1960s and early 1970s is now effectively lost. Even if you can find a tape drive that reads the now obsolete tapes, nobody knows what format the data on the tapes is stored in!

XML is an incredibly simple, well-documented, straightforward data format. XML documents are text, and any tool that can read a text file can read an XML document. Both XML data and markup are text, and the markup is present in the XML file as tags. You don't have to wonder whether every eighth byte is random padding, guess whether a four-byte quantity is a two's complement integer or an IEEE 754 floating point number, or try to decipher which integer codes map to which formatting properties. You can read the tag names directly to see exactly what's in the document. Similarly, since tags define element boundaries, you aren't likely to get tripped up by unexpected line ending conventions or the number of spaces mapped to a tab. All the important details about the document's structure are explicit. You don't have to reverse engineer the format or rely on questionable, and often unavailable, documentation.

A few software vendors may want to lock in their users with undocumented, proprietary binary file formats. However, in the long run we are all better off if we can use the cleanly documented, well-understood, easy to parse, text-based formats that XML provides. XML allows documents and data to move from one system to another with a reasonable hope that the receiving system can make sense out of it. Furthermore, validation lets the receiving side ensure that it gets what it expects. Java promised portable code. XML delivers portable data. In many ways, XML is the most portable and flexible document format designed since the ASCII text file.

## *How XML Works*

Example 1-1 shows a simple XML document. This particular XML document might appear in an inventory control system or a stock database. It marks up the data with tags and attributes describing the color, size, bar code number, manufacturer, and product name.

*Example 1-1: An XML Document*

```
<?xml version="1.0"?>
<product barcode="2394287410">
  <manufacturer>Verbatim</manufacturer>
  <name>DataLife MF 2HD</name>
  <quantity>10</quantity>
  <size>3.5"</size>
```

*Example 1-1: An XML Document (continued)*

```
  <color>black</color>
  <description>floppy disks</description>
</product>
```

This document is text and might well be stored in a text file. You can edit this file with any standard text editor, such as BBEdit, UltraEdit, Emacs, or vi. You do not need a special XML editor; in fact, we find that most general-purpose XML editors are far more trouble than they're worth and much harder to use than a simple text editor.

Then again, this document might not be a file at all. It might be a record in a database. It might be assembled on the fly by a CGI query to a web server and exist only in a computer's memory. It might even be stored in multiple files and assembled at runtime. Even if it isn't in a file, however, the document is a text document that can be read and transmitted by any software capable of reading and transmitting text.

Programs that actually try to understand the contents of the XML document, that is, do not merely treat it as any other text file, use an *XML parser* to read the document. The parser is responsible for dividing the document into individual elements, attributes, and other pieces. It passes the contents of the XML document to the application piece by piece. If at any point the parser detects a violation of XML rules, it reports the error to the application and stops parsing. In some cases the parser may read past the original error in the document so it can detect and report other errors that occur later in the document. However, once it has detected the first error, it no longer passes along the contents of the elements and attributes it encounters to the application.

Individual XML applications normally dictate precise rules about which elements and attributes are allowed where. You wouldn't expect to find a `G_Clef` element when reading a biology document, for instance. Some of these rules can be specified precisely using a DTD. A document may contain either the DTD itself or a pointer to a URI where the DTD is found. Some XML parsers notice these details and compare the document to its DTD as they read it to see if the document satisfies the specified constraints. Such a parser is called a *validating parser*. A violation of those constraints is a *validity error*, and the whole process of checking a document against a DTD is called *validation*. If a validating parser finds a validity error, it reports it to the application on whose behalf it parses the document. This application can then decide whether it wishes to continue parsing the document. However, validity errors, unlike well-formedness errors, are not necessarily fatal; an application may choose to ignore them. Not all parsers are validating parsers. Some merely check for well-formedness.

The application that receives data from the parser may be:

- A web browser, such as Netscape or Internet Explorer, that displays the document to a reader
- A word processor, such as StarOffice Writer, that loads the XML document for editing
- A database server, such as Oracle, that stores XML data in a database

- A drawing program, such as Corel Draw, that interprets XML as two-dimensional coordinates for the contents of a picture
- A spreadsheet, such as Gnumeric, that parses XML to find numbers and functions used in a calculation
- A personal finance program, such as Microsoft Money, that sees XML as a bank statement
- A syndication program that reads the XML document and extracts the headlines for today's news
- A program that you wrote in Java, C, Python, or some other language that does exactly what you want it to do
- Almost anything else

XML is an *extremely* flexible format for data. It can be used in all of these scenarios and many more. These examples are real. In theory, any data that can be stored in a computer can be stored in XML format. In practice, XML is suitable for storing and exchanging any data that can be plausibly encoded as text. Its use is unsuitable only for multimedia data, such as photographs, recorded sound, video, and other very large bit sequences.

## The Evolution of XML

XML is a descendant of the Standard Generalized Markup Language (SGML). The language that would eventually become SGML was invented by Charles Goldfarb, Ed Mosher, and Ray Lorie at IBM in the 1970s and developed by several hundred people around the world until its eventual adoption as ISO standard 8879 in 1986. SGML was intended to solve many of the same problems XML solves. It was and is a semantic and structural markup language for text documents. SGML is extremely powerful and achieved some success in the U.S. military and government, the aerospace sector, and other domains that needed ways of managing technical documents that were tens of thousands of pages long efficiently.

SGML's biggest success was HTML, an SGML application. However, HTML is just one SGML application. It does not have or offer the full power of SGML. Since HTML restricts authors to a finite set of tags designed to describe web pages in a fairly presentationally oriented way, it's really little more than a traditional markup language that has been adopted by web browsers. It simply doesn't lend itself to use beyond the single application of web page design. You would not use HTML to exchange data between incompatible databases or send updated product catalogs to retailer sites, for example. HTML is useful for creating web pages, but it isn't capable of much more than that.

The obvious choice for other applications that took advantage of the Internet, but were not simple web pages, was SGML. SGML's main problem is its complexity. The official SGML specification is more than 150 very technical pages. It covers many special cases and unlikely scenarios. It is so complex that almost no software has ever implemented it fully. Programs that implemented or relied on different subsets of SGML were often incompatible with one another. The special feature one program considered essential would be considered extraneous fluff and omitted by the next program.

In 1996 Jon Bosak, Tim Bray, C. M. Sperberg-McQueen, James Clark, and several others began work on a "lite" version of SGML. This version retained most of SGML's power, but trimmed many features that were redundant, too complicated to implement, confusing to end users, or that had simply not been proven useful over the previous 20 years of experience with SGML. The result, in February 1998, was XML 1.0, and it was an immediate success. Many developers who knew they needed a structural markup language but couldn't bring themselves to accept SGML's complexity adopted XML wholeheartedly. It was ultimately used in domains ranging from legal court filings to hog farming.

However, XML 1.0 was just the beginning. The next standard out of the gate was Namespaces in XML, an effort to allow conflict-free use of markup from different XML applications in the same document. A web page about books, for example, could have a `title` element that referred to the page's title and `title` elements that referred to the book's title, and the two would not conflict.

The Extensible Stylesheet Language, an XML application that transforms other XML documents into a form that is viewable in web browsers, was the next development. This language soon split into XSL Transformations (XSLT) and XSL Formatting Objects (XSL-FO). XSLT has become a general-purpose language for transforming one XML document into another for web page display and other purposes. XSL-FO is an XML application that describes the layout of both printed and web pages. This application rivals PostScript for its power and expressiveness.

However, XSL is not the only option for styling XML documents. The Cascading Stylesheet Language (CSS) was already in use for HTML documents when XML was invented, and it was a reasonable fit to XML, as well. With the advent of CSS Level 2, the W3C made styling XML documents an explicit goal for CSS and gave it equal importance to HTML. The preexisting Document Style Sheet and Semantics Language (DSSSL) was also adopted from its roots in the SGML world to style XML documents for print and use on the Web.

The Extensible Linking Language (XLL) defined more powerful linking constructs that could connect XML documents in a hypertext network, vastly overpowering HTML's `A` tag. It also divided into two separate standards: XLink, which described connections between documents, and XPointer, which addressed the individual parts of an XML document. At this point, it was noticed that both XPointer and XSLT were developing fairly sophisticated, yet incompatible, syntaxes to do exactly the same thing: identify particular elements of an XML document. Consequently, the addressing parts of both specifications were split off and combined into a third specification, XPath.

A similar phenomenon occurred when it was noticed that XML 1.0, XSLT, XML Schemas, and the Document Object Model (DOM) all had similar, but subtly different, conceptual models of the structure of an XML document. For instance, XML 1.0 considers a document's root element as its root, while XSLT uses a more abstract root that includes the root element and several other pieces. Thus the W3C XML Core Working Group began work on an XML Information Set that all these standards could rely on and refer to.

Another piece of the puzzle was a uniform interface for accessing the contents of the XML document from inside a Java, JavaScript, or C++ program. The simplest

API was to merely treat the document as an object that contained other objects. Indeed, work was already underway inside and outside the W3C to define such a Document Object Model for HTML. Expanding this effort to cover XML was not difficult.

Outside the W3C, Peter Murray-Rust, David Megginson, Tim Bray, and other members of the *xml-dev* mailing list recognized that XML parsers, while all compatible in the documents they could parse, were incompatible in their APIs. This observation led to the development of the Simple API for XML, SAX. SAX2 was released in 2000 to add greater configurability, namespace support, and several optional features.

Development of extensions to the core XML specification continues. Future directions include:

*XFragment*
: An effort to make sense out of XML document pieces that may not be considered well-formed documents in isolation.

*XML Schemas*
: An XML application that can describe the allowed content of documents conforming to a particular XML vocabulary.

*XHTML*
: A reformulation of HTML as a well-formed, modular, potentially valid XML application.

*XML Query Language*
: A language for finding the elements in a document that meet specified criteria.

*Canonical XML*
: A standard algorithm used for determining whether two XML documents are the same after throwing away insignificant details, such as whether single or double quotes are used around attribute values.

*XML Signatures*
: A standard means of digitally signing XML documents, embedding signatures in XML documents, and authenticating the resulting documents.

Many new extensions of XML remain to be invented. XML has proven itself a solid foundation for many other technologies.

# CHAPTER 2



# *XML Fundamentals*

This chapter shows you how to write simple XML documents. You'll see that an XML document is built from text content marked up with text tags, such as <SKU>, <Record_ID>, and <author>, that look superficially like HTML tags. However, in HTML you're limited to about a hundred predefined tags that describe web page formatting; in XML you can create as many tags as you need. Furthermore, these tags usually describe the type of content they contain, rather than formatting or layout information. In XML you don't say that something is a paragraph or an unordered list. You say that it's a book, a biography, or a calendar.

Although XML is looser than HTML in which tags it allows, it is much stricter about where those tags are placed and how they're written. In particular, all XML documents must be *well-formed*. Well-formedness rules specify constraints such as, "All opened tags must be closed" and "Attribute values must be quoted." These rules are unbreakable, which makes parsing XML documents easier and writing them a little harder, but still allows an almost unlimited flexibility of expression.

## *XML Documents and XML Files*

An XML document contains text, never binary data. It can be opened with any program that knows how to read a text file. Example 2-1 is close to the simplest XML document imaginable. It is nonetheless a well-formed XML document. XML parsers can read and understand it (at least as far as a computer program can be said to understand anything).

*Example 2-1: A Very Simple, Yet Complete, XML Document*

```
<person>
  Alan Turing
</person>
```

In the most common scenario, this document would be the entire content of a file named *person.xml*, or perhaps *2-1.xml*. However, XML is not picky about the filename. As far as the parser is concerned, this file could be called *person.txt*, *person*, or *Hey you, there's some XML in this here file!* Your operating system may not like these names, but an XML parser won't care. The document might not even be in a file. It could be a record or a field in a database. A CGI program could generate it on the fly in response to a browser query. It could even be stored in more than one file, though that's unlikely for such a simple document. If it's served by a web server, it will probably be assigned the MIME media type application/xml or text/xml. However, specific XML applications may use more specific MIME media types, such as application/mathml+xml, application/XSLT+xml, image/svg+xml, text/vnd.wap.wml, or text/html (in special cases).

## Elements, Tags, and Character Data

The document in Example 2-1 is composed of a single *element* whose type is `person`. This element is delimited by the *start tag* `<person>` and the *end tag* `</person>`. Everything between the element's start tag and end tag (exclusive) is the element's *content*. The content of this element is the text string:

```
Alan Turing
```

The whitespace is part of the content, though many applications will choose to ignore it. `<person>` and `</person>` are *markup*. The string `Alan Turing` and its surrounding whitespace are *character data*. The tag is the most common form of markup in an XML document, but there are other kinds we'll discuss later.

### Tag Syntax

Superficially, XML tags look like HTML tags. Start tags begin with a < and end tags begin with a </. Both of these are followed by the name of the element and are closed by a >. However, unlike HTML tags, you are allowed to make up new XML tags as you go along. To describe a person, use `<person>` and `</person>` tags. To describe a calendar, use `<calendar>` and `</calendar>` tags. The names of the tags reflect the type of content inside the element, not how that content will be formatted.

#### Empty elements

There's a special syntax for *empty elements*, elements without content. These elements can be represented by tags that begin with < but end with />. For instance, in XHTML, an XMLized reformulation of standard HTML, the line break and horizontal rule elements are written as `<br/>` and `<hr/>` instead of `<br>` and `<hr>`. These elements are exactly equivalent to `<br></br>` and `<hr></hr>`, however. You decide which form to use for empty elements. However, what you cannot do in XML and XHTML (unlike HTML) is use only the start tag, such as `<br>` or `<hr>`, without using matching end tags. That would be a well-formedness error.

#### Case sensitivity

XML, unlike HTML, is case sensitive. `<Person>` is not the same as `<PERSON>`, and neither is the same as `<person>`. If you open an element with a `<person>` tag, you can't close it with a </PERSON> tag. You're free to use upper- or lowercase, or both, as you choose. You just have to be consistent within any one element.

## XML Trees

XML documents are trees. To explain this concept, let's look at a slightly more complicated XML document. Example 2-2 is a person element containing information suitably marked up to show its meaning.

*Example 2-2: A More Complex XML Document Describing a Person*

```
<person>
  <name>
    <first_name>Alan</first_name>
    <last_name>Turing</last_name>
  </name>
  <profession>computer scientist</profession>
  <profession>mathematician</profession>
  <profession>cryptographer</profession>
</person>
```

### Parents and children

This XML document is still composed of one person element. However, now this element doesn't merely contain undifferentiated character data. It contains four *child elements*: a name element and three profession elements. The name element contains two child elements of its own, first_name and last_name.

The person element is called the *parent* of the name element and the three profession elements. The name element is the parent of the first_name and last_name elements. The name element and the three profession elements are sometimes called one another's *siblings*. The first_name and last_name elements are also siblings.

As in human society, any one parent may have multiple children. However, unlike human society, XML gives each child exactly one parent, not two. Each element (with one exception that we'll note shortly) has exactly one parent element. That is, it is completely enclosed by another element. If an element's start tag is inside an element, then its end tag must also be inside that element. Overlapping tags, as in <strong><em>this common example from HTML</strong></em>, are prohibited in XML. Since the em element begins inside the strong element, it must also finish inside the strong element.

### The root element

Every XML document has one element without a parent. This is the first element in the document that contains all other elements. In Example 2-1 and Example 2-2 the person element fills this role and is called the document's *root element*. It is sometimes also called the *document element*. Every well-formed XML document has exactly one root element. Since elements may not overlap and since all elements except the root have exactly one parent, XML documents form a data structure that programmers call a *tree*. Figure 2-1 diagrams this relationship for Example 2-2. Each gray box represents an element. Each black box represents character data. Each arrow represents a containment relationship.

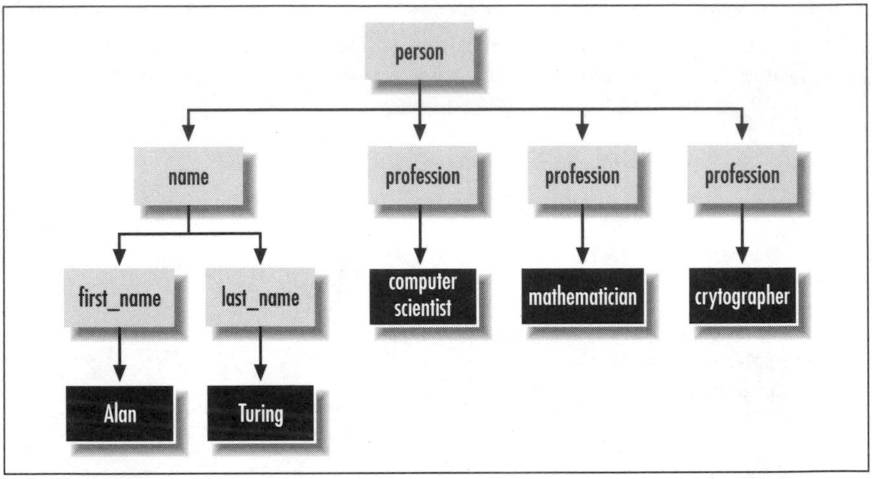


*Figure 2-1: A tree diagram for Example 2-2*

## *Mixed Content*

In Example 2-2, the contents of the `first_name`, `last_name`, and `profession` elements were character data: text that does not contain any tags. The contents of the `person` and `name` elements were child elements and some whitespace that most applications ignore. This dichotomy between elements that contain only character data and elements that contain only child elements (and possibly a little whitespace) is common in data-oriented documents. However, XML can also be used for free-form, narrative documents, such as business reports, magazine articles, student essays, short stories, and web pages, as shown in Example 2-3.

*Example 2-3: A Narrative-Organized XML Document*

```
<biography>
  <name><first_name>Alan</first_name> <last_name>Turing</last_name>
  </name> was one of the first people to truly deserve the name
  <emphasize>computer scientist</emphasize>. Although his contributions
  to the field are too numerous to list, his best-known are the
  eponymous <emphasize>Turing Test</emphasize> and
  <emphasize>Turing Machine</emphasize>.

  <definition>The <term>Turing Test</term> is to this day the standard
  test for determining whether a computer is truly intelligent. This
  test has yet to be passed. </definition>

  <definition>The <term>Turing Machine</term> is an abstract finite
  state automaton with infinite memory that can be proven equivalent
  to any any other finite state automaton with arbitrarily large memory.
```

```
  Thus what is true for a Turing machine is true for all equivalent
  machines no matter how implemented.
  </definition>

  <name><last_name>Turing</last_name></name> was also an accomplished
  <profession>mathematician</profession> and
  <profession>cryptographer</profession>. His assistance
  was crucial in helping the Allies decode the German Enigma
  machine. He committed suicide on <date><month>June</month>
  <day>7</day>, <year>1954</year></date> after being
  convicted of homosexuality and forced to take female
  hormone injections.
</biography>
```



This document's root element is `biography`. The `biography` contains `name`, `definition`, `profession`, and `emphasize` child elements. It also contains a lot of raw character data. Some elements, such as `last_name` and `profession`, contain only character data. Others, such as `name`, contain only child elements. Still others, such as `definition`, contain both character data and child elements. These elements are said to contain *mixed content*. Mixed content is common in XML documents used for anything organized as a written narrative, such as articles, essays, stories, books, novels, reports, and web pages. Mixed content is less common and harder to work with in the computer-generated and processed XML documents used for database exchange, object serialization, or persistent file formats. One of XML's strengths is the ease with which it can be adapted to the very different requirements of human-authored and computer-generated documents.

## Attributes

XML elements can have attributes. An attribute is a name-value pair attached to the element's start tag. Names are separated from values by an equals sign, and possibly optional whitespace. Values are enclosed in single or double quotation marks. For example, this `person` element has a `born` attribute with the value `1912/06/23` and a `died` attribute with the value `1954/06/07`:

```
<person born="1912/06/23" died="1954/06/07">
  Alan Turing
</person>
```

This next element is exactly the same to an XML parser. It simply uses single quotations instead of double quotations and puts some extra whitespace around the equals signs:

```
<person born = '1912/06/23' died = '1954/06/07'>
  Alan Turing
</person>
```

The whitespace around the equals signs is purely a matter of personal aesthetics. The single quotes may be useful in cases in which the attribute value itself contains a double quote.

Example 2-4 shows how attributes might be used to encode much of the same information given in Example 2-2's data-oriented document.

*Example 2-4: An XML Document That Describes a Person Using Attributes*

```
<person>
  <name first="Alan" last="Turing"/>
  <profession value="computer scientist"/>
  <profession value="mathematician"/>
  <profession value="cryptographer"/>
</person>
```

This example raises the question of when and whether one should use child elements or attributes to hold information. This is a subject of heated debate. Some informaticians maintain that attributes are for metadata about the element, while elements are for the information itself. Others point out that it's not always easy to identify what is data and what is metadata. Indeed the answer may depend on the uses to which the information is put.

The fact that each element may have no more than one attribute with a given name is undisputed. This is unlikely to be a problem for a birth or death date, but it would be an issue for a profession, name, address, or anything else of which an element might plausibly have more than one. Furthermore, attributes are quite limited in structure. An attribute's value is simply a text string. The division of a date into a year, month and day with slashes is at the limit of the substructure that can be reasonably encoded in an attribute. Consequently, an element-based structure is much more flexible and extensible. Nonetheless, attributes are certainly more convenient in some applications. Ultimately, if you're designing your own XML vocabulary, you decide when to use elements and when to use attributes.

Attributes are also useful in narrative-oriented documents, as Example 2-5 demonstrates. Here what belongs to elements or attributes is perhaps a little more obvious. The narrative's raw text is presented as character data inside elements. Additional information that annotates the data is presented as attributes. This information includes source references, image URLs, hyperlinks, and birth and death dates. Even here, however, there's more than one way to do it. For instance, the footnote numbers could be attributes of the footnote element rather than character data.

*Example 2-5: A Narrative XML Document That Uses Attributes*

```
<biography xmlns:xlink="http://www.w3.org/1999/xlink/namespace/">

  <image source="http://www.turing.org.uk/turing/pi1/bus.jpg"
  width="152" height="345"/>
  <person born='1912/06/23'
  died='1954/06/07'><first_name>Alan</first_name>
  <last_name>Turing</last_name> </person> was one of the first people
  to truly deserve the name <emphasize>computer scientist</emphasize>.
  Although his contributions to the field were too numerous to list,
  his best-known are the eponymous <emphasize xlink:type="simple"
  xlink:href="http://cogsci.ucsd.edu/~asaygin/tt/ttest.html">Turing
```

*Example 2-5: A Narrative XML Document That Uses Attributes (continued)*

```
  Test</emphasize> and <emphasize  xlink:type="simple"
  xlink:href="http://mathworld.wolfram.com/TuringMachine.html">Turing
  Machine</emphasize>.

  <last_name>Turing</last_name> was also an accomplished
  <profession>mathematician</profession> and
  <profession>cryptographer</profession>. His assistance
  was crucial in helping the Allies decode the German Enigma
  machine.<footnote source="The Ultra Secret, F.W. Winterbotham,
  1974">1</footnote>

  He committed suicide on <date><month>June</month> <day>7</day>,
  <year>1954</year></date> after being convicted of homosexuality
  and forced to take female hormone injections.<footnote
  source="Alan Turing: the Enigma, Andrew Hodges, 1983">2</footnote>

</biography>
```

XML Funda-
mentals

## XML Names

The XML specification can be quite legalistic and picky at times, but it tries to be efficient when possible. One way it tries to increase its efficiency is by reusing the same rules for different objects when possible. For example, the rules for XML element names are also the rules for XML attribute names and the names of several less common constructs. Generally, these names are referred to as *XML names*.

Element and other XML names may contain any alphanumeric character. These characters include the standard English letters A through Z and a through z, as well as the digits 0 through 9. XML names may also include non-English letters, numbers, and ideograms, such as ö, ç, ϑ, and ψ. They may also include these three punctuation characters:

_ Underscore

\- Hyphen

. Period

XML names may not contain other punctuation characters, such as quotation marks, apostrophes, dollar signs, carets, percent symbols, and semicolons. The colon is allowed, but its use is reserved for namespaces, as discussed in Chapter 4, *Namespaces*. XML names may not contain whitespace of any kind, whether a space, a carriage return, a line feed, or a nonbreaking space.

XML names may start only with letters, ideograms, or the underscore character. They may not start with a number, a hyphen, or a period. There is no limit to the length of an element or other XML name. The following elements are all well-formed:

- `<Drivers_License_Number>98 NY 32</Drivers_License_Number>`
- `<month-day-year>7/23/2001</month-day-year>`
- `<first_name>Alan</first_name>`
- `<_4-lane>I-610</_4-lane>`

- <téléphone>011 33 91 55 27 55 27</téléphone>
- <ονομα>Melina Merkouri</ονομα>

These elements are not well-formed:

- <Driver's_License_Number>98 NY 32</Driver's_License_Number>
- <month/day/year>7/23/2001</month/day/year>
- <first name>Alan</first name>
- <4-lane>I-610</4-lane>

## *Entity References*

The character data inside an element may not contain a raw unescaped opening angle bracket <. This character is always interpreted as the beginning of a tag. If you need to use this character in your text, you can escape it using the < *entity reference*. When a parser reads the document, it replaces the < entity reference with the actual < character. However, it does not confuse < with the start of a tag. For example:

```
<SCRIPT LANGUAGE="JavaScript">
  if (location.host.toLowerCase().indexOf("ibiblio") &lt; 0) {
    location.href="http://www.ibiblio.org/xml/";
  }
</SCRIPT>
```

The character data inside an element may not contain a raw unescaped ampersand & either. This character is always interpreted as the beginning of an entity or character reference. However, the ampersand may be escaped using the & entity reference like this:

```
<publisher>O'Reilly &amp; Associates</publisher>
```

Entity references such as & and < are considered markup. When an application parses an XML document, it replaces this particular markup with the actual characters the entity reference refers to. The result, O'Reilly & Associates in the previous example, is called *parsed character data*; that is, the character data that's left after the document is parsed and the entities are resolved.

XML predefines exactly five entity references:

<
: The less-than sign, or opening angle bracket (<)

&
: The ampersand (&)

>
: The greater-than sign, or closing angle bracket (>)

"
: The straight, double quotation marks (")

'
: The apostrophe, or single quote (')

Only **<** and **&** must be used in place of the literal characters in element content. The other references are optional. " and ' are useful inside attribute values, where a raw " or ' might be misconstrued as ending the attribute value. For example, this image tag uses the ' entity reference to fill in the apostrophe in O'Reilly:

```
<image source='oreilly_koala3.gif' width='122' height='66'
       alt='Powered by O&apos;Reilly Books'
/>
```

Although misinterpreting an unescaped greater-than sign > as closing a tag it wasn't meant to close is impossible, > is allowed for symmetry with <.

In addition to these five predefined entity references, you can define others in the document type definition. We'll discuss how to do this in Chapter 3, *Document Type Definitions.*



## *CDATA Sections*

When an XML document includes samples of XML or HTML source code, the < and & characters in those samples must be encoded as < and &. The more sections of literal code a document includes and the longer they are, the more tedious this encoding can become. To facilitate the process, you can enclose each sample of literal code in a *CDATA section.* A CDATA section is set off by a <![CDATA[ and ]]>. Everything between the <![CDATA[ and the ]]> is treated as raw character data. Less-than signs don't start tags. Ampersands don't start entity references. Everything is simply character data, not markup.

For example, in a Scalable Vector Graphics (SVG) tutorial written in XHTML, you might see something like this:

```
<p>You can use a default <code>xmlns</code> attribute to avoid
having to add the svg prefix to all your elements:</p>
     <![CDATA[
       <svg xmlns="http://www.w3.org/2000/svg"
            width="12cm" height="10cm">
         <ellipse rx="110" ry="130" cx="1cm" cy="1cm" />
         <rect x="4cm" y="1cm" width="3cm" height="6cm" />
       </svg>
     ]]>
```

The SVG source code was included directly in the XHTML file without having to carefully replace each < with <. The result is a sample SVG document, not an embedded SVG picture, as would happen if this example were not placed inside a CDATA section.

The only thing that cannot appear in a CDATA section is the CDATA section end delimiter ]]>.

CDATA sections are convenient for human authors, not programs. Parsers are not required to tell you whether a particular block of text came from a CDATA section, from normal character data, or from character data that contained entity references such as < and &. By the time you get access to the data, these differences may have been washed away.

## *Comments*

XML documents can be commented so coauthors can leave notes for each other documenting why they've done what they've done or items that remain to be done. XML comments are syntactically similar to HTML comments; they begin with `<!--` and end with the first occurrence of `-->`. For example:

```
<!-- I need to verify and update these links when I get a chance. -->
```

The double hyphen `--` should not appear anywhere inside the comment until the closing `-->`. In particular, a three-hyphen close like `--->` is specifically forbidden.

Comments may appear anywhere in the document's character data. They may also appear before or after the root element. (Comments are not elements, so this does not violate the tree structure or the one-root element rules for XML.) However, comments may not appear inside a tag or another comment.

XML parsers may or may not pass along information included in comments. They are certainly free to drop them out if they choose. Do not write documents or applications that depend on the availability of comments. Comments are strictly for making the raw source code of an XML document more legible to human readers. They are not intended for any computer program. If you need such a feature for a computer program, use a *processing instruction* instead.

## *Processing Instructions*

In HTML comments are sometimes abused to support nonstandard extensions. For instance, the contents of the `style` element are sometimes enclosed in a comment to protect it from display by a nonscript-aware browser. The Apache web server parses comments in *.shtml* files to recognize server-side includes. Unfortunately these documents may not survive being passed through various HTML editors and processors with their comments and associated semantics intact. Worse yet, it's possible for an innocent comment to be misconstrued as input to the application.

XML provides the processing instruction as an alternative means of passing information to particular applications that may read the document. A processing instruction begins with `<?` and ends with `?>`. Immediately following the `<?` is an XML name called the *target*, possibly the name of the application for which this processing instruction is intended, or perhaps just an identifier for this particular processing instruction. The rest of the processing instruction contains text in a format appropriate for the applications the instruction is intended for.

For example, HTML uses a Robots `META` tag to tell search engines and other robots whether and how they should index a page. The following processing instruction has been proposed as an equivalent for XML documents:

```
<?robots index="yes" follow="no"?>
```

The target of this processing instruction is `robots`. The syntax of this particular processing instruction is two pseudoattributes, one named `index` and one named `follow`, whose values are either `yes` or `no`. The semantics of this particular processing instruction are that if the `index` attribute has the value `yes`, then this page will be indexed by a search engine robot. If `index` has the value `no`, then it won't be. Similarly, if `follow` has the value `yes`, then links from this document will be followed. Otherwise, they won't be.

Other processing instructions may have totally different syntaxes and semantics. For instance, processing instructions can contain an unlimited amount of text. PHP includes large programs in processing instructions:

```
<?php
  mysql_connect("database.unc.edu", "clerk", "password");
  $result = mysql("CYNW", "SELECT LastName, FirstName FROM Employees
    ORDER BY LastName, FirstName");
  $i = 0;
  while ($i < mysql_numrows ($result)) {
     $fields = mysql_fetch_row($result);
     echo "<person>$fields[1] $fields[0] </person>\r\n";
     $i++;
  }
  mysql_close();
?>
```



Processing instructions are markup, but not elements. Consequently, like comments, processing instructions may appear anywhere in an XML document outside of a tag, including before or after the root element. The most common processing instruction, `xml-stylesheet` attaches stylesheets to documents. It always appears before the root element, as Example 2-6 demonstrates. In this example, the `xml-stylesheet` processing instruction tells browsers to apply the CSS stylesheet *person.css* to this document before showing it to the reader.

*Example 2-6: An XML Document with an xml-stylesheet Processing Instruction*

```
<?xml-stylesheet href="person.css" type="text/css"?>
<person>
  Alan Turing
</person>
```

The processing instruction name xml, in any combination of case, (that is, xml, XML, Xml, etc.) is resolved for use by the W3C. Otherwise, you're free to pick any legal XML name for your processing instructions.

## The XML Declaration

XML documents should, but do not have to, begin with an *XML declaration*. The XML declaration looks like a processing instruction with the name `xml` and `version`, `standalone`, and `encoding` attributes. Technically, it's not a processing instruction though, just the XML declaration; nothing more, nothing less. Example 2-7 demonstrates.

*Example 2-7: A Very Simple XML Document with an XML Declaration*

```
<?xml version="1.0" encoding="US-ASCII" standalone="yes"?>
<person>
  Alan Turing
</person>
```

XML documents do not have to have an XML declaration. However, if an XML document does have an XML declaration, then the declaration must be the first thing in the document. It must not be preceded by comments, whitespace, or processing instructions. The reason is that an XML parser uses the first five characters (`<?xml`) to make reasonable guesses about the encoding, such as whether the document uses a single- or multibyte character set. An invisible Unicode byte order mark is the only thing that may precede the XML declaration. We'll discuss this further in Chapter 5, *Internationalization*.

## *version*

The `version` attribute of the XML declaration always has the value 1.0. It is plausible that at some future time this value may change, and then the `version` attribute will be used to distinguish between documents that adhere to XML 1.0 and documents that adhere to a later version of the specification. However, it's also plausible that this will never happen. XML 1.0 is a fairly robust specification designed for extensibility. Most efforts to improve it—namespaces and schemas, for example—are built as layers on top of the infrastructure that XML 1.0 provides. They do not require breaking existing parsers or documents. Parsers that read XML 1.0 documents can still read documents that use namespaces, schemas, or hypothetical future developments. They may not understand the extra semantics that these new developments offer, but they can still read the documents. XML is designed to be both forward and backward compatible.

## *encoding*

So far we've been a little cavalier about encodings. We've said that XML documents are composed of pure text; but we haven't said what encoding that text uses. Is it ASCII? Latin-1? Unicode? Something else?

The short answer to this question is "Yes." The long answer is that, by default, XML documents are assumed to be encoded in the UTF-8 variable length encoding of the Unicode character set. This encoding is a strict superset of ASCII, so pure ASCII text files are also UTF-8 documents. However, most XML processors can handle a much broader range of encodings. All you have to do is give the name of the encoding in the XML declaration. Example 2-8 shows how you'd indicate that a document was written in the ISO 8859-1 (Latin-1) character set. This set includes characters needed for many non-English Western European languages, such as ö and ç.

*Example 2-8: An XML Document Encoded in Latin-1*

```
<?xml version="1.0" encoding="ISO-8859-1" standalone="yes"?>
<person>
  Erwin Schrödinger
</person>
```

The `encoding` attribute is optional in an XML declaration. If it is omitted, the Unicode character set is assumed. The parser may use the first several bytes of the file to guess which form of Unicode is in use.

Chapter 5 discusses the different encodings and proper handling of non-English XML documents in much greater detail.

### *standalone*

If the `standalone` attribute has the value `no`, then an application may have to read an external DTD (that is, a DTD in a file other than the one it's reading now) to determine the proper values for parts of the document. For instance, a DTD may provide default values for attributes a parser is required to report, though they aren't actually present in the document.

Documents that do not have DTDs, like all the documents in this chapter, can use the value `yes` for the `standalone` attribute. Documents that do have DTDs can also use the value `yes` for the `standalone` attribute if the DTD doesn't change the content of the document or if the DTD is purely internal. Chapter 3 provides details for documents with DTDs.

The `standalone` attribute is optional in an XML declaration. If it is omitted, the value `no` is assumed.



## *Checking Documents for Well-Formedness*

Every legal XML document, without exception, must be well-formed. This means it must adhere to a number of rules, including:

- Every start tag must have a matching end tag
- Elements may not overlap
- There must be exactly one root element
- Attribute values must be quoted
- An element may not have two attributes with the same name
- Comments and processing instructions may not appear inside tags
- No unescaped < or & signs may occur in the element's or attribute's character data

This list is not exhaustive. A document can be malformed in many ways. You'll find a complete list in Chapter 18, *XML 1.0 Reference*. Some of these malformations involve constructs we have not yet discussed, such as DTDs. Others are very unlikely to occur if you follow the examples in this chapter (for example, including whitespace between the opening < and the element name in a tag).

Whether the error is small or large, likely or unlikely, an XML parser reading a document must report it. It may report multiple well-formedness errors it detects in the document. However, the parser is not allowed to fix the document and make a best faith effort of providing what it thinks the author really meant. It can't fill in missing quotes around attribute values, insert an omitted end tag, or ignore the comment that's inside a start tag. The parser is required to return an error. The objective here is to avoid the bug-for-bug compatibility wars that plagued early web browsers and continues to this day. Consequently, before you publish an XML document, whether that document is a web page, input to a database or something else, you should check it for well-formedness.

The simplest way to check the document is by loading it into a web browser that understands XML documents, such as Opera or Mozilla. If the document is well-formed, the browser will display it. If it isn't, then it will show an error message.

Instead of loading the document into a web browser, you can use an XML parser directly. Most XML parsers are not intended for end users; they are class libraries designed to be embedded into a more user-friendly program like Internet Explorer. They provide a minimal command-line interface, if that; and that interface is often not well documented. Nonetheless, running a batch of files through a command-line interface is sometimes faster than loading each of them into a web browser. Once you learn about DTDs, you can use the same tools to validate documents.

Many XML parsers are available in a variety of languages. Here we'll demonstrate checking well-formedness with the Apache XML Project's Xerces-J, which you can download from *http://xml.apache.org/xerces-j/index.html*. This open source package is written in pure Java, so it should run across all major platforms. The procedure should be similar for other parsers, though details vary.

To use this parser you'll first need to install a Java 1.1 or later compatible virtual machine. Virtual machines for Windows, Solaris, and Linux are available from *http://java.sun.com/*. To install Xerces-J just add the *xerces.jar* and *xercesSamples.jar* files to your Java class path. In Java 2 you can simply put those *.jar* files into your *jre/lib/ext* directory.

The class that actually checks files for well-formedness is called `sax.SAXCount`. It's run from a Unix shell or DOS prompt, like any other standalone Java program. The command-line arguments are the URLs to or filenames of the documents you want to check. Here's the result of running *SAXCount* against the original version of Example 2-5. The first line of output locates the file's first problem. The rest of the output is an irrelevant stack trace:

```
D:\xian\examples\02>java sax.SAXCount 2-5.xml
[Fatal Error] 2-5.xml:3:30: The value of attribute "height" must not
contain the '<' character.
Stopping after fatal error: The value of attribute "height" must not
contain the '<' character.
at org.apache.xerces.framework.XMLParser.reportError(XMLParser.java:1282)
at org.apache.xerces.framework.XMLDocumentScanner.reportFatalXMLError(XM
LDocumentScanner.java:644)
at org.apache.xerces.framework.XMLDocumentScanner.scanAttValue(XMLDocume
ntScanner.java:519)
at org.apache.xerces.framework.XMLParser.scanAttValue(XMLParser.
java:1932)
at org.apache.xerces.framework.XMLDocumentScanner.scanElement(XMLDocumen
tScanner.java:1800)
at org.apache.xerces.framework.XMLDocumentScanner$ContentDispatcher.disp
atch(XMLDocumentScanner.java:1223)
at org.apache.xerces.framework.XMLDocumentScanner.parseSome(XMLDocumentS
canner.java:381)
at org.apache.xerces.framework.XMLParser.parse(XMLParser.java:1138)
at org.apache.xerces.framework.XMLParser.parse(XMLParser.java:1177)
at sax.SAXCount.print(SAXCount.java:135)
at sax.SAXCount.main(SAXCount.java:331)
```

As you can see, the program found an error. In this case the error message wasn't particularly helpful. The actual problem wasn't that an attribute value contained a < character. It was that the closing quote was missing from the attribute value. Still that information was sufficient to locate and fix the problem. Despite the long list of output in this example, *SAXCount* reports only the first error in the file, so you may have to run it multiple times until all mistakes are found and fixed. Once we fixed Example 2-5 to make it well-formed, *SAXCount* simply reported how long it took to parse the document and what it saw when it did:



```
D:\xian\examples\02>java sax.SAXCount 2-5.xml
2-5.xml: 140 ms (17 elems, 12 attrs, 0 spaces, 564 chars)
```

Once the document has been made well-formed, it can be passed to a web browser, a database, or whatever other program is waiting to receive it. Almost any nontrivial document crafted by hand contains well-formedness mistakes. That's why it's important to check your work before you publish it.

CHAPTER 3

# *Document Type Definitions*

While XML is extremely flexible, not all applications that need to read particular XML documents can afford such flexibility. Many programs can work with only some XML applications and not others. For example, Adobe Illustrator 9 can write Scalable Vector Graphics (SVG) files, but you wouldn't expect it to produce a Platform for Privacy Preferences (P3P) document. And within a particular XML application, ensuring that a given document indeed adheres to the rules of that XML application is often important. In XHTML `li` elements should only be children of `ul` or `ol` elements. Browsers may not know what to do with them, or may act inconsistently, if `li` elements appear in the middle of a `blockquote` or `p` element.

The solution to this dilemma is a document type definition (DTD). DTDs are written in a formal syntax that explains precisely which elements and entities may appear in the document and what the elements' contents and attributes are. A DTD can make statements such as, "A `ul` element contains only `li` elements," or "Every `employee` element must have a `social_security_number` attribute." Different XML applications can use different DTDs to specify what they do and do not allow.

Validating parsers compare documents to their DTDs and list places where the document differs from constraints specified in the DTD. The program can then decide what it wants to do about violations. Some programs may reject the document. Others may try to fix the document or reject only its invalid elements. Validation is an optional step in processing XML. Unlike a well-formedness error, a validity error is not necessarily a fatal error, though some applications may choose to treat it as one.

## *Validation*

A valid document includes a *document type declaration* that identifies the DTD the document satisfies. The DTD lists all elements, attributes, and entities the document uses and the contexts in which it uses them. The DTD may list items the document does not use, as well. Validity operates on the principle that everything not permitted is forbidden. Everything in the document must match a declaration in the DTD. If a document has a DTD and the document satisfies the DTD, then the document is considered *valid*. If it does not, it is *invalid*.

There are many things the DTD does not say:

- What the document's root element is
- How many instances of each kind of element appear in the document
- What the character data inside the elements looks like
- What the semantic meaning of an element is; for instance, whether it contains a date or a person's name

DTDs allow you to place constraints on the form an XML document takes, but there can be quite a bit of flexibility within those limits. A DTD never says anything about the length, structure, meaning, allowed values, or other aspects of an element's text content.

DTDs

Validity is optional. A parser reading an XML document may or may not check for validity. If it does check for validity, the program receiving data from the parser may not care about validity errors. In some cases, such as feeding records into a database, a validity error may be quite serious, indicating that a required field is missing. In other cases, rendering a web page, for example, a validity error may not be so important and can be worked around. Well-formedness is required of all XML documents. Validity is not. Your documents and your programs can use it as you find necessary.

## A Simple DTD Example

Recall Example 2-2 from the last chapter. This example described a person who had a name and three professions. The name element had a first and a last name. The particular person described in that example was Alan Turing. However, that information is not relevant for DTDs. A DTD describes only the general type, not the specific instance. A DTD for person documents would say that a `person` element contains one `name` child element and zero or more `profession` child elements. It would also say that the `name` element contains a `first_name` and a `last_name` child element. Finally, it would state that the `first_name`, `last_name`, and `profession` elements all contain text. Example 3-1 is a DTD that describes such a `person` element.

*Example 3-1: A DTD for the person Element*

```
<!ELEMENT person (name, profession*)>
<!ELEMENT name (first_name, last_name)>
<!ELEMENT first_name (#PCDATA)>
<!ELEMENT last_name (#PCDATA)>
<!ELEMENT profession (#PCDATA)>
```

This DTD would probably be stored in a file separate from the documents it describes. This allows it to be easily referenced from multiple XML documents. However, it can be included inside the XML document, if convenient, inside the document type declaration. If stored in a separate file, then that file would probably be named *person.dtd*, or something similar. The *.dtd* extension is fairly standard, though not specifically required by the XML specification. If a web server served this file, it would be given the MIME media type application/xml-dtd.

Each line of Example 3-1 is an *element declaration*. The first line declares the `person` element, the second line declares the `name` element, and the third line declares the `first_name` element. However, the line breaks aren't relevant, except for legibility. Although putting only one declaration on each line is customary, it's not required. Long declarations can even span multiple lines.

The first element declaration in Example 3-1 says that each `person` element must contain exactly one `name` child element, followed by zero or more `profession` elements. The asterisk after profession stands for "zero or more." Thus every person must have a name, and may or may not have one or more professions. However, the name must come before all professions. For example, this `person` element is valid:

```
<person>
  <name>
    <first_name>Alan</first_name>
    <last_name>Turing</last_name>
  </name>
</person>
```

However this `person` element is not valid because it omits the name:

```
<person>
  <profession>computer scientist</profession>
  <profession>mathematician</profession>
  <profession>cryptographer</profession>
</person>
```

This `person` element is invalid because a `profession` element comes before the `name`:

```
<person>
  <profession>computer scientist</profession>
  <name>
    <first_name>Alan</first_name>
    <last_name>Turing</last_name>
  </name>
  <profession>mathematician</profession>
  <profession>cryptographer</profession>
</person>
```

The `person` element may not contain any element except those listed in its content model. The only extra character data it can contain is whitespace. For example, this `person` element is invalid because it adds a `publication` element:

```
<person>
  <name>
    <first_name>Alan</first_name>
    <last_name>Turing</last_name>
  </name>
```

```
  <profession>mathematician</profession>
  <profession>cryptographer</profession>
  <publication>On Computable Numbers...</publication>
</person>
```

This **person** element is invalid because it adds text outside the allowed children:

```
<person>
  <name>
    <first_name>Alan</first_name>
    <last_name>Turing</last_name>
  </name>
  was a <profession>computer scientist</profession>,
  a <profession>mathematician</profession>, and a
  <profession>cryptographer</profession>
</person>
```

DTDs

In all these examples of invalid elements, you could change the DTD to make these elements valid. All examples are well formed, after all. However, they are not valid with the DTD in Example 3-1.

Example 3-1 placed the most complicated and highest-level declaration at the top. However, this is not required. For instance, Example 3-2 is an equivalent DTD that simply reorders the declarations. DTDs allow forward, backward, and circular references to other declarations.

*Example 3-2: An Alternate DTD for the person Element*

```
<!ELEMENT first_name (#PCDATA)>
<!ELEMENT last_name (#PCDATA)>
<!ELEMENT profession (#PCDATA)>
<!ELEMENT name (first_name, last_name)>
<!ELEMENT person (name, profession*)>
```

The `name` declaration says that each `name` element must contain exactly one `first_name` element followed by exactly one `last_name` element. All other variations are forbidden.

The remaining three declarations—`first_name`, `last_name`, and `profession`—all say that their elements must contain `#PCDATA`. This DTD keyword stands for parsed character data; that is, raw text possibly containing entity references such as `&` and `<`, but not containing any tags or child elements.

## The Document Type Declaration

A valid document includes a reference to the DTD to which it should be compared. This reference is given in the document's single *document type declaration*. A document type declaration looks like this:

```
<!DOCTYPE person SYSTEM "http://ibiblio.org/xml/dtds/person.dtd">
```

This declaration says that the document's root element is `person` and that the DTD for this document can be found at the URI *http://ibiblio.org/xml/dtds/person.dtd*.

URI stands for Uniform Resource Identifier. URIs are a superset of URLs, which include URLs and Uniform Resource Names (URNs). A URN allows you to identify a resource such as the DTD for Scalable Vector Graphics, irrespective of its location. Indeed, the resource might exist at multiple locations, all equally authoritative. In practice, the only URIs in wide use today are URLs.

The document type declaration is included in the prolog of the XML document after the XML declaration, but before the root element. The prolog is everything in the XML document before the root element start tag. Example 3-3 demonstrates.

*Example 3-3: A Valid person Document*

```
<?xml version="1.0" standalone="no"?>
<!DOCTYPE person SYSTEM "http://ibiblio.org/xml/dtds/person.dtd">
<person>
  <name>
    <first_name>Alan</first_name>
    <last_name>Turing</last_name>
  </name>
  <profession>computer scientist</profession>
  <profession>mathematician</profession>
  <profession>cryptographer</profession>
</person>
```

If the document resides at the same site as the DTD, you can use a relative URL instead of the absolute form:

```
<!DOCTYPE person SYSTEM "/dtds/person.dtd">
```

You can even use only the filename if the DTD is in the same directory as the document:

```
<!DOCTYPE person SYSTEM "person.dtd">
```

### *Public IDs*

Standard DTDs may actually be stored at multiple URLs. For example, if you draw an SVG picture on your laptop at the beach, you should probably validate your drawing without opening a network connection to the W3C's web site, where the official SVG DTD resides. Such DTDs may be associated with public IDs. The name of the public ID uniquely identifies the XML application in use. Generally, a URI is also given as a backup in case the validator does not recognize the public ID. To indicate that you're specifying a public ID, use the keyword `PUBLIC` in place of `SYSTEM`. This document type declaration refers to the Rich Site Summary (RSS) DTD standardized by Netscape:

```
<!DOCTYPE rss PUBLIC "-//Netscape Communications//DTD RSS 0.91//EN"
                "http://my.netscape.com/publish/formats/rss-0.91.dtd">
```

In practice, public IDs aren't used very often. Almost all XML parsers rely on the URI to actually validate the document.

## *Internal DTD Subsets*

When you first develop a DTD, it's often useful to keep the DTD and an example document in the same file so you can modify and check them simultaneously. Therefore, the document type declaration may actually contain the DTD between square brackets, rather than referencing it at an external URI. Example 3-4 demonstrates.

*Example 3-4: A Valid person Document with an Internal DTD*

```
<?xml version="1.0"?>
<!DOCTYPE person [
  <!ELEMENT first_name (#PCDATA)>
  <!ELEMENT last_name  (#PCDATA)>
  <!ELEMENT profession (#PCDATA)>
  <!ELEMENT name       (first_name, last_name)>
  <!ELEMENT person     (name, profession*)>
]>
<person>
  <name>
    <first_name>Alan</first_name>
    <last_name>Turing</last_name>
  </name>
  <profession>computer scientist</profession>
  <profession>mathematician</profession>
  <profession>cryptographer</profession>
</person>
```

Some document type declarations contain declarations directly and link in others using a `SYSTEM` or `PUBLIC` URI. This document type declaration declares the `profession` and `person` elements itself, but relies on the file *name.dtd* to contain the declaration of the `name` element:

```
<!DOCTYPE person SYSTEM "name.dtd" [
  <!ELEMENT profession (#PCDATA)>
  <!ELEMENT person (name, profession*)>
]>
```

The *internal DTD subset* is the part of the DTD between the brackets. All parts that come from outside this document are called the *external DTD subset*. Together, they comprise the complete DTD. As a general rule, the two different subsets must be compatible. Neither can override the element or attribute declarations the other makes. For example, there would be a problem if *name.dtd* also declared the `person` element. However, entity declarations can be overridden, with some important consequences for DTD structure and design that we'll see later when we discuss entities.

When you use an external DTD subset, you should give the `standalone` attribute of the XML declaration the value `no`:

```
<?xml version="1.0" encoding="UTF-8" standalone="no"?>
```

> The XML specification gives four very detailed rules explaining when the presence of an external DTD subset does and does not require the `standalone` attribute to have the value `no`. However, the net effect of these rules is that almost all XML documents that use external DTD subsets require `standalone` to have the value `no`. Since setting `standalone` to `no` is always permitted, even when it is not required, worrying about the uncommon cases is not worthwhile.

A validating processor is required to read the external DTD subset. A nonvalidating processor may read the subset, but is not required to, even if `standalone` has the value `no`. This means that if the external subset makes declarations with consequences for a document's content, (for instance, providing default values for attributes) then the document's content depends on which parser you use and how it's configured. This has led to much confusion. Though some of the earliest XML parsers did not resolve external entities, most parsers still in use can, and generally will, resolve the entities. You shouldn't choose to not read the external DTD subset unless efficiency is a major concern and you're very familiar with the structure of the documents you're parsing.

## *Validating a Document*

As a general rule, web browsers do not validate documents, but only check them for well-formedness. If you write your own programs to process XML, you can use the parser's API to validate documents. If you write documents by hand and want to validate them, you can use one of the online validators or run a command-line program to validate the document.

Online validators are probably the easiest way to validate your documents. Two are noteworthy:

- The Brown University Scholarly Technology Group's XML Validation Form at *http://www.stg.brown.edu/service/xmlvalid/*
- Richard Tobin's XML well-formedness checker and validator at *http://www.cogsci.ed.ac.uk/%7Erichard/xml-check.html*

First you must place the document and associated DTDs on a publicly accessible web server. Next, load one of the mentioned URLs in a browser and type the URL of the document you're checking into the online form. The validating server will retrieve your document and tell you what, if any, errors it found. Figure 3-1 shows the results of using the Brown validator on a simple invalid, but well-formed, document.

Most XML parser class libraries include a simple validator program you can use if you're comfortable installing and using command-line programs. In Xerces-J that program is *sax.SAXCount*. Use the `-v` flag to turn on validation. (By default

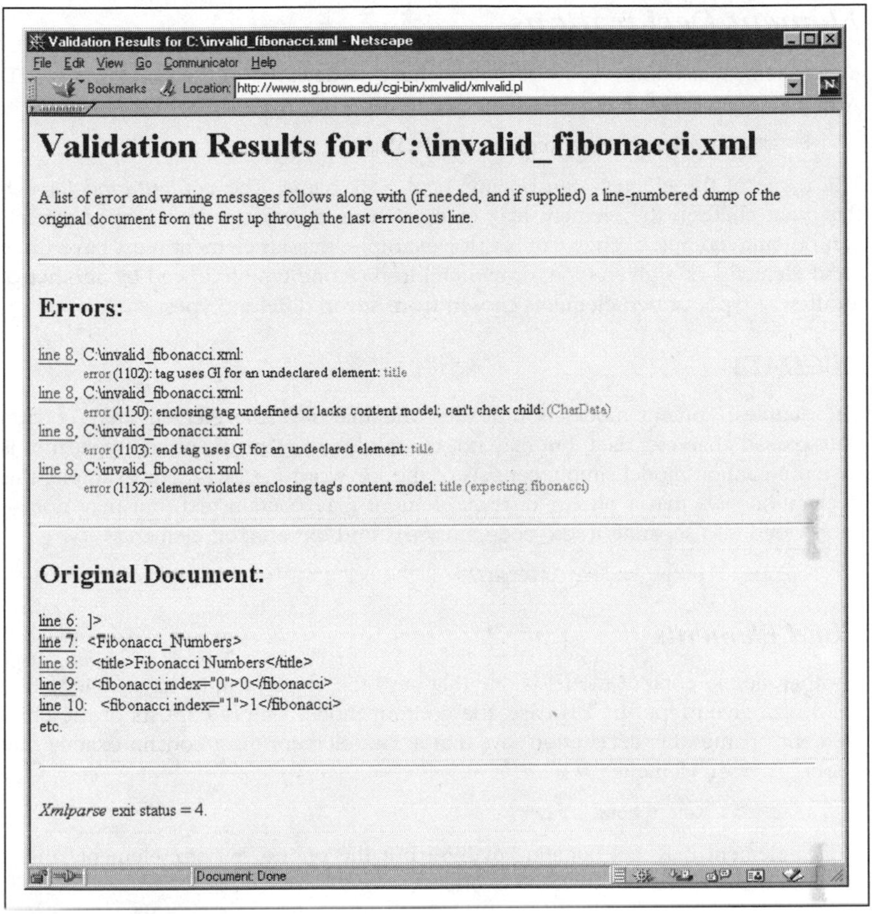


*Figure 3-1: Validity errors detected by the Brown University online validator*

*SAXCount* checks only for well-formedness.) Then pass the URLs or filenames of the documents you wish to validate to the *SAXCount* program on the command line like this:

```
C:\>java sax.SAXCount -v invalid_fibonacci.xml
[Error] invalid_fibonacci.xml:8:10: Element type "title" must be
declared.
[Error] invalid_fibonacci.xml:110:22: The content of element type
"Fibonacci_Numbers" must match "(fibonacci)*".
invalid_fibonacci.xml: 541 ms (103 elems, 101 attrs, 307 spaces,
1089 chars)
```

You can see from this output that two validity errors need to be fixed.

## *Element Declarations*

Every element used in a valid document must be declared in the document's DTD with an element declaration. Element declarations have this basic form:

```
<!ELEMENT element_name (content_model)>
```

The name of the element can be any legal XML name. The *content model* specifies what children the element may or must have in what order. Content models can be quite complex. They can say, for example, that an element must have three child elements of a given type, or two children of one type followed by another of a different type, or two elements chosen from seven different types.

### *#PCDATA*

The simplest content model is probably one that says the element may contain only parsed character data, but may not contain child elements of any type. In this case the content model simply consists of the keyword `#PCDATA`. For example, this declaration says that a `phone_number` element may contain text, but may not be subdivided into separate `area_code`, `number`, and `extension` elements:

```
<!ELEMENT phone_number (#PCDATA)>
```

### *Child Elements*

Another simple content model is one that says the element must have exactly one child of a given type. In this case, the content model simply consists of the child element's name; this declaration says that a `fax` element must contain exactly one `phone_number` element:

```
<!ELEMENT fax (phone_number)>
```

A `fax` element may not contain anything but the `phone_number` element, and it may not contain more or fewer than one.

### *Sequences*

In practice, a content model that lists exactly one child element is rare. Most elements contain either parsed character data or (potentially) multiple child elements. The simplest way to indicate multiple child elements is to separate them with commas. This is called a *sequence*. It indicates that the named elements must appear in the specified order. For example, this element declaration says that a `name` element must contain exactly one `first_name` child element followed by exactly one `last_name` child element:

```
<!ELEMENT name (first_name, last_name)>
```

Given this declaration, this `name` element is valid:

```
<name>
  <first_name>Madonna</first_name>
  <last_name>Ciccone</last_name>
</name>
```

However, this element is not because it flips the order of two elements:

```
<name>
  <last_name>Ciccone</last_name>
  <first_name>Madonna</first_name>
</name>
```

This element is invalid because it omits the `last_name` element:

```
<name>
  <first_name>Madonna</first_name>
</name>
```

This element is invalid because it adds a `middle_name` element:

```
<name>
  <first_name>Madonna</first_name>
  <middle_name>Louise</middle_name>
  <last_name>Ciccone</last_name>
</name>
```

DTDs

## *The Number of Children*

As these examples indicate, not all instances of a given element have exactly the same children. You can affix one of three suffixes to an element name in a content model to indicate how many instances of that element are expected at that position:

? Permits zero or one of the element

* Permits zero or more of the element

+ Permits one or more of the element

For example, this declaration says that a `name` element must contain a `first_name`, may or may not contain a `middle_name`, and may or may not contain a `last_name`:

```
<!ELEMENT name (first_name, middle_name?, last_name?)>
```

Given this declaration, all these `name` elements are valid:

```
<name>
  <first_name>Madonna</first_name>
  <last_name>Ciccone</last_name>
</name>
<name>
  <first_name>Madonna</first_name>
  <middle_name>Louise</middle_name>
  <last_name>Ciccone</last_name>
</name>
<name>
  <first_name>Madonna</first_name>
</name>
```

However, these names are not valid:

```
<name>
  <first_name>George</first_name>
  <!-- only one middle name is allowed -->
```

```
  <middle_name>Herbert</middle_name>
  <middle_name>Walker</middle_name>
  <last_name>Bush</last_name>
</name>
<name>
  <!-- first name must precede last name -->
  <last_name>Ciccone</last_name>
  <first_name>Madonna</first_name>
</name>
```

You can allow multiple middle names by placing an asterisk after the `middle_name`:

```
<!ELEMENT name (first_name, middle_name*, last_name?)>
```

If you want to require a `middle_name`, but still allow multiple middle names, use a plus sign instead:

```
<!ELEMENT name (first_name, middle_name+, last_name?)>
```

## *Choices*

Sometimes one instance of an element may contain one kind of child and another instance may contain a different child. This situation can be indicated with a *choice*. A choice is a list of element names separated by vertical bars. For example, this declaration says that a `methodResponse` element contains either a `params` child or a `fault` child:

```
<!ELEMENT methodResponse (params | fault)>
```

However, the element cannot contain both children at once. Each `methodResponse` element must contain one or the other.

Choices can be extended to an indefinite number of possible elements. For example, this declaration says that each `digit` element can contain exactly one of the child elements named `zero`, `one`, `two`, `three`, `four`, `five`, `six`, `seven`, `eight`, or `nine`:

```
<!ELEMENT digit
  (zero | one | two | three | four | five | six | seven | eight | nine)
>
```

## *Parentheses*

Individually, choices, sequences, and suffixes are fairly limited. However, they can be combined in arbitrarily complex fashions to describe essentially any reasonable content model. Either a choice or a sequence can be enclosed in parentheses. The parentheses can be suffixed with a `?`, `*`, or `+`. You can also nest the parenthesized item inside other choices or sequences.

Suppose you want to say that a `circle` element contains a `point` element and either a `radius` or a `diameter` element, but not both. This declaration specifies that:

```
<!ELEMENT circle (point, (radius | diameter))>
```

To continue with a geometry example, suppose a `point` element can be given in either Cartesian or polar coordinates. Then each point contains either an `x` and a `y` or an `r` and a `θ`. We declare this using two small sequences, each of which is parenthesized and combined in a choice:

```
<!ELEMENT point ((x, y) | (r, θ))>
```

Suppose you don't really care whether the `x` element comes before the `y` element, or vice versa, nor does it matter whether `r` comes before `θ`. Then you can expand the choice to cover all four possibilities:

```
<!ELEMENT point ((x, y) | (y, x) | (r, θ) | (θ, r) )>
```

As the number of elements in the sequence grows, the number of permutations grows more than exponentially. Thus, this technique isn't practical past two or three child elements. DTDs are not very useful when you want *n* instances of *A* and *m* instances of *B*, but don't really care what order they come in.

Suffixes can be applied to parenthesized elements, too. For instance, suppose a polygon is defined not by `point` elements, but by individual coordinates for each vertex, given in order. Here is a right triangle:

```
<polygon>
  <r>0</r>  <θ>0</θ>
  <x>0</x>  <y>10</y>
  <x>10</x> <y>0</y>
</polygon>
```

We want to say that a polygon is composed of three or more pairs of *x-y* or *r-θ* coordinates. An `x` is always followed by a `y`, and an `r` is always followed by a `θ`. This declaration does that:

```
<!ELEMENT polygon
  (((x, y) | (r, θ)), ((x, y) | (r, θ)), ((x, y) | (r, θ))+)>
```

The plus sign is applied to the parenthesized combination of `(x, y)` and `(r, θ)`, each of which is a parenthesized sequence.

To return to the name example, suppose you want to say that a name can contain just a first name, just a last name, or a first name and a last name with an indefinite number of middle names. This declaration achieves that goal:

```
<!element name (first_name | last_name
                | (first_name, middle_name*, last_name) ) >
```

## *Mixed Content*

In narrative documents a single element often contains both child elements and unmarked-up, nonwhitespace character data. Recall this `definition` element from Chapter 2, *XML Fundamentals*:

```
<definition>A <term>Turing Machine</term> is an abstract finite
state automaton with an infinite memory that can be proven equivalent
to any other finite state automaton with arbitrarily large memory.
Thus what is true for a Turing machine is true for all equivalent
machines no matter how implemented.
</definition>
```

The `definition` element contains some non-whitespace text and a `term` child. This is called *mixed content.* An element that contains mixed content is declared as follows:

```
<!ELEMENT definition (#PCDATA | term)*>
```

This declaration says that a `definition` element may contain parsed character data and `term` children. It does not specify in which order they appear or how many instances of each appear. This declaration allows a `definition` to have one `term` child, no `term` children, or 23 `term` children.

You can add any number of other child elements to the list of mixed content, though `#PCDATA` must always be first in the list. This declaration says that a `paragraph` element may contain any number of `name`, `profession`, `footnote`, `emphasize`, and `date` elements in any order, interspersed with parsed character data:

```
<!ELEMENT paragraph
  (#PCDATA | name | profession | footnote | emphasize | date )*
>
```

This is the *only* way to indicate that an element contains mixed content. You cannot say, for example, that there must be exactly one `term` child of the `definition` element and parsed character data. You cannot say that the parsed character data must all come after the `term` child. You cannot use parentheses around a mixed content declaration to make it part of a larger group. You can only say that the element contains any number of any elements from a particular list in any order and that it also contains undifferentiated parsed character data.

## *Empty Elements*

Some elements, called *empty elements*, do not have any content. Empty elements are sometimes written as a single standalone tag with a closing />:

```
<image source="bus.jpg" width="152" height="345"
       alt="Alan Turing standing in front of a bus"
/>
```

Empty elements are declared by using the keyword `EMPTY` for the content model:

```
<!ELEMENT image EMPTY>
```

## *ANY*

Very loose DTDs occasionally want to say that an element exists without indicating what it may or may not contain. In this case, you can use the keyword `ANY` as the content model. This declaration says that a `page` element can contain any content at all, including mixed content, child elements, and even other `page` elements:

```
<!ELEMENT page ANY>
```

The children that actually appear in the `page` elements' content in the document must still be declared in element declarations of their own. `ANY` does not allow you to use undeclared elements.

ANY is sometimes useful when you begin to design a DTD and document structure and don't yet have a clear picture of how everything fits together. However, using ANY in finished DTDs is extremely bad form. You'll probably see it used only when external DTD subsets and entities change in uncontrollable ways. However, this situation is actually quite rare. You'd really need ANY only if you were writing a DTD for an application, such as XSLT or RDF, that wraps content from arbitrary, unknown XML applications.

## Attribute Declarations

Besides declaring its elements, a valid document must declare all the elements' attributes. This is done with ATTLIST declarations. A single ATTLIST can declare multiple attributes for a single element type. However, if the same attribute is repeated on multiple elements, it must be declared separately for each element where it appears. Later in this chapter you'll see how to use parameter entity references to make this repetition less burdensome.

DTDs

For example, this ATTLIST declaration declares the source attribute of the image element:

```
<!ATTLIST image source CDATA #REQUIRED>
```

It says that the image element has an attribute named source. The value of the source attribute is character data, and instances of the image element in the document are required to provide a value for the source attribute.

A single ATTLIST declaration can declare multiple attributes for the same element. For example, this ATTLIST declaration declares not only the source attribute of the image element, but also the width, height, and alt attributes:

```
<!ATTLIST image source CDATA #REQUIRED
                width  CDATA #REQUIRED
                height CDATA #REQUIRED
                alt    CDATA #IMPLIED
>
```

This says that the source, width, and height attributes are required. However, the alt attribute is optional and may be omitted from particular image elements. All four attributes are declared to contain character data, the most generic attribute type.

This declaration has the same effect and meaning as four separate ATTLIST declarations, one for each attribute. Using one ATTLIST declaration per attribute is a matter of personal preference, but most experienced DTD designers prefer the multiple attribute form. Given judicious application of whitespace, this is no less legible than the alternative.

### Attribute Types

In merely well-formed XML, attribute values can be any string of text. The only restrictions are that occurrences of < or & must be escaped as < and &, and whichever type of quote mark, single or double, is used to delimit the value must also be escaped. However, a DTD permits somewhat stronger statements about an attribute value's content. Indeed, these statements are stronger than those that can be made about the element's contents. For instance, you can say that an attribute value must be unique within the document, a legal XML name token, or chosen from a fixed list of values.

Ten attribute types exist in XML:

- CDATA
- NMTOKEN
- NMTOKENS
- ENUMERATION
- ENTITY
- ENTITIES
- ID
- IDREF
- IDREFS
- NOTATION

Only these ten attribute types are allowed. A DTD cannot say that an attribute value must be an integer or a date, for example:

### *CDATA*

A CDATA attribute value can contain any string of text acceptable in a well-formed XML attribute value. This is the most general attribute type. You could use this type for an `alt` attribute of an `image` element because there's no particular form the text in such an attribute has to follow:

```
<!ATTLIST image alt CDATA #IMPLIED>
```

You would also use this type for other kinds of data, such as prices, URIs, email and snail mail addresses, and citations that have more structure than a simple string of text, but don't match any of the other attribute types:

```
<!ATTLIST sku
 list_price              CDATA #IMPLIED
 suggested_retail_price CDATA #IMPLIED
 actual_price            CDATA #IMPLIED
>
<!-- All three attributes should be in the form $XX.YY -->
```

---

***Datatyping with Schemas***

XML schemas do allow you to provide much stronger datatyping for attribute values such as URIs, prices, and addresses that DTDs have to lump together as CDATA.

---

### *NMTOKEN*

An XML *name token* is very close to an XML name. It must consist of the same characters as an XML name: alphanumeric and/or ideographic characters and the punctuation marks _, -, ., and :. Like an XML name, an XML name token may not contain whitespace. However, a name token differs from an XML name because all allowed characters can be the first character in a name token, while only letters, ideographs, and the underscore can be the first character of an XML name. Thus, 12 and .cshrc are legal XML name tokens, though they are not legal XML names. Every XML name is an XML name token, but not all XML name tokens are XML names.

The value of an attribute declared to have type `NMTOKEN` is an XML name token. For example, if you knew that the `year` attribute of a `journal` element should contain an integer such as 1990 or 2015, you might declare it to have `NMTOKEN` type, since all years are name tokens:

```
<!ATTLIST journal year NMTOKEN #REQUIRED>
```

This declaration still doesn't prevent the document author from assigning the year attribute values such as `99` or `March`, but it at least eliminates some possible wrong values, especially those containing whitespace, such as `1990 C.E.` or `Sally had a little lamb`.

### *NMTOKENS*

A `NMTOKENS` type attribute contains one or more XML name tokens separated by whitespace. You might use this attribute to describe the `dates` attribute of a `performances` element, if the dates were given in the form 08-26-2000:

```
<performances dates="08-21-2001 08-23-2001 08-27-2001">
  Kat and the Kings
</performances>
```

The appropriate declaration is:

```
<!ATTLIST performances dates NMTOKENS #REQUIRED>
```

On the other hand, you could not use this declaration for a list of dates in the form 08/27/2001 because the forward slash is not a legal name character.

### *Enumeration*

Enumeration is the only attribute type that is not an XML keyword. Rather, the content model is a list of all possible values for the attribute, separated by vertical bars. Each possible value must be an XML name token. The following declarations say that the value of the `month` attribute of a `date` element must be one of the 12 English month names, the value of a `day` attribute must be a number between 1 and 31, and the value of a `year` attribute must be an integer between 1970 and 2009:

```
<!ATTLIST date month (January | February | March | April | May | June
  | July | August | September | October | November | December) #REQUIRED
>
```

```
<!ATTLIST date day (1 | 2 | 3 | 4 | 5 | 6 | 7 | 8 | 9 | 10 | 11 | 12
  | 13 | 14 | 15 | 16 | 17 | 18 | 19 | 20 | 21 | 22 | 23 | 24 | 25
  | 26 | 27 | 28 | 29 | 30 | 31) #REQUIRED
>
<!ATTLIST date year (1970 | 1971 | 1972 | 1973 | 1974 | 1975 | 1976
  | 1977 | 1978 | 1979 | 1980 | 1981 | 1982 | 1983 | 1984 | 1985 | 1986
  | 1987 | 1988 | 1989 | 1990 | 1991 | 1992 | 1993 | 1994 | 1995 | 1996
  | 1997 | 1998 | 1999 | 2000 | 2001 | 2002 | 2003 | 2004 | 2005 | 2006
  | 2007 | 2008 | 2009 ) #REQUIRED
>
<!ELEMENT date EMPTY>
```

Given this DTD, this `date` element is valid:

```
<date month="January" day="22" year="2001"/>
```

However, these `date` elements are invalid:

```
<date month="01"      day="22" year="2001"/>
<date month="Jan"     day="22" year="2001"/>
<date month="January" day="02" year="2001"/>
<date month="January" day="2"  year="1969"/>
<date month="Janvier" day="22" year="2001"/>
```

We can pull this trick off here because all desired values are legal XML name tokens. However, we could not use the same trick if the possible values included whitespace or any punctuation besides the underscore, hyphen, colon, and period.

### *ID*

An `ID` type attribute must contain an XML name (not a name token) that is unique within the XML document. More precisely, no other `ID` type attribute in the document can have the same value; attributes of non-`ID` type are not even considered. Each element can have no more than one `ID` type attribute.

As the keyword suggests, `ID` type attributes are used to assign unique identifiers to elements. `ID` type attributes do not have to have the name "ID" or "id," though they very commonly do. This `ATTLIST` declaration says that every `employee` element must have a `social_security_number` ID attribute:

```
<!ATTLIST employee social_security_number ID #REQUIRED>
```

ID numbers are tricky because a number is not an XML name and therefore not a legal XML `ID`. The normal solution prefixes the values with an underscore or common letter. For example:

```
<employee social_security_number="_123-45-6789"/>
```

### *IDREF*

An `IDREF` type attribute refers to the `ID` type attribute of an element in the document. Thus, it must be an XML name. `IDREF` attributes are commonly used to establish many-to-many relationships between elements when simple containment won't suffice.

For example, imagine an XML document containing a list of project and employee elements. Every project has a project_id ID type attribute, and every employee has a social_security_number ID type attribute. Furthermore, each project has team_member child elements that identify who's working on the project, and each employee element has assignment children that indicate which projects that employee is assigned to. Since each project is assigned to multiple employees and some employees are assigned to more than one project, it's not possible to make the employees children of the projects or the projects children of the employees. The solution is to use IDREF type attributes in the following manner:

```
<project project_id="p1">
  <goal>Develop Strategic Plan</goal>
  <team_member person="ss123-45-6789"/>
  <team_member person="ss876-54-3210"/>
</project>

<project project_id="p2">
  <goal>Deploy Linux</goal>
  <team_member person="ss123-45-6789"/>
  <team_member person="ss876-12-3456"/>
</project>

<person social_security_number="ss123-45-6789">
  <name>Fred Smith</name>
  <assignment project_id="p1"/>
  <assignment project_id="p2"/>
</person>

<person social_security_number="ss876-54-3210">
  <name>Jill Jones</name>
  <assignment project_id="p1"/>
</person>

<person social_security_number="ss876-12-3456">
  <name>Sydney Lee</name>
  <assignment project_id="p2"/>
</person>
```

In this example, the project_id attribute of the project element and the social_security_number attribute of the person element should be declared to have type ID. The person attribute of the team_member element and the project_id attribute of the assignment element should have type IDREF. The relevant ATTLIST declarations look like this:

```
<!ATTLIST person  social_security_number ID #REQUIRED>
<!ATTLIST project project_id             ID #REQUIRED>

<!ATTLIST team_member person          IDREF #REQUIRED>
<!ATTLIST assignment  project_id      IDREF #REQUIRED>
```

These declarations constrain the person attribute of the team_member element and the project_id attribute of the assignment element to match the ID of something in the document. However, they do not constrain the person attribute of the team_member element to match only person IDs or constrain the person element's project_id attribute to match only project IDs. A team_member could validly, though not necessarily correctly, hold the ID of another project or the same project.

### *IDREFS*

An IDREFS type attribute contains a whitespace-separated list of XML names, each of which must be the ID of an element in the document. This attribute is used when one element needs to refer to multiple other elements. For instance, the previous project example could be rewritten to replace the assignment children of the person element with a a single assignments attribute. Similarly, the team_member children of the project element could be replaced by a team attribute, as in this declaration:

```
<project project_id="p1" team="ss123-45-6789 ss876-54-3210">
  <goal>Develop Strategic Plan</goal>
</project>

<project project_id="p2" team="ss123-45-6789 ss876-12-3456">
  <goal>Deploy Linux</goal>
</project>

<person social_security_number="ss123-45-6789" assignments="p1 p2">
  <name>Fred Smith</name>
</person>

<person social_security_number="ss876-54-3210" assignments="p1">
  <name>Jill Jones</name>
</person>

<person social_security_number="ss876-12-3456" assignments="p2">
  <name>Sydney Lee</name>
</person>
```

The appropriate declarations are:

```
<!ATTLIST person social_security_number ID     #REQUIRED
                 assignments            IDREFS #REQUIRED>
<!ATTLIST project project_id            ID     #REQUIRED
                  team                  IDREFS #REQUIRED>
```

### *ENTITY*

An ENTITY type attribute contains the name of an unparsed entity declared elsewhere in the DTD. For instance, a movie element might have an entity attribute identifying the MPEG or QuickTime file to play when the movie was activated:

```
<!ATTLIST movie source ENTITY #REQUIRED>
```

If the DTD declared an unparsed entity named X-Men-trailer, this movie element might be used to embed that video file in the XML document:

```
<movie source="X-Men-trailer"/>
```

We'll discuss unparsed entities again later.

### *ENTITIES*

An `ENTITIES` type attribute contains names of multiple unparsed entities declared elsewhere in the DTD, separated by whitespace. For instance, a `presentation` element might have an `ENTITIES` attribute identifying the JPEG files to show in the order they were to be shown:

```
<!ATTLIST slide_show slides ENTITIES #REQUIRED>
```

If the DTD declared unparsed entities named `slide1`, `slide2`, `slide3`, and so on through `slide10`, then you could use this `slide_show` element to embed the show in the XML document:

```
<slide_show slides="slide1 slide2 slide3 slide4 slide5 slide6
                    slide7 slide8 slide9 slide10"/>
```

### *NOTATION*

A `NOTATION` type attribute contains the name of a notation declared in the document's DTD. This attribute type is perhaps the rarest, and isn't much used in practice. In theory, you could use it to associate types with particular elements. These declarations define four notations for different image types and then specify that each `image` element must have a `type` attribute that selects exactly one of them:

```
<!NOTATION gif  SYSTEM "image/gif">
<!NOTATION tiff SYSTEM "image/tiff">
<!NOTATION jpeg SYSTEM "image/jpeg">
<!NOTATION png  SYSTEM "image/png">
<!ATTLIST  image type NOTATION (gif | tiff | jpeg | png) #REQUIRED>
```

The `type` attribute of each `image` element can have one of the four values `gif`, `tiff`, `jpeg`, or `png` but not any other value. This attribute has a slight advantage over the enumeration type, because the actual MIME media type of the notation is theoretically available. An enumeration type could not specify `image/png` or `image/gif` as an allowed value because the forward slash is not a legal character in XML names. In practice, no common software actually supports this scheme for indicating the element type.

## *Attribute Defaults*

Besides providing a datatype, each `ATTLIST` declaration includes a default declaration for that attribute. Four possibilities exist for this default:

`#IMPLIED`
: The attribute is optional. Each instance of the element may or may not provide a value for the attribute. No default value is provided.

`#REQUIRED`
: The attribute is required. Each instance of the element must provide a value for the attribute. No default value is provided.

`#FIXED`
: The attribute value is constant and immutable. This attribute has the specified value, whether or not the attribute is explicitly noted on an individual

instance of the element. In general, it is not included on individual instances, though it must have the specified value if it is included.

`Literal`
: The actual default value as a quoted string.

For example, this `ATTLIST` declaration says that `person` elements can, but do not have to, have `born` and `died` attributes:

```
<!ATTLIST person born CDATA #IMPLIED
                 died CDATA #IMPLIED
>
```

This `ATTLIST` declaration says that every `circle` element must have `center_x`, `center_y`, and `radius` attributes:

```
<!ATTLIST circle center_x NMTOKEN #REQUIRED
                 center_y NMTOKEN #REQUIRED
                 radius   NMTOKEN #REQUIRED
>
```

This `ATTLIST` declaration says that every `biography` element has an `xmlns:xlink` attribute, and that the attribute's value is `http://www.w3.org/1999/xlink`, even if the element's start tag does not explicitly include an `xmlns:xlink` attribute:

```
<!ATTLIST biography
   xmlns:xlink CDATA #FIXED "http://www.w3.org/1999/xlink">
```

This `ATTLIST` declaration says that every `web_page` element has a `protocol` attribute. If a particular `web_page` element doesn't have an explicit `protocol` attribute, then it has an implicit one with the value `http`:

```
<!ATTLIST web_page protocol NMTOKEN "http">
```

## *General Entity Declarations*

As you learned in Chapter 2, XML provides five entity references for your convenience:

<
: The less-than sign; the opening angle bracket (<)

&
: The ampersand (&)

>
: The greater-than sign; the closing angle bracket (>)

"
: Straight, double quotation marks (")

'
: The apostrophe; the single quote (')

The DTD can define many more entities. This is useful in both valid documents and in documents you don't plan to validate.

Entity references are defined with an `ENTITY` declaration in the DTD. This declaration gives the name of the entity, which must be an XML name, and the entity's replacement text. This entity declaration defines `&super;` as an abbreviation for *supercalifragilisticexpealidocious*:

```
<!ENTITY super "supercalifragilisticexpealidocious">
```

Once the definition is complete, you can use `&super;` anywhere you'd normally have to type the entire word (and probably misspell it).

Entities may contain markup as well as text. This declaration defines `&footer;` as an abbreviation for a standard web page footer that is repeated on many pages:

```
<!ENTITY footer '<hr size="1" noshade="true"/>
<font CLASS="footer">
<a href="index.html">O&apos;Reilly Home</a> |
<a href="sales/bookstores/">O&apos;Reilly Bookstores</a> |
<a href="order_new/">How to Order</a> |
<a href="oreilly/contact.html">O&apos;Reilly Contacts</a><br>
<a href="http://international.oreilly.com/">International</a> |
<a href="oreilly/about.html">About O&apos;Reilly</a> |
<a href="affiliates.html">Affiliated Companies</a>
</font>
<p>
<font CLASS="copy">
Copyright 2000, O&apos;Reilly &amp; Associates, Inc.<br/>
<a href="mailto:webmaster@oreilly.com">webmaster@oreilly.com</a>
</font>
</p>
'>
```

The entity replacement text must be well formed. For instance, you cannot put a start tag in one entity and place the corresponding end tag in another.

You must also be careful to use quotation marks inside the replacement text that differ from those that delimit it. Here we chose single quotes to surround the replacement text and double quotes internally. However, we did have to change the single quote in "O'Reilly" to the predefined general entity reference `'`. Replacement text may itself contain entity references that are resolved before the text is replaced. However, self-referential and circular references are forbidden.

General entities insert replacement text into the body of an XML document. They can also be used inside the DTD in places where they will eventually be included in the body of an XML document, for instance in a default attribute value or another entity's replacement text. However, they cannot be used to provide the text of the DTD itself. This declaration, for example, is illegal:

```
<!ENTITY coordinate  "((x, y) | (y, x) | (θ, r) | (r, θ))" >
<!ELEMENT polygon (&coordinate;, &coordinate;, &coordinate;+)>
```

Shortly, we'll see how to use a different kind of entity, the parameter entity, to achieve the result we're seeking here.

## *External Parsed General Entities*

The footer example is at the limits of what you can comfortably fit in a DTD. In practice, web sites prefer to store repeated content like this in external files and load it into their pages using PHP, server-side includes, or a similar mechanism. XML supports this technique through external general entity references, though in this case, the client, rather than the server, is responsible for integrating the different pieces of the document into a coherent whole.

An external parsed general entity reference is declared in the DTD using an `ENTITY` declaration. However instead of the actual replacement text, the `SYSTEM` keyword and a URI to the replacement text is given:

```
<!ENTITY footer SYSTEM "http://www.oreilly.com/boilerplate/footer.xml">
```

A relative URL is often used instead:

```
<!ENTITY footer SYSTEM "/boilerplate/footer.xml">
```

In either case, when the parser sees the general entity reference `&footer;` in the element's character data, the parser may replace it with the document found at *http://www.oreilly.com/boilerplate/footer.xml*. References to external parsed entities are not allowed in attribute values. Usually this shouldn't be too big a hassle because attribute values are generally small enough for easy inclusion in internal entities.

Notice we wrote that the parser *may* replace the entity reference with the document at the URL. We did not say it would replace the entity reference. In this area, parsers have some leeway in just how much of the XML specification they wish to implement. A validating parser must retrieve such an external entity. However, a nonvalidating parser may or may not choose to retrieve the entity.

Furthermore, not all text files can serve as external entities. To be loaded in by a general entity reference, the document must be potentially well formed when inserted into an existing document. This requirement does not mean the external entity itself must be well formed. In particular, the external entity may not have a single root element. However, if such a root element were wrapped around the external entity, the resulting document should be well formed. Thus, all elements that start inside the entity must finish inside the same entity. They cannot finish inside a different entity. Furthermore, the external entity does not have a prolog and therefore cannot have an XML declaration or a document type declaration.

### *Text Declarations*

Instead of an XML declaration, an external entity may have a text declaration. This looks much like an XML declaration. The main difference is that the encoding declaration in a text declaration is required, while the version information is optional. There is also no standalone declaration. The main purpose of the text declaration is to warn the parser if the external entity uses a different text encoding than the including document. Here is a common text declaration:

```
<?xml version="1.0" encoding="MacRoman"?>
```

However, you could also use this text declaration with no version attribute:

```
<?xml encoding="MacRoman"?>
```

Example 3-5 is a well-formed external entity that could be included from another document using an external general entity reference.

*Example 3-5: An External Parsed Entity*

```
<?xml encoding="ISO-8859-1"?>
<hr size="1" noshade="true"/>
<font CLASS="footer">
  <a href="index.html">O'Reilly Home</a> |
  <a href="sales/bookstores/">O'Reilly Bookstores</a> |
  <a href="order_new/">How to Order</a> |
  <a href="oreilly/contact.html">O'Reilly Contacts</a><br>
  <a href="http://international.oreilly.com/">International</a> |
  <a href="oreilly/about.html">About O'Reilly</a> |
  <a href="affiliates.html">Affiliated Companies</a>
</font>
<p>
  <font CLASS="copy">
    Copyright 2000, O'Reilly &amp; Associates, Inc.<br/>
    <a href="mailto:webmaster@oreilly.com">webmaster@oreilly.com</a>
  </font>
</p>
```

DTDs

## External Unparsed Entities and Notations

Not all data is XML. There are many ASCII text files that don't give two cents about escaping < as `<` or adhering to the other constraints that limit an XML document. Even more JPEG photographs, GIF line art, QuickTime movies, and MIDI sound files exist, none of which are well-formed XML. All, however, are necessary components of many documents.

XML suggests the *external unparsed entity* as the mechanism for embedding these things in your documents. The DTD specifies a name and URI for the entity containing the non-XML data. For example, this `ENTITY` declaration associates the name `turing_getting_off_bus` with the JPEG image at *http://www.turing.org.uk/turing/pi1/bus.jpg*:

```
<!ENTITY turing_getting_off_bus
         SYSTEM "http://www.turing.org.uk/turing/pi1/bus.jpg"
         NDATA jpeg>
```

### Notations

Since the data is not in XML format, the `NDATA` declaration specifies the type of the data. Here the name `jpeg` is used. XML does not recognize this name as an image in a format defined by the Joint Photographic Experts Group. Rather, this name identifies notation declared elsewhere in the DTD using a `NOTATION` declaration such as:

```
<!NOTATION jpeg SYSTEM "image/jpeg">
```

Here I've used the MIME media type image/jpeg as the external identifier for the notation. However, there is no standard or even a suggestion for exactly what this identifier should be. Individual applications must define their own requirements for the contents and meaning of notations.

## *Embedding Unparsed Entities in Documents*

The DTD only declares the existence, location, and type of the unparsed entity. To include the entity in the document in one or more locations, insert an element with an ENTITY type attribute whose value is the name of an unparsed entity declared in the DTD. Do not use an entity reference like &turing_getting_off_bus;. Entity references can only refer to parsed entities.

Suppose the image element and its source attribute are declared as follows:

```
<!ELEMENT image EMPTY>
<!ATTLIST image source ENTITY #REQUIRED>
```

Then this image element would refer to the photograph at *http://www.turing.org.uk/turing/pi1/bus.jpg*:

```
<image source="turing_getting_off_bus"/>
```

We should warn you that XML doesn't guarantee any particular behavior from an application that encounters an unparsed entity like this. It very well may not display the image to the user. Indeed, the parser may run in an environment where there's no user to display the image to. It may not even understand that it is an image. The parser may not load or make any sort of connection with the server where the actual image resides. At most, it tells the application on whose behalf it's parsing that there is an unparsed entity at a particular URI with a particular notation, and lets the application decide what, if anything, it wants to do with that information.

---

***Including Non-XML Content in XML Documents***

Unparsed general entities are not the only plausible way to embed non-XML content in XML documents. In particular, a simple URL, possibly associated with an XLink, does a fine job for many purposes, just as it does in HTML (which gets along just fine without unparsed entities). Including all the necessary information in a single empty element like <image source = "http://www.turing.org.uk/turing/pi1/bus.jpg"/> is arguably preferable to splitting the same information between the element where it's used and the DTD of the document it's used in. The only thing an unparsed entity really adds is the notation, but the notation is too nonstandard to be of much use.

In fact, many experienced XML developers, including this book's authors, feel strongly that unparsed entities are a complicated, confusing mistake that should never have been included in XML in the first place. Nonetheless, they are a part of the specification, so we describe them here.

---

## *Notations for Processing Instruction Targets*

Notations can also identify the exact target of a processing instruction. A processing instruction target must be an XML name, not a full path like */usr/local/bin/tex*. A notation can identify a short XML name such as tex with a more complete specification of the external program the processing instruction is intended for. For example, this notation associates the target `tex` with the more complete path */usr/local/bin/tex*:

```
<!NOTATION tex SYSTEM "/usr/local/bin/tex">
```

In practice, this technique isn't used or needed very often. Most applications that read XML files and pay attention to particular processing instructions simply recognize a particular target string, such as `php` or `robots`.

## Parameter Entities

Multiple elements often share all or part of the same attribute lists and content models. For instance, any element that's a simple XLink has `xlink:type` and `xlink:href`, and perhaps `xlink:show` and `xlink:actuate` attributes. In XHTML, a `th` and a `td` element contain roughly the same content. Repeating the same content models or attribute lists in multiple element declarations is tedious and error prone. Adding a newly defined child element to the declaration of some elements, while forgetting to include it in others, is entirely possible.

DTDs

For example, consider an XML application for residential real estate listings that needs separate elements for apartments, sublets, coops for sale, condos for sale, and houses for sale. The element declarations might look like this:

```
<!ELEMENT apartment (address, footage, rooms, baths, rent)>
<!ELEMENT sublet    (address, footage, rooms, baths, rent)>
<!ELEMENT coop      (address, footage, rooms, baths, price)>
<!ELEMENT condo     (address, footage, rooms, baths, price)>
<!ELEMENT house     (address, footage, rooms, baths, price)>
```

There's a lot of overlap and repeated text between the declarations. If you decide later that you need to add an additional element, such as `available_date`, then you need to add it to all five elements. It is preferable to define a constant that can hold the common parts of the content model for all five kinds of listings and refer to that constant from inside each element's content model. Then to add or delete something from all the listings, you only need to change the constant's definition.

An entity reference is the obvious candidate here. However, general entity references are not allowed to provide replacement text for a content model or attribute list, only for parts of the DTD that will be included in the XML document itself. Instead XML provides a new construct exclusively for use inside DTDs, the *parameter entity*, which is referred to by a *parameter entity reference*. Parameter entities behave and are declared almost exactly like a general entity. However, they use a % instead of an &, and they can be used only in a DTD, while general entities can be used only in the document content.

### Parameter Entity Syntax

A parameter entity reference is declared much like a general entity reference. However, an extra percent sign is placed between the `<!ENTITY` and the entity's name:

```
<!ENTITY % residential_content "address, footage, rooms, baths">
<!ENTITY % rental_content      "rent">
<!ENTITY % purchase_content    "price">
```

Parameter entities are dereferenced in the same way as a general entity reference, only with a percent sign instead of an ampersand:

```
<!ELEMENT apartment (%residential_content;, %rental_content;)>
<!ELEMENT sublet    (%residential_content;, %rental_content;)>
<!ELEMENT coop      (%residential_content;, %purchase_content;)>
<!ELEMENT condo     (%residential_content;, %purchase_content;)>
<!ELEMENT house     (%residential_content;, %purchase_content;)>
```

When the parser reads these declarations, it substitutes the entity's replacement text for the entity reference. Now to add an `available_date` element to the content model of all five listing types, you only need to add it to the `residential_content` entity like this:

```
<!ENTITY % residential_content "address, footage, rooms,
                                baths, available_date">
```

The same technique works equally well for attribute content models and element names and types. You'll see several examples of this technique in Chapter 4, *Namespaces*.

This trick is limited to external DTDs. Internal DTD subsets do not allow parameter entity references to be only part of a markup declaration. However, they can be used in internal DTD subsets to insert at least one entire markup declaration, typically through external parameter entities.

## *Redefining Parameter Entities*

Parameter entity references are particularly powerful because they can be redefined. If a document has both an external DTD subset and an internal DTD subset, the internal DTD subset can specify new replacement text for the entities. If the `ELEMENT` and `ATTLIST` content models in the external DTD are written indirectly with parameter entity references, instead of directly with literal names, the internal DTD subset may change the DTD for the document. A single document could add a `bedrooms` child element to the listings by redefining the `residential_content` entity like this:

```
<!ENTITY % residential_content "address, footage, rooms,
                                bedrooms, baths, available_date">
```

In the event of conflicting entity declarations, the first one encountered takes precedence. The internal DTD subset is read first. Thus, its definition of the `residential_content` entity takes precedence. When the external DTD subset is read, every declaration using the `residential_content` entity will contain a `bedrooms` child element it wouldn't have otherwise contained.

Modular XHTML, which we'll discuss in Chapter 7, *XML on the Web*, uses this technique heavily to allow particular documents to select only the subset of HTML that they actually need.

## *External DTD Subsets*

Real-world DTDs can be quite complex. The SVG DTD is more than a thousand lines long. The XHTML 1.0 strict DTD, the smallest of the three XHTML DTDs, is more than 1,500 lines long. And these are only medium-sized DTDs. The DocBook

XML DTD is more than 11,000 lines long. Working with, comprehending, and modifying such a large DTD is difficult when it's stored in a single monolithic file.

Fortunately DTDs can be broken up into independent pieces. For instance, the DocBook DTD is distributed in 28 separate pieces, covering different parts of the spec—one for tables, one for notations, one for entity declarations, and so on. These different pieces are then combined at validation time using *external parameter entity references.*

An external parameter entity is declared using a normal `ENTITY` declaration with a percent sign %, just like a normal parameter entity. However, rather than including the replacement text directly, the declaration contains the `SYSTEM` keyword followed by a URI to the DTD piece it wants to include. The following `ENTITY` declaration defines an external entity called `names`, whose content is taken from the file at the relative URI *names.dtd.* Then the parameter entity reference `%names;` inserts the contents of that file into the current DTD:

```
<!ENTITY % names SYSTEM "names.dtd">
%names;
```

You can use either relative or absolute URIs, as convenient. In most situations, relative URIs are more practical.

DTDs

## Conditional Inclusion

XML offers the `IGNORE` directive to "comment out" a section of declarations. For example, a parser ignores the following `production_note` element declaration as if it weren't in the DTD at all:

```
<![IGNORE[
  <!ELEMENT production_note (#PCDATA)>
]]>
```

This declaration may not seem particularly useful. After all, you could always use a real comment to comment out the declarations you want to temporarily remove from the DTD. If you prefer such an option, the `INCLUDE` directive will seem even more pointless. Its purpose is to indicate that the given declarations are actually used in the DTD.

```
<![INCLUDE[
  <!ELEMENT production_note (#PCDATA)>
]]>
```

This declaration has the same effect and meaning; it acts as if the `INCLUDE` directive were not present. However, now consider what happens if we don't use `INCLUDE` and `IGNORE` directly. Instead, suppose we define a parameter entity as follows:

```
<!ENTITY % notes_allowed "INCLUDE">
```

Then we use a parameter entity reference instead of the keyword:

```
<![%notes_allowed;[
  <!ELEMENT production_note (#PCDATA)>
]]>
```

The notes_allowed parameter entity can be redefined from outside this DTD. In particular, it can be redefined in the internal DTD subset of a document. This provides a switch that individual documents can use to turn the production_note declaration on or off. This technique is useful because it allows document authors to select only the functionality they need from the DTD.

# *Two DTD Examples*

Some of the best techniques for DTD design become apparent only when you look at larger documents. In this section we'll develop DTDs that cover the two different document formats for describing people, which were presented in Example 2-4 and Example 2-5 of the last chapter.

## *Data-Oriented DTDs*

Data-oriented DTDs are very straightforward. They use sequences heavily, occasionally use choices, and rarely use mixed content. Example 3-6 shows such a DTD. Since this example is small and since it's easier to understand when both the document and the DTD are on the same page, we've made this an internal DTD and included it in the document. However, we could easily put it in a separate file.

*Example 3-6: A Flexible, Yet Data-Oriented, DTD Describing People*

```
<?xml version="1.0"?>
<!DOCTYPE person [
  <!ELEMENT person (name+, profession*)>

  <!ELEMENT name EMPTY>
  <!ATTLIST name first CDATA #REQUIRED
                 last  CDATA #REQUIRED>
  <!-- The first and last attributes are required to be present
       but they may be empty. For example,
       <name first="Cher" last=""> -->

  <!ELEMENT profession EMPTY>
  <!ATTLIST profession value CDATA #REQUIRED>
]>
<person>
  <name first="Alan" last="Turing"/>
  <profession value="computer scientist"/>
  <profession value="mathematician"/>
  <profession value="cryptographer"/>
</person>
```

This DTD is completely contained inside the internal DTD subset and works from the top down. First, a person ELEMENT declaration states that each person must have one or more name children and zero or more profession children, in that order. This rule permits people to change their names or use aliases. It assumes that each person has at least one name, but may not have a profession.

This declaration also requires that all name elements precede all profession elements. Here the DTD is less flexible than it ideally would be; there's no particular reason why the names must come first. However, if we were to allow more random ordering, it would be hard to say that there must be at least one name. One of the weaknesses of DTDs is that it occasionally forces sequence order on you when all you really need is a constraint on the number of some element. Schemas are more flexible in this regard.

Both the name and profession elements are empty, so their declarations are very simple. The attribute declarations are a little more complex. In all three cases the form of attribute is open, so all three attributes are declared to have type CDATA. All three attributes are also required. However, note the use of comments to suggest a solution for edge cases, such as celebrities with no last names. Comments are an essential tool for making sense of otherwise obfuscated DTDs.

## *Narrative-Oriented DTDs*

DTDs

Narrative DTDs tend to be much looser and use mixed content models much more heavily than do DTDs that describe more database-like documents. Consequently, they tend to be written from the bottom up, starting with the smallest elements and building up to the largest. They also tend to use parameter entities to group similar content model and attribute lists.

Example 3-7 is a standalone DTD for biographies like the one shown in Example 2-5 of the last chapter. Notice that not everything it declares is actually present in Example 2-5. This is often the case with narrative documents. For instance, not all web pages contain unordered lists, but the XHTML DTD still needs to declare the ul element for XHTML documents that do include them. Also notice that a few attributes present in Example 2-5 have been made into fixed defaults. Thus they could be omitted from the document itself once it is attached to this DTD.

*Example 3-7: A Narrative-Oriented DTD for Biographies*

```
<!ATTLIST biography xmlns:xlink CDATA #FIXED "http://www.w3.org/1999/xlink">

<!ELEMENT person (first_name, last_name)>
<!-- Birth and death dates are given in the form yyyy/mm/dd -->
<!ATTLIST person born CDATA #IMPLIED
                 died CDATA #IMPLIED>

<!ELEMENT date   (month, day, year)>
<!ELEMENT month  (#PCDATA)>
<!ELEMENT day    (#PCDATA)>
<!ELEMENT year   (#PCDATA)>

<!-- xlink:href must contain a URI.
     xlink:type must have the value simple if it's present at all. -->
<!ATTLIST emphasize xlink:type (simple) #IMPLIED
                    xlink:href CDATA   #IMPLIED>

<!ELEMENT profession (#PCDATA)>
<!ELEMENT footnote   (#PCDATA)>

<!-- The source is given according to the Chicago Manual of Style
     citation conventions -->
<!ATTLIST footnote source CDATA #REQUIRED>
```

```
<!ELEMENT first_name (#PCDATA)>
<!ELEMENT last_name  (#PCDATA)>

<!ELEMENT image EMPTY>
<!ATTLIST image source CDATA   #REQUIRED
                width  NMTOKEN #REQUIRED
                height NMTOKEN #REQUIRED
                ALT    CDATA   #IMPLIED
>

<!ENTITY % top_level "( #PCDATA | image | paragraph | definition
                      | person | profession | emphasize | last_name
                      | first_name | footnote | date )*">

<!ELEMENT paragraph  %top_level; >
<!ELEMENT definition %top_level; >
<!ELEMENT emphasize  %top_level; >
<!ELEMENT biography  %top_level; >
```

The root `biography` element has a classic mixed content model. Since several elements can contain other elements in a fairly unpredictable fashion, we group all the possible top-level elements (elements that appear as the root element's immediate children) in a single `top_level` entity reference. Then we can make them all potential children of one another in a straightforward way. This step also makes adding new elements in the future much easier. This is important, since this one small example is almost certainly not broad enough to cover all possible biographies.

# Locating Standard DTDs

DTDs and validity are most important when you exchange data with others because they let you verify that you're sending what the receiver expects, and vice versa. Of course this arrangement works best if both ends of a conversation agree on which DTD and vocabulary they will use. Many standard DTDs exist for different professions and disciplines, and more are being created every day. Using an established DTD and vocabulary is often better than designing your own.

However, no agreed-upon, central repository that documents and links to such efforts exists. We do know of at least three attempts to create such a central repository:

- James Tauber's *schema.net* at *http://www.schema.net/*
- OASIS's *xml.org* at *http://www.xml.org/xmlorg_registry/*
- Microsoft's Biztalk initiative at *http://www.biztalk.org* (registration required)

However, none of these attempts have successfully established themselves as the standard place to list DTDs, and none of them cover more than a minority of the existing public DTDs. Indeed, probably the largest list of DTDs online does not even attempt to be a general repository; it is simply the result of collecting XML and SGML news for several years. You can find this site, Robin Cover's list of XML applications, at *http://www.oasis-open.org/cover/siteIndex.html#toc-applications.*

The W3C is one of the most prolific producers of standard XML DTDs. It has moved almost all its future development, including Scalable Vector Graphics (SVG), the Platform for Internet Content Selection (PICS), the Resource Description Framework (RDF), the Mathematical Markup Language (MathML), and even HTML itself, to XML. DTDs for these XML applications are generally published as appendixes to the specifications for the applications. The specifications are all found at *http://www.w3.org/TR/.*

However, XML isn't just for the Web, and far more activity goes on outside the W3C than inside it. Generally, within any one field, you should look to that field's standards bodies for DTDs relating to a specific area of interest. For example, the American Institute of Certified Public Accountants has published a DTD for XFRML, the Extensible Financial Reporting Markup Language. The Object Management Group (OMG) has published a DTD for describing Unified Modeling Language (UML) diagrams in XML. The Society of Automotive Engineers is working on XML applications to publish auto emissions information as required by the 1990 U.S. Clean Air Act. Chances are that in any industry that uses information technology heavily, some formal or informal group is already working on DTDs that cover parts of that industry.

CHAPTER 4

# *Namespaces*

Namespaces have two purposes in XML:

1. To distinguish between elements and attributes from different XML applications that share the same name
2. To group all related elements and attributes from a single XML application together so software can recognize them easily

The first purpose is easier to explain and grasp, but the second is more important in practice.

Namespaces are implemented by attaching a prefix to each element and attribute. Each prefix is mapped to a URI. Default URIs can also be provided for elements that don't have a prefix. Elements and attributes that are attached to the same URI are in the same namespace. Standard URIs identify elements from many XML applications.

## *The Need for Namespaces*

Some documents combine markup from multiple XML applications. For example, an XHTML document may contain both SVG pictures and MathML equations. An XSLT stylesheet contains both XSLT instructions and elements from the result tree vocabulary. And XLinks are always symbiotic with the elements of the document in which they appear, since XLink itself doesn't define any elements, only attributes.

In some cases, these applications may use the same name to refer to different things. For example, a `set` element in SVG is an abstract container used to attach a common property to a group of elements, while a `set` element in MathML represents a mathematical set, such as the set of all positive even numbers. You should know when you're working with a MathML `set` and when you're working with an SVG `set`; otherwise validation, rendering, indexing, and many other tasks will get confused and fail.

Consider Example 4-1. This example is a simple list of paintings that includes the title of each painting, the date each was painted, the artist who painted it, and a description:

*Example 4-1: A List of Paintings*

```
<?xml version="1.0" encoding="ISO-8859-1" standalone="yes"?>
<catalog>

  <painting>
    <title>Memory of the Garden at Etten</title>
    <artist>Vincent Van Gogh</artist>
    <date>November, 1888</date>
    <description>
      Two women look to the left. A third works in her garden.
    </description>
  </painting>

  <painting>
    <title>The Swing</title>
    <artist>Pierre-Auguste Renoir</artist>
    <date>1876</date>
    <description>
      A young girl on a swing. Two men and a toddler watch.
    </description>
  </painting>

  <!-- Many more paintings... -->

</catalog>
```

Now suppose Example 4-1 will be served as a web page and you want to make it accessible to search engines. Using the Resource Description Framework to embed metadata in the page is one possibility. This describes the page for any search engine or other robot that might come along. Using the Dublin Core metadata vocabulary (*http://purl.oclc.org/dc/*), a standard vocabulary for library catalog style information that can be encoded in XML or other syntaxes, an RDF description of this page might look something like:

```
<RDF>
  <Description about="http://ibiblio.org/examples/impressionists.xml">
    <title> Impressionist Paintings </dc:title>
    <creator> Elliotte Rusty Harold </creator>
    <description>
      A list of famous impressionist paintings organized
      by painter and date
    </description>
    <date>2000-08-22</date>
  </Description>
</RDF>
```

Here we've used the `Description` and `RDF` elements from RDF and the `title`, `creator`, `description`, and `date` elements from the Dublin Core. We have no choice about these names; they are established by their respective specifications. If we want standard software that understands RDF and the Dublin Core to understand our documents, we must use these names. Example 4-2 combines this description with the actual list of paintings.

*Example 4-2: A List of Paintings Including Catalog Information About the List*

```
<?xml version="1.0" encoding="ISO-8859-1" standalone="yes"?>
<catalog>

  <RDF>
    <Description
        about="http://ibiblio.org/examples/impressionists.xml">
      <title> Impressionist Paintings </title>
      <creator> Elliotte Rusty Harold </creator>
      <description>
        A list of famous impressionist paintings organized
        by painter and date
      </description>
      <date>2000-08-22</date>
    </Description>
  </RDF>

  <painting>
    <title>Memory of the Garden at Etten</title>
    <artist>Vincent Van Gogh</artist>
    <date>November, 1888</date>
    <description>
      Two women look to the left. A third works in her garden.
    </description>
  </painting>

  <painting>
    <title>The Swing</title>
    <artist>Pierre-Auguste Renoir</artist>
    <date>1876</date>
    <description>
      A young girl on a swing. Two men and a toddler watch.
    </description>
  </painting>

  <!-- Many more paintings... -->

</catalog>
```

Now we have a problem. Several elements have been overloaded with different meanings in various parts of the document. The `title` element is used for both the title of the page and the titles of the paintings. The `date` element is used for both the date when the page was written and the date when the painting was painted. One `description` element describes pages and another describes paintings.

This situation presents all sorts of problems. Validation is difficult because catalog and Dublin Core elements with the same name can have different content models.

For web browsers, you may want to hide the page description while showing the painting description, but not all stylesheet languages can distinguish between the two. Processing software may understand the date format used in the Dublin Core `date` element but not the free-form format used in the painting's `date` element.

We could change the element names and use `painting_title` instead of `title`, `date_painted` instead of `date`, and so on. However, this is inconvenient if you've already got a lot of documents marked up in the old version of the vocabulary. It also may not be possible to make this change in all cases, especially if the name collisions occur because of conflicts between two or more standard vocabularies, not because of conflicts between your vocabulary and a standard vocabulary. For instance, RDF barely avoids a collision with the Dublin Core over the `Description` and `description` elements.

In other cases, name conflicts might not occur, but it may still be important for software to quickly and decisively determine which XML application a given element or attribute belongs to. For instance, an XSLT processor needs to distinguish between XSLT instructions and literal result tree elements.

Namespaces

## *Namespace Syntax*

Namespaces disambiguate elements with the same name by assigning elements and attributes to URIs. Generally, all elements from one XML application will be assigned to one URI, and all the elements and attributes from a different XML application will be assigned to a different URI. The URIs partition the elements and attributes into disjoint sets. Elements with the same name but different URIs are different elements; elements with the same name and the same URIs are the same. There is usually a one-to-one mapping between namespaces and XML applications, though a few applications may use multiple namespaces to subdivide different parts of the application. For instance, XSL uses different namespaces for XSL Transformations (XSLT) and XSL Formatting Objects (XSL-FO).

### *Qualified Names, Prefixes, and Local Parts*

Since URIs frequently contain characters like /, %, and ~ that are not legal in XML names, short prefixes, such as `rdf` and `xsl`, stand in for them in element and attribute names. Each prefix is associated with exactly one URI. Names with prefixes associated with the same URI are in the same namespace. Names with prefixes associated with different URIs are in different namespaces. Elements and attributes in namespaces have names that contain exactly one colon:

```
rdf:description
xlink:type
xsl:template
```

Everything before the colon is called the *prefix*. Everything after the colon is called the *local part*. The complete name, including the colon, is called the *qualified name*, *QName*, or *raw name*. The prefix identifies the namespace to which the element or attribute belongs. The local part identifies the particular element or attribute within the namespace.

In a document containing both SVG and MathML `set` elements, one could be an `svg:set` element and the other a `mathml:set` element. This distinction would eliminate confusion between the elements. In an XSLT stylesheet that transformed documents into XSL formatting objects, the XSLT processor would recognize elements with the prefix `xsl` as XSLT instructions and elements with the prefix `fo` as literal result elements.

Prefixes may be composed from any legal XML name character except the colon. Prefixes beginning with the three letters "xml" (in any combination of case) are reserved for use by XML and its related specifications. Otherwise, you may name your prefixes in any convenient way. One further restriction namespaces add to XML 1.0 is that the local part may not contain colons. In short, the only legal use of a colon in XML is to separate a namespace prefix from the local part in a qualified name.

## *Binding Prefixes to URIs*

Each prefix in a qualified name must be associated with a URI. For example, all XSLT elements in XSLT 1.0 stylesheets are associated with the *http://www.w3.org/1999/XSL/Transform* URI. Customary ***prefix*** `xsl` is used in place of the longer URI *http://www.w3.org/1999/XSL/Transform.*

---

*URI Conventions*

You can't use the URI in the name directly. For one thing, the slashes in most URIs aren't legal characters in XML names. However, referring to the full name without assuming a particular prefix is occasionally useful. One convention used on many XML mailing lists and in XML documentation is to enclose the URI in curly braces and prefix it to the name. The qualified name `xsl:template` might be written as the full name `{http://www.w3.org/1999/XSL/Transform}template`. However, this form is only a convenience for communication among humans when the URI is important but the prefix isn't. Neither an XML parser nor an XSLT processor accepts or understands the long form.

---

Prefixes are bound to namespace URIs by attaching an `xmlns:`*`prefix`* attribute to the prefixed element or one of its ancestors. (*`prefix`* should be replaced by the actual prefix used.) For example, the `xmlns:rdf` attribute of this `rdf:RDF` element binds the prefix `rdf` to the namespace URI *http://www.w3.org/TR/REC-rdf-syntax#*:

```
<rdf:RDF xmlns:rdf="http://www.w3.org/TR/REC-rdf-syntax#">
 <rdf:Description about="http://ibiblio.org/examples/impressionists.xml">
    <title> Impressionist Paintings </title>
    <creator> Elliotte Rusty Harold </creator>
    <description>
      A list of famous impressionist paintings organized
      by painter and date
    </description>
```

```
    <date>2000-08-22</date>
  </rdf:Description>
</rdf:RDF>
```

Bindings have scope within the element in which they're declared and its contents. The `xmlns:rdf` attribute declares the `rdf` prefix for the `rdf:RDF` element and its child elements. An RDF processor will recognize `rdf:RDF` and `rdf:Description` as RDF elements because both have prefixes bound to the particular URI defined by the RDF specification. It will not consider the `title`, `creator`, `description`, and `date` elements RDF elements because they do not have prefixes bound to the *http://www.w3.org/TR/REC-rdf-syntax#* URI.

The prefix can be declared in the topmost element that uses the prefix, or in any ancestor thereof. This may be the document's root element or an element at a lower level. For instance, the Dublin Core elements could be attached to the *http://purl.org/dc/* namespace by adding an `xmlns:dc` attribute to the `rdf:Description` element, as shown in Example 4-3, since all Dublin Core elements in this document appear inside a single `rdf:Description` element. In documents that spread the elements out more, putting the namespace declaration in the root element start tag might be more convenient. If necessary, a single element can include multiple namespace declarations for different namespaces.

Namespaces

*Example 4-3: A Document Containing Both RDF and Dublin Core*

```
<?xml version="1.0" encoding="ISO-8859-1" standalone="yes"?>
<catalog>

  <rdf:RDF xmlns:rdf="http://www.w3.org/TR/REC-rdf-syntax#">
    <rdf:Description xmlns:dc="http://purl.org/dc/"
       about="http://ibiblio.org/examples/impressionists.xml">
      <dc:title> Impressionist Paintings </dc:title>
      <dc:creator> Elliotte Rusty Harold </dc:creator>
      <dc:description>
        A list of famous impressionist paintings organized
        by painter and date
      </dc:description>
      <dc:date>2000-08-22</dc:date>
    </rdf:Description>
  </rdf:RDF>

  <painting>
    <title>Memory of the Garden at Etten</title>
    <artist>Vincent Van Gogh</artist>
    <date>November, 1888</date>
    <description>
      Two women look to the left. A third works in her garden.
    </description>
  </painting>

  <painting>
    <title>The Swing</title>
    <artist>Pierre-Auguste Renoir</artist>
    <date>1876</date>
```

*Example 4-3: A Document Containing Both RDF and Dublin Core (continued)*

```
    <description>
      A young girl on a swing. Two men and a toddler watch.
    </description>
  </painting>

  <!-- Many more paintings... -->

</catalog>
```

A DTD for this document can include different content models for the `dc:description` and `description` elements. A stylesheet can attach different styles to `dc:title` and `title`. Software that sorts the catalog by date can pay attention to the `date` elements and ignore the `dc:date` elements.

In this example, the elements without prefixes such as `catalog`, `painting`, `description`, `artist`, and `title` are not in any namespace. Furthermore, unprefixed attributes, such as the `about` attribute of `rdf:Description` in the previous example, are never in a namespace. Being an attribute of an element in the *http://www.w3.org/TR/REC-rdf-syntax#* namespace is not sufficient to put the attribute in the *http://www.w3.org/TR/REC-rdf-syntax#* namespace. The only way an attribute belongs to a namespace is if it has a declared prefix, such as `xlink:type` and `xlink:href`.

It is possible to redefine a prefix within a document, so that the prefix refers to one namespace URI in one element but refers to a different namespace URI in another. In this case, the closest ancestor element that declares the prefix takes precedence. However, in most cases redefining prefixes is a very bad idea that only leads to confusion, not something you should actually do.

## *Namespace URIs*

Many XML applications have customary prefixes. For example, SVG elements often use the prefix `svg` and Resource Description Framework (RDF) elements often have the prefix `rdf`. However, these prefixes are simply conventions and can be changed based on necessity, convenience, or whim. Before a prefix can be used, it must be bound to a URI like *http://www.w3.org/2000/svg* or *http://www.w3.org/1999/02/22-rdf-syntax-ns#*. The URIs, not the prefixes, are standardized. The prefix can change as long as the URI stays the same. An RDF processor looks for the URI, not a particular prefix. As long as nobody outside the *w3.org* domain uses namespace URIs in the *w3.org* domain, and if the W3C can monitor what its people use for namespaces, all conflicts can be avoided.

Namespace URIs do not necessarily point to an actual document or page. In fact, they don't have to use the *http* scheme. They might even use another protocol, such as *mailto*, in which URIs don't even point to documents. However, if you define your own namespace using an *http* URI, placing documentation for the specification at the namespace URI would not be a bad idea. The W3C got tired of receiving broken link reports for the namespace URIs in their specifications, so they added simple pages at their namespace URIs. You are by no means required to do this, though. Many namespace URIs lead to 404-Not Found errors when you plug them into a web browser. Namespace URIs are purely formal identifiers; they are not the addresses of a page and are not meant to be followed as links.

Parsers compare namespace URIs on a character-by-character basis. If the URIs differ in even one normally insignificant place, then they define separate namespaces. For instance, *http://www.w3.org/1999/XSL/Transform*, *http://www.W3.ORG/1999/XSL/Transform*, *http://www.w3.org/1999/XSL/Transform/*, and *http://www.w3.org/1999/XSL/Transform/index.html* might all point to the same page. However, only the first is legal in XSLT stylesheets. If all four were used, they would create four separate namespaces.

## Setting a Default Namespace with the xmlns Attribute

You often know that all content of a particular element comes from a particular XML application. For instance, you're likely to only find other SVG elements inside a Scalable Vector Graphics (SVG) `svg` element. You can indicate that an unprefixed element and all its unprefixed descendant elements belong to a particular namespace by attaching an `xmlns` attribute with no prefix to the top element:

```
<svg xmlns="http://www.w3.org/2000/svg"
     width="12cm" height="10cm">
  <ellipse rx="110" ry="130" />
  <rect x="4cm" y="1cm" width="3cm" height="6cm" />
</svg>
```

Here, though no elements have prefixes, the `svg`, `ellipse`, and `rect` elements are in the *http://www.w3.org/2000/svg* namespace.

The attributes are a different story. Default namespaces apply only to elements, not to attributes. In this example the `width`, `height`, `rx`, `ry`, `x`, and `y` attributes are not in a namespace.

You can change the default namespace within a particular element by adding an `xmlns` attribute to the element. Example 4-4 is an XML document that initially sets the default namespace to *http://www.w3.org/1999/xhtml* for all the XHTML elements. This namespace declaration applies within most of the document. However, the `svg` element has an `xmlns` attribute that resets the default namespace to *http://www.w3.org/2000/svg* for itself and its content. The XLink information is included in attributes, however, so the attributes must be placed in the XLink namespace, using explicit prefixes.

*Example 4-4: An XML Document That Uses Default Namespaces*

```
<?xml version="1.0"?>
<html xmlns="http://www.w3.org/1999/xhtml"
      xmlns:xlink="http://www.w3.org/1999/xlink">
  <head><title>Three Namespaces</title></head>
  <body>
    <h1 align="center">An Ellipse and a Rectangle</h1>
    <svg xmlns="http://www.w3.org/2000/svg"
         width="12cm" height="10cm">
      <ellipse rx="110" ry="130" />
      <rect x="4cm" y="1cm" width="3cm" height="6cm" />
    </svg>
```

*Example 4-4: An XML Document That Uses Default Namespaces (continued)*

```
    <p xlink:type="simple" xlink:href="ellipses.html">
      More about ellipses
    </p>
    <p xlink:type="simple" xlink:href="rectangles.html">
      More about rectangles
    </p>
    <hr/>
    <p>Last Modified May 13, 2000</p>
  </body>
</html>
```

The default namespace does not apply to elements or attributes with prefixes, which still belong to whatever namespace their prefix is bound to. However, an unprefixed child element of a prefixed element may still belong to the default namespace.

### Attribute Declarations for xmlns

When namespaces are used only to identify the elements and attributes from a particular XML application, and not to distinguish different elements with the same name, a DTD can attach a fixed `xmlns` attribute to the primary container elements for an application to ensure that everything is placed in the right namespace without explicit `xmlns` attributes in the document. For example, this `ATTLIST` declaration fixes the default namespace of all `svg` elements as *http://www.w3.org/2000/*:

```
<!ATTLIST svg xmlns CDATA #FIXED "http://www.w3.org/2000/">
```

This allows you to omit `xmlns` attributes from all your `svg` elements.

A document does not need to be valid to take advantage of this omission. All that's required is that the parser read the DTD. All parsers read the internal DTD subset and process any `ATTLIST` declarations they find there. A few nonvalidating parsers may skip external DTD subsets and thus become confused. Ideally, you should use a parser that can validate so it can read the external DTD subset, though you might use it with validation turned off.

## How Parsers Handle Namespaces

Namespaces were added to XML 1.0 after the fact. However, care was taken to ensure backward compatibility. Thus, an XML 1.0 parser that does not know about namespaces should have no trouble reading a document that uses namespaces. Colons are legal characters in XML 1.0 element and attribute names. The parser simply reports that some names contain colons. The only possible problems occur when different qualified names resolve to the same full name, or when the same qualified name indicates a different full name in different parts of a document.

A namespace-aware parser does add a couple of checks to the normal well-formedness checks that it performs. Specifically, it ensures that all prefixes are mapped to URIs. It rejects documents that use unmapped prefixes, except for `xml` and `xmlns`, when used as specified in the XML 1.0 or Namespaces in XML specifications. It further rejects element or attribute names that contain more than one colon. Otherwise, it behaves almost exactly like a non-namespace-aware parser. Other software that sits on top of the raw XML parser, an XSLT engine, for example, may treat elements differently, depending on what namespace they belong to. However, the XML parser itself usually doesn't care, as long as all well-formedness and namespace constraints are met.

A possible exception occurs in the unlikely event that elements with different prefixes belong to the same namespace. In this case, a namespace-aware parser reports that the elements are the same, while a non-namespace-aware parser reports them as different. Equally unlikely is the case when two elements or attributes with the same qualified name are in different namespaces because the common prefix is bound to different URIs in different places in the document. Having two unprefixed names placed in different default namespaces is slightly more likely. In both these cases, a namespace-aware processor reports them as different, whereas a non-namespace-aware processor treats them as if they are the same. Many parsers let you turn namespace processing on or off as you see fit.

## *Namespaces and DTDs*

Namespaces are completely independent of DTDs and can be used in both valid and invalid documents. A document can have a DTD but not use namespaces or use namespaces but not have a DTD. It can use both namespaces and DTDs or neither namespaces nor DTDs. Namespaces do not change DTD syntax in any way or change the definition of validity. For instance, the DTD of a valid document using an element named `dc:title` must include an `ELEMENT` declaration that lays out the `dc:title` element's content properly:

```
<!ELEMENT dc:title (#PCDATA)>
```

The name of the element in the document must match the name of the element in the DTD, including the prefix, exactly. The DTD cannot omit the prefix and simply declare a `title` element. Prefixed attributes operate in a similar manner. For instance, if an element used in the document has `xlink:type` and `xlink:href` attributes, then the DTD must declare the `xlink:type` and `xlink:href` attributes, not simply `type` and `href`.

Conversely, if an element uses an `xmlns` attribute to set the default namespace and does not attach prefixes to elements, the names of the elements must be declared without prefixes in the DTD. The validator neither knows nor cares about namespaces. All it sees is that some element and attribute names happen to contain colons; and as far as it's concerned, such names are perfectly valid as long as they're declared.

### *Parameter Entity References for Namespace Prefixes*

Requiring DTDs to declare the prefixed names instead of the raw names or some combination of local part and namespace URIs makes it difficult to change the prefix in valid documents. The problem is that changing the prefix requires changing all declarations that use that prefix in the DTD as well. However, with a little forethought, parameter entity references can alleviate the pain quite a bit.

First, define both the namespace prefix and the colon that separates the prefix from the local name as parameter entities:

```
<!ENTITY % dc-prefix "dc">
<!ENTITY % dc-colon ":">
```

Second, define the qualified names as more parameter entity references:

```
<!ENTITY % dc-title       "%dc-prefix;%dc-colon;title">
<!ENTITY % dc-creator     "%dc-prefix;%dc-colon;creator">
<!ENTITY % dc-description "%dc-prefix;%dc-colon;description">
<!ENTITY % dc-date        "%dc-prefix;%dc-colon;date">
```

---

***Defining Qualified Names***

Do not omit this step and try to use the `dc-prefix` and `dc-colon` parameter entities directly in `ELEMENT` and `ATTLIST` declarations. This option would fail because XML parsers add extra space around the entity's replacement text when they're used outside another entity's replacement text.

---

Then use the entity references for the qualified name in all declarations:

```
<!ELEMENT %dc-title; (#PCDATA)>
<!ELEMENT %dc-creator; (#PCDATA)>
<!ELEMENT %dc-description; (#PCDATA)>
<!ELEMENT %dc-date; (#PCDATA)>
<!ELEMENT rdf:Description
  ((%dc-title; | %dc-creator; | %dc-description; | %dc-date; | )*)
>
```

Now a document that needs to change the prefix also changes the parameter entity definitions. In some cases, editing the DTD directly will change the definitions. In others, it may be done by overriding the definitions in the document's own internal DTD subset. For example, to change the prefix from `dc` to `dublin`, add this entity definition somewhere in your DTD before the normal definition:

```
<!ENTITY % dc-prefix "dublin">
```

If you wanted to use `xmlns` instead of explicit prefixes, redefine both the `dc-prefix` and `dc-colon` entities as the empty string:

```
<!ENTITY % dc-prefix "">
<!ENTITY % dc-colon  "">
```

# CHAPTER 5

# *Internationalization*



We've told you that XML documents contain text, but we haven't yet told you what kind of text they contain. In this chapter we rectify that omission. XML documents contain Unicode text. Unicode is a character set large enough to include all the world's living languages and a few dead ones. It can be written in a variety of encodings, including UCS-2 and the ASCII superset UTF-8. However, since Unicode text editors are relatively uncommon, XML documents may also be written in other character sets and encodings, which are converted to Unicode when the document is parsed. The encoding declaration specifies which character set a document uses. You can use character references, such as `θ` to insert Unicode characters like θ that aren't available in the legacy character set in which a document is written.

Computers don't really understand text. They don't recognize the Latin letter *Z*, the Greek letter γ, or the Han ideograph 齵. All a computer understands are numbers such as 90, 947, or 40,821. A *character set* maps particular characters, like *Z*, to particular numbers, like 90. These numbers are called *code points*. A *character encoding* determines how those code points are represented in bytes. For instance the code point 90 can be encoded as a signed byte, a little-endian unsigned short, a 4-byte, two's complement, big-endian integer, or in an even more complicated fashion.

A human script like Cyrillic may be written in multiple character sets, such as KOI8-R, Unicode, or ISO 8859-5. A character set like Unicode may then be encoded in multiple encodings, such as UTF-8, UCS-2, or UTF-16. In general, however, simpler character sets like ASCII and KOI8-R have only one encoding.

## *The Encoding Declaration*

Every XML document should have an encoding declaration as part of its XML declaration. The encoding declaration tells the parser what character set the document is written in. For example, this XML declaration says that the document uses the character encoding US-ASCII:

```
<?xml version="1.0" encoding="US-ASCII" standalone="yes"?>
```

This one states that the document uses the Latin-1 character set, though it uses the more official name ISO-8859-1:

```
<?xml version="1.0" encoding="ISO-8859-1"?>
```

When an XML parser reads a document, it translates characters from the document's native encoding, as specified by the encoding declaration, into Unicode. Not all parsers know how to convert all encodings, but most major parsers can handle the character sets you're most likely to encounter.

The encoding declaration may be omitted if and only if the document is written in either the UTF-8 or the UTF-16 encodings of Unicode. UTF-8 is a strict superset of ASCII, so ASCII files can be legal XML documents without an encoding declaration. Note, however, that this situation applies only to genuine, pure seven-bit ASCII files. It does not include the extended ASCII character sets that some editors produce with characters like ©, ç, or ".

## *Text Declarations*

XML documents may be composed of multiple parsed entities, as you learned in Chapter 3, *Document Type Definitions*. These external parsed entities may be DTD fragments or chunks of XML that will be inserted into the master document using external general entity references. In either case, the external parsed entity does not necessarily use the same character set as the master document. Indeed, one external parsed entity may be referenced in several different files, each of which is written in a different character set. Therefore specifying the character set for an external parsed entity independently of the character set the including document uses is important.

To accomplish this task, each external parsed entity should have a *text declaration*. If present, the text declaration must be the first thing in the external parsed entity. For example, this text declaration says that the associated entity is encoded in the KOI8-R character set:

```
<?xml version="1.0" encoding="KOI8-R"?>
```

The text declaration looks like an XML declaration. It has version info and an encoding declaration. However, a text declaration may not have a standalone declaration. Furthermore, the version info may be omitted. A legal text declaration that specifies the encoding as KOI8-R might look like this:

```
<?xml encoding="KOI8-R"?>
```

However, it is not a legal XML declaration.

Example 5-1 shows an external parsed entity containing several verses from Pushkin's *The Bronze Horseman* in a Cyrillic script.* The text declaration identifies

* *http://www.ocf.berkeley.edu/%7Eleong/Russkaya%20Literatura/Aleksandr%20Sergeevich%20Pushkin/Mednyi%20vsadnik/frame.htm*

the encoding as KOI8-R. Example 5-1 is not itself a well-formed XML document because it has no root element. It exists only for inclusion in other documents.

*Example 5-1: An External Parsed Entity with a Text Declaration Identifying the Character Set as KOI8-R*

```
<?xml version="1.0" encoding="KOI8-R"?>
<стих>Была ужасная пора,</стих>
<стих>Об ней свежо воспоминанье...</стих>
<стих>Об ней друзья мои, для вас</стих>
<стих>Начну свое повествованье.</стих>
<стих>Печален будет мой рассказ</стих>
```

External DTD subsets reside in external parsed entities, and thus may have text declarations. Indeed, they should have text declarations if they're written in a character set other than one of the Unicode's variants. Example 5-2 shows a DTD fragment written in KOI8-R that might be used to validate Example 5-1 after it is included as part of a larger document.

*Example 5-2: A DTD with a Text Declaration Identifying the Character Set as KOI8-R*

```
<?xml version="1.0" encoding="KOI8-R"?>
<!ELEMENT стих (#PCDATA)>
```

## *XML-Defined Character Sets*



An XML parser is required to handle the UF-16 and UTF-8 encodings or Unicode. However, XML processors are allowed to understand and process many other character sets. In particular, processors are recommended to recognize and be able to read these encodings:

| | |
|---|---|
| UTF-8 | UTF-16 |
| ISO-10646-UCS-2 | ISO-10646-UCS-4 |
| ISO-8859-1 | ISO-8859-2 |
| ISO-8859-3 | ISO-8859-4 |
| ISO-8859-5 | ISO-8859-6 |
| ISO-8859-7 | ISO-8859-8 |
| ISO-8859-9 | ISO-2022-JP |
| Shift_JIS | EUC-JP |

Many XML processors understand other legacy encodings. For instance, processors written in Java often understand all character sets available in a typical Java virtual machine. For a list, see *http://java.sun.com/products/jdk/1.3/docs/guide/intl/encoding.doc.html*. Furthermore, some processors may recognize aliases for these encodings; both Latin-1 and 8859_1 are sometimes used as synonyms for ISO-8859-1. However, using these names limits your document's portability. We recommend that you use standard names for standard encodings. For encodings whose standard name isn't given by the XML 1.0 specification, use one of the names registered with the Internet Assigned Numbers Authority (IANA) and listed at *ftp://ftp.isi.edu/in-notes/iana/assignments/character-sets*. However, knowing the name of a character set and saving a file in that set does not mean that your XML processor can read such a file. XML processors are only required to support UTF-8 and UTF-16. They are not required to support the hundreds of different legacy encodings used around the world.

## *Unicode*

Unicode is an international standard character set that can be used to write documents in almost any language you're likely to speak, learn, or encounter in your lifetime, barring abduction by aliens. Version 3.0.1, the current version as of winter 2000, contains 49,194 characters. Unicode easily covers the Latin alphabet, in which most of this book is written. Unicode also covers Greek-derived scripts, including ancient and modern Greek and the Cyrillic scripts used in Serbia and much of the former Soviet Union. Unicode covers several ideographic scripts, including the Han character set used for Chinese and Japanese, the Korean Hangul syllabary, and phonetic representations of these languages, including Katakana and Hiragana. It covers the right-to-left Arabic and Hebrew scripts. It covers various scripts native to the Indian subcontinent, including Devanagari, Thai, Bengali, and Tibetan. And that's still less than half of the scripts in Unicode 3.0. Probably less than one person in a thousand today speaks a language that cannot be reasonably represented in Unicode. In the future, Unicode will add still more characters, making this fraction even smaller. Unicode can potentially hold more than a million characters, but no one is willing to say in public where they think most of the remaining million characters will come from.*

The Unicode character set assigns characters to code points: that is, numbers. These numbers can then be encoded in a variety of schemes, including:

- UCS-2
- UCS-4
- UTF-8
- UTF-16

## *UCS-2 and UTF-16*

UCS-2, also known as ISO-10646-UCS-2, is perhaps the most natural encoding of Unicode. It represents each character as a two-byte, unsigned integer between 0 and 65,535. Thus the capital letter *A*, code point 65 in Unicode, is represented by the two bytes 00 and 41 (in hexadecimal). The capital letter *B*, code point 66, is represented by the two bytes 00 and 42. The two bytes 03 and A3 represent the capital Greek letter Σ, code point 931.

UCS-2 comes in two variations, big endian and little endian. In big-endian UCS-2, the most significant byte of the character comes first. In little-endian UCS-2, the order is reversed. Thus in big-endian UCS-2 the letter *A* is #x0041.† In little-endian

* Privately, some developers are willing to admit that they're preparing for a day when we're part of a Galactic Federation of thousands of intelligent species.

† For reasons that will become apparent shortly, this book has adopted the convention that **#x** precedes hexadecimal numbers. Every two hexadecimal digits map to one byte.

UCS-2, the bytes are swapped and *A* is #x4100. In big-endian UCS-2, the letter *B* is #x0042. In little-endian UCS-2, it's #x4200. In big-endian UCS-2, the letter Σ is #x03A3. In little-endian UCS-2, it's #xA303. In this book we use big-endian notation, but parsers cannot assume this. They must be able to determine the endianness from the document itself.

To distinguish between big-endian and little-endian UCS-2, a document encoded in UCS-2 customarily begins with Unicode character #xFEFF, the zero-width nonbreaking space, more commonly called the *byte order mark*. This character has the advantage of being invisible. Furthermore, if its bytes are swapped, the resulting #xFFFE character doesn't actually exist. Thus a program can look at the first two bytes of a UCS-2 document and tell immediately whether or not the document is big endian, depending on whether those bytes are #xFEFF or #xFFFE.

UCS-2 has three major disadvantages, however:

- Files containing mostly Latin text are about twice as large in UCS-2 as they are in a single-byte character set, such as ASCII or Latin-1.
- UCS-2 is not backward or forward compatible with ASCII. Tools that are accustomed to single-byte character sets often can't process a UCS-2 file in a reasonable way, even if the file only contains characters from the ASCII character set. For instance, a program written in C that expects the zero byte to terminate strings will choke on a UCS-2 file containing mostly English text because almost every other byte is zero.
- UCS-2 is limited to 65,536 characters.

The last problem isn't so important in practice, since Unicode currently defines fewer than 65,536 characters and nonetheless manages to cover most people's needs except for dead languages and fictional scripts, such as Phoenician and Klingon. Unicode does, however, provide a means of representing code points beyond 65,535 by recognizing certain two-byte sequences as half of a surrogate pair. A Unicode document that uses UCS-2 plus surrogate pairs is said to be in the UTF-16 encoding. Since no software currently supports or produces surrogate pairs, and since no scripts are encoded in Unicode with code points above 65,535, the distinction between UCS-2 and UTF-16 is mostly academic at this point.

The other two problems, however, are quite real. UTF-8 is an alternative encoding for Unicode that addresses both.

## *UTF-8*

UTF-8 is a variable-length encoding of Unicode. Characters 0 through 127, that is, the ASCII character set, are encoded in one byte each, exactly as they would be in ASCII. In ASCII, the byte with value 65 represents the letter *A*. In UTF-8 the byte with the value 65 also represents the letter *A*. There is a one-to-one identity mapping from ASCII characters to UTF-8 bytes. Thus, pure ASCII files are also acceptable UTF-8 files.

UTF-8 represents characters 128 to 2047, a range that covers the most common nonideographic scripts, in two bytes each. The remaining characters, mostly from Chinese, Japanese, and Korean, are represented in three bytes each. When characters with code points above 65,535 are added to Unicode, they will be encoded in four bytes each. For a file that's mostly Latin text, this system effectively halves the file size from what it would be in UCS-2. However, for a file that's primarily Japanese, Chinese, or Korean, the file size can grow by 50 percent. For other scripts, the file size is close to the same.

UTF-8 is probably the most broadly supported encoding of Unicode. For instance, it's how Java *.class* files store strings; it's the native encoding of the BeOS; and it's the default encoding an XML processor assumes unless told otherwise by a byte-order mark or an encoding declaration. Chances are pretty good that if a program tells you it's saving Unicode, it's really saving UTF-8.

## ISO Character Sets

Unicode has only recently become popular. Previously the space and processing costs associated with Unicode files prompted vendors to prefer smaller, single-byte character sets that could only handle English and a few other languages of interest, but not the full panoply of human language. The International Standards Organization (ISO) has standardized 14 of these character sets as ISO standard 8859. For all of these single-byte character sets, characters 0 through 127 are identical to the ASCII character set; characters 128 through 159 are the C1 controls; and characters 160 through 255 are the additional characters needed for scripts such as Greek, Cyrillic, and Turkish.

*ISO-8859-1 (Latin-1)*
: ASCII plus the accented letters and other characters needed for most Latin-alphabet Western European languages, including Danish, Dutch, Finnish, French, German, Icelandic, Italian, Norwegian, Portuguese, Spanish, and Swedish.

*ISO-8859-2 (Latin-2)*
: ASCII plus the accented letters and other characters needed to write most Latin-alphabet Central and Eastern European languages, including Czech, English, German, Hungarian, Polish, Romanian, Croatian, Slovak, Slovenian, and Sorbian.

*ISO-8859-3 (Latin-3)*
: ASCII plus the accented letters and other characters needed to write Esperanto, Maltese, and Turkish.

*ISO-8859-4 (Latin-4)*
: ASCII plus the accented letters and other characters needed to write most Baltic languages, including Estonian, Latvian, Lithuanian, Greenlandic, and Lappish. Now deprecated. New applications should use 8859-10 (Latin-6) or 8859-13 (Latin-7) instead.

*ISO-8859-5*
: ASCII plus the Cyrillic alphabet used for Russian and many other languages of the former Soviet Union and other Slavic countries, including Bulgarian, Byelorussian, Macedonian, Serbian, and Ukrainian.

*ISO-8859-6*

ASCII plus basic Arabic. However, the character set doesn't have the extra letters needed for non-Arabic languages written in the Arabic script, such as Farsi and Urdu.

*ISO-8859-7*

ASCII plus modern Greek. This set does not have the extra letters and accents necessary for ancient and Byzantine Greek.

*ISO-8859-8*

ASCII plus the Hebrew script used for Hebrew and Yiddish.

*ISO-8859-9 (Latin-5)*

Essentially the same as Latin-1, except six letters used in Icelandic have been replaced with six letters used in Turkish.

*ISO-8859-10 (Latin-6)*

ASCII plus accented letters and other characters needed to write most Baltic languages, including Estonian, Icelandic, Latvian, Lithuanian, Greenlandic, and Lappish.

*ISO-8859-11*

ASCII plus Thai.

*ISO-8859-13 (Latin-7)*

Yet another attempt to cover the Baltic region properly. Very similar to Latin-6, except for some question marks.

*ISO-8859-14 (Latin-8)*

ASCII plus the Celtic languages, including Gaelic and Welsh.

*ISO-8859-15 (Latin-9, Latin-0)*

A revised version of Latin-1 that replaces some unnecessary symbols, such as π, with extra French and Finnish letters. Instead of the international currency sign, these sets include the Euro sign €.

Various national standards bodies have produced other character sets to cover scripts and languages of interest within their geographic and political boundaries. For example, the Korea Industrial Standards Association developed the KS C 5601-1992 standard for encoding Korean. These national standard character sets can be used in XML documents as well, provided that you include the proper encoding declaration in the document and your parser knows how to translate these character sets into Unicode.

## Platform-Dependent Character Sets

In addition to the standard character sets discussed previously, many vendors have at one time or another produced proprietary character sets to meet the needs of their specific platform. Often, they contain special characters the vendor saw a need for, such as Apple's trademarked open apple  or the box-drawing characters like ╒ and ╡ used for cell boundaries in early DOS spreadsheets. Microsoft, IBM, and Apple are the three most prolific inventors of character sets. The single most common such set is probably Microsoft's Cp1252, a variant of Latin-1 that replaces the C1 controls with more graphic characters. Hundreds of such platform-dependent character sets are in use today. Documentation for these ranges from excellent to nonexistent.

Platform-specific character sets like these should be used only within a single system. They should never be placed on the wire or used to transfer data between systems. Doing so can lead to nasty surprises in unexpected places. For example, displaying a file that contains some of the extra Cp1252 characters ‹, ‰, ˆ, *f*, ", †, …, ‡, œ, Œ, •, ‘, ’, “, ”, –, —, Ÿ, š, ™, ›, and ~ on a VT-220 terminal can effectively disable the screen. Nonetheless these character sets are in common use and often seen on the Web even when they don't belong there. There's no absolute rule that says you can't use them for an XML document, provided that you include the proper encoding declaration and your parser understands it. The one advantage to using these sets is that existing text editors are likely to be much more comfortable with them than with Unicode and its friends. Nonetheless, we strongly recommend that you don't use them and stick to the documented standards that are much more broadly supported across platforms.

### *Cp1252*

The most common platform-dependent character set, and the one you're most likely to encounter on the Internet, is Cp1252, also (and incorrectly) known as *Windows ANSI.* This is the default character set used by most American and Western European Windows PCs, which explains its ubiquity. Cp1252 is a single-byte character set almost identical to the standard ISO-8859-1 character set—indeed, many Cp1252 documents are often incorrectly labeled as being Latin-1 documents. However, this set replaces the C1 controls between code points 128 and 159 with additional graphics characters, such as ‰, ‡, and Ÿ. These characters won't cause problems on other Windows systems. However, other platforms will have difficulty viewing them properly and may even crash in extreme cases. Cp1252 (and its siblings used in non-Western Windows systems) should be avoided.

### *MacRoman*

The Mac OS uses a different nonstandard, single-byte character set that's a superset of ASCII. The version used in the Americas and most of Western Europe is called MacRoman. Variants for other countries include MacGreek, MacHebrew, MacIceland, and so forth. Most Java-based XML processors can make sense out of these encodings if they're properly labeled, but most other non-Macintosh tools cannot. For instance, if the French sentence "Je l'ai cherché de tous bords, tous côtés" (I looked for him everywhere) is written on a Macintosh and then read on a PC, the PC user will see "Je lÕai cherchŽ de tous bords, tous c™tŽs," not the same thing at all. Generally the result is at least marginally intelligible if most of the text is ASCII, but it certainly doesn't lend itself to high fidelity or quality. Mac-specific character sets should also be avoided.

## *Converting Between Character Sets*

The ultimate solution to this character set morass is to use Unicode in either UTF-16 or UTF-8 format for all your XML documents. An increasing number of tools support one of these two formats natively; even the unassuming Notepad offers an option to save files in Unicode in Windows NT 4.0 and 2000. Microsoft Word 97 and later saves the text of its documents in Unicode, though unlike XML documents, Word files are hardly pure text. Much of the binary data in a Word file is not Unicode or any other kind of text. However, Word 2000 can actually save plain text files into Unicode and is the authors' Unicode editor of choice these days when we need to type a document in several different, complex scripts. To save Word 2000 as plain Unicode text, select the format Encoded Text from the Save As Type: Choice menu in Word's Save As dialog box. Then select one of the four Unicode formats in the resulting File Conversion dialog box.

Nonetheless, as we enter the third millennium, most of our tools are still adapted primarily for vendor-specific character sets that can't handle more than a few languages at one time. Thus, learning how to convert your documents from proprietary to more standard character sets is crucial.

Some of the better XML and HTML editors let you choose the character set you wish to save in and perform automatic conversions from the native character set you use for editing. On Unix, the native character set is likely one of the standard ISO character sets, and you can save into that format directly. On the Mac, you can avoid problems if you stick to pure ASCII documents. On Windows, you can go a little further and use Latin-1, if you're careful to stay away from the extra characters that aren't part of the official ISO 8859-1 specification. Otherwise you'll have to convert your document from its native, platform-dependent encoding to one of the standard platform-independent character sets.

François Pinard has written an open source character set conversion tool called *recode* for Linux and Unix, which you can download from *http://www.iro.umontreal.ca/contrib/recode/* as well as the usual GNU mirror sites. Wojciech Galazka has ported recode to DOS. See *ftp://ftp.simtel.net/pub/simtelnet/gnu/djgpp/v2gnu/rcode34b.zip*. You can also use the Java Development Kit's *native2ascii* tool at *http://java.sun.com/products/jdk/1.3/docs/tooldocs/win32/native2ascii.html*. First convert the file from its native encoding to Java's special ASCII-encoded Unicode format; then use the same tool in reverse to convert from the Java format to the encoding you actually want. For example, to convert the file *myfile.xml* from the Windows Cp1252 encoding to UTF-8, execute these two commands in sequence:

```
% native2ascii -encoding Cp1252 myfile.xml myfile.jtx
% native2ascii -reverse -encoding UTF-8 myfile.jtx myfile.xml
```

## *The Default Character Set for XML Documents*

Before an XML parser can read a document, it must know which character set and encoding the document uses. In some cases, external meta-information tells the parser what encoding the document uses. For instance, an HTTP header may include a Content-type header like this:

```
Content-type: text/html; charset=ISO-8859-1
```

However, XML parsers generally can't count on the availability of such information. Even if they can, they can't necessarily assume that it's accurate. Therefore an XML parser will attempt to guess the character set based on the first several bytes of the document. The main checks the parser makes include:

- If the first two bytes of the document bytes are #xFEFF, then the parser recognizes the bytes as the Unicode *byte-order mark*. It then guesses that the document is written in the big-endian, UCS-2 encoding of Unicode. With that knowledge it can read the rest of the document.
- If the first two bytes of the document are #xFFFE, however, then the parser recognizes the little-endian form of the Unicode byte-order mark. It now knows that the document is written in the little-endian, UCS-2 encoding of Unicode, and with that knowledge it can read the rest of the document.
- If the first four bytes of the document are #x3C3F786D, that is, the ASCII characters `<?xm`, then it guesses that the file is written in a superset of ASCII. In particular it assumes that the file is written in the UTF-8 encoding of Unicode. Even if it's wrong, this information is sufficient to continue reading the document until it gets to the encoding declaration and finds out what the character set really is.

Parsers that understand EBCDIC or UCS-4 may also apply similar heuristics to detect those encodings. However, UCS-4 isn't really used yet and is mostly of theoretical interest, and EBCDIC is a legacy family of character sets that shouldn't be used in new documents. Neither of these sets are important in practice.

## Character References

Unicode contains almost 50,000 different characters covering almost all of the world's written languages. Predefining entity references for each of these characters, most of which will never be used in any one document, would impose an excessive burden on XML parsers. Rather than pick and choose which characters are worthy of being encoded as entities, XML goes to the other extreme. It predefines entity references only for characters that have special meaning as markup in an XML document: <, >, &, ", and '. All these are ASCII characters that are easy to type in any text editor.

For other characters that may not be accessible from an ASCII text editor, XML lets you use *character references*. A character reference gives the number of the particular Unicode character it stands for, in either decimal or hexadecimal. Decimal character references look like `њ`; hexadecimal character references have an extra `x` after the `&#`; that is, they look like `њ`. Both of these references refer to the same character, њ, the Cyrillic small letter "nje" used in Serbian and Macedonian. For example, suppose you want to include the Greek maxim "σοφός εαυτόν γιγνωσκει" ("The wise man knows himself") in your XML document. However, you only have an ASCII text editor at your disposal. You can replace each Greek letter with the correct character reference like this:

```
<maxim>
  &#x3C3;&#x3BF;&#x3C6;&#x3CC;&#x3C2;
  &#x3AD;&#x3B1;&#x3C5;&#x3C4;&#x3CC;&#x3BD;
  &#x3B3;&#x3B9;&#x3B3;&#x3BD;&#x3CE;&#x3C3;&#x3BA;&#x3B5;&#x3B9;
</maxim>
```

To the XML processor, a document using character entity references referring to Unicode characters that don't exist in the current encoding is equivalent to a Unicode document in which all character references are replaced by the actual characters they refer to. In other words, this XML document is the same as the previous one:

```
<maxim>
  σοφός εαυτόν γιγνωσκει
</maxim>
```

Character references may be used in element content, attribute values, and comments. They may not be used in element and attribute names, processing instruction targets, or XML keywords, such as `DOCTYPE` or `ELEMENT`. They may be used in the DTD in attribute default values and entity replacement text. Tag and attribute names may be written in languages such as Greek, Russian, Arabic, or Chinese, but you must use a character set that allows you to include the appropriate characters natively. You can't insert these characters with character references. For instance, this is well-formed:

```
<λογος>
  &#x3C3;&#x3BF;&#x3C6;&#x3CC;&#x3C2;
</λογος>
```

This is not well-formed:

```
<&#x3BB;&#x3BF;&#x3B3;&#x3BF;&#x3C2;>
  &#x3C3;&#x3BF;&#x3C6;&#x3CC;&#x3C2;
</&#x3BB;&#x3BF;&#x3B3;&#x3BF;&#x3C2;>
```

Chapter 23, *Character Sets*, provides character codes in both decimal and hexadecimal for some of the most useful and widely used alphabetic scripts. The interested reader will find the complete set in *The Unicode Standard Version 3.0* by the Unicode Consortium (Addison Wesley, 2000). You can also view the code charts online at *http://www.unicode.org/charts/*.

If you use a particular group of character references frequently, you may find it easier to define them as entities; then refer to the entities instead. Example 5-3 shows a DTD defining the entities you might use to spell out the Greek words in the previous several examples.

*Example 5-3: A DTD That Defines General Entity References for Several Greek Letters*

```
<!ENTITY sigma                "&#x3C3;">
<!ENTITY omicron_with_tonos "&#x3CC;">
<!ENTITY phi                  "&#x3C6;">
<!ENTITY omicron              "&#x3BF;">
<!ENTITY final_sigma          "&#x3C2;">
<!ENTITY epsilon_with_tonos "&#x3AD;">
<!ENTITY alpha                "&#x3B1;">
<!ENTITY lambda               "&#x3C3;">
<!ENTITY upsilon              "&#x3C5;">
<!ENTITY tau                  "&#x3C4;">
<!ENTITY nu                   "&#x3BD;">
<!ENTITY gamma                "&#x3B3;">
```

*Example 5-3: A DTD That Defines General Entity References for Several Greek Letters (continued)*

```
<!ENTITY iota                "&#x3B9;">
<!ENTITY omega_with_tonos    "&#x3CE;">
<!ENTITY kappa               "&#x3BA;">
<!ENTITY epsilon             "&#x3B5;">
```

These entities can even be used in invalid documents, provided either that the declarations are made in the document's internal DTD subset, which all XML parsers are required to process, or that your parser reads the external DTD subset. By convention, DTD fragments that do nothing but define entities have the three-letter suffix *.ent.* Generally these fragments are imported into the document's DTD, using external parameter entity references. Example 5-4 shows how the maxim might be written using these entities, assuming they can be found at the relative URL *greek.ent.*

*Example 5-4: The Maxim Using Entity References Instead of Character References*

```
<?xml version="1.0" encoding="ISO-8859-1" standalone="no"?>
<!DOCTYPE maxim [

 <!ENTITY % greek_alphabet SYSTEM "greek.ent">
 %greek_alphabet;

]>
<maxim>
  &sigma;&omicron_with_tonos;&phi;&omicron;&final_sigma;
  &epsilon_with_tonos;&alpha;&upsilon;&tau;&omicron_with_tonos;&nu;
  &gamma;&iota;&gamma;&nu;&omega_with_tonos;&sigma;&kappa;&epsilon;&iota;
</maxim>
```

A few standard entity subsets are widely available for your own use. The XHTML 1.0 DTD includes three useful entity sets you can adopt in your own work:

*Latin-1 characters, http://www.w3.org/TR/xhtml1/DTD/xhtml-lat1.ent*
: The non-ASCII characters from 160 up in ISO-8859-1

*Special characters, http://www.w3.org/TR/xhtml1/DTD/xhtml-special.ent*
: Letters from ISO-8859-2 (Latin-2) that aren't also in Latin-1, such as Œ and various punctuation marks, such as the dagger, the Euro sign, and the em dash

*Symbols, http://www.w3.org/TR/xhtml1/DTD/xhtml-symbol.ent*
: The Greek alphabet (though accented characters are missing) and various punctuation marks, mathematical operators, and other symbols commonly used in mathematics

Chapter 23 provides complete charts showing of all characters in these entity sets. You can either use these directly from their relatively stable URLs at the W3C or copy them onto your own systems. For example, to use entities from the symbol set in a document, add the following to the document's DTD:

```
<!ENTITY % HTMLsymbol PUBLIC
   "-//W3C//ENTITIES Symbols for XHTML//EN"
   "http://www.w3.org/TR/xhtml1/DTD/xhtml-symbol.ent">
%HTMLsymbol;
```

Since these are fairly standard DTDs, they have both Public IDs and URLs. Other groups and individuals have written entity sets you can use similarly, though no canonical collection of entity sets that covers all of Unicode exists. Several slightly less polished sets covering most of the non-ASCII characters used in the various ISO-8859 character sets can be found at *http://www.oasis-open.org/cover/xml-ISOents.txt*. The full MathML DTD, available at *http://www.w3.org/TR/MathML2/appendixa.html*, also has several useful entity sets containing more mathematical symbols and the Greek, Cyrillic, and extended Latin alphabets.

## *xml:lang*

Since XML documents are written in Unicode, XML is an excellent choice for multilingual documents, such as an Arabic commentary on a Greek text (something that couldn't be done with almost any other character set). In such multilingual documents, it's useful to be able to identify which language a particular section of text is written in. For instance, a spellchecker that only knows English shouldn't try to check a French quote.

Each XML element may have an `xml:lang` attribute that specifies the language in which the content of that element is written. For example, the previous maxim might look like this:

```
<maxim xml:lang="el">
  &#x3C3;&#x3CC;&#3C6;&#3BF;&#3C2;
&#x3AD;&#3B1;&#3C5;&#3C4;&#x3CC;&#x3BD;
  &#x3B3;&#x3B9;&#x3B3;&#x3BD;&#X3CE;&#x3C3;&#x3BA;&#x3B5;&#x3B9;
</maxim>
```

This identifies it as Greek. The specific code used, `el`, comes from the Greek word for Greek, ελληνικά .

### *Language Codes*

The value of the `xml:lang` language attribute should be one of the two-letter language codes defined in ISO 639, *Codes for the Representation of Names of Languages*, found at *http://lcweb.loc.gov/standards/iso639-2/langhome.html*, if such a code exists for the language in question.

For languages that aren't listed in ISO-639, you can use a language identifier registered with IANA; currently, about 20 of these identifiers exist, including `i-navajo`, `i-klingon`, and `i-lux`. The complete list can be found at *ftp://ftp.isi.edu/in-notes/iana/assignments/languages/tags*. All identifiers begin with `i-`. For example:

```
<maxim xml:lang="i-klingon">Heghlu'meH QaQ jajvam</maxim>
```

If the language you need still isn't present in these two lists, you can create your own language tag, as long as it begins with the prefix `x-` or `X-` to identify it as a user-defined language code. For example, the title of this journal is written in J. R. R. Tolkien's fictional Quenya language:

```
<journal xml:lang="x-quenya">Tyalië Tyelelliéva</journal>
```

## Subcodes

For some purposes, knowing the language is not enough. You also need to know the region where the language is spoken. For instance, French has slightly different vocabulary, spelling, and pronunciation in France, Quebec, Belgium, and Switzerland. Although written identically with an ideographic character set, Mandarin and Cantonese are actually quite different, mutually unintelligible dialects of Chinese.

To handle these distinctions, the language code may be followed by any number of subcodes that further specify the language. Hyphens separate the language code from the subcode and subcodes from each other. If the language code is an ISO-639 code, the first subcode should be one of the two-letter country codes defined by ISO 3166, *Codes for the Representation of Names of Countries*, found at *http://www.ics.uci.edu/pub/ietf/http/related/iso3166.txt*. This `xml:lang` attribute indicates Canadian French:

```
<p xml:lang="fr-CA">Marie vient pour le fin de semaine.</p>
```

The language code is usually written in lowercase and the country code is written in uppercase. However, this is just a convention, not a requirement.

## ATTLIST Declarations of xml:lang

Although the XML 1.0 specification defines the `xml:lang` attribute, you still have to declare it in the DTDs of your valid documents. For example, this information declares the `maxim` element used several times in this chapter:

```
<!ELEMENT maxim (#PCDATA)>
<!ATTLIST maxim xml:lang NMTOKEN #IMPLIED>
```

Here I've used the `NMTOKEN` type. since all legal language codes are well-formed XML name tokens.

You may declare the `xml:lang` attribute in any convenient way. For instance, if you want to require its presence on the `maxim` element, you could make it `#REQUIRED`:

```
<!ATTLIST maxim xml:lang NMTOKEN #REQUIRED>
```

Or, if you wanted to allow only French and English text in your documents, you might specify it as an enumerated type with a default of English like this:

```
<!ATTLIST maxim xml:lang (en | fr) 'en'>
```

Unless you use an enumerated type, the parser will not check that the value you give it follows the rules outlined here. It's your responsibility to make sure you use appropriate language codes and subcodes.

# PART II

# *Narrative-Centric Documents*

# CHAPTER 6

# *XML as a Document Format*

XML is first and foremost a document format. It was always intended for web pages, books, scholarly articles, poems, short stories, reference manuals, tutorials, textbooks, legal pleadings, contracts, instruction sheets, and other documents that humans read. Its use as a syntax for computer data in applications such as order processing, object serialization, database exchange and backup, and electronic data interchange, is mostly a happy accident.

Most computer programmers are better trained to work with the rigid structures one encounters in data-oriented applications than in the more free-form environment of an article or story; most writers are more accustomed to the free-form format of a book, story, or article. XML is perhaps unique in addressing the needs of both communities equally well. This chapter describes by elucidation and example the structures encountered in documents that are meant to be read by people instead of computers. Subsequent chapters will look at web pages and then address technologies, such as XSLT, XLinks, and style sheets, that are primarily intended for use with documents that people will read. Once we've looked at these technologies, we'll examine XML as a format for relatively transitory data meant to be read by computers, rather than semipermanent documents intended for human consumption.



## *SGML's Legacy*

XML is a simplified form of the Standardized General Markup Language (SGML). The language that would eventually become SGML was invented by Charles F. Goldfarb, Ed Mosher, and Ray Lorie at IBM in the 1970s and developed by several hundred people around the world until its eventual adoption as ISO standard 8879 in 1986. SGML was intended to solve many of the same problems XML solves in much the same way XML solves them. It was and is a semantic and structural markup language for text documents. SGML is extremely powerful and achieved some success in the U.S. military, the U.S. government, the aerospace sector, and other domains that needed ways of efficiently managing technical documents that were tens of thousands of pages long.

SGML's biggest success was HTML, an SGML application. However, HTML is just one SGML application. It does not have anything close to the full power of SGML. SGML was also used to define other document formats, including DocBook and Text Encoding Initiative (TEI), both of which we'll discuss shortly.

However, SGML is very complicated. The official SGML specification is more than 150 very technical pages. It covers many special cases and unlikely scenarios. It is so complex that few software programs have ever implemented it fully; programs that implement or rely on different subsets of SGML are often incompatible. The special feature one program considers essential is often considered extraneous fluff and omitted by the next program. Nonetheless, experience with SGML has taught developers a lot about the proper design, implementation, and use of markup languages for a wide variety of documents. Much of that knowledge applies equally well to XML.

One thing all this should make clear is that XML documents aren't just used on the Web; XML can easily handle publishing needs in a variety of media, including books, magazines, journals, newspapers, and pamphlets. XML is particularly useful when you need to publish in any or all of these media. By applying different style sheets to the same source document, you can produce web pages, speaker's notes, and camera-ready copy for printing.

## *Narrative Document Structures*

All XML documents are trees. However, trees are general-purpose data structures. If you've been formally trained in computer science (and very possibly even if you haven't been), you've encountered binary trees, red-black trees, balanced trees, B-trees, and ordered trees. However, XML documents rarely match any of these structures. Instead XML documents are the most general sort of tree, with no particular restrictions on how nodes are ordered, how nodes are connected, and to which other nodes they connect. Narrative XML documents are even less likely than data-oriented XML documents to have an identifiable structure beyond their mere treeness.

So what does a narrative-oriented XML document look like? Of course it has a root element, which all XML documents have. Generally speaking this root element represents the document itself. For example, if the document is a book the root element is `book`. If the document is an article, the root element is `article`.

Large documents are generally broken up into sections, perhaps chapters for a book, sections for an article, or claims for a legal brief. Most of the document consists of these primary sections. In some cases, several different kinds of sections exist, for instance, one for the table of contents, one for the index, and one each for the chapters of a book.

Generally, the root element also contains elements providing meta-information about the document; that is, the work's title, the document's author, or the dates the document was written and last modified.

Placing the meta-information in one child of the root element and the main content of the work in another is another common pattern. This is how HTML documents are written. The root element is `html`. The meta-information goes in a `head` element and the main content goes in the `body` element. TEI also follows this pattern, as does DocBook.

Document sections can be further divided into subsections. The subsections themselves may be divided further. How many levels of subsection appear generally depends on how large the document is. An encyclopedia has many levels of sectioning, whereas a pamphlet or flier has almost none. Each section and subsection normally has a title. It may also have elements or attributes that indicate meta-information about the section, such as the author or date it was last modified.

Up to this point, mixed content is mostly avoided. Elements usually contain only child elements and ignorable whitespace. However, at some point inserting the document's actual text, the words that people read, is necessary. In most Western languages, this text will probably be divided into paragraphs and other block-level elements, such as headlines, figures, sidebars, and footnotes. Generic document DTDs, such as DocBook, won't be able to say any more about these items than this.

Paragraphs and other block-level items mostly contain words in a row, that is, text. Some of this text may be marked up with inline elements. For instance, you may wish to indicate that a particular string of text inside the block-level element is a date or a person, or that it is simply important. However, most text will not be annotated in this way.

One area in which different XML applications diverge is the question of whether block-level items may contain other block-level items. For instance, can a paragraph contain a list? Can a list item contain a paragraph? It's probably easier to work with more structured documents in which blocks can't contain other blocks (particularly other blocks of the same kind). However, a block often has a very good reason to contain other blocks. For instance, a long list item or quotation may contain several paragraphs.

This entire structure, from the root to the most deeply nested inline item, tends to be quite linear; that is, a person will read the words in pretty much the same order in which they appear in the document. If all the markup were suddenly removed and you were left with nothing but the raw text, the result would still be legible. The markup can be used to index or format the document, but it's not a fundamental part of the content.

Another important point about these types of XML documents: they are not only composed of words in a row, they're composed of *words*. They contain text intended for people to read. They do not contain numbers, dates, or money, except when these occur as part of the narrative's normal flow. The `#PCDATA` content of the tree's lowest level elements mostly has one type: string. If any element has a type other than string, it's usually meta-information about the document (figure number, date last modified, etc.), rather than the content of the document itself.

This goes a long way to explain why DTDs don't provide strong, or really any, datatyping. The documents that SGML was designed for didn't need it. XML documents that are doing jobs SGML wasn't designed for, such as tracking inventories or census data, do need datatyping, which is why various people and organizations have invented a plethora of schema languages. However, schemas don't add much to DTDs for these sorts of narrative documents.

Not all XML documents are like those we've described here. Not even all narrative-oriented XML documents fit this description. However, a surprising number of narrative-oriented XML applications do follow this basic pattern, perhaps with a nip here or a tuck there. The reason is that narratives follow this basic structure, which has proven its usefulness in the thousands of years since writing was invented. If you define your own DTDs for general narrative-oriented documents, you'll probably come up with something much like this structure. If you define your own DTDs for more specialized narrative-oriented documents, then the names of your elements may change to reflect your domain; for instance, if you were writing the next edition of the Boy Scout handbook, one of your subsections might be called `MeritBadge`. However, the basic hierarchy of document, meta-information, sections and subsections, block-level elements, and marked-up text would likely remain unchanged.

## *TEI*

The Text Encoding Initiative (TEI), (*http://www.tei-c.org/*), is an SGML application designed for the markup of classic literature, such as the Aeneid of Virgil or the collected works of Thomas Jefferson. TEI is a prime example of a narrative-oriented DTD. Since it is designed for scholarly analysis of text rather than casual reading or publishing, it includes elements for both common document structures (chapter, scene, stanza, etc.) and for typographical elements, grammatical structure, the position of illustrations on the page, and so forth. These structures and elements aren't important to most readers, but they are crucial to TEI's intended audience of humanities scholars. For many academic purposes, one manuscript of the Aeneid is not necessarily the same as the next. Transcription errors and emendations made by various monks in the Middle Ages can be important.

TEI is an SGML application. It uses several features of SGML not found in XML, including the `&` connector and tag minimization. However, XML is clearly the wave of the future. Thus, like most evolving SGML applications, TEI is moving to XML. A light version of the TEI DTD is available for authors who prefer to work in pure XML. It's not quite as complete as the SGML version, but it's very close for many practical uses.

Example 6-1 shows a fairly simple TEI Lite document that uses the XML version of the TEI DTD. The content comes from the book you're reading now. Although a complete TEI-encoded copy of this manuscript would be much longer, this simple example demonstrates the basic features of most TEI documents that represent books. (Besides prose, TEI can be used for plays, poems, missals, and essentially any other form of written literature.)

*Example 6-1: A TEI Document*

```
<?xml version="1.0" encoding="UTF-8" standalone="no"?>
<!DOCTYPE TEI.2 SYSTEM "xteilite.dtd">
```

*Example 6-1: A TEI Document (continued)*

```
<TEI.2>

  <teiHeader>
    <fileDesc>
      <titleStmt>
        <title>XML in a Nutshell</title>
        <author>Harold, Elliotte Rusty</author>
        <author>Means, W. Scott</author>
      </titleStmt>
      <publicationStmt><p></p></publicationStmt>
      <sourceDesc><p>Early manuscript draft</p></sourceDesc>
    </fileDesc>
  </teiHeader>

  <text id="HarXMLi">

    <front>
      <div type='toc'>
        <head>Table Of Contents</head>
        <list>
          <item>Introducing XML</item>
          <item>XML as a Document Format</item>
          <item>XML as a "better" HTML</item>
        </list>
      </div>

    </front>

    <body>

      <div1 type="chapter">
        <head>Introducing XML</head>
        <p></p>
      </div1>

      <div1 type="chapter">
        <head>XML as a Document Format</head>
        <p>
          XML is first and foremost a document format. It was always
          intended for web pages, books, scholarly articles, poems,
          short stories, reference manuals, tutorials, texts, legal
          pleadings, contracts, instruction sheets, and other documents
          that human beings would read. Its use as a syntax for computer
          data in applications like syndication, order processing,
          object serialization, database exchange and backup, electronic
          data interchange, and so forth is mostly a happy accident.
       </p>

       <div2 type="section">
         <head>SGML's Legacy</head>
         <p></p>
       </div2>
```

Document Format

*Example 6-1: A TEI Document (continued)*

```
        <div2 type="section">
          <head>TEI</head>
          <p></p>
        </div2>

        <div2 type="section">
          <head>DocBook</head>
          <p>
            DocBook (<hi>http://www.oasis-open.org/docbook/</hi>) is an
            SGML application designed for new documents, not old ones.
            It's especially common in computer documentation. Several
            O'Reilly books have been written in DocBook including
            <bibl><author>Norm Walsh</author>'s <title>DocBook: The
            Definitive Guide</title></bibl>. Much of the <abbr
            expan='Linux Documentation Project'>LDP</abbr>
            (<hi>http://www.linuxdoc.org/</hi>) corpus is written in
            DocBook.
          </p>
        </div2>

      </div1>

      <div1 type="chapter">
        <head>XML as a "better" HTML</head>
        <p></p>
      </div1>
    </body>

    <back>
      <div1 type="index">
        <list>
          <head>INDEX</head>
          <item>SGML, 46, 87-88</item>
          <item>DocBook, 93-98</item>
          <item>TEI, 90-93</item>
          <item>Text Encoding Initiative, See TEI</item>
        </list>
      </div1>
    </back>

  </text>
</TEI.2>
```

The root element of all TEI documents is `TEI.2`. This root element is always divided into two parts: a header represented by a `teiHeader` element and the document's main content represented by a `text` element. The header contains information about the source document, for instance which exact medieval manuscript the text was copied from, the encoding of the document, or keywords describing the document.

The text element is itself divided into three parts:

*Frontmatter in the front element*
: The frontmatter includes the preface, table of contents, dedication page, and pictures of the cover. Each of these elements is represented by a `div` element with a `type` attribute, whose value identifies the division as a table of contents, preface, title page, etc. Each division contains other elements that lay out that division's content.

*Body in the body element*
: The body includes individual chapters that make up the document. Each of these elements is represented by a `div1` element with a `type` attribute that identifies this particular division as a volume, book, part, chapter, poem, act, etc. Each `div1` element has a `header` child giving the title of the volume, book, part, or chapter.

*Backmatter in the back element*
: The backmatter includes the index and glossary.

These may be subdivided further. `div1`s can contain `div2`s. `div2`s can contain `div3`s. `div3`s can contain `div4`s, and so on up to `div7`. However, for any given work, a smallest division exists. This division contains paragraphs represented by `p` elements for prose or stanzas represented by `lg` elements for poetry. Stanzas are broken up further into individual lines represented by `l` elements.

Both lines and paragraphs contain mixed content. That is, they contain plain text. However, parts of this text may be marked up further by elements indicating that particular words or characters are peoples' names (`name`), corrections (`corr`), illegible (`unclear`), misspellings (`sic`), etc.

This structure closely reflects the structure of the actual documents encoded in TEI. This is true of most narrative-oriented XML applications that need to handle fairly generic documents. TEI is a very representative example of typical XML document structure.

**Document Format**

## DocBook

DocBook (*http://www.oasis-open.org/docbook/*) is an SGML application designed for new, not old, documents. Its use is especially common in computer documentation. Several O'Reilly books have been written in DocBook, including Norman Walsh and Leonard Muellner's *DocBook: The Definitive Guide*. Much of the Linux Documentation Project (*http://www.linuxdoc.org/*) corpus is written in DocBook.

The current version of DocBook, 4.1.2, is available as both an SGML and an XML application. The XML version is not quite the same as the SGML version, but it's very close for most practical uses. The DocBook maintainers have announced plans to move to a single DTD that is completely compatible with both SGML and XML in Version 5.0. Example 6-2 shows a simple DocBook XML document based on the book you're reading now. Needless to say, the full version of this document would be much longer.

*Example 6-2: A DocBook Document*

```
<?xml version="1.0" encoding="UTF-8" standalone="no"?>
<!DOCTYPE book PUBLIC "-//Norman Walsh//DTD DocBk XML V3.1.7//EN"
                      "docbook/docbookx.dtd">
<book>
  <title>XML in a Nutshell</title>

  <bookinfo>
    <author>
      <firstname>Elliotte Rusty</firstname>
      <surname>Harold</surname>
    </author>
    <author>
      <firstname>W. Scott</firstname>
      <surname>Means</surname>
    </author>
  </bookinfo>

  <toc>
    <tocchap><tocentry>Introducing XML</tocentry></tocchap>
    <tocchap><tocentry>XML as a Document Format</tocentry></tocchap>
    <tocchap><tocentry>XML as a "better" HTML</tocentry></tocchap>
  </toc>

  <chapter>
    <title>Introducing XML</title>
    <para></para>
  </chapter>

  <chapter>
    <title>XML as a Document Format</title>

   <para>
     XML is first and foremost a document format. It was always intended
     for web pages, books, scholarly articles, poems, short stories,
     reference manuals, tutorials, texts, legal pleadings, contracts,
     instruction sheets, and other documents that human beings would
     read. Its use as a syntax for computer data in applications like
     syndication, order processing, object serialization, database
     exchange and backup, electronic data interchange, and so forth is
     mostly a happy accident.
   </para>

   <sect1>
     <title>SGML's Legacy</title>
     <para></para>
   </sect1>

   <sect1>
     <title>TEI</title>
     <para></para>
   </sect1>
```

*Example 6-2: A DocBook Document (continued)*

```
  <sect1>
    <title>DocBook</title>
    <para>
      <ulink url="http://www.oasis-open.org/docbook/">DocBook</ulink>
      is an SGML application designed for new documents, not old ones.
      It's especially common in computer documentation. Several
      O'Reilly books have been written in DocBook including
      <citation>Norman Walsh and Leonard Muellner's<title>DocBook: The
      Definitive Guide</title></citation>. Much of the <ulink
      url="http://www.linuxdoc.org/">Linux Documentation Project
      </ulink> corpus is written in DocBook. </para>
  </sect1>

</chapter>

<chapter>
  <title>XML as a "better" HTML</title>
  <para></para>
</chapter>

<index>
  <indexentry>
    <primaryie>SGML, 46, 87-88</primaryie>
  </indexentry>
  <indexentry>
    <primaryie>DocBook, 93-98</primaryie>
  </indexentry>
  <indexentry>
    <primaryie>TEI, 90-93</primaryie>
  </indexentry>
  <indexentry>
    <primaryie>Text Encoding Initiative</primaryie>
    <seeie>TEI</seeie>
  </indexentry>
</index>

</book>
```

DocBook offers many advantages to technical authors. First, it's open, nonproprietary, and can be created with any text editor. Writing open source documentation for open source software in closed and proprietary tools such as Microsoft Word would feel a little silly. If your documents are written in DocBook, they aren't tied to any one platform, vendor, or application software. They're portable across essentially any plausible environment you can imagine.

Second, not only is DocBook theoretically editable with basic text editors; its simplicity makes such editing practical, as well. If you need help, free tools, including an emacs major mode, are available at *http://www.nwalsh.com/emacs/docbookide/index.html.* Third, like many good XML applications, DocBook is modular. You can use the pieces you need and ignore the rest. If you need tables, a very powerful tables module is available. If you don't need tables, you don't need to know about or use this module. Other modules cover various entity sets and equations.

DocBook is an authoring format, not a format for finished presentation. Before a person reads a DocBook document, it should be converted to one of several formats, including:

- HTML
- XSL Formatting Objects
- Rich Text Format (RTF)
- $\TeX$

For example, if you wanted high-quality printed documentation for a program, you could convert the DocBook document to $\TeX$, use the standard $\TeX$ tools to convert the resulting $\TeX$ file to a DVI and/or PostScript file, and print that file. If you just wanted to read it on your computer, then you'd probably convert it to HTML and load it into your web browser. For other purposes, you'd pick a different format. When using DocBook, you get all these formats essentially for free. Producing multiple output documents in different formats from a single DocBook source document is very easy. Indeed this benefit isn't just limited to DocBook. Most carefully thought-out XML input formats are equally simple to publish in other formats, as desired.

## Document Permanence

XML documents intended for computers to read are often transitory. If you create a Simple Object Access Protocol (SOAP) document that represents a request to a Windows server running Next Generation Windows Services (NGWS), then that document exists for the time it takes the client to send it to the server and for the server to parse it into its internal data structures. After that process is finished, the document will be discarded. It probably won't be around for two minutes, much less two years. The document is an ephemeral communication between two systems, with no more permanence than the billions of other messages computers exchange on a daily basis, most of which are never even stored to disk, much less archived for posterity.

Some applications do store more permanent computer-oriented data in XML. For instance, XML is the native file format of the Gnumeric spreadsheet. This format, however, is really only understood by Gnumeric and perhaps the other GNOME applications. It's designed to meet the specific needs of that one program. Exchanging data with other applications, including ones that haven't even been invented, is a secondary concern.

XML documents meant for humans tend to be more permanent and less software bound, however. If you encode the Declaration of Independence in XML, you want people to be able to read it in 2 years, in 200 years, or in 2,000 years. You also want them to read it with any convenient tool, including ones not yet invented. These requirements have important implications for both the XML applications you design to hold the data and the tools you use to read and write them.

The first rule is that the format should be very well documented. There should be a DTD, and that DTD should be well commented. Furthermore, a significant amount of prose documentation should also exist. Prose documentation can't substitute for the DTD's formal documentation, but it's an invaluable assist in understanding the DTD.

Standard formats, such as DocBook and TEI, should be preferred to custom, one-off XML applications. You should avoid proprietary DTDs that are owned by any one person or company and whose future may depend on the fortunes of that individual or company. Even DTDs that come from nonprofit consortia, such as OASIS or TEI, should be licensed liberally enough so that intellectual property restrictions won't allow anyone to throw any roadblocks in your path. At least one purveyor of DTDs has actually filed for patents on its DTDs. These DTDs should be avoided like the plague. Stick to DTDs that may be freely copied and shared and that can be retrieved from many different locations.

Once you've settled on a standard DTD, try to avoid modifying it if you possibly can. If you absolutely must modify it, then document your changes in excruciating, redundant detail. Include comments in both your DTDs and documents explaining what you've done. Use the parameter entities built into the DTDs to add new element types or subtract old ones, rather than modifying the DTD files themselves.

Conversely, the format shouldn't be too hard to reverse-engineer if the documentation is lost. Make sure to use full names for elements and attributes throughout the document. DocBook's `para` element is superior to TEI's `p` element. `Paragraph` would be even better.

All of the document's inherent structure should be indicated by markup alone. It should not be left for the user to infer, nor should it be encoded using separators such as whitespace. Here's an example of what not to do from SVG:

```
<polygon style="fill: blue; stroke: green; stroke-width: 12"
         points="350,75  379,161 469,161 397,215 423,301 350,250
                 277,301 303,215 231,161 321,161" />
```

The `style` attribute contains three separate and barely related items. Understanding this element requires parsing the non-XML CSS format. The `points` attribute is even worse. This attribute is a long list of numbers, but it contains no information about what each number is. You can't, for instance, determine which are the *x* and which are the *y* coordinates. An approach like the next example is preferable:

```
<polygon fill="blue" stroke="green" stroke-width="12">
  <point x="350" y="75"/>
  <point x="379" y="161"/>
  <point x="469" y="161"/>
  <point x="397" y="215"/>
  <point x="423" y="301"/>
  <point x="350" y="250"/>
  <point x="277" y="301"/>
  <point x="303" y="215"/>
  <point x="231" y="161"/>
  <point x="321" y="161"/>
</polygon>
```

The attribute-based style syntax is actually allowed in SVG. However, the debate over which form to use for coordinates was quite heated in the W3C SVG working group. The group ultimately decided, wrongly in our opinion, that the more verbose form would never be adopted because of its size, even though most members felt it maintained the spirit of XML better. We think that the working group overemphasized the importance of document size in an era of exponentially growing hard disks and network bandwidth. It also ignored the ease with which the second format could be compressed for transport or storage.

Stylesheets are important. We're all familiar with the injunction to separate style from content. You've heard enough warnings about not including mere style information, such as italics and font choices, in your XML documents. However, be careful not to go the other way and include content in your stylesheets. Author names, titles, copyrights, and other information that changes between documents belongs in the document, not the stylesheet, even if it includes meta-information about the document rather than the actual content of the document.

Always remember that you're not just writing for the next couple of months or years, but possibly for the next couple of thousands of years. Have pity on the poor historian who's going to have to decipher your markup with limited tools and information.

## *Transformation and Presentation*

The markup in a typical XML document describes the document's structure, but it tends not to describe the document's presentation; that is, it says how the document is organized, but not how it looks. Though XML documents are text, and a person could read them in native form if they really wanted to, an XML document is usually rendered into another format before it is presented to a human audience. One key idea of markup languages in general, and XML in particular, is that the input format does not need to be the same as the output format. To put it another way, what you see is not what you get, nor is it what you want to get. The input markup language is designed for the convenience of the writer. The output language is designed for the convenience of the reader.

Of course this design requires a means of transforming the input format into the output format. Most XML documents undergo a transformation before they are presented to the reader. The transformation may be to a different XML vocabulary, such as XHTML or XSL-FO, or it may be to a non-XML format, such as PostScript or RTF.

XML's semiofficial transformation language is the Extensible Stylesheet Language Transformations (XSLT). An XSLT document contains a list of templates. Each template has a pattern noting which elements and other nodes it matches. An XSLT processor reads the input document. When it sees something in the input document that matches a template in the stylesheet, it outputs the template's contents. Part of the template's content is normally an instruction that tells the processor to include content from the input in the output. This instruction allows, for example, the text of the output document to be the same while all the markup is changed. For instance, you could write a stylesheet that transforms DocBook documents into TEI documents. XSLT will be discussed in more detail in Chapter 8, *XSL Transformations*.

However, XSLT is not the only transformation language you can use with XML documents. Other style sheet languages, such as the Document Style Sheet and Semantics Language (DSSSL) (*http://www.netfolder.com/DSSSL/*), are available, as are a variety of proprietary tools, such as OmniMark (*http://www.omnimark.com/*). Most of these tools have particular strengths and weaknesses for specific kinds of documents. Custom programs written in a variety of programming languages, such as Java, C++, Perl, and Python, can use various APIs, such as SAX, DOM, and JDOM, to transform documents. These languages are sometimes useful when you need something more than a mere transformation; for instance, interpreting certain elements as database queries and actually inserting the results of those queries into the output document or asking the user to answer questions in the middle of the transformation. However, when choosing which tool to use, the biggest single factor to consider is which language and syntax you're most comfortable with. De linguis non disputandum est.

There are also many different choices for the output format from a transformation. A PostScript file can be printed on paper, overhead transparencies, slides, or even T-shirts. You can view a PDF document in all these media and on the screen. However, for screen display, PDF is vastly inferior to simple HTML, which is broadly accessible across platforms and very easy to generate from source XML documents via XSLT. Generating a PDF or a PostScript file normally requires an additional step in which special software converts a custom XML output format like XSL-FO to what you actually want.

Providing a descriptive style sheet that states how to format each element in the original document is an alternative to using a transformation-based presentation. This is the realm of Cascading Stylesheets (CSS). CSS works particularly well for narrative documents, which only require a list of which fonts, styles, or sizes to apply to each element's content. When all markup is stripped from the document, what remains is more or less a plain text version of what you want to see. No reordering or rearrangement is necessary. This approach does not work as well for data-oriented documents. In these documents, raw content may be nothing more than an undifferentiated mass of numbers, dates, or other information that's hard to understand without the context and annotations provided by the markup. In this case, a combination approach, in which a transformation produces a new document containing rearranged and annotated information, is appropriate. A CSS style sheet can then apply style rules to the elements in the transformed document.

CHAPTER 7

# *XML on the Web*

XML began as an effort to bring the full power and structure of SGML to the Web in a form that was simple enough for nonexperts to use. Like most great inventions, XML turned out to have uses far beyond what its creators originally envisioned. Indeed there's a lot more XML off the Web than on it. Nonetheless, XML is still a very attractive language in which to write and serve web pages. Since XML documents must be well-formed and parsers must reject malformed documents, XML pages are less likely to have annoying cross-browser incompatibilities. Since XML documents are highly structured, they're much easier for robots to parse. Since XML tag and attribute names reflect the nature of the content they hold, search engine spiders can more easily determine the true meaning of a page.

XML on the Web comes in two flavors. The first is XHTML, an XMLized variant of HTML 4.0 that tightens up HTML to match XML's syntax. For instance, XHTML requires that all start tags correspond to a matching end tag and that all attribute values be quoted. XHTML also adds a few bits of syntax to HTML, such as the XML declaration and empty element tags that end with `/>`. Most XHTML can be displayed quite well in legacy browsers, with a few notable exceptions.

The second flavor of XML on the Web is the direct display of XML documents that use arbitrary vocabularies in web browsers. Generally, such a document's formatting is supplied by either a CSS stylesheet or an XSLT stylesheet that transforms the document to HTML (perhaps XHTML). This flavor requires an XML-aware browser and is not well supported by the installed base of web clients.

A third option is to mix raw XML vocabularies, such as MathML and SVG, with XHTML. This is accomplished using XHTML 1.1, also known as Modular XHTML. Modular XHTML lets you embed RDF cataloging information, MathML equations, and SVG pictures inside your XHTML documents. Namespaces sort out which elements belong to which application.

# *XHTML*

XHTML is an official W3C recommendation. It defines an XML-compatible version of HTML, or rather, it redefines HTML as an XML application instead of an SGML application. Just by looking at an XHTML document, you might not even realize that anything is different about it. It still uses the same `<p>`, `<li>`, `<table>`, `<h1>`, and other tags you're familiar with. Elements and attributes have the same familiar names they have in HTML. The syntax is still basically the same.

The difference is not so much in what's allowed, but in what's not allowed. Although `<p>` is a legal XHTML tag, `<P>` is not. `<table border="0" width="515">` is legal XHTML; `<table border=0 width=515>` is not. A paragraph prefixed with a `<p>` and suffixed with a `</p>` is legal XHTML, but a paragraph that omits the closing `</p>` tag is not. Most existing HTML documents require substantial editing before they become well-formed and valid XHTML documents. However, once they are valid XHTML documents, they are automatically valid XML documents that can be manipulated with the same editors, parsers, and other tools you use to work with an XML document.

## *Moving from HTML to XHTML*

Most changes required to turn an existing HTML document into an XHTML document involve making the document well-formed. For instance, given an existing HTML document, you'll probably have to make at least some of these changes to turn it into XHTML:

- Add missing end tags, such as `</p>` and `</li>`.
- Rewrite elements so they nest rather than overlap. For example, change `<p><em>an emphasized paragraph</p></em>` to `<p><em>an emphasized paragraph</em></p>`.
- Make the case of closing tags the same as the start tags they match (preferably by making them all lowercase). For example, change `<CODE>text</code>` to `<code>text</code>`.
- Put quotes around attribute values. For example, change `<p align=center>` to `<p align="center">`.
- Make sure all attributes have values. For example, change `<input type="checkbox" checked>` to `<input type="checkbox" checked="checked">`.
- Replace any occurrences of `&` or `<` in character data or attribute values with `&` and `<`. For instance, change `A&P` to `A&P` and `<a href="http://www.google.com/search?client=googlet&q=Java%20XML">` to `<a href="http://www.google.com/search?client=googlet&q=Java%20XML">`.
- Make sure the document has a single root element, preferably `html`.
- Change empty tags like `<hr>` to `<hr/>` or `<hr></hr>`.

- Add hyphens to comments so `<! this is a comment>` becomes `<!-- this is a comment -->`.
- Encode the document in UTF-8 or UTF-16 or add an XML declaration that specifies which character set it is encoded in.

However, XHTML doesn't merely require well-formedness; it also requires validity. To create a valid XHTML document, you need to make these changes as well:

- Add a `DOCTYPE` declaration to the document pointing to one of the three XHTML DTDs.
- Make all element and attribute names lowercase.
- Make any other changes you have to make to your markup so the document validates against the DTD. For example, eliminate nonstandard elements, such as `marquee`, add required attributes, such as the `alt` attribute of `img`, or move child elements out from inside elements where they're not allowed, such as a `blockquote` inside a `p`.

In addition, the XHTML specification imposes several requirements that, strictly speaking, are not required for either well-formedness or validity. However, they do make parsing XHTML documents a little easier:

- The document's root element must be `html`.
- A `DOCTYPE` declaration that uses a PUBLIC ID to identify one of the three XHTML DTDs must be present.
- The root element of the document must have an `xmlns` attribute identifying the default namespace as `http://www.w3.org/1999/xhtml`.

Finally, you may, if you wish, add an XML declaration or an `xml-stylesheet` processing instruction to your document's prolog.

Example 7-1 shows an HTML document from the O'Reilly web site that exhibits many of the validity problems you'll find on the Web today. In fact, this page is much neater than most. Nonetheless, not all attribute values are quoted. The `noshade` attribute of the `HR` element doesn't even have a value, and no document type declaration exists. Tags are a mix of upper- and lowercase, mostly uppercase. The `DD` elements are missing end tags, and some character data inside the second definition element is not part of a `DT` or a `DD`.

*Example 7-1: A Standard HTML Document*

```
<HTML><HEAD>
  <TITLE>O'Reilly Shipping Information</TITLE>
</HEAD>
<BODY BGCOLOR="#ffffff" VLINK="#0000CC" LINK="#990000" TEXT="#000000">
<table border=0 width=515>
<tr>
<td>
<IMG SRC="/www/graphics_new/generic_ora_header_wide.gif" BORDER=0>
<H2>U.S. Shipping Information </H2>
<HR size="1" align=left noshade>
<DL>
```

*Example 7-1: A Standard HTML Document (continued)*

```
<DT> <B>UPS Ground Service (Continental US only -- 5-7 business
days):</B></DT>
<DD>
<PRE>
$  5.95 - $ 49.99 ......................... $ 4.50
$ 50.00 - $ 99.99 ......................... $ 6.50
$100.00 - $149.99 ......................... $ 8.50
$150.00 - $199.99 ......................... $10.50
$200.00 - $249.99 ......................... $12.50
$250.00 - $299.99 ......................... $14.50
</PRE>
<DT> <B>Federal Express:</B></DT>
(Shipping within 24 hours of receipt of order by O'Reilly)
<DD>
<PRE>
<EM>1 or 2 books</EM>:
Economy 2-day ............................. $ 8.75
Overnight Standard (Afternoon Delivery) ... $12.75
Overnight Priority (Morning Delivery) ..... $16.50

</PRE>
</DL>
<b>Alaska and Hawaii:</b> add $10 to Federal Express rates.
<P>
<A HREF="int-ship.html"><b>International Shipping Information</b></A>
<P>
<CENTER>
<HR SIZE="1" NOSHADE>
<FONT SIZE="1" FACE="Verdana, Arial, Helvetica">
<A HREF="http://www.oreilly.com/">
<B>O'Reilly Home</B></A> <B> | </B>
<A HREF="http://www.oreilly.com/sales/bookstores">
<B>O'Reilly Bookstores</B></A> <B> | </B>
<A HREF="http://www.oreilly.com/order_new/">
<B>How to Order</B></A> <B> | </B>
<A HREF="http://www.oreilly.com/oreilly/contact.html">
<B>O'Reilly Contacts<BR></B></A>
<A HREF="http://www.oreilly.com/international/">
<B>International</B></A> <B> | </B>
<A HREF="http://www.oreilly.com/oreilly/about.html">
<B>About O'Reilly</B></A> <B> | </B>
<A HREF="http://www.oreilly.com/affiliates.html">
<B>Affiliated Companies</B></A><p>
<EM>&copy; 2000, O'Reilly &amp; Associates, Inc.</EM>
</FONT>
</CENTER>
</td>
</tr>
</table>

</BODY>
</HTML>
```

Example 7-2 shows this document after it's been converted to XHTML. All of the previously noted problems and a few more besides have been fixed. A number of deprecated presentational attributes, such as the **size** and **noshade** attributes of **hr** had to be replaced with CSS styles. We've also added the necessary document type and namespace declarations. HTML and XML browsers and parsers can all read this document now.

*Example 7-2: A Valid XHTML Document*

```
<!DOCTYPE html PUBLIC "-//W3C//DTD XHTML 1.0 Strict//EN"
    "http://www.w3.org/TR/xhtml1/DTD/xhtml1-strict.dtd">
<html xmlns="http://www.w3.org/1999/xhtml">
<head>
<meta name="generator" content="HTML Tidy, see www.w3.org" />
<style type="text/css">
  body      {backgroundColor: #FFFFFF; color: #000000}
  a:visited {color: #0000CC}
  a:link    {color: #990000}
</style>
<title>O'Reilly Shipping Information</title>
</head>
<body>
<table border="0" width="515">
<tr>
<td><img src="/www/graphics_new/generic_ora_header_wide.gif"
style="border-width: 0" alt="O'Reilly"/>
<h2>U.S. Shipping Information</h2>

<hr style="height: 1; text-align: left"/>
<dl>
<dt><b>UPS Ground Service (Continental US only -- 5-7 business
days):</b></dt>

<dd>
<pre>
$  5.95 - $ 49.99 .......................... $ 4.50
$ 50.00 - $ 99.99 .......................... $ 6.50
$100.00 - $149.99 .......................... $ 8.50
$150.00 - $199.99 .......................... $10.50
$200.00 - $249.99 .......................... $12.50
$250.00 - $299.99 .......................... $14.50
</pre>
</dd>

<dt><b>Federal Express:</b></dt>

<dd>(Shipping within 24 hours of receipt of order by O'Reilly)</dd>

<dd>
<pre>
<em>1 or 2 books</em>:
Economy 2-day ............................ $ 8.75
```

*Example 7-2: A Valid XHTML Document (continued)*

```
Overnight Standard (Afternoon Delivery) ... $12.75
Overnight Priority (Morning Delivery) ..... $16.50

</pre>
</dd>
</dl>

<b>Alaska and Hawaii:</b> add $10 to Federal Express rates.

<p><a href="int-ship.html"><b>International Shipping
Information</b></a></p>

<div style="font-size: xx-small; font-face: Verdana, Arial, Helvetica; text-
align: center">
<hr style="height: 1"/>
<a
href="http://www.oreilly.com/"><b>O'Reilly Home</b></a> <b>|</b> <a
href="http://www.oreilly.com/sales/bookstores"><b>O'Reilly
Bookstores</b></a> <b>|</b> <a
href="http://www.oreilly.com/order_new/"><b>How to Order</b></a>
<b>|</b> <a href="http://www.oreilly.com/oreilly/contact.html"><b>
O'Reilly Contacts<br />
</b></a> <a href="http://www.oreilly.com/international/"><b>
International</b></a> <b>|</b> <a
href="http://www.oreilly.com/oreilly/about.html"><b>About
O'Reilly</b></a> <b>|</b> <a
href="http://www.oreilly.com/affiliates.html"><b>Affiliated
Companies</b></a></div>

<p style="font-size: xx-small; font-family: Verdana, Arial, Helvetica"><em>
&copy; 2000, O'Reilly &amp; Associates, Inc.</em></p>
</td>
</tr>
</table>
</body>
</html>
```



Making all these changes can be tedious for large documents or collections of many documents. Fortunately, there's an open source tool that can do most of the work for you. Dave Ragget's Tidy (*http://www.w3.org/People/Raggett/tidy/*) is a C program that has been ported to most major operating systems and can convert some pretty nasty HTML into valid XHTML. For example, to convert the file *bad.html* to *good.xml*, you would type:

```
% tidy --output-xhtml yes bad.html good.xml
```

Tidy fixes as much as it can and warns you about what it can't fix so you can fix it manually. For example, it tells you that a required `alt` attribute is missing from an `img` element.

### *Three DTDs for XHTML*

XHTML comes in three flavors, depending on which DTD you choose:

*Strict*
: The W3C-recommended form of XHTML. It includes all basic elements and attributes, such as `p` and `class`. However, it does not include deprecated elements and attributes, such as `applet` and `center`. It also forbids the use of presentational attributes, such as the `body` element's `bgcolor`, `vlink`, `link`, and `text`. These capabilities are provided by CSS instead. Strict XHTML is identified with this `DOCTYPE` declaration:

```
<!DOCTYPE html PUBLIC "-//W3C//DTD XHTML 1.0 Strict//EN"
                      "DTD/xhtml1-strict.dtd" >
```

Example 7-2 used this DTD.

*Transitional*
: A looser form of XHTML for when you can't easily do without deprecated elements and attributes such as `applet` and `bgcolor`. It is identified with this `DOCTYPE` declaration:

```
<!DOCTYPE html PUBLIC "-//W3C//DTD XHTML 1.0 Transitional//EN"
                      "DTD/xhtml1-transitional.dtd" >
```

*Frameset*
: The same as the transitional DTD, except it also allows frame-related elements such as `frameset` and `iframe`. It is identified with this `DOCTYPE` declaration:

```
<!DOCTYPE html PUBLIC "-//W3C//DTD XHTML 1.0 Frameset//EN"
                      "DTD/xhtml1-frameset.dtd" >
```

All three DTDs use the same *http://www.w3.org/1999/xhtml* namespace. You should choose the strict DTD unless you've got a specific reason to use another one.

## *Browser Support for XHTML*

Current web browsers deal with XHTML inconsistently. Certainly they don't require it, as they accept such a wide variety of malformed, invalid, and out-and-out mistaken HTML. However, some common browsers do have some problems when they encounter certain common XHTML constructs.

### *The XML declaration and processing instructions*

Some browsers display processing instructions and the XML declaration inline. These should be omitted if possible.

Few, if any, browsers recognize or respect the XML declaration's encoding declaration. Furthermore, many browsers won't automatically recognize UTF-8 or UCS-2 Unicode text. If you use a non-ASCII character set, you should also include a `meta` element in the header identifying the character set:

```
<meta http-equiv="Content-type"
      content='text/html; charset="UTF-8"'></meta>
```

### *Empty elements*

Browsers deal inconsistently with both forms of empty-element syntax. Some browsers understand `<hr/>` but not `<hr></hr>` (typically rendering it as two horizontal lines rather than one), while others recognize `<hr></hr>` but not `<hr/>` (typically omitting the horizontal line completely). The most consistent effect seems to be achieved by using an empty-element tag with an optional attribute, such as `class` or `id`, as in `<hr class="empty" />`. There's no real reason for the `class` attribute here, except that its presence keeps browsers from choking on the `/>`. Other attributes that the DTD allows would serve equally well.

On the other hand, if a particular instance of an element is empty, but not all instances of the element have to be empty—for instance, a `p` that doesn't contain text—you should use the two-tag syntax, such as `<p></p>`, rather than the empty-element syntax `<p/>`.

### *Entity references*

Embedded scripts often contain reserved characters like `&` or `<`, so the document that contains them is not well-formed. However, most JavaScript and VBScript interpreters won't recognize `&` or `<` in place of the operators they represent. If the script can't be rewritten without these operators (for instance, by changing a less-than comparison to a greater-than or equal-to comparison with the arguments flipped), then you should move to external scripts instead of embedded ones.

Furthermore, most non-XML aware browsers don't recognize the `'` predefined entity reference. If possible, you should avoid using this reference and use the literal `'` character instead. The only place where this character might be a problem is inside attribute values that are enclosed in single quotes because they contain double quotes. However, most browsers do recognize the `"` entity reference for the `"` character, so you can enclose attribute values in double quotes and escape double quotes that are part of attribute values as `"`.

### *Other unsupported features*

A few other subtle differences exist between how browsers handle XHTML and how XHTML expects to be handled. For instance, XHTML allows character references and CDATA sections, though few current browsers understand these constructs. However, you're unlikely to encounter these when converting from HTML to XHTML, and you can generally do without them if you write XHTML from scratch.

Internet Explorer 5.5 and later, as well Netscape 6.0 and later and Mozilla 5.0 and later can parse and display valid XHTML without difficulty and without requiring page authors to jump through these hoops. However, since relatively few users have upgraded their browsers to the level XHTML requires, user-friendly web designers will be jumping through these hoops for years to come.



## *Direct Display of XML in Browsers*

Ultimately, one hopes that browsers will be able to display not just XHTML documents, but any XML document. Since it's too much to ask that browsers provide semantics for all XML applications, both current and yet-to-be-invented, stylesheets will be attached to each document to provide instructions about how each element will be rendered.

The current major stylesheet languages are:

- Cascading Stylesheets Level 1 (CSS1)
- Cascading Stylesheets Level 2 (CSS2)
- XSL Transformations 1.0

Eventually, more versions of these languages, including at least CSS3 and XSLT 1.1, will be available. However, let's begin by looking at how well the current style languages are supported by existing browsers.

## The xml-stylesheet Processing Instruction

The stylesheet associated with a document is indicated by an `xml-stylesheet` processing instruction in the document's prolog: after the XML declaration but before the root element start tag. This processing instruction uses pseudo-attributes to describe the stylesheet; they look like attributes but aren't because `xml-stylesheet` is a processing instruction and not an element.

### The required href and type pseudo-attributes

Two pseudo-attributes for `xml-stylesheet` processing instructions are required. The `href` pseudo-attribute gives the URL, possibly relative, where the stylesheet can be found. The `type` pseudo-attribute specifies the MIME media type of the stylesheet: text/css for cascading stylesheets, text/xml or application/xml for XSLT stylesheets. In Example 7-3, the `xml-stylesheet` processing instruction tells browsers to apply the CSS stylesheet *person.css* to this document before showing it to the reader.

*Example 7-3: A Very Simple, Yet Complete XML Document*

```
<?xml version="1.0"?>
<?xml-stylesheet href="person.css" type="text/css"?>
<person>
  Alan Turing
</person>
```

There are four optional pseudo-attributes in addition to these two required ones:

- `media`
- `charset`
- `alternate`
- `title`

### The media pseudo-attribute

The `media` pseudo-attribute contains a short string identifying the medium this stylesheet should be used for, such as paper, computer monitors, or television. It can be either a single medium or a comma-separated list. Recognized values include:

`screen`
: Computer monitors

`tty`
: Teletypes, terminals, xterms, and other monospaced, text-only devices

`tv`
: Televisions, WebTVs, video game consoles, etc.

`projection`
: Slides, transparencies, and laptop presentations shown to an audience on a large screen

`handheld`
: PDAs, cell phones, GameBoys, etc.

`print`
: Paper

`braille`
: Tactile feedback devices for the sight impaired

`aural`
: Screen readers and speech synthesizers

`all`
: All listed mediums and any that aren't yet invented

For example, this `xml-stylesheet` processing instruction says that the CSS stylesheet at the URL *http://www.ibiblio.org/xml/style/titus.css* should be used for television, projection, and print:

```
<?xml-stylesheet href="http://www.ibiblio.org/xml/style/titus.css"
                 type="text/css" media="tv, projection, print"?>
```

### *The charset pseudo-attribute*

The `charset` pseudo-attribute specifies which character set the stylesheet is written in, using the same values as the encoding declaration. For example, to say that the CSS stylesheet *koran.css* is written in the ISO 8859-6 character set, use this processing instruction:

```
<?xml-stylesheet href="koran.css" type="text/css" charset="ISO-8859-6"?>
```

### *The alternate and title pseudo-attributes*

The `alternate` pseudo-attribute specifies whether this stylesheet is the primary one for its media type or an alternate one for special cases. The default value is no, which indicates that it is the primary stylesheet. If `alternate` has the value `yes`, the browser may give the user a choice from among the alternate stylesheets. If it does offer a choice, it uses the `title` pseudo-attribute's value to tell the user how the style sheets differ. These three `xml-stylesheet` processing instructions offer the user a choice between large, small, and medium text:

```
<?xml-stylesheet href="big.css" type="text/css"
                 alternate="yes" title="Large fonts"?>
```

```
<?xml-stylesheet href="small.css" type="text/css"
                 alternate="yes" title="Small fonts"?>
<?xml-stylesheet href="medium.css" type="text/css" title="Normal fonts"?>
```

Browsers that cannot ask the user to choose a stylesheet simply pick the first nonalternate sheet that most closely matches the environment's media type.

## *Internet Explorer*

Microsoft Internet Explorer 4.0 (IE4) includes an XML parser that users can access from VBScript or JavaScript. IE uses the parser internally to support channels and the Active Desktop. Your own JavaScript and VBScript programs can use this parser to read XML data and insert it into the web page. However, anything more straightforward, such as displaying a page of XML from a specified URL, is beyond IE4's capabilities. Furthermore, IE4 doesn't understand any stylesheet language when applied to XML.

Internet Explorer 5 (IE5) and later does understand XML, though its parser is a little buggy and rejects some documents it shouldn't reject, most embarrassingly the XML 1.0 specification itself. IE5 can display XML files directly, with or without an associated stylesheet. If no stylesheet is provided, IE5 uses a default, built-in XSLT stylesheet that displays the XML document's tree structure with a little DHTML to allow the user to collapse and expand nodes in the tree. Figure 7-1 shows IE5 displaying Example 6-1 from the last chapter.

IE5 also supports parts of CSS Level 1 and some of CSS Level 2. However, the support is inconsistent. Some aspects of CSS that work for HTML documents fail when applied to XML documents. IE 5.5 improves coverage of CSS, though it still doesn't support all CSS properties and selectors.

IE5 and IE5.5 support their own custom version of XSLT, based on a very early working draft of the XSLT specification. They do *not* support XSLT 1.0. You can tell the difference by looking at the namespace of the stylesheet. A stylesheet written for IE5 uses the *http://www.w3.org/TR/WD-xsl* namespace, whereas a stylesheet designed for standard-compliant XSLT processors uses the *http://www.w3.org/1999/XSL/Transform* namespace. Despite superficial similarities, these two languages are not compatible. A stylesheet written for IE will not work with other XSLT processors, and a stylesheet written with standard XSLT 1.0 will not work in IE.

## *Netscape and Mozilla*

Netscape 4.x and earlier do not provide significant support for displaying XML in the browser. Netscape 4.0.6 and later do use XML internally for some features, such as "What's Related." However, the parser used isn't accessible to the page author, even through JavaScript.

Mozilla and Netscape 6.0 do fully support display of XML in the browser. CSS Level 2 is mostly supported. Mozilla can read an XML web page, download the associated CSS stylesheet, apply it to the document, and display the result to the end user, automatically and just as XML on the Web was always meant to work.

*Figure 7-1: A Document viewed using IE5's built-in stylesheet*

Mozilla and Netscape do not support XSLT at all, not even partially. Since Mozilla is open source, there's an ongoing third-party effort to add support for XSLT to Mozilla. Eventually this may be merged back into the main code base, but not in time for Netscape 6.0.

In addition, there are also third-party efforts to support SVG graphics and MathML equations in Mozilla. These efforts probably won't be ready for the first release of Mozilla, but they will be available shortly thereafter.



## Alternative Approaches

Authoring your web pages in XML does not necessarily require serving them in XML. Fourth-generation and earlier browsers that don't support XML in any significant way will be with us for years. Servicing users with these browsers requires standard, ordinary HTML that works in browsers dating back to Mosaic 1.0.

Writing the pages in XML, but serving them in HTML, is a popular option. When the server receives a request for an XML document, it automatically converts the document to HTML and sends the converted document instead. More sophisticated servers can cache the converted documents. They can also recognize browsers that can handle XML and send them the raw data.

The preferred way to perform this conversion is with an XSLT stylesheet and a Java servlet. Indeed most XSLT engines like XT and SAXON include servlets that do exactly this. However, other schemes are possible, such as using PHP or CGI instead of a servlet. The key is to make sure that browsers receive only what they know how to read and display. We'll talk more about XSLT in the next chapter.

## *Authoring Compound Documents with Modular XHTML*

XHTML 1.1 divides the three XHTML DTDs into individual modules. Parameter entities connect the modules by including or leaving out particular modules. The modules include:

*Structure Module,* `%xhtml-struct.module;`
: Absolute bare minimum of elements needed for an HTML document: `html`, `head`, `title`, and `body`.

*Text Module,* `%xhtml-text.module;`
: Basic elements that contain text and other inline elements: `abbr`, `acronym`, `address`, `blockquote`, `br`, `cite`, `code`, `dfn`, `div`, `em`, `h1`, `h2`, `h3`, `h4`, `h5`, `h6`, `kbd`, `p`, `pre`, `q`, `samp`, `span`, `strong`, and `var`.

*Hypertext Module,* `%xhtml-hypertext.module;`
: Elements used for linking: the `a` element.

*List Module,* `%xhtml-list.module;`
: Elements used for lists: `dl`, `dt`, `dd`, `ul`, `ol`, and `li`.

*Applet Module,* `%xhtml-applet.module;`
: Elements needed for Java applets: `applet` and `param`.

*Presentation Module,* `%xhtml-pres.module;`
: Presentation-oriented markup: `b`, `big`, `hr`, `i`, `small`, `sub`, `sup`, and `tt` .

*Edit Module,* `%xhtml-edit.module;`
: Elements for revision tracking: `del` and `ins`.

*Bidirectional Text Module,* `%xhtml-bdo.module;`
: The `bdo` element used to indicate directionality when text in left-to-right languages, such as English and French, is mixed with text in right-to-left languages, such as Hebrew and Arabic.

*Basic Forms Module,* `%xhtml-basic-form.module;`
: Forms as defined in HTML 3.2 using the `form`, `input`, `select`, `option`, and `textarea` elements.

*Forms Module,* `%xhtml-form.module;`
: Forms as defined in HTML 4.0 using the `form`, `input`, `select`, `option`, `textarea`, `button`, `fieldset`, `label`, `legend`, and `optgroup` elements.

*Basic Tables Module,* `%xhtml-basic-table.module;`
: Minimal table support, including only the `table`, `caption`, `th`, `tr`, and `td` elements.

*Tables Module*, `%xhtml-table.module;`
: More complete table support, including not only the `table`, `caption`, `th`, `tr`, and `td` elements, but also the `col`, `colgroup`, `tbody`, `thead`, and `tfoot` elements.

*Image Module*, `%xhtml-image.module;`
: The `img` element.

*Client-side Image Map Module*, `%xhtml-csismap.module;`
: The `map` and `area` elements and extra attributes for several other elements needed to support client-side image maps.

*Server-side Image Map Module*, `%xhtml-ssismap.module;`
: This module doesn't provide new elements, but it adds the `ismap` attribute to the `img` element.

*Object Module*, `%xhtml-object.module;`
: The `object` element used to embed executable content, such as Java applets and ActiveX controls, in web pages.

*Param Module*, `%xhtml-param.module;`
: The `param` element used to pass parameters from web pages to their embedded executable content, such as Java applets and ActiveX controls.

*Frames Module*, `%xhtml-frames.module;`
: The elements needed to implement frames, including `frame`, `frameset`, and `noframes`.

*Iframe Module* `%xhtml-iframe.mod;`
: The `iframe` element used for inline frames.

*Intrinsic Events*, `%xhtml-events.module;`
: Attributes to support scripting, such as `onsubmit` and `onfocus`, that are attached to elements declared in other modules.

*Meta-information Module*, `%xhtml-meta.module;`
: The `meta` element used in headers.

*Scripting Module*, `%xhtml-script.module;`
: Elements that support JavaScript and VBScript: `script` and `noscript`.

*Stylesheet Module*, `%xhtml-style.module;`
: The `style` element used to define Cascading Stylesheets.

*Link Module*, `%xhtml-link.module;`
: The `link` element that specifies relationships to various external documents, such as stylesheets, bases, and translations.

*Base Module*, `%xhtml-base.module;`
: The `base` element that specifies which URL relative URLs are resolved against.

*Target Module*, `%xhtml-target.module;`
: The `target` attribute used to specify the destination frame or a window of a link inside a frame.

*Style Attribute Module*, `%xhtml-inlstyle.module;`
: The `style` attribute that attaches CSS styles to individual elements in the document.

*Name Identification Module,* `%xhtml-nameident.module;`
: The `name` attribute is a deprecated earlier version of the `id` attribute.

*Legacy Module,* `%xhtml-legacy.module;`
: Deprecated elements and attributes, including the `basefont`, `center`, `font`, `s`, `strike`, and `u` elements.

*Ruby Module,* `%xhtml11-ruby.module;`
: The `ruby`, `rbc`, `rtc`, `rb`, `rt`, and `rp` elements used in East Asian text to place small amounts of text next to the body text, generally indicating pronunciation.

## *Mixing XHTML into Your Applications*

The advantage to dividing HTML into all these different modules is that you can pick and choose the pieces you want. If your documents use tables, include the table module. If your documents don't use tables, leave it out. You get only the functionality you actually need.

For example, suppose you're designing a DTD for a catalog. Each item in the catalog is a `catalog_entry` element. Each `catalog_entry` contains a `name`, a `price`, an `item_number`, a `color`, a `size`, and various other common elements you'll likely find in catalogs. Furthermore, each `catalog_entry` contains a `description` of the item. The `description` contains formatted narrative text and looks something like this:

```
<catalog_entry>
  <name>Aluminum Duck Drainer</name>
  <price>34.99</price>
  <item_number>54X8</item_number>
  <color>silver</color>
  <size>XL</size>
  <description>
    <p>
     This sturdy <strong>silver</strong> colored
     sink stopper dignifies the <em>finest
     kitchens</em>. It makes a great gift for
    </p>
    <ul>
      <li>Christmas</li>
      <li>Birthdays</li>
      <li>Mother's Day</li>
    </ul>
    <p>and all other occasions!</p>
  </description>
</catalog_entry>
```

Writing this markup is easy enough. The tricky part is validating it. Rather than reinventing a complete DTD to describe all the formatting that's needed in straightforward narrative descriptions, you can reuse XHTML. The XHTML 1.1 DTD heavily uses parameter entity references to define content models and attribute lists for the different elements. Three entity references are of particular note:

`%Inline.mix;`

A choice containing elements, such as `em`, `a`, and `q`, that don't generally require a line break; it resolves to:

```
br | span | em | strong | dfn | code | samp | kbd | var | cite | abbr |
acronym | q | tt | i | b | big | small | sub | sup | bdo | a | img | map
| applet | ruby | input | select | textarea | label | button | ins | del
| script | noscript
```

`%Block.mix;`

A choice containing elements, such as `b`, `blockquote`, and `ul`, that generally require a line break; it resolves to:

```
h1 | h2 | h3| h4 |h5 | h6| ul| ol| dl| p | div | pre| blockquote |
address | hr | table | form | fieldset | ins | del | script | noscript
```

`%Flow.mix;`

A choice containing both the `Inline.mix;` and `Block.mix;` elements; it resolves to:

```
h1 | h2 | h3 | h4 | h5 | h6 | ul | ol | dl | p | div | pre | blockquote |
address | hr | table | form | fieldset | br | span | em | strong | dfn |
code | samp | kbd | var | cite | abbr | acronym | q | tt | i | b | big |
small | sub | sup | bdo | a | img | map | applet | ruby | input | select
| textarea | label | button | ins | del | script | noscript
```

You can declare that the `description` element contains essentially any legal XHTML fragment in this manner:

```
  <!ENTITY % xhtml PUBLIC "-//W3C//DTD XHTML 1.1//EN"
"xhtml/xhtml11.dtd">
  %xhtml;
  <!ELEMENT description (#PCDATA | %Flow.mix;)*>
```

If you wanted to require `description` to contain only block elements at the top level, you'd declare as follows:

```
  <!ENTITY % xhtml PUBLIC "-//W3C//DTD XHTML 1.1//EN"
"xhtml/xhtml11.dtd">
  %xhtml;
  <!ELEMENT description ((%Block.mix;)*)>
```

The first two lines import the main XHTML DTD from a relative URL, in particular a directory called *xhtml*. This directory must contain the DTD modules bundled with three separate W3C specifications:

- XHTML 1.1—Module-based XHTML (*http://www.w3.org/TR/xhtml11/*)
- Modularization of XHTML (*http://www.w3.org/TR/xhtml-modularization*)
- Ruby Annotation (*http://www.w3.org/TR/ruby*)

The second line uses an entity reference defined in that DTD to set the content model for the `description` element.

Unfortunately this DTD goes a little too far. It includes not only the pieces of HTML you want, such as `p`, `em`, and `ul`, but also a lot of elements you don't want in a printed catalog, such as `a`, `applet`, and `img`. However, you can omit these elements. The main XHTML DTD imports each module inside an `INCLUDE/IGNORE` block like this one for the hypertext module:

```
<!-- Hypertext Module (required) ................................ -->
<!ENTITY % xhtml-hypertext.module "INCLUDE" >
<![%xhtml-hypertext.module;[
<!ENTITY % xhtml-hypertext.mod
     PUBLIC "-//W3C//ELEMENTS XHTML 1.1 Hypertext 1.0//EN"
            "xhtml-hypertext-1.mod" >
%xhtml-hypertext.mod;]]>
```

If the **`%xhtml-hypertext.module;`** parameter entity reference was defined previously as `IGNORE` instead of `INCLUDE`, that declaration takes precedence, and all the elements and attributes defined in the hypertext module, specifically the `a` element, are left out of the resulting DTD.

Let's say you want just the Structure, Basic Text, and List modules. Use a driver DTD that redefines the parameter entity references for the other modules as `IGNORE`. Example 7-4 demonstrates this idea.

*Example 7-4: Catalog DTD Using Basic XHTML and Omitting Elements*

```
<!ELEMENT catalog (catalog_entry*)>
<!ELEMENT catalog_entry (name, price, item_number, color, size, description)>
<!ELEMENT name (#PCDATA)>
<!ELEMENT size (#PCDATA)>
<!ELEMENT price (#PCDATA)>
<!ELEMENT item_number (#PCDATA)>
<!ELEMENT color (#PCDATA)>

<!-- throw away the modules we don't need -->
<!ENTITY % xhtml-hypertext.module "IGNORE" >
<!ENTITY % xhtml-ruby.module      "IGNORE" >
<!ENTITY % xhtml-edit.module      "IGNORE" >
<!ENTITY % xhtml-pres.module      "IGNORE" >
<!ENTITY % xhtml-applet.module    "IGNORE" >
<!ENTITY % xhtml-param.module     "IGNORE" >
<!ENTITY % xhtml-bidi.module      "IGNORE" >
<!ENTITY % xhtml-form.module      "IGNORE" >
<!ENTITY % xhtml-table.module     "IGNORE" >
<!ENTITY % xhtml-image.module     "IGNORE" >
<!ENTITY % xhtml-csismap.module   "IGNORE" >
<!ENTITY % xhtml-ssismap.module   "IGNORE" >
<!ENTITY % xhtml-meta.module      "IGNORE" >
<!ENTITY % xhtml-script.module    "IGNORE" >
<!ENTITY % xhtml-style.module     "IGNORE" >
<!ENTITY % xhtml-link.module      "IGNORE" >
<!ENTITY % xhtml-base.module      "IGNORE" >
<!ENTITY % xhtml-target.module    "IGNORE" >

<!-- import the XHTML DTD, at least those parts we aren't ignoring.
     You will probably need to change the system ID to point to
     whatever directory you've stored the DTD in.
-->
```

*Example 7-4: Catalog DTD Using Basic XHTML and Omitting Elements (continued)*

```
<!ENTITY % xhtml11.mod PUBLIC "-//W3C//DTD XHTML 1.1//EN"
                        "xhtml-modularization/DTD/xhtml11.dtd">
%xhtml11.mod;

<!ELEMENT description (%Block.mix;)+)>
```

## Mixing Your Applications into XHTML

An even more important feature of Modular XHTML is that it allows you to add new elements that HTML doesn't support. For instance, to include SVG pictures in your documents, just import the SVG DTD and redefine the `Misc.extra` parameter entity to allow the SVG root element `svg`. (This step only lets you include SVG pictures in your XML documents. It doesn't magically give the browser the ability to render these pictures.) You can add these new elements by redefining any of three parameter entity references:

`%Inline.extra;`
: Place the root elements of your application here if you want them added to the content model of all inline elements, such as `span`, `em`, `code`, and `textarea`.

`%Block.extra;`
: Place the application's root elements here if you want them added to the content model of all block elements, such as `div`, `h1`, `p`, and `pre`.

`%Misc.extra;`
: Place the application's root elements here if you want them added to the content model of both block and inline elements.

The definition of each of these parameter entities should be a list of the elements you want to add to the content model, separated by a vertical bar and beginning with a vertical bar. For instance, to include MathML equations as both inline and block elements, import the MathML DTD and redefine the `Misc.extra` parameter entity to include the MathML root element `math` like this:

```
<!ENTITY % Misc.extra "| math">
```

If you want to allow block-level MathML equations and SVG pictures, import their respective DTDs and redefine the `Block.extra` parameter entity like this:

```
<!ENTITY % Block.extra "| math | svg">
```

Order is important here. The MathML DTD and the `Block.extra` declaration both have to be parsed before the XHTML DTD is parsed. Example 7-5 demonstrates this idea with a DTD that mixes MathML 1.0 and XHTML and throws in a namespace declaration for good measure.

*Example 7-5: A DTD That Mixes MathML into XHTML and MathML*

```
<!ENTITY % mathml SYSTEM "mathml/mathml.dtd">
%mathml;

<!-- MathML 1.0.1 doesn't know about namespaces -->
<!ATTLIST math xmlns CDATA #FIXED "http://www.w3.org/TR/REC-MathML/">
```

```
<!ENTITY % Misc.extra "| math">

<!ENTITY % xhtml PUBLIC "-//W3C//DTD XHTML 1.1//EN" "xhtml/xhtml11.dtd">
%xhtml;
```

You can also mix new elements, such as `math`, into individual elements like `p` without changing all other block elements. The content model for each XHTML element is defined by a parameter entity named `*Element*.content` (e.g., `%p.content;`, `%em.content;`, and `%td.content;`). The following code looks like the standard definition of `p.content`:

```
<!ENTITY % p.content
     "( #PCDATA | %Inline.mix; )*" >
```

To add the `math` element to this block element, but not to every other block element, redefine `p.content` like this:

```
<!ENTITY % p.content "( #PCDATA | %Inline.mix; | math )*" >
```

The XHTML 1.1 DTD is quite sophisticated. You can play more tricks by mixing and matching different parts of the DTD, mostly by defining and redefining different parameter entity references. The easiest way to learn about these references is by reading the raw DTDs. The comments in the DTD are often more descriptive and accurate than the prose specification.

## *Mixing Your Own XHTML*

The XHTML 1.1 DTD does not include all available modules. For instance, frames and the legacy presentational elements are deliberately omitted and cannot easily be turned on. This is the W3C's not-so-subtle way of saying that you shouldn't use these elements in the first place. If you do want to use them, you must create your own complete DTD using the individual modules you require.

To do this, you must first define the namespace URI and prefix for your elements and attributes. The W3C provides a template you can adapt for this purpose at *http://www.w3.org/TR/xhtml-modularization/DTD/templates/template-qname-1.mod*. Example 7-6 demonstrates a DTD fragment that defines names for the `today` and `quoteoftheday` elements that one of the authors uses on his web sites. The module is based on the W3C-provided template.

*Example 7-6: A DTD Fragment Used to Define the today Element's Names and Namespaces*

```
<!-- ....................................................... -->
<!-- CafeML Qualified Names Module ......................... -->
<!-- file: cafe-qname-1.mod

     This is an extension of XHTML, a reformulation of HTML as
     a modular XML application.

     This DTD module is identified by the PUBLIC and SYSTEM identifiers:
```

*Example 7-6: A DTD Fragment Used to Define the today Element's Names and Namespaces (continued)*

```
PUBLIC "-//Elliotte Rusty Harold//ELEMENTS CafeML Qualified Names 1.0//EN"
       "cafe-qname-1.mod"

     Revisions:
     (none)
     ............................................................. -->

<!-- NOTES:  Using the CafeML Qualified Names Extension

     This is a module for a markup language 'CafeML',
     which currently declares two extension element types, <quoteoftheday>
     and <today>. The parameter entity naming convention uses uppercase
     for the entity name and lowercase for namespace prefixes, hence
     this example uses 'CAFEML' and 'cafeml' respectively.

     Please note the three case variants:

         'CafeML'   the human-readable markup language name
         'CAFEML'   used as a parameter entity name prefix
         'cafeml'   used as the default namespace prefix

     The %NS.prefixed; conditional section keyword must be declared
     as "INCLUDE" in order to allow prefixing be used.
-->

<!-- end of NOTES section -->


<!-- :::::::::::::::::::::::::::::::::::::::::::::::::::::::::::::::: -->

<!-- CafeML Qualified Names

     This module is contained in two parts, labeled Section 'A' and 'B':

       Section A declares parameter entities to support namespace-
       qualified names, namespace declarations, and name prefixing
       for CafeML.

       Section B declares parameter entities used to provide
       namespace-qualified names for all CafeML element types.

     The recommended 12 step program for creating conforming
     modules is enumerated below, and spans both the CafeML Qualified
     Names Template and CafeML Extension Template modules.
-->

<!-- Section A: XHTML XML Namespace Framework :::::::::::::::::::: -->

<!-- 1. Declare the two parameter entities used to support XLink,
        first the parameter entity container for the URI used to
        identify the XLink namespace:
-->
```

XML on the Web

*Example 7-6: A DTD Fragment Used to Define the today Element's Names and Namespaces (continued)*

```
<!ENTITY % XLINK.xmlns "http://www.w3.org/1999/xlink" >

<!-- This contains the XLink namespace declaration attribute.
-->
<!ENTITY % XLINK.xmlns.attrib
     "xmlns:xlink  %URI.datatype;           #FIXED '%XLINK.xmlns;'"
>

<!-- 2. Declare a parameter entity %CAFEML.xmlns; containing the
        namespace URI for the CafeML namespace:
-->
<!ENTITY % CAFEML.xmlns  "http://www.ibiblio.org/xml/cafeml/" >

<!-- 3. Declare a parameter entity %CAFEML.prefix; containing the
        default namespace prefix string(s) to use when prefixing
        is enabled. This may be overridden in the DTD driver or
        the internal subset of an document instance when prefixing
        of only the non-XHTML markup is desired.

     NOTE: As specified in [XMLNAMES], the namespace prefix serves
     as a proxy for the URI reference, and is not in itself significant.
-->
<!ENTITY % CAFEML.prefix  "cafe" >

<!-- 4. Declare a %CAFEML.prefixed; conditional section keyword, used
        to activate namespace prefixing. The default value should
        inherit '%NS.prefixed;' from the DTD driver, so that unless
        overridden, the default behaviour follows the overall DTD
        prefixing scheme.
-->
<!ENTITY % NS.prefixed "IGNORE" >
<!ENTITY % CAFEML.prefixed "%NS.prefixed;" >

<!-- 5. Declare a parameter entity %CAFEML.pfx; containing the
        colonized prefix (eg., '%CAFEML.prefix;:') used when
        prefixing is active, an empty string when it is not.
-->
<![%CAFEML.prefixed;[
<!ENTITY % CAFEML.pfx  "%CAFEML.prefix;:" >
]]>
<!ENTITY % CAFEML.pfx  "" >

<!-- 6. Declare a parameter entity %CAFEML.xmlns.extra.attrib;
        that when %CAFEML.prefixed; is 'INCLUDE' recursively
        contains all non-CafeML namespace declaration attributes
        for namespaces embedded in CafeML.

        When %CAFEML.prefixed; is 'IGNORE', this should be declared
        as '%XLINK.xmlns.attrib;', or an empty string if XLink is
        not used in the DTD.
-->
```

*Example 7-6: A DTD Fragment Used to Define the today Element's Names and Namespaces (continued)*

```
<![%CAFEML.prefixed;[
<!ENTITY % CAFEML.xmlns.extra.attrib ""
>
]]>
<!ENTITY % CAFEML.xmlns.extra.attrib
     "%XLINK.xmlns.attrib;"
>

<!-- 7. Declare a parameter entity %CAFEML.xmlns.attrib; containing
        all XML namespace declaration attributes used by CafeML,
        the form dependent on whether prefixing is active. Neither
        XHTML nor XLink should be included here.
-->
<![%CAFEML.prefixed;[
<!ENTITY % CAFEML.xmlns.attrib
     "xmlns:%CAFEML.prefix;  %URI.datatype;   #FIXED '%CAFEML.xmlns;'
      %CAFEML.xmlns.extra.attrib;"
>
]]>
<!ENTITY % CAFEML.xmlns.attrib
     "xmlns        %URI.datatype;           #FIXED '%CAFEML.xmlns;'
      %CAFEML.xmlns.extra.attrib;"
>

<!-- 8. Declare a parameter entity that recursively aggregates all
        previous namespace declaration attributes by including the
        %CAFEML.xmlns.extra.attrib; parameter entity into that of its
        embedding vocabulary, in this case XHTML.

        NOTE: this conditional section is controlled by %NS.prefixed;
        so that CafeML's default namespace attribute won't appear on
        XHTML elements when only CafeML prefixing is active.
-->
<![%NS.prefixed;[
<!ENTITY % XHTML.xmlns.extra.attrib
     "%CAFEML.xmlns.attrib;" >
]]>
<!ENTITY % XHTML.xmlns.extra.attrib
     "%XLINK.xmlns.attrib;"
>

<!-- Section B: CafeML Qualified Names :::::::::::::::::::::::::::: -->

<!-- 9. This section declares parameter entities used to provide
        namespace-qualified names for all CafeML element types.
-->

<!-- template-1.mod -->
<!ENTITY % CAFEML.quoteoftheday.qname  "%CAFEML.pfx;quoteoftheday" >
<!ENTITY % CAFEML.today.qname   "%CAFEML.pfx;today" >

<!-- end of cafe-qname-1.mod -->
```

Next, define the elements and attributes with these names in a module you created. The W3C provides a template for this purpose at *http://www.w3.org/TR/xhtml-modularization/DTD/templates/template-1.mod.* This template uses the same techniques and follows the same patterns as XHTML's built-in modules; for example, it uses parameter entity references that resolve to `INCLUDE` or `IGNORE`.

Example 7-7 demonstrates a DTD fragment that defines the `today` and `quoteoftheday` elements. The `today` element can contain any block-level content through the `Block.mix` parameter entity and has a required `date` attribute. The `quoteoftheday` element always contains exactly one `blockquote` element, followed by exactly one `p` element with no attributes.

*Example 7-7: A DTD Fragment Used to Define the today and quoteoftheday Elements*

```
<!-- ........................................................... -->
<!-- CafeML Extension Module ....................................... -->
<!-- file: CafeML-1.mod

    This is an extension of XHTML, a reformulation of HTML as
    a modular XML application.

    The Extensible Hypertext Markup Language (XHTML)
    Copyright 1998-2000 W3C (MIT, INRIA, Keio), All Rights Reserved.
    Revision: $Id: ch07 1.50 2001/01/04 21:36:48 aschirmer Exp judyh $ SMI

    This DTD module is identified by the PUBLIC and SYSTEM identifiers:

      PUBLIC "-//Elliotte Rusty Harold//ENTITIES CafeML Extension 1.0//EN"
             "CafeML-1.mod"

     Revisions:
     (none)
     ........................................................... -->

<!-- Extension CafeML

     [This module declares two extension element
     types, <today> and <quoteoftheday>. The parameter entity naming
     convention uses uppercase for the entity name and lowercase
     for namespace prefixes, hence this example uses 'CAFEML' and
     'cafe' respectively.]

     This module declares parameter entities used to provide
     namespace-qualified names for all CafeML element types,
     as well as an extensible framework for attribute-based
     namespace declarations on all element types.

     The %NS.prefixed; conditional section keyword must be
     declared as "INCLUDE" in order to allow prefixing to be used.
     By default, foreign (i.e., non-XHTML) namespace modules should
     inherit %NS.prefixed; from XHTML, but this can be overridden
     when prefixing of only the non-XHTML markup is desired.
```

*Example 7-7: A DTD Fragment Used to Define the today and quoteoftheday Elements (continued)*

```
     XHTML's default value for the 'namespace prefix' is an empty
     string. The Prefix value can be redeclared either in a DTD
     driver or in a document's internal subset as appropriate.

     NOTE: As specified in [XMLNAMES], the namespace prefix serves as
     a proxy for the URI reference, and is not in itself significant.
-->

<!-- ................................................................. -->

<!-- 10. Declare the xmlns attributes used by CAFEML dependent on whether
         CafeML's prefixing is active. This should be used on all CafeML
         element types as part of CafeML's common attributes.

        If the entire DTD is namespace-prefixed, CafeML should inherit
        %NamespaceDecl.attrib;, otherwise it should declare default
        xmlns attributes on its own element types.
-->
<![%NS.prefixed;[
<!ENTITY % CAFEML.NamespaceDecl.attrib "%NamespaceDecl.attrib;" >
]]>
<!ENTITY % CAFEML.NamespaceDecl.attrib "%CAFEML.xmlns.attrib;" >

<!-- now include the module's various markup declarations ........ -->

<!ENTITY % CAFEML.Common.attrib
     "%CAFEML.NamespaceDecl.attrib;
      id             ID                         #IMPLIED"
>

<!-- 11. In the attribute list for each element, declare the XML Namespace
         declarations that are legal in the document instance by including
         the %NamespaceDecl.attrib; parameter entity in the ATTLIST of
         each element type.
-->

<!ENTITY % CAFEML.today.qname  "today" >
<!ELEMENT %CAFEML.today.qname;  ( %Block.mix; )* >
<!ATTLIST %CAFEML.today.qname;
      %CAFEML.Common.attrib;
      date CDATA #REQUIRED
>

<!ENTITY % CAFEML.quoteoftheday.qname  "quoteoftheday" >
<!ELEMENT %CAFEML.quoteoftheday.qname;  ( %blockquote.element;,
                                          %p.element; ) >
<!ATTLIST %CAFEML.quoteoftheday.qname;
      %CAFEML.Common.attrib;
>

<!-- end of CafeML-1.mod -->
```

XML on the Web

Next, replace the standard XHTML DTD that imports only the normal XHTML modules with a new one that imports the standard modules you want with any new modules you've defined. Again, the W3C offers a template for this purpose, which you can download from *http://www.w3.org/TR/xhtml-modularization/DTD/templates/template.dtd*. This template is a minimal DTD that makes the necessary imports and declares the necessary parameter entity references that all other modules depend on. Example 7-8 is a DTD based on this template. It merges in the `today` element module defined in Example 7-7 and the standard XHTML basic tables module.

*Example 7-8: An XHTML DTD That Mixes in the Cafe DTD*

```
<!-- ............................................................... -->
<!-- XHTML + CafeML DTD  ........................................... -->
<!-- file: CafeML.dtd
-->

<!-- CafeML DTD
-->
<!-- Please use this formal public identifier to identify it:

         "-//Elliotte Rusty Harold//DTD XHTML CafeDTD//EN"
-->
<!ENTITY % XHTML.version  "-//W3C//DTD XHTML CafeDTD//EN" >

<!-- Bring in any qualified name modules outside of XHTML -->
<!ENTITY % cafe-qname-1.mod "">
%MODULE-qname.mod;

<!-- Define any extra prefixed namespaces that this DTD relies upon -->
<!ENTITY NS.prefixed.extras.attrib "" >

<!-- Define the Content Model file for the framework to use -->
<!ENTITY % xhtml-model.mod "http://www.w3.org/TR/xhtml11/DTD/xhtml11-model-1.
mod">

<!-- Bi-directional text support
     This feature-test entity is used to declare elements and attributes
     used for internationalization support. Set it to INCLUDE
     or IGNORE as appropriate for your markup language.
-->
<!ENTITY % XHTML.bidi              "IGNORE" >

<!-- ::::::::::::::::::::::::::::::::::::::::::::::::::::::::::::::: -->

<!-- Pre-Framework Redeclaration placeholder  .................... -->
<!-- This serves as a location to insert markup declarations
     into the DTD prior to the framework declarations.
     I use it to add the quoteoftheday and today elements to
     the content model of all block level elements.
-->

<!ENTITY % Block.extra "| %CAFEML.quoteoftheday.qname;
                       | %CAFEML.today.qname;">
```

```
<!ENTITY % xhtml-prefw-redecl.module "IGNORE" >
<![%xhtml-prefw-redecl.module;[
%xhtml-prefw-redecl.mod;
<!-- end of xhtml-prefw-redecl.module -->]]>

<!-- The events module should be included here if you need it. In this
     skeleton it is IGNOREd.
-->
<!ENTITY % xhtml-events.module "IGNORE" >

<!-- Modular Framework Module ................................... -->
<!ENTITY % xhtml-framework.module "INCLUDE" >
<![%xhtml-framework.module;[
<!ENTITY % xhtml-framework.mod
     PUBLIC "-//W3C//ENTITIES XHTML 1.1 Modular Framework 1.0//EN"
            "xhtml11-framework-1.mod" >
%xhtml-framework.mod;]]>

<!-- Post-Framework Redeclaration placeholder ................... -->
<!-- This serves as a location to insert markup declarations
     into the DTD following the framework declarations.
-->
<!ENTITY % xhtml-postfw-redecl.module "IGNORE" >
<![%xhtml-postfw-redecl.module;[
%xhtml-postfw-redecl.mod;
<!-- end of xhtml-postfw-redecl.module -->]]>

<!-- Text Module (required) ................................. -->
<!ENTITY % xhtml-text.module "INCLUDE" >
<![%xhtml-text.module;[
<!ENTITY % xhtml-text.mod
     PUBLIC "-//W3C//ELEMENTS XHTML 1.1 Text 1.0//EN"
            "xhtml11-text-1.mod" >
%xhtml-text.mod;]]>

<!-- Hypertext Module (required) ................................ -->
<!ENTITY % xhtml-hypertext.module "INCLUDE" >
<![%xhtml-hypertext.module;[
<!ENTITY % xhtml-hypertext.mod
     PUBLIC "-//W3C//ELEMENTS XHTML 1.1 Hypertext 1.0//EN"
            "xhtml11-hypertext-1.mod" >
%xhtml-hypertext.mod;]]>

<!-- Lists Module (required) .................................. -->
<!ENTITY % xhtml-list.module "INCLUDE" >
<![%xhtml-list.module;[
<!ENTITY % xhtml-list.mod
     PUBLIC "-//W3C//ELEMENTS XHTML 1.1 Lists 1.0//EN"
            "xhtml11-list-1.mod" >
%xhtml-list.mod;]]>
```

*Example 7-8: An XHTML DTD That Mixes in the Cafe DTD (continued)*

```
<!-- Your modules can be included here. Use the basic form defined above,
     and be sure to include the public FPI definition in your catalog file
     for each module that you define. You may also include W3C-defined
     modules at this point.
-->

<!-- CafeML Module (custom module)  ...................... -->
<!ENTITY % cafeml.module "INCLUDE" >
<![%cafeml.module;[
<!ENTITY % cafeml.mod
     PUBLIC "-//Cafe con Leche//XHTML Extensions today 1.0//EN"
            "CafeML-1.mod" >
%cafeml.mod;]]>

<!-- Basic Tables Module (optional)  ...................... -->
<!ENTITY % xhtml-basic-table.module "INCLUDE" >
<![%xhtml-basic-table.module;[
<!ENTITY % xhtml-basic-table.module
     PUBLIC "-//W3C//ELEMENTS XHTML Basic Tables 1.0//EN"
            "xhtml-basic-table-1.mod" >
%xhtml-basic-table.mod;]]>

<!-- Document Structure Module (required)  ...................... -->
<!ENTITY % xhtml-struct.module "INCLUDE" >
<![%xhtml-struct.module;[
<!ENTITY % xhtml-struct.mod
     PUBLIC "-//W3C//ELEMENTS XHTML 1.1 Document Structure 1.0//EN"
            "xhtml11-struct-1.mod" >
%xhtml-struct.mod;]]>

<!-- end of XHTML + CafeML DTD  ..........................................
-->
<!-- .............................................................. -->
```

## Prospects for Improved Web Search Methods

Part of the XML hype is that web search engines will finally understand what a document means by looking at its markup. For instance, you can search for the movie *Sneakers* and get back hits about it without sorting through "Internet Wide Area 'Tiger Teamers' mailing list," "Children's Side Zip Sneakers Recalled by Reebok," "Infant's 'Little Air Jordan' Sneakers Recalled by NIKE," "Sneakers.com—Athletic Shoes from Nike, Reebok, Adidas, Fila, New," and the 32,395 other results that Google pulled up on this search that had nothing to do with the movie.*

In practice, this development is still vapor, mostly because few web pages are available on the frontend in XML, though an increasing number of backends are available in XML. The search engine robots see only the frontend HTML. As this situation slowly changes, and as search engines get smarter, we should see more useful results. Meanwhile, it's possible to add XML hints to your HTML pages that

* In fairness to Google, four of the first ten hits it returned were about the movie.

knowledgeable search engines can employ by using the Resource Description Framework (RDF), the Dublin Core, and the `robots` processing instruction.

## RDF

The Resource Description Framework (RDF), (*http://www.w3.org/RDF/*) is an XML encoding for a particularly simple data model. An RDF document describes resources. Each resource has zero or more properties. Each property has a name and a value, and the value may itself be another resource.

An RDF document's root element is an `RDF` element. Each resource the `RDF` element describes is represented as a `Description` element whose `about` attribute contains a URI, or other identifier, pointing to the resource described. Each child element of the `Description` element represents a property of the resource. Contents of that child element are the value of that property. All RDF elements, such as `RDF` and `Description`, are placed in the *http://www.w3.org/1999/02/22-rdf-syntax-ns#* namespace. Property values normally come from other namespaces.

Suppose we want to say that the book *XML in a Nutshell* has the authors W. Scott Means and Elliotte Rusty Harold. In other words, we want to say that the resource identified by the URI *urn:isbn:0596000588* has one author property with the value `W. Scott Means` and another author property with the value `Elliotte Rusty Harold`. Example 7-9 demonstrates.

*Example 7-9: An RDF Document Naming the Authors of XML in a Nutshell*

```
<rdf:RDF xmlns:rdf="http://www.w3.org/1999/02/22-rdf-syntax-ns#">

  <rdf:Description about="urn:isbn:0596000588">
    <author>Elliotte Rusty Harold</author>
    <author>W. Scott Means</author>
  </rdf:Description>

</rdf:RDF>
```

In this simple example, the values of the author properties are merely text. However, they could be XML or other RDF elements. Other topics relating to RDF include containers, schemas, and nested properties. However, this example is a sufficient description for web metadata.

## Dublin Core

The Dublin Core, *http://purl.org/dc/*, is a standard set of ten information items with specified semantics that reflect the sort of data you'd be likely to find in a card catalog or annotated bibliography. These items include:

*Title*
: The name by which the resource is known. For example, the title of this book is *XML in a Nutshell.*

*Creator*
: The person or organization who created the resource, e.g., a painter, author, illustrator, or composer. For example, the creators of this book are W. Scott Means and Elliotte Rusty Harold.

*Subject*

The subject normally contains a list of keywords, probably from another vocabulary, such as the Dewey Decimal System or Yahoo categories, identifying the topics of the resource. Using the Library of Congress Subject Headings vocabulary, the subject of this book is "XML (Document markup language)."

*Description*

Typically a small amount of text describing the content of the resource in prose; it may also include a picture, table of contents, or other description of the resource. For example, a description of this book might be "A brief tutorial on and quick reference to XML and related technologies and specifications."

*Publisher*

The name of the person, company or organization that makes the resource available. For example, this book's publisher is O'Reilly & Associates.

*Contributor*

A person or organization that contributed to the resource but is not the resource's primary creator. For example, the editor of this book, Laurie Petrycki, might be identified as a contributor, as would the artist who drew the picture on the cover and the designers who laid out the book.

*Date*

The date the book was created or published, normally given in the form YYYY-MM-DD. For example, this book's date might be 2001.01.18.

*Type*

The abstract kind of resource, such as image, text, sound, or software. For example, a description of this book would have the type text.

*Format*

For hard objects like books, the format describes the resource's physical dimensions. For example, the paper version of *XML in a Nutshell* has the dimensions 6" x 9". For digital objects such as web pages, the Format is possibly the MIME media type. An online version of this book would have the Format text/html.

*Identifier*

A formal identifier for the resource, such as an ISBN number, a URI, or a Social Security number. This book's identifier is 0596000588.

*Source*

The resource from which the present resource was derived. For instance, the French translation of this book might reference the original English edition as its source.

*Language*

The language in which this resource is written, typically an ISO 639 language code, optionally suffixed with a hyphen and an ISO 3166 country code. For instance, the language for this book is en-US. The language for this book's French translation might be fr-FR.

*Relation*

A reference to a resource that is in some way related to the current resource. A relation generally uses a formal identifier, such as a URI or an ISBN number. For instance, a reference might refer to the web page for this book.

*Coverage*

The location, time, or jurisdiction the resource covers. For instance, the coverage of this book might be the United States, Canada, Australia, the United Kingdom, and Ireland. The coverage of the French translation of this book might be France, Quebec, Haiti, Belgium, and Switzerland. The coverage will generally be listed in a formal syntax, such as country codes.

*Rights*

Information about copyright, patent, trademark, and other restrictions on the content of the resource. A rights statement about this book may say "Copyright 2000 O'Reilly & Associates."

Dublin Core can be encoded in various forms, including HTML `META` tags and RDF. Here we concentrate on its encoding in RDF. Typically, each resource is described with an `rdf:Description` element. This element contains child elements for as many of the Dublin Core information items as are known about the resource. The name of each element matches the name of one of the 15 Dublin Core properties. These elements are placed in the *http://www.purl.org/dc/* namespace. Example 7-10 shows an RDF-encoded Dublin Core description of this book.

*Example 7-10: An RDF-Encoded Dublin Core Description for XML in a Nutshell*

```
<?xml version="1.0" encoding="UTF-8" standalone="yes"?>
<rdf:RDF xmlns:rdf="http://www.w3.org/1999/02/22-rdf-syntax-ns#"
         xmlns:dc="http://www.purl.org/dc/">

  <rdf:Description about="urn:isbn:0596000588">
    <dc:Title>XML in a Nutshell</dc:Title>
    <dc:Creator>W. Scott Means</dc:Creator>
    <dc:Creator>Elliotte Rusty Harold</dc:Creator>
    <dc:Subject>XML (Document markup language)</dc:Subject>.
    <dc:Description>
      A brief tutorial on and quick reference to XML and
      related technologies and specifications
    </dc:Description>
    <dc:Publisher>O'Reilly &amp; Associates</dc:Publisher>
    <dc:Contributor>Laurie Petrycki</dc:Contributor>
    <dc:Date>2001-01-23</dc:Date>
    <dc:Type>text</dc:Type>
    <dc:Format>6" x 9"</dc:Format>
    <dc:Identifier>0596000588</dc:Identifier>
    <dc:Language>en-US</dc:Language>
    <dc:Relation>http://www.oreilly.com/catalog/xmlnut/</dc:Relation>
    <dc:Coverage>US UK ZA CA AU NZ</dc:Coverage>
    <dc:Rights>Copyright 2000 O'Reilly &amp; Associates</dc:Rights>
  </rdf:Description>

</rdf:RDF>
```

No standard exists yet for how an RDF document should be associated with the XML document it describes. One possibility is for the `rdf:RDF` element to be embedded in the document it describes, for instance as a child of the DocBook source's `BookInfo` element for this book. Having servers provide this meta-information through an extra-document channel in another possibility. A standard protocol that would allow search engines to request this information for any page on the site, for example, could be defined. A convention could be adopted that permits the URL *xyz/meta.rdf* to contain the RDF-encoded Dublin Core metadata for any URL *xyz* on a given web site.

## *Robots*

In HTML the robot's `META` tag tells search engines and other robots whether they may index a page. The following processing instruction has been proposed (*http://homepages.go.com/~wunder0/robots-pi.html*) as an equivalent for XML documents:

```
<?robots index="yes" follow="no"?>
```

Robots look for this instruction in the prolog of any XML document they encounter. The syntax of this particular processing instruction is two attributes, one named `index` and one named `follow`, whose values are either `yes` or `no`. If the `index` attribute has the value `yes`, then a search engine robot indexes this page. If `index` has the value `no`, the robot does not index the page. Similarly, if `follow` has the value `yes`, links from this document are followed. If `follow` has the value no, they won't be.

CHAPTER 8

# XSL Transformations

The Extensible Stylesheet Language (XSL) is divided into two parts: XSL Transformations (XSLT) and XSL Formatting Objects (XSL-FO). This chapter describes XSLT. Chapter 13, *XSL Formatting Objects (XSL-FO)*, covers XSL-FO.

XSLT is an XML application that specifies rules by which one XML document is transformed into another. An XSLT document—that is, an XSLT stylesheet—contains templates. An XSLT processor compares the elements in an input XML document to the templates in a stylesheet. When it finds a matching template, it writes the template's contents into an output tree. When it completes this step, it may serialize the output tree further into an XML document or another format, such as plain text or HTML.

This chapter describes the templates and other elements that appear in an XSLT stylesheet. XSLT uses the XPath syntax to identify matching elements. We will introduce a few pieces of XPath in this chapter, but most of it will be covered in Chapter 9, *XPath*.

## An Example Input Document

To demonstrate XSL transformations, we first need a document to transform. Example 8-1 shows the document used in this chapter. The root element is `people`, which contains two `person` elements. The `person` elements have roughly the same structure (a name followed by professions and hobbies) with some notable differences. For instance, Alan Turing has three professions, but Richard Feynman has only one. Feynman has a `middle_initial` and a `hobby`, but Turing doesn't. Still, these variations clearly use the same basic structure. A DTD that permitted both would be easy to write.



*Example 8-1: An XML Document Describing Two People*

```
<?xml version="1.0"?>
<people>
```

```
  <person born="1912" died="1954">
    <name>
      <first_name>Alan</first_name>
      <last_name>Turing</last_name>
    </name>
    <profession>computer scientist</profession>
    <profession>mathematician</profession>
    <profession>cryptographer</profession>
  </person>

  <person born="1918" died="1988">
    <name>
      <first_name>Richard</first_name>
      <middle_initial>M</middle_initial>
      <last_name>Feynman</last_name>
    </name>
    <profession>physicist</profession>
    <hobby>Playing the bongoes</hobby>
  </person>

</people>
```

Example 8-1 is an XML document. For purposes of this example, it will be stored in a file called *people.xml*. It doesn't have a DTD. However, this fact is tangential: XSLT works equally well with valid and invalid (but well-formed) documents. This document doesn't use namespaces either, though it could. XSLT works just fine with namespaces. Unlike validation, XSLT does pay attention to the actual namespace URIs instead of the prefixes. Thus it is possible to use one prefix for an element in the input document and different prefixes for the same namespace in the stylesheet and output documents.

## *xsl:stylesheet and xsl:transform*

An XSLT stylesheet is an XML document. It can and generally should have an XML declaration. It can have a document type declaration, though most stylesheets do not. The root element of this document is either `stylesheet` or `transform`. These are synonyms for each other. You can use either `stylesheet` or `transform` as you prefer. There is absolutely no difference between them, aside from the name. They both have the same possible children and attributes. They both mean the same thing to an XSLT processor.

The `stylesheet` and `transform` elements, like all other XSLT elements, are in the *http://www.w3.org/1999/XSL/Transform* namespace. This namespace is customarily mapped to the `xsl` prefix, so you write `xsl:transform` or `xsl:stylesheet` rather than `transform` or `stylesheet`.

This namespace URI must be exactly correct. If even a single character is wrong, the stylesheet processor outputs the stylesheet itself instead of the transformed input document. There's a reason for this (see Section 2.3 of the XSLT specification, *Literal Result Element as Stylesheet*, if you really want to know), but the bottom line is that this weird behavior looks very much like a bug in the XSLT processor if you don't expect it. If you do see your stylesheet processor spitting your stylesheet back out at you, the problem almost certainly stems from an incorrect namespace URI.

Internet Explorer 5.0 and 5.5 partially support a very out-of-date working draft of XSLT. They do not support XSLT 1.0, and indeed no XSLT stylesheets in this book work in IE5. Stylesheets that are meant for Microsoft XSLT can be identified by their use of the *http://www.w3.org/TR/WD-xsl* namespace. Good XSLT developers don't use *http://www.w3.org/TR/WD-xsl* or associate with developers who do.

Along with the `xmlns:xsl` attribute declaring this prefix mapping, the root element must have a `version` attribute with the value `1.0`. In XSLT 1.1 the value of this attribute will be changed to 1.1 for stylesheets that require new features only available in XSLT 1.1. XSLT 1.1 processors will still be able to process XSLT 1.0 stylesheets that use `version="1.0"`, however. Thus a minimal XSLT stylesheet, with only the root element and nothing else, is as shown in Example 8-2.

*Example 8-2: A Minimal XSLT Stylesheet*

```
<?xml version="1.0"?>
<xsl:stylesheet version="1.0"
                xmlns:xsl="http://www.w3.org/1999/XSL/Transform">

</xsl:stylesheet>
```

Surprisingly, this is a completely acceptable XSLT stylesheet, and an XSLT processor can apply it to an XML document to produce an output document. Example 8-3 shows the effect of applying this stylesheet to Example 8-1.

*Example 8-3: people.xml Transformed by the Minimal XSLT Stylesheet*

```
<?xml version="1.0" encoding="utf-8"?>




    Alan
    Turing

  computer scientist
  mathematician
  cryptographer
```

*Example 8-3: people.xml Transformed by the Minimal XSLT Stylesheet (continued)*

```
    Richard
    P
    Feynman

  physicist
  Playing the bongoes
```

You can see that the output consists of a text declaration plus the input document text. In this case, the output is a well-formed, external parsed entity; but is not itself a complete XML document.

Markup from the input document has been stripped. The net effect of applying an empty stylesheet, such as Example 8-2, to any input XML document is to reproduce the content but not the markup of the input document. To change that, we need to add templates to the stylesheet telling the XSLT processor how to handle the specific elements in the input document. In the absence of specific templates, an XSLT processor falls back on built-in template rules that have the effect shown here.

## Stylesheet Processors

An XSLT processor is a piece of software that reads an XSLT stylesheet, reads an input XML document, and converts the input document into an output document according to the instructions given in the stylesheet. An XSLT processor can be built into a web browser like MSXML is built into Internet Explorer 5.5. It can be built into a web or application server, as in the Apache XML Project's Cocoon (*http://xml.apache.org/cocoon/*). Or it can be a standalone program run from the command line, such as Michael Kay's SAXON (*http://users.iclway.co.uk/mhkay/saxon/*) or the Apache XML Project's Xalan (*http://xml.apache.org/xalan/*).

### Command-Line Processors

The exact details of how to install, configure, and run the XSLT processor vary from processor to processor. Generally, you must install the processor in your path, or possibly add its *jar* file to your class path if it's written in Java. Then pass in the names of the input file, stylesheet file, and output file on the command line. For example, using Xalan, Example 8-3 is created in this fashion:

```
% java org.apache.xalan.xslt.Process -IN people.xml -XSL minimal.xsl -OUT
8-3.txt
========= Parsing file:D:/books/xian/examples/08/minimal.xsl ==========
Parse of file:D:/books/xian/examples/08/minimal.xsl took 771 milliseconds
========= Parsing people.xml ==========
Parse of people.xml took 90 milliseconds
=============================
Transforming...
transform took 20 milliseconds
XSLProcessor: done
```

For exact details, consult the documentation that comes with your XSLT processor.

### The xml-stylesheet Processing Instruction

XML documents that will be served directly to web browsers can have an `xml-stylesheet` processing instruction in their prolog telling the browser where to find the associated stylesheet for the document, as discussed in the last chapter. If this stylesheet is an XSLT stylesheet, the `type` pseudo-attribute should have the value `text/xml`. For example, this `xml-stylesheet` processing instruction says that browsers should apply the stylesheet found at the absolute URL *http://www.oreilly.com/styles/people.xsl*. Relative URLs can also be used:

```
<?xml version="1.0"?>
<?xml-stylesheet type="text/xml"
                 href="http://www.oreilly.com/styles/people.xsl"?>
<people>
  ...
```

## Templates

To control which output is created from which input, you add templates to your XSLT stylesheet. Each template is represented by an `xsl:template` element. This element has a `match` attribute that contains an XPath pattern identifying the input it matches. The simplest pattern is an element name. Thus this template says that every time a `person` element is seen, the stylesheet processor should emit the text "A Person":

```
<xsl:template match="person">A Person</xsl:template>
```

Example 8-4 is a complete stylesheet that uses this template.

*Example 8-4: A Very Simple XSLT Stylesheet*

```
<?xml version="1.0"?>
<xsl:stylesheet version="1.0"
                xmlns:xsl="http://www.w3.org/1999/XSL/Transform">

  <xsl:template match="person">A Person</xsl:template>

</xsl:stylesheet>
```

When you apply this stylesheet to the document in Example 8-1, you get this output:

```
<?xml version="1.0" encoding="utf-8"?>


  A Person


  A Person
```

Two `person` elements were in the input document. Each time the processor saw one, it emitted the text "A Person." The whitespace outside the `person` elements was preserved, but everything inside the `person` elements was replaced by the contents of the template.

The text "A Person" is called *literal data characters*, a fancy way of saying "plain text that is copied from the stylesheet into the output document." A template may also contain literal result elements, such as markup, that are copied from the stylesheet to the output document. For instance, Example 8-5 wraps the text "A Person" between the <p> and </p> tags:

*Example 8-5: A Simple XSLT Stylesheet with Literal Result Elements*

```
<?xml version="1.0"?>
<xsl:stylesheet version="1.0"
                xmlns:xsl="http://www.w3.org/1999/XSL/Transform">

  <xsl:template match="person">
    <p>A Person</p>
  </xsl:template>

</xsl:stylesheet>
```

The output from this stylesheet is:

```
<?xml version="1.0" encoding="utf-8"?>


  <p>A Person</p>

  <p>A Person</p>
```

The <p> and </p> tags were copied from the input to the output. The only major restriction on the markup you may output is that it must be well-formed XML because the stylesheet must be well-formed XML. For instance, you cannot write a template rule like this:

```
<xsl:template match="person">
  A Person<p>
</xsl:template>
```

Here the <p> tag has no matching end tag, and therefore the stylesheet is malformed. Any other markup you include in your XSLT stylesheet must be similarly well-formed. Empty element tags must end with `/>`; attribute values must be quoted; less-than signs must be escaped as `<`; and all entity references must be declared in a DTD, except for the five predefined ones. XSLT makes no exceptions to the rules of well-formedness.

## *Calculating the Value of an Element with xsl:value-of*

The output text is usually more closely related to the input text than it was in the last couple of examples. Other XSLT elements can select particular content from the input document and insert it into the output document.

One of the most generally useful elements is `xsl:value-of`. This element calculates the string value of a particular input element and inserts it into the output.

The element's value is the text content of the element after all tags have been removed. A `select` attribute containing an XPath expression identifies the element whose value is taken.

For example, suppose you just want to extract the names of all people in the input document. Then you might use a stylesheet like that in Example 8-6. Here the person template outputs only the value of the `name` child element of the matched `person` between the <p> and </p> tags.

*Example 8-6: A Simple XSLT Stylesheet That Uses xsl:value-of*

```
<?xml version="1.0"?>
<xsl:stylesheet version="1.0"
                xmlns:xsl="http://www.w3.org/1999/XSL/Transform">

  <xsl:template match="person">
    <p>
      <xsl:value-of select="name"/>
    </p>
  </xsl:template>

</xsl:stylesheet>
```

When an XSLT processor applies this stylesheet to Example 8-1, it outputs this text:

```
<?xml version="1.0" encoding="utf-8"?>


    <p>
        Alan
        Turing
      </p>


    <p>
        Richard
        P
        Feynman
      </p>
```

## Applying Templates with xsl:apply-templates

By default, an XSLT processor reads the input XML document from top to bottom, starting at the document's root and working its way down using preorder traversal. Templates are activated in the order they match elements encountered during this traversal. This means that a template for a parent will be activated before the templates matching the parent's children.

However, a template can change the order of traversal. That is, it can specify which element or elements should be processed next and specify that an element or elements should be processed in the middle of processing another element. It can even prevent particular elements from being processed. In fact, Examples 8-4 through 8-6 all implicitly prevent processing of each `person` element's child elements. Instead, they provide their own instructions about what the XSLT processor is and is not to do with those children.

The `xsl:apply-templates` element lets you make your choice of processing order explicit. Its `select` attribute contains an XPath expression, telling the XSLT processor which nodes to process at that point in the output tree.

For example, suppose you want to list names of people in the input document, but you want to put the last names first, regardless of the order in which the names occur in the input document, and you don't want to output the professions or hobbies. First, you need a name template that looks like this:

```
<xsl:template match="name">
  <xsl:value-of select="last_name"/>,
  <xsl:value-of select="first_name"/>
</xsl:template>
```

This template alone isn't enough, however, because if it were all there was in the stylesheet, then the output would include the names along with the professions and hobbies. You also need a person template that says to apply templates only to `name` children, but not to other child elements, such as `profession` or `hobby`. This template makes this specification:

```
<xsl:template match="person">
  <xsl:apply-templates select="name"/>
</xsl:template>
```

Example 8-7 shows the complete stylesheet.

*Example 8-7: A Simple XSLT Stylesheet That Uses xsl:apply-templates*

```
<?xml version="1.0"?>
<xsl:stylesheet version="1.0"
               xmlns:xsl="http://www.w3.org/1999/XSL/Transform">

  <xsl:template match="name">
    <xsl:value-of select="last_name"/>,
    <xsl:value-of select="first_name"/>
  </xsl:template>

  <xsl:template match="person">
    <xsl:apply-templates select="name"/>
  </xsl:template>

</xsl:stylesheet>
```

When an XSLT processor applies this stylesheet to Example 8-1, it outputs this result:

```
<?xml version="1.0" encoding="utf-8"?>


  Turing,
    Alan

  Feynman,
    Richard
```

The order of templates in the stylesheet doesn't matter. Only the order of the elements in the input document matters.

Applying templates is also important when the child elements have templates of their own, even if you don't need to reorder the elements. For example, suppose you want a template for the root `people` element that wraps the entire document in an HTML header and body. This template needs to use `xsl:apply-templates` to indicate where it wants the root element's children to be placed. That template might look like this:

```
<xsl:template match="people">
  <html>
    <head><title>Famous Scientists</title></head>
    <body>
      <xsl:apply-templates select="person"/>
    </body>
  </html>
</xsl:template>
```

This template tells the XSLT processor to replace every `people` element in the input document (of which there is only one) with an `html` element. This `html` element contains literal character data and several literal result elements, of which one is a `body` element. The `body` element contains an `xsl:apply-templates` child element that tells the XSLT processor to process all `person` children of the current `people` element and insert the output of any matched templates into the output document's `body` element.

If you'd rather apply templates to all types of children of the `people` element, rather than just `person` children, you can omit the `select` attribute as demonstrated in Example 8-8. You can also use the more complicated XPath expressions discussed in the next chapter to be more precise about which elements you do and do not want to apply templates to.

*Example 8-8: An XSLT Stylesheet That Generates a Complete HTML Document*

```
<?xml version="1.0"?>
<xsl:stylesheet version="1.0"
                xmlns:xsl="http://www.w3.org/1999/XSL/Transform">

  <xsl:template match="people">
    <html>
      <head><title>Famous Scientists</title></head>
      <body>
        <xsl:apply-templates/>
      </body>
    </html>
  </xsl:template>

  <xsl:template match="name">
    <p><xsl:value-of select="last_name"/>,
    <xsl:value-of select="first_name"/></p>
```

XSL Transformations

*Example 8-8: An XSLT Stylesheet That Generates a Complete HTML Document (continued)*

```
  </xsl:template>

  <xsl:template match="person">
    <xsl:apply-templates select="name"/>
  </xsl:template>

</xsl:stylesheet>
```

When an XSLT processor applies this stylesheet to Example 8-1, it outputs the well-formed HTML document shown in Example 8-9. Look closely at this example and you may spot an important change that was not explicitly caused by the instructions in the stylesheet.

*Example 8-9: HTML Document Produced by Applying Example 8-8 to Example 8-1*

```
<html>
<head>
<title>Famous Scientists</title>
</head>
<body>

  <p>Turing,
    Alan</p>

  <p>Feynman,
    Richard</p>

</body>
</html>
```

The difference between Example 8-9 and the previous output examples is that the text declaration disappeared! Although an XSLT element is available to specify whether you do or do not want a text declaration preceding your output (`xsl:output`), we haven't used that element here. Instead, the XSLT processor noticed that the root output element was `html` and adjusted itself accordingly. Since HTML output is such a common case, XSLT uses special rules to handle it. Besides omitting the text declaration, the processor uses HTML empty element syntax, such as `<br>`, instead of XML empty element syntax, such as `<br/>`, in the output document. (The input document and stylesheet must still be well-formed XML.) The XSLT processor will make about half a dozen other changes when it knows it's outputting HTML, all designed to make the output more acceptable to existing web browsers than is well-formed XML.

## *The Built-in Template Rules*

There are seven kinds of nodes in an XML document: the root node, element nodes, attribute nodes, text nodes, comment nodes, processing instruction nodes, and namespace nodes. For each of the seven types of nodes, XSLT provides a default built-in template rule that says what to do with that node if the stylesheet author has not provided more specific instructions. These rules use special wildcard XPath expressions to match all nodes of a given type. Together these template rules largely determine which nodes are activated when.

### The Default Template Rule for Text and Attribute Nodes

The most basic built-in template rule copies the value of text and attribute nodes into the output document. It looks like the following:

```
<xsl:template match="text()|@*">
  <xsl:value-of select="."/>
</xsl:template>
```

The `text()` function is an XPath expression matching all text nodes, just as `first_name` is an XPath expression matching all `first_name` element nodes. `@*` is an XPath expression matching all attribute nodes. The vertical bar combines these two expressions so it selects both text and attribute nodes. The contents of this template say that whenever a text or attribute node is matched, the processor should output the value of that node. For a text node, this value is simply the text in the node. For an attribute, this value is the attribute node value, but not the name.

Example 8-10 is an XSLT stylesheet that pulls the birth and death dates out of the `born` and `died` attributes in Example 8-1. The default template rule for attributes takes the value of the attributes, but an explicit rule selects these values.

*Example 8-10: An XSLT Stylesheet That Reads Attributes*

```
<?xml version="1.0"?>
<xsl:stylesheet version="1.0"
                xmlns:xsl="http://www.w3.org/1999/XSL/Transform">

  <xsl:template match="people">
    <html>
      <head><title>Famous Scientists</title></head>
      <body>
        <dl>
          <xsl:apply-templates/>
        </dl>
      </body>
    </html>
  </xsl:template>

  <xsl:template match="person">
    <dt><xsl:apply-templates select="name"/></dt>
    <dd><ul>
      <li>Born: <xsl:apply-templates select="@born"/></li>
      <li>Died: <xsl:apply-templates select="@died"/></li>
    </ul></dd>
  </xsl:template>

</xsl:stylesheet>
```

XSL Transformations

When an XSLT processor applies this stylesheet to Example 8-1, it outputs the well-formed HTML document shown in Example 8-11.

*Example 8-11: HTML Document Produced by Applying Example 8-10 to Example 8-1*

```
<html>
   <head>
      <title>Famous Scientists</title>
   </head>
   <body>
      <dl>


         <dt>
            Alan
            Turing

         </dt>
         <dd>
            <ul>
               <li>Born: 1912</li>
               <li>Died: 1954</li>
            </ul>
         </dd>


         <dt>
            Richard
            P
            Feynman

         </dt>
         <dd>
            <ul>
               <li>Born: 1918</li>
               <li>Died: 1988</li>
            </ul>
         </dd>


      </dl>
   </body>
</html>
```

It's important to note that though this template states what should happen when an attribute node is reached, by default the XSLT processor never reaches attribute nodes, and therefore never outputs an attribute's value. Attribute values are output only if a specific rule applies templates to them, and none of the default rules apply these templates because attributes are not considered to be children of their parents. In other words, if element `E` has an attribute `A`, then `E` is the parent of `A`, but `A` is not the child of `E`. Applying templates to children of an element with `<xsl:apply-templates/>`, does not apply templates to attributes of the element. To apply the templates, the `xsl:apply-templates` element must contain an XPath expression specifically matching attributes.

## The Default Template Rule for Element and Root Nodes

The most important template rule guarantees that children are processed. The rule is as follows:

```
<xsl:template match="*|/">
  <xsl:apply-templates/>
</xsl:template>
```

The asterisk `*` is an XPath wildcard expression that matches all element nodes, regardless of what name they have or what namespace they're in. The forward slash `/` is an XPath expression that matches the root node. The root node is the first node the processor selects for processing, and therefore the processor executes this template first (unless a nondefault template also matches the root node). Again, the vertical bar combines these two expressions so it selects both the root node and element nodes. In isolation, this rule means that the XSLT processor eventually finds and applies templates to all nodes except attribute and namespace nodes because every nonattribute, nonnamespace node is either the root node, a child of the root node, or a child of an element. Only attribute and namespace nodes are not children of their parents. (You can think of them as disinherited nodes.)

Of course, specific templates may override the default behavior. For example, when including a template matching `person` elements in your stylesheet, children of the matched `person` elements are not necessarily processed unless your own template says to process them.

## The Default Template for Comment and Processing Instruction Nodes

The default template rule for comments and processing instructions is as follows:

```
<xsl:template match="processing-instruction()|comment()"/>
```

This rule matches all comments and processing instructions. However, it does not output anything into the result tree. Unless you provide specific rules matching comments or processing instructions, no part of these items will be copied from the input document to the output document.

## The Default Template for Namespace Nodes

A similar template rule matches namespace nodes and instructs the processor to not copy any part of the namespace node to the output. This rule is truly built-in and must be implemented in the XSLT processor's source code; it can't even be written in an XSLT stylesheet because there is no such thing as an XPath expression that matches a namespace node. That is, no `namespace()` function in XPath exists. The XSLT inserts any necessary namespace declarations in the output document automatically, without any special assistance from namespace templates.

## Modes

Sometimes the same input content needs to appear multiple times in the output document, formatted according to a different template each time. For instance, titles of chapters in a book would be formatted one way in the chapters themselves and a different way in the book's table of contents. Both `xsl:apply-templates` and `xsl:template` elements can have optional `mode` attributes that connect different templates to different uses. A `mode` attribute on `xsl:template` element identifies in which mode that template should be activated. An `xsl:apply-templates` element with a `mode` attribute only activates templates with matching `mode` attributes. Example 8-12 demonstrates this activation with a stylesheet that begins the output document with a list of people's names. This action is accomplished in the `toc` mode. Then a separate template and a separate `xsl:apply-templates` element in the default mode (really no mode at all) output the complete contents of all `person` elements.

*Example 8-12: A Stylesheet That Uses Modes*

```
<?xml version="1.0"?>
<xsl:stylesheet version="1.0"
                xmlns:xsl="http://www.w3.org/1999/XSL/Transform">

  <xsl:template match="people">
    <html>
      <head><title>Famous Scientists</title></head>
      <body>
        <ul><xsl:apply-templates select="person" mode="toc"/></ul>
        <xsl:apply-templates select="person"/>
      </body>
    </html>
  </xsl:template>

  <!-- Table of Contents Mode Templates -->
  <xsl:template match="person" mode="toc">
    <xsl:apply-templates select="name" mode="toc"/>
  </xsl:template>

  <xsl:template match="name" mode="toc">
    <li><xsl:value-of select="last_name"/>,
    <xsl:value-of select="first_name"/></li>
  </xsl:template>

  <!-- Normal Mode Templates -->
  <xsl:template match="person">
    <p><xsl:apply-templates/></p>
  </xsl:template>

</xsl:stylesheet>
```

Example 8-13 shows the output displayed when this stylesheet is applied to *people.xml*. The people template in Example 8-12 applies templates to its `person` children twice. It applies the templates the first time in the `toc` mode. This selects the first person template in the stylesheet that outputs each person in the form `<li>Turing, Alan</li>`. It doesn't specify a mode the second time. This selects the second person template in the stylesheet, which outputs all the `person` character data wrapped in a `p` element.

*Example 8-13: Output from a Stylesheet That Uses Modes to Process Each Person Twice with Different Templates*

```
<html>
<head>
<title>Famous Scientists</title>
</head>
<body>
<ul>
<li>Turing,
   Alan</li>
<li>Feynman,
   Richard</li>
</ul>
<p>

      Alan
      Turing

    computer scientist
    mathematician
    cryptographer
  </p>
<p>

      Richard
      P
      Feynman

    physicist
    Playing the bongoes
  </p>
</body>
</html>
```

For every mode you use in the stylesheet, the XSLT processor adds one default template rule to its set of built-in rules. This rule applies to all element and root nodes in the specified node and applies templates to their children in the same mode (since the usual built-in template rule for element and root nodes doesn't have a mode). For instance, the extra default rule for Example 8-10 looks like this:

```
<xsl:template match="*|/" mode="toc">
  <xsl:apply-templates mode="toc"/>
</xsl:template>
```

## Attribute Value Templates

Including known attribute values in the output document as the literal content of a literal result element is easy. For example, this template rule wraps each input `person` element in an HTML `span` element that has a `class` attribute with the value `person`:

```
<xsl:template match="person">
  <span class="person"><xsl:apply-templates/></span>
</xsl:template>
```

However, the process is trickier if the attribute's value is not known when the stylesheet is written, and instead must be read from the input document. The solution is to use an *attribute value template.* An attribute value template is an XPath expression enclosed in curly braces that's placed in the attribute value in the stylesheet. When the processor outputs that attribute, it replaces the attribute value template with its value. For example, suppose you want to write a name template that changes the input `name` elements to empty elements with `first_name`, `middle_initial`, and `last_name` attributes like this:

```
<name first="Richard" initial="P" last="Feynman"/>
```

This template accomplishes that task:

```
<xsl:template match="name">
  <name first="{first_name}"
        initial="{middle_initial}"
        last="{last_name}" />
</xsl:template>
```

The value of the `first` attribute in the stylesheet is replaced by the value of the `first_name` element from the input document; the value of the `initial` attribute is replaced by the value of the `middle_initial` element from the input document; and the value of the `last` attribute is replaced by the value of the `last_name` element from the input document.

## XSLT and Namespaces

XPath expressions that match and select elements identify these elements based on their local name and namespace URI. They do not consider the namespace prefix. Most commonly, the same namespace prefix is mapped to the same URI in both the input XML document and the stylesheet. However, this is not required. Consider Example 8-14. This example is exactly the same as Example 8-1, except that now all elements are placed in the namespace *http://namespaces.oreilly.com/people.*

*Example 8-14: Document Describing Two People Using a Default Namespace*

```
<?xml version="1.0"?>
<people xmlns="http://namespaces.oreilly.com/people">

  <person born="1912" died="1954">
    <name>
      <first_name>Alan</first_name>
```

*Example 8-14: Document Describing Two People Using a Default Namespace (continued)*

```
      <last_name>Turing</last_name>
    </name>
    <profession>computer scientist</profession>
    <profession>mathematician</profession>
    <profession>cryptographer</profession>
  </person>

  <person born="1918" died="1988">
    <name>
      <first_name>Richard</first_name>
      <middle_initial>P</middle_initial>
      <last_name>Feynman</last_name>
    </name>
    <profession>physicist</profession>
    <hobby>Playing the bongoes</hobby>
  </person>

</people>
```

Except for the built-in templates, none of the templates mentioned so far in this chapter will work on this document! Consider this template from Example 8-8:

```
<xsl:template match="name">
  <p><xsl:value-of select="last_name"/>,
  <xsl:value-of select="first_name"/></p>
</xsl:template>
```

The template tries to match a `name` element in the default namespace, but the `name` elements in Example 8-13 aren't in the default namespace; they're in the *http://namespaces.oreilly.com/people* namespace. This template no longer applies. To make it fit, we could declare that the default namespace in the stylesheet is in fact *http://namespaces.oreilly.com/people*. However, that declaration would change the default namespace for matched elements like `name` and literal result elements like `p`. Since we don't want to do that here, (you might want to if the input and output vocabularies were the same) we instead map the prefix `pe` to the namespace URI *http://namespaces.oreilly.com/people*. Then instead of matching `name`, we match `pe:name`. The fact that the input document doesn't use the prefix `pe` is irrelevant, as long as the namespace URIs match up. Example 8-15 demonstrates by rewriting Example 8-8 to work with Example 8-14 instead.

*Example 8-15: XSLT Stylesheet for Documents Using the http://namespaces.oreilly.com/people Namespace*

```
<?xml version="1.0"?>
<xsl:stylesheet version="1.0"
                xmlns:xsl="http://www.w3.org/1999/XSL/Transform"
                xmlns:pe="http://namespaces.oreilly.com/people">

  <xsl:template match="pe:people">
    <html>
      <head><title>Famous Scientists</title></head>
```

*Example 8-15: XSLT Stylesheet for Documents Using the http://namespaces.oreilly.com/people Namespace (continued)*

```
      <body>
        <xsl:apply-templates/>
      </body>
    </html>
  </xsl:template>

  <xsl:template match="pe:name">
    <p><xsl:value-of select="pe:last_name"/>,
    <xsl:value-of select="pe:first_name"/></p>
  </xsl:template>

  <xsl:template match="pe:person">
    <xsl:apply-templates select="pe:name"/>
  </xsl:template>

</xsl:stylesheet>
```

The output is the same as you get by applying Example 8-8 to Example 8-1 because in both cases, the result tree uses the default namespace exclusively, though it generally doesn't have to.

## Other XSLT Elements

XSLT does much more than what we've covered in this introductory chapter. Other features yet to be discussed include:

- Named templates
- Numbering and sorting output elements
- Conditional processing
- Iteration
- Extension elements and functions
- Importing other stylesheets

Chapter 20, *XSLT Reference*, will discuss the elements that provide these features. Since XSLT is itself Turing complete and since it can invoke extension functions written in other languages, such as Java, chances are very good that you can use XSLT to perform whatever transformations you need.

Besides these additional elements, you can do much more by simply expanding the XPath expressions and patterns used in the `select` and `match` attributes of elements you're already familiar with. These techniques will be explored in the next chapter.

The techniques outlined in this chapter lay the foundation for all subsequent, advanced work with XSLT. The key to transforming XML documents with XSLT is to match templates to elements in the input document. These templates contain both literal result data and XSLT elements that instruct the processor where to get more data. This simple idea is the basis for everything you do with XSLT.

CHAPTER 9

# XPath

XPath is a non-XML language used to identify particular parts of XML documents. XPath lets you write expressions that refer to the document's first `person` element, the seventh child element of the third `person` element, the `ID` attribute of the first `person` element whose contents are the string "Fred Jones," all `xml-stylesheet` processing instructions in the document's prolog, and so forth. XPath indicates nodes by position, relative position, type, content, and several other criteria. XSLT uses XPath expressions to match and select particular elements in the input document for copying into the output document or further processing. XPointer uses XPath expressions to identify the particular point in or part of an XML document that an XLink links to.

XPath expressions can also represent numbers, strings, or Booleans, so XSLT stylesheets carry out simple arithmetic for numbering and cross referencing figures, tables, and equations. String manipulation in XPath lets XSLT perform tasks like making the title of a chapter uppercase in a headline, but mixed case in a reference in the body text.

## The Tree Structure of an XML Document

An XML document is a tree made up of nodes. Some nodes contain other nodes. One root node ultimately contains all other nodes. XPath is a language for picking nodes and sets of nodes out of this tree. From the perspective of XPath, there are seven kinds of nodes:

- The root node
- Element nodes
- Text nodes
- Attribute nodes

- Comment nodes
- Processing instruction nodes
- Namespace nodes

Note the constructs not included in this list: CDATA sections, entity references, and document type declarations. XPath operates on an XML document after these items have merged into the document. For instance, XPath cannot identify the first CDATA section in a document or tell whether a particular attribute value was included directly in the source element start tag or merely defaulted from the declaration of the attribute in the DTD.

Consider the document in Example 9-1. This document exhibits all seven types of nodes. Figure 9-1 is a diagram of this document's tree structure.

*Example 9-1: The Example XML Document Used in This Chapter*

```
<?xml version="1.0"?>
<?xml-stylesheet type="text/xsl" href="people.xsl"?>
<!DOCTYPE people [
 <!ATTLIST homepage xlink:type CDATA #FIXED "simple"
                  xmlns:xlink CDATA #FIXED "http://www.w3.org/1999/xlink">
 <!ATTLIST person id ID #IMPLIED>
]>
<people>

  <person born="1912" died="1954" id="p342">
    <name>
      <first_name>Alan</first_name>
      <last_name>Turing</last_name>
    </name>
    <!-- Did the word computer scientist exist in Turing's day? -->
    <profession>computer scientist</profession>
    <profession>mathematician</profession>
    <profession>cryptographer</profession>
    <homepage xlink:href="http://www.turing.org.uk/"/>
  </person>

  <person born="1918" died="1988" id="p4567">
    <name>
      <first_name>Richard</first_name>
      <middle_initial>&#x4D;</middle_initial>
      <last_name>Feynman</last_name>
    </name>
    <profession>physicist</profession>
    <hobby>Playing the bongoes</hobby>
  </person>

</people>
```

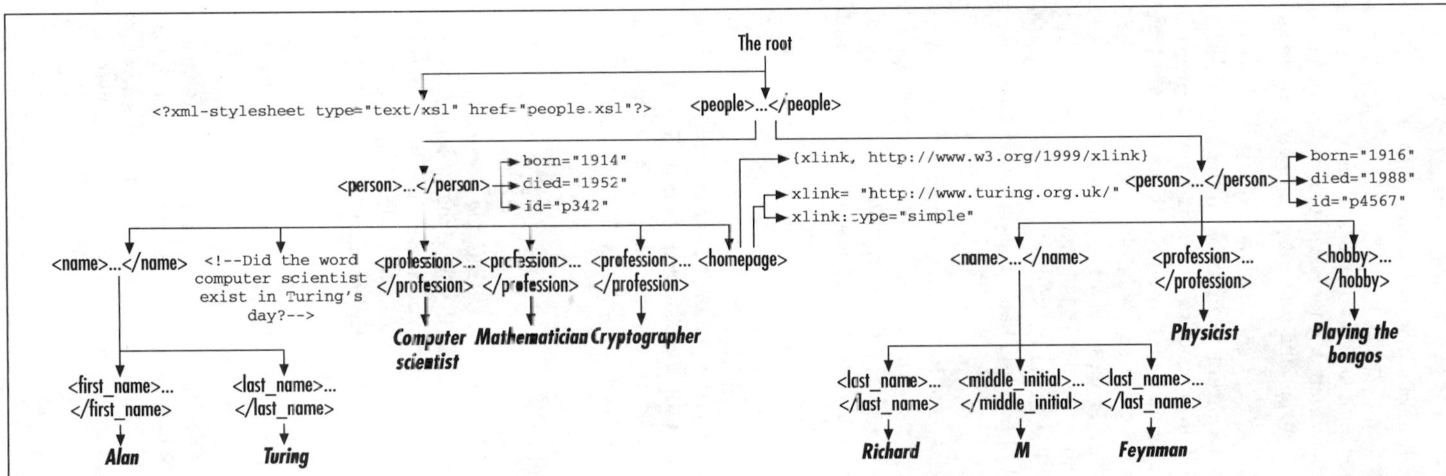


*Figure 9-1: The tree structure of Example 9-1*

The XPath data model has several inobvious features. First, the tree's root node is *not* the same as its root element. The tree's root node contains the entire document, including the root element and comments and processing instructions that occur before the root element start tag or after the root element end tag. In Example 9-1, the root node contains the `xml-stylesheet` processing instruction and the root element `people`.

The XPath data model does not include everything in the document. In particular, the XML declaration and DTD are *not* addressable via XPath. However, if the DTD provides default values for any attributes, then XPath recognizes those attributes. The `homepage` element has an `xlink:type` attribute supplied by the DTD. Similarly, any references to parsed entities are resolved. Entity references, character references, and CDATA sections are not individually identifiable, though any data they contain is addressable. For example, XSLT does not enable you to make all text in CDATA sections bold because XPath doesn't know what text is and isn't part of a CDATA section.

Finally, `xmlns` attributes are reported as namespace nodes. They are not considered attribute nodes, though a non-namespace aware parser will see them as such. Furthermore these nodes are attached to every element and attribute node for which that declaration has scope. They are not just attached to the single element where the namespace is declared.

## Location Paths

The most useful XPath expression is a *location path*. A location path uses at least one location step to identify a set of nodes in a document. This set may be empty, contain a single node, or contain several nodes. These nodes can be element, attribute, namespace, text, comment, processing instruction, root nodes, or any combination of them.

### The Root Location Path

The simplest location path is the one that selects the document's root node. This path is simply the forward slash `/`. (You'll notice that a lot of XPath syntax was deliberately chosen to be similar to the syntax used by the Unix shell. Here `/` is the root of a Unix filesystem and `/` is the root node of an XML document.) For example, this XSLT template uses the XPath pattern `/` to match the entire input document tree and wrap it in an `html` element:

```
<xsl:template match="/">
  <html><xsl:apply-templates/></html>
</xsl:template>
```

The forward slash `/` is an absolute location path because no matter what the context node is, no matter where you were in the input document when this template was applied, it always means the same thing: the root node of the document. It is relative to the document you process, but not to anything within that document.

## *Child Element Location Steps*

The second simplest location path is a single element name. This selects all child elements with the specified name. For example, the XPath `profession` refers to all `profession` child elements of the context node. Exactly which elements they are depends on what the context node is, so this is a relative XPath. If the context node is the Alan Turing `person` element in Example 9-1, then the location path `profession` refers to that element's three `profession` child elements:

```
<profession>computer scientist</profession>
<profession>mathematician</profession>
<profession>cryptographer</profession>
```

However, if the context node is the Richard Feynman `person` element in Example 9-1, then the XPath `profession` refers to its single `profession` child element:

```
<profession>physicist</profession>
```

If the context node is the `name` child element of Richard Feynman or Alan Turing's `person` element, then this XPath doesn't refer to anything at all because neither of these elements has `profession` child elements.

In XSLT, the context node for an XPath expression used in the `select` attribute of `xsl:apply-templates` and similar elements is the currently matched node. Consider the simple stylesheet in Example 9-2. Look at the template for the `person` element. The XSLT processor activates this template twice, once for each `person` node in the document. The first time this template rule is activated, the context node is set to Alan Turing's `person` element. The second time this template rule is activated, the context node is set to Richard Feynman's `person` element. When the same template is activated with a different context node, the XPath expression in `<xsl:value-of select="name"/>` refers to a different element, and the output produced is therefore different.

*Example 9-2: A Very Simple Stylesheet for Example 9-1*

```
<?xml version="1.0"?>
<xsl:stylesheet version="1.0"
                xmlns:xsl="http://www.w3.org/1999/XSL/Transform">

  <xsl:template match="people">
    <xsl:apply-templates select="person"/>
  </xsl:template>

  <xsl:template match="person">
    <xsl:value-of select="name"/>
  </xsl:template>

</xsl:stylesheet>
```

When other systems, such as XPointer, use XPath, other means are provided for determining the context node.

## *Attribute Location Steps*

Attributes are also part of XPath. To select a particular attribute of an element, use an at sign @ followed by the name of the attribute you want. For example, the XPath expression `@born` selects the `born` attribute of the context node. Example 9-3 is a simple XSLT stylesheet that generates an HTML table of names and birth and death dates from documents such as Example 9-1.

*Example 9-3: An XSLT Stylesheet Using Root, Child Element, and Attribute Location Steps*

```
<?xml version="1.0"?>
<xsl:stylesheet version="1.0"
                xmlns:xsl="http://www.w3.org/1999/XSL/Transform">

  <xsl:template match="/">
    <html>
      <xsl:apply-templates select="people"/>
    </html>
  </xsl:template>

  <xsl:template match="people">
    <table>
      <xsl:apply-templates select="person"/>
    </table>
  </xsl:template>

  <xsl:template match="person">
    <tr>
      <td><xsl:value-of select="name"/></td>
      <td><xsl:value-of select="@born"/></td>
      <td><xsl:value-of select="@died"/></td>
    </tr>
  </xsl:template>

</xsl:stylesheet>
```

The stylesheet in Example 9-3 has three templates. The first template has a match pattern that matches the root node, `/`. The XSLT processor activates this template and sets the context node to the root node. Then it outputs the start tag `<html>`. This is followed by an `xsl:apply-templates` element that selects nodes matching the XPath expression `people`. If the input document is Example 9-1, then exactly one such node, the root element, is present. This element is selected and its template, the one with the match pattern of `people`, is applied. The XSLT processor sets the context node to the root `people` element and then begins processing the `people` template. It outputs a `<table>` start tag and then encounters an `xsl:apply-templates` element that selects nodes matching the XPath expression `person`. Two child elements of this context node match the XPath expression `person`, so they're each processed in turn using the `person` template. When it begins processing each `person` element, the XSLT processor sets the context node context node to that element. It outputs that element's `name` child element value and `born` and `died` attribute values, wrapped in a table row and three table cells. The net result is:

```
<html>
   <table>
      <tr>
         <td>
            Alan
            Turing

         </td>
         <td>1912</td>
         <td>1954</td>
      </tr>
      <tr>
         <td>
            Richard
            P
            Feynman

         </td>
         <td>1918</td>
         <td>1988</td>
      </tr>
   </table>
</html>
```

## *The comment(), text(), and processing-instruction() Location Steps*

Though element, attribute, and root nodes account for at least 90 percent of what you need to do with XML documents, four kinds of nodes still need to be addressed: namespace nodes, text nodes, processing instruction nodes, and comment nodes. Namespace nodes are rarely invoked explicitly. Instead, the stylesheet uses its own `xmlns` attributes and prefixes, and the processor handles any necessary conversion between input namespace prefixes and stylesheet namespace prefixes (as long as the URIs match). On output, the XSLT processor inserts `xmlns` attributes as necessary to make namespaces in the output document correct. The other three node types have special functions to match them:

- `comment()`
- `text()`
- `processing-instruction()`

Since comments and text nodes don't have names, the `comment()` and `text()` functions match any comment or text node that's an immediate child of the context node. Each comment is a separate comment node. Each text node contains the maximum possible contiguous run of text not interrupted by a tag. Entity references and CDATA sections are resolved into text and markup and do not interrupt text nodes.

By default XSLT stylesheets do process text nodes but do not process comment nodes. You can add a comment template to an XSLT stylesheet so it will process comments, too. This template replaces each comment with the text "Comment Deleted" in italic:

```
<xsl:template match="comment()">
  <i>Comment Deleted</i>
</xsl:template>
```

With no arguments, the `processing-instruction()` function selects all the context node's processing instruction children. If it has an argument, it selects only the processing instruction children with the specified target. For example, the XPath expression `processing-instruction('xml-stylesheet')` selects all processing instruction children of the context node whose target is `xml-stylesheet`.

## *Wildcards*

Wildcards allow you to match different element and node types at the same time. There are three wild cards: `*`, `node()`, and `@*`.

The asterisk `*` matches any element node, regardless of type. For example, this XSLT template says that all elements should have their child elements processed but should not produce any output:

```
<xsl:template match="*"><xsl:apply-templates select="*"/></xsl:template>
```

The `*` does not match attributes, text nodes, comments, or processing instruction nodes. Thus in this example, output comes only from child elements that have their own templates that override this one.

You can put a namespace prefix in front of the asterisk. In this case, only elements in the same namespace are matched. For example, `svg:*` matches all elements with the same namespace URI as the `svg` prefix is mapped to. As usual, the URI, not the prefix, matters. The prefix may differ in the stylesheet and the source document, as long as the namespace URI is the same.

The `node()` wild card matches all nodes: element nodes, text nodes, attribute nodes, processing instruction nodes, namespace nodes, and comment nodes.

The `@*` wild card matches all attribute nodes. For example, this XSLT template copies the values of all attributes of a `person` element in the document to an `attributes` element in the output:

```
<xsl:template match="person">
  <attributes><xsl:apply-templates select="@*"/></attributes>
</xsl:template>
```

As with elements, you can attach a namespace prefix to the wild card to match only attributes in a specific namespace. For instance, `@xlink:*` matches all XLink attributes, provided that the prefix `xlink` is mapped to the `http://www.w3.org/1999/xlink` namespace. Again, the URI, not the actual prefix, matters.

### *Multiple Matches with |*

You may want to match more than one type of element or attribute, but not all types. For example, you may want an XSLT template that applies to the profession and hobby elements, but not to the name, person, or people elements. You can combine individual location steps with the vertical bar | to indicate that you want to match any of the named elements. For instance, profession|hobby matches profession and hobby child elements of the context node. first_name|middle_initial|last_name matches first_name, middle_initial, and last_name child elements of the context node. @id|@xlink:type matches id and xlink:type attributes of the context node. *|@* matches elements and attributes, but does not match text nodes, comment nodes, or processing instruction nodes. This XSLT template applies to all the nonempty leaf elements (elements that don't contain any other elements) of Example 9-1:

```
<xsl:template match="first_name|last_name|profession|hobby">
  <xsl:value-of select="text()"/>
</xsl:template>
```

## *Compound Location Paths*

The XPath expressions you've seen so far—element names, @ plus an attribute name, /, comment(), text(), node(), and processing-instruction()—are all single location steps. You can combine these location steps with the forward slash to move down the hierarchy from the matched node to other nodes. You can also use a period to refer to the current node, a double period to refer to the parent node, and a double forward slash to refer to descendants of the context node. With the exception of //, these are all similar to Unix shell syntax for navigating a hierarchical file system.

### *Building Compound Location Paths from Location Steps with /*

The forward slash / combines different location steps to make a compound location path. Each step in the path is relative to the one that preceded it. If the path begins with /, then the first step in the path is relative to the root node. Otherwise, it is relative to the context node. For example, consider the XPath expression /people/person/name/first_name. This expression begins at the root node, selects all people element children of the root node, selects all person element children of those nodes, then all name children of those nodes, and finally, all first_name children of the nodes. Applied to Example 9-1, the expression indicates these two elements:

```
<first_name>Alan</first_name>
<first_name>Richard</first_name>
```

To indicate only textual content of those two nodes, we must go one step further. The XPath expression /people/person/name/first_name/text() selects the strings "Alan" and "Richard" from Example 9-1.

These two XPath expressions both began with /, so they're absolute location paths that start at the root. Relative location paths can also count down from the context node. For example, the XPath expression person/@id selects the id attribute of the person child element of the context node.

## *Selecting from All Descendants with //*

A double forward slash // selects from all descendants of the context node as well as the context node itself. At the beginning of an XPath expression, it selects from all descendants of the root node. For example, the XPath expression //name selects all name elements in the document.

## *Selecting the Parent Element with ..*

A double period .. indicates the parent of the current node. For example, the XPath expression //@id identifies all id attributes in the document. The expression //@id selects all the id attributes of any element in the document. The expression person//@id selects all the id attributes of any element that is contained in the person child element of the context node. Therefore, //@id/.. identifies all elements in the document that have id attributes. The XPath expression //middle_initial/../first_name identifies all first_name elements that are siblings of middle_initial elements in the document. Applied to Example 9-1, this expression selects <first_name>Richard</first_name>, but not <first_name>Alan</first_name>.

## *Selecting the Current Element with .*

The single period indicates the current node. In XSLT this is most commonly used when you need to take the value of the currently matched element. For example, this template copies the content of each comment in the input document to an italicized span element in the output document:

```
<xsl:template match="comment()">
  <span class="comment"><i><xsl:value-of select="."></i></span>
</xsl:template>
```

The ., the value of the select attribute of xsl:value-of, stands for the matched node. This works equally well for element nodes, attribute nodes, and all the other kinds of nodes. For example, this template matches name elements from the input document and copies their value into strongly emphasized text in the output document:

```
<xsl:template match="name">
  <strong><xsl:value-of select="."></strong>
</xsl:template>
```

# Predicates

In general an XPath expression may refer to more than one node. Sometimes this is what you want, but sometimes you need to winnow the node set further to select only some of the nodes the expression returns. Each step in a location path may have a predicate that selects from the node list that is current at that step in the expression. The predicate contains a boolean expression, which is tested for each node in the context node list. If the expression is false, that node is deleted from the list; otherwise, it's retained.

For example, suppose you want to find all profession elements whose value is physicist. The XPath expression //profession[.="physicist"] finds these elements. Here the period stands for the string value of the current node, the same as the value returned by xsl:value-of. You can use single instead of double quotes around the string, which is often useful when the XPath expression appears inside an already-quoted attribute value; for example, <xsl:template match="//profession[.='physicist']">.

Use the XPath expression //person [profession="physicist"] to ask for all person elements that have a profession child element with the value "physicist." If you want to find the person element with id p4567, put an @ in front of the attribute name, as in //person[@id="p4567"].

As well as the equals sign, XPath supports a full complement of relational operators, including <, >, >=, <=, and !=. The expression //person[@born<=1976], for example, locates all the document's person elements with a born attribute whose numeric value is less than or equal to 1976. Note that if < or <= is used inside an XML document, you still must escape the less-than sign as <; for example <xsl:apply-templates select="//person[@born<=1976]"/> is one example. XPath doesn't get special exemptions from the normal well-formedness rules of XML. On the other hand, if the XPath expression appears outside an XML document, as it may in some uses of XPointer, you may not need to escape the less-than sign.

XPath also provides Boolean and and or operators to combine expressions logically. For example, the XPath expression //person[@born<=1920 and @born>=1910] selects all person elements with born attribute values between 1910 and 1920, inclusive. //name[first_name="Richard" or first_name="Dick"] selects all name elements that have a first_name child with the value Richard or Dick.

In some cases the predicate may not be a boolean, but converting it to one can be straightforward. Predicates that evaluate to numbers are true if they're equal to the position of the context node, false otherwise. Predicates that indicate node sets are true if the node set is nonempty and false if it's empty. String values are true if the string isn't the empty string, false if it is. For example, suppose you want to select only the name elements in the document that have a middle_initial child element. The XPath expression //name selects all name elements. The XPath expression //name[middle_initial] selects all name elements and then checks each one to see if it has a middle_initial child element. Only those that do are retained. When applied to Listing 9-1, this expression indicates Richard M. Feynman's name element, but not Alan Turing's.

Any or all location steps in a location path can have predicates. For example, the XPath expression `/people/person[@born < 1950]/name[first_name = "Alan"]` first selects all `people` child elements of the root element (of which there's exactly one in Example 9-1). Then it chooses all `person` elements whose `born` attribute has a value numerically less than 1950 from those elements. Finally, it selects all `name` child elements that have a `first_name` child element with the value `Alan` from that group of elements.

## *Unabbreviated Location Paths*

Up to this point we've used what are called *abbreviated location paths*. These paths are much easier to type, less verbose, and more familiar to most people. They're also the kind of XPath expression that works best for XSLT match patterns. However, XPath also offers an unabbreviated syntax for location paths that is more verbose, but perhaps less cryptic and definitely more flexible.

Every location step in a location path has two required parts, an axis and a node test, and one optional part, the predicates. The axis tells you which direction to travel from the context node to look for the next nodes. The node test tells you which nodes to include along that axis, and the predicates further winnow the nodes according to an expression.

In an abbreviated location path, the axis and the node test are combined. However, they're separated by a double colon `::` in an unabbreviated location path. For example, the abbreviated location path `people/person/@id` is composed of three location steps. The first step selects `people` element nodes along the child axis, the second selects `person` element nodes along the child axis, and the third selects `id` nodes along the attribute axis. When rewritten using the unabbreviated syntax, the same location path is `child::people/child::person/attribute::id`.

These full, unabbreviated location paths may be absolute if they start from the root node, just as abbreviated paths can be. The full form `/child::people/child::person`, for example, is equivalent to the unabbreviated form `/people/person`. Unabbreviated location paths may also have predicates. For example, the abbreviated path `/people/person[@born < 1950]/name[first_name = "Alan"]` becomes `/child::people/child::person[@born < 1950]/child::name[first_name = "Alan"]` in the full form.

Overall the unabbreviated form is verbose and not used much in practice. It isn't even allowed in XSLT match patterns. However, it does offer one crucial ability that makes it essential to know. The unabbreviated form is the only way to access most of the axes from which XPath expressions can choose nodes. The abbreviated syntax lets you walk along the child, parent, self, attribute, and descendant-or-self axes. The unabbreviated syntax adds eight more axes:

*Ancestor axis*
: All element nodes that contain the context node; the parent node, the parent's parent, the parent's parent's parent, etc., up through the root node in reverse document order

*Following-sibling axis*
: All nodes that follow the context node and are contained in the same parent element node in document order

*Preceding-sibling axis*
: All nodes that precede the context node and are contained in the same parent element node in reverse document order

*Following axis*
: All nodes that follow the end of the context node in document order

*Preceding axis*
: All nodes that precede the start of the context node in reverse document order

*Namespace axis*
: All namespaces in scope on the context node, whether declared on the context node or one of its ancestors

*Descendant axis*
: All the context node's descendants, not including the context node itself

*Ancestor-or-self axis*
: All the context node's ancestors and the context node itself

Using the full, unabbreviated syntax, Example 9-4 demonstrates several of these axes. The example produces a list of `person` elements that look more or less like this (after accounting for whitespace):

```
<dt>Richard M Feynman</dt>
<dd>
  <ul>
    <li>physicist</li>
    <li>Playing the bongoes</li>
  </ul>
</dd>
```

*Example 9-4. An XSLT Stylesheet That Uses Unabbreviated XPath Syntax*

```
<?xml version="1.0"?>
<xsl:stylesheet version="1.0"
                xmlns:xsl="http://www.w3.org/1999/XSL/Transform">

  <xsl:template match="/">
    <dl>
      <xsl:apply-templates select="descendant::person"/>
    </dl>
  </xsl:template>

  <xsl:template match="person">
    <dt><xsl:value-of select="child::name"/></dt>
    <dd>
      <ul>
        <xsl:apply-templates select="child::name/following-sibling::*"/>
      </ul>
    </dd>
  </xsl:template>
```

*Example 9-4: An XSLT Stylesheet That Uses Unabbreviated XPath Syntax (continued)*

```
  <xsl:template match="*">
    <li><xsl:value-of select="self::*"/></li>
  </xsl:template>

  <xsl:template match="homepage"
                xmlns:xlink="http://www.w3.org/1999/xlink">
    <li><xsl:value-of select="attribute::xlink:href"/></li>
  </xsl:template>

</xsl:stylesheet>
```

The first template matches the root node. It applies templates to all descendants of the root node that are `person` elements; that is, it moves from the root node along the `descendant` axis with a node test of `person`.

The second template matches `person` elements. It places the value of the `name` child of each `person` element in a `dt` element. (The location path used here, `child::name`, could have been rewritten in the abbreviated syntax as the single word `name`.) Next, it applies templates to all elements that follow the name element at the same level of the hierarchy. It begins at the context node `person` element, then moves along the child axis to find the `name` element. From there it moves along the `following-sibling` axis looking for elements of any type (`*`) after the `name` element that are also children of the same `person` element. No abbreviated equivalent exists for the `following-sibling` axis, so this really is the simplest way to make the statement.

The third template matches any element not matched by another template; it simply wraps that element in an `li` element. The XPath `self::*` selects the value of the currently matched element, the context node. This expression could have been abbreviated as a single period.

The fourth and final template matches `homepage` elements. In this case you need to select the value of `xlink:href` attribute, so move from the context `homepage` node along the attribute axis. The node test looks for the `xlink:href` attributes. Specifically, it looks for an attribute with the local name `href` whose prefix is mapped to the *http://www.w3.org/1999/xlink* namespace URI.

## General XPath Expressions

So far we've focused on the very useful subset of XPath expressions called location paths. Location paths identify a set of nodes in an XML document and are used in XSLT match patterns and select expressions. However, location paths are not the only possible type of an XPath expression. XPath expressions can also return numbers, booleans, and strings. For instance, all legal XPath expressions include:

- `3.141529`
- `2+2`
- `'Rosalind Franklin'`
- `true()`

- `32.5 < 76.2E-21`
- `position()=last()`

XPath expressions that aren't node sets can't be used in the `match` attribute of an `xsl:template` element. However, they can be used as values for the `select` attribute of `xsl:value-of` elements and in location path predicates.

## *Numbers*

No pure integers exist in XPath. All numbers are eight-byte, IEEE 754 floating point doubles, even if they don't have an explicit decimal point. This format is identical to Java's `double` primitive type. Besides representing floating-point numbers ranging from 4.94065645841246544e-324 to 1.79769313486231570e+308 (positive or negative) and zero, this type includes special representations of positive and negative infinity and a special not a number value (NaN) used as the result of operations, such as dividing zero by zero.

XPath provides the five basic arithmetic operators familiar to any programmer:

+
: Addition

-
: Subtraction

*
: Multiplication

*div*
: Division

*mod*
: Taking the remainder

The more common forward slash couldn't be used for division because it's already used to separate location steps in a location path. Consequently, a new operator was chosen. Java's `%` operator was also replaced by the word `mod`. Aside from these minor differences in syntax, all five operators behave exactly as they do in Java. For instance, 2+2 is 4, 6.5 div 1.5 is 4.33333333, 6.5 mod 1.5 is 0.5, and so on. Placing the element `<xsl:value-of select="6*7"/>` in an XSLT template would insert the string `42` into the output document when the template was processed. More often, you'll perform simple arithmetic on numbers read from the input document. For instance, this template divides the value of the `id` attribute by 10 and inserts the result into the output:

```
<xsl:template match="person">
  <xsl:value-of select="@id div 10"/>
</xsl:template>
```

## *Strings*

XPath strings are ordered sequences of Unicode characters like "Fred," "Ethel," "كريم" or "Ξηνο." String literals may be enclosed in either single or double quotes, as convenient. The quotes are not themselves part of the string. The only restriction XPath places on a string literal is that it does not contain the type of quote that delimits it. If the string contains single quotes, it must be enclosed in double quotes. and vice versa. String literals may contain whitespace, including tabs, carriage returns, line feeds, backslashes, and other characters that would be illegal in many programming languages. However, if the XPath expression is part of an XML document, some of these possibilities may be ruled out by XML's well-formedness rules, depending on context.

You can use the = and != comparison operators to check whether two strings are the same. You can also use the relational <, >, <=, and >= operators to compare strings, but unless both strings clearly represent numbers (e.g., -7.5 or 54.2) the results will probably not make sense. In general, you can't define a real notion of string order in Unicode without detailed knowledge of the text being ordered.

Other operations on strings are provided by XPath functions and are discussed in the following sections.

## *Booleans*

A boolean is a value that has exactly two states: true or false. Every boolean must have one of these binary values. XPath does not provide boolean literals. If you use `<xsl:value-of select="true"/>` in an XSLT stylesheet, then the XSLT processor looks for a child element of the context node named `true`. However, the XPath functions `true()` and `false()` can substitute for the missing literals quite easily.

Booleans, however, are usually created by comparisons between other objects, most commonly numbers. XPath provides all the usual relational operators, including =, !=, <, >, >=, and <=. The `and` and `or` operators can also be used to combine boolean expressions according to the usual rules of boolean logic.

Booleans are most commonly used in predicates of location paths. In the location path `//person[profession="physicist"]`, `profession="physicist"` is a boolean. It is either true or false; there is no other possibility. Booleans are also commonly used in the `test` attribute of `xsl:if` and `xsl:when` elements. For example, this XSLT template includes the `profession` element in the output if and only if its contents are "physicist" or "computer scientist":

```
<xsl:template match="profession">
  <xsl:if test=".='computer scientist' or .='physicist'">
    <xsl:value-of select="."/>
  </xsl:if>
</xsl:template>
```

This XSLT template italicizes the `profession` element if and only if its content is the string "computer scientist":

```
<xsl:template match="profession">
  <xsl:choose>
    <xsl:when test=".='computer scientist'">
      <i><xsl:value-of select="."/></i>
    </xsl:when>
    <xsl:otherwise>
      <xsl:value-of select="."/>
```

```
      </xsl:otherwise>
    </xsl:choose>
  </xsl:template>
```

Finally, a `not()` function reverses the sense of its boolean argument. For example, if `.='computer scientist'` is true, then `not(.='computer scientist')` is false, and vice versa.

## *XPath Functions*

XPath provides many functions you may find useful in predicates or in raw expressions. All of these functions are discussed in Chapter 19, *XPath Reference*. For example, the `position()` function returns the current node's position in the context node list as a number. This XSLT template uses the `position()` function to calculate the number of the `person` being processed, relative to other nodes in the context node list:

```
<xsl:template match="person">
  Person <xsl:value-of select="position()"/>,
  <xsl:value-of select="name"/>
</xsl:template>
```

Each XPath function returns one of these four types:

- boolean
- number
- node set
- string

There are no void functions in XPath. Otherwise, XPath is not as strongly typed as languages such as Java or C. You can often use these types as a function argument, regardless of which type the function expects, and the processor will convert it the best it can. If you insert a boolean where a string is expected, the processor will substitute one of the two strings `true` and `false` for the boolean. The one exception is functions that expect to receive node sets as arguments. XPath cannot convert strings, booleans, or numbers to node sets.

Functions are identified by the parentheses at the end of function names. Sometimes these functions take arguments between the parentheses. The `round()` function takes a single number as an argument. It returns the number rounded to the nearest integer. For example, `<xsl:value-of select="round(3.14)"/>` inserts 3 into the output tree.

Other functions take more than one argument. For instance, the `starts-with()` function takes two arguments, both strings. It returns `true` if the first string starts with the second string. For example, this `xsl:apply-templates` element selects all `name` elements whose last name begins with T:

```
<xsl:apply-templates select="name[starts-with(last_name, 'T')]"/>
```

In this example the first argument to the `starts-with()` function is actually a node set, not a string. The XPath processor converts that node set to its string

XPath

value (the text content of the last_name element) before checking to see whether it starts with T.

Some XSLT functions have variable length argument lists. The concat() function takes as arguments any number of strings and returns one string formed by concatenating all those strings together in order. For instance, concat("a", "b", "c", "d") returns "abcd".

Besides the functions defined in XPath and discussed in this chapter, most uses of XPath like XSLT and XPointer define more functions that are useful in their particular context. You use these extra functions just like built-in functions when you use those applications. XSLT even lets you write extension functions in Java and other languages that can do almost anything, for example, make SQL queries against a remote database server and return the result of the query as a node set.

## *Node Set Functions*

Node set functions either operate on or return information about node sets, ordered collections of XPath nodes. You've already encountered the position() function. Two related functions are last() and count(). The last() function returns the number of nodes in the context node set, which is the same as the position of the last node in the set. The count() function is similar, except that it returns the number of nodes in its node set argument rather than in the context node list. For example, count(//name) tells you how many name elements exist in the document. Example 9-5 uses the position() and count() functions to list people in the document in the form "Person 1 of 10, Person 2 of 10, Person 3 of 10, etc." In the second template the position() function tells you which person element is currently being processed, and the count() function tells you how many total person elements exist in the document.

*Example 9-5: An XSLT Stylesheet That Uses the position() and count() Functions*

```
<?xml version="1.0"?>
<xsl:stylesheet version="1.0"
                xmlns:xsl="http://www.w3.org/1999/XSL/Transform">

  <xsl:template match="people">
    <xsl:apply-templates select="person"/>
  </xsl:template>

  <xsl:template match="person">
    Person <xsl:value-of select="position()"/>
    of <xsl:value-of select="count(//person)"/>:
    <xsl:value-of select="name"/>
  </xsl:template>

</xsl:stylesheet>
```

The id() function takes a string containing one or more IDs separated by whitespace as an argument and returns a node set containing all nodes in the document that have those IDs. These are nodes with attributes declared to have type ID in the DTD, not necessarily nodes with attributes named `ID` or `id`. Thus in Example 9-1, `id('p342')` indicates Alan Turing's `person` element and `id('p342 p4567')` indicates both Alan Turing and Richard Feynman's `person` elements.

The `id()` function is most commonly used in the abbreviated XPath syntax. It allows you to form absolute location paths that don't start from the root. For example, `id('p342')/name` refers to Alan Turing's `name` element, regardless of where Alan Turing's `person` element is in the document, as long as it hasn't changed ID. This function is especially useful in XPointers, where it takes the place of HTML's named anchors.

Finally, three node set functions are related to namespaces. The `local-name()` function takes as an argument a node set, most often containing just a single node, and returns the local name of the first node in that set. The `namespace-uri()` function takes a node set as an argument and returns the namespace URI of the set's first node. Finally, the `name()` function takes a node set as an argument and returns the prefixed name of the first node in that set. In all three functions the argument may be omitted, in which case the context node is evaluated. For instance, when applied to Example 9-1 the XPath expression, `local-name(//homepage/@xlink:href)` is `href`; `namespace-uri(//homepage/@xlink:href)` is `http://www.w3.org/1999/xlink`; and `name(//homepage/@xlink:href)` is `xlink:href`.

## *String Functions*

XPath includes functions for basic string operations, such as finding a string's length or changing letters from uppercase to lowercase. It doesn't have the full power of the string libraries in Python or Perl; for example, there's no regular expression support. However, XPath is sufficient for many simple manipulations you need for XSLT or XPointer.

The `string()` function converts any type of argument to a string in a reasonable fashion. Booleans are converted to the string `true` or the string `false`. Node sets are converted to the string value of the first node in the set. This value is the same value calculated by the `xsl:value-of` element; the string value of the element is the complete Unicode text of the element after all entity references are resolved and tags, comments, and processing instructions have been stripped out. Numbers are converted to strings in the format used by most programming languages such as "1987," "299792500," "2.71828," or "2.998E+10."

> In XSLT, the `xsl:number` element provides precise control over formatting so you can insert separators between groups, change the decimal separator, use non-European digits, and make similar adjustments.

The normal use of most of the remaining string functions is to manipulate or address the text content of XML elements or attributes. If `date` attributes were given in the format MM/DD/YYYY, then the string functions would allow you to target the month, day, and year separately.

The `starts-with()` function takes two string arguments. It returns `true` if the first argument starts with the second argument. For example, `starts-with('Richard', 'Ric')` is `true`, but `starts-with('Richard', 'Rick')` is `false`. There is no corresponding `ends-with()` function.

The `contains()` function also takes two string arguments. However, it returns `true` if the first argument contains the second argument—that is, if the second argument is a substring of the first argument—regardless of position. For example, `contains('Richard','ar')` is `true`, but `contains('Richard','art')` is `false`.

The `substring-before()` function takes two string arguments and returns the substring of the first argument string that precedes the second argument's initial appearance. If the second string doesn't appear in the first string, then `substring-before()` returns the empty string. For example, `substring-before('MM/DD/YYYY','/')` is `'MM'`. The `substring-after()` function also takes two string arguments, but returns the substring of the first argument string that follows the second argument's initial appearance. If the second string doesn't appear in the first string, `substring-after()` returns the empty string. For example, `substring-after('MM/DD/YYYY','/')` is `'DD/YYYY'`, `substring-before(substring-after('MM/DD/YYYY','/')','/')` is DD. and `substring-after(substring-after('MM/DD/YYYY', '/')', '/')` is YYYY.

If you know the position of the substring you want in a given string, then use the `substring()` method instead. This method takes three arguments: the string from which the substring is copied, the position in the string from which to start extracting, and the number of characters to copy for the substring. The third argument may be omitted, in which case the substring contains all characters from the specified start position to the end of the string. For example, `substring('MM/DD/YYYY',1,2)` is MM; `substring('MM/DD/YYYY',4,2)` is DD; and `substring('MM/DD/YYYY', 7)` is YYYY.

The `string-length()` function returns a number giving the length of the string value of its argument, or of the context node if no argument is included. In Example 9-1, `string-length(//name[position()=1])` is 29. If that value seems long, remember that all whitespace characters are included in the count. If it seems short, remember that markup characters are not included in the count.

Theoretically, you could use these functions to trim and normalize whitespace in element content. However, since this process would be relatively complex and is such a common need, XPath provides the `normalize-space()` function to do this. In Example 9-1 the value of `string(//name[position()=1])` is:

```
      Alan
      Turing
```

This example contains a lot of extra whitespace that was inserted only to make the XML document neater. However, `normalize-space(string(//name[position()=1]))` is more reasonable:

```
Alan Turing
```

Though a more powerful string manipulation library would be useful, XSLT is really designed for transforming the element structure of an XML document. It's not meant to have the general power of a language like Perl, which can handle arbitrarily complicated and varying string formats.

## *Boolean Functions*

The boolean functions are straightforward and few in number. They all return a boolean with the value `true` or `false`. The `true()` function always returns `true` and the `false()` function always returns `false`. These functions substitute for boolean literals in XPath.

The `not()` function reverses the sense of its boolean argument. For example, `not(@id>400)` is almost always equivalent to `(@id<=400)`. (NaN is a special case.)

The `boolean()` function converts its single argument to a boolean and returns the result. If the argument is omitted, it converts the context node. Numbers are converted to `false` if they're zero or NaN (not a number); all other numbers are `true`. Node sets are `false` if they're empty and `true` if they contain at least one node. Strings are `false` if they have zero length and `true` otherwise. Note that according to this rule, the string `"false"` is in fact `true`.

## *Number Functions*

XPath includes a few simple numeric functions used for summing groups of numbers and finding the nearest integer to a number. It doesn't have the full power of the math libraries in Java or FORTRAN, for instance, there's no square root or exponentiation function—but it's got enough to do most basic math you need for XSLT or the simpler requirements of XPointer.

The `number()` function can take any type as an argument and convert it to a number. If the argument is omitted, it converts the context node. Booleans are converted to 1 if true and 0 if false. Strings are converted in a plausible fashion. For instance, the string "7.5" is converted to the number 7.5 and the string "8.5E2" is converted to the number 8,500. The string "Fred" is converted to NaN. Node sets are converted to numbers by first converting them to their string values and then converting the resulting string to a number. The detailed rules are more complex, but as long as the object you convert can be reasonably interpreted as a single number, the `number()` function will probably do what you expect. If the object you convert can't be reasonably interpreted as a single number, then the `number()` function returns NaN.

The `round()`, `floor()`, and `ceiling()` functions all take a single number as an argument. The `floor()` function returns the greatest integer less than or equal to its argument. The `ceiling()` function returns the smallest integer greater than or equal to its argument. The `round()` function returns its argument rounded to the nearest integer. When rounding numbers like 1.5 and –3.5 that are equally close to two integers, `round ()` returns the larger of the two.

The `sum()` function takes a node set as an argument. It converts each node in the set to its string value, then converts each of those strings to a number. Finally, it adds the numbers and returns the result.

CHAPTER 10

# *XLinks*

XLinks are an attribute-based syntax for attaching links to XML documents. XLinks can be simple Point A-to-Point B links, like the links you're accustomed to from HTML's `A` element. XLinks can also be bidirectional, linking two documents in both directions so you can go from A to B or B to A. XLinks can even be multidirectional, presenting many different paths between any number of XML documents. The documents don't have to be XML documents; XLinks can be placed in an XML document that lists connections between other documents that may or may not be XML documents themselves. Web graffiti artists take note: these third-party links let you attach links to pages you don't even control, like the home page of the *New York Times* or the CIA. At its core, XLink is nothing more and nothing less than an XML syntax for describing directed graphs in which the vertices are documents at particular URIs and the edges are the links between the documents. What you put in that graph is up to you.

At most, current web browsers support simple XLinks that do little more than duplicate the functionality of HTML's `A` element. Many browsers don't support XLinks at all. However, custom applications may do much more. Since XLinks are so powerful, it shouldn't surprise you that you can do more with them than simply make blue underlined links on web pages. XLinks can describe tables of contents or indexes. They can connect textual emendations to the text they describe. They can indicate possible paths through online courses or virtual worlds. Different applications interpret different sets of XLinks differently. Just as no one browser really understands the semantics of all the various XML applications, no one program can process all collections of XLinks.

This chapter is based on the July 3, 2000 Candidate Recommendation of the XLink's specification. However, there are known issues with this draft and some details described here are likely to change. The most current version of the XLink specification can be found at *http://www.w3.org/TR/xlink/*.

## *Simple Links*

A simple link defines a one-way connection between two resources. The source, the connection's *starting resource*, is itself the link element. The target or *ending resource* of the connection is identified by a URI. The link goes from the starting resource to the ending resource. The starting resource is always an XML element. The ending resource may be an XML document, a particular element in an XML document, a group of elements in an XML document, a span of text in an XML document, or something that isn't even a part of an XML document, such as an MPEG movie or a PDF file. The URI may be something other than a URL, such as a book's ISBN number (e.g., *urn:isbn:1565922247*).

A simple XLink is encoded in an XML document as an element of arbitrary type that has an `xlink:type` attribute with the value `simple` and an `xlink:href` attribute. The attribute's value is the link target's URI. The `xlink` prefix must be mapped to the *http://www.w3.org/1999/xlink* namespace URI. For example, suppose this `novel` element appears in a list of children's literature and we want to link it to the novel's actual text available from the URL *ftp://archive.org/pub/etext/etext93/wizoz10.txt*:

```
<novel>
  <title>The Wonderful Wizard of Oz</title>
  <author>L. Frank Baum</author>
  <year>1900</year>
</novel>
```

We give the `novel` element an `xlink:type` attribute with the value `simple`, an `xlink:href` attribute that contains the URL to link to, and an `xmlns:xlink` attribute that associates the prefix `xlink` with the namespace URI `http://www.w3.org/1999/xlink`. The result is as follows:

```
<novel xmlns:xlink= "http://www.w3.org/1999/xlink"
       xlink:type = "simple"
       xlink:href = "ftp://archive.org/pub/etext/etext93/wizoz10.txt">
  <title>The Wonderful Wizard of Oz</title>
  <author>L. Frank Baum</author>
  <year>1900</year>
</novel>
```

This establishes a simple link from this `novel` element to the plain text file found at *ftp://archive.org/pub/etext/etext93/wizoz10.txt*. Browsers are free to interpret this link as they like. However, the most natural interpretation, and the one implemented by the few experimental browsers that do support simple XLinks, is to make it a blue, underlined hypertext link that replaces the current page with the file the user links to when the user clicks on it. Other schemes are possible, however.

XLinks are fully namespace aware. The `xlink` prefix is customary, though it can be changed. However it must be mapped to the URI *http://www.w3.org/1999/xlink*. This mapping can be done on the XLink element itself, as in the `novel` example, or on any ancestor of that element up to, and including, the document's root element. Future examples in this and the next chapter use the `xlink` prefix exclusively and assume that the prefix was properly declared on an ancestor element.

Every XLink element must have an `xlink:type` attribute telling you what kind of link (or part of a link) it is. The `xlink:type` attribute has six possible values:

- `simple`
- `extended`
- `locator`
- `arc`
- `title`
- `resource`

Simple XLinks are the only links that are similar to HTML links. The remaining five kinds of XLink elements are discussed in later sections.

The `xlink:href` attribute identifies the resource that is linked to. It always contains a URI. Both relative and absolute URLs can be used, as they are in HTML links. However, the URI need not be a URL. For example, if we wanted to link to the print edition of *The Wonderful Wizard of Oz* with the ISBN number 0688069444, we would have written the `novel` element like this:

```
<novel xmlns:xlink= "http://www.w3.org/1999/xlink"
       xlink:type = "simple"
       xlink:href = "urn:isbn:0688069444">
  <title>The Wonderful Wizard of Oz</title>
  <author>L. Frank Baum</author>
  <year>1900</year>
</novel>
```

## *Link Behavior*

So far, we've been careful to talk in the abstract. We've said that an XLink describes a connection between two resources, but we haven't said much about how that connection is presented to the end user or what it makes software reading the document do. We haven't addressed these questions because they don't have just one answer. For instance, when the browser encounters a `novel` element that uses an `http` URL, clicking the link should probably load the text of the novel from the URL into the current window, thereby replacing the document that contained the link. Then again, maybe it should open a new window and show the user the new document in that window. The proper behavior for a browser encountering the `novel` element that uses an `isbn` URN is even less clear. Perhaps it should reserve the book with the specified ISBN at the local library so the user can walk in and pick it up. Or perhaps it should order the book from an online bookstore. In other cases, something else may be called for. For instance, the content of some links is embedded directly in the linking document, as in this `image` element:

```
<image width="152" height="345" xlink:type="simple"
       xlink:href="http://www.turing.org.uk/turing/pi1/bus.jpg" />
```

Here, the author probably intends for the browser to download and display the image as soon as it finds the link. Rather than opening a new window for the image or replacing the current document with the image, the image should be embedded into the current document.

Just as XML is more flexible than HTML in the documents it describes, XLink is also more flexible in the links it describes. An XLink indicates a connection between two documents, but it's up to the application reading the XLink to decide what that connection means. It's not necessarily a blue, underlined phrase the user clicks on in a browser to jump from the first source document to the target. It may indeed be an underlined phrase, just as an XML document may be a web page, but it may be something else.

Page authors can offer suggestions to browsers about how links should be handled by using the `xlink:show` and `xlink:actuate` attributes. The `xlink:show` attribute tells a browser, or other application, what to do when the link is activated; for example, whether to show the linked content in the same window or to display it by opening a new window. The `xlink:actuate` attribute tells the browser when to show the content, for example, whether it should follow the link as soon as it sees it or whether it should wait for an explicit user request.

## *xlink:show*

The optional `xlink:show` attribute has five possible values that suggest the context in which the application loading an XLinked resource should display that resource:

`new`
: Opens a new window and shows the content at the link's URI (the ending resource) in that window.

`replace`
: Shows the ending resource in the current window, replacing the current document.

`embed`
: Embeds the ending resource in the current document at the location of the link element.

`other`
: Do something other than opening a new window, replacing the document in the existing window, or embedding the resource in the existing document. Exactly what this behavior may be is specified by other, nonstandard markup that a particular application understands.

`none`
: Specifies no behavior.

All five values are only suggestions that browsers, or other applications following XLinks, are free to ignore. For example, a web spider would not open a window for any link and might ignore embedded links and treat the other four types identically. Some browsers with unusual GUIs might open a new panel in an existing window for `xlink:show="replace"` rather than create a completely new window. Custom behavior is allowed if it makes sense in the context of the application.

## *xlink:actuate*

The optional `xlink:actuate` attribute has four possible values that suggest when an application reading a document that contains XLinks should follow them:

`onLoad`
: The link should be followed as soon as the application sees it.

`onRequest`
: The link should be followed when the user asks to follow it.

`other`
: Other markup in the document, not specified by XLink, determines when to follow the link.

`none`
: No details are available about when or whether to follow this link. Indeed following the link may not have any plausible meaning, as in the earlier example in which the link pointed to a book's ISBN number rather than a URL where the book could be found.

All four of these values are only suggestions that browsers or other applications following XLinks are free to ignore. For example, a web spider would use its own algorithms to decide when to follow and not follow a link. When faced with the same attributes, different behavior is allowed, as long as it makes sense to the application reading the document.

A traditional simple link, such as that provided by HTML's `a` element and indicated by the first novel example, would be encoded as follows:

```
<novel xlink:type="simple"
       xlink:href="ftp://archive.org/pub/etext/etext93/wizoz10.txt"
       xlink:actuate="onRequest" xlink:show="replace">
  <title>The Wonderful Wizard of Oz</title>
  <author>L. Frank Baum</author>
  <year>1900</year>
</novel>
```

This code says to wait for an explicit user request to follow the link (e.g., click on the content of the link) and then replace the existing document with the document found at *ftp://archive.org/pub/etext/etext93/wizoz10.txt*. On the other hand, if you used XLinks to embed images in documents, you'd want them traversed immediately and then embedded in the originating document. This syntax would be appropriate:

```
<image xlink:type="simple"
       xlink:actuate="onLoad" xlink:show="embed"
       xlink:href="http://www.turing.org.uk/turing/pi1/bus.jpg"
       width="152" height="345" />
```

Both `xlink:show` and `xlink:actuate` are optional. An application should be prepared to do something reasonable if they're missing.

## *Link Semantics*

A link describes a connection between two resources. These resources may not be XML documents, but even if they are, the relationships they have with each other can vary. For example, links can indicate parent-child, previous-next, employer-employee, or customer-supplier relationships. XLink elements can have `xlink:title` and `xlink:role` attributes to specify the meaning of the connection between the resources. The `xlink:title` attribute contains a small amount of plain text describing the remote resource, such as what a tooltip might show when the user moves the cursor over the link. The `xlink:role` attribute contains a URI pointing to a longer description of the remote resource.

For example, this `novel` element uses the `xlink:title` attribute to specify that the text comes from Project Gutenberg, whereas the `xlink:role` attribute points to the Project Gutenberg home page:

```
<novel xlink:type="simple"
 xlink:href="ftp://archive.org/pub/etext/etext93/wizoz10.txt"
 xlink:title= "The complete text of the novel from Project Gutenberg"
 xlink:role="http://promo.net/pg/" >
  <title>The Wonderful Wizard of Oz</title>
  <author>L. Frank Baum</author>
  <year>1900</year>
</novel>
```

As with almost everything related to XLink, exactly what browsers or other applications will do with this information, or how they'll present it to readers, remains to be determined.

## *Extended Links*

While a simple link describes one unidirectional connection between an XML element and a remote resource, an extended link describes a collection of resources and paths between those resources. Each path connects exactly two resources. Any individual resource may be connected to another resource, two other resources, no resources, all other resources, or any subset of other resources in the collection. It may even connect back to itself. In computer science terms, an *extended link* is a directed, labeled graph in which the paths are arcs, the documents are vertices, and the labels are URIs.

Simple links are easy to understand by analogy to HTML links. However, no obvious analogy exists for extended links. What the links look like, how applications treat them, and what user interfaces present them to people is all undecided. No simple visual metaphors, such as "click on the blue underlined text to jump to a new page," have been invented for extended links, and no browsers support such metaphors. How they'll be used and what user interfaces will be designed for them remains to be seen.

In XML, an extended link is represented by an extended link element, an element of arbitrary type that has an `xlink:type` attribute with the value `extended`. For example, consider this extended link element that refers to the novel *The Wonderful Wizard of Oz*:

```
<novel xlink:type="extended">
  <title>The Wonderful Wizard of Oz</title>
  <author>L. Frank Baum</author>
  <year>1900</year>
</novel>
```

Most extended links contain local resources, remote resources, and arcs between those resources. A remote resource is represented by a locator element, which is any type of element that has an `xlink:type` attribute with the value `locator`. A local resource is represented by a resource element, any type of element that has an `xlink:type` attribute with the value `resource`. An arc element, any type of element that has an `xlink:type` attribute with the value `arc`, represents a connection between two resources.

## *Locators*

Each locator element has an `xlink:type` attribute with the value `locator` and an `xlink:href` attribute containing a URI for the resource it locates. For example, this `novel` element for *The Wonderful Wizard of Oz* contains three locator elements that identify particular editions of the book:

```
<novel xlink:type = "extended">
  <title>The Wonderful Wizard of Oz</title>
  <author>L. Frank Baum</author>
  <year>1900</year>
  <edition xlink:type="locator" xlink:href="urn:isbn:0688069444" />
  <edition xlink:type="locator" xlink:href="urn:isbn:0192839306" />
  <edition xlink:type="locator" xlink:href="urn:isbn:0700609857" />
</novel>
```

Usually each locator element also has an `xlink:label` attribute that serves as the element's ID. This attribute's value can be any XML name that does not contain a colon (i.e., a name without a namespace prefix). In the previous example, we could add labels based on the ISBN number like this:

```
<novel xlink:type = "extended">
  <title>The Wonderful Wizard of Oz</title>
  <author>L. Frank Baum</author>
  <year>1900</year>
  <edition xlink:type="locator" xlink:href="urn:isbn:0688069444"
                                  xlink:label="ISBN0688069444"/>
  <edition xlink:type="locator" xlink:href="urn:isbn:0192839306"
                                  xlink:label="ISBN0192839306"/>
  <edition xlink:type="locator" xlink:href="urn:isbn:0700609857"
                                  xlink:label="ISBN0700609857"/>
</novel>
```

The number alone could not be used because XML names may not start with a digit. In most cases, the labels are unique within the extended link, but they don't have to be.

Locators may also have the optional semantic attributes **xlink:title** and **xlink:role** to provide more information about the remote resource. These attributes have the same meanings they have for simple XLinks. The **xlink:title** attribute contains a small amount of text describing the remote resource, and the **xlink:role** attribute contains a URI pointing to a longer description of the remote resource. The **edition** elements could provide the publisher's name and URL using these attributes:

```
<novel xlink:type = "extended">
  <title>The Wonderful Wizard of Oz</title>
  <author>L. Frank Baum</author>
  <year>1900</year>
  <edition xlink:type="locator" xlink:href="urn:isbn:0688069444"
           xlink:title="William Morrow"
           xlink:role="http://www.williammorrow.com/"
           xlink:label="ISBN0688069444"/>
  <edition xlink:type="locator" xlink:href="urn:isbn:0192839306"
           xlink:title="Oxford University Press"
           xlink:role="http://www.oup-usa.org/"
           xlink:label="ISBN0192839306"/>
  <edition xlink:type="locator" xlink:href="urn:isbn:0700609857"
           xlink:title="University Press of Kansas"
           xlink:role="http://www.kansaspress.ku.edu/"
           xlink:label="ISBN0700609857"/>
</novel>
```

## *Arcs*

Paths between resources are called *arcs*. Arcs are represented by arc elements, that is, elements of arbitrary type that have an **xlink:type** attribute with the value **arc**. Each arc element should have an **xlink:from** and an **xlink:to** attribute. The **xlink:from** attribute identifies the link's source and the **xlink:to** attribute identifies the link's target. These attributes do not contain URIs, as you might expect. Rather, they contain a name matching the value of the **xlink:label** attribute of one of the locator elements in the extended link.

Example 10-1 shows an extended link that contains the first three novels in the Wizard of Oz series (*The Wonderful Wizard of Oz*, *The Marvelous Land of Oz*, and *Ozma of Oz*) and uses arcs to connect from the first novel to the second, from the second to the third, and then back again. In this example, the root **series** element is the extended link element; each **novel** element is a locator element; and the **next** and **previous** elements are arc elements.

*Example 10-1: An Extended Link with Three Locators and Four Arcs*

```
<series xlink:type="extended" xmlns:xlink="http://www.w3.org/1999/xlink">
  <author>L. Frank Baum</author>

  <!-- locator elements -->
  <novel xlink:type="locator" xlink:label="oz1"
        xlink:href="ftp://archive.org/pub/etext/etext93/wizoz10.txt">
    <title>The Wonderful Wizard of Oz</title>
    <year>1900</year>
```

*Example 10-1: An Extended Link with Three Locators and Four Arcs (continued)*

```
  </novel>
  <novel xlink:type="locator" xlink:label="oz2"
         xlink:href="ftp://archive.org/pub/etext/etext93/ozland10.txt">
    <title>The Marvelous Land of Oz</title>
    <year>1904</year>
  </novel>
  <novel xlink:type="locator" xlink:label="oz3"
         xlink:href="ftp://archive.org/pub/etext/etext93/wizoz10.txt">
    <title>Ozma of Oz</title>
    <year>1907</year>
  </novel>

  <!-- arcs -->
  <next     xlink:type="arc" xlink:from="oz1" xlink:to="oz2" />
  <next     xlink:type="arc" xlink:from="oz2" xlink:to="oz3" />
  <previous xlink:type="arc" xlink:from="oz2" xlink:to="oz1" />
  <previous xlink:type="arc" xlink:from="oz3" xlink:to="oz2" />

</series>
```

Figure 10-1 diagrams this extended link. Resources are represented by books and arcs are represented by arrows. However, though we can understand the link in this sort of abstract way, it doesn't really tell us anything about how a browser might present links to users and how users might choose which links to follow. This extended link might be interpreted as nothing more than the order in which to print these documents. All details of interpretation are left up to the application.

*Figure 10-1: An extended link with three resources and four arcs between them*

### *Multiple arcs from one arc element*

A single arc element occasionally defines multiple arcs. If multiple elements share the same label, then an arc element using that label in its `xlink:to` or `xlink:from` attribute defines arcs between all resources that share that label. Example 10-2 shows an extended link containing locator elements for three different online bookstores and one edition of *The Wonderful Wizard of Oz*. Each `bookstore` element has the label `buy`, and a single `purchase` arc element connects all of elements. Figure 10-2 shows this extended link's graph structure.



*Example 10-2: An Extended Link with One Arc Element, but Three Arcs*

```
<book xlink:type="extended" xmlns:xlink="http://www.w3.org/1999/xlink">

  <author>L. Frank Baum</author>
  <title>The Wonderful Wizard of Oz</title>

  <!-- locator elements -->
  <edition xlink:type="locator" xlink:href="urn:isbn:0192839306"
           xlink:title="Oxford University Press"
           xlink:role="http://www.oup-usa.org/"
           xlink:label="ISBN0192839306"/>

  <store xlink:type="locator"
         xlink:href="http://www.amazon.com/exec/obidos/ASIN/0192839306"
         xlink:label="buy">Amazon</store>

  <store xlink:type="locator" xlink:href=
   "http://www1.fatbrain.com/asp/bookinfo/bookinfo.asp?theisbn=0192839306"
    xlink:label="buy">Fatbrain</store>

  <store xlink:type="locator" xlink:href=
"http://shop.bn.com/booksearch/isbninquiry.asp?isbn=0192839306"
    xlink:label="buy">Barnes &amp; Noble</store>

  <!-- arcs -->
  <purchase xlink:type="arc" xlink:from="ISBN0192839306" xlink:to="buy" />

</book>
```

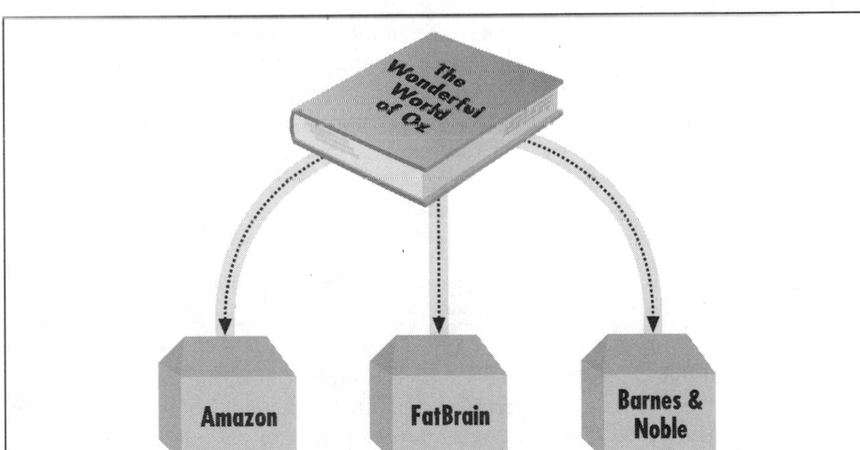


*Figure 10-2: One arc element can generate several arcs*

If an arc element does not have an xlink:to attribute, then it uses all resources in the extended link as sources. If an arc element does not have an xlink:from attribute, it uses all resources in the extended link as targets.

However, it is an error for more than one arc element to define an arc between the same two resources, whether implicitly or explicitly. If an extended link contains *N* resources and an arc element, such as <edition xlink:type="arc"/>, with neither an xlink:to or xlink:from attribute, then it cannot contain other arc elements because this one arc element defines all $N^2$ possible arcs between the extended links' resources.

### *Arc titles*

Each arc element may optionally have an xlink:title attribute, like all other XLink elements. This attribute contains a small amount of text describing the arc intended for humans to read. In Example 10-1, we might give these titles to the arcs:

```
<next     xlink:type="arc" xlink:from="oz1" xlink:to="oz2"
          xlink:title="Next" />
<next     xlink:type="arc" xlink:from="oz2" xlink:to="oz3"
          xlink:title="Next" />
<previous xlink:type="arc" xlink:from="oz2" xlink:to="oz1"
          xlink:title="Previous" />
<previous xlink:type="arc" xlink:from="oz3" xlink:to="oz2"
          xlink:title="Previous" />
```

When processing an extended link, a browser might show the title to the users as the link's contents so they could choose which arc they wanted to follow from their current position. Or the contents might appear in a pop-up menu when a user was on one of the referenced pages. XLink does not require or suggest any specific user interface for arcs or arc titles.

### *Arc roles*

Arc elements cannot have xlink:role attributes. However they can have xlink:arcrole attributes, which should contain a URI pointing to the arc's description. More specifically, this URI should point to a resource that indicates which relationship the arc describes; e.g., parent-child or employer-employee. However, there's really no way to validate this information beyond checking to see that xlink:arcrole contains a legal URI, and even that URI is not strictly required. In Example 10-2, we might add an xlink:arcrole attribute to the purchase arc that pointed to the relative URL *purchase_details.txt*:

```
<purchase xlink:type="arc" xlink:from="ISBN0192839306" xlink:to="buy"
          xlink:arcrole="purchase_details.txt" />
```

The *purchase_details.txt* file might then contain the text, "will be bought from." This text would indicate that the link's source is bought from the target of the link; for example, "*The Wonderful Wizard of Oz* will be bought from Amazon," "*The Wonderful Wizard of Oz* will be bought from Fatbrain," or "*The Wonderful Wizard of Oz* will be bought from Barnes & Noble." However, though this use is suggested, XLink processors do not enforce it, and indeed they could not be asked to enforce this use since it would require that they understand what they read. The `xlink:arcrole` attribute is optional. You don't have to include it on your arcs, and XLink processors don't have to do anything with it, even if you do.

### Local Resources

Locators represent remote resources: resources that are not part of the document that contains the extended link. Extended links can also contain local resources, in which the extended link element contains the data. A resource element represents each such resource. This is an element of arbitrary type that has an `xlink:type` attribute with the value `resource`. In Example 10-1, the `series` extended link element contains an `author` child element. Giving this element an `xlink:type="resource"` attribute makes it a local resource:

```
<author xlink:type="resource">L. Frank Baum</author>
```

A resource element generally has the same attributes as a locator element, that is, `xlink:label`, `xlink:role`, and `xlink:title`. These attributes have the same semantics as they do for locator elements. For example, the label may be used so arcs can connect to and from resources. An arc can connect a resource to a resource, a resource to a locator, a locator to a resource, or a locator to a locator. Arcs don't care whether resources are local or remote. To link to or from this resource, it needs an `xlink:label` attribute:

```
<author xlink:type="resource" xlink:label="baum">L. Frank Baum</author>
```

To establish links from this local resource to all the books, simply add these three arc elements:

```
<book xlink:type="arc" xlink:from="baum" xlink:to="oz1" />
<book xlink:type="arc" xlink:from="baum" xlink:to="oz2" />
<book xlink:type="arc" xlink:from="baum" xlink:to="oz3" />
```

To move in the other direction, simply reverse the values of the `xlink:from` and `xlink:to` attributes.

### Title Elements

As you've seen, extended link elements, locator elements, arc elements, and resource elements can all have `xlink:title` attributes that provide a short blurb of text identifying the link. However, these attributes aren't always enough. In a document that is a large, extended link, you should mark up the titles using XHTML or another vocabulary. Thus, a title can instead (or in addition) be provided as a title type child element, an element whose `xlink:type` attribute has the value `title`.

Suppose you want to provide a complete description of each edition of *The Wonderful Wizard of Oz* rather than simply list its publisher. In this case, give the `edition` element a title type element containing any convenient markup, such as:

```
<edition xlink:type="locator" xlink:href="urn:isbn:0700609857"
         xlink:title="University Press of Kansas"
         xlink:role="http://www.kansaspress.ku.edu/"
         xlink:label="ISBN0700609857">
  <publisher_info xlink:type="title">
```

```
      <ul>
        <li>The Kansas Centennial Edition</li>
        <li>Illustrated by Michael McCurdy</li>
        <li>Foreword by Ray Bradbury</li>
        <li>1999</li>
        <li>216 pages</li>
        <li>SRP: $24.95</li>
      </ul>
    </publisher_info>
  </edition>
```

You may use any markup you choose inside the `title` element, as long as it's well-formed XML. XLink doesn't constrain the markup in any way. How the application interprets that markup is its own business. Here we've used basic HTML that a browser might be able to render. However, this is far enough past the bleeding edge that exact browser behavior, even when browsers do support extended XLinks, is hard to predict.

## *Linkbases*

One of XLinks' most revolutionary features is its ability to define links between documents you don't control. For instance, Example 10-1 is an extended link that describes and links three documents that neither of this book's authors has anything to do with. Links between purely remote resources are called *third-party links*. A third-party link is created when an arc's `xlink:from` and `xlink:to` attributes both contain labels for locator elements. Links from a remote resource to a local resource are called *inbound links*. An inbound link is created when an arc's `xlink:from` attribute contains the label of a locator element and its `xlink:to` attribute contains the label of a resource element. Links from a local resource to a remote resource are called *outbound links*. An outbound link is established when an arc's `xlink:from` attribute contains the label of a resource element and its `xlink:to` attribute contains the label of a locator element. Simple links are also outbound links.

An XML document that contains inbound or third-party links is called a *linkbase*. A linkbase establishes links from documents other than the linkbase itself, including documents the linkbase's author does not own and cannot control. How a browser or other application loads a linkbase and discovers its links is still an open question. The process probably involves visiting a web site that provides the linkbase. When the browser sees the extended link that attempts to establish links from a third web site, it should ask the users whether they wish to accept the suggested links. It might even use the `xlink:role` and `xlink:title` attributes to help users make this decision. However, if past experience with cookies, Java applets, and ActiveX controls is any guide, then the initial user interfaces are likely to be poor and the choices offered limited.

Once a browser loads a linkbase and goes to a page referenced as the starting resource of at least one of the linkbase's links, it should inform users of the referenced page and give them a means to traverse the link. The user interface for this activity remains to be designed. Perhaps it will be a pop-up window showing the third-party links associated with a page. Or maybe it will simply embed the links in the page but use a different underlining color. Users could still activate the links the same way they activate a normal HTML link.

If this scheme is adopted, it would be useful if the starting resource of the link didn't have to be an entire document, but could be just part of it, such as a specific paragraph, personal name, or book title. You can attach an XPointer to the URI-identifying starting resource of the link that chooses a particular part of or point in the starting document. The next chapter, *XPointers*, discusses this topic in greater detail.

## DTDs for XLinks

For a document containing XLinks to be valid, all XLink attributes the document uses must be declared in a DTD, just like any other attributes. Some attributes can usually be declared `#FIXED`, so that they do not need to be explicitly included in the document itself. For example, this DTD fragment describes the `novel` element seen earlier:

```
<!ELEMENT novel  (title, author, year)>
<!ATTLIST novel  xmlns:xlink CDATA    #FIXED
'http://www.w3.org/1999/xlink'
                 xlink:type (simple) #FIXED 'simple'
                 xlink:href  CDATA    #REQUIRED>
<!ELEMENT title  (#PCDATA)>
<!ELEMENT author (#PCDATA)>
<!ELEMENT year   (#PCDATA)>
```

Given this DTD to fill in the fixed attributes `xmlns:xlink` and `xlink:type`, a `novel` element only needs an `xlink:href` attribute to be a complete simple XLink:

```
<novel xlink:href = "urn:isbn:0688069444">
  <title>The Wonderful Wizard of Oz</title>
  <author>L. Frank Baum</author>
  <year>1900</year>
</novel>
```

Documents that contain many XLink elements often use parameter entity references to define common attributes. Suppose `novel`, `anthology`, and `nonfiction` are all simple XLink elements. Their XLink attributes could be declared in a DTD like this:

```
<!ENTITY % simplelink
  "xlink:type (simple) #FIXED 'simple'
   xlink:href  CDATA   #REQUIRED
   xmlns:xlink CDATA   #FIXED 'http://www.w3.org/1999/xlink'
   xlink:role  NMTOKEN #IMPLIED
   xlink:title CDATA   #IMPLIED
   xlink:actuate (onRequest | onLoad | other | none) 'onRequest'
   xlink:show (new | replace | embed | other | none) 'new'"
>
<!ATTLIST anthology  %simplelink;>
<!ATTLIST novel      %simplelink;>
<!ATTLIST manual     %simplelink;>
```

Similar techniques can be applied to declarations of attributes for extended XLinks.

CHAPTER 11

# XPointers

XPointers are a non-XML syntax used for locating points in or ranges across XML documents. An XPointer is attached to the end of the URI as its fragment identifier to indicate a particular part of an XML document, rather than the entire document. XPointer syntax builds on the XPath syntax used by XSLT and covered in Chapter 9, *XPath*. To the four fundamental XPath datatypes—boolean, node set, number, and string—XPointer adds points and ranges, as well as the functions needed to work with these types. It also adds a shorthand syntax for particularly useful and common forms of XPath expressions.

---

This chapter is based on the June 7, 2000 Candidate Recommendation of XPointer. However, there are known issues with this draft, and some details described here are likely to change. The most current version of the XPointer recommendation can be found at *http://www.w3.org/TR/xptr*.

---

## XPointers on URLs

A URL that identifies a document typically looks something like *http://java.sun.com:80/products/jndi/index.html*. The scheme, *http* in this example, tells you what protocol the application should use to retrieve the document. The authority, *java.sun.com:80,* tells you what host the application should retrieve the document from. The authority may also contain the port to connect to on that host and the username and password to use. The path, */products/jndi/index.html*, tells you which file in which directory to ask the server for. This file may not always be a real file in an actual filesystem, but it should be a complete document that the server knows how to generate and return. You're already familiar with this, and XPointer doesn't change any of it.

You probably also know that some URLs contain fragment identifiers that identify the particular named anchor inside the document identified by the URL's path. The sharp sign # separates this anchor from the path. If we added the fragment *download* to the previous URL, it would become *http://java.sun.com:80/products/jndi/index.html#download.* When a web browser follows a link to this URL, it would look for a named anchor in the document at *http://java.sun.com:80/products/jndi/index.html* with the name *download,* such as this one:

```
<a name="download"></a>
```

It would then scroll the browser window to the position in the document where the anchor with the right name was found. This scheme is simple and straightforward and it works well for HTML's simple needs. However, it has one major drawback: to link to a particular point in a document, you must be able to modify the document to insert a named anchor at the point you'd like to link to. XPointer tries to eliminate this restriction by allowing you to specify where you want to link to using full XPath expressions as fragment identifiers. Furthermore, XPointer expands on XPath by providing operations to select particular points in or ranges of an XML document. These points and ranges do not necessarily coincide with any one node or set of nodes in an XML document. For instance, an XPointer can describe the range of text currently selected by the mouse in an editor.

An XPointer is simply an XPath expression, often a location path, enclosed in the parentheses of `xpointer()`. These are all legal XPointers:

```
xpointer(/)
xpointer(//first_name)
xpointer(id('sec-intro'))
xpointer(/people/person/name/first_name/text())
xpointer(//middle_initial[position()=1]/../first_name)
xpointer(//profession[.="physicist"])
xpointer(/child::people/child::person[@id<4000])
xpointer(/child::people/child::person/attribute::id)
```

Not all of these XPointers necessarily refer to a single element. Depending on which document the XPointer is evaluated in relation to, an XPointer may identify zero, one, or more than one node. Most commonly the identified nodes are elements, but they can also be attribute nodes, text nodes, or points or ranges, two new node types XPointer introduces that XPath doesn't have.

XPointers can identify multiple elements by stringing them together. If you want to indicate all `first_name` and `last_name` elements in the document, use this XPointer:

```
xpointer(//first_name)xpointer(//last_name)
```

To indicate all `first_name`, `last_name`, and `middle_initial` elements, use this XPointer:

```
xpointer(//first_name)xpointer(//last_name)xpointer(//middle_initial)
```

No special separator character or whitespace is required between the individual `xpointer()` parts.

## *XPointers in Links*

What an XPointer points to obviously depends on which document it's applied to. The URL the XPointer is attached to specifies this document. If you want a URL that points to the first name element in the document at *http://www.ibiblio.org/xml/people.xml*, type:

```
http://www.ibiblio.org/xml/people.xml#xpointer(//name[position()=1])
```

If the XPointer uses characters that cannot be included in a URI according to the URI specification, such as the left angle bracket < or the double quote mark ", then the characters must be escaped, as required by the URI specification, before the XPointer is attached to the URI; each such character is replaced by a percent sign, followed by the hexadecimal value of each byte in the character in the UTF-8 encoding of Unicode. Thus < would be written as %3C and " would appear as %22.

In HTML, a element's URLs can contain an XPointer fragment identifier:

```
<a href =
"http://www.ibiblio.org/xml/people.xml#xpointer (//name[position()=1])">
  The name of a person
</a>
```

If a browser followed this link, it would probably load the entire document at *http://www.ibiblio.org/xml/people.xml* and then scroll the window to the beginning of the document's first name element. However, no browsers yet support XPointer, so exact behavior is open for debate. In some situations it might make sense for the browser to show only the specific element or elements the XPointer referred to rather than the entire document.

Since XPath can only locate nodes in a well-formed XML document, XPointers can only point into XML documents. You can't use them to link into non-well-formed HTML, plain text files, or other non-XML documents. However, linking from HTML documents, printing XPointers in books, painting them on the sides of buildings, or communicating them in any way text can be communicated is acceptable.

XPointers are more frequently used in XLinks. This simple link points to the first book child of the bookcoll child of the testament root element in the document at the relative URL *ot.xml*:

```
<link xlink:type="simple"
      xlink:href=
"ot.xml#xpointer(/testament/bookcoll/book[position( )=1])"
>
  Genesis
</link>
```

In extended links, an XPointer can help identify the starting and ending resources of an arc. This extended XLink establishes an arc between the last v element in the document at the relative URL *ot.xml* and the first v element of the document at the relative URL *nt.xml*. It then establishes a link from *nt.xml*'s first v element to *ot.xml*'s last v element:

```
<link xlink:type="extended" xmlns:xlink="http://www.w3.org/1999/xlink">

  <testament xlink:type="locator" xlink:label="ot"
```

```
              xlink:href="ot.xml#xpointer(//v[position()=last()])"/>
  <testament xlink:type="locator" xlink:label="nt"
              xlink:href="nt.xml#xpointer(//v[position()=1])" />

  <next      xlink:from="ot" xlink:to="nt"/>
  <previous xlink:from="nt" xlink:to="ot"/>

</link>
```

Links can even be purely internal; they can link from one place in a document to another place in the same document. The `slide` element shown in the next example contains simple XLinks that point to the previous and next `slide` elements:

```
<slide xmlns:xlink="http://www.w3.org/1999/xlink">

  <point>Acme Wonder Goo is a delicious dessert topping!</point>
  <point>Acme Wonder Goo is a powerful floor cleaner!</point>
  <point>It's two products in one!</point>

  <previous xlink:type="simple" xlink:href=
 "#xpointer(ancestor::slide/preceding-sibling::slide[position()=1])">
    Back
  </previous>
  <next xlink:type="simple" xlink:href=
 "#xpointer(ancestor::slide/following-sibling::slide[position()=1])">
    Back
  </next>
</slide>
```

Since the XPath expressions used in this example are themselves relative, the current node is the link element itself, the `previous` and `next` elements.

## Bare Names

XPointers provide many convenient extensions to XPath. The *bare name* is one of the simplest. A bare name XPointer is similar to an HTML named anchor; it identifies the element it points at by its name. However, an ID attribute of the element being pointed at, rather than a special `a` element with a `name` attribute, supplies this name. To link to an element with a bare name, append the usual fragment separator # to the URL, followed by the ID of the element you're linking to. For example, the URL *http://www.w3.org/TR/1999/REC-xpath-19991116.xml#NT-AbsoluteLocationPath* links to the element in the XPath 1.0 specification that has an ID type attribute with the value *NT-AbsoluteLocationPath*.

The ID attribute is an attribute declared to have ID type in the document's DTD. It does not have to be named `ID` or `id`. Bare names cannot link to elements in documents that don't have DTDs because such documents cannot have ID type attributes.

Suppose you wanted to link to the Motivation and Summary section of the *Namespaces in XML* recommendation at *http://www.w3.org/TR/1999/REC-xml-names-19990114/xml-names.xml*. A quick peek at this document's source code reveals that it has an `id` attribute with the value `sec-intro` and that this attribute is declared to have ID type in the associated DTD. Its start tag looks like this:

```
<div1 id='sec-intro'>
```

Therefore *http://www.w3.org/TR/1999/REC-xml-names-19990114/xml-names.xml#sec-intro* is a URL that points to this section. To make this work, the name should not be enclosed in `xpointer()`. The ID value alone is sufficient. This link is just a convenient shorthand for an XPointer using an XPath expression that uses the `id()` function. The same URL could have been written as *http://www.w3.org/TR/1999/REC-xml-names-19990114/xml-names.xml#xpointer(id('sec-intro'))*.

## *Child Sequences*

Many XPointers descend exclusively along the child axis, selecting elements by their position relative to their siblings; `xpointer(/child::*[position()=1]/child::*[position()=2]/child::*[position()=3])` selects the third child element of the second child element of the document's root element. Since this is so common, XPointer allows you to abbreviate this syntax by providing only the numbers of the child elements, separated by forward slashes. This abbreviation is called a *child sequence*. The previous XPointer could be rewritten as a child sequence in the more compact form `/1/2/3`. A child sequence should not be enclosed in `xpointer()` like a normal XPath expression.

The aforementioned Motivation and Summary section of the *Namespaces in XML* recommendation at *http://www.w3.org/TR/1999/REC-xml-names-19990114/xml-names.xml* is given as a `div` element. This `div` element is the first child element of the root element's second child element. Therefore the URL *http://www.w3.org/TR/1999/REC-xml-names-19990114/xml-names.xml#/1/2/1* points to this section.

## *Points*

XPaths, bare names, and child sequences let you point only to entire nodes or sets of nodes. However sometimes you may want to point to something that isn't a node, such as the third word of the second paragraph or the year in a `date` attribute that looks like `date="01/03/1950"`. XPointer adds points and ranges to the XPath syntax to make this possible. Points can also be positions inside comments, processing instructions, or attribute values. Points cannot be located inside an entity reference, though they can be inside the entity's replacement text. A range is the span of parsed character data between two points.

A point is identified by its *container node* and a nonnegative index into that node. If the node, such as a document or element node, contains child nodes, then points exist before and after each of its children. If the node, such as a comment, processing instruction, attribute, namespace, or text node, does not contain child nodes, then a point is present before and after each character in the node's string value. Consider the document in Example 11-1. It contains a `novel` element with seven child nodes, three of which are element nodes and four of which are text nodes containing only whitespace.

*Example 11-1: A Novel Document*

```
<?xml version="1.0"?>
<?xml-stylesheet type="text/css" value="novel.css"?>
<!-- You may recognize this from the last chapter -->
<novel copyright="public domain">
  <title>The Wonderful Wizard of Oz</title>
  <author>L. Frank Baum</author>
  <year>1900</year>
</novel>
```

Eight points are located directly inside the `novel` element, numbered from 0 to 7, one immediately after and one immediately before each tag. Figure 11-1 identifies these points.

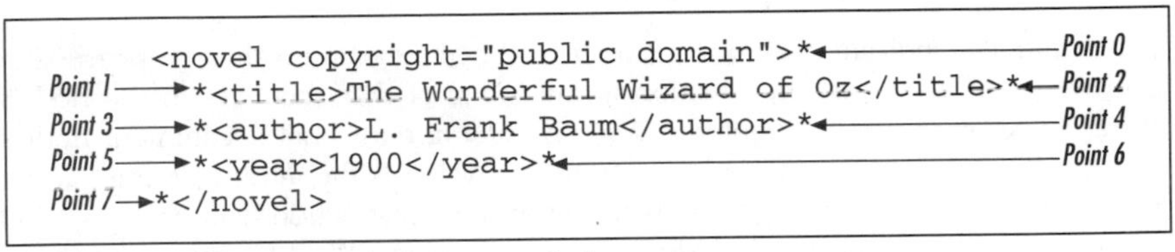


*Figure 11-1: The points inside the novel element*

Five points are present inside the text node child of the `year` element:

- Point 0 between <year> and 1
- Point 1 between 1 and 9
- Point 2 between 9 and 0
- Point 3 between 0 and 0
- Point 4 between 0 and </year>

Notice that the points occur between the characters of the text and don't identify the characters themselves. Points are zero dimensional. They identify a location, but have no extension, not even a single character. To indicate at least one character, specify a range between two points.

To point at a point with an XPointer, use the `point()` node test in an XPath expression. First, the XPath expression selects the container node. Then you attach one more location step with a `point` node test and a predicate, indicating which point you want. For example, the XPointer `xpointer(//title[position()=1]/text()/point()[position()=3])` initially finds the document's first `title` element. Then it takes its text node child. Within this text node, it selects the point between the third and fourth characters. If this XPointer were applied to Example 11-1, it would point to the space after `The`.

If the containing node is a document or element node, then the points an XPointer points at are before or after other child nodes, rather than before or after individual characters. This XPointer indicates the point immediately preceding the `<title>` tag:

```
xpointer(/novel/point()[position()=1]))
```

This next XPointer points to the same point, though it's a little tricky because it requires you to count the number of whitespace characters in a text node:

```
xpointer(/novel/text()[position()=1]/point()[position()=3])
```

XPointer adds two functions to XPath that facilitate selection of the point immediately before or immediately after an element or text node, `start-point()` and `end-point()`. This XPointer is a third way of identifying the same point:

```
xpointer(start-point()(//title))
```

This XPointer indicates the point immediately after the `</author>` tag:

```
xpointer(end-point()(//author))
```

If multiple `title` and `author` elements in the document were present, then these functions would select multiple points.

Points can also indicate positions inside a comment, attribute value, or processing instruction. In each case the position is the index of that character in the node's string value. Recall from Chapter 8, *XSL Transformations*, that a comment node's value is the comment's text, an attribute node's value is the attribute value, and a processing instruction node's value is the processing instruction data. Suppose you want to indicate the point right before the word `may` in `<!-- You may recognize this from the last chapter -->`. The letter *m* is the sixth character of the comment's value. Therefore the point immediately before it has index 5. This XPointer finds it:

```
xpointer(/comment()[position()=1]/point()[position()=5])
```

Processing instructions are similar, except you don't count the processing instruction target or subsequent whitespace. Suppose you wanted to point to the point between the `"` and the *n* in `"novel.css"`. The `"` is the data's 23rd character and the *n* is the 24th, so this XPointer selects the point between them:

```
xpointer(/processing-instruction()[position()=1]/point()[position()=23])
```

Processing instructions can only have pseudo-attributes, so you can't use the attribute axis to select the `value` attribute of the `xml-stylesheet` processing instruction or any points inside it. However, you can do this for genuine attributes, such as the `copyright` attribute of the `novel` element in Example 11-1. This XPointer selects the point between the `"` and the `p` in `copyright="public domain"`:

```
xpointer(/novel/@copyright/point()[position()=0]))
```

Notice that the attribute name is not included in the attribute's string value, so position 0 locates the point at the beginning of the attribute value.

In all cases, it's an error if a `point()` node test points before the beginning of the containing node (i.e., has a negative index) or after the end of the containing node. However, an application is free to decide what to do in the face of such an error. No specific behavior is required. In a web browser the results might be similar to following a link to a named anchor that no longer exists; that is, the document would be loaded and positioned at its start and the fragment identifier would be ignored.

## Ranges

A *range* is the span of parsed character data between two points. It may or may not represent a well-formed chunk of XML. For example, a range can include an element's start tag but not its end tag. This makes ranges suitable for representing the text a user selects with the mouse. Ranges are created with four functions that XPointer adds to XPath:

- `range()`
- `range-inside()`
- `range-to()`
- `string-range()`

XPointers

### The range() Function

The `range()` function takes an XPath expression that returns a location set as an argument. For each node in this location set, the `range()` function returns a range that covers that node exactly; the range's start point is the point immediately before the node and its end point is the point immediately after the node. If the node is an element, then the range begins right before the element's start tag and finishes right after its end tag. Consider this XPointer:

```
xpointer(range-inside(//title))
```

When applied to Example 11-1, it selects a range that covers the single `title` element exactly. If more than one `title` element in the document were present, it would return one range for each such `title` element. If there were no `title` elements in the document, then it wouldn't return any range.

Now consider this XPointer:

```
xpointer(range(/novel/*))
```

If applied to Example 11-1, it returns three ranges, one covering each of the `novel` root element's three child elements.

### The range-inside() Function

The `range-inside()` function takes an XPath expression that returns a location set as an argument. For each node in this location set, it returns a range covering the contents of that node exactly. For anything except an element node this range is the same as that returned by `range()`. For an element node, this range includes everything inside the element, but not the element's start or end tag. For example, when applied to Example 11-1, `xpointer(range(//title))` returns a range covering `The Wonderful Wizard of Oz`, but not `<title>The Wonderful Wizard of Oz</title>`.

### The range-to() Function

The `range-to()` function is evaluated in respect to a context node and takes a location set as an argument. The start points of the context nodes are the start points of the ranges it returns. The end points of the node in the argument are the end points of the ranges. If either the context node list or the argument indicates multiple nodes, then the `range-to()` function returns multiple ranges.

Suppose you wanted to produce a single range that covered everything between `<title>` and `</year>` in Example 11-1. This XPointer produces the range by starting with the start point of the `title` element and continuing to the end point of the `year` element:

```
xpointer(/title/range-to(year))
```

Ranges do not necessarily have to cover well-formed fragments of XML. For instance, the start tag of an element can be included and the end tag left out. This XPointer selects `<title>The Wonderful Wizard of Oz`:

```
xpointer(/title/range-to(/title/text()))
```

It starts at the start point of the `title` element, but finishes at the end point of the `title` element's text node child, thereby omitting the end tag.

## *The string-range() Function*

The `string-range()` function is unusual. Rather than operating on a location set and including various tags, comments, and processing instructions, it operates on the text of a document after all markup has been stripped from it. Tags are ignored.

The `string-range()` function takes an XPath expression identifying nodes and a string as arguments to match against the text of those nodes. It returns a range that starts at the first occurrence of the matched string and returns a range covering the matched string. Matches are case sensitive; this XPointer produces ranges for all occurrences of the word "Wizard" in the document's `title` elements:

```
xpointer(string-range(//title, "Wizard"))
```

You can also specify an offset and a length to the function so that strings start a certain number of characters from the beginning of the match and continue for a specified number of characters. This XPointer selects the first 12 characters after the "Wizard" in the `title` elements:

```
xpointer(string-range(//title, "Wizard", 6, 12))
```

All characters for a string range are taken from the document's character data, never from the markup.

# CHAPTER 12

# *Cascading Stylesheets (CSS)*



Most properly designed XML tags describe the semantic meaning of the content they contain. Ultimately this content needs to be formatted and displayed to users. For this to occur, there must be a step when formatting information is applied to the XML document and the semantic markup is transformed into presentational markup. There are a variety of choices for the syntax of this presentation layer. Two are particularly noteworthy:

- Cascading Stylesheets (CSS)
- XSL Formatting Objects (XSL-FO)

CSS is a non-XML syntax used to describe the appearance of particular elements in a document. CSS is a very straightforward language. No transformation is performed; the document's parsed character data is presented more or less as it appears in the XML document, though you can always transform the document with XSLT and then apply a CSS stylesheet to it if you need to rearrange a document's content before showing it to the user. A CSS stylesheet does not change the XML document's markup at all. It merely applies rules to the markup that already exists.

In contrast, XSL-FO is a complete XML application that describes the layout of text on a page. It has elements that represent pages, blocks of text on the pages, graphics, and horizontal rules. Users do not normally work with this application directly. Instead they write an XSLT stylesheet that transforms the document's native markup into XSL-FO. The application rendering the document reads the XSL-FO and displays it to the user.

In this and the next chapter, we'll demonstrate features of the two major stylesheet languages by applying them to the simple, well-formed XML document shown in Example 12-1. This document does not have a document type declaration and is not valid, though a DTD could be added easily. In general, DTDs don't impact stylesheets, except by changing the document's content through entity declarations, default attribute values, etc.

*Example 12-1: Marjorie Anderson's Recipe for Southern Cornbread*

```
<?xml version="1.0" encoding="ISO-8859-1" standalone="yes"?>
<?xml-stylesheet type="text/css" href="recipe.css"?>
<recipe source="Marjorie Anderson">
  <dish>Southern Corn Bread</dish>
  <ingredients>
    <ingredient>
      <quantity>1 cup</quantity>
      <component>flour</component>
    </ingredient>
    <ingredient>
      <quantity>4 tablespoons</quantity>
      <component>Royal Baking Powder</component>
    </ingredient>
    <ingredient>
      <quantity>1/2 teaspoon</quantity>
      <component>salt</component>
    </ingredient>
    <ingredient>
      <quantity>1 cup</quantity>
      <component>corn meal</component>
    </ingredient>
    <ingredient>
      <quantity>1 1/2 cups</quantity>
      <component>whole milk</component>
    </ingredient>
    <ingredient>
      <quantity>4 tablespoons</quantity>
      <component>melted butter</component>
    </ingredient>
  </ingredients>

  <directions>
    <step>Sift flour, baking powder, sugar &amp; salt together.</step>
    <step>Add 1 cup corn meal.</step>
    <step>
      Beat egg in cup and add beaten egg and 1 1/2 cups whole
       milk to make a batter. Stir well.
    </step>
    <step>
      Add melted shortening and beat until light and thoroughly mixed.
    </step>
    <step>
      Pour into greased shallow pan or greased muffin rings.
    </step>
    <step>
      Bake in hot oven at <temperature>425º F</temperature> for
      <duration>25 minutes</duration>.
    </step>
    <step optional="yes">
      Cut into squares if cooked in shallow pan.
    </step>
  </directions>
```

```
  <story>
    After my mother-in-law <person>Marjorie Anderson</person> died,
    Beth and I found this recipe written on the "extra recipes"
    page in a local cookbook in her cupboard.
    This was published by The Episcopal Churchwomen,
    Church of Ascension, <city>Mt. Sterling</city>,
    <state>Kentucky</state>.
  </story>

</recipe>
```

CSS

## The Three Levels of CSS

As of the year 2001, there are three versions of CSS. CSS Level 1 was an early W3C Recommendation from 1996 used only for HTML, though the extension to XML was obvious. The CSS Level 1 specification was incomplete and led to inconsistent browser implementations.

CSS Level 2 is the current recommendation, and this chapter focuses on it. CSS Level 2 places XML on an equal footing with HTML. Indeed, CSS Level 2 often works better with XML than with HTML because in XML, CSS styles don't have to interact with predefined rendering semantics. CSS Level 2 is generally a superset of CSS Level 1; all CSS Level 1 stylesheets are also CSS Level 2 stylesheets that mean the same thing.

The W3C is now working on CSS Level 3. When complete, it will modularize the CSS specification to allow software to implement particular CSS functionality subsets without having to implement everything. For instance, an audio browser could implement audio stylesheets but ignore the visual formatting model. CSS Level 3 also adds several features to CSS, including multicolumn layouts, better support for non-Western languages such as Arabic and Chinese, XML namespace support, more powerful selectors, and paged media. However, browsers have not yet implemented CSS Level 3.

## CSS Syntax

CSS syntax isn't XML syntax, but the syntax is so trivial that it hardly matters. A CSS stylesheet is simply a list of the elements to which you should apply the styles, normally one to a line. If the element is in a namespace, then the qualified name, such as `recipe:dish`, must be used. Each element name is followed by the list of styles you want to apply to that element. Comments can be inserted using the `/*...*/` style comments familiar to C programmers. Whitespace isn't particularly significant, so it can be used to format the stylesheet. Example 12-2 is a simple CSS stylesheet for the recipe document in Example 12-1. Figure 12-1 shows the recipe document as rendered and displayed by the Opera 4.0 browser with this stylesheet.

*Example 12-2: A CSS Stylesheet for Recipes*

```
/* Defaults for the entire document */
recipe  {font-family: "New York", "Times New Roman", serif;
         font-size: 12pt }

/* Make the dish look like a headline */
dish    {
  display: block;
  font-family: Helvetica, Arial, sans-serif;
  font-size: 20pt;
  font-weight: bold;
  text-align: center
}

/* A bulleted list */
ingredient  {display: list-item}

/* Format these two items as paragraphs */
directions, story {
  display: block;
  margin-top: 12pt;
  margin-left: 4pt
}
```

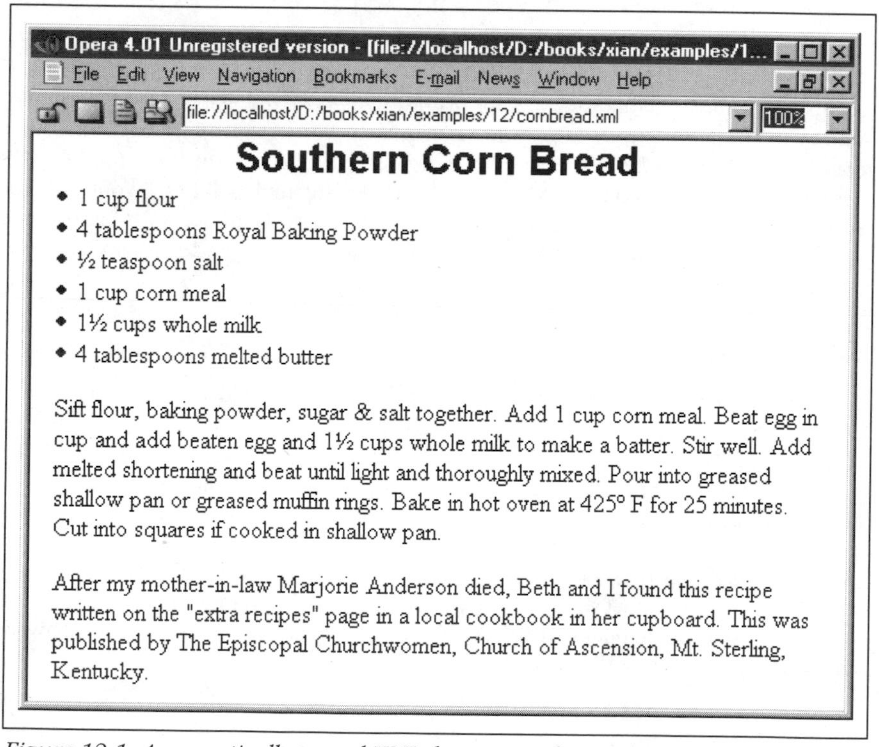


*Figure 12-1: A semantically tagged XML document after application of a CSS stylesheet*

This stylesheet has four style rules. Each rule names the element or elements it formats, followed by a pair of curly braces containing the style properties to apply to those elements. Each property has a name, such as `font-family`, and a value, such as `"New York", "Times New Roman", serif`. Semicolons separate the properties. Neither the names nor the values are case sensitive; `font-family` is the same as `FONT-FAMILY` or `Font-Family`. CSS Level 2 defines more than a hundred different style properties. However, you don't need to know them all. Reasonable default values are provided for all properties you don't set.

For example, the first rule applies to the `recipe` element and says that it should be formatted using the New York font at a 12-point size. If New York isn't available, then Times New Roman is chosen instead. If that font isn't available, then any convenient serif font will suffice. These styles also apply to all `recipe` element descendants; the styles *cascade* down the tree. Since `recipe` is the root element, it sets the default font for the entire document.

The second rule makes the `dish` element look like a heading, as you can see in Figure 12-1. It's set to a much larger sans serif font, made bold, and centered. Furthermore, its `display` style is set to `block`. This means that a line break will appear between it and its next and previous sibling elements. The third rule formats the ingredients as a bulleted list, while the fourth rule formats both the `directions` and `story` elements as relatively straightforward paragraphs with a little extra whitespace around their top and lefthand sides.

Not all elements in the document have style rules, and not all need them. For example, the `step` element is not specifically styled. Rather, it simply inherits a variety of styles from its ancestor elements `directions` and `recipe` and uses some defaults. A different stylesheet could add a rule for the `step` element that overrides the styles it inherits. The following rule would set its font to 10-point Palatino:

```
step  {font-family: Palatino, serif; font-size: 10pt }
```

## *Associating Stylesheets with XML Documents*

CSS stylesheets are intended primarily for use in web pages. Web browsers find the stylesheet for a document by looking for `xml-stylesheet` processing instructions in the XML document's prolog. This processing instruction should have a `type` pseudo-attribute with the value `text/css` and an `href` pseudo-attribute whose value is an absolute or relative URL locating the stylesheet document. This processing instruction attaches the stylesheet in Listing 12-2 (*recipe.css*) to the file in Example 12-1 (*cornbread.xml*) if both are found in the same directory:

```
<?xml-stylesheet type="text/css" href="recipe.css"?>
```

Including the required `type` and `href` pseudo-attributes, the `xml-stylesheet` processing instruction can have up to six pseudo-attributes:

`type`
: The stylesheet's MIME media type; `text/css` for CSS and `text/xml` (not `text/xsl`!) for XSLT.

`href`
: The absolute or relative URL where the stylesheet can be found.

`charset`
: This pseudo-attribute contains the name of the character set in which the stylesheet is written, such as UTF-8 or ISO-8859-7. This name does not have to be the same as the character set the document is written in. The names used are the same ones used for the XML declaration's `encoding` pseudo-attribute.

`title`
: This pseudo-attribute names the stylesheet. If more than one stylesheet is available for a document, the browser may present readers with a list of titles of all available stylesheets and ask them to choose one.

`media`
: Printed pages, television screens, and computer displays are all fundamentally different media that require different styles. For example, comfortable reading on screen requires much larger fonts than does a printed page. This pseudo-attribute specifies which media types this stylesheet should apply to. Nine values are possible:

- `screen`
- `tty`
- `tv`
- `projection`
- `handheld`
- `print`
- `braille`
- `aural`
- `all`

You can make a single document attractive in many different environments by including several `xml-stylesheet` processing instructions, each pointing to a different stylesheet and using a different media type.

`alternate`
: This pseudo-attribute must be assigned one of the two values `yes` or `no`. `yes` means this pseudo-attribute is an alternate stylesheet, and is not normally used. `no` means this pseudo-attribute is the primary stylesheet to use unless the users indicate they want a different one. The default is `no`.

This group of `xml-stylesheet` processing instructions could be placed in the recipe document prolog to make it more accessible on a broader range of devices:

```
<?xml-stylesheet type="text/css" href="recipe.css" media="screen"
          alternate="no"  title="For Web Browsers" charset="US-ASCII"?>
<?xml-stylesheet type="text/css"
          href="printable_recipe.css" media="print"
          alternate="no" title="For Printing" charset="ISO-8859-1"?>
<?xml-stylesheet type="text/css" href="big_recipe.css" media="projection"
          alternate="no" title="For presentations" charset="UTF-8"?>
<?xml-stylesheet type="text/css" href="tty_recipe.css" media="tty"
          alternate="no" title="For Lynx" charset="US-ASCII"?>
<?xml-stylesheet type="text/css" href="small_recipe.css" media="handheld"
          alternate="no" title="For Palm Pilots" charset="US-ASCII"?>
```

## Selectors

CSS provides very limited abilities to select the elements to which a given rule applies. Many stylesheets use only element names and lists of element names separated by commas, as shown in Example 12-2. However CSS provides other basic selectors you can use, though they're by no means as powerful as XSLT's XPath syntax.

### The Universal Selector

The asterisk matches any element; it applies the specified rule to everything in the document that does not have a more specific conflicting rule. For example, this rule says that all elements in the document should use a large font:

```
* {font-size: large}
```

CSS

### Matching Descendants, Children, and Siblings

An element name `A` followed by another element name `B` matches all `B` elements that are descendants of `A` elements. This rule matches `quantity` elements that are descendants of `ingredients` elements, but not other ones that appear elsewhere in the document:

```
ingredients quantity {font-size: medium}
```

If the two element names are separated by a greater-than sign >, then the second element must be an immediate child of the first for the rule to apply, This rule gives `quantity` children of `ingredient` elements the same `font-size` as the `ingredient` element:

```
ingredient > quantity {font-size: inherit}
```

If the two element names are separated by a plus sign +, then the second element must be the next element immediately after the first element. This style rule sets the `border-top-style` property of only the first `story` element following a `directions` element:

```
directions + story {border-top-style: solid}
```

### Attribute Selectors

Square brackets allow you to select elements with particular attributes or attribute values. This rule hides all `step` elements that have an `optional` attribute:

```
step[optional] {display: none}
```

This rule hides all elements that have an `optional` attribute, regardless of their type:

```
*[optional] {display: none}
```

Use an equals sign to select an element by a given attribute's value. This rule hides all `step` elements that have an `optional` attribute with the value `yes`:

```
step[optional="yes"] {display: none}
```

You can also select elements that contain a given word as part of a specified attribute's value by using the ~= operator. The word must be complete and whitespace must separate it from other words in the attribute value, as in a `NMTOKENS` or `ENTITIES` attribute. This is not a substring match. This rule bolds all `recipe` elements whose `source` attribute contains the word "Anderson":

```
recipe[source~="Anderson"] {font-weight: bold}
```

Finally, if you only want to match against the first word in the whitespace-separated list of attribute values, instead of any word, use |=. This rule makes all `recipe` elements whose `source` attribute starts with the word "Marjorie" bold:

```
recipe[source|="Marjorie"] {font-weight: bold}
```

CSS also provides a special syntax for selecting elements with a given ID value, even when you don't know the exact name of the ID type attribute. Simply separate the ID from the element name with a sharp sign #. This rule applies to the single `step` element whose ID type attribute has the value `P833`:

```
step#P833 { font-weight: 800 }
```

## *Pseudo-class Selectors*

Pseudo-class selectors match elements according to a condition not involving their name. There are seven of these. They are all separated from the element name by a colon. For example, the `first-child` pseudo-class matches the first child element of the named element. When applied to Example 12-1, this rule italicizes only the first `step` element:

```
directions:first-child {font-style: italic}
```

The `link` pseudo-class matches the named element if that element is the source of an unvisited link. This rule makes all links in the document blue and underlined:

```
*:link {color: blue; text-decoration: underline}
```

The previous example isn't yet well supported for XML documents because most browsers don't yet recognize XLinks. Matching the attributes by name, as this rule does, is probably wiser:

```
*[xlink:type="simple"] {color: blue; text-decoration: underline}
```

The `visited` pseudo-class applies to all visited links of the specified type. This rule marks all visited links as purple and underlined:

```
*:visited {color: purple; text-decoration: underline}
```

The `active` pseudo-class applies to all elements that the user is currently activating, by clicking the mouse, for example. Exactly what it means to activate an element depends on context, and indeed not all applications allow you to activate elements. Even those that do, don't necessarily allow you to activate all elements. This rule marks all active elements as red and blinking:

```
*:active {color: red; text-decoration: blink}
```

Note, however, that the CSS2 specification specifically allows browsers to ignore the request to make elements blink. This is a good thing.

The hover pseudo-class applies to all activatable elements on which the cursor is currently positioned but which the user has not yet activated. This rule marks all these elements as green and underlined:

```
*:hover {color: green; text-decoration: underline}
```

The focus pseudo-class applies to all activatable elements that currently have the focus. This rule draws a one-pixel red border around the element with the focus, assuming such an element exists:

```
*:focus {border: 1px solid red }
```

Finally, the lang pseudo-class matches all elements in the specified language as determined by the xml:lang attribute. This rule uses the David New Hebrew font for all elements written in Hebrew (more properly, all elements whose xml:lang attribute has the value he):

```
*:lang(he) {font-family: "David New Hebrew"}
```

CSS

## *Pseudo-element Selectors*

Pseudo-element selectors match things that aren't actually elements. Like pseudo-class selectors a colon attaches them to an element selector. There are four of these selectors:

- first-letter
- first-line
- before
- after

The first-letter pseudo-element selects the first letter of a given element and applies special formatting to it. This rule makes the first letter of the story element a drop cap:

```
story:first-letter {
  font-size: 200%;
  font-weight: bold;
  float: left;
  padding-right: 3pt
}
```

The first-line pseudo-element applies formatting to all characters in the first line of a block-level element. If the browser window is resized so that characters move in or out of the first line, then the formatting changes to match. This rule formats the first line of the story element in small capitals instead of lowercase letters:

```
story:first-line {font-variant: small-caps}
```

The before and after pseudo-elements select the points immediately before and after the specified element. You can't really apply font or text styles to a zero-width point, but you can insert text at that point using the content property. For example, this rule inserts the string "Ingredients! " before the ingredients element:

```
ingredients:before {content: "Ingredients! "}
```

This rule places the number of the step in front of each `step` element in the form 1., 2., 3., . . . :

```
step:before {
  content: counter(step) ". ";
  counter-increment: step;
}
```

## The Display Property

`Display` is one of the most important CSS properties. This property identifies how the element as a whole will be laid out on a page. There are 18 legal values for this property. However, the two primary values are `inline` and `block`. The display property can also create lists and tables or hide elements completely.

### Inline Elements

Setting the display to `inline`, the default value, places the element in the next available position from left to right, much as each word in this paragraph is added. The exact direction can change for right-to-left languages, such as Hebrew, or top-to-bottom languages like traditional Chinese. Hard line breaks won't be placed between each inline element. If necessary, the text may be wrapped from one line to the next. In Example 12-1 and Example 12-2, the `quantity`, `step`, `person`, `city`, and `state` elements were all formatted as inline. This format was the default and didn't need to be specified explicitly.

### Block Elements

In contrast to inline elements, an element set to `display: block` is separated from its siblings, generally by a line break. For example, in HTML paragraphs and headings are block elements. In Example 12-1 and Example 12-2, the `dish`, `directions`, and `story` elements were all formatted with `display: block`.

### List Elements

An element whose `display` property is set to `list-item` is also formatted as a block-level element. However, a bullet is inserted at the beginning of the block. The `list-style-type`, `list-style-image`, and `list-style-position` properties control which character or image is used for a bullet and exactly how the list is indented. For example, this rule would format the steps as a numbered list rather than render them as a single paragraph:

```
step {
  display: list-item;
  list-style-type: decimal;
  list-style-position: inside
}
```

### Hidden Elements

An element whose `display` property is set to `none` is not included in the rendered document the reader sees. It is invisible and does not occupy space or affect the placement of other elements. For example, this style rule hides the `story` element completely:

```
story {display: none}
```

### *Table Elements*

Ten `display` values identify elements as parts of a table:

- `table`
- `inline-table`
- `table-row-group`
- `table-header-group`
- `table-footer-group`
- `table-row`
- `table-column-group`
- `table-column`
- `table-cell`
- `table-caption`

These display values have the obvious meanings by analogy with HTML 4.0 table tags. Their use should be consistent with one another and with other elements in the document. For instance, an element formatted as a table-row should have a parent element formatted as a table and child elements formatted as table-cells. These three rules format the ingredients as a simple table:

```
ingredients          { display: table      }
ingredient           { display: table-row  }
quantity, component  { display: table-cell }
```

## *Pixels, Points, Picas, and Other Units of Length*

Many CSS properties represent lengths. Some of the most important properties include:

- `border-width`
- `font-size`
- `line-height`
- `margin-left`, `margin-top`, `margin-right`, and `margin-bottom`
- `left`
- `top`
- `height`
- `width`

CSS

CSS provides many different units you can use to specify length. They fall into two groups:

- Absolute units of length, such as inches, centimeters, millimeters, points, and picas
- Relative units, such as ems, exes, pixels, and percentages

Absolute units of length are appropriate for printed media (paper), but should be avoided in other media. Relative units should be used for all other media, except for pixels, which probably shouldn't be used at all. This style rule sets the **dish** element to be exactly one-half centimeter high:

```
dish { height: 0.5 cm}
```

However, documents intended for display on screen media, such as television sets and computer monitors, should not be set to fixed sizes. For one thing, the size of an inch or other absolute unit can vary, depending on the monitor's resolution. Also, not all users like the same defaults, and what looks good on one monitor may be illegible on another. Instead you should use units that are relative to something, such as an em, which is relative to the width of the uppercase letter *M* in the current font, or ex, which is relative to the height of the lowercase letter *x* in the current font. This rule sets the **line-height** property of the **story** element to one-and-a-half times the height of the letter *x*:

```
story { line-height: 1.5ex}
```

Pixel is also a relative unit, though what it's relative to is the size of a pixel on the current display. This size is generally in the vicinity of a point, but it can vary from system to system. We don't recommend using pixels unless you need to line something up with a bitmapped graphic displayed at an exact 1:1 ratio. Web pages formatted with pixel lengths invariably look too small or too large on some users' monitors.

Specifying lengths as percentages of another length is a very useful technique. What the length is a percentage of varies from property to property. For instance, if the **line-height** is given as a percentage, then it's calculated with respect to the same element's **font-height**. These two rules set the **dish** element's **font-height** to 0.5 centimeters and its **line-height** to 0.75 centimeters:

```
dish  { font-height: 0.5cm }
dish  { line-height: 150% }
```

## *Font Properties*

Fonts are one of the most basic things designers want to set with CSS. Is the text italic? Is it bold? What typeface and size are used? CSS provides properties to set all these basic characteristics of text. In particular, you can set these properties:

`font-family`
: This property lists font names, separated by commas, in order of preference. The last name in the list should always be one of the generic names **serif**, **sans-serif**, **monospace**, **cursive**, or **fantasy**. Multiword names, such as *Times New Roman*, should be enclosed in quotes.

`font-style`
: The value `italic` indicates that an italic version of the font should be used, if available. The value `oblique` suggests that the text should be slanted algorithmically rather than using a specially designed italic font. The default is `normal` (no italicizing or slanting). An element can also be set to `inherit` the parent element's `font-style`.

`font-size`
: This property specifies the size of the font. The size should be specified as one of the values `xx-small`, `x-small`, `small`, `medium`, `large`, `x-large`, or `xx-large`. Alternately it can be a percentage of the parent element's `font-size`. It can also be specified as a length, such as `0.2cm` or `12pt`, but this should only be done for print media.

`font-variant`
: If this property is set to `small-caps`, then the text is rendered in smaller capitals LIKE THIS instead of using normal lowercase letters.

`font-weight`
: This property determines how bold or light the text is. It's generally specified as one of the keywords `normal` (the default), `bold`, `bolder`, or `lighter`. It can also be set to any multiple of 100 from `100` (lightest) to `900` (darkest). However, not all browsers necessarily provide nine different levels of boldness.

`font-stretch`
: This property lets you adjust the space between letters to make the text more or less compact. Legal values include `normal` (the default), `wider`, `narrower`, `ultra-condensed`, `extra-condensed`, `condensed`, `semi-condensed`, `semi-expanded`, `expanded`, `extra-expanded`, and `ultra-expanded`.

This style rule uses all these properties to make the `dish` element a suitably impressive headline:

```
dish {
  font-family: Helvetica, Arial, sans-serif;
  font-size: x-large;
  font-style: italic;
  font-variant: small-caps;
  font-weight: 900;
  font-stretch: semi-expanded
}
```

## Text Properties

Text properties cover aspects of text formatting other than what can be adjusted merely by changing the font. These aspects include whether the text is indented and how the paragraph is aligned. The most common of these properties include:

`text-indent`
: The `text-indent` property specifies how far in to indent the first line of the block. (Indents of all lines are generally applied via margin properties.) Hanging indents can be specified by making `text-indent` negative. This

property applies only to block-level elements. This style rule indents the `story` element's first line by half an inch from the left side:

```
story { text-indent: 0.5in }
```

`text-align`
: The `text-align` property can be set to `left`, `right`, `center`, or `justify` to align the text with the left or right edge of the block, center the text in the block, or spread the text out across the block. This property only applies to block-level elements.

`text-decoration`
: The `text-decoration` property can be set to `underline`, `overline`, `line-through`, or `blink` to produce the obvious effects. Fortunately, however, browsers and other user agents may ignore requests to make text blink.

`text-transform`
: The `text-transform` property has three main values: `capitalize`, `uppercase`, and `lowercase`. Uppercase changes all text to capital letters LIKE THESE. Lowercase changes all text to lowercase letters like these. Capitalize simply uppercases the first letter of each word Like This, but leaves the other letters alone. This property's default value is `none`, which performs no transformation. The value can also be set to `inherit` to use the same transform as the parent element.

---

Changing the case in English is fairly straightforward, but is more complicated in other languages. Specifically, software written by native English speakers tends to do a very poor job of changing the case in ligature-heavy European languages, such as Maltese, or context-sensitive languages, such as Arabic. Outside of English text, it's best to make the transformations directly in the source document rather than rely on the stylesheet engine to correctly decide which letters to capitalize.

---

`white-space`
: The `white-space` property determines whether text is wrapped. It has only four legal values: `normal`, `pre`, `nowrap`, and `inherit`. `normal` is the default and simply means to wrap the text wherever convenient, much like in this paragraph. `pre` means to preserve all line breaks and whitespace in the document, as does the `pre` element in HTML. `nowrap` means that runs of whitespace can be condensed, but that line breaks will not be inserted. Finally, `inherit` simply takes on the same behavior as the parent element.

## *Colors*

CSS has several properties for changing the color of various items:

`color`
: The color of the text itself (black on this page)

`background-color`
: The color of the background behind the text (white on this page)

`border-color`
: The color of a visible box surrounding the text

CSS uses a 24-bit color space to specify colors, much like HTML. Remember, however, that just because you can specify a color doesn't mean any given device can render it. A black-and-white printer won't print red, no matter how you identify it. It might give you some nice shades of gray, though. Like many other properties, color depends on the medium in which the document is presented.

The simplest way to choose a color is through one of these 16 named constants: `aqua`, `black`, `blue`, `fuchsia`, `gray`, `green`, `lime`, `maroon`, `navy`, `olive`, `purple`, `red`, `silver`, `teal`, `white`, and `yellow`. Some other colors are defined to be the same as a part of the user interface. For instance, `WindowText` is the same color as text in windows on the local system.

Beyond this small list, you can specify the color of an item by indicating the three components—red, green, and blue—of each color, much as you do for background colors on HTML pages. Each component is given as a number between 0 and 255, with 255 representing the maximum amount of the color. Numbers can be given in decimal or hexadecimal. These rules make the `dish` element pure red, the `story` element pure green, and the `directions` element pure blue:

```
dish       { color: #FF0000 }
story      { color: #00FF00 }
directions { color: #0000FF }
```

If you prefer, you can specify the color as decimals separated by commas inside an `rgb()`function. For example, white is `rgb(255,255,255)`. Black is `rgb(0,0,0)`. Colors in which each component is equal form various shades of gray. These rules make the `ingredient` element a light shade of gray, and its `quantity` child element a darker shade of gray:

```
ingredient { color: rgb(43,43,43) }
quantity   { color: rgb(21,21,21) }
```

You can even give the color as percentages of each color from 0 to 100 percent. The previous rules can be rewritten like this:

```
ingredient { color: rgb(16.9%,16.9%,16.9%) }
quantity   { color: rgb(8.2%,8.2%,8.2%) }
```

CHAPTER 13

# *XSL Formatting Objects (XSL-FO)*

Most properly designed XML tags describe the semantic meaning of the content they contain. Ultimately this content needs to be formatted and displayed to users. To format and display this content, a step that applies formatting information to the XML document and transforms the semantic markup into presentational markup is required. A variety of choices for this presentation layer's syntax are available. Two are particularly noteworthy:

- Cascading Stylesheets (CSS)
- XSL Formatting Objects (XSL-FO)

Chapter 12, *Cascading Stylesheets (CSS)*, covered the first choice, CSS. This chapter discusses the second option, XSL-FO. In contrast to CSS, XSL-FO is a complete XML application used to describe the precise layout of text on a page. It has elements that represent pages, blocks of text on the pages, graphics, and horizontal rules. Most of the time, however, you don't write XSL-FO directly. Instead, you write an XSLT stylesheet that transforms your document's native markup into XSL-FO. The application rendering the document reads the XSL-FO and displays it to the user. Since no major browsers currently support direct rendering of XSL-FO documents, a third step, in which another processor transforms the XSL-FO into a third format, such as PDF or TeX, is usually necessary.

---

> This chapter is based on the November 21, 2000 Candidate Recommendation of the XSL Formatting Object specification. However, there are known issues with this draft, and some details described here are likely to change. The most current version of the XSL-FO specification can be found at *http://www.w3.org/TR/xsl/*.

---

Once again, we demonstrate the features of XSL-FO by applying it to the simple, well-formed XML document shown in Example 12-1 in the last chapter and repeated here in Example 13-1 for convenience.

*Example 13-1: Marjorie Anderson's Recipe for Southern Cornbread*

```
<?xml version="1.0" encoding="ISO-8859-1" standalone="yes"?>
<?xml-stylesheet type="text/css" href="recipe.css"?>
<recipe source="Marjorie Anderson">
  <dish>Southern Corn Bread</dish>
  <ingredients>
    <ingredient>
      <quantity>1 cup</quantity>
      <component>flour</component>
    </ingredient>
    <ingredient>
      <quantity>4 tablespoons</quantity>
      <component>Royal Baking Powder</component>
    </ingredient>
    <ingredient>
      <quantity>1/2 teaspoon</quantity>
      <component>salt</component>
    </ingredient>
    <ingredient>
      <quantity>1 cup</quantity>
      <component>corn meal</component>
    </ingredient>
    <ingredient>
      <quantity>1 1/2 cups</quantity>
      <component>whole milk</component>
    </ingredient>
    <ingredient>
      <quantity>4 tablespoons</quantity>
      <component>melted butter</component>
    </ingredient>
  </ingredients>

  <directions>
    <step>Sift flour, baking powder, sugar &amp; salt together.</step>
    <step>Add 1 cup corn meal.</step>
    <step>
      Beat egg in cup and add beaten egg and 1 1/2 cups whole
       milk to make a batter. Stir well.
    </step>
    <step>
      Add melted shortening and beat until light and thoroughly mixed.
    </step>
    <step>
      Pour into greased shallow pan or greased muffin rings.
    </step>
    <step>
      Bake in hot oven at <temperature>425º F</temperature> for
      <duration>25 minutes</duration>.
    </step>
```

*Example 13-1: Marjorie Anderson's Recipe for Southern Cornbread (continued)*

```
    <step optional="yes">
      Cut into squares if cooked in shallow pan.
    </step>
  </directions>

  <story>
    After my mother-in-law <person>Marjorie Anderson</person> died,
    Beth and I found this recipe written on the "extra recipes"
    page in a local cookbook in her cupboard.
    This was published by the The Episcopal Churchwomen,
    Church of Ascension, <city>Mt. Sterling</city>,
    <state>Kentucky</state>.
  </story>

</recipe>
```

# XSL Formatting Objects

In contrast to CSS, XSL Formatting Objects (XSL-FO) is a very complex XML application used to describe the precise appearance of a page's data. Most of the time, however, you don't write XSL-FO directly. Instead, you write an XSLT stylesheet that transforms an input XML document into XSL-FO. Since no major browsers support direct rendering of XSL-FO documents, a third step is usually necessary. In this step, another processor transforms the XSL-FO into a third format, such as PDF or $\TeX$.

An XSL-FO document describes the layout of a series of nested boxes or areas that are placed on at least one page. These boxes contain text, or occasionally an external image or a horizontal rule. There are four kinds of boxes:

- Block areas
- Inline areas
- Line areas
- Glyph areas

Block and inline areas are created by particular elements in the formatting objects document. The formatter creates line and inline areas as necessary. The rendering engine generally decides exactly where to place the boxes and how big to make them based on their contents. However, you can specify properties for these boxes that adjust their relative and absolute position, spacing, and size on a page. Most of the time, as in this figure, the individual boxes won't overlap one another. However, setting the absolute position properties `left`, `top`, `width`, and `height` on the boxes can force them to overlap.

Each box has a content area in which its content, generally text, but possibly an image or a rule, is placed. This content area is surrounded by a padding area of blank space. An optional border can surround the padding. The size of the area is the combined size of border, padding, and content. The box may also have a margin that adds blank space outside the box's area, as diagramed in Figure 13-1.

Text properties, such as font family, font size, alignment, and font weight can be applied by attaching the appropriate properties to one of the boxes containing the

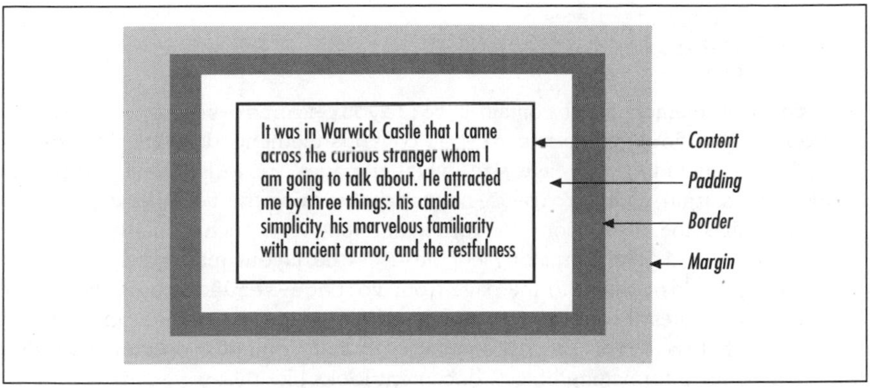


*Figure 13-1: Content, padding, border, and margin of an XSL-FO area*

text. Text takes on the properties specified on the nearest enclosing box. Attaching attributes to the elements that generate the boxes sets the properties. These properties usually have the same semantics as CSS properties of the same name. Only the syntax for applying the properties to particular ranges of text differs.



The elements in the XSL-FO document do not map to the boxes on the page in a one-to-one fashion. Instead the XSL-FO document contains a slightly more abstract representation of the document. The formatting software uses these elements to decide what boxes to create and where to place them. In the process it splits the large blocks the XSL-FO document describes with `fo:block` elements into smaller line and glyph areas. It may also split single block areas described by the XSL-FO document into multiple block areas if a page break is required in the middle of a large block. However, XSL-FO does let you prevent these breaks if necessary. The formatter also generates the correct number of pages for the content that's found. In short, the XSL-FO document contains instructions and hints that the formatter uses to decide what items to place where on which pages; but you do not need to specify each box's exact position.

## *The Structure of an XSL-FO Document*

`fo:root` is the root element of all XSL-FO documents. This element normally declares the `fo` prefix that must be mapped to the `http://www.w3.org/1999/XSL/Format` namespace URI. As always, the prefix can change if the URI stays the same. In this chapter we assume that the prefix `fo` is associated with `http://www.w3.org/1999/XSL/Format`. A typical XSL-FO document looks like this:

```
<?xml version="1.0" encoding="UTF-8"?>
<fo:root xmlns:fo="http://www.w3.org/1999/XSL/Format">
  <!-- Formatting Object elements -->
</fo:root>
```

This document isn't normally written directly, as it is here. Instead, it's formed by an XSLT template, such as this one:

```
<xsl:template match="/">
  <fo:root>
```

```
      <xsl:apply-templates/>
    </fo:root>
  </xsl:template>
```

The `fo:root` element must contain a `fo:layout-master-set` and a `fo:page-sequence`. The `fo:layout-master-set` contains elements describing the overall page layout, including the page size, whether pages are in landscape or portrait mode, and margin width. `fo:page-sequence` contains the actual text placed on the pages and the instructions for formatting that text, such as italic, 20 points high, and justified. The formatting engine uses the layout master set to create a page. Next, it adds content to the page from `fo:page-sequence` until the page is full. Then it creates the next page in the sequence and places the next batch of content on that page. This process continues until all content is positioned. Adding these elements, a formatting objects document looks like this:

```
<?xml version="1.0" encoding="UTF-8"?>
<fo:root xmlns:fo="http://www.w3.org/1999/XSL/Format">

  <fo:layout-master-set>
    <!-- page masters -->
  </fo:layout-master-set>

  <fo:page-sequence>
    <!-- data to place on the page -->
  </fo:page-sequence>

</fo:root>
```

## Master Pages

XSL-FO 1.0 defines only one kind of master page, the `fo:simple-page-master`. This master page represents a standard rectangular page with a fixed width, fixed height, and margins on all four sides. This master page also has a name given by a `master-name` attribute. For example, this element describes a master page named `first` that represents an 8.5" x 11" page with 1" margins on all four sides:

```
<fo:simple-page-master margin-right="1in"  margin-left="1in"
                       margin-bottom="1in" margin-top="1in"
                       page-width="8.5in"  page-height="11in"
                       master-name="first">
  <!-- Separate parts of the page go here -->
</fo:simple-page-master>
```

The part of the page inside the margins is divided into five regions: the start, end, before, after, and body regions. The writing direction determines where these regions fall on a page. In left-to-right, top-to-bottom languages such as English, start is on the lefthand side, end is on the righthand side, before is on top, and after is on bottom, as diagrammed in Figure 13-2. However, if the text were Hebrew, then the start region would be on the righthand side of the page and the end region would be on the lefthand side. If the text were traditional Chinese, then the start would be on top, the end on the bottom, the before on the lefthand side, and the after on the righthand side. Other combinations are possible.

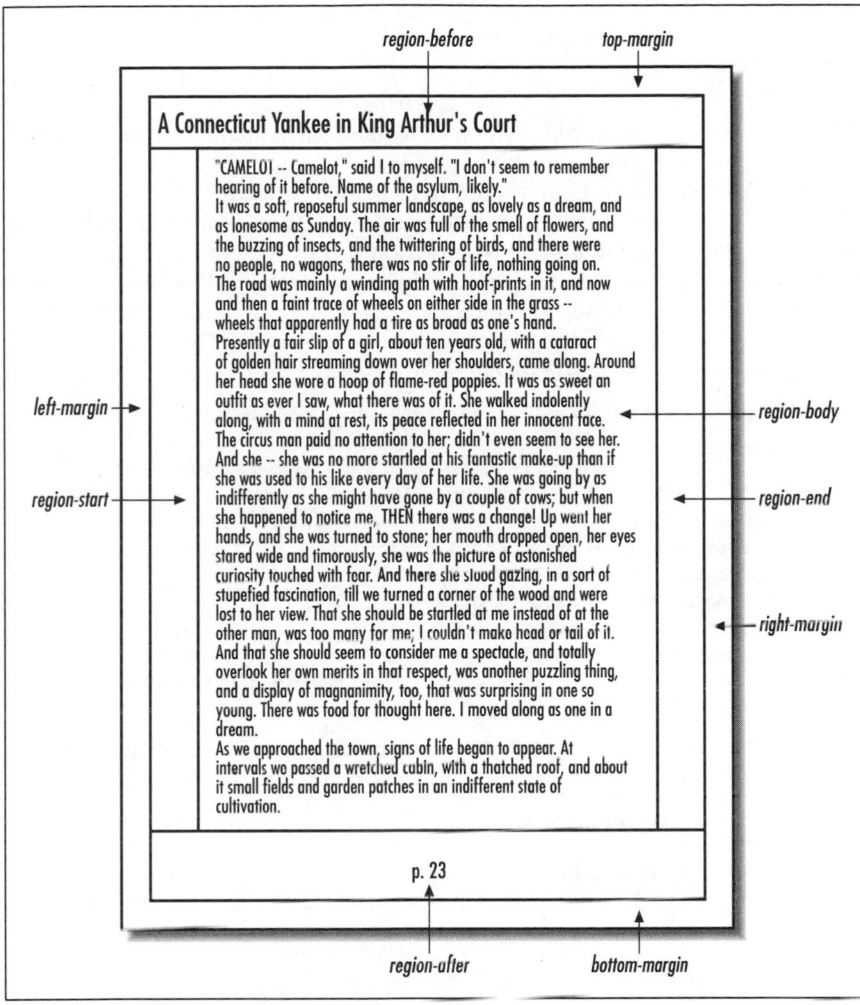


*Figure 13-2: The five regions in a left-to-right, top-to-bottom writing system*



These regions are represented by `fo:region-start`, `fo:region-end`, `fo:region-before`, `fo:region-after`, and `fo:region-body` child elements of the `fo:simple-page-master` element. You can place different content into each of the five sections. The after region often contains a page number, and the before region may contain the book or chapter title.

The body region and its corresponding `fo:region-body` element are required. The other four elements are optional. By default the body region takes up the entire page, and the other four regions have zero area. To specify this simplest page, add an empty `fo:region-body` child element to the `fo:simple-page-master` element:

```
<fo:simple-page-master margin-right="1in"  margin-left="1in"
                       margin-bottom="1in" margin-top="1in"
```

```
                         page-width="8.5in"  page-height="11in"
                         master-name="first">
    <fo:region-body/>
  </fo:simple-page-master>
```

However you can add extent attributes to the four nonbody regions to specify the height of the before and after regions and the width of the start and end regions. Then the region body should have margin properties that are at least as large as each region's extent to push it away from each nonbody region. Otherwise, content placed in the body is drawn on top of content placed in the other four regions. For example, this fo:simple-page-master element has half-inch margins on each side, representing the unprintable area on many common printers. The start and end regions are half an inch wide. The before and after regions are one inch wide. The body has margins that match the region sizes:

```
  <fo:simple-page-master margin-right="0.5in"  margin-left="0.5in"
                         margin-bottom="0.5in" margin-top="0.5in"
                         page-width="8.5in"    page-height="11in"
                         master-name="first">
    <fo:region-body/>
    <fo:region-before extent="0.5in"/>
    <fo:region-after  extent="0.5in"/>
    <fo:region-start  extent="0.5in"/>
    <fo:region-end    extent="0.5in"/>
    <fo:region-body   margin-top="1.0in"  margin-bottom="1.0in"
                      margin-left="0.5in" margin-right="0.5in"/>
  </fo:simple-page-master>
```

The details of the layout-master set are usually fixed in the stylesheet. Here's the revised XSLT template that includes a full fo:layout-master-set:

```
<xsl:template match="/">
  <fo:root>
    <fo:layout-master-set>
      <fo:simple-page-master margin-right="1in"  margin-left="1in"
                             margin-bottom="1in" margin-top="1in"
                             page-width="8.5in"  page-height="11in"
                             master-name="first">
        <fo:region-body/>
      </fo:simple-page-master>
    </fo:layout-master-set>

    <fo:page-sequence master-name="first">
      <!-- data to place on the page -->
    </fo:page-sequence>

  </fo:root>
</xsl:template>
```

## *Flowing Content into the Pages*

Next, we add a fo:flow child to the fo:page-sequence where the actual text of the transformed document appears. The formatter instantiates a page based on the master page named by the fo:page-sequence's master-name attribute, fills it with content from the `fo:flow` element until the page is full, then instantiates a second page. It then fills the page with more content from `fo:flow`, instantiates a third page, and continues this process until it's used up all data in `fo:flow`.

The `fo:flow` element must contain block-level formatting object elements. The most basic of these elements is `fo:block`. Others include `fo:block-container`, `fo:list-block`, `fo:table`, and `fo:table-and-caption`. We begin with the element `fo:block`. `fo:block` can contain a combination of raw text and formatting objects, such as `fo:external-graphic`, `fo:inline`, `fo:page-number`, `fo:footnote`, and other `fo:block` elements. For the moment, we'll restrict ourselves to parsed character data. Here's a basic `fo:flow` for the recipe:

```
<fo:flow>
  <fo:block>Southern Corn Bread</fo:block>

  <fo:block>1 cup flour</fo:block>
  <fo:block>4 tablespoons Royal Baking Powder</fo:block>
  <fo:block>1/2 teaspoon salt</fo:block>
  <fo:block>1 cup corn meal</fo:block>
  <fo:block>1 1/2 cups whole milk</fo:block>
  <fo:block>4 tablespoons melted butter</fo:block>

  <fo:block>
    Sift flour, baking powder, sugar &amp; salt together.
    Add 1 cup corn meal.
    Beat egg in cup and add beaten egg and 1 1/2 cups whole
    milk to make a batter. Stir well.
    Add melted shortening and beat until light and thoroughly mixed.
    Pour into greased shallow pan or greased muffin rings.
    Bake in hot oven at 425º F for 25 minutes.
    Cut into squares if cooked in shallow pan.
  </fo:block>

  <fo:block>
    After my mother-in-law Marjorie Anderson died,
    Beth and I found this recipe written on the "extra recipes"
    page in a local cookbook in her cupboard.
    This was published by the The Episcopal Churchwomen,
    Church of Ascension, Mt. Sterling, Kentucky.
  </fo:block>

</fo:flow>
```

Here's an XSLT template that produces the content of this `fo:flow` element (modulo insignificant whitespace) through judicious use of the default templates:

```
<xsl:template match="dish|ingredient|directions|story">
  <fo:block><xsl:apply-templates/></fo:block>
</xsl:template>
```

## *Generating the Finished Document*

We now have the minimum set of pieces needed to put together a full XSL-FO document. Example 13-2 is an XSLT stylesheet that transforms documents such as Example 13-1 into XSL-formatting objects documents.

*Example 13-2: An XSLT-to-XSL-FO Transform*

```
<?xml version="1.0" encoding="UTF-8"?>
<xsl:stylesheet version="1.0"
                xmlns:xsl="http://www.w3.org/1999/XSL/Transform"
                xmlns:fo="http://www.w3.org/1999/XSL/Format">

  <xsl:template match="/">
    <fo:root>
      <fo:layout-master-set>
        <fo:simple-page-master margin-right="1in"  margin-left="1in"
                               margin-bottom="1in" margin-top="1in"
                               page-width="8.5in"  page-height="11in"
                               master-name="first">
          <fo:region-body/>
        </fo:simple-page-master>
      </fo:layout-master-set>

      <fo:page-sequence master-name="first">

        <fo:flow>
          <xsl:apply-templates/>
        </fo:flow>

      </fo:page-sequence>

    </fo:root>
  </xsl:template>

  <xsl:template match="dish|ingredient|directions|story">
    <fo:block><xsl:apply-templates/></fo:block>
  </xsl:template>

</xsl:stylesheet>
```

Example 13-3 shows the complete XSL-FO document produced by running the cornbread recipe through an XSLT engine like Xalan or SAXON with this stylesheet. The whitespace is a little off because of the way XSLT treats whitespace in the transform document. However, this won't be significant when the document is rendered.

*Example 13-3: An XSL-FO Document Describing a Recipe for Cornbread*

```
<?xml version="1.0" encoding="utf-8"?><fo:root xmlns:fo="http://www.w3.org/
1999/XSL/Format"><fo:layout-master-set><fo:simple-page-master margin-
right="1in" margin-left="1in" margin-bottom="1in" margin-top="1in" page-
width="8.5in" page-height="11in" master-name="first"><fo:region-body/></
fo:simple-page-master></fo:layout-master-set><fo:page-sequence master-
name="first"><fo:flow>
  <fo:block>Southern Corn Bread</fo:block>

    <fo:block>
      1 cup
      flour
    </fo:block>
```

*Example 13-3: An XSL-FO Document Describing a Recipe for Cornbread (continued)*

```
    <fo:block>
      4 tablespoons
      Royal Baking Powder
    </fo:block>
    <fo:block>
      1/2 teaspoon
      salt
    </fo:block>
    <fo:block>
      1 cup
      corn meal
    </fo:block>
    <fo:block>
      1 1/2 cups
      whole milk
    </fo:block>
    <fo:block>
      4 tablespoons
      melted butter
    </fo:block>


  <fo:block>
    Sift flour, baking powder, sugar &amp; salt together.
    Add 1 cup corn meal.

      Beat egg in cup and add beaten egg and 1 1/2 cups whole
       milk to make a batter. Stir well.


      Add melted shortening and beat until light and thoroughly mixed.


      Pour into greased shallow pan or greased muffin rings.


      Bake in hot oven at 425º F for
      25 minutes.


      Cut into squares if cooked in shallow pan.

  </fo:block>

  <fo:block>
    After my mother-in-law Marjorie Anderson died,
    Beth and I found this recipe written on the "extra recipes"
    page in a local cookbook in her cupboard.
    This was published by The Episcopal Churchwomen,
    Church of Ascension, Mt. Sterling,
    Kentucky.
```

```
  </fo:block>

</fo:flow></fo:page-sequence></fo:root>
```

The final step in this process converts the formatting objects document into another format that can be viewed on screen or paper. To complete this step, run a formatting program, such as the Apache XML Project's open source FOP (*http://xml.apache.org/fop/*) or RenderX's payware XEP (*http://www.renderx.com/*). Both are Java programs that run on most platforms. As of late 2000, both programs have significant holes in their coverage, and neither is close to a finished product. Then again, neither is XSL-FO. After installing FOP in your class path, use this command line to transform the file *cornbread.fo* into a PDF document:

```
% java org.apache.fop.apps.CommandLine cornbread.fo cornbread.pdf
```

Figure 13-3 shows the final result of this process.

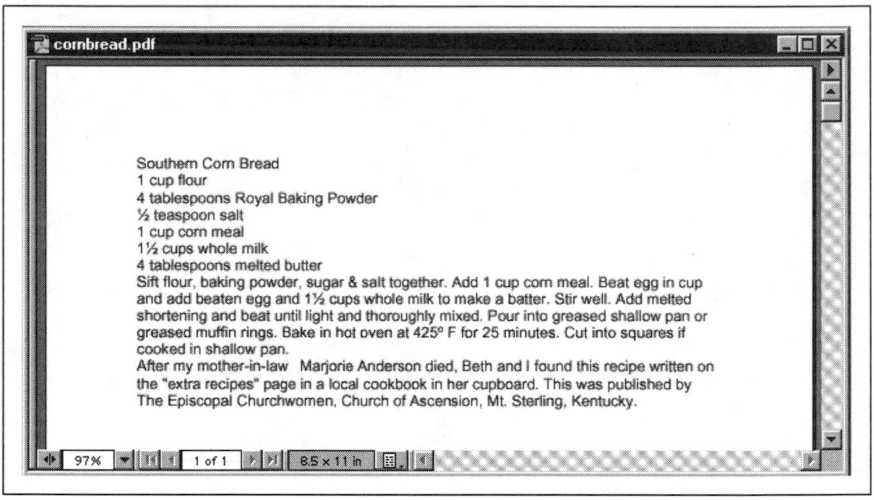


*Figure 13-3: The recipe document after conversion from XSL-FO to PDF*

Other ways to view XSL-FO documents may be available in the future. Various developers are working on software to convert XSL-FO to Scalable Vector Graphics and TeX. Others are writing programs based on the Java 2D API that can view XSL-FO documents directly. Some of these programs may be publicly available by the time you read this book.

## *XSL-FO Properties*

The finished document shown in Figure 13-3 is quite Spartan. It simply breaks the original XML document into a few separate paragraphs. After much work, it still hasn't reached the polish that was achieved much more simply with CSS in Example 12-2 and Figure 12-1. To add the sparkle of different fonts, bold headlines, bulleted lists, and other desirable features, we must set the relevant properties on individual formatting objects to specify these qualities. These properties are set through optional attributes of the formatting object elements, such as `fo:block`. The good news is that most of the property names and semantics are the same as they are for CSS. For example, to make the text in a `fo:block` element bold, give it a `font-weight` attribute with the value `bold`:

```
<fo:block font-weight="bold">Southern Corn Bread</fo:block>
```

The similarity with the equivalent CSS rule is obvious:

```
dish {font-weight: bold}
```

The property name and property value are the same. The meaning of the property is the same. Similarly, you can use all `font-weight` keywords and values, such as `lighter` and `100`, `200`, `300`, or `400`, that you learned for CSS. Only the syntactic details of how the value `bold` is assigned to the property `font-weight` and how that property is then attached to the `dish` element has changed. When XSL-FO and CSS converge, they do so closely.

Many other properties come across from CSS by straight extrapolation. In Example 12-2 in Chapter 12, the `dish` element was formatted with this rule:

```
dish    {
  display: block;
  font-family: Helvetica, Arial, sans-serif;
  font-size: 20pt;
  font-weight: bold;
  text-align: center
}
```

In XSL-FO, it is formatted with this XSLT template:

```
<xsl:template match="dish">
  <fo:block font-family="Helvetica, Arial, sans-serif" font-size="20pt"
            font-weight="bold" text-align="center">
    <xsl:apply-templates/>
  </fo:block>
</xsl:template>
```

Similarly the margins on the various elements are set by margin properties on their respective blocks:

```
<xsl:template match="directions|story">
  <fo:block margin-top="12pt" margin-left="4pt">
    <xsl:apply-templates/>
  </fo:block>
</xsl:template>
```

In a few cases, CSS properties become XSL-FO elements rather than attributes. To format the ingredients as a bulleted list, use the `fo:list-block`, `fo:list-item`, `fo:list-item-label`, and `fo:list-item-body` elements, as in this XSLT template:

```
<xsl:template match="ingredient">
  <fo:list-item>
            <!-- Unicode Bullet Character -->
    <fo:list-item-label>&#x2022;</fo:list-item-label>
    <fo:list-item-body><xsl:apply-templates/></fo:list-item-body>
  </fo:list-item>
</xsl:template>
```

XSL-FO

We now have the pieces needed to put together a more attractive XSL-FO document. Example 13-4 is an XSLT stylesheet that transforms documents like Example 13-1 into XSL-FO documents.

*Example 13-4: An XSLT-to-XSL-FO Transform*

```
<?xml version="1.0" encoding="UTF-8"?>
<xsl:stylesheet version="1.0"
                xmlns:xsl="http://www.w3.org/1999/XSL/Transform"
                xmlns:fo="http://www.w3.org/1999/XSL/Format">

  <xsl:template match="/">
    <fo:root>
      <fo:layout-master-set>
        <fo:simple-page-master margin-right="1in"  margin-left="1in"
                               margin-bottom="1in" margin-top="1in"
                               page-width="8.5in"  page-height="11in"
                               master-name="first">
          <fo:region-body/>
        </fo:simple-page-master>
      </fo:layout-master-set>

      <fo:page-sequence master-name="first">

        <fo:flow>
          <xsl:apply-templates/>
        </fo:flow>

      </fo:page-sequence>

    </fo:root>
  </xsl:template>

  <xsl:template match="recipe">
    <fo:block font-family="Times, 'Times New Roman', serif"
              font-size="12pt">
      <xsl:apply-templates/>
    </fo:block>
  </xsl:template>

  <xsl:template match="dish">
    <fo:block font-family="Helvetica, Arial, sans-serif" font-size="20pt"
              font-weight="bold" text-align="center">
      <xsl:apply-templates/>
    </fo:block>
  </xsl:template>

  <xsl:template match="directions|story">
    <fo:block margin-top="12pt" margin-left="4pt">
      <xsl:apply-templates/>
    </fo:block>
  </xsl:template>
```

*Example 13-4: An XSLT-to-XSL-FO Transform (continued)*

```
  <xsl:template match="ingredients">
    <fo:list-block><xsl:apply-templates/></fo:list-block>
  </xsl:template>

  <xsl:template match="ingredient">
    <fo:list-item>
              <!-- Unicode Bullet Character -->
      <fo:list-item-label>
        <fo:block>&#x2022;</fo:block>
      </fo:list-item-label>
      <fo:list-item-body>
        <fo:block><xsl:apply-templates/></fo:block>
      </fo:list-item-body>
    </fo:list-item>
  </xsl:template>

</xsl:stylesheet>
```

Example 13-5 shows the XSL-FO document produced by applying this transform to the cornbread recipe in Example 13-1. The whitespace has been cleaned up a little by hand, but it won't affect the final rendered result.

*Example 13-5: An XSL-FO Document Describing a Recipe for Cornbread*

```
<?xml version="1.0" encoding="utf-8"?>
<fo:root xmlns:fo="http://www.w3.org/1999/XSL/Format">
  <fo:layout-master-set>
    <fo:simple-page-master margin-right="1in" margin-left="1in"
      margin-bottom="1in" margin-top="1in" page-width="8.5in"
      page-height="11in" master-name="first">
      <fo:region-body/>
    </fo:simple-page-master>
  </fo:layout-master-set>
  <fo:page-sequence master-name="first"><fo:flow>
  <fo:block>Southern Corn Bread</fo:block>

    <fo:block>
      1 cup
      flour
    </fo:block>
    <fo:block>
      4 tablespoons
      Royal Baking Powder
    </fo:block>
    <fo:block>
      1/2 teaspoon
      salt
    </fo:block>
    <fo:block>
      1 cup
      corn meal
    </fo:block>
```

*Example 13-5: An XSL-FO Document Describing a Recipe for Cornbread (continued)*

```
    <fo:block>
      1 1/2 cups
      whole milk
    </fo:block>
    <fo:block>
      4 tablespoons
      melted butter
    </fo:block>


  <fo:block>
    Sift flour, baking powder, sugar &amp; salt together.
    Add 1 cup corn meal.

      Beat egg in cup and add beaten egg and 1 1/2 cups whole
       milk to make a batter. Stir well.


      Add melted shortening and beat until light and thoroughly mixed.


      Pour into greased shallow pan or greased muffin rings.


      Bake in hot oven at 425º F for
      25 minutes.


      Cut into squares if cooked in shallow pan.

  </fo:block>

  <fo:block>
    After my mother-in-law Marjorie Anderson died,
    Beth and I found this recipe written on the "extra recipes"
    page in a local cookbook in her cupboard.
    This was published by The Episcopal Churchwomen,
    Church of Ascension, Mt. Sterling,
    Kentucky.
  </fo:block>

</fo:flow></fo:page-sequence></fo:root>
```

This document must run through a formatter and a PDF file must be produced for viewing. Figure 13-4 shows the final result of this process.

XSL-FO does add some properties that CSS doesn't provide. To name just a few, XSL-FO has properties to control hyphenation, properties to insert leaders, properties to specify the number of columns on a page, and properties to determine where page breaks occur and which paragraphs must be kept together. CSS has none of these. For the most part, XSL-FO's properties are a superset of CSS's properties.

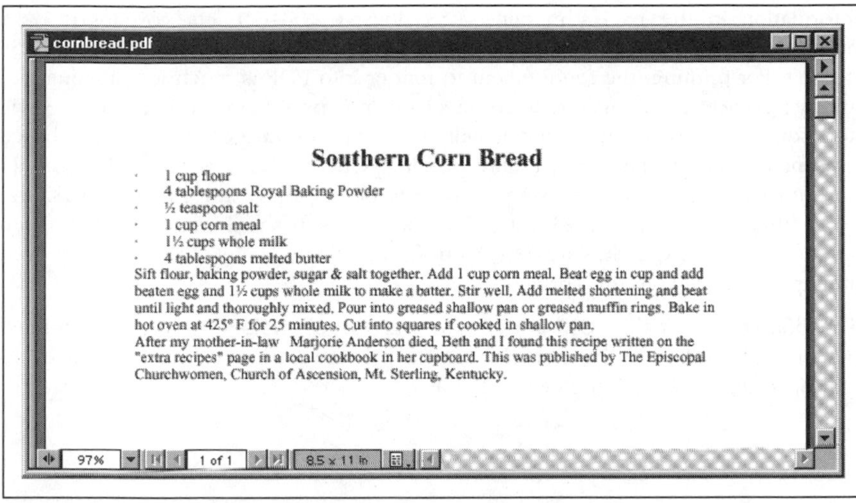


*Figure 13-4: The recipe document converted from XSL Formatting Objects to PDF*



## Choosing Between CSS and XSL-FO

CSS is a very straightforward, easy-to-learn, user-friendly language used to format web pages. To the extent that CSS has a reputation for being buggy and difficult to use, that's mostly because of inconsistent, nonstandard browser implementations. Opera 5.0 and Netscape/Mozilla 6.0 provide extensive support for most features of CSS Level 2 with only a few minor bugs. Internet Explorer's support is weaker, but improving.

It's hard to imagine any web site you can't produce by using XSLT to transform a document into HTML and then applying a CSS stylesheet. Alternately, you can transform the XML document into another XML document, and apply the CSS stylesheet to it. If the element content in the original XML document is exactly what you want to display in the output document, in the correct order, you can even omit the XSLT transformation step, as we did in Example 12-1 and Example 12-2 in Chapter 12.

Most importantly, CSS is a finished, complete specification. While additions to it, including a CSS Level 3, are inevitable, web designers already understand CSS Level 2 well and current browsers already support it. XSL-FO, by contrast, is still in a state of rapid change. It is not supported directly by any browser. To view an XSL-FO document, you must first convert it into the inconvenient PDF format. PDF does not adjust to the wide variety of monitors and screen sizes in use today as well as HTML. Viewing it inside a web browser requires a special plug-in. The limited third-party tools that support XSL-FO are alpha quality at best, do not support the latest working drafts of XSL-FO, and leave out many pieces of versions they do support. Personally, we see little reason to use anything other than CSS on the Web.

On the other hand, XSL-FO does go beyond CSS in ways that are crucial for high-quality printing. For example, XSL-FO offers multiple column layouts, but CSS doesn't. XSL-FO lets you condition formatting on what's actually in the document; CSS doesn't. XSL-FO allows you to place footnotes, running headers, and other information in the page's margins; CSS doesn't. XSL-FO lets you insert page numbers and automatically cross-reference to particular pages by number, but CSS doesn't. For printing, the requirement to render into PDF is much less limiting and annoying since the ultimate delivery mechanism is paper anyway. CSS Level 3 will add some of these features, but it will still focus on ease-of-use and web-based presentation rather than high-quality printing. Once XSL-FO is finished, it should be the clear choice for professionally typeset books, magazines, newspapers, and other printed matter rendered from XML documents. It should be competitive with solutions such as Quark XPress, TeX, troff, and FrameMaker. CSS does not even attempt to compete in this space.

The bottom line is this: CSS is right for web pages, XSL-FO is right for printed matter; and XSLT is taking a crucial step to prepare an input document for eventual presentation with either CSS or XSL-FO.

# PART III

# *Data-Centric Documents*

CHAPTER 14

# *XML as a Data Format*



Despite its document-centric roots, XML is evolving as the data format of choice for the transmission and storage of information on the Internet. Like the ASCII standard made Latin text portable across disparate systems, XML promises to make complex data structures portable between different programming languages and computer architectures. Though the basic language structures are the same, using XML to describe program data instead of human-readable documents presents a unique set of challenges. This chapter lists XML's most common data-centric applications and gives an overview of the tools and technologies used to implement them.

## *Programming Applications of XML*

Before XML, individual programmers had to determine how data would be formatted whenever they needed to store or transmit program data. In most cases, the data was never intended for use outside the original program, so programmers would store it in the most convenient format they could devise. A few de facto file formats evolved over the years (RTF, CSV, and the ubiquitous Windows *.ini* file format), but the data written by one program could usually be read only by that same program. In fact, it was often possible for only that specific *version* of the same program to read the data.

The rapid proliferation of XML and free XML tools throughout the programming community has given developers an obvious choice when the time comes to select a data storage or transmission format for their application. For all but the most trivial applications, the benefits of using XML to store and retrieve data far outweigh the additional overhead of including an XML parser in your application. The unique strengths of using XML as a software data format include:

- Simple syntax: easy to generate and parse.
- Support for nesting: tags easily allow programs to represent structures with nested elements.

- Easy to debug: human-readable data format is easy to mimic and simulate with a basic text editor.
- Language and platform independent: XML and Unicode guarantee that your datafile will be portable across virtually every popular computer architecture and language combination in use today.

Besides these basic strengths, XML sometimes actually enables new types of applications that would have been previously impossible (or very costly) to implement.

## *Mixed Environments*

Modern enterprise applications often involve software running on different computer systems under various operating systems. Choosing a communication protocol involves finding the lowest common denominator available on each system. With the large number of XML parsers that can be freely integrated with your application, XML is becoming a popular format for enterprise data sharing.

Imagine a typical enterprise application that needs to display data from a mainframe to users connected to a corporate web site. In this case, XML acts as the "glue" to connect a web server with a legacy application on a mainframe. The simple XML interface application accepts requests from the web server, calls the legacy application, and converts the result to XML. Using a technology like XSLT, the web server can then transform the XML into any one of a number of acceptable web formats. By adopting XML as the common language of your enterprise, reusing existing data in new ways becomes easier.

## *Communications*

Building flexible communications protocols that link disparate systems has always been a major effort in computer science. With the proliferation of computer networking and the Internet, the importance of building distributed systems has become even higher. In much the same way that the HTTP protocol allows web clients to view content on web servers, standards such as the Simple Object Access Protocol (SOAP) aim to make software services available to any software client on the Internet.

## *Object Serialization*

Like the issue of communications, the question of where and how to store the state of persistent objects has been answered in various ways over the years. With the popular adoption of object-oriented languages, such as C++ and Java, the language and runtime environment frequently handle object serialization mechanics. Unfortunately, most of these technologies predate XML.

Most existing serialization methods are highly language and architecture specific. The serialized object is most often stored in a binary format that is not human readable. These files are intolerant to corruption and maintaining compatibility, as the object's structure changes frequently and requires custom work on the part of the programmer.

The features that make XML popular as a communications protocol also make it popular as a format for serializing object contents. Viewing the object's contents, making manual modifications, and even repairing damaged files is easy. XML's flexible nature allows the file format to expand ad infinitum while maintaining backward compatibility with older file versions.

### Data Storage/Retrieval

In application, the line between an XML file and a relational database is often blurred. Though XML is too verbose and slow to search for high-performance database applications, it may be used as a simple, self-contained data store for small databases.

Combined with DHTML, XML datafiles are used to offload some nontransactional data search and retrieval applications from busy web servers down to the desktop web browser. On the server side, XML is used as an alternate delivery mechanism for query results. Products such as Microsoft's SQL Server 2000 and Oracle's Oracle8i include native support for XML as a data retrieval format.

## Describing Data

From the beginning, XML's primary purpose was to allow users to define new data formats unambiguously and share those formats with others. The DTD mechanism provides a definitive way to identify documents with data drawn from the same problem space. By ensuring that an XML document is well-formed and valid (given a specific DTD), any application that expects data conforming to the same DTD can understand it immediately. Consider the following sample document:

```
<?xml version="1.0"?>
<!DOCTYPE smil PUBLIC "-//W3C//DTD SMIL 1.0//EN"
               "http://www.w3.org/TR/REC-smil/SMIL10.dtd">
<smil>
    <head>
    <layout>
        <root-layout width="300" height="200" background-color="white" />
        <region id="text_region" left="75" top="50" width="150"
height="100" />
    </layout>
    </head>
    <body>
        <text region="text_region" src="Hello.txt" dur="3s"/>
        <text region="text_region" src="World!!!.txt" begin="1s"
dur="3s"/>
    </body>
</smil>
```

The DOCTYPE declaration indicates that this document conforms to Version 1.0 of the Synchronized Multimedia Integration Language (SMIL) specification and that any SMIL-enabled player can interpret it. The absolute URL *http://www.w3.org/TR/REC-smil/SMIL10.dtd* points to the W3C site's copy of the official SMIL DTD. The SMIL DTD guarantees that this document conforms to the official SMIL standard.

> ### *"Valid" Isn't Necessarily Correct*
>
> It is important to remember that constraints that a DTD can place on an XML document are not particularly rigorous. Most applications have domain-specific constraints that must be observed. Among other things, a DTD *can* enforce:
>
> - Relationships between elements
> - Types, names, and possibly values of element attributes
> - Contents of elements
>
> However, it cannot enforce element datatypes, sizes, or values. For instance, the following XML snippet could be valid according to its DTD:
>
> ```
> <integer_val>Illegal Value</integer_val>
> ```
>
> However, to an application expecting an integer value, this document is definitely not valid. The inherent ambiguity of XML 1.0 is being addressed by the XML Schema Working Group.

## *Resource Description Framework (RDF)*

At the present stage in the Web's evolution, most traffic on the Internet is between human consumers using web browsers and content providers (web servers). As businesses move more of their daily operations online, this producer/consumer mix will begin to shift. The Resource Description Framework is intended to support growth of computer-to-computer peer services.

The RDF essentially defines a language used to describe objects and the services they provide in machine-readable format. An XML application includes facilities for describing objects, their properties, and relationships to one another. The eventual vision for RDF is that software applications will be able to consistently and unambiguously describe their information products, services, and content for use by crawlers and autonomous agents.

## *XML Schemas*

The XML Schema language is intended to supplement the basic DTD mechanism included in XML Version 1.0 with a much more rigorous framework for declaring the structure and contents of XML documents. Besides basic element and attribute relationship facilities built into XML 1.0, schemas allow application writers to enforce specific datatype restrictions on their documents' contents. It also provides support for the construction of user-defined complex datatypes, data ranges, and masks. In conjunction with standards like RDF, XML Schemas are intended to help developers create machine-oriented services that can be accessed over the Internet.

Consider the following XML fragment:

```
<!ELEMENT birthday (#PCDATA)>
. . .
<birthday>Green</birthday>
```

Since XML 1.0 doesn't support the inclusion of semantic information about the format of character data, the XML parse wouldn't know that the value `Green` was supposed to be a date field. The new XML Schema language allows extended information about the type of character data to be included with structural information:

```
<element name="birthday" type="date">
```

If the erroneous element from the previous example were included in a document with this schema rule, the XML parser could flag it as a violation of the datatype included in the `birthday` element definition.

## *Support for Programmers*

XML is itself nothing but a passive format used to encode data. To take advantage of it, programmers must incorporate XML generation and parsing technology into their applications. Fortunately, XML's relatively simple grammatical structure has made many excellent, and usually free, libraries available. Despite the wide variety of languages and platforms supported by these parsers, most provide access to the underlying XML data using one of two API models: the W3C Document Object Model (DOM) or the Simple API for XML (SAX). Thoroughly understanding these two technologies will help developers select the right tools for their application. Chapter 16, *Document Object Model (DOM)*, and Chapter 17, *SAX*, explore these two technologies in more detail.

### *Document Object Model (DOM)*

Like HTML, XML is a hierarchical data format. Data elements can be nested within other data elements, and data elements can have attributes attached to them. The Document Object Model defines an object hierarchy that can fully describe an XML or HTML document as a recursive list of lists. DOM's most significant feature is that the entire document must be parsed and stored in memory to create this data structure. This feature has implications for very large documents or applications in which the entire document may not be available before processing must occur. In addition, many implementations of the DOM are memory-intensive, and some incur 100 percent memory usage over the original document's size. The DOM is very useful for applications that require repeated, random access to different sections of a document.

### *Simple API for XML (SAX)*

Members of the XML-DEV mailing list developed the Simple API for XML collaboratively, primarily to provide a lightweight alternative to the DOM. In contrast to the DOM, SAX provides an event-driven model for parsing XML documents. Instead of constructing a full image of the document in memory, a SAX parser uses a callback mechanism to notify the client application when different XML syntax constructs are recognized. The parser does not maintain any state, which means that very large documents can be processed without consuming large quantities of memory.

CHAPTER 15

# Programming Models

This chapter briefly explains the most popular programming models in use today for parsing and manipulating XML data. It also attempts to explain how some features of the XML language itself are used in real-world applications.

## Event- Versus Object-Driven Models

The two most popular programming APIs for working with XML are the Simple API for XML (SAX) and the Document Object Model (DOM). The fundamental difference between these two technologies lies in the way the XML document data is made available to the client application. SAX is an event-driven model, which means that the client application is continuously notified as document features are recognized by the parser. The DOM model, on the other hand, is object based; the entire XML document is parsed and stored as a hierarchical arrangement of objects that the client application can then access randomly.

The nature of the client application dictates which approach (event or object driven) is appropriate. If the XML data is used as a real-time messaging protocol, for instance, an event-driven model would probably be appropriate. For an application that uses an XML document as a simple database, however, the object model would be more suitable. Table 15-1 outlines the basic differences between SAX and DOM.

*Table 15-1: SAX and DOM Differences*

| *SAX* | *DOM* |
|---|---|
| Doesn't store data from the XML document during parsing. | Constructs an in-memory copy of the document tree. |
| Has no support for modifying or writing XML document data. | The in-memory document tree can be modified. |
| Document data becomes available as it is parsed. | The entire document must be parsed before the document tree is available to the client application. |

## *Programming Language Support*

Both the SAX and DOM APIs are implemented for most popular programming languages and environments. Though SAX and DOM are by far the most popular XML APIs, several other parsing models don't fit precisely into the event-driven or tree-driven model. The following sections explain how to access XML parsing technologies from most popular programming languages. For an up-to-date listing of XML parsers available for use in your language of choice, check the current list on XML.com at *http://www.xml.com/pub/Guide/XML_Parsers*.

### *C*

Very few parsers are available for the C programming language, as its popularity has waned somewhat with the advent of modern, object-oriented languages, such as C++ and Java. James Clark's expat parser is written in C available for use under either the Mozilla Public License Version 1.1 or the GNU General Public License.

Expat uses a callback mechanism that is very similar to the Simple API for XML (SAX) model. A C program implements callback functions to handle the XML document data it is interested in, then registers them with the parser library.

### *C++*

You can access XML parsing functionality from C++ in several ways. When writing C++ with a COM-enabled compiler, you can import a COM-based XML parser. A few native C++ parsers, such as Apache Xerces-C++, also exist. Xerces includes support for DOM 1.0 and SAX 1.0 libraries, which can be accessed from within a C++ application.

The DOM library is implemented as a set of C++ classes that conform to the DOM 1.0 IDL. A client application then calls an implementation-specific parsing function to generate the document object hierarchy.

The SAX library provides a set of interfaces that can be subclassed by a client application. After the parser is invoked, the application-specific overridden methods are called with the XML document data as it is parsed.



### *Perl*

At least one parser module exists for Perl, based on the C language expat parser discussed previously. It exposes both a tree-based access method and an event-driven interface that calls Perl routines as XML language structures are recognized. For access to the latest Perl XML parser packages, check the Comprehensive Perl Archive Network at *http://www.cpan.org*.

### *Python*

Python developers have already integrated XML support into the base language distribution. The latest release of Python includes the XML package with support for the SAX and DOM XML APIs. An interface to the expat parser called *pyexpat* is also available.

### *Java*

Java is one of the most popular languages for implementing and using XML parsers. Several full-featured implementations of SAX, DOM, and other XML APIs are available for use in Java programs. Full Java implementations of SAX and DOM parsers are available from IBM's Alphaworks division, Sun Microsystems, and the Apache Project.

### *COM*

The most widely used COM-based parser is Microsoft's MSXML parser, which originally shipped as part of Microsoft's Internet Explorer 5.0 web browser. The most recent release of MSXML includes both DOM and SAX implementations that can be used from any COM-enabled programming environment.

## *Non-Standard Extensions*

The DOM standard is deliberately designed to be programming-language and platform neutral. The result of this requirement is that many practical usage details are not standardized and must be improvised by each specific implementation. For instance, since each programming language has different file handling facilities, the interface used for invoking the DOM parser to create the document hierarchy is different in a Java-based library than in one written for C++. This shortcoming will be addressed in DOM 3.0.

Many vendors have released extended versions of the basic DOM model that incorporate features missing from the DOM Level 1 implementation. The Microsoft XML parser that shipped with Internet Explorer 5.0 (MSXML) provided many extended methods beyond those defined by the actual DOM specification. While these extensions simplify tasks within a client program, the trade-off is greater dependency on a specific vendor's DOM implementation. See Chapter 16, *Document Object Model (DOM)*, for more information about using the Document Object Model.

The SAX standard, on the other hand, has not been approved formally by any standards body. The members of the XML-DEV mailing list defined it as an alternative to the DOM for applications in which in-memory document trees are inappropriate or inefficient. Besides the variations required to accommodate the callback model within different programming environments, many implementations provide extended access to XML document information that is not available via the core interface. See Chapter 17, *SAX*, for more information about the Simple API for XML.

## *Transformations*

Another facility available to the XML programmer is a form of XML transformation library. The Extensible Stylesheet Language Transformation language (XSLT) covered in Chapter 8, *XSL Transformations*, is the most popular tool currently available for transforming XML to HTML, XML, or any other regular language that can be expressed in XSLT. In some cases, using a transformation to perform pre- or post-processing on XML data when processing it with either DOM or SAX might be simpler or more efficient. For instance, XSLT could be used as a preprocessor for a screen-scraping application that accepts XHTML documents. A script could be written to extract the meaningful features from the XHTML document and pour them into an application-specific XML format.

## Processing Instructions

Both SAX and DOM provide the client application access to XML processing instructions. Processing instructions are not considered to be part of an XML document's content, but instead provide a mechanism for document authors to communicate with XML-aware applications behind the scenes. The processing instruction's most widely recognized application is its ability to embed stylesheet references inside XML documents. The following XML fragment shows a stylesheet reference:

```
<?xml version="1.0"?>
<?xml-stylesheet type="text/xml" href="test.xsl"?>
```

An XSL-aware application, such as Internet Explorer 5.5, would be capable of recognizing the XML author's intention to display the document using the `test.xsl` stylesheet. Applications that do not understand the processing instruction are still able to parse and use the information in the XML document while ignoring the unfamiliar processing instruction.

The furniture example from Chapter 18, *XML 1.0 Reference*, gives a hypothetical application of processing instructions. A processing instruction in the *bookcase.xml* file signals the furniture example's processor to verify the parts list from the document against the true list of parts required to build the furniture item:

```
<parts_list>
    <part_name id="A" count="1">END PANEL</part_name>
    <part_name id="B" count="2">SIDE PANEL</part_name>
    <part_name id="C" count="1">BACK PANEL</part_name>
    <part_name id="D" count="4">SHELF</part_name>
    <part_name id="E" count="8">HIDDEN CONNECTORS</part_name>
    <part_name id="F" count="8">CONNECTOR SCREWS</part_name>
    <part_name id="G" count="22">7/16" TACKS</part_name>
    <part_name id="H" count="16">SHELF PEGS</part_name>
</parts_list>

<?furniture_app    verify_parts_list?>
```

This processing instruction is meaningless unless the parsing application understands the given type of processing instruction.

## Links and References

Like HTML, the ability to create links between and within documents is important to XML's long-term success, particularly on the World Wide Web. The XLink specification, sponsored by the W3C, defines the semantics of how these links can be created. Unlike simple HTML links, XLinks can express sophisticated relationships between the source and target elements of a link.

If your XML application requires the ability to encode relationships between various parts of an XML document, or between different documents, you should consider implementing this functionality using the XLinks recommendation. Not only would you save yourself the effort of defining a new (and incompatible) linking scheme, your documents will be intelligible to new XML authoring tools and browsers as XLinks support becomes more widespread.

## *Notations*

The notation syntax of XML provides a way for the document author to specify the type of an external unparsed entity within the XML document's framework. If your application requires access to external data that cannot be represented in XML, consider declaring a notation name and using it where appropriate when declaring external unparsed entities. For example, if an XML application were an annotated Java source code format, the compiled bytecode could be referenced as an external unparsed entity.

Denoting that the contents of a particular element can be interpreted according to grammar that is not compatible with XML is another use of an XML notation:

```
<!NOTATION DOS PUBLIC "-//MS/DOS Batch File/">
. . .
<batch_code lang="DOS">
  echo Hello, world!
</batch_code>
```

The text contained by the `batch_code` element is marked as a distinct grammar, indicated by use of the public identifier in the XML notation declaration. Applications that read this document and recognized the public identifier could interpret the foreign element data correctly, based on its type.

Categorizing processing instructions is the other use of notations important to custom XML applications. For instance, the previous `furniture_app` processing instruction example could have been declared as a notation in the DTD:

```
<!NOTATION furniture_app SYSTEM "http://namespaces.oreilly.com/furniture">
```

Then the furniture document processing application could verify that the processing instruction was actually intended for itself, and not for another application that used a processing instruction with the same name.

## *What You Get Is Not What You Saw*

The XML specification provides several loopholes that permit XML parsers to play fast and loose with your document's literal contents, while retaining the semantic meaning. Comments, whitespace, and entity references, respectively, can be omitted, collapsed, and silently replaced by the parser without any warning to the client application. While reconstructing an XML document with exactly the same logical structure and content is possible, guaranteeing that it will match the original in a byte-by-byte comparison is not.

Authors of simple XML processing tools that act on data without storing or modifying it might not consider these constraints particularly restrictive. The ability to reconstruct an XML document precisely from in-memory data structures, however, becomes more critical for authors of XML editing tools and content management solutions. While no parser is required to make all comments, whitespace, and entity references available from the parse stream, many do or can be made to do so with the proper configuration options.

CHAPTER 16

# *Document Object Model (DOM)*

The Document Object Model is a W3C recommendation that describes a programming language neutral object model used to store hierarchical documents in memory. The most recent standard, DOM Level 2, provides models for manipulating XML documents, HTML documents, and stylesheets. We limit our coverage of the DOM to the parts applicable to processing XML documents.

> This chapter is based on the Document Object Model (DOM) Level 2 Core Specification, which was released on November 13, 2000. The version of this recommendation, along with any errata that have been reported, is available on the W3C web site (*http://www.w3.org/TR/DOM-Level-2-Core/*).

The Document Object Model is intended to be operating system- and language-neutral; therefore all DOM interfaces are specified using the Interface Description Language (IDL) notation defined by the Object Management Group organization (*www.omg.org*). To conform to the language of the specification, this chapter and Chapter 21, *DOM Reference*, will use IDL terminology when discussing interface specifics. For example, the word "attribute" in IDL-speak refers to what would be a member variable in C++. This should not be confused with the XML term "attribute," which is a name-value pair that appears within an element open tag.

The language-independent IDL interface must then be translated (according to the rules set down by the OMG) into a specific language binding. Take the following interface, for example:

```
interface NodeList {
  Node                item(in unsigned long index);
  readonly attribute unsigned long    length;
};
```

This interface would be expressed as a Java inteface like this:

```
package org.w3c.dom;

    public interface NodeList {
        public Node item(int index);

        public int getLength();

    }
```

The same interface would be exposed in ECMAScript this way:

```
Object NodeList
    The NodeList object has the following properties:
      length
        This read-only property is of type Number.
    The NodeList object has the following methods:
      item(index)
        This method returns a Node object.
        The index parameter is of type Number.
        Note: This object can also be dereferenced using square
        bracket notation (e.g. obj[1]). Dereferencing with an
        integer index is equivalent to invoking the item method
        with that index.
```

## *DOM Core*

The DOM Core interfaces provide generic access to all supported document content types. For example, the DOM defines a set of HTML-specific interfaces that expose specific document structures, such as tables, paragraphs, and <img> tags, directly. Besides using these specialized interfaces, you can access the same information using the generic interfaces defined in the core.

Since XML is designed as a venue for creating new, unique, structured markup languages, standards bodies cannot define application-specific interfaces in advance. Instead, the DOM Core interfaces are provided to manipulate document elements in a completely application-independent manner.

The DOM Core is further segregated into the Fundamental and Extended Interfaces. The Fundamental Interfaces are relevant to both XML and HTML documents, whereas the Extended Interfaces deal with XML-only document structures, such as entity declarations and processing instructions. All DOM Core interfaces are derived from the Node interface, which provides a generic set of interfaces for accessing a document or document fragment's structure and content.

DOM

## *DOM Strengths and Weaknesses*

Like all programming tools, the DOM is better for addressing some classes of problems than others. Since the DOM object hierarchy stores references between the various nodes in a document, you must read and parse a document fully before it is available to a DOM application. This step also demands that the entire document be stored in memory, often with a significant amount of overhead. Some early DOM implementations added up to 100 percent of the original document's size.

This memory usage model makes the DOM unsuitable for document transformation applications or applications that require incremental parsing of the data, such as a messaging protocol. Although DOM provides some methods for modifying the structure of a document in memory, it does not provide explicit support for parsing documents or serializing new documents to external storage. This random-access aspect of the DOM makes it an excellent tool for document editing, data retrieval, or navigation.

## *Parsing a Document with DOM*

Though the DOM standard doesn't specify an actual interface for parsing a document, most implementations provide a simple parsing interface that accepts a reference to an XML document file, stream, or URI. After this interface successfully parses and validates the document (if it is a validating parser), it generally provides a mechanism for getting a reference to the `Document` interface's instance for the parsed document. The following code fragment shows how to parse a document using the Apache Xerces XML DOM parser:

```
// create a new parser
DOMParser dp = new DOMParser();

// parse the document and get the DOM Document interface
dp.parse("http://www.w3.org/TR/2000/REC-xml-20001006.xml");
Document doc = dp.getDocument();
```

The application can then access the parsed document via the generic `Node` interface or one of the specialized subclasses of `Node`.

## *The Node Interface*

The `Node` interface is the DOM Core class hierarchy's root. Though never instantiated directly, it is the root interface of all specific interfaces, and you can use it to extract information from any DOM object without knowing its actual type. Accessing a document's complete structure and content using only the methods and properties exposed by the `Node` interface is possible. This interface contains information about the type, location, name, and value of the underlying document data fragment.

### *Node Type*

Since the `Node` interface is never instantiated directly, the `nodeType` attribute contains a value that indicates the given instance's true type. Table 16-1 shows the node type values and their corresponding DOM interfaces.

*Table 16-1: DOM Node Types and Interfaces*

| *Node Type* | *DOM Interface* |
|---|---|
| `ELEMENT_NODE` | `Element` |
| `ATTRIBUTE_NODE` | `Attr` |
| `TEXT_NODE` | `Text` |
| `CDATA_SECTION_NODE` | `CDATASection` |

*Table 16-1: DOM Node Types and Interfaces (continued)*

| *Node Type* | *DOM Interface* |
|---|---|
| ENTITY_REFERENCE_NODE | EntityReference |
| ENTITY_NODE | Entity |
| PROCESSING_INSTRUCTION_NODE | ProcessingInstruction |
| COMMENT_NODE | Comment |
| DOCUMENT_NODE | Document |
| DOCUMENT_TYPE_NODE | DocumentType |
| DOCUMENT_FRAGMENT_NODE | DocumentFragment |
| NOTATION_NODE | Notation |

Based on the nodeType, it is possible to cast a generic Node reference safely to a specific interface for further processing.

## Document Structure

Although the DOM doesn't specify how a document is parsed, it does specify how the document's syntax structures are encoded as DOM objects. A document is stored as a hierarchical tree structure, with each item in the tree linked to its parent, children, and siblings:

```
<sample bogus="value"><text_node>Test data.</text_node></sample>
```

Figure 16-1 shows how the preceding short sample document would be stored by a DOM parser.

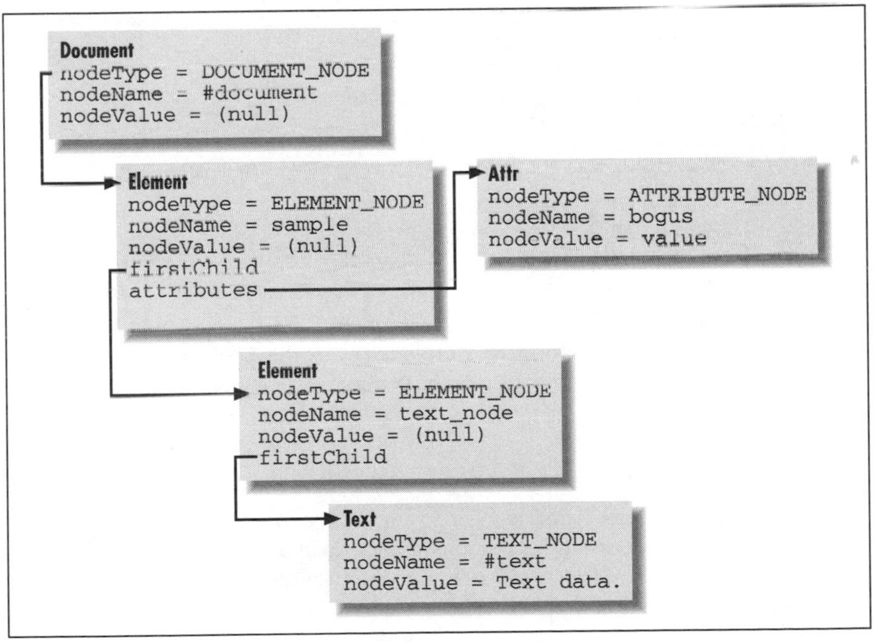


*Figure 16-1: Document storage and linkages*

### Traversing Documents Using the Node Interface

Each Node-derived object in a parsed DOM document contains references to its parent, child, and sibling nodes. These references enable an application to enumerate document data using any number of standard tree traversal algorithms.

## Specific Node Types

Though accessing the data from the original XML document using only the Node interface is possible, the DOM Core provides a number of node-type specific interfaces that simplify common programming tasks. These specific node types can be divided into two broad types: structural nodes and content nodes.

### Structural Nodes

Within an XML document, a number of syntax structures exist that are not formally part of the content. The following interfaces provide access to the portions of the document that are not related to character or element data.

#### DocumentType

The DocumentType interface provides access to the XML document type defenition's notations, entities, internal subset, public ID, and system ID. Since a document can have only one <!DOCTYPE> tag, only one DocumentType node can exist for a given document. It is accessed via the doctype member of the Document interface. The IDL for the DocumentType interface is as follows:

```
interface DocumentType : Node {
  readonly attribute DOMString          name;
  readonly attribute NamedNodeMap       entities;
  readonly attribute NamedNodeMap       notations;
  // Introduced in DOM Level 2:
  readonly attribute DOMString          publicId;
  // Introduced in DOM Level 2:
  readonly attribute DOMString          systemId;
  // Introduced in DOM Level 2:
  readonly attribute DOMString          internalSubset;
};
```

Using additional fields available from DOM Level 2, fully reconstructing a parsed document using only the information provided with the DOM framework is now possible. No programmatic way to modify DocumentType node contents currently exists.

#### ProcessingInstruction

This node type provides direct access to an XML name processing instruction's contents. Though processing instructions appear in the document's text, they are not considered part of the document content data per se. The following IDL describes the ProcessingInstruction node's attributes:

```
interface ProcessingInstruction : Node {
  readonly attribute DOMString          target;
```

```
        attribute DOMString        data;
  // raises(DOMException) on setting

};
```

Though processing instructions resemble normal XML tags, remember that the only syntactically defined part is the target name, which is an XML token. The remaining data (up to the terminating >) is free-form. See Chapter 15, *Programming Models*, for more information about uses (and misuses) of XML processing instructions.

### *Notation*

XML notations formally declare the format for external unparsed entities and processing instruction targets. The list of all available notations is stored in a `NamedNodeMap` within the document's `DOCTYPE` node, which is accessed from the `Document` interface. The IDL for the `Notation` interface is as follows:

```
interface Notation : Node {
  readonly attribute DOMString        publicId;
  readonly attribute DOMString        systemId;
};
```

### *Entity*

The name of the `Entity` interface is somewhat ambiguous, but its meaning becomes clear once you realize an `EntityReference` interface that is also part of the DOM Core. The `Entity` interface provides access to the unparsed entity declaration's notation name, public ID, and system ID. The IDL for this interface is as follows:

```
interface Entity : Node {
  readonly attribute DOMString        publicId;
  readonly attribute DOMString        systemId;
  readonly attribute DOMString        notationName;
};
```

All members of this interface are read-only and cannot be changed at runtime.

## *Content Nodes*

The actual data conveyed by an XML document is contained completely within the document element. The following node types map directly to the XML document's nonstructural parts, such as character data, elements, and attribute values.



### *Document*

Each parsed document causes the creation of a single `Document` node in memory, which is returned through the `DOMImplementation` interface. This node provides access to the document type information and the single, top-level `Element` node that contains the entire body of the parsed document. It also provides access to the class factory methods that allow an application to create new content nodes that were not created by parsing a document. The following IDL shows all attributes and methods of the Document interface:

```
interface Document : Node {
  readonly attribute DocumentType      doctype;
  readonly attribute DOMImplementation  implementation;
  readonly attribute Element           documentElement;
  Element              createElement(in DOMString tagName)
                                        raises(DOMException);
  DocumentFragment     createDocumentFragment();
  Text                 createTextNode(in DOMString data);
  Comment              createComment(in DOMString data);
  CDATASection         createCDATASection(in DOMString data)
                                        raises(DOMException);
  ProcessingInstruction createProcessingInstruction(in DOMString target,
                                                    in DOMString data)
                                        raises(DOMException);
  Attr                 createAttribute(in DOMString name)
                                        raises(DOMException);
  EntityReference      createEntityReference(in DOMString name)
                                        raises(DOMException);
  NodeList             getElementsByTagName(in DOMString tagname);
  // Introduced in DOM Level 2:
  Node                 importNode(in Node importedNode,
                                  in boolean deep)
                                        raises(DOMException);
  // Introduced in DOM Level 2:
  Element              createElementNS(in DOMString namespaceURI,
                                      in DOMString qualifiedName)
                                        raises(DOMException);
  // Introduced in DOM Level 2:
  Attr                 createAttributeNS(in DOMString namespaceURI,
                                        in DOMString qualifiedName)
                                        raises(DOMException);
  // Introduced in DOM Level 2:
  NodeList             getElementsByTagNameNS(in DOMString namespaceURI,
                                             in DOMString localName);
  // Introduced in DOM Level 2:
  Element              getElementById(in DOMString elementId);
};
```

The various `create...()` methods are important for applications that wish to modify the structure of a document that was previously parsed. Note that nodes created using one `Document` instance can be inserted only into that same document tree legally. DOM Level 2 provides a new `importNode()` method that allows movement of a node, and possibly its children, from one document to another.

Besides the various node creation methods, some methods can locate specific XML elements or lists of elements. The `getElementsByTagName()` and `getElementsByTagNameNS()` methods return a list of all XML elements with the name, and possibly namespace, specified. The `getElementById()` method returns the single element with the given ID attribute.

### *DocumentFragment*

Applications that allow real-time editing of XML documents sometimes need to temporarily park document nodes outside the hierarchy of the parsed document. A visual editor that wants to provide clipboard functionality is one example. When the time comes to implement the cut function, it is possible to temporarily move the cut nodes to a `DocumentFragment` node without deleting them, rather than having to leave them in place within the live document. Then when they need to be pasted back into the document, they can be moved back.

### *Element*

`Element` nodes are the most frequently encountered node type in a typical XML document. These nodes are parents for the `Text`, `Comment`, `EntityReference`, and `CDATASection` nodes that comprise the document's body. They also allow access to the `Attr` objects that contain the element's attributes. The following IDL shows all access functions supported by the `Element` interface:

```
interface Element : Node {
  readonly attribute DOMString        tagName;
  DOMString          getAttribute(in DOMString name);
  void               setAttribute(in DOMString name,
                                  in DOMString value)
                                        raises(DOMException);
  void               removeAttribute(in DOMString name)
                                        raises(DOMException);
  Attr               getAttributeNode(in DOMString name);
  Attr               setAttributeNode(in Attr newAttr)
                                        raises(DOMException);
  Attr               removeAttributeNode(in Attr oldAttr)
                                        raises(DOMException);
  NodeList           getElementsByTagName(in DOMString name);
  // Introduced in DOM Level 2:
  DOMString          getAttributeNS(in DOMString namespaceURI,
                                    in DOMString localName);
  // Introduced in DOM Level 2:
  void               setAttributeNS(in DOMString namespaceURI,
                                    in DOMString qualifiedName,
                                    in DOMString value)
                                        raises(DOMException);
  // Introduced in DOM Level 2:
  void               removeAttributeNS(in DOMString namespaceURI,
                                       in DOMString localName)
                                        raises(DOMException);
  // Introduced in DOM Level 2:
  Attr               getAttributeNodeNS(in DOMString namespaceURI,
                                        in DOMString localName);
  // Introduced in DOM Level 2:
  Attr               setAttributeNodeNS(in Attr newAttr)
                                        raises(DOMException);
  // Introduced in DOM Level 2:
  NodeList           getElementsByTagNameNS(in DOMString namespaceURI,
                                            in DOMString localName);
```

```
    // Introduced in DOM Level 2:
    boolean             hasAttribute(in DOMString name);
    // Introduced in DOM Level 2:
    boolean             hasAttributeNS(in DOMString namespaceURI,
                                       in DOMString localName);
  };
```

### *Attr*

Since XML attributes may contain either text values or entity references, the DOM stores element attribute values as `Node` sub-trees. The following XML fragment shows an element with two attributes:

```
<!ENTITY bookcase_pic SYSTEM "bookcase.gif" NDATA gif>
. . .
<picture src="bookcase_pic" alt="3/4 view of bookcase"/>
```

Note that the `nodeValue` of the `Attr` node gives the flattened text value from the `Attr` node's children. The following IDL shows the attributes and methods supported by the `Attr` interface:

```
interface Attr : Node {
  readonly attribute DOMString        name;
  readonly attribute boolean          specified;
           attribute DOMString        value;
  // raises(DOMException) on setting

  // Introduced in DOM Level 2:
  readonly attribute Element          ownerElement;
};
```

Besides the attribute name and value string attributes, the `Attr` node includes a flag that indicates whether this particular attribute instance was included explicitly in the XML document or inherited from the `<!ATTLIST>` declaration of the DTD. There is also a back pointer to the `Element` node that owns this attribute object.

### *Comment*

DOM parsers are not required to make the contents of XML comments available after parsing, and relying on comment data in your application is a poor programming practice at best. If your application requires access to metadata that should not be part of the basic XML document, consider using processing instructions instead.

### *EntityReference*

If an XML document contains references to general entities within the body of its elements, the DOM-compliant parser may pass these references along as `EntityReference` nodes. This behavior is not guaranteed because the parser is free to expand any entity or character reference included with the actual Unicode character sequence it represents.

### Text

The character data of an XML document is stored within Text nodes. Text nodes are children of either Element or Attr nodes. After parsing, every contiguous block of character data from the original XML document is translated directly into a single Text node. The following IDL describes the Text interface:

```
interface Text : CharacterData {
  Text               splitText(in unsigned long offset)
                                        raises(DOMException);
};
```

The splitText method provides a way to split a single Text node into two nodes at the given point. This split would be useful if an editing application wished to insert additional markup nodes into an existing island of character data. After the split, you could insert additional nodes into the resulting gap.

### CDATASection

<![CDATA[]]> sections provide a simplified way to include characters that would normally be considered markup in your XML document. These sections are stored within a DOM document hierarchy as CDATASection nodes.

## The DOMImplementation Interface

This interface could be considered to be the highest level interface in the DOM. It exposes the hasFeature() method, which allows a programmer using a given DOM implementation to detect if specific features are available. In DOM Level 2, it also provides facilities for creating new DocumentType nodes which can then be used to create new Document instances.

## A Simple DOM Application

Example 16-1 illustrates how you might use these interfaces in a typical programming situation. This application takes a document that uses the *furniture.dtd* sample DTD from Chapter 18, *XML 1.0 Reference*, and validates that the parts list included in the document matches the actual parts used within the document:

*Example 16-1: Parts Checker Application*

```
/**
 * PartsCheck.java
 *
 * DOM Usage example from the O'Reilly _XML in a Nutshell_ book.
 *
 */

// we'll use the Apache Software Foundation's Xerces parser.
import org.apache.xerces.parsers.*;
import org.apache.xerces.framework.*;
```

DOM

*Example 16-1: Parts Checker Application (continued)*

```
// import the DOM interfaces
import org.w3c.dom.*;
import org.xml.sax.*;

// get the necessary java support classes
import java.io.*;
import java.util.*;

/**
 * This class is designed to check the parts list of an XML document that
 * represents a piece of furniture for validity. It uses the DOM to
 * analyze the actual furniture description and then check it against the
 * parts list that is embedded in the document.
 */
public class PartsCheck {
  // contains the true part count, keyed by part number
  HashMap m_hmTruePartsList = new HashMap();

  /**
   * The main function that allows this class to be invoked from the command
   * line.  Check each document provided on the commandline for validity.
   */
  public static void main(String[] args) {
    PartsCheck pc = new PartsCheck();

    try {
      for (int i = 0; i < args.length; i++) {
        pc.validatePartsList(args[i]);
      }
    } catch (Exception e) {
      System.err.println(e);
    }
  }


  /**
   * Given a system identifier for an XML document, this function
   * compares the actual parts used to the declared parts
   * list within the document.
   *
   * It prints warnings to standard error if the lists don't agree.
   */
  public void validatePartsList(String strXMLSysID) throws IOException,
      SAXException
  {
    // create a new parser
    DOMParser dp = new DOMParser();

    // parse the document and get the DOM Document interface
    dp.parse(strXMLSysID);
    Document doc = dp.getDocument();
```

*Example 16-1: Parts Checker Application (continued)*

```
    // get an accurate parts list count
    countParts(doc.getDocumentElement(), 1);

    // compare it to the parts list in the document
    reconcilePartsList(doc);
  }

  /**
   * Updates the true parts list by adding the count to the current count
   * for the part number given.
   */
  private void recordPart(String strPartNum, int cCount)
  {
    if (!m_hmTruePartsList.containsKey(strPartNum)) {
      // this part isn't listed yet
      m_hmTruePartsList.put(strPartNum, new Integer(cCount));
    } else {
      // update the count
      Integer cUpdate = (Integer)m_hmTruePartsList.get(strPartNum);
      m_hmTruePartsList.put(strPartNum,
      new Integer(cUpdate.intValue() + cCount));
    }
  }

  /**
   * Counts the parts referenced by and below the given node.
   */
  private void countParts(Node nd, int cRepeat)
  {
    // start the local repeat count at 1
    int cLocalRepeat = 1;
    Node ndTemp;

    if ((ndTemp = nd.getAttributes().getNamedItem("repeat")) != null) {
      // this node specifies a repeat count for its children
      cLocalRepeat = Integer.parseInt(ndTemp.getNodeValue());
    }

    if ((ndTemp = nd.getAttributes().getNamedItem("part_num")) != null) {
      // start the count at 1
      int cCount = 1;
      String strPartNum = ndTemp.getNodeValue();

      if ((ndTemp = nd.getAttributes().getNamedItem("count")) != null) {
        // more than one part needed by this node
        cCount = Integer.parseInt(ndTemp.getNodeValue());
      }

      // multiply the local count by the repeat passed in from the parent
      cCount *= cRepeat;
```

DOM

```
      // add the new parts count to the total
      recordPart(strPartNum, cCount);
    }

    // now process the children
    NodeList nl = nd.getChildNodes();
    Node ndCur;

    for (int i = 0; i < nl.getLength(); i++) {
      ndCur = nl.item(i);

      if (ndCur.getNodeType() == Node.ELEMENT_NODE) {
        // recursively count the parts for the child, using the local repeat
        countParts(ndCur, cLocalRepeat);
      }
    }
  }

  /**
   * This method reconciles the true parts list against the list in the
   * document.
   */
  private void reconcilePartsList(Document doc)
  {
    Iterator iReal = m_hmTruePartsList.keySet().iterator();

    String strPartNum;
    int cReal;
    Node ndCheck;

    // loop through all of the parts in the true parts list
    while (iReal.hasNext()) {
      strPartNum = (String)iReal.next();
      cReal = ((Integer)m_hmTruePartsList.get(strPartNum)).intValue();

      // find the part list element in the document
      ndCheck = doc.getElementById(strPartNum);

      if (ndCheck == null) {
        // this part isn't even listed!
        System.err.println("missing <part_name> element for part #" +
            strPartNum + " (count " + cReal + ")");
      } else {
        Node ndTemp;

        if ((ndTemp = ndCheck.getAttributes().getNamedItem("count")) != null)
{
          int cCheck = Integer.parseInt(ndTemp.getNodeValue());

          if (cCheck != cReal) {
```

*Example 16-1: Parts Checker Application (continued)*

```
          // counts don't agree
          System.err.println("<part_name> element for part #" +
             strPartNum + " is incorrect:  true part count = " + cReal +
             " (count in document is " + cCheck + ")");
        }
      } else {
        // they didn't provide a count for this part!
        System.err.println("missing count attribute for part #" +
            strPartNum + " (count " + cReal + ")");
      }
    }
  }
 }
}
```

When this application is run over the *bookcase.xml* sample document from Chapter 18, it generates the following output:

```
missing count attribute for part #HC (count 8)

<part_name> element for part #A is incorrect:  true part count = 2 (count
in document is 1)
```

To compile and use this sample application, download and install the Xerces Java Parser from the Apache-XML project (http://*xml.apache.org/xerces-j*). The code was compiled and tested with Sun's JDK Version 1.2.2.

DOM

CHAPTER 17

# *SAX*

SAX, the Simple API for XML, is a straightforward, event-based API for parsing XML documents. Many different XML parsers, including Xerces, MSXML, the Oracle XML Parser for Java, and Ælfred implement the SAX API. SAX was originally defined as a Java API and is intended primarily for parsers written in Java. Therefore this chapter focuses on the Java version of the API. However, SAX has been ported to most other major object-oriented languages, including C++, Python, Perl, and Eiffel. The translation from Java is usually fairly obvious.

The SAX API is unique among XML APIs because it's an event-based push model rather than a tree-based pull model. As the XML parser reads an XML document, it sends your program information from the document in real time. Each time the parser sees a start tag, an end tag, character data, or a processing instruction, it tells your program. You do not have to wait for the entire document to be read before acting on the data at the beginning of the document. The document is presented to your program one piece at a time from top to bottom. You can either save the pieces you're interested in until the entire document has been read or process the information as soon as you receive it. Most importantly, the entire document does not have to reside in memory. This feature makes SAX the API of choice for very large documents that do not fit into available memory.

---

This chapter covers SAX2 exclusively. In 2001 all major parsers that support SAX support SAX2. The major change in SAX2 from SAX1 is the addition of namespace support. This addition necessitated changing the names and signatures of almost every method and class in SAX. The old SAX1 methods and classes are still available, but they're now deprecated and you shouldn't use them.

---

SAX is primarily a collection of interfaces in the `org.xml.sax` package. One such interface is `XMLReader`. This interface represents the XML parser. It declares methods to parse a document and configure the parsing process, for instance, by turning validation on or off. To parse a document with SAX, first create an instance of `XMLReader` with the `XMLReaderFactory` class in the `org.xml.sax.helpers` package. This class has a static `createXMLReader()` method that produces the parser-specific implementation of the `XMLReader` interface. The system property `org.xml.sax.driver` specifies the concrete class to instantiate:

```
try {
  XMLReader parser = XMLReaderFactory.createXMLReader();
  // parse the document...
}
catch (SAXException e) {
  // couldn't create the XMLReader
}
```

The call to `XMLReaderFactory.createXMLReader()` is wrapped in a `try-catch` block that catches `SAXException`. This is the generic runtime exception superclass for almost anything that can go wrong while parsing an XML document. In this case, it means that either the `org.xml.sax.driver` system property wasn't set, or that it was set to the name of the class that Java couldn't find in the class path.

You can choose which concrete class to instantiate by passing its name as a string to the `createXMLReader()` method. This code fragment instantiates the Xerces parser by name:

```
try {
  XMLReader parser =
   XMLReaderFactory.createXMLReader("org.apache.xerces.parsers
SAXParser");
  // parse the document...
}
catch (SAXException e) {
  // couldn't create the XMLReader
}
```

Now that you've created a parser, you're ready to parse some documents with it. Pass the system ID of the document you want to parse to the `parse()` method. The system ID is either an absolute or a relative URL encoded in a string. For example, this code fragment parses the document at *http://www.slashdot.org/slashdot.xml*:

```
try {
  XMLReader parser = XMLReaderFactory.createXMLReader();
  parser.parse("http://www.slashdot.org/slashdot.xml");
}
catch (SAXException e) {
  // couldn't create the XMLReader or well-formedness error
}
```

The `parse()` method throws a `SAXException` if the document it attempts to parse is malformed. Otherwise, it returns `void`. To receive information from the parser as it reads the document, you must configure it with a `ContentHandler`.

## The ContentHandler Interface

`ContentHandler`, shown in stripped-down form in Example 17-1, is an interface in the `org.xml.sax` package. You implement this interface in a class of your own devising. Next, you configure an `XMLReader` with an instance of your implementation. As the `XMLReader` reads the document, it invokes the methods in your object to tell it what's in the XML document. You can respond to these method invocations in any way you see fit.

---

Note that this class has no relation to the moribund `java.net.ContentHandler` class. However, you may encounter a name conflict if you import both `java.net.*` and `org.xml.sax.*` in the same class. It's better to import just the `java.net` classes you actually need, rather than the entire package.

---

*Example 17-1: The org.xml.sax.ContentHandler Interface*

```
package org.xml.sax;

public interface ContentHandler {

    public void setDocumentLocator(Locator locator);
    public void startDocument() throws SAXException;
    public void endDocument() throws SAXException;
    public void startPrefixMapping(String prefix, String uri)
     throws SAXException;
    public void endPrefixMapping(String prefix) throws SAXException;
    public void startElement(String namespaceURI, String localName,
     String qualifiedName, Attributes atts) throws SAXException;
    public void endElement(String namespaceURI, String localName,
     String qualifiedName) throws SAXException;
    public void characters(char[] ch, int start, int length)
     throws SAXException;
    public void ignorableWhitespace(char[] ch, int start, int length)
     throws SAXException;
    public void processingInstruction(String target, String data)
     throws SAXException;
    public void skippedEntity(String name) throws SAXException;

}
```

Every time the `XMLReader` reads another piece of the document, it calls a method in its `ContentHandler`. Suppose a parser reads the simple document shown in Example 17-2.

*Example 17-2: A Simple XML Document*

```
<?xml version="1.0" encoding="ISO-8859-1"?>
<!DOCTYPE person SYSTEM "person.dtd">
<person xmlns="http://xml.oreilly.com/person">
```

*Example 17-2: A Simple XML Document (continued)*

```
  <name:name xmlns:name="http://xml.oreilly.com/name">
    <name:first>Sydney</name:first>
    <name:last>Lee</name:last>
  </name:name>
  <assignment project_id="p2"/>
</person>
```

The parser will call these methods in its `ContentHandler` with these arguments in this order. The values of the arguments passed to each method are given after each method name:

1. 
```
setDocumentLocator(Locator locator)
locator: org.apache.xerces.readers.DefaultEntityHandler@1f953d
```
2. 
```
startDocument()
```
3. 
```
startPrefixMapping(String prefix, String namespaceURI)
prefix: ""
namespaceURI: "http://xml.oreilly.com/person"
```
4. 
```
startElement(String namespaceURI, String localName, String qualifiedName,
Attributes atts)
namespaceURI: "http://xml.oreilly.com/person"
localName: "person"
qualifiedName: "person"
atts: {} (no attributes, an empty list)
```
5. 
```
characters(char[] ch, int start, int end)
ch: <?xml version="1.0" encoding="ISO-8859-1"?>
<!DOCTYPE person SYSTEM "person.dtd">
<person xmlns="http://xml.oreilly.com/person">
  <name:name xmlns:name="http://xml.oreilly.com/name">
    <name:first>Sydney</name:first>
    <name:last>Lee</name:last>
  </name:name>
  <assignment project_id="p2"/>
</person>
start: 128
end: 3
```
6. 
```
startPrefixMapping(String prefix, String uri)
prefix: "name"
uri: "http://xml.oreilly.com/name")
```
7. 
```
startElement(String namespaceURI, String localName, String qualifiedName,
Attributes atts)
namespaceURI: "http://xml.oreilly.com/name"
localName: "name"
qualifiedName: "name:name"
atts: {} (no attributes, an empty list)
```
8. 
```
characters(char[] ch, int start, int end)
ch: <?xml version="1.0" encoding="ISO-8859-1"?>
<!DOCTYPE person SYSTEM "person.dtd">
<person xmlns="http://xml.oreilly.com/person">
  <name:name xmlns:name="http://xml.oreilly.com/name">
```

```
    <name:first>Sydney</name:first>
    <name:last>Lee</name:last>
  </name:name>
  <assignment project_id="p2"/>
</person>
start: 183
end: 5
```

9. startElement(String namespaceURI, String localName, String qualifiedName, Attributes atts)

```
namespaceURI: "http://xml.oreilly.com/name"
localName: "first"
qualifiedName: "name:first"
atts: {} (no attributes, an empty list)
```

10. characters(char[] ch, int start, int end)

```
ch: <?xml version="1.0" encoding="ISO-8859-1"?>
<!DOCTYPE person SYSTEM "person.dtd">
<person xmlns="http://xml.oreilly.com/person">
  <name:name xmlns:name="http://xml.oreilly.com/name">
    <name:first>Sydney</name:first>
    <name:last>Lee</name:last>
  </name:name>
  <assignment project_id="p2"/>
</person>
start: 200
end: 6
```

11. endElement(String namespaceURI, String localName, String qualifiedName)

```
namespaceURI: "http://xml.oreilly.com/name"
localName: "first"
qualifiedName: "name:first"
```

12. characters(charp[] ch, int start, int end)

```
ch: <?xml version="1.0" encoding="ISO-8859-1"?>
<!DOCTYPE person SYSTEM "person.dtd">
<person xmlns="http://xml.oreilly.com/person">
  <name:name xmlns:name="http://xml.oreilly.com/name">
    <name:first>Sydney</name:first>
    <name:last>Lee</name:last>
  </name:name>
  <assignment project_id="p2"/>
</person>
start: 219
end: 5
```

13. startElement(String namespaceURI, String localName, String qualifiedName, Attributes atts)

```
namespaceURI: "http://xml.oreilly.com/name"
localName: "last"
qualifiedName: "name:last"
atts: {} (no attributes, an empty list)
```

14. characters(char[] ch, int start, int end)

```
ch: <?xml version="1.0" encoding="ISO-8859-1"?>
<!DOCTYPE person SYSTEM "person.dtd">
<person xmlns="http://xml.oreilly.com/person">
```

```
  <name:name xmlns:name="http://xml.oreilly.com/name">
    <name:first>Sydney</name:first>
    <name:last>Lee</name:last>
  </name:name>
  <assignment project_id="p2"/>
</person>
start: 235
end: 3
```

15. `endElement(String namespaceURI, String localName, String qualifiedName)`

```
namespaceURI: "http://xml.oreilly.com/name"
localName: "last"
qualifiedName: "name:last"
```

16. `characters(char[] ch, int start, int end)`

```
ch: <?xml version="1.0" encoding="ISO-8859-1"?>
<!DOCTYPE person SYSTEM "person.dtd">
<person xmlns="http://xml.oreilly.com/person">
  <name:name xmlns:name="http://xml.oreilly.com/name">
    <name:first>Sydney</name:first>
    <name:last>Lee</name:last>
  </name:name>
  <assignment project_id="p2"/>
</person>
start: 250
end: 3
```

17. `endElement(String namespaceURI, String localName, String qualifiedName)`

```
namespaceURI: "http://xml.oreilly.com/name"
localName: "name"
qualifiedName: "name:name"
```

18. `endPrefixMapping(String prefix)`

```
prefix: "name"
```

19. `characters(char[] ch, int start, int end)`

```
ch: <?xml version="1.0" encoding="ISO-8859-1"?>
<!DOCTYPE person SYSTEM "person.dtd">
<person xmlns="http://xml.oreilly.com/person">
  <name:name xmlns:name="http://xml.oreilly.com/name">
    <name:first>Sydney</name:first>
    <name:last>Lee</name:last>
  </name:name>
  <assignment project_id="p2"/>
</person>
start: 265
end: 3
```

20. `startElement(String namespaceURI, String localName, String qualifiedName, Attributes atts)`

```
namespaceURI: "http://xml.oreilly.com/person"
localName: "assignment"
qualifiedName: "assignment
atts: {project_id="p2"}
```

21. ```
    endElement(String namespaceURI, String localName, String qualifiedName)
    namespaceURI: "http://xml.oreilly.com/person"
    localName: "assignment"
    qualifiedName: "assignment"
    ```
22. ```
    characters(char[] ch, int start, int end)
    ch: <?xml version="1.0" encoding="ISO-8859-1"?>
    <!DOCTYPE person SYSTEM "person.dtd">
    <person xmlns="http://xml.oreilly.com/person">
      <name:name xmlns:name="http://xml.oreilly.com/name">
        <name:first>Sydney</name:first>
        <name:last>Lee</name:last>
      </name:name>
      <assignment project_id="p2"/>
    </person>
    start: 297
    end: 1
    ```
23. ```
    endElement(String namespaceURI, String localName, String qualifiedName)
    namespaceURI: "http://xml.oreilly.com/person"
    localName: "person"
    qualifiedName: "person"
    ```
24. ```
    endPrefixMapping(String prefix)
    prefix: ""
    ```
25. ```
    endDocument()
    ```

Some pieces of this are not deterministic. Note that the `char` array passed to each call to `characters()` actually contains the entire document! The specific text block the parser really returns is indicated by the second two arguments to `characters()`. This is an optimization that Xerces-J performs. Other parsers are free to pass different `char` arrays as long as they set the `start` and `length` arguments to match. Indeed, the parser is also free to split a long run of plain text across multiple calls to `characters()`, so you cannot assume that `characters()` necessarily returns the longest possible contiguous run of plain text. Other details that may change from parser to parser include attribute order within a tag and whether or not a `Locator` object is provided by calling `setDocumentLocator()`.

Suppose you want to count the number of elements, attributes, processing instructions, and characters of plain text that exist in a given XML document. To do this, first write a class that implements the `ContentHandler` interface. The current count of each of the four items of interest is stored in a field. The field values are initialized to zero in the `startDocument()` method, which is called exactly once for each document parsed. Each callback method in the class increments the relevant field. The `endDocument()` method reports the total for that document. Example 17-3 is such a class.

*Example 17-3: The XMLCounter ContentHandler*

```
import org.xml.sax.*;

public class XMLCounter implements ContentHandler {

  private int numberOfElements;
```
```

*Example 17-3: The XMLCounter ContentHandler (continued)*

```
  private int numberOfAttributes;
  private int numberOfProcessingInstructions;
  private int numberOfCharacters;

  public void startDocument() throws SAXException {
    numberOfElements = 0;
    numberOfAttributes = 0;
    numberOfProcessingInstructions = 0;
    numberOfCharacters = 0;
  }

  // We should count either the start tag of the element or the end tag,
  // but not both. Empty elements will still be reported by each of these
  // methods.
  public void startElement(String namespaceURI, String localName,
   String qualifiedName, Attributes atts) throws SAXException {
    numberOfElements++;
    numberOfAttributes += atts.getLength();
  }

  public void endElement(String namespaceURI, String localName,
   String qualifiedName) throws SAXException {}

  public void characters(char[] text, int start, int length)
   throws SAXException {
    numberOfCharacters += length;
  }

  public void ignorableWhitespace(char[] text, int start, int length)
   throws SAXException {
    // We don't count the ignorable white space
  }

  public void processingInstruction(String target, String data)
   throws SAXException {
    numberOfProcessingInstructions++;
  }

  // Now that the document is done, we can print out the final results
  public void endDocument() throws SAXException {
    System.out.println("Number of elements: " + numberOfElements);
    System.out.println("Number of attributes: " + numberOfAttributes);
    System.out.println("Number of processing instructions: "
     + numberOfProcessingInstructions);
    System.out.println("Number of characters of plain text: "
     + numberOfCharacters);
  }

  // Do-nothing methods we have to implement to fulfill the interface
  // requirements but which don't need to do anything:
  public void setDocumentLocator(Locator locator) {}

  public void startPrefixMapping(String prefix, String uri)
```

*Example 17-3: The XMLCounter ContentHandler (continued)*

```
   throws SAXException {}
  public void endPrefixMapping(String prefix) throws SAXException {}
  public void skippedEntity(String name) throws SAXException {}
```

---

In this case, we need to override most methods in the `ContentHandler` interface. However, if you only really want to provide one or two `ContentHandler` methods, you may want to subclass the `DefaultHandler` class instead. This class implements all methods in the `ContentHandler` interface with do-nothing methods, so you only have to override methods you're genuinely interested in.

---

Next, build an **`XMLReader`** and configure it with an instance of this class. Finally, parse the documents you want to count, as in Example 17-4.

*Example 17-4: The DocumentStatistics Driver Class*

```
import org.xml.sax.*;
import org.xml.sax.helpers.*;
import java.io.IOException;

public class DocumentStatistics {

  public static void main(String[] args) {

    XMLReader parser;
    try {
     parser = XMLReaderFactory.createXMLReader();
    }
    catch (SAXException e) {
      // fall back on Xerces parser by name
      try {
        parser = XMLReaderFactory.createXMLReader(
         "org.apache.xerces.parsers.SAXParser");
      }
      catch (SAXException ee) {
        System.err.println("Couldn't locate a SAX parser");
        return;
      }
    }

    if (args.length == 0) {
      System.out.println(
       "Usage: java EventReporter URL1 URL2...");
    }

    // Install the Content Handler
    parser.setContentHandler(new XMLCounter());

    // start parsing...
    for (int i = 0; i < args.length; i++) {
```

*Example 17-4: The DocumentStatistics Driver Class (continued)*

```
        // command line should offer URIs or file names
        try {
          parser.parse(args[i]);
        }
        catch (SAXParseException e) { // well-formedness error
          System.out.println(args[i] + " is not well formed.");
          System.out.println(e.getMessage()
           + " at line " + e.getLineNumber()
           + ", column " + e.getColumnNumber());
        }
        catch (SAXException e) { // some other kind of error
          System.out.println(e.getMessage());
        }
        catch (IOException e) {
          System.out.println("Could not report on " + args[i]
           + " because of the IOException " + e);
        }

      }

    }

}
```

Running the program in Example 17-4 across the document in Example 17-2 results in the following output:

```
D:\books\xian\examples\17>java DocumentStatistics 17-2.xml
Number of elements: 5
Number of attributes: 1
Number of processing instructions: 0
Number of characters of plain text: 29
```

This generic program works on any well-formed XML document. Most SAX programs are more specific and only work with certain XML applications. They look for particular elements or attributes in particular places and respond to them accordingly. They may rely on patterns that are enforced by a validating parser. Still, this behavior comprises the fundamentals of SAX.

The complicated part of most SAX programs is the data structure you must build to store information returned by the parser until you're ready to use it. Sometimes this information can be as complicated as the XML document itself, in which case you may be better off using DOM, which at least provides a ready-made data structure for an XML document. You usually want only some information, though, and the data structure you construct should be less complex than the document itself.

SAX

## SAX Features and Properties

SAX uses properties and features to control parser behavior. Each feature and property has a name that's an absolute URI. Like namespace URIs, these URIs are only used to name things and do not necessarily point to a real page you can load into a web browser. Features are either true or false; that is, they're Booleans. Properties have values of an unspecified `Object` type.

The *http://xml.org/sax/features/validation* feature controls whether or not a parser validates. If this feature is true, then the parser will report validity errors in the document to the registered `ErrorHandler`. Otherwise it won't. This feature is turned off by default. To turn a feature on, pass the feature's name and value to the `XMLReader`'s `setFeature()` method:

```
try {
  parser.setFeature("http://xml.org/sax/features/validation", true);
}
catch (SAXNotSupportedException e) {
  System.out.println("This is not a validating parser");
}
catch (SAXNotRecognizedException e) {
  System.out.println("This parser does not recognize the" +
   + "http://xml.org/sax/features/validation feature");
}
```

Not all parsers validate. If you try to turn on validation in a parser that doesn't validate or set any other feature the parser doesn't support, `setFeature()` throws a `SAXNotSupportedException`. If you try to set a feature the parser is not familiar with, `setFeature()` throws a `SAXNotRecognizedException`. All SAX2-compliant parsers should at least recognize the *http://xml.org/sax/features/validation* feature, if not always implement it. However, parsers may define their own custom features that other parsers may not recognize.

You can check a feature's current value using `XMLReader`'s `getFeature()` method. This method returns a `boolean` and throws the same exceptions for the same reasons as `setFeature()`. If you want to know whether the parser validates, you can ask in the following manner:

```
try {
  boolean isValidating =
   parser.getFeature("http://xml.org/sax/features/validation");
}
catch (SAXNotSupportedException e) {
  System.out.println(
   "This is not a validating parser");
}
catch (SAXNotRecognizedException e) {
  System.out.println("Parser does not recognize the" +
   + "http://xml.org/sax/features/validation feature");
}
```

Properties are similar to features, but they allow a broader choice than a simple boolean on/off, true/false dichotomy. Each property value is an object of unspecified type. For example, if you want to know the literal string of data parsed to produce the current SAX event, you can ask by reading the *http://xml.org/sax/properties/xml-string* property with the `getProperty()` method:

```
try {
  String tag = parser.getProperty(
   "http://xml.org/sax/properties/xml-string");
}
```

```
catch (SAXNotSupportedException e) {
  System.out.println("This parser does not provide the original data");
}
catch (SAXNotRecognizedException e) {
  System.out.println("Parser does not recognize the " +
   "http://xml.org/sax/properties/xml-string property");
}
```

You can change a property value by invoking the `setProperty()` method with two arguments. The first is the URI of the property to set. The second is the object specifying the value for the property. For example, this code fragment attempts to set the *http://xml.org/sax/handlers/LexicalHandler* property to a new instance of the `MyLexicalHandlerClass`. The parser reports lexical events (comments, CDATA sections, and entity references) to the `org.xml.sax.ext.LexicalHandler` implementation object named by this property:

```
try {
  parser.setProperty(
    "http://xml.org/sax/handlers/LexicalHandler",
    new MyLexicalHandlerClass()
  );
}
catch (SAXException e) {
  System.out.println("This parser does not provide lexical events.");
}
```

Not all features and properties can be set at all times. For example, you cannot suddenly decide to start validating when the parser is already halfway through a document. An attempt to do so will fail and throw a `SAXNotSupportedException`. However, you can change a parser's features in between documents; after parsing one document, but before parsing the next. You can read most feature and property values at any time.

SAX

# PART IV

# *Reference*

CHAPTER 18

# *XML 1.0 Reference*

This chapter is intended to serve as a comprehensive, but easily understood, reference to the Extensible Markup Language (XML) 1.0 W3C Recommendation (Second Edition), dated 6 October 2000. We have made every effort to cover the contents of the official W3C document exhaustively. If you are implementing an XML parser, editor, or tool, however, you should also review the latest revision of the recommendation on the web at *http://www.w3.org/TR/REC-xml*.

## *How to Use This Reference*

This chapter consists of a comprehensive XML example application, followed by detailed reference sections that describe every feature of the 1.0 specification. The syntax elements of a valid XML document are introduced in the rough order they appear in an XML document. Each entry explains the syntactic structure, where it can be used, and the applicable validity and well-formedness constraints. Each section contains a description of the XML language structure, an informal syntax, and an example of the syntax's usage where appropriate.

Every XML document is broken into two primary sections: the prolog and the document element. A few documents may also have comments or processing instructions that follow the root element in a sort of *epilog* (an unofficial term). The prolog contains structural information about the particular type of XML document you are writing, including the XML declaration and document type declaration. The prolog is optional, and if a document is not valid, it can be omitted completely. The only required structure in a well-formed XML document is the top-level document element itself.

## *Annotated Sample Documents*

These examples are intended for use as a mnemonic aid for XML syntax and a quick map from a specific instance of an XML language construct to its corresponding XML syntax structure. The example document and DTD also use features exposed by the XML 1.0 specification and the XML Namespaces standard.

The following XML application describes the construction of a piece of furniture. Four files make up this application:

*bookcase.xml*
: A document shown in Figure 18-1 uses the `furniture.dtd` application to describe a simple bookcase.

*furniture.dtd*
: An XML Document Type Definition shown in Figure 18-2 provides a simple grammar for describing components and assembly details for a piece of furniture.

*bookcase_ex.ent*
: An external entity file shown in Figure 18-3 contains additional bookcase specific elements for the bookcase.xml document.

*parts_list.ent*
: Figure 18-4 contains an external parsed general entity example that contains the parts list for the bookcase example document.

Each distinct language construct is enclosed in a box, with the relevant reference section as a callout. By locating a construct in the sample, then locating the associated reference section, you should be able to quickly identify and understand any unfamiliar XML syntax you encounter.

## Key to XML Syntax

For each section of this reference that maps directly to an XML language structure, an informal syntax reference describes that structure's form. The following conventions are used within these syntax blocks:

| *Format* | *Meaning* |
|---|---|
| **DOCTYPE** | Bold text indicates literal characters that must appear as written within the document (e.g., **DOCTYPE**). |
| *encoding-name* | Italicized text indicates that the user must replace the text with real data. The item indicates what type of data should be inserted (e.g., *encoding-name* = en-us). |
| \| | The vertical bar \| indicates that only one out of a list of possible values can be selected. |
| [ ] | Square brackets indicate that a particular portion of the syntax is optional. |

## Well-Formedness

Well-formedness refers to an XML document's physical organization. Certain lexical rules must be obeyed before an XML parser can consider a document well-formed. These rules should not be confused with validity constraints, which determine whether or not a particular document is valid when parsed using the document structure rules contained in its DTD. The BNF grammar rules must also

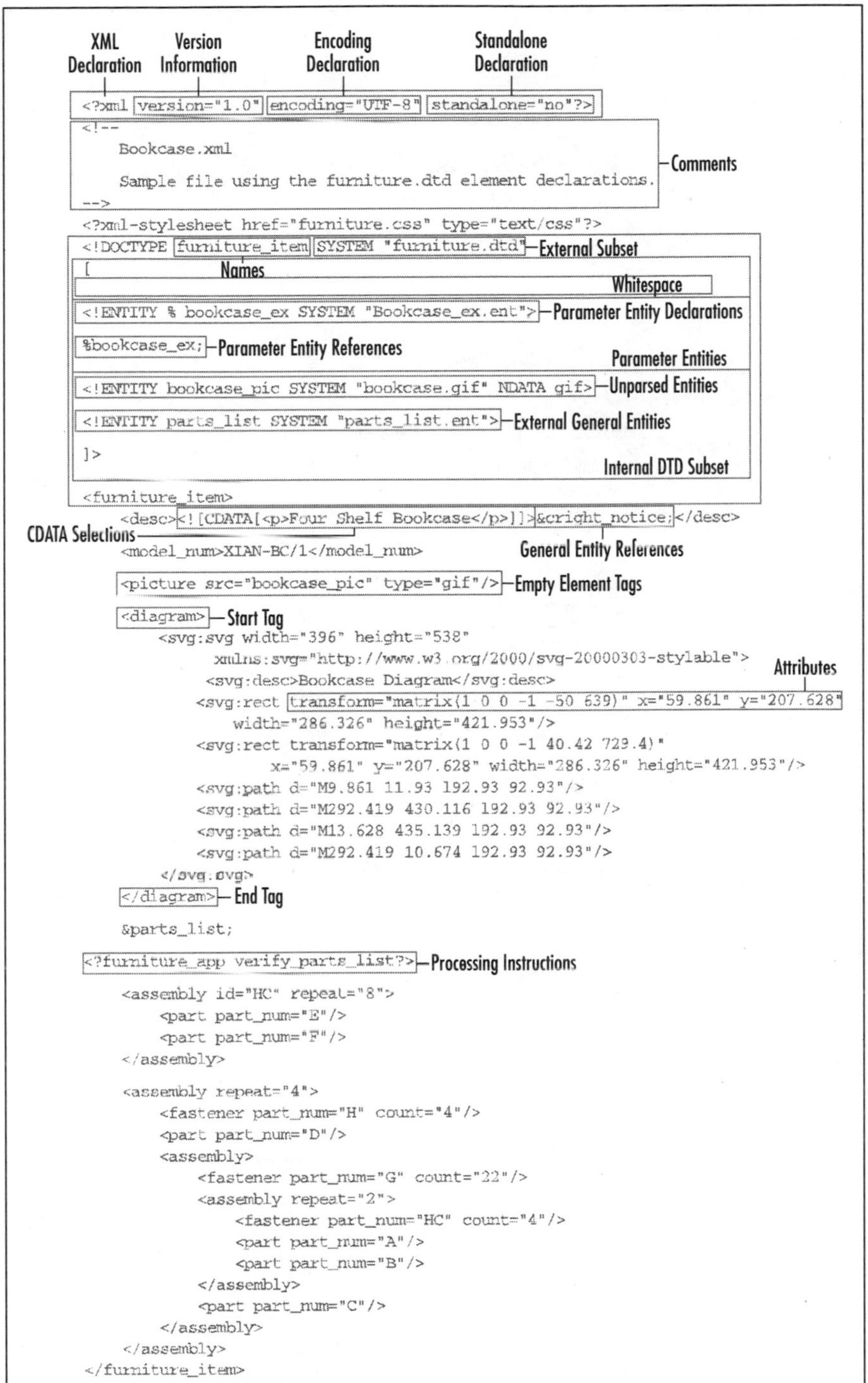


*Figure 18-1: bookcase.xml*

```
<!--
    furniture.dtd

    A vocabulary for describing furniture.
-->

<!ELEMENT furniture_item (desc, %extra_tags; user_tags?, parts_list,
assembly+)>

<!ATTLIST furniture_item
    xmlns CDATA #FIXED "http://namespaces.oreilly.com/furniture/"
>

<!ELEMENT p (#PCDATA)>

<!ELEMENT desc (#PCDATA | p)* >
<!ATTLIST desc
    xml:lang NMTOKEN 'en'
    xml:space (default|preserve) 'preserve'
>
<!ELEMENT user_tags ANY>
<!ELEMENT parts_list (part_name+)>
<!ELEMENT part_name (#PCDATA)>
<!ATTLIST part_name
    id ID #REQUIRED
    count CDATA "1"
>
<!ELEMENT assembly (fastener*, (assembly | part), (assembly | part)+) >
<!ATTLIST assembly
    id ID #IMPLIED
    repeat CDATA "1"
>
<!ELEMENT fastener EMPTY >
<!ATTLIST fastener
    part_num IDREF #REQUIRED
    count CDATA "1"
>
<!ELEMENT part EMPTY>
<!ATTLIST part
    part_num IDREF #REQUIRED
    count CDATA "1"
>
<!ENTITY % private 'IGNORE'>
<!ENTITY % public 'INCLUDE'>
<![ %private; [
  <!ENTITY cright_notice "&#xa9; 2000 Furniture Makers. DO NOT
DISTRIBUTE">
]]>
<![ %public; [
 <!ENTITY cright_notice "&#xa9; 2000 Furniture Makers.">
]]>
```

Element Type Declaration
Mixed Element Type
xml:lang
xml:space
Enumeration Type
Any Element Type
Constrained Child Nodes
Attribute List Declaration
Simple Attribute Type
Empty Element
Default Values
Character References
General Entity Declarations
Internal General Entities
Conditional Sections

*Figure 18-2: furniture.dtd*

```
<!ENTITY % extra_tags "model_num, picture, diagram,">
<!ELEMENT model_num (#PCDATA)>
<!ELEMENT picture EMPTY>
<!ATTLIST picture
    src ENTITY #REQUIRED
>

<!NOTATION dos SYSTEM "dos_batch">
<!NOTATION perl SYSTEM "perl">

<!ELEMENT batch_script (#PCDATA)>

<!ATTLIST batch_script
    lang NOTATION (dos | perl) #IMPLIED         —Notation Attribute Type
>

<!ELEMENT diagram ANY>
<!ELEMENT svg:svg (svg:desc, (svg:rect | svg:path)+)>
<!ATTLIST svg:svg
    width CDATA "1"
    height CDATA "1"
    xmlns:svg CDATA #FIXED "http://www.w3.org/2000/svg-20000303-stylable"
>

<!ELEMENT svg:desc (#PCDATA)>

<!ELEMENT svg:rect EMPTY>
<!ATTLIST svg:rect
    transform CDATA "1"
    x CDATA "1"
    y CDATA "1"
    width CDATA "1"
    height CDATA "1"
>

<!ELEMENT svg:path EMPTY>
<!ATTLIST svg:path
    d CDATA "1"
>

<!NOTATION gif SYSTEM "images/gif">         —Notation Declaration
```

*Figure 18-3: bookcase_ex.ent*

```
<parts_list>
        <part_name id="A" count="1">END PANEL</part_name>
        <part_name id="B" count="2">SIDE PANEL</part_name>
        <part_name id="C" count="1">BACK PANEL</part_name>
        <part_name id="D" count="4">SHELF</part_name>
        <part_name id="E" count="8">HIDDEN CONNECTORS</part_name>
        <part_name id="F" count="8">CONNECTOR SCREWS</part_name>
        <part_name id="G" count="22">7/16&quot; TACKS</part_name>
        <part_name id="H" count="16">SHELF PEGS</part_name>
</parts_list>
                                   Predefined Character References
```

*Figure 18-4: parts_list.ent*

be satisfied. The following list contains all well-formedness constraints recognized by XML Version 1.0 parsers, including actual text from the 1.0 specification:

---

## *PEs in Internal Subset*

### *Text from Specification*

In the internal DTD subset, parameter entity references can occur only where markup declarations can occur, not within markup declarations. (This does not apply to references that occur in external parameter entities or to the external subset.)

### *Description*

It is only legal to use parameter entity references to build markup declarations within the external DTD subset.

---

## *[E109]-External Subset*

### *Text from Specification*

The external subset, if any, must match production for extSubset.

### *Description*

The `extSubset` production constrains what type of declaration may be contained in the external subset.

---

## *[E109]PE Between Declarations*

### *Text from Specification*

The replacement text of a parameter entity reference in a DeclSep must match the production extSubsetDecl.

### *Description*

The replacement text of parameter entities may contain declarations that might not be allowed if the replacement text appeared directly. Parameter entity references in the internal subset parameter cannot appear within declarations, but this rule does not apply to declarations included via parameter entities.

---

## *Element Type Match*

### *Text from Specification*

The Name in an element's end-tag must match the element type in the start-tag.

### *Description*

Proper element nesting is strictly enforced, and every open tag must be matched by a corresponding close tag.

## Unique Att Spec

### Text from Specification

No attribute name may appear more than once in the same start-tag or empty-element tag.

### Description

Attribute names must be unique within a given element.

## No External Entity References

### Text from Specification

Attribute values cannot contain direct or indirect entity references to external entities.

### Description

XML parsers do not replace references to external parsed entities within attribute values.

## No < in Attribute Values

### Text from Specification

The replacement text of any entity referred to directly or indirectly in an attribute value [E83] (other than "<") must not contain a <.

### Description

This restriction should simplify the task of parsing XML data. Since attribute values can't appear to contain element data, simple parsers need not track literal strings.

## Legal Character

### Text from Specification

Characters referred to using character references must match the production for Char.

### Description

The character you try to make the XML parser generate must be a real character. A few character values in Unicode are not valid stand-alone characters.

## Entity Declared

### Text from Specification

In a document without any DTD, a document with only an internal DTD subset which contains no parameter entity references, or a document with standalone='yes', [E34] for an entity reference that does not occur within the external subset or a parameter entity, the Name given in the entity reference must match that in an entity declaration that does not occur within the external subset or a parameter entity, except that well-formed documents need not declare any of the following entities: amp, lt, gt, apos, quot. [E29] The declaration of a parameter entity must precede any reference to it. Similarly, the declaration of a general entity must precede any reference to it which appears in a default value in an attribute-list declaration. Note that if entities are declared in the external subset or in external parameter entities, a non-validating processor is not obligated to read and process their declarations; for such documents, the rule that an entity must be declared is a well-formedness constraint only if standalone='yes'.

### *Description*

This long constraint lists the only situations in which an entity reference may appear without a corresponding entity declaration. Since a nonvalidating parser is not obliged to read and parse the external subset, the parser must give the document the benefit of the doubt, if an entity could possibly have been declared.

---

## *Parsed Entity*

### *Text from Specification*

An entity reference must not contain the name of an unparsed entity. Unparsed entities may be referred to only in attribute values declared to be of type ENTITY or ENTITIES.

### *Description*

Since unparsed entities can't be parsed, don't try to force the parser to parse them.

---

## *No Recursion*

### *Text from Specification*

A parsed entity must not contain a recursive reference to itself, either directly or indirectly.

### *Description*

Be careful how you structure your entities; make sure you don't inadvertently create a circular reference:

```
<!ENTITY a "&b;">
<!ENTITY b "&c;">
<!ENTITY c "&a;"> <!--wrong!-->
```

---

## *In DTD*

### *Text from Specification*

Parameter entity references may only appear in the DTD.

### Description

This constraint is self evident because the % character has no significance outside of the DTD. Therefore, it is perfectly legal to have an element like this in your document:

```
<ok>%noproblem;</ok>
```

The text `%noproblem;` is passed on by the parser without generating an error.

# Validity

The following list contains all validity constraints that are enforced by a validating parser. It includes actual text from the XML 1.0 specification and a short explanation of what the constraint actually means.

---

## Root Element Type

### Text from Specification

The Name in the document type declaration must match the element type of the root element.

### Description

The name provided in the `<!DOCTYPE` declaration determines the document element's name.

---

## Proper Declaration/PE Nesting

### Text from Specification

Parameter entity replacement text must be properly nested with markup declarations. That is to say, if either the first character or the last character of a markup declaration (markupdecl above) is contained in the replacement text for a parameter entity reference, both must be contained in the same replacement text.

### Description

This constraint means you can't create a parameter entity that completes one DTD declaration and begins another; the following XML fragment would violate this constraint:

```
<!ENTITY % finish_it ">">
<!ENTITY % bad "won't work" %finish_it; <!--wrong!-->
```

---

## Standalone Document Declaration

### Text from Specification

The standalone document declaration must have the value "no" if any external markup declarations contain declarations of: attributes with default values, if elements to which these attributes apply appear in the document without specifications of values for these attributes, or entities (other than amp, lt, gt, apos, quot), if references to those entities appear in the document, or attributes with values subject to normalization, where the attribute appears in the document with a value which will change as a result of normalization, or element types with element content, if white space occurs directly within any instance of those types.

### *Description*

You can read this laundry list of potential standalone flag violations as, "if you have an external subset in your DTD, ensure that your document doesn't depend on anything in it if you say `standalone='yes'` in your XML declaration." A more succinct interpretation would be, "if your document has an external DTD subset, just set standalone to `no`."

---

## *Element Valid*

### *Text from Specification*

An element is valid if there is a declaration matching elementdecl where the Name matches the element type, and one of the following holds: The declaration matches EMPTY and the element has no content. The declaration matches children and the sequence of child elements belongs to the language generated by the regular expression in the content model, with optional white space (characters matching the nonterminal S) between [E59] the start-tag and the first child element, between child elements, or between the last child element and the end-tag. Note that a CDATA section containing only white space does not match the nonterminal S, and hence cannot appear in these positions. The declaration matches Mixed and the content consists of character data and child elements whose types match names in the content model. The declaration matches ANY, and the types of any child elements have been declared.

### *Description*

If you have an element declaration, make sure the actual elements in your document match the rules set down in the DTD.

---

## *Attribute Value Type*

### *Text from Specification*

The attribute must have been declared; the value must be of the type declared for it. (For attribute types, see Attribute List Declarations.)

### *Description*

If you declare an attribute for an element, make sure that every instance of that attribute has a valid value.

## Unique Element Type Declaration

### Text from Specification

No element type may be declared more than once.

### Description

Unlike entity declarations, only one declaration may exist for a particular element type.

## Proper Group/PE Nesting

### Text from Specification

Parameter entity replacement text must be properly nested with [E11] parenthesized groups. That is to say, if either of the opening or closing parentheses in a choice, seq, or Mixed construct is contained in the replacement text for a parameter entity, both must be contained in the same replacement text. [E19]

For interoperability, if a parameter entity reference appears in a choice, seq, or Mixed construct, its replacement text should contain at least one non-blank character, and neither the first nor last non-blank character of the replacement text should be a connector (| or ,).

### Description

This constraint restricts the way parameter entities can be used to construct element declarations. It prevents the XML author from hiding significant syntax elements inside parameter entities.

## No Duplicate Types

### Text from Specification

The same name must not appear more than once in a single mixed-content declaration.

### Description

Don't list the same element type name more than once in the same mixed-content declaration.

## ID

### Text from Specification

Values of type ID must match the Name production. A name must not appear more than once in an XML document as a value of this type; i.e., ID values must uniquely identify the elements which bear them.

### *Description*

No two attribute values for attributes declared as type ID can have the same value. This constraint is not restricted by element type, but is global across the entire document.

## *One ID per Element Type*

### *Text from Specification*

No element type may have more than one ID attribute specified.

### *Description*

Each element can have at most one ID type attribute.

## *ID Attribute Default*

### *Text from Specification*

An ID attribute must have a declared default of #IMPLIED or #REQUIRED.

### *Description*

For obvious reasons, you can't declare an `ID` attribute to be `#FIXED`.

## *IDREF*

### *Text from Specification*

Values of type IDREF must match the Name production, and values of type IDREFS must match Names; each Name must match the value of an ID attribute on some element in the XML document; i.e., IDREF values must match the value of some ID attribute.

### *Description*

`ID` references must refer to actual `ID`s that exist within the document.

## *Entity Name*

### *Text from Specification*

Values of type ENTITY must match the Name production, and values of type ENTITIES must match Names; each Name must match the name of an unparsed entity declared in the DTD.

### *Description*

Attributes declared to contain entity references must contain references to unparsed entities that have been declared in the DTD.

## Name Token

### Text from Specification

Values of type NMTOKEN must match the Nmtoken production; values of type NMTOKENS must match Nmtokens.

### Description

If an attribute is declared to contain a name or list of names, the values must be legal XML name tokens.

## Notation Attributes

### Text from Specification

Values of this type must match one of the notation names included in the declaration; all notation names in the declaration must be declared.

### Description

Attributes that must contain notation names have to contain names that reference actual notations declared in the DTD.

## [E7]One Notation Per Element Type

### Text from Specification

No element type may have more than one NOTATION attribute specified.

### Description

A given element can have only one attribute declared with the `NOTATION` attribute type.

## [E68]No Notation on Empty Element

### Text from Specification

For compatibility, an attribute of type NOTATION must not be declared on an element declared EMPTY.

### Description

Empty elements cannot have `NOTATION` attributes to maintain compatibility with SGML.

## Enumeration

### Text from Specification

Values of this type must match one of the Nmtoken tokens in the declaration.

### *Description*

Assigning a value to an enumerated type attribute that isn't listed in the enumeration is illegal in the DTD.

---

## *Required Attribute*

### *Text from Specification*

If the default declaration is the keyword #REQUIRED, then the attribute must be specified for all elements of the type in the attribute-list declaration.

### *Description*

Required attributes must have a value assigned to them.

---

## *Attribute Default Legal*

### *Text from Specification*

The declared default value must meet the lexical constraints of the declared attribute type.

### *Description*

If you provide a default attribute value, it must obey the same rules that apply to a normal attribute value within the document.

---

## *Fixed Attribute Default*

### *Text from Specification*

If an attribute has a default value declared with the #FIXED keyword, instances of that attribute must match the default value.

### *Description*

If you choose to provide an explicit value for a `#FIXED` attribute in your document, it must match the default value given in the attribute declaration.

---

## *[E90]Proper Conditional Section/PE Nesting*

### *Text from Specification*

If any of the "<![", "[", or "]]>" of a conditional section is contained in the replacement text for a parameter entity reference, all of them must be contained in the same replacement text.

### *Description*

If you use a parameter entity to contain the beginning of a conditional section, it must also contain the end of the section.

## *Entity Declared*

### *Text from Specification*

In a document with an external subset or external parameter entities with "standalone='no'", the Name given in the entity reference must match that in an entity declaration. For interoperability, valid documents should declare the entities amp, lt, gt, apos, quot, in the form specified in 4.6 Predefined Entities. The declaration of a parameter entity must precede any reference to it. Similarly, the declaration of a general entity must precede any [E92]attribute-list declaration containing a default value with a direct or indirect reference to that general entity.

### *Description*

Parameter and general entity declarations must precede any references to these entities. All entity references must refer to previously declared entities. Declaring the five predefined general entities (`amp`, `lt`, `gt`, `apos`, and `quot`) is also a good idea.

## *Notation Declared*

### *Text from Specification*

The Name must match the declared name of a notation.

### *Description*

External unparsed entities must use a notation that is declared in the document.

## *[E22]Unique Notation Name*

### *Text from Specification*

Only one notation declaration can declare a given Name.

### *Description*

Declaring two notations with the same name is illegal.

# *Global Syntax Structures*

The following syntax structures are common to the entire XML document. Unless otherwise noted within a subsequent reference item, the following structures can appear anywhere within an XML document.

## *Whitespace*

*Whitespace* is defined as a space, tab, or empty line (which is composed of a carriage return, line feed, or combination of the two). Whitespace serves the same purpose in XML as it does in most programming and natural languages: to separate tokens and language elements from one another. XML has simplified the task of determining which whitespace is significant to an application and which space is not. To an XML parser, all whitespace is significant and will be passed to the client application. Consider the following example:

```
<p>
  This sentence has extraneous
  line breaks.
</p>
```

After parsing, the character data from this example element is passed to the underlying application as:

```

  This sentence has extraneous
  line breaks.
```

Though XML specifies that all whitespace be preserved for use by the client application, an additional facility is available to the XML author to further hint that an element's character data's space and formatting should be preserved. For more information, see the discussion of the `xml:space` attribute in this chapter.

## *Names*

To ease the burden of XML parser writers, XML names must adhere to the following lexical conventions:

- Begin with a letter, _, or : character.
- After the first character, be composed only of letters, digits, ., -, _, and : characters.

According to the XML 1.0 specification, you may use the : character freely within your names, although the character is now officially reserved as part of the Namespaces in XML Recommendation. Even if you do not intend to use namespaces within your document, you should only use the colon for namespace scoping to retain compatibility with newer XML parsers. See Chapter 4, *Namespaces*, for a detailed explanation of XML namespaces.

## *Character References*

### *Syntax*

```
&#decimal-number;
&#xhexadecimal-number;
```

### *Description*

All XML parsers are considered to be based on the Unicode character set, no matter what the external encoding of the XML file is. It is theoretically possible to author documents directly in Unicode, but most text editing, storage, and delivery systems still use the ASCII character set. To allow XML authors to include Unicode characters in their documents without forcing them to abandon their existing editing tools, XML provides the *character reference* mechanism.

A character reference allows an author to insert a Unicode character, by number, into the output stream produced by the parser to an XML application. Consider an XML document that includes the following character data:

```
&#xa9; 2000 O'Reilly &#38; Associates
```

In this example, the parser would replace the character reference with the actual Unicode character and pass it to the client application:

```
© 2000 O'Reilly & Associates
```

### Predefined character entities

Besides user-defined entity references, XML includes the five named entity references shown in Table 18-1 that can be used without being declared. These references are a subset of those available in HTML documents.

*Table 18-1: Predefined Entities*

| *Entity* | *Character* | *XML Declaration* |
|---|---|---|
| < | < | <!ENTITY lt "<"> |
| > | > | <!ENTITY gt ">"> |
| & | & | <!ENTITY amp "&"> |
| ' | ' | <!ENTITY apos "'"> |
| " | " | <!ENTITY quot """> |

Though the parser must recognize these entities whether or not they have been declared, you can declare them in your DTD without generating errors.

The presence of these "special" predefined entities creates a conundrum within an XML document. Because it is possible to use these references without declaring them, it is possible to have a valid XML document that includes references to entities that were never declared. The XML specification actually encourages document authors to declare these entities to maintain the integrity of the entity declaration-reference rule. In practical terms, declaring these entities only adds unnecessary complexity to your document.

## *CDATA (Character Data) Sections*

XML documents consist of markup and character data. The < or & characters cannot be included inside normal character data without using a character or entity reference, such as & or &. Using a reference, the resulting < and & characters are not be recognized as markup by the parser, but will become part of the datastream to the parser's client application.

For large blocks of character data, particularly if the data contains markup, such as an HTML or XML fragment, the CDATA section can be used. Within a CDATA block, every character between the opening and closing tag is considered character data. Thus, special characters can be included in a CDATA section with impunity, except for the CDATA closing sequence ]]>. If you must include large sections of text with characters that might be mistaken for markup, you should use the CDATA section. For example:

```
<![CDATA[unescaped character & markup data]]>
```

CDATA blocks cannot be nested. The character sequence `]]>` cannot appear within data that is being escaped or the CDATA block will be closed prematurely. This situation should not be a problem ordinarily, but if your application includes XML documents as unparsed character data, you should be aware of this constraint. If you need to include the CDATA closing sequence in your data, close the open CDATA section, include the closing characters using character references to escape them, then reopen the CDATA section to contain the rest of the character data.

## *Entity References*

An XML entity can be best understood as a macro replacement facility, in which the replacement can either be parsed (the text becomes part of the XML document) or unparsed. If unparsed, the entity declaration points to external binary data that cannot be parsed. Additionally, the replacement text for parsed entities can come from a string or the contents of an external file. During parsing, a parsed entity reference is replaced by the substitution text that is specified in the entity declaration. The replacement text is then reparsed until no more entity or character references remain.

To simplify document parsing, two distinct types of entities are used in different situations: general and parameter. The basic syntax for referencing both entity types is almost identical, but specific rules apply to where each type can be used.

### Parameter entities

*Syntax*

```
%entity_name;
```

*Description*

Parameter entities are recognized only within the DTD, and can be used to help organize complex documents. Within the document's body, the `%` character has no significance and does not need to be escaped.

### General entities

*Syntax*

```
&entity_name;
```

*Description*

General entities are recognized and replaced only within XML character data, not within the DTD.

Entity references are not recognized within CDATA blocks. If you want the XML parser to expand your entity reference, then include the reference outside the CDATA block.

## Comments

### Syntax

```
<!-- comment text -->
```

### Description

Comments can appear anywhere in your document or DTD, outside of other markup tags. XML parsers are not required to preserve contents of comment blocks, so they should be used only to store information that is not a part of your application. In reality, most information you might consider storing in a comment block probably should be made an official part of your XML application. Rather than storing data that will be read and acted on by an application in a comment, as is frequently done within HTML documents, you should store it within the element structure of the actual XML document. Enhancing the readability of a complex DTD or temporarily disabling blocks of markup are effective uses of comments.

*Comment Block Exception*

The character sequence `--` cannot be included within a comment block, except as part of the tag closing text. Because comments cannot be nested, commenting out a comment block is impossible. If you habitually comment out unused parts of your document during development, be aware of this common problem.

## Processing Instructions

### Syntax

```
<?target[ processing-instruction data]?>
```

### Description

Processing instructions provide an escape hatch that allows an XML application to include instructions that are not part of the XML markup or character data. The processing instruction target can be any legal XML name, except <mono>xml</mono> in any combination of upper and lower case (see Chapter 2, *XML Fundamentals*). Linking to a stylesheet to provide formatting instructions for a document is a common use of this mechanism. According to the principles of XML, formatting instructions should remain separate from the actual content of a document, but some mechanism must associate the two. Processing instructions are significant only to applications that recognize them.

The notation facility is used to indicate exactly what type of processing instruction is included, and each individual XML application must decide what to do with the additional data. No action is required by an XML parser when it recognizes that a particular processing instruction matches a declared notation. Applications that do not recognize the public or system identifiers of a given processing instruction should realize that they could not properly interpret the data portion of a processing instruction.

## *XML Declaration*

### *Syntax*

```
<?xml version="1.0"[ encoding="encoding-name"][ standalone="yes|no"]?>
```

### *Description*

The XML declaration serves several purposes: telling the parser what version of the specification was used, how the document is encoded, and whether or not the document is completely self-contained or has references to external entities.

The XML declaration, if included, must be the first thing that appears in your XML document. Nothing, except possibly a Unicode byte-order mark, can appear before this structure's initial < character.

> ### *Character Encoding Auto-Detection*
>
> The XML declaration must be the very first item in your document so the XML parser can determine which character encoding you used to store your document. A chicken-and-egg problem exists, involving the XML declaration's `encoding="..."` clause: the parser can't parse the clause if it doesn't know what character encoding your document uses. However, since the first five characters of your document must be the string `<?xml`, the parser can read the first few bytes of your document and, in most cases, determine the character encoding without reading the `encoding` declaration.

### Version information

#### *Syntax*

```
... version="1.0" ...
```

#### *Description*

The version information attribute indicates which version of the XML specification the document conforms to. Currently this string must always equal `"1.0"`.

### Encoding declaration

#### *Syntax*

```
... encoding="encoding-name" ...
```

*Description*

The encoding declaration indicates which character-encoding scheme was used to store the document. Although all XML documents are ultimately handled as Unicode by the parser, the external storage scheme may be anything from an ASCII text file using the Latin-1 character set (ISO-8859-1) to a file with native Japanese characters.

XML parsers may also recognize other encodings, but the XML specification only requires that they recognize UTF-8 and UTF-16 encoded documents. Check the documentation for your parser implementation of choice to see if it supports additional encodings beyond the defaults. For a thorough discussion of character-encoding schemes, see Chapter 23, *Character Sets*.

### Standalone declaration

*Syntax*

```
... standalone="yes|no" ...
```

*Description*

If your document is completely self contained (the DTD, if there is one, is contained completely within the original document), then the `standalone="yes"` declaration can be used. If this declaration is not given, the value no is assumed, and all external entities are read and parsed. It is possible to convert any document in which `standalone="no"` to a standalone document by replacing each external entity reference with the text contained in the external entity file. This replacement would be particularly useful if an XML document were to be transmitted across a network or to some secondary storage device where having a self-contained copy of the document would be more convenient.

From the standpoint of an XML application developer, this flag has no effect on how your document is parsed. If it is given, it must be accurate. Setting `standalone="yes"` when your document does require DTD declarations that are not present in the main document file is a violation of XML validity rules.

# *DTD (Document Type Definition)*

Chapter 2 explained the difference between well-formed and valid documents. Well-formed documents that include and conform to a given DTD are considered valid. Documents that include a DTD and violate the rules of that DTD are invalid. The DTD is comprised of the `<!DOCTYPE` declaration and both the internal subset (declarations contained directly within the document) and the external subset (declarations that are included from outside the main document).

## *Parameter Entities*

Parameter entities provide a method to reference and/or change commonly used constructs within the DTD. They are intended to support the replacement of commonly used DTD expressions with a single reference. The replacement text's source can be either a literal string or the contents of an external file. Parameter entities simplify maintenance of large, complex documents by allowing authors to build libraries of commonly used entity declarations.

### Parameter entity declarations

*Syntax*

```
<!ENTITY % name "Replacement text.">
<!ENTITY % name SYSTEM
    "http://www.oreilly.com/catalog/xmlnut/    examples/sample.ent">
<!ENTITY % name PUBLIC "-//OREILLY//XML IN A NUTSHELL//EN"
    "sample.ent">
```

*Description*

Parameter entities are declared within the document's DTD and must be declared before they are used. The declaration provides two key pieces of information:

— The name of the entity, which is used when it is referenced

— The replacement text, either directly or indirectly through a link to an external entity

Be aware that an XML parser performs some preprocessing on the replacement text before it is used in an entity reference. Most importantly, parameter entity references in the replacement text are themselves expanded recursively before the final version of the replacement text is stored. Character references are also replaced immediately with the specified character. This replacement can lead to unexpected side effects, particularly when constructing parameter entities that declare other parameter entities. For full disclosure of how entity replacement is implemented by an XML parser, and what kinds of unexpected side effects can occur, see Appendix D of the XML 1.0 specification.

### Parameter entity references

*Syntax*

```
%name;
```

*Description*

When an XML parser encounters a parameter entity reference within your document's DTD, it replaces the reference with the entity's text. Whether the replacement text is included as a literal or included from an external entity, the parser then continues parsing the replacement text as if it had always been a part of the document. This parsing has interesting implications for nested entity references:

```
<!ENTITY % YEAR "2001">
<!ENTITY COPYRIGHT "&#xa9; %YEAR;">
. . .
<copyright_notice>&COPYRIGHT;</copyright_notice>
```

After the necessary entity replacements are made, the previous example would yield the following canonical element:

```
<copyright_notice>© 2001</copyright_notice>
```

*Entity Reference Locations*

XML treats parameter entity references differently, depending on where they appear within the DTD. References within the literal value of an entity declaration (such as `Copyright © %YEAR;`) are valid only as part of the external subset. Within the internal subset, parameter entity references may occur only where a complete markup declaration could exist; within the internal subset, parameter references can be used only to include markup declarations.

Parameter entity references are recognized only within the DTD; therefore, the `%` character has no significance within character data and does not need to be escaped.

## General Entities

General entities are declared within the document type definition, then referenced within the document's text and attribute content. When the document is parsed, the entity's replacement text is substituted for the entity reference. The parser then resumes parsing, starting with the text that was just replaced.

### General entity declarations

General entities are declared within the DTD, using a superset of the syntax used to declare parameter entities. Besides the ability to declare internal parsed entities and external parsed entities, you can declare external unparsed entities and associate an XML notation name with them:

```
<!ENTITY name "Replacement text.">
<!ENTITY name SYSTEM
    "http://www.oreilly.com/catalog/xmlnut/examples/sample.ent">
<!ENTITY name PUBLIC
    "-//OREILLY//XML IN A NUTSHELL//EN" "sample.ent">
<!ENTITY name SYSTEM
    "http://www.oreilly.com/catalog/covers/xmlnut.s.gif" NDATA GIF>
<!ENTITY name PUBLIC "-//OREILLY//XML IN A NUTSHELL//EN"
    "xmlnut.s.gif" NDATA GIF>
```

### Internal general entities

Internal entities are used when the replacement text can be stored efficiently inline as a literal string. The replacement text within an internal entity is included completely in the entity declaration itself, obviating the need for an external file to contain the replacement text. This situation closely resembles the string replacement macro facilities found in many popular programming languages and environments.

### External general entities

There are two types of external entities: parsed and unparsed. When a parsed entity is referenced, the contents of the external entity are included in the document and the XML parser resumes parsing, starting with the newly included text. When an unparsed entity is referenced, the parser supplies the application with the unparsed entity's URI, but does not insert that data into the document or parse it. What to do with that URI is up to the application. Any entity declared with an XML notation name associated with it is an external unparsed entity, and any references to it within the document must be attribute values.

When creating files that contain external parsed entities, you must include a text declaration if the entity file uses a character encoding other than UTF-8 or UTF-16:

```
<?xml[ version="1.0"] encoding="encoding-name"?>
```

This declaration would be followed by the replacement text of the external parsed entity.

---

*Entity Restrictions*

External parsed entities may contain only document content or a completely well-formed subset of the DTD. This restriction is significant because it indicates that external parameter entities cannot be used to play token-pasting games by splitting XML syntax constructs into multiple files, then expecting the parser to reassemble them.

---

### General Entity References

General entity references are recognized only within the content of an XML document, using the following syntax:

```
&name;
```

---

*Recursive Entity Expansion*

The sequence of operations that occurs when a parsed general entity is included by the XML parser can lead to interesting side effects. Remember that the entity's replacement text is, in turn, read by the parser; if character or general entity replacements exist in the entity replacement text, they are also parsed and included as parsing continues. Though this recursive entity expansion can be exploited to create very unclear XML, it is best to design your XML application to remove dependencies on this effect.

---

## Unparsed Entities

It is necessary at times to include data in your XML document that should not be parsed. For instance, your XML document may need to include pointers to graphics files that will be used by an application. These files are logically part of the document, but should not be parsed. The XML language allows you to declare external unparsed entities that can be included as attribute values within the content of your document.

To include unparsed entities, you must first declare a notation that will be referenced in the actual entity declaration:

```
<!NOTATION gif SYSTEM "images/gif">
```

Then declaring the entity itself is possible:

```
<!ENTITY bookcase_pic SYSTEM "bookcase.gif" NDATA gif>
```

As an unparsed general entity, it can be referenced only as an attribute value:

```
<picture src="bookcase_pic"/>
```

When an XML parser parses this element, the information contained in the entity and notation declarations can be used to identify the actual type of data stored in the external entity; a program could choose to display a GIF entity on the screen, once the actual format is known.

## External Subset

The document type declaration can include part or all of the document type definition from at least one external file. This external portion of the DTD is referred to as the external DTD subset. Each piece of the external DTD subset may contain markup declarations, conditional sections, and parameter entity references. As an external parsed entity, it must include a text declaration if the character encoding is not UTF-8 or UTF-16:

```
<?xml [ version="1.0"] encoding="encoding-name"?>
```

This declaration is then followed by a series of complete DTD markup statements, including `<!ELEMENT`, `<!ATTLIST`, `<!ENTITY`, `<!NOTATION`, conditional sections, and processing instructions:

```
<?xml version="1.0"?>
<!ELEMENT furniture_item (desc, %extra_tags; user_tags?, parts_list,
assembly+)>

<!ATTLIST furniture_item
    xmlns CDATA #FIXED "http://namespaces.oreilly.com/furniture/"
>
...
```

## Internal DTD Subset

The internal DTD subset is the portion of the document type definition included directly within the document type declaration between the `[` and `]` characters. The internal DTD subset can contain markup declarations and parameter entity references, but not conditional sections. A single document may have both internal and external DTD subsets, which, taken together, form the complete document type definition. The following example shows the internal subset, which appears between the `[` and `]` characters:

```
<!DOCTYPE furniture_item SYSTEM "furniture.dtd"
[
<!ENTITY % bookcase_ex SYSTEM "Bookcase_ex.ent">

%bookcase_ex;

<!ENTITY bookcase_pic SYSTEM "bookcase.gif" NDATA gif>
]>
```

## *Element Type Declaration*

Element type declarations provide a template for the actual element instances that appear within an XML document. This declaration determines what type of content, if any, can be contained within elements with the given name. The following sections describe the various element content options available.

### Empty element type

*Syntax*

```
<!ELEMENT name EMPTY>
```

*Description*

Elements that are declared to be empty cannot contain content or nested elements. Within the document, empty elements use one of the following two syntax forms:

```
<name/>
<name></name>
```

### Any element type

*Syntax*

```
<!ELEMENT name ANY>
```

*Description*

This content specifier acts as a wildcard, allowing elements of this type to contain character data or instances of valid element types that are declared in the DTD.

### Mixed content element type

*Syntax*

```
<!ELEMENT name (#PCDATA [ | name]+)>
```

*Description*

Element declarations that include the `#PCDATA` token can include text content mixed with other nested elements that are declared in the optional portion of the element declaration. If the `#PCDATA` token is used, it is not possible to limit the number of times or sequence in which other nested elements are mixed with the parsed character data.

## Constrained child nodes

*Syntax*

```
<!ELEMENT name (child_node_regexp)['?' | '*' | '+']>
```

*Description*

XML provides a simple regular expression syntax that can be used to limit the order and number of occurrences of child elements within a parent element. This language includes the following operators:

| *Operator* | *Meaning* |
|---|---|
| Name | Matches an element of the given name |
| ( ... ) | Evaluates the expression within the parentheses first |
| ? | Indicates that the preceding name or expression can occur zero or one times at this point in the document |
| * | Indicates that the preceding name or expression can occur zero or more times at this point in the document |
| + | Indicates that the preceding name or expression must occur one or more times at this point in the document |

## Attribute list declaration

*Syntax*

```
<!ATTLIST element_name [attribute_name attribute_type default_decl]*>
```

*Description*

In a valid XML document you must declare the attribute names, types, and default values that are used with each element type.

The element name must match an element that was declared using the `<!ELEMENT` declaration syntax. The attribute name must obey the rules for XML identifiers, and no duplicate attribute names may exist within a single declaration.

## Simple attribute types

The following simple attribute types determine what types of values may be assigned to the declared attributes within the document's body. Including the specified keyword in proper position of the attribute type declaration specifies the type. The following table lists the various attribute types and their meanings:

| *Attribute Type* | *Meaning* |
|---|---|
| CDATA | Simple character data. |
| ID | A unique `ID` value within the current XML document. No two `ID` attribute values within a document can have the same value. |
| IDREF, IDREFS | A single reference to an element `ID`, `IDREF`, or a list of `ID`s, `IDREFS`, separated by spaces. Every `ID` token must refer to a valid `ID` located somewhere within the document that appears as the `ID` type attribute's value. |

| *Attribute Type* | *Meaning* |
|---|---|
| ENTITY, ENTITIES | A single reference to a declared unparsed external entity, ENTITY, or a list of references, ENTITIES, separated by spaces. |
| NMTOKEN, NMTOKENS | A single name token value, NMTOKEN, or a list of name tokens, NMTOKENS, separated by spaces. |

## NOTATION attribute type

### *Syntax*

... **NOTATION (***notation [| notation]****) ...

### *Description*

The notation attribute mechanism is provided to allow XML document authors to indicate that the character content of some elements obey the rules of some formal language other than XML. The following short example document shows how notations might be used to specify the type of programming language stored in the code_fragment element:

```
<?xml version="1.0"?>
<!DOCTYPE code_fragment
[
<!NOTATION java_code PUBLIC "Java source code">
<!NOTATION c_code PUBLIC "C source code">
<!NOTATION perl_code PUBLIC "Perl source code">
<!ELEMENT code_fragment (#PCDATA)>
<!ATTLIST code_fragment
          code_lang NOTATION (java_code | c_code | perl_code)
#REQUIRED>

]>
<code_fragment code_lang="c_code">
    main() { printf("Hello, world."); }
</code_fragment>
```

## Enumeration attribute type

### *Syntax*

... **(***name_token [| name_token]****) ...

### *Description*

This syntax limits the possible values of the given attribute to one of the name tokens from the provided list:

```
<!ELEMENT door EMPTY>
<!ATTLIST door
          state (open | closed | missing) "open">
. . .
<door state="closed"/>
```

## Default values

You may also include a default value within the attribute type declaration that will be provided to the XML parser for every element that doesn't include an explicit value for the given attribute. The following table shows various forms of the attribute default value clause and their meanings:

| *Default Value Clause* | *Explanation* |
|---|---|
| #REQUIRED | A value must be provided for this attribute. |
| #IMPLIED | A value may or may not be provided for this attribute. |
| [#FIXED ] "*default value*" | If this attribute has no explicit value, the XML parser substitutes the given default value. If the `#FIXED` token is provided, this attribute's value must match the given default value. In either case, the parent element always has an attribute with this name. |

The `#FIXED` modifier indicates that the attribute may contain only the value given in the attribute declaration. Although it is completely redundant, including an explicit attribute and value in an element is legal, even when the attribute was declared as `#FIXED`. The only restriction is that the attribute value must match the default value given in the `#FIXED` declaration exactly.

### Special attributes

Some attributes are significant to XML and must be declared and implemented in a particular way.

**`xml:space`**

The `xml:space` attribute indicates to an XML application whether or not the whitespace within the specified element is significant:

```
<!ATTLIST element_name xml:space (default|preserve)
  default_decl>
<!ATTLIST element_name xml:space (default) #FIXED 'default' >
<!ATTLIST element_name xml:space (preserve) #FIXED 'preserve' >
```

**`xml:lang`**

For an element's character content, the `xml:lang` attribute allows a document author to specify the human language for an element's character content. If used in a valid XML document, the document type definition must include an attribute type declaration that includes the `xml:lang` attribute name. See Chapter 5, *Internationalization*, for an explanation of language support in XML.

## *Notation Declaration*

### *Syntax*

```
<!NOTATION notation_name SYSTEM "system-literal">
<!NOTATION notation_name PUBLIC "pubid-literal">
<!NOTATION notation_name PUBLIC "pubid-literal" "system-literal">
```

### *Description*

Notation declarations are used to provide information to an XML application about the format of the document's unparsed content. Notations are used by unparsed external entities, processing instructions, and some attribute values.

Notation information serves no purpose within the XML document, but is preserved by the XML parser for use by the client application. The public and system identifiers are available to the parser client application so that it may correctly interpret non-XML data and processing instructions.

## *Conditional Sections*

The conditional section markup provides support for conditionally including and excluding content at parse time within an XML document's external subset. Conditional sections are not allowed within a document's internal subset. The following example illustrates a likely application of conditional sections:

```
<!ENTITY % debug 'IGNORE' >
<!ENTITY % release 'INCLUDE' >

<!ELEMENT addend (#PCDATA)>
<!ELEMENT result (#PCDATA)>

<![%debug;[
<!ELEMENT sum (addend+, result)>
]]>
<![%release;[
<!ELEMENT sum (result)>
]]>
```

# *Document Body*

Elements are an XML document's lifeblood. They provide the structure for character data and attribute values that make up a particular instance of an XML document type definition. The `<!ELEMENT` and `<!ATTLIST` declarations from the DTD restrict the possible contents of an element within a valid XML document. Combining elements and/or attributes that violate these restrictions generates an error in a validating parser.

## *Start Tags and End Tags*

### *Syntax*

```
<element_name [attribute_name="attribute value"]*> …</element_name>
```

### *Description*

Elements that are allowed to have content (either character data, other elements, or both) must start with an element start tag and end with an element end tag.

## *Empty-Element Tags*

### *Syntax*

```
<empty_element></empty_element>
<element_name [attribute_name="attribute value"]*/>
```

### Description

Empty elements have no content, and are written using either the start and end tag syntax mentioned previously, or are written using the empty-element syntax. The two forms are functionally identical, but the empty element syntax is more succinct and more frequently used.

---

## Attributes

### Syntax

```
attribute_name="attribute value"
attribute_name='attribute value'
```

### Description

Elements may include attributes. The order of attributes within an element tag is not significant. Attribute values must appear within either single or double quotations. Attribute values within a document must conform to the rules explained in the "Well-Formedness" section of this chapter.

Note that whitespace may appear around the = character.

The value that appears in the quoted string is tested for validity, depending on the attribute type provided in the `<!ATTLIST` declaration for the element type. Attribute values can contain general entity references, but cannot contain references to external parsed entities. See the "Well-Formedness" section of this chapter for more information about attribute value restrictions.

# XML Document Grammar

The Extended Backus-Naur Form (EBNF) grammar, shown in Example 18-1, was collected from the XML 1.0 Recommendation, Second Edition. It brings all XML language productions together in a single location, and describes the syntax that is understood by XML-1.0-compliant parsers.

*Example 18-1: Extended Backus-Naur Form (EBNF) Grammar*

```
document ::= prolog element Misc*
Char ::= #x9 | #xA | #xD | [#x20-#xD7FF] | [#xE000-#xFFFD]
    | [#x10000-#x10FFFF]
S ::= (#x20 | #x9 | #xD | #xA)+
NameChar ::= Letter | Digit| '.' | '-' | '_' | ':'
    | CombiningChar | Extender
EntityValue ::= '"' ([^%&"] | PEReference| Reference)* '"'
    |  "'" ([^%&'] | PEReference | Reference)* "'"
CharData ::= [^<&]* - ([^<&]* ']]>' [^<&]*)
Comment ::= '<!--' ((Char - '-') | ('-'(Char - '-')))* '-->'
PI ::= '<?' PITarget (S(Char* - (Char* '?>' Char*)))? '?>'
CDSect ::= CDStart CData CDEnd
prolog ::= XMLDecl? Misc*(doctypedecl Misc*)?
XMLDecl ::= '<?xml' VersionInfo EncodingDecl? SDDecl? S? '?>'
VersionInfo ::= S 'version' Eq ("'" VersionNum "'"
    | '"' VersionNum'"')[E15]
```

```
Eq ::= S? '=' S?
VersionNum ::= ([a-zA-Z0-9_.:] | '-')+
Misc ::= Comment | PI| S
doctypedecl ::= '<!DOCTYPE' S Name(S ExternalID)? S?
   ('[' (markupdecl | DeclSep)*']' S?)? '>'
DeclSep ::= PEReference | S
markupdecl ::= elementdecl | AttlistDecl | EntityDecl
   | NotationDecl | PI | Comment
extSubset ::= TextDecl? extSubsetDecl
extSubsetDecl ::= ( markupdecl | conditionalSect | DeclSep)*
SDDecl ::= S 'standalone' Eq(("'" ('yes' | 'no') "'")
   | ('"' ('yes' | 'no') '"'))
LanguageID ::= Langcode ('-' Subcode)*
element ::= EmptyElemTag| STag content ETag
STag ::= '<' Name (S Attribute)* S? '>'
Attribute ::= Name Eq AttValue
ETag ::= '</' Name S?'>'
content ::= CharData? ((element| Reference | CDSect| PI | Comment)
   CharData?)*
EmptyElemTag ::= '<' Name (S Attribute)* S? '/>'
elementdecl ::= '<!ELEMENT' S Name S contentspec S?'>'
contentspec ::= 'EMPTY' | 'ANY' | Mixed| children
children ::= (choice | seq)('?' | '*' | '+')?
cp ::= (Name | choice| seq) ('?' | '*' | '+')?
choice ::= '(' S? cp ( S? '|' S? cp )+ S? ')'
seq ::= '(' S? cp ( S? ',' S? cp )* S? ')'
Mixed ::= '(' S? '#PCDATA' (S?'|' S? Name)* S?')*'
   | '(' S? '#PCDATA' S? ')'
AttlistDecl ::= '<!ATTLIST' S Name AttDef* S? '>'
AttType ::= StringType | TokenizedType| EnumeratedType
StringType ::= 'CDATA'
TokenizedType ::= 'ID'
EnumeratedType ::= NotationType| Enumeration
DefaultDecl ::= '#REQUIRED' | '#IMPLIED'| (('#FIXED' S)? AttValue)
conditionalSect ::= includeSect | ignoreSect
includeSect ::= '<![' S? 'INCLUDE' S? '[' extSubsetDecl']]>'
ignoreSect ::= '<![' S? 'IGNORE' S? '[' ignoreSectContents*']]>'
ignoreSectContents ::= Ignore ('<![' ignoreSectContents ']]>' Ignore)*
Ignore ::= Char* - (Char*('<![' | ']]>') Char*)
CharRef ::= '&#' [0-9]+ ';' | '&#x' [0-9a-fA-F]+ ';'
Reference ::= EntityRef | CharRef
EntityDecl ::= GEDecl | PEDecl
GEDecl ::= '<!ENTITY' S Name S EntityDef S?'>'
PEDecl ::= '<!ENTITY' S '%' S Name S PEDef S? '>'
EntityDef ::= EntityValue | (ExternalID NDataDecl?)
PEDef ::= EntityValue | ExternalID
ExternalID ::= 'SYSTEM' S SystemLiteral| 'PUBLIC' S PubidLiteral
   S SystemLiteral
TextDecl ::= '<?xml' VersionInfo? EncodingDecl S? '?>'
extParsedEnt ::= TextDecl? content
EncodingDecl ::= S 'encoding' Eq('"' EncName '"' | "'" EncName"'" )
NotationDecl ::= '<!NOTATION' S Name S (ExternalID | PublicID) S? '>'
Letter ::= BaseChar | Ideographic
```

*Example 18-1: Extended Backus-Naur Form (EBNF) Grammar (continued)*

```
BaseChar ::= [#x0041-#x005A] | [#x0061-#x007A] | [#x00C0-#x00D6]
    | [#x00D8-#x00F6] | [#x00F8-#x00FF] | [#x0100-#x0131] | [#x0134-#x013E]
    | [#x0141-#x0148] | [#x014A-#x017E] | [#x0180-#x01C3] | [#x01CD-#x01F0]
    | [#x01F4-#x01F5] | [#x01FA-#x0217] | [#x0250-#x02A8] | [#x02BB-#x02C1]
    | #x0386 | [#x0388-#x038A] | #x038C | [#x038E-#x03A1] | [#x03A3-#x03CE]
    | [#x03D0-#x03D6] | #x03DA | #x03DC| #x03DE | #x03E0 | [#x03E2-#x03F3]
    | [#x0401-#x040C] | [#x040E-#x044F] | [#x0451-#x045C] | [#x045E-#x0481]
    | [#x0490-#x04C4] | [#x04C7-#x04C8] | [#x04CB-#x04CC] | [#x04D0-#x04EB]
    | [#x04EE-#x04F5] | [#x04F8-#x04F9] | [#x0531-#x0556] | #x0559
    | [#x0561-#x0586] | [#x05D0-#x05EA] | [#x05F0-#x05F2] | [#x0621-#x063A]
    | [#x0641-#x064A] | [#x0671-#x06B7] | [#x06BA-#x06BE] | [#x06C0-#x06CE]
    | [#x06D0-#x06D3] | #x06D5 | [#x06E5-#x06E6] | [#x0905-#x0939] | #x093D
    | [#x0958-#x0961] | [#x0985-#x098C] | [#x098F-#x0990] | [#x0993-#x09A8]
    | [#x09AA-#x09B0] | #x09B2 | [#x09B6-#x09B9] | [#x09DC-#x09DD]
    | [#x09DF-#x09E1] | [#x09F0-#x09F1] | [#x0A05-#x0A0A] | [#x0A0F-#x0A10]
    | [#x0A13-#x0A28] | [#x0A2A-#x0A30] | [#x0A32-#x0A33] | [#x0A35-#x0A36]
    | [#x0A38-#x0A39] | [#x0A59-#x0A5C] | #x0A5E | [#x0A72-#x0A74]
    | [#x0A85-#x0A8B] | #x0A8D | [#x0A8F-#x0A91] | [#x0A93-#x0AA8]
    | [#x0AAA-#x0AB0] | [#x0AB2-#x0AB3] | [#x0AB5-#x0AB9] | #x0ABD
    | #x0AE0 | [#x0B05-#x0B0C] | [#x0B0F-#x0B10] | [#x0B13-#x0B28]
    | [#x0B2A-#x0B30] | [#x0B32-#x0B33] | [#x0B36-#x0B39] | #x0B3D
    | [#x0B5C-#x0B5D] | [#x0B5F-#x0B61] | [#x0B85-#x0B8A] | [#x0B8E-#x0B90]
    | [#x0B92-#x0B95] | [#x0B99-#x0B9A] | #x0B9C | [#x0B9E-#x0B9F]
    | [#x0BA3-#x0BA4] | [#x0BA8-#x0BAA] | [#x0BAE-#x0BB5] | [#x0BB7-#x0BB9]
    | [#x0C05-#x0C0C] | [#x0C0E-#x0C10] | [#x0C12-#x0C28] | [#x0C2A-#x0C33]
    | [#x0C35-#x0C39] | [#x0C60-#x0C61] | [#x0C85-#x0C8C] | [#x0C8E-#x0C90]
    | [#x0C92-#x0CA8] | [#x0CAA-#x0CB3] | [#x0CB5-#x0CB9] | #x0CDE
    | [#x0CE0-#x0CE1] | [#x0D05-#x0D0C] | [#x0D0E-#x0D10] | [#x0D12-#x0D28]
    | [#x0D2A-#x0D39] | [#x0D60-#x0D61] | [#x0E01-#x0E2E] | #x0E30
    | [#x0E32-#x0E33] | [#x0E40-#x0E45] | [#x0E81-#x0E82] | #x0E84
    | [#x0E87-#x0E88] | #x0E8A | #x0E8D | [#x0E94-#x0E97] | [#x0E99-#x0E9F]
    | [#x0EA1-#x0EA3] | #x0EA5 | #x0EA7| [#x0EAA-#x0EAB] | [#x0EAD-#x0EAE]
    | #x0EB0 | [#x0EB2-#x0EB3] | #x0EBD | [#x0EC0-#x0EC4] | [#x0F40-#x0F47]
    | [#x0F49-#x0F69] | [#x10A0-#x10C5] | [#x10D0-#x10F6] | #x1100
    | [#x1102-#x1103] | [#x1105-#x1107] | #x1109 | [#x110B-#x110C]
    | [#x110E-#x1112] | #x113C | #x113E | #x1140 | #x114C | #x114E | #x1150
    | [#x1154-#x1155] | #x1159 | [#x115F-#x1161] | #x1163| #x1165 | #x1167
    | #x1169 | [#x116D-#x116E] | [#x1172-#x1173] | #x1175 | #x119E | #x11A8
    | #x11AB | [#x11AE-#x11AF] | [#x11B7-#x11B8] | #x11BA | [#x11BC-#x11C2]
    | #x11EB| #x11F0 | #x11F9 | [#x1E00-#x1E9B] | [#x1EA0-#x1EF9]
    | [#x1F00-#x1F15] | [#x1F18-#x1F1D] | [#x1F20-#x1F45] | [#x1F48-#x1F4D]
    | [#x1F50-#x1F57] | #x1F59 | #x1F5B | #x1F5D | [#x1F5F-#x1F7D]
    | [#x1F80-#x1FB4] | [#x1FB6-#x1FBC] | #x1FBE | [#x1FC2-#x1FC4]
    | [#x1FC6-#x1FCC] | [#x1FD0-#x1FD3] | [#x1FD6-#x1FDB] | [#x1FE0-#x1FEC]
    | [#x1FF2-#x1FF4] | [#x1FF6-#x1FFC] | #x2126 | [#x212A-#x212B]
    | #x212E | [#x2180-#x2182] | [#x3041-#x3094] | [#x30A1-#x30FA]
    | [#x3105-#x312C] | [#xAC00-#xD7A3]
Ideographic ::= [#x4E00-#x9FA5] | #x3007 | [#x3021-#x3029]
```

*Example 18-1: Extended Backus-Naur Form (EBNF) Grammar (continued)*

```
CombiningChar ::= [#x0300-#x0345] | [#x0360-#x0361] | [#x0483-#x0486]
    | [#x0591-#x05A1] | [#x05A3-#x05B9] | [#x05BB-#x05BD] | #x05BF
    | [#x05C1-#x05C2] | #x05C4 | [#x064B-#x0652] | #x0670| [#x06D6-#x06DC]
    | [#x06DD-#x06DF] | [#x06E0-#x06E4] | [#x06E7-#x06E8] | [#x06EA-#x06ED]
    | [#x0901-#x0903] | #x093C | [#x093E-#x094C] | #x094D | [#x0951-#x0954]
    | [#x0962-#x0963] | [#x0981-#x0983] | #x09BC | #x09BE | #x09BF
    | [#x09C0-#x09C4] | [#x09C7-#x09C8] | [#x09CB-#x09CD] | #x09D7
    | [#x09E2-#x09E3] | #x0A02| #x0A3C | #x0A3E | #x0A3F | [#x0A40-#x0A42]
    | [#x0A47-#x0A48] | [#x0A4B-#x0A4D] | [#x0A70-#x0A71] | [#x0A81-#x0A83]
    | #x0ABC| [#x0ABE-#x0AC5] | [#x0AC7-#x0AC9] | [#x0ACB-#x0ACD]
    | [#x0B01-#x0B03] | #x0B3C | [#x0B3E-#x0B43] | [#x0B47-#x0B48]
    | [#x0B4B-#x0B4D] | [#x0B56-#x0B57] | [#x0B82-#x0B83] | [#x0BBE-#x0BC2]
    | [#x0BC6-#x0BC8] | [#x0BCA-#x0BCD] | #x0BD7 | [#x0C01-#x0C03]
    | [#x0C3E-#x0C44] | [#x0C46-#x0C48] | [#x0C4A-#x0C4D] | [#x0C55-#x0C56]
    | [#x0C82-#x0C83] | [#x0CBE-#x0CC4] | [#x0CC6-#x0CC8] | [#x0CCA-#x0CCD]
    | [#x0CD5-#x0CD6] | [#x0D02-#x0D03] | [#x0D3E-#x0D43] | [#x0D46-#x0D48]
    | [#x0D4A-#x0D4D] | #x0D57 | #x0E31 | [#x0E34-#x0E3A] | [#x0E47-#x0E4E]
    | #x0EB1 | [#x0EB4-#x0EB9] | [#x0EBB-#x0EBC] | [#x0EC8-#x0ECD]
    | [#x0F18-#x0F19] | #x0F35 | #x0F37 | #x0F39 | #x0F3E| #x0F3F
    | [#x0F71-#x0F84] | [#x0F86-#x0F8B] | [#x0F90-#x0F95] | #x0F97
    | [#x0F99-#x0FAD] | [#x0FB1-#x0FB7] | #x0FB9| [#x20D0-#x20DC] | #x20E1
    | [#x302A-#x302F] | #x3099| #x309A
Digit ::= [#x0030-#x0039] | [#x0660-#x0669] | [#x06F0-#x06F9]
    | [#x0966-#x096F] | [#x09E6-#x09EF] | [#x0A66-#x0A6F] | [#x0AE6-#x0AEF]
    | [#x0B66-#x0B6F] | [#x0BE7-#x0BEF] | [#x0C66-#x0C6F] | [#x0CE6-#x0CEF]
    | [#x0D66-#x0D6F] | [#x0E50-#x0E59] | [#x0ED0-#x0ED9] | [#x0F20-#x0F29]
Extender ::= #x00B7 | #x02D0 | #x02D1 | #x0387 | #x0640| #x0E46 | #x0EC6
    | #x3005 | [#x3031-#x3035] | [#x309D-#x309E] | [#x30FC-#x30FE]
```

CHAPTER 19

# XPath Reference

XPath is a non-XML syntax used for expressions that identify particular nodes and groups of nodes in an XML document. It is used by both XPointer and XSLT, and by some proposals for a future XML Query Language.

## The XPath Data Model

XPath views each XML document as a tree of nodes. Each node has one of seven types:

*root*
: Each document has exactly one root node, which is the root of the tree. This node includes as children one comment node for each comment outside the document element, one processing instruction node for each processing instruction outside the document element, and exactly one element node for the document element. It does not contain any representation of the XML declaration or the document type declaration. The root node has no parent node. The root node's value is the value of the document element.

*element*
: An element node represents an element. It has a name, a namespace URI, a parent node, and a list of child nodes, which may include other element nodes, comment nodes, processing instruction nodes, and text nodes. An element also has a list of attributes and a list of in-scope namespaces, none of which are considered to be children of the element. The value of an element node is the complete, parsed text between the element's start and end tags that remains after all tags, comments, and processing instructions are removed.

*attribute*
: An attribute node represents an attribute. It has a name, a namespace URI, a value, and a parent element. However, although elements are parents of attributes, attributes are not children of their parent elements. The biological

metaphor breaks down here. `xmlns` and `xmlns:`*`prefix`* attributes are not represented as attribute nodes. An attribute node's value is the normalized attribute value.

*text*

Each text node represents a maximum possible contiguous run of text between tags, processing instructions, and comments. A text node has a parent node but does not have children. A text node's value is the text of the node.

*namespace*

A namespace node represents a namespace in scope on an element or attribute. In general, each namespace declaration by an `xmlns` or `xmlns:`*`prefix`* attribute produces multiple namespace nodes in the document tree. Like attribute nodes, each namespace node has a parent element but is not the child of that parent.

*processing instruction*

A processing instruction node represents a processing instruction. It has a target, data, a parent node, and no children.

*comment*

A comment node represents a comment. It has a parent node and no children.

The XML declaration and the document type declaration are not included in XPath's view of an XML document. All entity references, character references, and CDATA sections are resolved before the XPath tree is built. The references themselves are not included as a separate part of the tree.

## Datatype

Each XPath expression evaluates to one of four types:

*Boolean*

A binary value that is either true or false. In XPath, booleans are most commonly produced by using the comparison operators =, `!=`, <, >, <=, and >=. XPath does not offer boolean literals. However, the `true()` and `false()` functions fill that need.

*Number*

All numbers in XPath are IEEE 754-compliant, 64-bit floating-point numbers. This is the same as the `double` type in Java. Numbers range from 4.94065645841246544e-324d to 1.79769313486231570e+308d, and are either positive or negative. Numbers also include the special values `Inf` (positive infinity), `-Inf` (negative infinity), and `NaN` (not a number) used for the results of illegal operations, such as dividing by zero. XPath provides all the customary operators for working with numbers, including:

`+` Addition.

`-` Subtraction; however, this operator should always be surrounded by whitespace to avoid accidental misinterpretation as part of an XML name.

`*` Multiplication.

`div` Division.

`mod` Taking the remainder.

*String*

An XPath string is a sequence of zero or more Unicode characters. XPath does allow Unicode surrogate pairs in strings. String literals are enclosed in either single or double quotes, as convenient. Unlike Java, XPath does not allow strings to be concatenated with the plus sign. However, the `concat()` function serves this purpose.

*Node set*

A node set is a collection of zero or more nodes from an XML document. Location paths produce most node sets. Generally, a single node set can contain every kind of node: root, element, attribute, namespace, comment, processing instruction, and text. However, most node sets contain a single type of node.

Some standards that use XPath also define additional datatypes. For instance, XSLT defines a result tree fragment type that represents the string form of a node set that includes markup. XPointer defines a location set type that extends node sets to include points and ranges.

## Location Paths

Node sets are returned by location path expressions. Location paths consist of location steps. Each location step contains an axis and a node test separated by a double colon. That is, a location step looks like this:

```
axis::node-test
```

The axis specifies in which direction from the context node the processor searches for nodes. The node test specifies which nodes along that axis are selected. These are some location steps with different axes and node tests:

```
child::set
descendant-or-self::node()
ancestor-or-self::*
attribute::xlink:href
```

Each location step may be suffixed with one or more predicates enclosed in square brackets that further winnow the node set. For example:

```
child::set[position()=2]
descendant-or-self::node()[.='Eunice']
ancestor-or-self::*[position()=2][.="Celeste"]
attribute::xlink:href[starts-with('http')]
```

Each individual location step is itself a relative location path. The context node against which the relative location path is evaluated is established by some means external to XPath; for example, by the current matched node in an XSLT template.

Location steps can be combined by separating them with forward slashes. Each step in the resulting location path sets the context node (or nodes) for the next path in the step. For example:

```
ancestor-or-self::*/child::*[position()=1]
child::document/child::set[position()=2]/following-sibling::*
descendant::node()[.='Eunice']/attribute::ID
```

An absolute location path is formed by prefixing a forward slash to a relative location path. This sets the context node for the first step in the location path to the root of the document. For example, these are all absolute location paths:

```
/descendant::ship/ancestor-or-self::*/child::*[position()=1]
/child::document/child::set[position()=2]/following-sibling::*
/descendant::node()[.='Eunice']/attribute::ID
```

An abbreviated syntax is available for particularly common location paths. This is the syntax allowed in XSLT match patterns. In this syntax, the five axes use this shorthand:

`.` The current node

`..` The parent node

*`name`*
: The child element or elements with the specified name

*`/name`*
: The element or elements with the specified name that are descendants of the context node or the context node itself

`@`*`name`*
: The attribute of the context node with the specified name

Using the abbreviated syntax, these examples could be rewritten in the following manner:

```
/set
//node()
ancestor-or-self::*
@xlink:href
/set[position()=2]
//node()[.='Eunice']
ancestor-or-self::*[position()=2][.="Celeste"]
@xlink:href[starts-with('http')]
ancestor-or-self::*/*[position()=1]
/document/set[position()=2]/following-sibling::*
//descendantnode()[.='Eunice']/@ID
//ship/ancestor-or-self::*/*[position()=1]
```

Notice that not all location steps can be rewritten using the abbreviated syntax. In particular, only the child, self, attribute, descendant-or-self, and parent axes can be abbreviated. The remaining axes must be spelled out in full.

## Axes

Each XPath location step moves along an axis from a context node. The context node is a particular root, element, attribute, comment, processing instruction, namespace, or text node in the XML document. (In practice it's almost always an element node or the root node.) The context node may be a node selected by the previous location step in the location path, or it may be determined by extra-XPath rules, such as which node is matched by an `xsl:template` element.

However the context node is determined, it has some relationship to every other node in the document. The various axes divide the document into different, overlapping sets, depending on their relationship to the context node. There are exactly 13 axes you can use in an XPath location step:

`child`
: All children of the context node. This is the default axis, and can be omitted in an abbreviated location path. Only root and element nodes have children. Attribute and namespace nodes are not children of any node; though they do have parent nodes.

`descendant`
: All nodes contained inside the context node, that is, a child node, a child of a child node, a child of a child of a child node, and so on. Only root and element nodes have descendants. Like the `child` axis, the `descendant` axis never contains attribute or namespace nodes. This axis cannot be used in an abbreviated location path.

`descendant-or-self`
: Any descendant of the context node or the context node itself. This axis may be abbreviated as the forward slash `/` (which is always preceded by another forward slash representing the root node or separating this step from the previous step).

`parent`
: The element or root node that immediately contains the context node. Only the root node does not have a parent node. This axis may be written as the double period `..` in an abbreviated location path, but cannot be used in XSLT `match` attributes.

`ancestor`
: The root node and all element nodes that contain the context node. The root node itself has no ancestors. This axis cannot be used in an abbreviated location path.

`ancestor-or-self`
: All ancestors of the context node, as well as the node itself. This axis cannot be used in an abbreviated location path.

`following-sibling`
: All nodes that follow the end of the context node and have the same parent node. Attribute and namespace nodes do not have siblings. This axis cannot be used in an abbreviated location path.

`preceding-sibling`
: All nodes that precede the start of the context node and have the same parent node. Attribute and namespace nodes do not have siblings. This axis cannot be used in an abbreviated location path.

`following`
: All nodes that begin after the context node ends, except for attribute nodes and namespace nodes. This axis cannot be used in an abbreviated location path.

`preceding`
: All nodes that end before the context node begins, except for attribute nodes and namespace nodes. This axis cannot be used in an abbreviated location path.

`attribute`
: All attributes of the context node; the axis is empty if the context node is not an element node. This axis does not contain `xmlns` attributes used to declare namespaces. It may be abbreviated as `@` in abbreviated location paths.

`namespace`
: All namespaces in scope (not merely declared) on the context node; this axis is empty if the context node is not an element node.

`self`
: The context node itself. It may be abbreviated as a single period `.` in abbreviated location paths.

## *Node Tests*

Each location step has at least an axis and a node test. The node test further refines the nodes selected by the location step. A double colon `::` separates the axis from the node test. There are seven kinds of node tests:

*`name`*
: An XML name matches all elements with the same name. However, along the attribute axis it matches all attributes with the same name, instead. As usual, if the name is prefixed, only the URI the prefix is mapped to matters, not the prefix itself.

*`prefix`*`:*`
: Along the element axis, this node test matches all element nodes whose namespace URIs are the same as the namespace URI to which this prefix is mapped, regardless of name. Along the attribute axis, this node test matches all attribute nodes whose namespace URIs are the same as the namespace URI to which this prefix is mapped.

`comment()`
: All comment nodes.

`text()`
: All text nodes. Each text node is a maximum contiguous run of text between other types of nodes.

`processing-instruction()`
`processing-instruction('`*`target`*`')`
: With no arguments, this node test selects all processing instructions. With a single string argument `target`, it selects all processing instructions that have the specified target.

`node()`
: This node test selects all nodes, regardless of type: attribute, namespace, element, text, comment, processing instruction, and root.

`*`
: This test normally selects all element nodes, regardless of name. However, if the axis is the attribute axis, then it selects all attribute nodes. If the axis is the namespace axis, then it selects all namespace nodes.

## Predicates

Each location test may have zero or more *predicates*. A predicate is an XPath expression enclosed in square brackets that follows the node test in the location step. This expression most commonly, but not necessarily, returns a boolean value. In the following location path:

```
/person[position()=1]/profession[.="physicist"][position()<3]
```

`[position() 1]`, `[.="physicist"]`, and `[position()<3]` are predicates. An XPath processor works from left to right in an expression. After it has evaluated everything that precedes the predicate, it's left with a context node set that may contain no nodes, one node, or more than one node. The predicate is evaluated against each node in the context node set. If the expression returns true, then that node is retained in the set. If the expression returns false, then the node is removed from the set. If the expression returns a number, then the node being evaluated is left in the set if and only if the number is the same as the position of that node in the context node set. If the expression returns a non-boolean, non-number type, then that return value is converted to a boolean using the `boolean()` function described later to determine whether it retains the node in the set.

## XPath Functions

XPath 1.0 defines 27 built-in functions for use in XPath expressions. Various technologies that use XPath, such as XSLT and XPointer, also extend this list with functions they need. XSLT even allows user-defined extension functions.

Every function is evaluated in the context of a particular node list, generally given by the location step it's a part of. The higher level specification in which XPath is used, such as XSLT or XPointer, decides exactly how this context node list is determined. In some cases the function operates on the context node or the context node list. In other cases it operates on the argument, if present, and the context node, if no argument exists. The context node is ignored in other cases.

In the following sections, each function is described with at least one signature in this form:

```
return-type function-name(type argument, type argument, ...)
```

Compared to languages like Java, XPath argument lists are quite loose. Some XPath functions take a variable number of arguments, and fill in the arguments that are omitted with default values or the context node.

Furthermore, XPath is weakly typed. If you pass an argument of the wrong type to an XPath function, it generally converts that argument to the appropriate type using the `boolean()`, `string()`, or `number()` functions described later. The exceptions to the weak-typing rule are the functions that take a node set as an argument. Standard XSLT 1.0 provides no means of converting anything that isn't a node set into a node set. In some cases a function can operate equally well on multiple argument types. In this case, its type is given simply as `object`.

## *boolean()*

### *Signature*

```
boolean boolean(object o)
```

### *Description*

The `boolean()` function converts its argument to a boolean as follows:

- Zero and NaN are converted to false. All other numbers are converted to true.
- Empty node sets are converted to false. Nonempty node sets are converted to true.
- Empty strings are converted to false. Nonempty strings are converted to true.

## *ceiling()*

### *Signature*

```
number ceiling(number x)
number ceiling(object o)
```

### *Description*

The `ceiling()` function returns the smallest integer greater than or equal to `x`. For example, `ceiling(3.141592)` is 4. `ceiling(-3.141592)`is –3. Before the ceiling is calculated, non-number types are converted to numbers as if by the `number()` function.

## *concat()*

### *Signature*

```
string concat()
string concat(string s1)
string concat(string s1, string s2)
string concat(string s1, string s2, string s3)
...
```

### *Description*

This function concatenates its arguments in order from left to right and returns the combined string. It may take any number of arguments. Non-strings may be passed to this function as well, in which case they're converted to strings automatically as if by the `string()` function.

## *contains()*

### *Signature*

```
boolean contains(string s1, string s2)
boolean contains(object o1, object o2)
```

### Description

This function returns true if `s2` is a substring of `s1`; that is, if `s1` contains `s2`; false otherwise. For example, `contains("A very Charming cat", "Charm")` is true, but `contains("A very Charming cat", "Marjorie")` is false. The test is case sensitive. Nonstrings may also be passed to this function, in which case they're automatically converted to strings as if by the `string()` function.

---

## *count()*

### Signature

```
number count(node-set set)
```

### Description

The `count()` function returns the number of nodes in the argument node set; that is, the length of the set.

---

## *false()*

### Signature

```
boolean false()
```

### Description

The `false()` function always returns false. It makes up for the lack of boolean literals in XPath.

---

## *floor()*

### Signature

```
number floor(number x)
number floor(object o)
```

### Description

The `floor()` function returns the greatest integer less than or equal to `x`. For example, `floor(3.141592)` is 3. `floor(-3.141592)`is -4. Before their floor is calculated, non-number types are converted to numbers as if by the `number()` function.

---

## *id()*

### Signature

```
node-set id(string IDs)
node-set id(node-set IDs)
node-set id(object IDs)
```

### *Description*

The `id()` function returns a node set containing all elements in the document with any of the specified IDs. If the argument is a string, then this string is interpreted as a white-space separated list of IDs and the function returns a node set containing any elements that have an ID matching with one of these IDs. If the argument is a node set, then each node in the set is converted to a string, and the returned node set contains all the elements whose ID matches any of those strings. Finally, if the argument is any other type, then it's converted to a string, as by the `string()` function, and it returns the same result as passing that string value to `id()` directly.

---

## *lang()*

### *Signature*

```
boolean lang(string languageCode)
```

### *Description*

The `lang()` function returns true if the context node is written in the language specified by the `languageCode` argument; false otherwise. The nearest `xml:lang` attribute on the context node or one of its ancestors determines the language of any given node. If no such `xml:lang` attribute exists, then `lang()` returns false.

This function does not perform a simple string comparison. The `lang()` function takes account of country and other subcodes before making its determination.

---

## *last()*

### *Signature*

```
number last()
```

### *Description*

The `last()` function returns the size of (i.e., the number of nodes in) the context node list.

---

## *local-name()*

### *Signature*

```
string local-name()
string local-name(node-set nodes)
```

### *Description*

With no arguments, this function returns the context node's local name, that is, the part of the name after the colon. With an argument that's a node set, it returns the local name of the first node in the node set. If the node set is empty, or if the context node or the set's first node is not an element or attribute node (i.e., it does not have a name), then it returns the empty string.

## *name()*

### *Signature*

```
string name()
string name(node-set nodes)
```

### *Description*

With no arguments, this function returns the qualified (prefixed) name of the context node. With a node set as an argument, it returns the qualified name of the first node in the node set. If the node set is empty, or if the context node or the set's first node is not an element or attribute node (i.e., it does not have a name), then it returns the empty string.

## *namespace-uri()*

### *Signature*

```
string namespace-uri()
string namespace-uri(node-set nodes)
```

### *Description*

With no arguments, this function returns the namespace URI of the context node. With a node set as an argument, it returns the namespace URI of the first node in the node set. If this node does not have a namespace URI (i.e., it's not an element or an attribute node; or it is an element or attribute node, but is not in any namespace, or the node set is empty), then it returns the empty string.

## *normalize-space()*

### *Signature*

```
string normalize-space()
string normalize-space(string s)
string normalize-space(object o)
```

### *Description*

The `normalize-space()` function strips all leading and trailing whitespace from its argument and replaces each run of whitespace with a single space character. Among other effects, this removes all line breaks. If the argument is omitted, it normalizes the string value of the context node. A nonstring may be passed to this function, in which case it's automatically converted to a string, as if by the `string()` function, and that string is normalized and returned.

## *not()*

### *Signature*

```
boolean not(boolean b)
boolean not(object o)
```

### Description

The `not()` function inverts its argument; that is, false becomes true and true becomes false. For example, `not(3 > 2)` is false and `not(2+2=5)` is true. Non-booleans are converted as by the `boolean()` function before being processed.

## number()

### Signature

```
number number()
number number(object o)
```

### Description

The `number()` function converts its argument to a number according to these rules:

- A string is converted by first stripping leading and trailing whitespace and then picking the IEEE 754 value that is closest (according to the IEEE 754 round-to-nearest rule) to the mathematical value represented by the string. If the string does not seem to represent a number, it is converted to NaN. Exponential notation (e.g., 75.2E-12) is recognized.
- True booleans are converted to 1; false booleans are converted to 0.
- Node sets are first converted to a string, as if by the `string()` function. The resulting string is then converted to a number.

If the argument is omitted, then it converts the context node.

## position()

### Signature

```
number position()
```

### Description

The `position()` function returns a number equal to the position of the current node in the context node set. For most axes it counts forward from the context node. However, if the axis in use is ancestor, ancestor-or-self, preceding, or preceding-sibling, then it counts backward from the context node instead.

## round()

### Signature

```
number round(number x)
number round(object o)
```

### Description

The `round()` function returns the integer closest in value to `x`. For example, `round(3.141592)` returns 3. `round(-3.141592)` returns –3. If two integers are equally close to **x**, then the one that is closer to positive infinity is returned. For example, `round(3.5)` returns 4 and `round(-3.5)` returns –3. Non-number types are converted to numbers as if by the `number()` function, before rounding.



## *starts-with()*

### *Signature*

```
boolean starts-with(string s1, string s2)
boolean starts-with(object o1, object o2)
```

### *Description*

This function returns true if `s1` starts with `s2`; false otherwise. For example, `starts-with("Charming cat", "Charm")` is true; but `starts-with ("Charming cat", "Marjorie")` is false. The test is case sensitive. Non-strings may be passed to this function as well, in which case they're automatically converted to strings, as if by the `string()` function, before the test is made.

## *string()*

### *Signature*

```
string string()
string string(object o)
```

### *Description*

The `string()` function converts an object to a string according to these rules:

- A node set is converted to the string value of the first node in the node set. If the node set is empty, it's converted to the empty string.
- A number is converted to a string as follows:
  - NaN is converted to the string `NaN`.
  - Positive Inf is converted to the string `Infinity`.
  - Negative Inf is converted to the string `-Infinity`.
  - Integers are converted to their customary English form with no decimal point and no leading zeroes. A minus sign is used if the number is negative, but no plus sign is used for positive numbers.
  - Non-integers (numbers with nonzero fractional parts) are converted to their customary English form with a decimal point, at least one digit before the decimal point, and at least one digit after the decimal point. A minus sign is used if the number is negative, but no plus sign is used for positive numbers.
- A boolean with the value true is converted to the English word "true." A boolean with the value false is converted to the English word "false." Lowercase is always used.

The object to be converted is normally passed as an argument, but if omitted, the context node is converted instead.

> The XPath specification specifically notes that the "string function is not intended for converting numbers into strings for presentation to users." The primary problem is that it's not localizable and not attractive for large numbers. If you intend to show a string to an end user, use the `format-number()` function and/or `xsl:number` element in XSLT instead.

## *string-length()*

### *Signature*

```
number string-length(string s)
number string-length(object o)
number string-length()
```

### *Description*

The `string-length()` function returns the number of characters in its argument. For example, `string-length("Charm")` returns 5. If the argument is omitted, it returns the number of characters in the string value of the context node. A non-string may be passed to this function, in which case it's automatically converted to a string, as if by the `string()` function, and that string's length is returned.

## *substring()*

### *Signature*

```
string substring(string s, number index, number length)
string substring(string s, number index)
string substring(object s, object index, object length)
string substring(object s, object index)
```

### *Description*

The `substring()` function returns the substring of `s` starting at `index` and continuing for `length` characters. The first character in the string is at position 1 (not 0, as in Java and JavaScript). For example, `substring('Charming cat', 1, '5')` returns `"Charm"`. If `length` is omitted, then the substring to the end of the string is returned. For example, `substring('Charming cat', 10)` returns `"cat"`. As usual, any type of object may be passed to this function in place of the normal argument, in which case it is automatically converted to the correct type.

## *substring-after()*

### *Signature*

```
string substring-after(string s1, string s2)
string substring-after(object o1, object o2)
```

### Description

The `substring-after()` function returns the substring of `s1` that follows the first occurrence of the `s2` in `s1`, or the empty string, if `s1` does not contain `s2`. For example, `substring-after('Charming cat', 'ing')` returns `"cat"`. The test is case sensitive. As usual, non-string objects may be passed to this function, in which case they're automatically converted to strings, as if by the `string()` function.

---

## substring-before()

### Signature

```
string substring-before(string s1, string s2)
string substring-before(object o1, object o2)
```

### Description

The `substring-before()` function returns the substring of `s1` that precedes the first occurrence of the `s2` in `s1`, or the empty string if `s1` does not contain `s2`. For example, `substring-before('Charming cat', 'ing')` returns `"Charm"`. The test is case sensitive. Again, non-string objects may be passed to this function, in which case they're automatically converted to strings, as if by the `string()` function.

---

## sum()

### Signature

```
number sum(node-set nodes)
```

### Description

The `sum()` function converts each node in the node set to a number, as if by the `number()` function, adds up those numbers, and returns the sum.

---

## translate()

### Signature

```
string translate(string s1, string s2, string s3)
string translate(object o1, object o2, object o3)
```

### Description

The `translate()` function looks in `s1` for any characters found in `s2`. It replaces each character with the corresponding character from `s3`. For example, `translate("XML in a Nutshell", " ", "_")` replaces the spaces with underscores and returns `"XML_in_a_Nutshell."` If `s3` is shorter than `s2`, then characters in `s1` and `s2` with no corresponding character in `s3` are simply deleted. For example, `translate("XML in a Nutshell", " ", "")` deletes the spaces and returns `"XMLinaNutshell"`. Once again, non-string objects may be passed to this function, in which case they're automatically converted to strings, as if by the `string()` function.

## *true()*

### *Signature*

```
boolean true()
```

### *Description*

The `true()` function simply returns true. It makes up for the lack of boolean literals in XPath.

# CHAPTER 20



# *XSLT Reference*

Extensible Stylesheet Language Transformations (XSLT) is a functional programming language used to specify how an input XML document is converted into another text document, possibly though not necessarily another XML document. An XSLT processor reads both an input XML document and an XSLT stylesheet (which is itself an XML document because XSLT is an XML application) and produces a result tree as output. This result tree may then be serialized into a file or written onto another stream.

## *The XSLT Namespace*

All standard XSLT elements are in the *http://www.w3.org/1999/XSL/Transform* namespace. In this chapter, we assume that this URI is mapped to the **xsl** prefix using an appropriate **xmlns:xsl** declaration somewhere in the stylesheet. This mapping is normally declared on the root element like this:

```
<xsl:stylesheet version="1.0"
                xmlns:xsl="http://www.w3.org/1999/XSL/Transform">

  <!-- XSLT top-level elements go here -->

</xsl:stylesheet>
```

## *XSLT Elements*

XSLT defines 35 elements, which break down into three categories:

- Two root elements:

  ```
  xsl:stylesheet
  xsl:transform
  ```

- Thirteen top-level elements. These elements may appear as immediate children of the root and include:

  ```
  xsl:apply-imports
  xsl:attribute-set
  xsl:decimal-format
  xsl:import
  xsl:include
  xsl:key
  xsl:namespace-alias
  xsl:output
  xsl:param
  xsl:preserve-space
  xsl:strip-space
  xsl:template
  xsl:variable
  ```

- Twenty instruction elements. These elements appear in the content of elements that contain templates. Here we don't mean the **`xsl:template`** element. We mean the content of that and several other elements, such as **`xsl:for-each`** and **`xsl:message`**, that are composed of literal result elements, character data, and XSLT instructions that are processed to produce part of the result tree. These elements are:

  ```
  xsl:apply-imports
  xsl:apply-templates
  xsl:attribute
  xsl:call-template
  xsl:choose
  xsl:comment
  xsl:copy
  xsl:copy-of
  xsl:element
  xsl:fallback
  xsl:for-each
  xsl:if
  xsl:message
  xsl:number
  xsl:otherwise
  xsl:processing-instruction
  xsl:text
  xsl:value-of
  xsl:variable
  xsl:when
  ```

Most XSLT processors also provide various nonstandard extension elements and allow you to write your own extension elements in languages such as Java and JavaScript.

Elements in this section are arranged alphabetically from **`xsl:apply-imports`** to **`xsl:with-param`**. Each element begins with a synopsis in the following form:

```
<xsl:elementName
   attribute1 = "allowed attribute values"
   attribute2 = "allowed attribute values"
>
```

```
  <!-- Content model -->
</xsl:elementName>
```

Most attribute values are one of the following types:

*expression*
: An XPath expression. In cases where the expression is expected to return a value of a particular type, such as node set or number, it is prefixed with the type and a hyphen; for example, `node-set-expression` or `number-expression`. However, XPath is weakly typed, and in most cases, any supplied type will be converted to the requested type. For instance, an attribute that should contain a string might in fact contain a number or a node set. The processor automatically converts this number or set to a string, according to the rules given in the last chapter for XPath's `string()` function. The only exception to this rule is `node-set-expression`. XSLT does not convert other types to node sets automatically. If an attribute requires a `node-set-expression`, then setting its value to another type of expression, such as a boolean or string, is an error.

*QualifiedName*
: An XML name, such as `set` or `mathml:set`. If the name is in a nondefault namespace, then it has a prefix.

*pattern*
: An XPath location path expression using only the child, descendant-or-self, and/or attribute axes.

*langcode*
: An RFC 1766 language code, such as `en` or `fr-CA`.

*string*
: An arbitrary string of text.

*char*
: A single Unicode character.

*enumerated type*
: One value in a finite list of values. The values shown here are separated by vertical bars, as in an enumerated content model in an `ATTLIST` declaration.

*URI*
: A relative or absolute URI. Relative URIs are relative to the location of the style sheet itself.

Potentially nonempty elements have content models given in a comment in the form they might appear in an `ELEMENT` declaration. If an element can contain a template, we use the word "template" to stand in for that large number of possible elements that may appear.

---

## *xsl:apply-imports*

### *Syntax*

```
<xsl:apply-imports />
```

### *Description*

The `xsl:apply-imports` instruction processes the current node using only templates that were imported into the stylesheet with `xsl:import`. A template rule that overrides a template rule in an imported stylesheet can invoke the overridden template rule with `xsl:apply-imports`.

## *xsl:apply-templates*

### *Syntax*

```
<xsl:apply-templates
  select = "node-set-expression"
  mode   = "QualifiedName">
  <!-- (xsl:sort | xsl:with-param)* -->
</xsl:apply-templates>
```

### *Description*

The `xsl:apply-templates` instruction tells the processor to search for and apply the highest priority template in the stylesheet that matches each node identified by the `select` attribute.

### *Attributes*

`select`, *optional*

Contains an XPath expression that returns a node set. Each node in this set will be processed further. If the `select` attribute is omitted, then all child nodes of the context node should be processed.

`mode`, *optional*

If the `mode` attribute is present, then only templates that have a matching `mode` attribute will be applied. If the `mode` attribute is absent, then only templates without a `mode` attribute will be applied.

### *Contents*

The `xsl:apply-templates` element may have `xsl:sort` child elements to specify the order in which the selected nodes will be processed.

The `xsl:apply-templates` element may have `xsl:with-param` child elements to pass parameter values to the matched templates.

## *xsl:attribute*

### *Syntax*

```
<xsl:attribute
  name      = "QualifiedName"
  namespace = "URI">
  <!-- template for the attribute value -->
</xsl:attribute>
```

### *Description*

The `xsl:attribute` instruction adds an attribute to an element in the result tree. This element can be a child of an `xsl:attribute-set` element, an `xsl:element` instruction, or a literal result element. In each case, all `xsl:attribute` elements must precede all literal result elements and other instructions that insert content into the output element.

### *Attributes*

`name`, *required, attribute value template*
: The name of the attribute this instruction creates.

`namespace`, *optional, attribute value template*
: The namespace URI of the attribute. If a nonempty namespace URI is specified, then the name should contain a prefix and a local part. If this attribute is omitted, then the attribute is not in a namespace and the name must not be prefixed.

### *Contents*

The contents of this element are a template. Plain text must be the result of instantiating this template. The value of the attribute added to the result tree is given by instantiating the template and normalizing the result.

XSLT Reference

---

## *xsl:attribute-set*

### *Syntax*

```
<xsl:attribute-set
  name = "QualifiedName"
  use-attribute-sets = "QualifiedNames">
  <!-- xsl:attribute* -->
</xsl:attribute-set>
```

### *Description*

The `xsl:attribute-set` top-level element defines a collection of attributes that can be applied to elements elsewhere in the stylesheet. For instance, you could define an attribute set that includes the necessary attributes to create a simple XLink and then attach the set to each element you want to be a simple XLink.

### *Attributes*

`name`, *required*
: The `name` attribute gives a name for the set, by which `xsl:element` and other `xsl:attribute-set` elements can load this attribute set.

`use-attribute-sets`, *optional*
: The `use-attribute-sets` attribute adds attributes from a different attribute set into this attribute set. More than one attribute set can be loaded by separating multiple names with whitespace. The attributes defined in all loaded sets and all attributes defined by child `xsl:attribute` elements are merged so that no attribute appears in the set more than once. It is an error if an attribute set uses itself directly or indirectly.

### *Contents*

This element contains zero or more `xsl:attribute` elements. Each such element adds one attribute to the set.

## *xsl:call-template*

### *Syntax*

```
<xsl:call-template
   name = "QualifiedName">
   <!-- xsl:with-param* -->
</xsl:call-template>
```

### *Description*

The `xsl:call-template` instruction invokes a template by name. The current node and context node list are the same for the called template as for the calling template. Templates may be called recursively; an `xsl:template` element may contain an `xsl:call-template` element that calls that very `xsl:template` element. This technique is useful for doing things you'd accomplish with loops in a traditional procedural programming language.

### *Attributes*

`name`, *required*

The name of the `xsl:template` element to call.

### *Contents*

This element contains zero or more `xsl:with-param` elements that pass parameters to the named template.

## *xsl:choose*

### *Syntax*

```
<xsl:choose>
  <!-- (xsl:when+, xsl:otherwise?) -->
</xsl:choose>
```

### *Description*

The `xsl:choose` element selects zero or one of a sequence of alternatives.

### *Contents*

This element contains one `xsl:when` element, each of which has a test condition. The contents of the first `xsl:when` child whose test condition is true are output.

The `xsl:choose` element may have an optional `xsl:otherwise` element whose contents are output only if no test conditions of any `xsl:when` elements are true.

If no `xsl:otherwise` element exists and none of the test conditions in any of the `xsl:when` child elements is true, then this element will not produce output.

## *xsl:comment*

### *Syntax*

```
<xsl:comment>
  <!-- template -->
</xsl:comment>
```

### Description

The `xsl:comment` instruction inserts a comment into the result tree.

### Contents

The content of `xsl:comment` is a template that will be instantiated to form the text of the comment inserted into the result tree. The result of instantiating this template must only be text nodes that do not contain the double hyphen -- that signals the end of a comment.



## xsl:copy

### Syntax

```
<xsl:copy
  use-attribute-sets = "QualifiedName1 QualifiedName2...">
  <!-- template -->
</xsl:copy>
```

### Description

The `xsl:copy` element copies the current node from the source document into the output document. It copies the node itself, and any namespace nodes the node possesses. However, it does not copy the node's children or attributes.

### Attributes

`use-attribute-sets`, *optional*
: A whitespace-separated list of `xsl:attribute-set` element names. These attribute sets are merged, and all attributes in the merged set are added to the copied element. The `use-attribute-sets` attribute can be used only when the copied node is an element node.

### Contents

If the current node is an element node, attributes can be added via `xsl:attribute` children. If the current node is the root node or an element node (a node that can have children), then `xsl:copy` may contain a template that specifies the content of the element inserted into the result tree. All `xsl:attribute` elements must precede the output template.

## xsl:copy-of

### Syntax

```
<xsl:copy-of
   select = "expression" />
```

### Description

The `xsl:copy-of` instruction inserts the result tree fragment identified by the `select` attribute into the output document. This instruction copies the specific nodes identified by the expression, and all those nodes' children, attributes, namespaces, and descendants. This is how it differs from `xsl:copy`. If the expression selects something other than a node set or a result tree fragment, such as a number, then the expression is converted to its string value and the string is output.

### *Attributes*

`select`, *required*

An XPath expression identifying the object to copy into the result tree.

---

## *xsl:decimal-format*

### *Syntax*

```
<xsl:decimal-format
   name                = "QualifiedName">
   decimal-separator  = "char"
   grouping-separator = "char"
   infinity           = "string"
   minus-sign         = "char"
   NaN                = "string"
   percent            = "char"
   per-mille          = "char"
   zero-digit         = "char"
   digit              = "char"
   pattern-separator  = "char"/>
```

### *Description*

The `xsl:decimal-format` top-level element defines a pattern by which the `format-number()` function can convert floating-point numbers into text strings. The defaults work well for English, but details may change for other languages and locales, such as French or Chinese.

### *Attributes*

`name`, *optional*

The string by which the `format-number()` function identifies the `xsl:decimal-format` element to use. If this attribute is omitted, then this element establishes the default decimal format used by the `format-number()` function.

`decimal-separator`, *optional*

The character used to separate the integer part from the fractional point in a floating-point number. This character is a period (decimal point) in English and a comma in French. It may be something else in other languages.

`grouping-separator`, *optional*

The character used to separate groups of digits (e.g., the comma that separates every three digits in English).

`infinity`, *optional*

The string that represents IEEE 754 infinity; `infinity` by default.

`minus-sign`, *optional*

The character prefixed to negative numbers; a hyphen by default.

`NaN`, *optional*

The string that represents IEEE 754 Not a Number; `NaN` by default.

`percent`, *optional*
: The character that represents a percent; `%` by default.

`per-mille`, *optional*
: The character that represents a per mille; `‰` by default.

`zero-digit`, *optional*
: The character that represents zero; `0` by default. Digits 1 through 9 will be represented by the nine subsequent Unicode values after this one. For instance, setting `zero-digit` to `A` would set 1 to `B`, 2 to `C`, 3 to `D`, and so on. This is also the character used to represent 0 in format patterns.

`digit`, *optional*
: The character that represents a digit in a format pattern; `#` by default.

`pattern-separator`, *optional*
: The character that separates positive and negative subpatterns in a format pattern; `;` by default.

XSLT Reference

---

## *xsl:element*

### *Syntax*

```
<xsl:element
  name                   = "QualifiedName"
  namespace              = "URI"
  use-attribute-sets = "QualifiedName1 QualifiedName2...">
  <!-- template -->
</xsl:element>
```

### *Description*

The `xsl:element` instruction inserts an element into the result tree. The element's name is given by the `name` attribute. The element's namespace URI, if any, is given by the optional `namespace` attribute. Attributes can be added via `xsl:attribute` children or by referencing an `xsl:attribute-set` declared elsewhere in the stylesheet from the `use-attribute-sets` attribute. Finally the element's contents are determined by instantiating the template contained in the `xsl:element` element's content.

### *Attributes*

`name`, *required, attribute value template*
: The name of the element this instruction creates.

`namespace`, *optional, attribute value template*
: The namespace URI of the element this instruction creates. If this attribute is omitted, then the attribute is not in any namespace and the name must not be prefixed.

`use-attribute-sets`, *optional*
: A whitespace-separated list of names of `xsl:attribute-set` elements declared as top-level elements elsewhere in the stylesheet. These attribute sets are merged, and all attributes in the merged set are added to the element.

### Contents

The contents of this element are a template. Once instantiated, this template forms the content of the element inserted into the result tree.

## xsl:fallback

### Syntax

```
<xsl:fallback>
  <!-- template -->
</xsl:fallback>
```

### Description

The `xsl:fallback` instruction normally appears as a child of an extension element. If the processor does not recognize the extension element, then it instantiates the contents of all the element's `xsl:fallback` children in order. If the processor does recognize the element in which the `xsl:fallback` element appears, then the contents of the `xsl:fallback` element will not be output.

### Contents

The contents of this element are a template that is instantiated and output if and only if the XSLT processor does not recognize the `xsl:fallback` element's parent element.

## xsl:for-each

### Syntax

```
<xsl:for-each
   select = "node-set-expression">
   <!-- (xsl:sort*, template) -->
</xsl:for-each>
```

### Description

The `xsl:for-each` instruction iterates over the nodes identified by its `select` attribute and applies templates to each one.

### Attributes

`select`, *required*

An XPath node set expression identifying the nodes to apply templates to.

### Contents

Normally, the order in which the selected nodes are processed is the order in which they appear in the document. However, nodes can be sorted using `xsl:sort` child elements. The first such element is the primary sort key; the second is the secondary sort key; and so on.

The `xsl:for-each` element must also contain a template that is instantiated once for each member of the node set returned by the node set expression in the `select` attribute.

## *xsl:if*

### *Syntax*

```
<xsl:if
  test = "boolean-expression">
  <!-- template -->
</xsl:if>
```

### *Description*

The `xsl:if` instruction contains a template that is instantiated if and only if the XPath expression contained in its `test` attribute is `true`. There is no `xsl:else` or `xsl:else-if` element. For these purposes, use `xsl:choose` instead.



### *Attributes*

`test`, *required*
: An XPath expression returning a boolean. If this expression is true, the contents of the `xsl:if` element are instantiated. If it's false, they're not.

### *Contents*

A template that is instantiated only if the `test` attribute evaluates to true.

## *xsl:import*

### *Syntax*

```
<xsl:import
  href = "URI" />
```

### *Description*

The `xsl:import` top-level element imports the XSLT stylesheet found at the URI given by the `href` attribute. Source documents are processed using the combination of templates in the imported and importing stylesheets. In the event of a conflict between templates in the two stylesheets, the ones in the importing stylesheet take precedence. In the event of a conflict between imported stylesheets, the last one imported takes precedence.

All `xsl:import` elements must be immediate children of the root `xsl:stylesheet` element. Furthermore, they must appear before all other top-level elements.

An imported stylesheet may itself import another stylesheet. A stylesheet may not import a stylesheet that was already imported, directly or indirectly. That is, it's an error if A imports B, which imports A, thus creating a circular reference.

### *Attributes*

`href`, *required*
: The relative or absolute URI of the stylesheet to import. Relative URIs are resolved relative to the base URI of the importing stylesheet.

## *xsl:include*

### *Syntax*

```
<xsl:include
   href = "URI" />
```

### *Description*

The `xsl:include` top-level element copies the contents of the `xsl:stylesheet` or `xsl:transform` element found at the URI given by the `href` attribute. Unlike `xsl:import`, whether a template or other rule comes from the including or the included stylesheet has absolutely no effect on the precedence of the various rules.

An included stylesheet may include another stylesheet. A stylesheet may not include a stylesheet that was already included, directly or indirectly; it is an error if A includes B, which includes A.

### *Attributes*

`href`, *required*

The relative or absolute URI of the stylesheet to include. Relative URIs are resolved relative to the including stylesheet's base URI.

## *xsl:key*

### *Syntax*

```
<xsl:key
   name  = "QualifiedName"
   match = "pattern"
   use   = "expression" />
```

### *Description*

The `xsl:key` top-level element defines one or more *keys* that can be referenced from elsewhere in the stylesheet using the `key()` function. Each key has a name, a string value, and a node.

### *Attributes*

`name`, *required*

The key's name.

`match`, *required*

An XSLT match pattern, like that used by `xsl:template`, specifying which nodes have this key. If this pattern matches more than one node in the source document, then a single `xsl:key` element may define many keys, all with the same name and possibly the same value, but with different nodes.

`use`, *required*

An XPath expression that is converted to a string to give the value of keys defined by this element. The expression is evaluated with respect to each key's node; if `match` identifies multiple nodes, then `use` may produce different values for each key.

## *xsl:message*

### *Syntax*

```
<xsl:message
  terminate = "yes" | "no">
  <!-- template -->
</xsl:message>
```

### *Description*

The `xsl:message` instruction sends a message to the XSLT processor. Which messages the processor understands and what it does with messages it does understand is processor dependent. Printing debugging information on `stderr` or `stdout` is one common use of `xsl:message`.

### *Attributes*

`terminate`, *optional*

If the attribute is present and has the value `yes`, then the XSLT processor should halt after the message is delivered and acted on.

### *Contents*

An `xsl:message` element's content is a template instantiated to create an *XML fragment*. The result is then delivered to the XSLT processor as the message.

> The XSLT specification does not define *XML fragment*, and various XSLT processors interpret it differently. It may be a result tree fragment or an XML fragment, as defined by the now moribund XML Fragment Interchange working draft. It may be something else. Clarification from the W3C is necessary.

## *xsl:namespace-alias*

### *Syntax*

```
<xsl:namespace-alias
   stylesheet-prefix = "prefix"
   result-prefix     = "prefix" />
```

### *Description*

The top-level `xsl:namespace-alias` element declares that one namespace URI in the stylesheet should be replaced by a different namespace URI in the result tree. Aliasing is particularly useful when you're transforming XSLT into XSLT using XSLT; and consequently which names belong to the input, which belong to the output, and which belong to the stylesheet is not obvious.

### Attributes

`stylesheet-prefix`, *required*

The prefix used inside the stylesheet itself. May be set to `#default` to indicate that the nonprefixed default namespace should be used.

`result-prefix`, *required*

The prefix used in the result tree. May be set to `#default` to indicate that the nonprefixed default namespace should be used.

---

## xsl:number

### Syntax

```
<xsl:number
   value  = "number-expression"
   count  = "pattern"
   from   = "pattern"
   level  = "single" | "multiple" | "any"
   format = "letter or digit"
   lang   = "langcode"
   letter-value = "alphabetic" | "traditional"
   grouping-separator = "char"
   grouping-size = "number" />
```

### Description

The `xsl:number` instruction inserts a formatted integer into the result tree.

### Attributes

`value`, *optional*

An XPath expression returning the number to be formatted. If necessary, the result of the expression is rounded to the nearest integer. The `value` attribute is often omitted, in which case the number is calculated from the position of the current node in the source document. The position is calculated as specified by the `level`, `count`, and `from` attributes.

`level`, *optional*

This attribute can be set to `single`—all preceding siblings of the current node's ancestor that matches the `count` pattern; `multiple`—the sum total of all preceding siblings of all the current node's ancestors that match the `count` pattern; or `any`—all nodes in the document that match the `count` pattern and precede the current node. The default is `single`.

`count`, *optional*

This attribute contains a pattern that specifies which nodes should be counted at those levels. The default is to count all nodes of the same node type (element, text, attribute, etc.) and name as the current node.

`from`, *optional*

This attribute contains a pattern identifying the node from which counting starts; that is, it says which node is number 1.

format, *optional, attribute value template*

This attribute determines how the list is numbered. Format tokens and sequences they produce include:

*1* 1, 2, 3, 4, 5, 6, . . .

*01* 01, 02, 03, 04, 05, 06, 07, 08, 09, 10, 11, 12, . . .

*A* A, B, C, D, . . . ,Z, AA, AB, AC, . . .

*a* a, b, c, d, . . . ,z, aa, ab, ac, . . .

*i* i, ii, iii, iv, v, vi, vii, viii, ix, x, xi, . . .

*I* I, II, III, IV, V, VI, VII, VIII, IX, X, XI, XII, . . .

You can also change the starting point; for instance, setting the format token to 5 would create the sequence 5, 6, 7, 8, 9, . . . .

lang, *optional, attribute value template*

The RFC 1766 language code describing the language in which the number should be formatted (e.g., en or fr).

letter-value, *optional, attribute value template*

The default is traditional. However, you can set this attribute to alphabetic to indicate that a format of I should start the sequence I, J, K, L, M, N, . . . rather than I, II, III, IV, V, VI, . . . .

grouping-separator, *optional, attribute value template*

The character that separates groups of digits. For instance, in English the comma customarily separates every three digits, as in 2,987,667,342. In French a space is used instead, so this number would be formatted as 2 987 667 342.

grouping-size, *optional, attribute value template*

The number of digits in each group. In most languages, including English, digits are divided into groups of three. However, a few languages use groups of four.

XSLT Reference

## *xsl:otherwise*

### *Syntax*

```
<xsl:otherwise>
  <!-- template -->
</xsl:otherwise>
```

### *Description*

The xsl:otherwise element only appears as the last child element of an xsl:choose element. It serves as the default result in the event that no xsl:when element in the same xsl:choose element is instantiated.

### *Contents*

The contents are a template that is instantiated if and only if none of the xsl:choose element's xsl:when sibling elements is true.

# *xsl:output*

## *Syntax*

```
<xsl:output
  method     = "xml" | "html" | "text"
  version    = "NMTOKEN"
  encoding    = "encoding_name"
  omit-xml-declaration   = "yes" | "no"
  standalone    = "yes" | "no"
  doctype-public    = "PUBLIC_ID"
  doctype-system     = "SYSTEM_ID"
  cdata-section-elements  = "element_name_1 element_name_2..."
  indent    = "yes" | "no"
  media-type    = "string" />
```

## *Description*

The top-level `xsl:output` element helps determine the exact formatting of the XML document produced when the result tree is stored in a file, written onto a stream, or otherwise serialized into a sequence of bytes. It has no effect on the production of the result tree itself.

## *Attributes*

`method`, *optional*
: The default method is `xml`, which simply means that the serialized output document will be a well-formed external parsed entity or XML document. If `method` is set to `html`, or if the `method` attribute is not present and the root element of the output tree is `html`, in any combination of case, then the processor attempts to generate HTML that is more compatible with existing browsers. For example, empty element tags like `<br/>` are converted to `<br>`. The `text` method outputs only the contents of the text nodes in the output tree. It strips all markup. XSLT processors may also recognize and support other values, such as `TeX` or `RTF`, but none do so yet.

`version` , *optional*
: A name token that identifies the output method's version. In practice, this has no effect on the output.

`encoding`, *optional*
: The name of the encoding the outputter should use, like ISO-8859-1 or UTF-16.

`omit-xml-declaration`, *optional*
: If this attribute has the value `yes`, then no XML declaration is included. If it has the value `no` or is not present, then an XML declaration is included.

`standalone`, *optional*
: This attribute sets the `standalone` attribute's value in the XML declaration. Like that attribute, it must have the value `yes` or `no`.

`doctype-public`, *optional*
: The public identifier used in the document type declaration.

`doctype-system`, *optional*
: The system identifier used in the document type declaration.

cdata-section-elements, *optional*

A whitespace-separated list of qualified element names in the result tree whose contents should be emitted using CDATA sections rather than character references.

indent, *optional*

If this attribute has the value yes, then the processor is allowed (but not required) to insert extra whitespace to attempt to "pretty-print" the output tree. The default is no.

media-type, *optional*

The output's MIME media type, such as text/html or text/xml.



# *xsl:param*

## *Syntax*

```
<xsl:param
  name   = "QualifiedName"
  select = "expression">
  <!-- template -->
</xsl:param>
```

## *Description*

An xsl:param element binds a name to a value. A top-level xsl:param element provides a default value to use if the named parameter is not supplied when a template is called. The xsl:param element may also appear inside an xsl:template element to receive values of the parameters passed in with xsl:with-param when the template is called. It also provides a default value that is good only inside that template to use when the caller does not provide a value for the parameter. If an xsl:apply-templates or xsl:call-template passes in a parameter value using xsl:with-param when the template is invoked, then this value overrides any default value the xsl:param element may have.

## *Attributes*

name, *required*

The parameter's name.

select, *optional*

An XPath expression that provides the parameter's value. If xsl:param has a select attribute, then it must be an empty element. If xsl:param does not have a select attribute, then the value is taken from the element's contents.

## *Contents*

An xsl:param element's content is a template that is instantiated to produce a result tree fragment. This result tree fragment then becomes the parameter's value. A nonempty xsl:param element must not have a select attribute.

## *xsl:preserve-space*

### *Syntax*

```
<xsl:preserve-space
   elements="QualifiedName_1 QualifiedName_2..." />
```

### *Description*

The top-level `xsl:preserve-space` element specifies which elements in the source document will not have whitespace stripped from them before they are transformed. Whitespace stripping removes text nodes that contain only whitespace (the space character, the tab character, the carriage return, and the linefeed). By default whitespace is preserved in an element unless its name is listed in the `elements` attribute of an `xsl:strip-space` element. This element allows you to override the list given in `xsl:strip-space`; if an element is listed in both `xsl:strip-space` and `xsl:preserve-space`, then its whitespace is preserved.

### *Attributes*

`elements`, *required*

A whitespace-separated list of elements in which space should be preserved. Besides element names, the `elements` attribute can contain an asterisk to indicate that whitespace should be preserved in all elements or a namespace prefix followed by a colon and an asterisk to indicate that whitespace should be preserved in all elements in the given namespace.

## *xsl:processing-instruction*

### *Syntax*

```
<xsl:processing-instruction
  name = "target">
  <!-- template -->
</xsl:processing-instruction>
```

### *Description*

The `xsl:processing-instruction` element inserts a processing instruction into the result tree.

### *Attributes*

`name`, *required, attribute value template*

The processing instruction's target.

### *Contents*

The `xsl:processing-instruction` element's contents are a template that is instantiated to produce the processing instruction data. This template may include XSLT instructions, provided that the result of instantiating this template is well-formed processing instruction data.

## *xsl:sort*

### *Syntax*

```
<xsl:sort
   select     = "string-expression"
   data-type  = "text" | "number"
   lang       = "langcode"
   order      = "ascending" | "descending"
   case-order = "upper-first" | "lower-first" />
```

### *Description*

The `xsl:sort` instruction appears as a child of either `xsl:apply-templates` or `xsl:for-each`. It changes the order of the context node list from document order to another order, such as alphabetic. You can perform multiple key sorts (e.g., sort first by last name, then by first name, then by middle name) using multiple `xsl:sort` elements in descending order of the keys' importance.

### *Attributes*

`select`, *optional*
: The key to sort by. If `select` is omitted, then the sort key is set to the value of the current node.

`data-type`, *optional, attribute value template*
: By default, sorting is purely alphabetic. However, alphabetic sorting leads to strange results with numbers. For instance, 10, 100, and 1000 all sort before 2, 3, and 4. You can specify numeric sorting by setting the `data-type` attribute to `number`.

`lang`, *optional, attribute value template*
: Sorting is language dependent. Setting the `lang` attribute to an RFC 1766 language code changes the language. The default language is system dependent.

`order`, *optional*
: The order by which strings are sorted. This order can be either `descending` or `ascending`. The default is ascending order.

`case-order`, *optional, attribute value template*
: The `case-order` attribute can be set to `upper-first` or `lower-first` to specify whether uppercase letters sort before lowercase letters, or vice versa. The default depends on the language.

## *xsl:strip-space*

### *Syntax*

```
<xsl:strip-space
   elements="QualifiedName_1 QualifiedName_2..." />
```

### *Description*

The top-level `xsl:strip-space` element specifies which elements in the source document have whitespace stripped from them before they are transformed. Whitespace stripping removes all text nodes that contain only whitespace (the space character, the tab character, the carriage return, and the line feed). By default whitespace is not stripped from an element unless its name is listed in the `elements` attribute of an `xsl:strip-space` element.

This element does not trim leading or trailing whitespace, or otherwise normalize whitespace in elements that contain even a single nonwhitespace character.

### Attributes

`elements`, *required*

A whitespace-separated list of elements in which space should be stripped. Besides element names, the `elements` attribute can contain an asterisk to indicate that whitespace should be stripped in all elements, or a namespace prefix followed by a colon and asterisk to indicate that whitespace should be stripped in all elements in the given namespace.

---

## xsl:stylesheet

### Syntax

```
<xsl:stylesheet
  xmlns:xsl="http://www.w3.org/1999/XSL/Transform"
  id = "ID"
  extension-element-prefixes = "prefix1 prefix2..."
  exclude-result-prefixes = "prefix1 prefix2..."
  version = "1.0">
  <!-- (xsl:import*, top-level-elements) -->
</xsl:stylesheet>
```

### Description

The `xsl:stylesheet` element is the root element for XSLT stylesheets.

### Attributes

`xmlns:xsl`, *technically optional but de facto required*

A standard namespace declaration that maps the prefix `xsl` to the namespace URI `http://www.w3.org/1999/XSL/Transform`. The prefix can be changed if necessary.

`version`, *required*

Currently this attribute always has the value `1.0`. However, XSLT 1.1 will probably be released in 2001 with a concurrent updating of this number.

`id`, *optional*

Any XML name that's unique within this document's ID attributes.

`extension-element-prefixes`, *optional*

A whitespace-separated list of namespace prefixes used by this document's extension elements.

`exclude-result-prefixes`, *optional*

A whitespace-separated list of namespace prefixes whose declarations should not be copied into the output document.

### Contents

Any `xsl:import` elements, followed by any other top-level elements in any order.

## *xsl:template*

### *Syntax*

```
<xsl:template
  match    = "pattern"
  priority = "number"
  name     = "Qualified_Name"
  mode     = "Qualified_Name">
  <!-- (xsl:param*, template) -->
</xsl:template>
```



### *Description*

The `xsl:template` top-level element is the key to all of XSLT. The `match` attribute contains a pattern against which nodes are compared as they're processed. If the pattern matches a node, then the contents are instantiated and inserted into the output tree.

### *Attributes*

`match`, *optional*

A pattern against which nodes can be compared. This pattern is a location path using only the child, attribute, and descendant-or-self axes.

`name`, *optional*

A name by which this template can be invoked from an `xsl:call-template` element, rather than by node matching.

`priority`, *optional*

A number. If more than one template with the same import precedence matches a given node, the one with the highest priority is chosen. If this attribute is not present, then the template's priority is calculated in the following way:

- Templates with match patterns composed of just an element or attribute name (e.g. `person` or `@profession`) have priority 0.
- Templates with match patterns composed of just the `processing-instruction()` function (e.g., `processing-instruction()` or `processing-instruction('robots')`) have priority 0.
- Templates with match patterns in the form `prefix:*` have priority –0.25.
- Templates with match patterns that just have a node test (`*`, `@*`, `comment()`, `node()`, `text()`) have priority –0.5. (This means that built-in template rules have priority –0.5. However, they are also imported before all other template rules, and thus never override any explicit template rule, regardless of priority.)
- All other patterns (`person[name='Feynman']`, `people/person/@profession`, `person/text()`, etc.) have priority 0.5.

It is an error if two or more templates match a node and have the same priority. However, in this case most XSLT processors choose the last template occurring in the stylesheet rather than signaling the error.

`mode`, *optional*

The template's mode. If the `xsl:template` element has a mode, then this template is matched only when the calling instruction's `mode` attribute matches this `mode` attribute's value.

### *Contents*

The template that should be instantiated when this element is matched or called by name.

---

## *xsl:text*

### *Syntax*

```
<xsl:text
   disable-output-escaping = "yes" | "no">
   <!-- #PCDATA -->
</xsl:text>
```

### *Description*

The `xsl:text` instruction is used inside templates to indicate that its contents should be output as text. Its contents are pure text, not elements.

### *Attributes*

`disable-output-escaping`, *optional*

By setting the `disable-output-escaping` attribute to `yes`, you indicate that characters such as < and &, which are normally replaced by character or entity references such as `<` or `<`, should instead be output as the literal characters themselves. Note that the `xsl:text` element's content in the stylesheet must still be well-formed, and any < or & characters must be written as `<` or `&` or the equivalent character references. However, when the output document is serialized, these references are replaced by the actual represented characters rather than references that represent them.

---

## *xsl:transform*

### *Syntax*

```
<xsl:transform
  xmlns:xsl="http://www.w3.org/1999/XSL/Transform"
  id = "ID"
  extension-element-prefixes = "prefix1 prefix2..."
  exclude-result-prefixes = "prefix1 prefix2..."
  version = "1.0">
  <!-- (xsl:import*, top-level-elements) -->
</xsl:transform>
```

### *Description*

The `xsl:transform` element is a seldom-used synonym for the `xsl:stylesheet` root element. It has the same attributes and contents as `xsl:stylesheet`, and is used in exactly the same way as `xsl:stylesheet`. See the element's description of the `xsl:stylesheet` for the discussion of its attributes and content.

## *xsl:value-of*

### *Syntax*

```
<xsl:value-of
   select = "expression"
   disable-output-escaping = "yes" | "no" />
```

### *Description*

The `xsl:value-of` element computes the string value of an XPath expression and inserts it into the result tree. The values of the seven different kinds of nodes are:

*element*
: The text content of the element after all entity references are resolved and all tags are stripped

*text*
: The text of the node

*attribute*
: The normalized value of the attribute

*root*
: The value of the root element

*processing instruction*
: The processing instruction data (<?, ?>, and the target are not included)

*comment*
: The text of the comment (<!-- and --> are not included)

*namespace*
: The namespace URI

You can also take values of things that aren't nodes. The value of a node set is the value of the first node in the set. The value of a string expression is the string. The value of a number expression is the string form of the number. The value of a boolean expression is the string `true` or the string `false`.

### *Attributes*

`select`, *required*
: The XPath expression whose value is inserted into the result tree.

`disable-output-escaping`, *optional*
: If this attribute has the value `yes`, then when the output document is serialized, characters such as < and & in the value are not replaced with entity or character references. This may result in a malformed document.

## *xsl:variable*

### *Syntax*

```
<xsl:variable
  name   = "QualifiedName"
  select = "expression">
  <!-- template -->
</xsl:variable>
```

### *Description*

The top-level `xsl:variable` element binds a name to a value of any type (string, number, node set, etc.). This variable can then be dereferenced elsewhere by using the form `$`*`name`* in an attribute value template.

---

The word *variable* is a little misleading. Once the value of an `xsl:variable` is set, it cannot be changed. An `xsl:variable` is more like a named constant than a traditional variable.

---

### *Attributes*

`name`, *required*
: The variable's name.

`select`, *optional*
: An XPath expression that sets the value of the variable. If `xsl:variable` has a `select` attribute, then it must be an empty element.

### *Contents*

A template that is instantiated to produce the variable's value as a result tree fragment. If an `xsl:variable` is not an empty element, it must not have a `select` attribute. If `xsl:variable` is empty and does not have a `select` attribute, then its value is the empty string.

---

## *xsl:when*

### *Syntax*

```
<xsl:when
  test = "boolean-expression">
  <!-- template -->
</xsl:when>
```

### *Description*

The `xsl:when` element appears only as a child of an `xsl:choose` element.

### *Attributes*

`test`, *required*
: An XPath expression that evaluates to either true or false. The `xsl:when` contents are inserted into the result tree if and only if this is the first `xsl:when` element in the `xsl:choose` element whose `test` attribute evaluates to true.

### *Contents*

The template to be instantiated and inserted into the result tree if the `test` attribute is true.

## *xsl:with-param*

### *Syntax*

```
<xsl:with-param
  name   = "QualifiedName"
  select = "expression">
  <!-- template -->
</xsl:with-param>
```

### *Description*

The `xsl:with-param` element passes a named parameter to a template that expects it. This can either be a child of `xsl:apply-templates` or `xsl:call-template`. An `xsl:template` element receives the parameter via an `xsl:param` element with the same name. If a template expects to receive a particular parameter and doesn't get it, then it can take the default from an `xsl:param` element instead.

### *Attributes*

`name`, *required*
: The name of the parameter.

`select`, *optional*
: An XPath expression evaluated to form the value of the parameter. If `xsl:with-param` has a `select` attribute, then it must be an empty element. If `xsl:with-param` does not have a `select` attribute, then the value is taken from the element's contents.

### *Contents*

A template that is instantiated and passed as the parameter's value. If `xsl:with-param` is not an empty element, it must not have a `select` attribute. If `xsl:with-param` is empty and does not have a `select` attribute, then its value is the empty string.

# *XSLT Functions*

XSLT uses the XPath syntax heavily and supports all functions defined in XPath. In addition, it defines ten extra functions. Most XSLT processors also make several extension functions available and allow you to write your own extension functions in Java or other languages. The extension API is nonstandard and processor dependent, though XSLT 1.1 will probably add standard bindings for extension functions written in Java and JavaScript.

XPath and XSLT functions are weakly typed. Although one type or another is occasionally preferred, you can usually pass in any type and the processor will make an effort to convert it. When this seems particularly likely, the type of each argument or the return value is listed as `object`. Functions that only take node sets as arguments are an exception to the weak typing rule. Other datatypes, including strings, numbers, and booleans cannot be converted to node sets automatically. However, many XSLT processors, including SAXON and MSXML, bundle an extension function to convert strings to node sets, and a standard version of such a function will probably be added in XSLT 1.1.

XPath and XSLT functions also use optional arguments that are filled in with defaults if omitted. In the following sections, we list the most common and useful variations of each function.

## *current()*

### *Syntax*

```
node-set current()
```

### *Description*

The `current()` function returns a node set containing a single node, the current node. Outside of an XPath predicate, the current node and the context node (represented by a period in the abbreviated XPath syntax) are identical. However, in a predicate, the current node may change based on other contents in the predicate, while the context node stays the same.

## *document()*

### *Syntax*

```
node-set document(string uri)
node-set document(node-set uris)
node-set document(string uri, node-set base)
node-set document(node-set uris, node-set base)
```

### *Description*

The `document()` function loads the XML document at the URI specified by the first argument and returns a node set containing that document's root node. The URI is normally given as a string but may be given as another type that is converted to a string. If the URI is given as a node set, then each node in the set is converted to a string, and the returned node set includes root nodes of all documents referenced by the URI argument.

If the URI contains a fragment identifier, then the node set returned may indicate something other than the root node and contain more than one node. If an error occurs while retrieving a document, then an empty node set is returned.

The `document()` function may also take a node set as an optional second argument, in which case the first node (in document order) in this set is used as the base URI with which to resolve relative URIs given in the first argument. If the second argument is omitted, then base URIs are resolved relative to the stylesheet's location.

## *element-available()*

### *Syntax*

```
boolean element-available(string qualifiedElementName)
```

### *Description*

`element-available()` returns `true` if and only if the argument identifies an XSLT element the processor recognizes. If the qualified name maps to a non-null namespace URI, then it refers to an extension element; otherwise, it refers to a standard XSLT element. Assuming use of a fully conformant processor, you don't need to use this to test for standard elements; just use it for extension elements.

## *format-number()*

### *Syntax*

```
string format-number(number x, string pattern)
string format-number(number x, string pattern, string decimalFormat)
```

### *Description*

The `format-number()` function converts the number `x` to a string using the pattern specified by the second argument and the `xsl:decimal-format` element named by the third argument (or the default decimal format, if the third argument is omitted).

This function's behavior is modeled after the `java.text.DecimalFormat` class in Java 1.1 (not 1.2 or 1.3). See *http://java.sun.com/products/jdk/1.1/docs/api/java.text.DecimalFormat.html* for full documentation of the pattern passed as the second argument.

The pattern specifies whether leading and trailing zeroes should be printed, whether the number's fractional part is printed, the number of digits in a group, and the leading and trailing suffixes for negative and positive numbers. The patterns are described using an almost Backus-Naur-Form grammar, given here:

```
pattern     ->  subpattern{;subpattern}
subpattern  ->  {prefix}integer{.fraction}{suffix}
prefix      ->  '\\u0000'..'\\uFFFD' - specialCharacters
suffix      ->  '\\u0000'..'\\uFFFD' - specialCharacters
integer     ->  '#'* '0'* '0'
fraction    ->  '0'* '#'*
```

The first line is not pure BNF. The first subpattern is used for positive numbers. The second subpattern, which may not be present, is used for negative numbers. If it's not present, negative numbers use the positive format, but are prefixed with a minus sign. Table 20-1 defines the symbols used in the grammar.

*Table 20-1: Symbols Used in the Pattern Grammar*

| *Symbol* | *Meaning* |
|---|---|
| 0 | A digit, including leading or trailing zeroes; may be set to a different character using the `zero-digit` attribute of `xsl:decimal-format`. |
| # | A digit, except for leading or trailing zero; may be set to a different character using the `digit` attribute of `xsl:decimal-format`. |
| . | A decimal separator; may be set to a different character using the `decimal-separator` attribute of `xsl:decimal-format`. |
| , | A grouping separator; may be set to a different character using `xsl:decimal-format`'s `grouping-separator` attribute. |
| ; | Separates the positive and negative format patterns in a format string; may be set to a different character using the `pattern-separator` attribute of `xsl:decimal-format`. |

*Table 20-1: Symbols Used in the Pattern Grammar (continued)*

| *Symbol* | *Meaning* |
|---|---|
| - | A default negative prefix; may be set to a different character using `xsl:decimal-format`'s `minus-sign` attribute. |
| % | Divides by 100 and shows as percentage; may be set to a different character using `xsl:decimal-format`'s `percent` attribute. |
| X | Indicates that any other character can be used in the prefix or suffix. |
| ' | Used to quote special characters in a prefix or suffix. |
| X* | Indicates zero or more occurrences of X. |
| (X \| Y) | Indicates either X or Y. |
| X..Y | Indicates any character from X through Y, inclusive. |
| S – T | Indicates characters in S, but not in T. |

For instance, #,##0.### is a common decimal format pattern. The # mark indicates any digit character except a leading or trailing zero. The comma is the grouping separator. The period is the decimal separator. The 0 is a digit that is printed even if it's a nonsignificant zero. This pattern is interpreted as follows:

1. The integer part contains as many digits as necessary.
2. The grouping separator separates every three digits.
3. If the integer part only contains zeroes, a single zero is placed before the decimal separator.
4. Up to three digits are printed after the decimal point. However, any trailing zeros are not printed.
5. No separate pattern is included for negative numbers. Thus negative numbers are printed the same as positive numbers, but prefixed with a minus sign.

---

## *function-available()*

### *Syntax*

```
boolean function-available(string qualifiedName)
```

### *Description*

`function-available()` returns true if the argument identifies a function in the processor's function library, false otherwise. If the qualified name maps to a non-null namespace URI, then it refers to an extension function; otherwise, it refers to a built-in function from XPath or XSLT. Assuming you're using a fully conformant processor, however, you need not use this to test for standard functions, only for extension functions.

---

## *generate-id()*

### *Syntax*

```
string generate-id(node-set node)
string generate-id()
```

### *Description*

The `generate-id()` function returns a string that can be used as the value of an ID type attribute. This function always produces the same string for the same node and a different string for a different node. If the node set contains more than one node, then only the first node in the set is considered. If the argument is omitted, then the node set is set to the context node. If the node set is empty, then the empty string is returned.



---

## *key()*

### *Syntax*

```
node-set key(string keyName, object value)
node-set key(string keyName, string value)
node-set key(string keyName, node-set values)
```

### *Description*

The `key()` function returns a node set containing all nodes in the source document that have a key with the name given by the first argument and the value given by the second argument. If the second argument is a node set, then the node set returned contains all nodes that have a key with the specified name and a value that matches that of any node in the second argument. Otherwise, the returned node set contains all nodes that have a key with the specified name and a value that matches the second argument's string value. Key names and values are assigned to nodes using the `xsl:key` element.

---

## *system-property()*

### *Syntax*

```
object system-property(string qualifiedPropertyName)
```

### *Description*

The `system-property()` function returns the value of the named property. The type of the returned object is processor and property dependent. If the processor does not recognize the property name, then it returns an empty string.

XSLT processors are required to recognize and return values for these three properties:

`xsl:version`
: A number specifying the version of XSLT implemented by the processor; this is currently always 1.0, but may become 1.1 during this book's life span.

`xsl:vendor`
: A string identifying the XSLT processor's vendor; for instance, `Apache Software Foundation` for Xalan or `SAXON 5.4.1 from Michael Kay of ICL` for SAXON.

`xsl:vendor-url`

A string containing a URL for the XSLT processor's vendor; for instance, `http://xml.apache.org/xalan` for Xalan or `http://users.iclway.co.uk/mhkay/saxon/index.html` for SAXON.

Implementations may also recognize and return values for other, processor-dependent properties.

---

## *unparsed-entity-uri()*

### *Syntax*

```
string unparsed-entity-uri(string entityName)
```

### *Description*

The `unparsed-entity-uri()` function returns the URI of the unparsed entity with the specified name declared in the source document's DTD or the empty string, if no unparsed entity with that name exists.

# CHAPTER 21

# *DOM Reference*



The Document Object Model (DOM) is a language- and platform-independent object framework for manipulating structured documents (see Chapter 16, *Document Object Model (DOM)*, for additional information on IDL). The current W3C recommendation specifies what is called the Level 2 DOM. The full Level 2 DOM is designed to support editing of HTML documents, with several classes and methods specific to HTML document structures. This larger DOM is built on top of a smaller, but complete, subset called the Core DOM. Only the Core DOM is required to support editing of XML documents.

This reference section documents the Level 1 and Level 2 Core DOM objects, using the language-neutral OMG IDL object descriptions. Included with each IDL description is the language-specific binding for the Java programming language. Level 2-only constructs are indicated using the ❷ symbol after the given attribute or method name.

> This chapter is based on the Document Object Model (DOM) Specification, which was released on November 13, 2000. The latest version of this recommendation, along with any errata that have been reported, is available on the W3C web site (*http://www.w3.org*).

The DOM structures a document as a hierarchy of `Node` objects. The `Node` interface is the base interface for every member of a DOM document tree. It exposes attributes common to every type of document object and provides a few simple methods to retrieve type-specific information without resorting to downcasting. This interface also exposes all methods used to query, insert, and remove objects from the document hierarchy. The `Node` interface makes it easier to build general-purpose tree manipulation routines that are not dependent on specific document element types.

## *Object Hierarchy*

The following table shows the DOM object hierarchy:

| *Object* | *Permitted Child Objects* |
|---|---|
| `Document` | `Element` (one is the maximum)<br>`ProcessingInstruction`<br>`Comment`<br>`DocumentType` (one is the maximum) |
| `DocumentFragment` | `Element`<br>`ProcessingInstruction`<br>`Comment`<br>`Text`<br>`CDATASection`<br>`EntityReference` |
| `DocumentType` | None (leaf node) |
| `EntityReference` | `Element`<br>`ProcessingInstruction`<br>`Comment`<br>`Text`<br>`CDATASection`<br>`EntityReference` |
| `Element` | `Element`<br>`Text`<br>`Comment`<br>`ProcessingInstruction`<br>`CDATASection`<br>`EntityReference` |
| `Attr` | `Text`<br>`EntityReference` |
| `ProcessingInstruction` | None (leaf node) |
| `Comment` | None (leaf node) |
| `Text` | None (leaf node) |
| `CDATASection` | None (leaf node) |
| `Entity` | `Element`<br>`ProcessingInstruction`<br>`Comment`<br>`Text`<br>`CDATASection`<br>`EntityReference` |
| `Notation` | None (leaf node) |

## *Object Reference*

This section details the XML DOM Level 2 Core objects. The reference sections detail the descriptions, attributes, and methods of each object in the language-independent IDL specification. Java examples and bindings for items are presented to illustrate usage.

## Attr

The Attr interface represents the value assigned to an attribute of an XML element. Since the attributes NamedNodeList attribute of the Element interface is the only access to Attr objects within the DOM, the parentNode, previousSibling, and nextSibling attributes always return null. Although the Attr interface inherits the Node base interface, many basic Node methods are not applicable.

An XML element can acquire an attribute in several ways. An element has an attribute value if:

- The XML document explicitly provides an attribute value.
- The document DTD specifies a default attribute value.
- An attribute is added programmatically using the setAttribute() or setAttributeNode() methods of the Element interface.

Though an Attr node is not officially part of the DOM document tree, it can be the parent of a value subtree. An Attr object can have EntityReference objects as children. The value attribute provides the expanded DOMString representation of this attribute. To determine if any entity replacements were made, it is necessary to check the Attr node for child nodes.

### *Java example*

```
//Get the element's size attribute as an Attr object
Attr attrName = elem.getAttributeNode("size");
```

### *Attributes*

The following attributes are defined for the Attr object.

#### name: *DOMString*

The name of the attribute. Read-only.

*Java binding*

```
Public String getName();
```

*Java example*

```
// Dump element attribute names
Attr attr;

for (int i = 0; i < elem.getAttributes().getLength(); i++) {
    // temporarily alias the attribute
    attr = (Attr)elem.getAttributes().item(i);
    System.out.println(attr.getName());
    }
```

#### ownerElement: *Element* ❷

This property provides a link to the Element object that owns this attribute. If the attribute is currently unowned, it equals null. Read-only.

*Java binding*

```
public Element getOwnerElement();
```

**specified:** *boolean*

Indicates whether this attribute was explicitly set in the XML source for the parent element or is a default value specified in the DTD. Read-only.

*Java binding*

```
public boolean getSpecified();
```

*Java example*

```
// Dump element attribute names
for (int i = 0; i < elem.getAttributes().getLength(); i++) {
    // temporarily alias the attribute
    attr = (Attr)elem.getAttributes().item(i);
    // only show attributes that were explicitly included in the XML
    source file
     // (i.e. ignore default attributes from the DTD.)
     if (attr.getSpecified()) {
         System.out.println(attr.getName());
    }
}
```

**value:** *DOMString*

This attribute provides a simple way to set and retreive the `Attr` object's text value. When used to get the text value, the attribute includes the expanded value of any general entity references. When used to set the value, it creates a child `Text` node that contains the string value. Attempting to set the value on a read-only node raises the `NO_MODIFICATION_ALLOWED_ERR` `DOM` exception.

*Java bindings*

```
public String getValue();
public void setValue(String value);
```

*Java example*

```
// Make all attribute values lowercase
Attr attr;

for (int i = 0; i < elem.getAttributes().getLength(); i++) {
    attr = (Attr)elem.getAttributes().item(i);
    attr.setValue(attr.getValue().toLowerCase());
}
```

## *CDATASection*

The `CDATASection` interface contains the unparsed, unescaped data contained within `CDATA` blocks in an XML document. Though this interface inherits the `Text` interface, adjacent `CDATASection` blocks are not merged by the `normalize()` method of the `Element` interface.

### *Java example*

```
// Open an XML source file
try {
    FileInputStream fis = new FileInputStream("phone_list.xml");
    StringBuffer sb = new StringBuffer();

    // read the XML source file into memory
    int ch;
    while ((ch = fis.read()) != -1) {
        sb.append((char)ch);
    }

    // now, create a CDATASection object to contain it within
    // an element of our document using the CDATA facility
    CDATASection ndCDATA = doc.createCDATASection(sb.toString());
} catch (IOException e) {
    ...
```

`CDATASection` is a pure subclass of the `Text` interface and has no attributes or methods of its own. See the `Text` interface section of this chapter for a list of applicable methods for accessing character data in nodes of this type.

## *CharacterData*

The `CharacterData` interface is completely abstract, extending the basic `Node` interface only to support manipulation of character data. Every DOM object type that deals with text data inherits, directly or indirectly, from this interface.

This interface's string-handling facilities are similar to those found in most modern programming languages. Like C/C++ string-processing routines, all `CharacterData` routines are 0 based.

### *Java example*

```
// Create a new, unattached Text node
Text ndText = doc.createTextNode("The truth is out there.");

// cast it to the CharacterData interface
CharacterData ndCD = (CharacterData)ndText;
```

### *Attributes*

The following attributes are defined for `CharacterData`:

**data:** *DOMString*

This attribute allows access to the "raw" data of the `CharacterData` node. Though a given DOM implementation cannot arbitrarily limit the amount of character data that can be stored in a `CharacterData` node, you may need to use the `substringData` method to retrieve the data in manageable sections because of implementation constraints.

*Exceptions*

*NO_MODIFICATION_ALLOWED_ERR*
Raised on a write attempt when the `data` attribute is read-only for this DOM object type.

*DOMSTRING_SIZE_ERR*
Raised if the read value that would be returned is too large to be contained by a `DOMString` type in the given implementation.

***Java bindings***

```
public String getData() throws DOMException;
public void setData(String data) throws DOMException;
```

***Java example***

```
// Quote the CharacterData node contents
CharacterData ndCD = (CharacterData)doc.createTextNode("Unquoted text.");
...
ndCD.setData('\"' + ndCD.getData() + '\"');
```

---

**length:** *unsigned long*

The size of the `DOMString` stored in the `data` attribute. For all methods of this interface that take an `index` parameter, the valid range for the index is `0 <= index < length`. This value can be 0, since having an empty `CharacterData` node is possible. Read-only.

***Java binding***

```
public long getLength();
```

***Java example***

```
// Display the contents of a CharacterData node
CharacterData ndCD = (CharacterData)doc.createTextNode("This string has
                          30 characters.");

System.out.println("The string \'" + ndCD.getData() + "\' has "
              + Long.toString(ndCD.getLength()) + " characters.");
```

## *Methods*

The following methods are defined for `CharacterData`.

---

**appendData:** *arg*

This method appends contents of the `arg` parameter to the current contents of the `data` attribute.

***Arguments***

*arg: DOMString*
The string to append.

*Exceptions*

*NO_MODIFICATION_ALLOWED_ERR*
: Raised if this node is read-only.

*Java binding*

```
public void appendData(String arg) throws DOMException;
```

*Java example*

```
// Append to an existing string
// Create a new Text object and reference the CharacterData interface
CharacterData ndCD = (CharacterData)doc.createTextNode("The truth is ");

// flip a coin
ndCD.appendData((Math.random() < 0.5) ? "out there." : "in here.");

System.out.println(ndCD.getData());
```

---

## deleteData: *offset, count*

Truncates the `DOMString` in the `data` attribute. This method removes `count` characters, starting at the `offset` position.

*Arguments*

*offset: unsigned long*
: The position in the `data` attribute to remove `count` characters.

*count: unsigned long*
: The count of characters to remove. If the `offset` + `count` is >= the `length` attribute; the remainder, starting at position `offset`, is deleted.

*Exceptions*

*INDEX_SIZE_ERR*
: Raised if the `offset` parameter is not a valid zero based index into the `data DOMString`.

*NO_MODIFICATION_ALLOWED_ERR*
: Raised if the node is read-only.

*Java binding*

```
public void deleteData(long offset, long count)
               throws DOMException;
```

*Java example*

```
// Create a new Text object and reference the CharacterData interface
CharacterData ndCD = (CharacterData)doc.createTextNode("The truth is
                       not out there.");

// change of heart
ndCD.deleteData(12, 4);

System.out.println(ndCD.getData());
```

### insertData: *offset, arg*

This method takes a string, splits the `data` attribute's current contents at the given `offset`, then inserts the string from the `arg` parameter between the two substrings.

***Arguments***

*offset: unsigned long*
: The zero-based offset in the `data` attribute where the insertion is made.

*arg: DOMString*
: The string to be inserted.

***Exceptions***

*INDEX_SIZE_ERR*
: Raised if the `offset` parameter is not a valid, zero-based index into the `data DOMString`.

*NO_MODIFICATION_ALLOWED_ERR*
: Raised if the node is read-only.

***Java binding***

```
public void insertData(long offset, String arg) throws
  DOMException;
```

***Java example***

```
// Insert data into a string
boolean fCynical = true;

// create a new Text object, and reference the CharacterData interface
CharacterData ndCD = (CharacterData)doc.createTextNode("The truth is
                      out there.");

...

// check for cynicism
if (fCynical) {
    ndCD.insertData(12, " not");
}

System.out.println(ndCD.getData());
```

### replaceData: *offset, count, arg*

Replaces a substring within the `data` attribute with another string value `arg` using the specifed `offset` and `count` parameters.

***Arguments***

*offset: long*
: The offset of the beginning of the replacement region.

*count: long*
: The number of characters to replace. If `offset` + `count` is >= the `length` attribute, everything beyond the `offset` character position is replaced.

*arg: DOMString*
: The replacement string.

The `replaceData` operation is the equivalent of the following code fragment:

```
cdNode.deleteData(offset, count);
 cdNode.insertData(offset, arg);
```

***Exceptions***

*INDEX_SIZE_ERR*
: Raised if the `offset` parameter is not a valid, zero-based index into the `data DOMString`.

*NO_MODIFICATION_ALLOWED_ERR*
: Raised if the node is read-only.

***Java binding***

```
public void replaceData(long offset, long count,
                        String arg) throws DOMException;
```

***Java example***

```
 // Create a new Text object and reference the CharacterData interface
CharacterData ndCD = (CharacterData)doc.createTextNode("The truth is
                     not out there.");

// replace the truth
String strFind = "truth";
String strReplace = "dog";

ndCD.replaceData(ndCD.getData().indexOf(strFind), strFind.length(),
                 strReplace);

System.out.println(ndCD.getData());
```

## substringData: *offset, count*

Returns a `DOMString` that contains a subset of the string stored in the `data` attribute. The `offset` and `count` arguments define the substring. Though the `offset` argument must represent a valid position within the node data, the end point of the substring could fall past the end of the `data` attribute. If this happens, the method returns everything between the `offset` position and the end of the `data` string.

***Arguments***

*offset: unsigned long*
: Zero-based, starting offset of the substring to return. A valid offset must be >= 0 and < the `length` attribute of the node.

*count: unsigned long*
: Count of characters to return.

*Exceptions*

*INDEX_SIZE_ERR*
: Raised if the given offset is < 0, >= the `length` attribute, or if the `count` parameter is negative.

*DOMSTRING_SIZE_ERR*
: Raised if the value that would be returned is too large to be contained by a `DOMString` type in the given implementation.

### *Java binding*

```
public String substringData(unsigned long offset, unsigned long count)
                 throws DOMException;
```

### *Java example*

```
// Get a reference to the CharacterData interface
CharacterData ndCD = (CharacterData)doc.createTextNode("The truth is
                       out there.");

// we only want the "truth"
String strTruth = ndCD.substringData(4, 5);

System.out.println("The substring is '" + strTruth + '\'');
```

## *Comment*

This object contains the text of an XML comment (everything between the opening `<!--` and closing `-->`.) It inherits from `CharacterData`.

> The DOM specification does not require XML parsers to preserve the original document comments after the document is parsed. Some implementations strip comments as part of the parsing process.

### *Java example*

```
// Create a comment
Comment ndComment = doc.createComment("Document was parsed by DOM utility.");

// and add it to the document
doc.appendChild(ndComment);
```

## *Document*

The `Document` interface represents an entire, well-formed XML document. Once the `Document` object is created via the `DOMImplementation` interface, you can access every aspect of the underlying XML document through the various tree navigation methods exposed by the `Node` interface, the parent of the `Document` interface.

In DOM documents, document elements cannot exist outside of a parent document. For this reason, the Document interface exposes several factory methods used to create new document elements.

### *Attributes*

The following attributes are defined for the Document object.

---

#### doctype: *DocumentType*

This attribute returns an instance of the DocumentType interface representing the DTD for this document. If no DTD was declared in the document, this property is null. Read-only.

***Java binding***

```
public DocumentType getDoctype();
```

***Java example***

```
// Get the parsed DTD information for this document
DocumentType docType = docIn.getDoctype();

if (docType == null) {
    System.out.println("warning: no DTD provided");
}
```

---

#### documentElement: *Element*

This attribute points to the single Element node that is the root of the XML document tree. Read-only.

***Java binding***

```
public Element getDocumentElement();
```

***Java example***

```
// Identify the root element
Element elRoot = docIn.getDocumentElement();
System.out.println("This is a '" + elRoot.getTagName() + "' document.");
```

---

#### implementation: *DOMImplementation*

Returns a reference to the DOMImplementation that is responsible for this document. It is conceivable (but unlikely) that a single application might use DOM objects from multiple DOM implementations. Read-only.

***Java binding***

```
public DOMImplementation getImplementation();
```

***Java example***

```
// Ensure the support of DOM Level 1 XML
DOMImplementation di = doc.getImplementation();
if (!di.hasFeature("XML", "1.0")) {
    return false;
}
```

### *Methods*

The following methods are defined for the Document object.

---

#### createAttribute: *name*

This function creates an `Attr` object with the given name. `Attr` nodes construct complex element attributes that can include `EntityReference` objects and text data. See the `Attr` section earlier in this chapter for more information about creating and attaching `Attr` nodes to XML elements.

***Argument***

*name: DOMString*
  The name of the XML attribute.

***Return value***

The new `Attr` object.

***Exceptions***

*INVALID_CHARACTER_ERR*
  Indicates that the name you passed in to `createAttribute()` doesn't conform to a valid XML tag name. See Chapter 2, *XML Fundamentals*, for the XML restrictions on name construction.

***Java binding***

```
public Attr createAttribute(String name) throws DOMException;
```

***Java example***

```
// Create an entity reference
EntityReference er = doc.createEntityReference("name_entity");

// must create an Attribute object to include an explicit
// entity reference
Attr attr = doc.createAttribute("name");

// append the entity reference
attr.appendChild(er);
```

---

#### createAttributeNS: *namespaceURI*, *qualifiedName* ❷

This method serves the same purpose as the `createAttribute` method, but includes support for XML namespaces. See Chapter 4, *Namespaces,* for more information about namespaces.

***Arguments***

*namespaceURI: DOMString*
  The URI associated with the namespace prefix in the `qualifiedName` parameter.

*qualifiedName: DOMString*
  The name of the attribute to instantiate; include the namespace prefix associated with the namespace URI given in the `namespaceURI` parameter.

### *Return value*

The new Attr object is returned with the following attribute values:

| *Attribute* | *Value* |
|---|---|
| Node.nodeName | The complete, fully qualified name given in the qualifiedName parameter. |
| Node.namespaceURI | The given namespace URI. |
| Node.prefix | The namespace prefix, which is parsed from the qualifiedName parameter. |
| Node.localName | The local part of the qualified name, located to the right of the : character. |
| Attr.tagName | The qualifiedName. |

### *Exceptions*

*INVALID_CHARACTER_ERR*
: Indicates that the name you passed in to createAttributeNS() doesn't conform to a valid XML tag name. See Chapter 2 for the XML restrictions on name construction.

*NAMESPACE_ERR*
: Raised if the qualifiedName is malformed, has a prefix but no namespaceURI, or if the reserved xml namespace prefix was used incorrectly.

### *Java binding*

```
public Attr createAttributeNS(String namespaceURI, String qualifiedName)
                throws DOMException;
```

## createCDATASection: *data*

Creates a new CDATASection node that contains the data text. CDATASection nodes contain non-XML text content that would be inconvenient or impractical to quote using the standard XML entities, such as &, <, or >.

### *Argument*

*data: DOMString*
: The text contained by the new CDATASection object.

### *Exceptions*

*NOT_SUPPORTED_ERR*
: Occurs if you try to call this method on an HTML document.

### *Java binding*

```
public CDATASection createCDATASection(String data) throws DOMException;
```

### *Java example*

```
// Use CDATASection to embed XML characters
CDATASection cds = doc.createCDATASection("
<xml_example>This is sample text.</xml_example>
");
```

### createComment: *data*

Returns a new `Comment` node containing the specified string. See the `Comment` object reference earlier in this chapter for special restrictions that apply to the contents of `Comment` nodes.

*Argument*

*data: DOMString*
The comment text.

> ***Comment Text Restriction***
>
> The XML specification indicates that the `--` characters must not appear in the comment text, for compatibility reasons. Despite this warning, some DOM implementations don't flag comments containing double hyphens as syntax errors.

***Java binding***

```
public Comment createComment(String data);
```

***Java example***

```
// Create a timestamp comment
StringBuffer sb = new StringBuffer();
Date dtNow = new Date();

sb.append("\tModified " + dtNow.toString() + '\n');

Comment cmt = doc.createComment(sb.toString());
```

### createDocumentFragment()

Returns an empty `DocumentFragment` object. See the `DocumentFragment` reference later in this chapter for a discussion of a document fragment's uses and limitations.

***Java binding***

```
public DocumentFragment createDocumentFragment();
```

### createElement: *tagName*

Creates a new, empty `Element` node for use within the parent document. The element type (XML tag) is given as an argument to the method. The resulting `Element` node belongs to the parent `Document` object, but is not part of the document element hierarchy. See the `Node` section later in this chapter for more information about how the document hierarchy manipulation methods are used.

*Argument*

*tagName: DOMString*
The XML tag name used to create the new `Element` node. This tag is assigned to the `nodeName` attribute of the resulting `Element` node.

*Return value*

The new `Element` object.

*Exceptions*

*INVALID_CHARACTER_ERR*
: Indicates that the name you passed in to `createElement()` doesn't conform to a valid XML tag name. See Chapter 2 for the XML restrictions on name construction.

*Java binding*

```
public Element createElement(String tagName) throws DOMException;
```

*Java example*

```
// Create the new my_tag Element
Element elOut = doc.createElement("my_tag");
```

---

### createElementNS: *namespaceURI, qualifiedName* ❷

This method serves the same purpose as the `createElement` method, but includes support for XML namespaces. See Chapter 4 for more information about namespaces.

*Arguments*

*namespaceURI: DOMString*
: The URI associated with the namespace prefix in the `qualifiedName` parameter.

*qualifiedName: DOMString*
: The name of the element to instantiate, including the namespace prefix associated with the namespace URI given in the `namespaceURI` parameter.

*Return value*

The new `Element` object is returned with the following attribute values:

| *Attribute* | *Value* |
|---|---|
| `Node.nodeName` | The complete, fully qualified name given in the `qualifiedName` parameter |
| `Node.namespaceURI` | The given namespace URI |
| `Node.prefix` | The namespace prefix, which is parsed from the `qualifiedName` parameter |
| `Node.localName` | The local part of the qualified name, located to the right of the `:` character |
| `Element.tagName` | The full element tag name, which is the same as the `qualifiedName` |

*Exceptions*

*INVALID_CHARACTER_ERR*
: Indicates that the name you passed in to `createElementNS()` doesn't conform to a valid XML tag name. See Chapter 2 for the XML restrictions on name construction.

*NAMESPACE_ERR*

Raised if the `qualifiedName` is malformed, has a prefix but no `namespaceURI`, or if the reserved `xml` namespace prefix was used incorrectly.

***Java binding***

```
public Element createElementNS(String namespaceURI, String qualifiedName)
                    throws DOMException;
```

---

### createEntityReference: *name*

Creates an `EntityReference` object.

***Argument***

*name: DOMString*

The name of the XML entity to be referenced. The name must match an XML entity declaration that is valid in the current document.

***Exceptions***

*INVALID_CHARACTER_ERR*

Indicates that the name you passed in to `createEntityReference()` doesn't conform to a valid XML tag name. See Chapter 2 for the XML restrictions on name construction.

*NOT_SUPPORTED_ERR*

This exception would be generated if you attempted to create an entity reference using an HTML document.

***Java binding***

```
public EntityReference createEntityReference(String name)
                              throws DOMException;
```

***Java example***

```
// Create an entity reference
EntityReference er = doc.createEntityReference("name_entity");
```

---

### createProcessingInstruction: *target, data*

Creates a new `ProcessingInstruction` node with the given *target* name and *data* values. The processing instruction target name "xml" (case insensitive) is reserved by the XML working group, and can't be used by an application.

***Arguments***

*target: DOMString*

The target name of the processing instruction. This name identifies the application that will interpret the data portion of the instruction.

*data:DOMString*

The application-specific data for the resulting `ProcessingInstruction` node.

*Exceptions*

*INVALID_CHARACTER_ERR*

Indicates that the name you passed in to `createProcessingInstruction` doesn't conform to a valid XML tag name. See Chapter 2 for the XML restrictions on name construction.

*NOT_SUPPORTED_ERR*

Generated if you attempt to create a `ProcessingInstruction` using an HTML document.

***Java binding***

```
public ProcessingInstruction createProcessingInstruction(String target,
                                String data) throws DOMException;
```

***Java example***

```
// Add the application-specific processing instruction
ProcessingInstruction pi = doc.createProcessingInstruction("my_app",
            "action=\"save\"");
```

## createTextNode: *data*

Creates a new `Text` node that contains the given `data` string.

***Argument***

*data: DOMString*

The string that will be the contents of the new node.

***Java binding***

```
public Text createTextNode(String data);
```

***Java example***

```
// Create a new node that contains character data
Text txtDesc = doc.createTextNode("Character data contents for a new
                                Element.");
```

## getElementById: *elementID* ❷

This method returns the `Element` node with the given value for its ID attribute.

> It is important to not confuse attributes that have the name ID with ID attributes. *ID attributes* are attributes that were declared with the ID attribute type within the document type definition. See the "Attribute List Declaration" section in Chapter 18, *XML 1.0 Reference*, for more information about ID attributes.

***Argument***

*elementID: DOMString*

The unique ID value for the desired element.

*Return value*

A single `Element` object that has the requested ID attribute or `null`, if no match is found.

*Java binding*

```
public Element getElementById(String elementId);
```

### getElementsByTagName: *tagName*

This function returns a list of `Element` nodes from the current document whose `tagName` attribute matches the given `tagName` parameter. The nodes are returned in the same order in which they would be encountered in a preorder traversal of the document tree. A preorder traversal conforms to the order that XML elements appear in the source document.

*Argument*

*tagName: DOMString*
The name of the tag to use as a filter. The special name * matches any tag.

*Java binding*

```
public NodeList getElementsByTagName(String tagName);
```

*Java example*

```
// Get a list of all phone numbers in the document
NodeList nl = doc.getElementsByTagName("phone_number");
```

### getElementsByTagNameNS: *namespaceURI, localName* ❷

Like the `getElementsByTagName()` method, this method returns a list of `Element` nodes (a `NodeList` object) that match the criteria given in the `namespaceURI` and `localName` parameters. The resulting list contains all elements matching the namespace URI and local name restrictions, as they would be encountered in a preorder traversal of the document tree.

*Arguments*

*namespaceURI: DOMString*
The namespace URI of the elements to be matched. The special * value matches any namespace.

*localName: DOMString*
The local name part of the elements to be matched. The special value * matches any local name.

*Java binding*

```
public NodeList getElementsByTagNameNS(String namespaceURI,
                                       String localName);
```

### hasAttribute: *name* ❷

This method determines whether an `Element` instance has a value that is valid for a particular attribute. It will return `true` if the attribute is given either explicitly within the XML document or as a default; otherwise, it returns `false`.

***Argument***

*name: DOMString*

The name of the attribute to find.

***Java binding***

```
public boolean hasAttribute(String name);
```

---

## hasAttributeNS: *namespaceURI, localName* ❷

This method determines whether an `Element` instance has a value valid for a particular namespace-enabled attribute. It returns `true` if the attribute is given either explicitly within the XML document or as a default; otherwise, it returns `false`.

***Arguments***

*namespaceURI: DOMString*

The namespace URI of the attribute to find.

*localName: DOMString*

The local name to search for.

***Java binding***

```
public boolean hasAttributeNS(String namespaceURI, String localName);
```

---

## importNode: *importedNode, deep* ❷

This method's name is somewhat deceptive. It creates a copy of a `Node` object from another document that can be inserted within the current document's node hierarchy. Specifics of this copy operation vary, depending on the type of copied node.

| *Node Type* | *Result* | *Effect of deep Flag* |
|---|---|---|
| `ATTRIBUTE_NODE` | Copies the source attribute and all its children. The `ownerElement` attribute is set to `null` and the `specified` flag is set to `true`. | None. |
| `DOCUMENT_FRAGMENT_NODE` | Creates an empty `DocumentFragment` node. | Fully copies the children of the source `DocumentFragment` node. |
| `DOCUMENT_NODE` | Cannot be imported. | N/A. |
| `DOCUMENT_TYPE_NODE` | Cannot be imported. | N/A. |
| `ELEMENT_NODE` | Copies only the attribute nodes with the `specified` flag set to the new element. | Recursively copies all the source element's children. |
| `ENTITY_NODE` | Copies the `publicId`, `systemId`, and `notationName` attributes. | Recursively copies all of the `Entity` node's children. |

| *Node Type* | *Result* | *Effect of deep Flag* |
|---|---|---|
| ENTITY_REFERENCE_NODE | Copies only the `EntityReference` node. Its value, if any, is taken from the DTD of the document doing the import. | None. |
| NOTATION_NODE | Imports the `notation` node, but since in Level 2 the `DocumentType` interface is read-only, it cannot be included in the target document. | None. |
| PROCESSING_INSTRUCTION_NODE | Copies the `target` and `data` values. | None. |
| TEXT_NODE, CDATA_SECTION_NODE, COMMENT_NODE | Copies the `data` and `length` attributes. | None. |

The new (copied) node object is returned based on the arguments.

***Arguments***

*importedNode: Node*
: The node duplicated for use in the current document hierarchy.

*deep: boolean*
: Whether to copy the single node given or the entire subtree of its children. For details, see the previous table.

***Exceptions***

*NOT_SUPPORTED_ERR*
: Thrown if an attempt is made to import an unsupported `Node` type, such as a `Document` node.

***Java Binding***

```
public Node importNode(Node importedNode, boolean deep)
    throws DOMException;
```

## *DocumentFragment*

The `DocumentFragment` is a lightweight container used to temporarily store XML document fragments. Since it has no properties or methods of its own, it can only provide the same functionality exposed by the `Node` object. It is intended to serve as a container for at least one well-formed XML sub-tree.

This object's most obvious application is in the case of clipboard or drag-and-drop operations in a visual editor. The user may elect to select several sub-trees that appear at the same level of the tree to be copied:

```
<xml_example>
    <caption><filename>sample.xml</filename> before DocumentFragment copy
operation</caption>
    <document>
        <parent>
            <child_1></child_1>
```

```
            <child_2></child_2>
        </parent>
        <parent>
        </parent>
    </document>
</xml_example>
```

If the user decides to copy the two child nodes to the clipboard, the DOM application would:

- Create a DocumentFragment object.
- Attach copies of the child nodes to the new object using the cloneNode() and appendChild() methods.

```
<xml_example>
    <caption>DocumentFragment object on clipboard.</caption>
    <DocumentFragment frame="dashed">
        <child_1></child_1>
        <child_2></child_2>
    </DocumentFragment>
</xml_example>
```

Then, when the user decides to paste the copied nodes to a new location, the new DocumentFragment node is passed to this target node's appendChild() method. During the copy operation, the DocumentFragment node itself is ignored, and only the children are attached to the target node.

```
<xml_example>
    <caption><filename>sample.xml</filename> after DocumentFragment copy
operation</caption>
    <document>
        <parent>
            <child_1></child_1>
            <child_2></child_2>
        </parent>
        <parent>
            <child_1></child_1>
            <child_2></child_2>
        </parent>
    </document>
</xml_example>
```

### *Java example*

```
// Create a Document Fragment object
DocumentFragment dfNorm = doc.createDocumentFragment();
```

## *DocumentType*

The Document interface includes a single attribute, docType, that points either to a description of the DTD for the current document or to null if none exists:

```
// get document type information
    DocumentType dtDoc = doc.getDoctype();
```

### *Attributes*

The DocumentType object contains the following attributes.

---

**entities:** *NamedNodeMap*

This attribute provides a list of all general entities declared in the document's DTD. If the same entity is declared more than once within a single document, only the first occurrence is preserved in this NamedNodeMap. Note that parameter entity declarations are not available through the DocumentType interface. Each member of this list implements the Entity interface. Read-only.

***Java binding***

```
public NamedNodeMap getEntities();
```

***Java example***

```
// Dump the document entities
NamedNodeMap nnm = doc.getDoctype().getEntities();

Entity ndEnt;
for (int i = 0; i < nnm.getLength(); i++) {
    ndEnt = (Entity)nnm.item(i);

    System.out.println(ndEnt.getNodeName());

    if (ndEnt.getPublicId() != null) {
        System.out.println("\tPublic Identifier: " +
                           ndEnt.getPublicId());
    }

    if (ndEnt.getSystemId() != null) {
        System.out.println("\tSystem Identifier: " +
                           ndEnt.getSystemId());
    }

    if (ndEnt.getNotationName() != null) {
        System.out.println("\tNotation Name: " +
                           ndEnt.getNotationName());
    }
}
```

---

**internalSubset:** *DOMString*

This attribute contains the document's internal subset as a string value. The content's actual format depends on the level of support provided by a particular XML parser. Read-only.

***Java binding***

```
public String getInternalSubset();
```

---

**name:** *DOMString*

The name of the DTD, which is the XML name following the XML DOCTYPE keyword in the source document. Read-only.

*Java binding*

```
public String getName();
```

*Java example*

```
// Display document type information
DocumentType dtDoc = doc.getDoctype();

System.out.println("This is a " + dtDoc.getName() + " document.");
```

## notations: *NamedNodeMap*

A NamedNodeMap containing a list of XML notation declarations for the current document. Each member of this list implements the `Notation` interface, and the list itself is read-only.

*Java binding*

```
public NamedNodeMap getNotations();
```

*Java example*

```
// Dump the document notations
NamedNodeMap nnm = doc.getDoctype().getNotations();
Notation ndNotation;
for (int i = 0; i < nnm.getLength(); i++) {
    ndNotation = (Notation)nnm.item(i);

    System.out.println(ndNotation.getNodeName());
    if (ndNotation.getPublicId() != null) {
        System.out.println("\tPublic Identifier: " +
                           ndNotation.getPublicId());
    }
    if (ndNotation.getSystemId() != null) {
        System.out.println("\tSystem Identifier: " +
                           ndNotation.getSystemId());
    }
}
```

## publicId: DOMString

The public identifier of the external subset. Read-only.

*Java binding*

```
public String getPublicId();
```

## systemId: DOMString

The system identifier (URI) of this document's external subset. Read-only.

*Java binding*

```
public String getSystemId();
```

## *DOMException*

For languages and runtime platforms that support them, structured exceptions provide a way to separate the code that deals with abnormal or unexpected problems from the normal flow of execution. For languages that don't support exceptions, such as ECMAScript or Perl, these conditions are reported to your program as error codes from the method that recognized the condition.

The `ExceptionCode` is an integer value that indicates what type of exception was detected. The following `ExceptionCodes` are defined, with unused numeric codes reserved for future use by the W3C:

### INDEX_SIZE_ERR [unsigned short, value: 1]

An index outside the expected range was passed to a method that accepts an index. The expected range for most collections is 0 <= index < collection.length.

*Java binding*

```
public static final short INDEX_SIZE_ERR = 1;
```

### DOMSTRING_SIZE_ERR [unsigned short, value: 2]

The `DOMString` that would be returned from a method is too large.

*Java binding*

```
public static final short DOMSTRING_SIZE_ERR = 2;
```

### HIERARCHY_REQUEST_ERR [unsigned short, value: 3 ]

The node insertion you requested violates the document structure's integrity. For example, the insertion would cause a node to become one of its own children.

*Java binding*

```
public static final short HIERARCHY_REQUEST_ERR = 3;
```

### WRONG_DOCUMENT_ERR [unsigned short, value: 4 ]

An attempt to insert a node from one document directly into another. A given implementer of the DOM framework determines whether this insertion generates an error.

*Java binding*

```
public static final short WRONG_DOCUMENT_ERR = 4;
```

### INVALID_CHARACTER_ERR [unsigned short, value: 5 ]

An invalid character was used in a name, such as trying to create an `Element` object with the name `"my element"`, as spaces are not allowed.

*Java binding*

```
public static final short INVALID_CHARACTER_ERR = 5;
```

### NO_DATA_ALLOWED_ERR [unsigned short, value: 6 ]

Data was assigned to a `Node` that doesn't support data, like an `Element` node.

***Java binding***

```
public static final short NO_DATA_ALLOWED_ERR = 6;
```

### NO_MODIFICATION_ALLOWED_ERR [unsigned short, value: 7 ]

A node that cannot be modified was modified.

***Java binding***

```
public static final short NO_MODIFICATION_ALLOWED_ERR = 7;
```

### NOT_FOUND_ERR [unsigned short, value: 8 ]

A node was modified in a context in which it could not be found.

***Java binding***

```
public static final short NOT_FOUND_ERR = 8;
```

### NOT_SUPPORTED_ERR [unsigned short, value: 9 ]

If the specific implementation of the DOM you use chose not to implement an optional feature, this exception would be thrown.

***Java binding***

```
public static final short NOT_SUPPORTED_ERR = 9;
```

### INUSE_ATTRIBUTE_ERR [unsigned short, value: 10 ]

An attempt was made to add an attribute that is already in use elsewhere. This error could occur if you acquire an attribute via the `getAttributeNode()` method and tried to add the same object instance to another element using the `setAttributeNode()` method. You would first need to create a new `Attr` object, probably using the `cloneNode()` method.

***Java binding***

```
public static final short INUSE_ATTRIBUTE_ERR = 10;
```

### INVALID_STATE_ERR [unsigned short, value: 11 ] ❷

An attempt was made to use an object that is no longer usable.

***Java binding***

```
public static final short INVALID_STATE_ERR = 11;
```

### SYNTAX_ERR [unsigned short, value: 12 ] ❷

An invalid or illegal string was specified.

***Java binding***

```
public static final short SYNTAX_ERR = 12;
```

### INVALID_MODIFICATION_ERR [unsigned short, value: 13 ] ❷

An attempt was made to change the type's underlying object.

*Java binding*

```
public static final short INVALID_MODIFICATION_ERR = 13;
```

**NAMESPACE_ERR [unsigned short, value: 14 ] ❷**

An attempt was made to use a method that supports XML namespaces in a way that would violate namespace rules. This error could occur if a qualified name were given to a method without a corresponding namespace URI.

*Java binding*

```
public static final short NAMESPACE_ERR = 14;
```

**INVALID_ACCESS_ERR [unsigned short, value: 15 ] ❷**

The underlying object does not support a parameter or operation.

*Java binding*

```
public static final short INVALID_ACCESS_ERR = 15;
```

## *DOMImplementation*

The `DOMImplementation` interface provides global information about the DOM implementation you currently use. The only way to obtain a reference to the `DOMImplementation` interface is through the `getImplementation()` method of the `Document` object.

### *Java example*

```
// Check for DOM Level 1 support
DOMImplementation di = doc.getImplementation();
// make sure that DOM Level 1 XML is supported
if (!di.hasFeature("XML", "1.0")) {
    return null;
}
```

### *Methods*

The `DOMImplementation` object defines the following methods:

**createDocument:** *namespaceURI, qualifiedName, doctype* ❷

Creates a new, empty `Document` object with the given document type. It also creates the single, top-level document element using the given qualified name and namespace URI.

*Arguments*

*namespaceURI: DOMString*
: The namespace URI used to create the top-level document element. Can be `null` if no namespace is used.

*qualifiedName: DOMString*
: The namespace-aware qualified name of the top-level document element to be created. The prefix given in this parameter is associated with the namespace URI given in the `namespaceURI` parameter.

*doctype: DOMString*

The document type definition object to be associated with the new document. If this parameter is not null, the `DocumentType` node's `ownerDocument` attribute is set to point to the new document object.

***Exceptions***

*INVALID_CHARACTER_ERR*

Indicates that the `qualifiedName` parameter has a malformed XML identifier.

*NAMESPACE_ERR*

Raised if an inconsistency exists between the values given for the `namespaceURI` and the `qualifiedName` parameters. Passing in a qualified name with a namespace prefix and not passing in a namespace URI is illegal. This can also be generated if a reserved namespace prefix, such as `"xml"`, is given with an incorrect namespace URI.

*WRONG_DOCUMENT_ERR*

Raised if the `DocumentType` node passed in the `doctype` parameter is already associated with another document object. New `DocumentType` objects must be created using the new `createDocumentType` method of the `DOMImplementation` interface.

***Java binding***

```
public Document createDocument(String namespaceURI,
    String qualifiedName, DocumentType doctype) throws DOMException;
```

---

## createDocumentType: *qualifiedName, publicId, systemId* ❷

Creates an empty `DocumentType` node that is not associated with any document. No entity declarations or notations are available in this new, empty `DocumentType` object. No support currently exists in the DOM to populate this object.

***Arguments***

*qualifiedName: DOMString*

The qualified name of the document type to be created.

*publicId: DOMString*

The external subset's public identifier.

*systemId: DOMString*

The system identifier (URI) of the external subset to be created.

***Return value***

A new `DocumentType` object with the `ownerDocument` attribute set to `null`.

***Exceptions***

*INVALID_CHARACTER_ERR*

Indicates that the `qualifiedName` parameter has a malformed XML identifier.

*NAMESPACE_ERR*

Raised if the qualified name is malformed.

***Java binding***

```
public DocumentType createDocumentType(String qualifiedName,
        String publicId, String systemId) throws DOMException;
```

**hasFeature:** *feature, version*

Tests to see if the DOM implementation supports a given named feature package. Returns `true` if the particular version of the specified feature is available; otherwise, returns `false`.

***Arguments***

*feature: DOMString*

The package name of the feature to test. The following feature names are valid:

`XML`

Supports DOM Level 1.0 or 2.0 Core objects.

`HTML`

Supports DOM Level 1.0 or 2.0 HTML objects.

*version: DOMString*

The DOM version level of the specified feature to test. If no version number is specified, the function returns `true` if any version is supported.

***Java binding***

```
public boolean hasFeature(String feature, String version);
```

***Java example***

```
// Make sure that DOM Level 1 XML is supported
if (!di.hasFeature("XML", "1.0")) {
    return null;
}
```

The HTML-specific DOM objects are beyond the scope of this book, but are extremely useful tools for building applications that perform transformations on HTML documents. An excellent reference to the HTML DOM objects can be found in the book *Dynamic HTML: The Definitive Reference*, by Danny Goodman (O'Reilly & Associates, 1998).

## *Element*

The `Element` object type provides access to the XML document's structure and data. Every XML element is translated into a single `Element` node. The document's root element is accessible through the `documentElement` property of the

Document object. From this node, it is possible to recreate the full structure of the original XML document by traversing the element tree.

This interface extends the basic Node interface to allow access to the XML attributes of the document element. Two sets of methods allow access to attribute values, either as Attr object trees or as simple DOMStrings.

*Java example*

```
// Get the XML document's root element
Element elem = doc.getDocumentElement();
```

## *Attributes*

The Element object defines one attribute that contains the XML tag name.

---

**tagName:** *DOMString*

The XML tag name from the original document.

*Java binding*

```
public String getTagName();
```

*Java example*

```
// Show the name of the root element tag
Element elem = doc.getDocumentElement();
System.out.println("This is a " + elem.getTagName() + " document.");
```

## *Methods*

The following methods are defined for this object:

---

**getAttribute:** *name*

Returns the attribute specified by the name parameter as a DOMString. See the value topic for a complete explanation of how an attribute value is determined. Returns an empty string if no attribute is set and if no default attribute value was specified in the DTD.

*Java binding*

```
public String getAttribute(String name);
```

*Java example*

```
// Check for the name attribute
Element elem = doc.getDocumentElement();

if (elem.getAttribute("name") == "") {
    System.out.println("warning: " + elem.getTagName() +
                    " element: no name attribute");
}
```

---

**getAttributeNS:** *namespaceURI, localName* ❷

Returns an attribute as a DOMString, based on the namespace and local part of the qualified name.

***Arguments***

*namespaceURI: DOMString*
The namespace URI of the attribute to return.

*localName: DOMString*
The local name portion of the qualified attribute name to return.

***Return value***

Returns an empty string if no attribute is set and if no default attribute value was specified in the DTD.

***Java binding***

```
public String getAttributeNS(String namespaceURI, String localName);
```

---

## getAttributeNode: *name*

Retrieves the `Attr` for the `name` attribute. Returns a reference to the attribute object if it is found, otherwise `null`.

***Arguments***

*name: DOMString*
Name of the attribute to retrieve.

***Java binding***

```
public Attr getAttributeNode(String name);
```

***Java example***

```
// Use the id attribute
Attr attr;

if ((attr = elem.getAttributeNode("id")) == null) {
    System.out.println("warning: element " + elem.getTagName() +
                       ": no id attribute provided.");
}
```

---

## getAttributeNodeNS: *namespaceURI, localName* ❷

Retrieves the `Attr` object for the attribute specified by the given namespace URI and local name. Returns a reference to the attribute object if it is found, otherwise returns `null`.

***Arguments***

*namespaceURI: DOMString*
Namespace URI of the target attribute.

*localName: DOMString*
Local name of the target attribute. The local name is the part of the name to the right of the `:` in a qualified name.

***Java binding***

```
public Attr getAttributeNodeNS(String namespaceURI, String localName);
```

## getElementsByTagName: *name*

This function returns a `NodeList` of all child `Element` nodes whose `tagName` attribute matches the given `name` parameter. The nodes are returned in the same order they would be encountered in a preorder traversal of the document tree. A preorder traversal conforms to the order the XML elements appear in the source document.

***Argument***

*name: DOMString*
: The name of the tag to use as a filter. The special name `*` matches any tag.

***Java binding***

```
public NodeList getElementsByTagName(String name);
```

***Java example***

```
// Find every address element in the document
Element elem = doc.getDocumentElement();
NodeList nlAddrs = elem.getElementsByTagName("address");
```

## getElementsByTagNameNS: *namespaceURI, localName* ❷

Like the `getElementsByTagName` method, this method returns a list of `Element` nodes that match the criteria given in the `namespaceURI` and `localName` parameters. The resulting list contains all elements matching the namespace URI and local name restrictions, as they would be encountered in a preorder traversal of the document tree.

***Arguments***

*namespaceURI: DOMString*
: The namespace URI of elements to be matched. The special `*` value matches any namespace.

*localName: DOMString*
: The local name part of elements to be matched. The special value `*` matches any local name.

***Java binding***

```
public NodeList getElementsByTagNameNS(String namespaceURI,
                                       String localName);
```

## hasAttribute: *name* ❷

Returns `true` if an attribute with the given name has been set or has a default value. Returns `false` if the attribute isn't defined.

***Argument***

*name: DOMString*
: The name of the attribute to be identified.

***Java binding***

```
public boolean hasAttribute(String name);
```

### hasAttributeNS: *namespaceURI, localName* ❷

Returns `true` if an attribute with the given `namespaceURI` and `localName` has been set or has a default value. Returns `false` if the attribute isn't defined.

***Arguments***

*namespaceURI: DOMString*
The namespace URI of the attribute to be identified.

*localName: DOMSTring*
The local name of the attribute to be identified.

***Java binding***

```
public boolean hasAttribute(String namespaceURI, String localName);
```

### normalize

Traverses the sub-tree of the current `Element`, combining adjacent `Text` nodes into a single node.

> This method was moved to the `Node` interface as part of the DOM Level 2 specification. It is still accessible from the `Element` interface, as it inherits from the `Node` interface.

***Java binding***

```
public void normalize();
```

***Java example***

```
// Merge all adjacent text nodes below this element
elem.normalize();
```

### removeAttribute: *name*

Removes the named element attribute from this element's `attributes` collection. If the attribute to be removed has a default value declared in the DTD, subsequent attempts to retrieve the attribute value return the default value.

***Argument***

*name: DOMString*
Name of the attribute to remove.

***Exceptions***

*NO_MODIFICATION_ALLOWED_ERR*
Raised if the element is read-only.

***Java binding***

```
public void removeAttribute(String name) throws DOMException;
```

*Java example*

```
// Remove the unique ID
...
elem.removeAttribute("id");
...
```

---

### removeAttributeNS: *namespaceURI, localName* ❷

This method uses the given namespace URI and local name parameters to remove the desired attribute from the element's `attributes` collection.

*Arguments*

*namespaceURI: DOMString*
: Namespace URI of the target attribute.

*localName: DOMString*
: Local name part of the target attribute. The local name is the part to the right of the final `:` in a qualified name.

*Exceptions*

*NO_MODIFICATION_ALLOWED_ERR*
: Raised if the element is read-only.

*Java binding*

```
public void removeAttributeNS(String namespaceURI, String localName)
              throws DOMException;
```

---

### removeAttributeNode: *oldAttr*

Removes the referenced attribute node from this element's `attributes` collection. If the attribute to be removed has a default value declared in the DTD, subsequent attempts to retrieve the attribute value return the default value.

*Argument*

*oldAttr: Attr*
: Name of the attribute to remove.

*Exceptions*

*NO_MODIFICATION_ALLOWED_ERR*
: Raised if the node is read-only.

*NOT_FOUND_ERR*
: Raised if no attribute name matching the `oldAttr` parameter is found in the map.

*Java binding*

```
public Attr removeAttributeNode(Attr oldAttr) throws DOMException;
```

*Java example*

```
// Find and remove temporary attributes
Attr attr;
```

*Java example*

```
if ((attr = elem.getAttributeNode("temp")) != null) {
    // remove it
    elem.removeAttributeNode(attr);
}
```

---

**setAttribute:** *name, value*

This method sets the attribute specified by the `name` parameter to the `DOMString` passed in the `value` argument. The string is not parsed for entity references and is set as a `Text` node child of the corresponding member of the `attributes` collection. If an attribute with the given name already exists, the value is set to the `value` argument.

***Arguments***

*name: DOMString*
The attribute name to set or modify.

*value: DOMString*
The new attribute value.

***Exceptions***

*INVALID_CHARACTER_ERR*
Indicates that the attribute name you passed in doesn't represent a valid XML attribute name.

*NO_MODIFICATION_ALLOWED_ERR*
Raised if the element is read-only.

***Java binding***

```
public void setAttribute(String name, String value) throws DOMException;
```

***Java example***

```
// Check for the name attribute
if (elem.getAttribute("name") == "") {
    // oh well, set a reasonable default
    elem.setAttribute("name", elem.getTagName());
}
```

---

**setAttributeNS:** *namespaceURI, qualifiedName, value* ❷

This method is the namespace-enabled version of the basic `setAttribute` method. The namespace URI and the qualified name update the `attributes` collection of the element in question.

***Arguments***

*namespaceURI: DOMString*
The namespace URI of the attribute value to set.

*qualifiedName: DOMString*
The qualified name (including namespace prefix) of the new value to set.

*value: DOMString*
The new attribute value.

*Exceptions*

*INVALID_CHARACTER_ERR*

Indicates that the attribute name you passed in doesn't represent a valid XML attribute name.

*NO_MODIFICATION_ALLOWED_ERR*

Raised if the element is read-only.

*NAMESPACE_ERR*

Raised if the `namespaceURI` and `qualifiedName` parameters would violate rules concerning namespaces. If the qualified name includes a prefix, the namespace URI cannot be `null` or an empty string. If the reserved "xml" or "xmlns" prefixes are used, the namespace URI must match the corresponding specified system URI. See Chapter 4 for more information about namespaces and prefixes.

*Java binding*

```
public void setAttributeNS(String namespaceURI, String qualifiedName,
                           String value) throws DOMException;
```

---

### setAttributeNode: *newAttr*

Sets or replaces the attribute in the `Node` interface's `attributes` collection with the given `Attr` object. The attribute name is retrieved from the `name` attribute of the new attribute object. If an `Attr` object with the given name in the `attributes` collection already exists, this method returns a reference to the old `Attr` object. Otherwise, it returns `null`.

*Argument*

*newAttr: Attr*

The new `Attr` object to set.

*Exception*

*WRONG_DOCUMENT_ERR*

Raised if the `newAttr` node was created in a document different than the parent node.

*NO_MODIFICATION_ALLOWED_ERR*

Raised if the new parent node is read-only.

*INUSE_ATTRIBUTE_ERR*

Raised if another `Element` already uses the new `Attr` node. Each element must have a distinct `Attr` object.

*Java binding*

```
public Attr setAttributeNode(Attr newAttr) throws DOMException;
```

*Java example*

```
// Make sure you have an id attribute to work with
Attr attr;

if ((attr = elem.getAttributeNode("id")) == null) {
    // add a default, unique id
    attr = doc.createAttribute("id");
```

*Java example*

```
    elem.setAttributeNode(attr);

    // continue processing
}
```

**setAttributeNodeNS:** *newAttr* ❷

Sets or replaces the attribute in the element's `attributes` collection that matches the namespace URI and the given `Attr` object's local name. This operation is identical to the `setAttributeNode` method, except that it considers namespace differences between attributes. If an `Attr` object with the given name in the `attributes` collection already exists, this method returns a reference to the old `Attr` object. Otherwise it returns `null`.

***Argument***

*newAttr: Attr*
: The new `Attr` object to set.

***Exceptions***

*WRONG_DOCUMENT_ERR*
: Raised if the `newAttr` node was created in a different document than the parent node.

*NO_MODIFICATION_ALLOWED_ERR*
: Raised if the new parent node is read-only.

*INUSE_ATTRIBUTE_ERR*
: Raised if another `Element` already uses the `newAttr` node. Each element must have a unique `Attr` object.

***Java binding***

```
public Attr setAttributeNodeNS(Attr newAttr) throws DOMException;
```

## *Entity*

The `Entity` object represents a given general XML entity's replacement value. Depending on whether a given DOM implementation is validating or nonvalidating and whether it chooses to expand entity references in-line during parsing, `Entity` objects may not be available to the DOM user.

### *Java example*

```
// Locate the my_entity entity declaration
Entity ndEnt = (Entity)doc.getDoctype().getEntities().
    getNamedItem("my_entity");
```

### *Attributes*

The following read-only attributes are defined for the `Entity` object.

### notationName: *DOMString*

If this entity is unparsed, `notationName` is the entity's notation name. For parsed entities, this attribute is `null`.

#### *Java binding*

```
public String getNotationName();
```

#### *Java example*

```
// Find out if it's a parsed entity
boolean fParsedEnt = ndEnt.getNotationName() == null;
```

### publicId: *DOMString*

The public identifier URL (URI) given for this entity, or `null` if none was specified.

#### *Java binding*

```
public String getPublicId();
```

#### *Java example*

```
// Locate the my_entity entity declaration
Entity ndEnt = (Entity)doc.getDoctype().getEntities().getNamedItem("my
entity");

// if my_entity type was found and there is a public-ID (URL)...
if (ndEnt != null && ndEnt.getPublicId() != null) {
    try {
        // ...get the URL protocol
        URL urlSys = new URL(ndEnt.getPublicId());
        System.out.println("Entity " + ndEnt.getNodeName() +
                           ": protocol " + urlSys.getProtocol());
    } catch (MalformedURLException e) {
    }
}
```

### systemId: *DOMString*

The system identifier URL (URI) given for this entity, or `null` if none was specified.

#### *Java binding*

```
public String getSystemId();
```

#### *Java example*

```
// Get the Public ID or System ID for this entity
Entity ndEnt = (Entity)doc.getDoctype().getEntities().getNamedItem("my_
entity");

String strURL = ndEnt.getPublicId();

// if can't find the public URL
if (strURL == null) {
```

*Java example*

```
    // find the system URL
    strURL = ndEnt.getSystemId();
}
```

## *EntityReference*

`EntityReference` nodes appear within the document hierarchy wherever an XML general entity reference is embedded within the source document. Depending on the DOM implementation, a corresponding `Entity` object in the `entities` collection of the `docType` attribute of the `Document` object may exist. If such an entity exists, then the child nodes of both the `Entity` and `EntityReference` represent the replacement text associated with the given entity.

*Java example*

```
// Create a new entity reference
EntityReference ndER = doc.createEntityReference("my_entity");
```

## *NamedNodeMap*

The `NamedNodeMap` interface provides a mechanism used to retrieve `Node` objects from a collection by name. Though this interface exposes the same methods and attributes as the `NodeList` class, they are not related. While it is possible to enumerate the nodes in a `NamedNodeMap` using the `item()` method and `length` attribute, the nodes are not guaranteed to be in any particular order.

*Java example*

```
// Get an element's attributes
NamedNodeMap nnm = elem.getAttributes();
```

### *Attributes*

The NamedNodeMap defines one attribute.

**length**: *unsigned long*

The total number of `Node` objects in the list.

*Java binding*

```
public long getLength();
```

*Java example*

```
// Iterate over the attribute list
for (int i = 0; i < nnm.getLength(); i++) {
    ...
}
```

### *Methods*

The following methods are defined for the **NamedNodeMap** object.

---

**getNamedItem:** *name*

Returns a reference to the node with the given **nodeName** property specified by **name**.

***Argument***

*name: DOMString*

Name of the node to retrieve.

***Java binding***

```
public Node getNamedItem(String name);
```

***Java example***

```
// Check to see if an ID attribute exists
// in this map, and add it if necessary
if (nnm.getNamedItem("id") == null) {
    // get the document
    Document doc = elem.getOwnerDocument();
    // create a new attribute Node
    Attr attrID = doc.createAttribute("id");

    // set the attribute value
    attrID.appendChild(doc.createTextNode(makeUniqueID(elem)));
    // ... and add it to the NamedNodeMap
    nnm.setNamedItem(attrID);
}
```

---

**getNamedItemNS:** *namespaceURI, localName* ❷

Extends the basic **getNamedItem** method to include support for namespaces. Instead of finding an item in the list based only on the local part of the node name, it is possible to incorporate the namespace URI into the search.

***Arguments***

*namespaceURI: DOMString*

Namespace URI of the node to retrieve.

*localName: DOMString*

Local name of the node to retrieve.

***Java binding***

```
public Node getNamedItemNS(String namespaceURI, String localName);
```

---

**item:** *index*

Returns a reference to the **Node** object at position **index**. If the given index is < 0 or >= the **length** attribute of the **NodeList**, this function returns **null**.

*Argument*

*index: unsigned long*
Zero-based index of the list of the Node to return.

*Java binding*

```
public Node item(long index);
```

*Java example*

```
// Remove the last attribute from the list
if (nnm.getLength() > 0) {
    nnm.removeNamedItem(nnm.item(nnm.getLength()-1).getNodeName());
}
```

---

### removeNamedItem: *name*

Removes the Node object with the nodeName property that matches the name parameter, and returns a reference to the removed object. If the node you plan to remove is an Attr node and if it has a defined default value, the node will be replaced immediately with a new Node object set to the default value.

*Argument*

*name: DOMString*
The nodeName value of the node to be removed.

*Exceptions*

*NOT_FOUND_ERR*
Raised if no node matching the name parameter is found in the map.

*Java binding*

```
public Node removeNamedItem(String name) throws DOMException;
```

*Java example*

```
// Remove the ID node attribute
NamedNodeMap nnm = elem.getAttributes();


if (nnm.removeNamedItem("id") == null) {
    System.err.println("no ID attribute found");
}
```

---

### removeNamedItemNS: *namespaceURI, localName* ❷

Removes the Node object with the matching namespaceURI and localName properties and returns a reference to the removed object. If the node you plan to remove is an Attr node, and if it has a defined default value, a new Node object set to the default value will replace the node immediately.

*Arguments*

*namespaceURI: DOMString*
Namespace URI of the node to retrieve.

*localName: DOMString*
Local name of the node to retrieve.

*Exception*

*NOT_FOUND_ERR*

Raised if no node matching the namespaceURI and localName parameter is found in the map.

*Java binding*

```
public Node removeNamedItemNS(String namespaceURI, String localName);
```

### setNamedItem: *arg*

Inserts the Node object given into the list, using its nodeName attribute. Since many DOM node types expose the same, hardcoded value for this property, only storing one of them in a single NamedNodeMap is possible. Each subsequent insertion overwrites the previous node entry. See the nodeName topic for a discussion of these special name values.

This method returns a reference to the Node object that the new node replaces. If no node with the same nodeName value is currently in the map, this method returns null.

*Argument*

*arg: Node*

The Node object to be stored in the map. The value of the nodeName property is used as the lookup key. A node with the same nodeName value as the new node is replaced with the node referenced by arg.

*Exceptions*

*WRONG_DOCUMENT_ERR*

Raised if a document different than the creator of the target NamedNodeMap created the arg node.

*NO_MODIFICATION_ALLOWED_ERR*

Raised if the NamedNodeMap is read-only.

*INUSE_ATTRIBUTE_ERR*

Raised if the arg node is an Attr node that is already in use by another element's attributes map.

*Java binding*

```
public Node setNamedItem(Node arg) throws DOMException;
```

*Java example*

```
// Check to see if an ID attribute exists
// in this map, and add it if necessary
if (nnm.getNamedItem("id") == null) {
    // get the document
    Document doc = elem.getOwnerDocument();
    // create a new attribute Node
    Attr attrID = doc.createAttribute("id");

    // set the attribute value
    attrID.appendChild(doc.createTextNode(makeUniqueID(elem)));
```

*Java example (continued)*

```
    // ... and add it to the NamedNodeMap
    nnm.setNamedItem(attrID);
}
```

### setNamedItemNS: *arg* ❷

Identical in function to the basic `setNamedItem` method, except that it considers namespace properties in the `Node` object. A reference to the replaced `Node` object is returned.

***Argument***

*arg: Node*

The `Node` object to be stored in the map. The values of the `namespaceURI and localName` properties are used as the lookup key. If another node with identical values for these two properties exist, the new node replaces it.

***Exceptions***

*WRONG_DOCUMENT_ERR*

Raised if a document different than the creator of the target `NamedNodeMap` created the `arg` node.

*NO_MODIFICATION_ALLOWED_ERR*

Raised if the `NamedNodeMap` is read-only.

*INUSE_ATTRIBUTE_ERR*

Raised if the `arg` node is an `Attr` node already in use by another element's `attributes` map.

***Java binding***

```
public Node setNamedItemNS(Node arg) throws DOMException;
```

## *Node*

The `Node` interface is the base interface for every member of a DOM document tree. It exposes attributes common to every type of document object and provides simple methods to retrieve type-specific information without resorting to downcasting. For instance, the `attributes` list provides access to the an `Element` object's attributes, but would have no meaning for a `ProcessingInstruction` node.

This interface also exposes all methods for querying, inserting, and removing objects from the document hierarchy. The `Node` interface makes building general-purpose tree manipulation routines that are not dependent on specific document element types easier.

***Attributes***

The following attributes provide information about where the `Node` object is located within the document tree. These attributes are read-only. Additional methods allow the insertion and removal of nodes from the document tree.

### attributes: *NamedNodeMap*

Has meaning only for `Element` objects. It provides access to a list of `Attr` objects in a `NamedNodeMap`. For all other object types, it returns `null`.

***Java binding***

```
public NamedNodeMap getAttributes();
```

***Java example***

```
// List the attributes of an Element node
NamedNodeMap nnm = doc.getDocumentElement().getAttributes();

if (nnm != null) {

    for (int i = 0; i < nnm.getLength(); i++) {
        // print the attribute and value
        System.out.println(nnm.item(i).getNodeName() + " = \"" +
                           nnm.item(i).getNodeValue() + "\"");
    }
}
```

### childNodes: *NodeList*

Returns a `NodeList` containing a reference to every child of this `Node`.

***Java binding***

```
public NodeList getChildNodes();
```

***Java example***

```
// List the text contents of an element
NodeList nlChildren = elem.getChildNodes();
Node ndChild;

for (int iNode = 0; iNode < nlChildren.getLength(); iNode++) {
    ndChild = nlChildren.item(iNode);

    if (ndChild.getNodeType() == Node.TEXT_NODE) {
        System.out.println(ndChild.getNodeValue());
    }
}
```

### firstChild: *Node*

Points to the head of the linked list of children of this node. If no child nodes exist, it returns `null`.

***Java binding***

```
public Node getFirstChild();
```

## *Dynamic Tree References*

Throughout the DOM, several places return lists or collections of nodes that represent the current state of the document tree. These references are all live; any modifications to the document hierarchy, made by inserting or removing nodes, are reflected in the list immediately.

Whether due to multithreading or unforeseen side effects of procedure calls, be aware that the contents of the list being used could change. To reduce the likelihood of difficult-to-find bugs resulting from stale values, request values, such as the length of a list, directly from the `NodeList` or `NamedNodeMap` objects. This option is better than storing values in intermediate variables.

***Java example***

```
// List the contents of a node
for (Node nd = ndDump.getFirstChild(); nd != null;
     nd = nd.getNextSibling()) {
    if (nd.getNodeValue() != null) {
        System.out.println(nd.getNodeValue());
    }
}
```

### lastChild: *Node*

Returns a pointer to the end of a given `Node` object's linked list of child nodes. If no children exist, it returns `null`.

***Java binding***

```
public Node getLastChild();
```

***Java example***

```
// List the value of a node in reverse order
for (Node nd = ndDump.getLastChild(); nd != null;
     nd = nd.getPreviousSibling()) {
    if (nd.getNodeValue() != null) {
        System.out.println(nd.getNodeValue());
    }
}
```

### localName: *DOMString* ❷

Returns the local part of the fully qualified node name. This part of the name is to the right of the final `:` in a namespace-qualified name.

***Java binding***

```
public String getLocalName();
```

### namespaceURI: *DOMString* ❷

The namespace URI given to this `Node` object at creation time; returns `null` if no namespace was given. This value is not computed, but is the value given at create time by one of the `create*NS()` methods of the `Document` interface.

#### *Java binding*

```
public String getNamespaceURI();
```

### nextSibling: *Node*

Returns the next node in the sibling list. If this node is the end of the list, `nextSibling` returns `null`.

#### *Java binding*

```
public Node getNextSibling();
```

#### *Java example*

```
// List the contents of a node
for (Node nd = ndDump.getFirstChild(); nd != null;
     nd = nd.getNextSibling()) {
    if (nd.getNodeValue() != null) {
        System.out.println(nd.getNodeValue());
    }
}
```

### nodeName: *DOMString*

Intended to represent the underlying DOM object's name. Depending on the object type, this attribute may map to another attribute of the object or a constant string:

| *Object Type* | *nodeName* |
|---|---|
| `Element` | Tag Name |
| `Attr` | Attribute name |
| `Text` | `"#text"` |
| `CDATASection` | `"#cdata-section"` |
| `EntityReference` | Name of entity referenced |
| `Entity` | Entity name |
| `ProcessingInstruction` | Target |
| `Comment` | `"#comment"` |
| `Document` | `"#document"` |
| `DocumentType` | Document type name |
| `DocumentFragment` | `"#document-fragment"` |
| `Notation` | Notation name |

#### *Java binding*

```
public String getNodeName();
```

DOM Reference

### *Java example*

```
// Print the document root tag name
Node ndDoc = (Node)doc.getDocumentElement();
System.out.println("Document root element type: " + ndDoc.getNodeName());
```

## nodeType: *unsigned short*

Contains a value that indicates the true type of the object referenced through the Node interface. The following table shows this attribute's possible values, along with the actual object types they represent:

| *Constant Name* | *Object Type* | *Constant Value* |
|---|---|---|
| ELEMENT_NODE | Element | 1 |
| ATTRIBUTE_NODE | Attr | 2 |
| TEXT_NODE | Text | 3 |
| CDATA_SECTION_NODE | CDATASection | 4 |
| ENTITY_REFERENCE_NODE | EntityReference | 5 |
| ENTITY_NODE | Entity | 6 |
| PROCESSING_INSTRUCTION_NODE | ProcessingInstruction | 7 |
| COMMENT_NODE | Comment | 8 |
| DOCUMENT_NODE | Document | 9 |
| DOCUMENT_TYPE_NODE | DocumentType | 10 |
| DOCUMENT_FRAGMENT_NODE | DocumentFragment | 11 |
| NOTATION_NODE | Notation | 12 |

The parent-child and sibling relationships between document nodes can be visualized as two doubly linked lists. One list links parents to children, while the other links nodes that exist at the same level.

### *Java binding*

```
public short getNodeType();
```

### *Java example*

```
// Check to see if a node is an Element type node
public boolean isElement(Node nd) {
    return nd.getNodeType() == Node.ELEMENT_NODE;
}
```

## nodeValue: *DOMString*

Intended to provide a reasonable string value for the underlying DOM object. Depending on the nodeType, this property may be read-only, read/write, or null.

| *Object Type* | *nodeValue* |
|---|---|
| Element | null |
| Attr | Attribute value |
| Text | Text node content |

| *Object Type* | *nodeValue* |
|---|---|
| CDATASection | CDATA Section content |
| EntityReference | null |
| Entity | null |
| ProcessingInstruction | Entire content, excluding the target |
| Comment | Comment content |
| Document | null |
| DocumentType | null |
| DocumentFragment | null |
| Notation | null |

### *Exceptions*

*NO_MODIFICATION_ALLOWED_ERR*
: Indicates the `nodeValue` attribute is read-only for this DOM object type.

*DOMSTRING_SIZE_ERR*
: This exception is raised if the value that would be returned is too large to be contained by a `DOMString` type in the given implementation.

### *Java bindings*

```
public String getNodeValue() throws DOMException;
public void setNodeValue(String nodeValue) throws DOMException;
```

### *Java example*

```
// If this node is a text node, make the value lowercase
if (nd.getNodeType() == Node.TEXT_NODE) {
    // make it lowercase
    nd.setNodeValue(nd.getNodeValue().toLowerCase());
}
```

## ownerDocument: *Document*

Returns a reference to the `Document` used to create this `Node` object. Since the `Document` object is the only mechanism exposed for creating new nodes, even newly created, empty nodes have the `ownerDocument` property set. This attribute can be `null` only for `Document` nodes and `DocumentType` nodes that are not yet part of a document.

### *Java binding*

```
public Document getOwnerDocument();
```

### *Java example*

```
// Add my two cents
Document doc = elem.getOwnerDocument();
Text txtAdd = doc.createTextNode("My $.02");
elem.appendChild(txtAdd);
```

## parentNode: *Node*

Provides a reference to the parent of this node. All node types, except `Document`, `DocumentFragment`, and `Attr`, may have a parent node. Every node within a `Document` hierarchy has a parent. Nodes that are not part of the document tree, such as new nodes and nodes removed from the document using the `replaceChild()` or `removeChild()` methods, have a `parentNode` attribute of `null`.

***Java binding***

```
Node getParentNode();
```

***Java example***

```
// Unlink an element from the document tree
elem.getParentNode().removeChild(elem);
```

### prefix: *DOMString* ❷

The namespace prefix of this `Node`, used for nodes that support namespace prefixes. For `ELEMENT_NODE` and `ATTRIBUTE_NODE` type nodes, changing the namespace prefix also affects the `nodeName`, `tagName`, and `name` attributes. Since these properties hold the qualified name of the node, changing the prefix also updates it.

***Exceptions***

*INVALID_CHARACTER_ERR*
: Raised if the `prefix` includes an illegal character.

*NO_MODIFICATION_ALLOWED_ERR*
: Indicates that the `prefix` attribute is read-only for this DOM object type.

*NAMESPACE_ERR*
: Raised if the `prefix` is malformed, according to the rules of namespace identifier formation. This exception is also be raised if the `namespaceURI` attribute is `null`, or if an attempt was made to violate the XML rules of identifier formation. Such an attempt includes invalid use of the `xml` or `xmlns` identifier. For more information about namespaces, see Chapter 4.

***Java bindings***

```
public String getPrefix();
public void setPrefix(String prefix) throws DOMException;
```

### previousSibling: *Node*

Returns the preceding node in the sibling list. If this node is the head of the sibling list, it returns `null`.

***Java binding***

```
public Node getPreviousSibling();
```

***Java example***

```
// List the value of a node in reverse order
for (Node nd = ndDump.getLastChild(); nd != null;
     nd = nd.getPreviousSibling()) {
    if (nd.getNodeValue() != null) {
        System.out.println(nd.getNodeValue());
    }
}
```

### *Methods*

The following methods are defined for node interface objects:

#### appendChild: *newchild*

Appends the newchild node to the end of the child list. If newchild is already linked into the document tree, it is unlinked before the append is performed. This method returns a reference to the newchild node.

***Argument***

*newchild: Node*

The node to append. If the node is a DocumentFragment node, the children of newchild are appended to the end of the node's child list in sequence.

***Exceptions***

*HIERARCHY_REQUEST_ERR*

Raised if the insert operation violates at least one document structure rule. For instance, the node doesn't allow children or doesn't allow children of the newchild node type. This exception is also raised if the operation creates a circular reference (i.e., it tries to insert a node's parent as a node's child).

*WRONG_DOCUMENT_ERR*

Raised if the newchild node is created in a different document than that of the new parent node.

*NO_MODIFICATION_ALLOWED_ERR*

Raised if the new parent node is read-only.

***Java binding***

```
public Node appendChild(Node newChild) throws DOMException;
```

***Java example***

```
// Move the first child to the end of the child node list
if (elem.getFirstChild() != null) {
    elem.appendChild(elem.removeChild(elem.getFirstChild()));
}
```

#### cloneNode: *deep*

Returns a copy of the node without a parent node. If the cloned node is specified as deep (true), the subtree under the node is also copied. Otherwise, the cloned node does not contain child nodes.

***Argument***

*deep: boolean*

If true, child nodes are copied to the cloned node. If false, only the original node is copied.

***Java binding***

```
public Node cloneNode(boolean deep);
```

### *Java example*

```
// Make a copy of this element and all children
elem.cloneNode(true);
```

## hasAttributes ( )

Indicates whether an `Element` node has any attributes. Returns `true` if the node has attributes, otherwise it returns `false`.

### *Java binding*

```
public boolean hasAttributes();
```

## hasChildNodes ( )

This method provides a quick way to determine if a node has children. Returns `true` if the node has any children, otherwise it returns `false`.

### *Java binding*

```
public boolean hasChildNodes();
```

## insertBefore: *newchild, refchild*

Inserts the `Node` object `newchild` into the child list of the parent node that invokes it. The `refchild` parameter allows you to specify where to insert the new node in the list. If `refchild` is `null`, the new node is inserted at the end of the child list. If it is not `null`, the new node is inserted into the list in front of the specified node. If the `newchild` node is already part of the document tree, it is unlinked before it is inserted in its new position. Also, if the `newchild` node references a `DocumentFragment` object, each of its children are inserted, in order, before the `refchild` node. A reference to the `newchild` node is returned.

### *Arguments*

*newchild: Node*
: The new node to insert.

*refchild: Node*
: The node that follows the new node in the child list, or `null`, if the new node is inserted at the end of the child list.

### *Exceptions*

*HIERARCHY_REQUEST_ERR*
: Raised if the insert operation would violate at least one document structure rule. For instance, the node doesn't allow children or doesn't allow children of the `newchild` node type. This exception is also raised if the operation creates a circular reference (i.e., it tries to insert a node's parent as a node's child).

*WRONG_DOCUMENT_ERR*
: Raised if the `newchild` node was created in a document different than that of the new parent node.

*NO_MODIFICATION_ALLOWED_ERR*
: Raised if the new parent node is read-only.

*NOT_FOUND_ERR*

Raised if the node pointed to by **refchild** is not a child of the node performing the insert.

***Java binding***

```
public Node insertBefore(Node newChild, Node refChild)
            throws DOMException;
```

***Java example***

```
// Insert a new node at the head of the child list of a parent node
ndParent.insertBefore(ndNew, ndParent.getFirstChild());
```

---

## isSupported: *feature, version* ❷

Checks to see if a particular DOM feature is available for this implementation. For more information about the feature names, see the **hasFeature** method of the DOMImplementation object earlier in this chapter. This method returns **true** if the feature is available, **false** if it is not.

***Arguments***

*feature: DOMString*

The name of the feature to test for. See detail of the **hasFeature** method of the DOMImplementation object for a list of this parameter's valid values.

*version: DOMString*

The version number of the feature to test. For DOM Level 2, Version 1, this string should be 2.0. If the version is not specified, this method tests for any version of the feature.

***Java binding***

```
public boolean supports(String feature, String version);
```

---

## normalize ( ) ❷

Recursively combines all adjacent Text nodes into a single node. It also removes empty Text nodes from the document tree. This operation is useful for operations that require absolute references within a document, or if two documents must be compared.

***Java binding***

```
public void normalize();
```

---

## removeChild: *oldchild*

Unlinks the oldchild node from the child list of a given node and returns a reference to the now detached Node object.

***Argument***

*oldchild: Node*

The node to be removed.

*Exceptions*

*NO_MODIFICATION_ALLOWED_ERR*
Raised if the parent node is read-only.

*NOT_FOUND_ERR*
Raised if the oldchild node is not a child of this node.

*Java binding*

```
public Node removeChild(Node oldChild) throws DOMException;
```

*Java example*

```
// Unlink an element and all its children
// from the document tree
elem.getParentNode().removeChild(elem);
```

---

### replaceChild: *newchild, oldchild*

Replaces the child node `oldchild` with `newchild`. If `newchild` is currently linked into the document tree, it is removed before the replace is performed. The method returns a reference to the `oldchild` node.

*Arguments*

*newchild: Node*
The node to be inserted.

*oldchild: Node*
The node being replaced.

*Exceptions*

*HIERARCHY_REQUEST_ERR*
This exception is raised if the insert operation violates at least one document structure rule. For instance the node doesn't allow children, or doesn't allow children of the `newchild` node type. This exception is also raised if the operation creates a circular reference (i.e., it tries to insert a node's parent as a node's child).

*WRONG_DOCUMENT_ERR*
Raised if the `newchild` node was created in a different document than the new parent node.

*NO_MODIFICATION_ALLOWED_ERR*
Raised if the new parent node is read-only.

*NOT_FOUND_ERR*
Raised if the node pointed to by `oldchild` is not a child of the node performing the replacement.

*Java binding*

```
public Node replaceChild(Node newChild, Node oldChild)
                throws DOMException;
```

*Java example*

```
// Replace an old node with a new one
ndOld.getParentNode().replaceChild(ndNew, ndOld);
```

## *NodeList*

The `NodeList` interface allows DOM classes to expose an ordered collection of nodes. A `NodeList` represents a read-only, zero-based array of `Node` objects. Since no mechanism exists for creating, adding, or removing nodes from a `NodeList`, DOM users cannot use this class as a general-purpose utility class.

### *Java example*

```
// List the text contents of an element
NodeList nlChildren = elem.getChildNodes();
Node ndChild;

for (int iNode = 0; iNode < nlChildren.getLength(); iNode++) {
    ndChild = nlChildren.item(iNode);

    if (ndChild.getNodeType() == Node.TEXT_NODE) {
        System.out.println(ndChild.getNodeValue());
    }
}
```

### *Attributes*

The `NodeList` interface defines one attribute.

#### length: *unsigned long*

The total number of `Node` objects in the list.

*Java binding*

```
public long getLength();
```

### *Methods*

The NodeList interface defines one method.

#### item: *index*

Returns a reference to the `Node` object at position `index`, or `null` if the index is invalid. If the index given is < 0 or >= the `length` attribute of the `NodeList`, this function returns `null`.

*Argument*

*index: unsigned long*
Zero-based index into the list of the `Node` to return.

*Java binding*

```
public Node item(long index);
```

## ProcessingInstruction

This interface provides access to the contents of an XML processing instruction. Processing instructions provide a mechanism for embedding commands to an XML processing application that is in line with the XML content.

### Java example

```
// Add an application-specific processing instruction
ProcessingInstruction pi = doc.createProcessingInstruction("my_app",
        "action=\"save\"");
```

### Attributes

The interface defines two attributes.

#### data: *DOMString*

Returns the data portion of this processing instruction. The data portion is identified starting at the first nonwhitespace character after the `target` token and ending at the closing `?>`.

*Write exceptions*

*NO_MODIFICATION_ALLOWED_ERR*
    Raised if the node is read-only.

*Java bindings*

```
public String getData();
public void setData(String data) throws DOMException;
```

*Java example*

```
// Check the application's data attribute
if (pi.getTarget() == "MY_APPLICATION") {
    // check the data attribute for my own application-specific info
    if (pi.getData() == "CHECK_SIBLINGS") {
        // check the siblings
        ...
    }

    pi.setData("SIBLINGS_CHECKED");
}
```

#### target: DOMString

Returns the target portion of this processing instruction. The target is the first whitespace-delimited token within the processing instruction block.

Processing instructions are meant to embed application-specific instructions for automatic content generation, parsing, etc., within the XML stream. The instruction's `target` portion is the flag that allows different processing applications to coexist. Applications that use processing instructions for formatting should ignore processing instructions they do not recognize.

*Java binding*

```
public String getTarget();
```

### *Java example*

```
// Check to see if your application is targeted
if (pi.getTarget() == "MY_APPLICATION") {
    // do my application-specific processing here
}
```

---

## *Text*

`Text` nodes contain the nonmarkup character data contained within the XML document. After the XML document is parsed, exactly one `Text` node exists for each uninterrupted block of nonmarkup text:

```
<text_node>This is text.</text_node>
```

### *Methods*

The following method is defined for the `Text` interface.

**splitText:** *offset*

Splits a `Text` node into two adjacent `Text` nodes. The contents of the original node are divided at the given split offset, with the second substring used as the new node's value. The first substring remains in the original node. If the node is currently linked into the DOM tree, the new node with the split content becomes the next sibling of the original node. A new `Text` node containing the second part of the split data is returned.

*Argument*

*offset (unsigned long)*
    Zero-based offset where the split occurs.

*Exceptions*

*INDEX_SIZE_ERR*
    Raised if the offset given is < 0, >= the `length` attribute.

*NO_MODIFICATION_ALLOWED_ERR*
    Raised if the element is read-only.

#### *Java binding*

```
public Text splitText(long offset) throws DOMException;
```

#### *Java example*

```
// Make one Text node
long = doc.createTextNode("This text is split.");

// and split it
Text ndSplit = ndText.splitText(9);
```

> `Text` is a subclass of the `CharacterData` interface. See the `CharacterData` interface section in this chapter for a list of applicable methods for accessing character data in nodes of this type.

CHAPTER 22

# SAX Reference

SAX, the Simple API for XML, is a straightforward, event-based API used to parse XML documents. David Megginson, SAX's primary author, has placed SAX in the public domain. SAX is bundled with all parsers that implement the API, including Xerces, MSXML, the Oracle XML Parser for Java, and Ælfred. However, you can also get it and the full source code from *http://www.megginson.com/SAX*.

SAX was originally defined as a Java API and is intended primarily for parsers written in Java, so this chapter will focus on its Java implementation. However, its port to other object-oriented languages, such as C++, Python, Perl, and Eiffel, is obvious.

> This chapter covers SAX2 exclusively. In 2001, all major parsers that support SAX support SAX2. The major change from SAX1 to SAX2 was the addition of namespace support. This addition necessitated changing the names and signatures of almost every method and class in SAX. The old SAX1 methods and classes are still available, but they're now deprecated and you shouldn't use them.

## The org.xml.sax Package

The `org.xml.sax` package contains the core interfaces and classes that comprise the Simple API for XML.

### The Attributes Interface

An object that implements the `Attributes` interface represents a list of attributes on a start tag. The order of attributes in the list is not guaranteed to match the order in the document itself. `Attributes` objects are passed as arguments to the `startElement()` method of `ContentHandler`. You can access particular attributes in three ways:

- By number
- By namespace URI and local name
- By qualified (prefixed) name

This list does not include namespace declaration attributes (`xmlns:*`) unless the *http://xml.org/sax/features/namespace-prefixes* feature is true. It is false by default.

If the namespace-prefixes feature is false, qualified name access may not be available; if the *http://xml.org/sax/features/namespaces* feature is false, namespace-qualified name access may not be available:

```
package org.xml.sax;

public interface Attributes {

  public int    getLength();
  public String getURI(int index);
  public String getLocalName(int index);
  public String getQName(int index);
  public int    getIndex(String uri, String localName);
  public int    getIndex(String qualifiedName);
  public String getType(int index);
  public String getType(String uri, String localName);
  public String getType(String qualifiedName);
  public String getValue(String uri, String localName);
  public String getValue(String qualifiedName);
  public String getValue(int index);

}
```

## The ContentHandler Interface

`ContentHandler` is the key piece of SAX. Almost every SAX program needs to use this interface. `ContentHandler` is a callback interface. An instance of this interface is passed to the parser via the `setContentHandler()` method of `XMLReader`. As the parser reads the document, it invokes the methods in its `ContentHandler` to tell the program what's in the document:

```
package org.xml.sax;

public interface ContentHandler {

  public void setDocumentLocator(Locator locator);
  public void startDocument() throws SAXException;
  public void endDocument() throws SAXException;
  public void startPrefixMapping(String prefix, String uri)
   throws SAXException;
  public void endPrefixMapping(String prefix) throws SAXException;
  public void startElement(String namespaceURI, String localName,
   String qualifiedName, Attributes atts) throws SAXException;
```

SAX Reference

```
  public void endElement(String namespaceURI, String localName,
   String qualifiedName) throws SAXException;
  public void characters(char[] text, int start, int length)
   throws SAXException;
  public void ignorableWhitespace(char[] text, int start, int length)
   throws SAXException;
  public void processingInstruction(String target, String data)
   throws SAXException;
  public void skippedEntity(String name) throws SAXException;

}
```

## *The DTDHandler Interface*

By passing an instance of the `DTDHandler` interface to the `setDTDHandler()` method of `XMLReader`, you can receive notification of notation and unparsed entity declarations in the DTD. You can store this information and use it later to retrieve information about the unparsed entities you encounter while reading the document:

```
package org.xml.sax;

public interface DTDHandler {

  public void notationDecl(String name, String publicId, String systemId)
   throws SAXException;
  public void unparsedEntityDecl(String name, String publicId,
   String systemId, String notationName) throws SAXException;

}
```

## *The EntityResolver Interface*

By passing an instance of the `EntityResolver` interface to the `setEntityResolver()` method of `XMLReader`, you can intercept parser requests for external entities, such as the external DTD subset or external parameter entities, and redirect those requests to substitute different entities. For example, you could replace a reference to a remote copy of a standard DTD with a local one or find the sources for particular public IDs in a catalog. Most SAX programs do not need to implement this interface, but it is useful for applications that build XML documents from databases or input sources that don't look like traditional XML files. The interface is also useful for applications that use URI types other than URLs:

```
package org.xml.sax;

public interface EntityResolver {

  public InputSource resolveEntity(String publicId, String systemId)
   throws SAXException, IOException;

}
```

## The ErrorHandler Interface

By passing an instance of the ErrorHandler interface to the setErrorHandler() method of XMLReader, you can provide custom handling for particular classes of errors the parser detects. For example, you can choose whether to stop parsing when a validity error is detected. The SAXParseException passed to each of the three methods in this interface provides details about the specific cause and location of the error:

```
package org.xml.sax;

public interface ErrorHandler {

  public void warning(SAXParseException exception) throws SAXException;
  public void error(SAXParseException exception) throws SAXException;
  public void fatalError(SAXParseException exception)
   throws SAXException;

}
```

Warnings represent possible problems the parser has noticed that are not technically violations of XML's well-formedness or validity rules. For instance, a parser might issue a warning if an xml:lang attribute's value was not a legal ISO-639 language code. The most common kind of error is a validity problem. The parser should report it, but it should continue processing. A fatal error violates well-formedness. The parser should not continue parsing after reporting such an error.



## The Locator Interface

Unlike most other interfaces in the org.xml.sax package, you do not have to implement the Locator interface. Instead, the parser has the option to provide an implementation. If it does so, it will pass its implementation to the setLocator() method in your ContentHandler instance before it calls startDocument(). You can save a reference to this object in a field in your ContentHandler class like this:

```
private Locator locator;

public void setDocumentLocator(Locator locator) {
  this.locator = locator;
}
```

Once you've found the locator, you can then use it inside any other ContentHandler method, such as startElement() or characters(), to determine in exactly which document and at which line and column the event took place. For instance, the locator allows you to determine that a particular start tag began on the third column of the document's seventeenth line at the URL *http://www.slashdot.org/slashdot.xml*:

```
package org.xml.sax;

public interface Locator {

  public String getPublicId();
```

```
    public String getSystemId();
    public int    getLineNumber();
    public int    getColumnNumber();

  }
```

## The XMLFilter Interface

An XMLFilter is an XMLReader that obtains its events from another XMLReader, rather than reading it from a source such as InputStream. Filters can sit between the original source of XML and the application and modify data in the original source before passing it to the application:

```
  package org.xml.sax;

  public interface XMLFilter extends XMLReader {

    public void      setParent(XMLReader parent);
    public XMLReader getParent();

  }
```

## The XMLReader Interface

The XMLReader interface represents the actual XML parser that reads at least one XML document. You should generally not implement this interface yourself. Instead, use the org.xml.sax.helpers.XMLReaderFactory class to build a parser-specific implementation. Then use this parser's various set methods to configure the parsing process. Finally, invoke the parse() method to read the document while calling back to methods in your own implementations of ContentHandler, ErrorHandler, EntityResolver, and DTDHandler, as the document is read:

```
  package org.xml.sax;

  public interface XMLReader {

    public boolean getFeature(String name)
     throws SAXNotRecognizedException, SAXNotSupportedException;
    public void    setFeature(String name, boolean value)
     throws SAXNotRecognizedException, SAXNotSupportedException;
    public Object  getProperty(String name)
     throws SAXNotRecognizedException, SAXNotSupportedException;
    public void    setProperty(String name, Object value)
     throws SAXNotRecognizedException, SAXNotSupportedException;

    public void           setEntityResolver(EntityResolver resolver);
    public EntityResolver getEntityResolver();
    public void           setDTDHandler(DTDHandler handler);
    public DTDHandler     getDTDHandler();
    public void           setContentHandler(ContentHandler handler);
    public ContentHandler getContentHandler();
    public void           setErrorHandler(ErrorHandler handler);
    public ErrorHandler   getErrorHandler();
```

```
    public void parse(InputSource input) throws IOException, SAXException;
    public void parse(String systemId) throws IOException, SAXException;

}
```

## *The InputSource Class*

The InputSource class is an abstraction of a data source from which the raw bytes for an XML document are read. It can wrap a system ID, a public ID, an InputStream, or a Reader:

```
package org.xml.sax;

public class InputSource {

    public InputSource();
    public InputSource(String systemId);
    public InputSource(InputStream byteStream);
    public InputSource(Reader reader);

    public void        setPublicId(String publicId);
    public String      getPublicId();
    public void        setSystemId(String systemId);
    public String      getSystemId();
    public void        setByteStream(InputStream byteStream);
    public InputStream getByteStream();
    public void        setEncoding(String encoding);
    public String      getEncoding();
    public void        setCharacterStream(Reader reader);
    public Reader      getCharacterStream();

}
```

SAX Reference

## *SAXExceptions*

Most exceptions thrown by SAX methods are instances of the SAXException class or one of its subclasses. The single exception to this rule is the parse() method of XMLReader which may throw a raw IOException if a purely I/O related error occurs; for example, if a socket is broken before the parser finishes reading the document from the network.

Besides the usual exception methods, such as getMessage() and printStackTrace(), that SAXException inherits from or overrides in its superclasses, SAXException adds a getException() method to return the nested exception that caused the SAXException to be thrown in the first place:

```
package org.xml.sax;

public class SAXException extends Exception {

    public SAXException(String message);
    public SAXException(Exception ex);
    public SAXException(String message, Exception ex);
```

```
    public String    getMessage();
    public Exception getException();
    public String    toString();

}
```

### *SAXParseException*

If a well-formedness error is encountered while parsing a document, the parser throws a `SAXParseException`, which is a subclass of `SAXException`. `SAXParseExceptions` are also passed as arguments to the methods of the `ErrorHandler` interface, where you can decide whether or not you want to throw them.

Besides the methods it inherits from its superclasses, this class adds methods to get the line number, column number, system ID, and public ID of the document where the error was detected:

```
package org.xml.sax;

public class SAXParseException extends SAXException {

  public SAXParseException(String message, Locator locator);
  public SAXParseException(String message, Locator locator, Exception e);
  public SAXParseException(String message, String publicId,
   String systemId, int lineNumber, int columnNumber);
  public SAXParseException(String message, String publicId,
   String systemId, int lineNumber, int columnNumber, Exception e);

  public String getPublicId();
  public String getSystemId();
  public int    getLineNumber();
  public int    getColumnNumber();

}
```

### *SAXNotRecognizedException*

A `SAXNotRecognizedException` is thrown if you attempt to set a property or feature the parser has never heard of. Besides the single constructor, all its methods are inherited from superclasses:

```
package org.xml.sax;

public class SAXNotRecognizedException extends SAXException {

  public SAXNotRecognizedException(String message);

}
```

### *SAXNotSupportedException*

A SAXNotSupportedException is thrown if you attempt to set a property or feature that the parser recognizes, but is not prepared to implement. Besides the single constructor, all of its methods are inherited from superclasses:

```
package org.xml.sax;

public class SAXNotSupportedException extends SAXException {

  public SAXNotSupportedException(String message);

}
```

## *The org.xml.sax.helpers Package*

The org.xml.sax.helpers package contains support classes for the core SAX classes. These classes include factory classes used to build instances of particular org.xml.sax interfaces and default implementations of those interfaces.

### *The AttributesImpl Class*

AttributesImpl is a default implementation of the Attributes interface that SAX parsers may use. The Attributes object passed to the startElement() method in your ContentHandler may be an instance of this class. However, depending on the parser, it may be an instance of some other class, so you should check its type with instanceof before attempting to use the unique methods of this class not declared in the Attributes interface.

Besides the methods of the Attributes interface, this class offers manipulator methods so the list of attributes can be modified or reused. These methods allow you to take a persistent snapshot of an Attributes object in startElement() and construct or modify an Attributes object in a SAX driver or filter:

```
package org.xml.sax.helpers;

public class AttributesImpl implements Attributes {

    public AttributesImpl();
    public AttributesImpl(Attributes atts);

    public int    getLength();
    public String getURI(int index);
    public String getLocalName(int index);
    public String getQName(int index);
    public String getType(int index);
    public String getValue(int index);
    public int    getIndex(String uri, String localName);
    public int    getIndex(String qualifiedName);
    public String getType(String uri, String localName);
    public String getType(String qualifiedName);
    public String getValue(String uri, String localName);
    public String getValue(String qualifiedName);
```

SAX Reference

```
    public void   clear();
    public void   setAttributes(Attributes atts);
    public void   addAttribute(String uri, String localName,
     String qualifiedName, String type, String value);
    public void   setAttribute(int index, String uri, String localName,
     String qualifiedName, String type, String value);
    public void   removeAttribute(int index)
    public void   setURI(int index, String uri)
    public void   setLocalName(int index, String localName)
    public void   setQName(int index, String qualifiedName);
    public void   setType(int index, String type);
    public void   setValue(int index, String value);

}
```

## *The DefaultHandler Class*

`DefaultHandler` is a convenience class that implements the `EntityResolver`, `DTDHandler`, `ContentHandler`, and `ErrorHandler` interfaces with mostly do-nothing methods. You can subclass this `DefaultHandler` and override methods for events you actually want to respond to. You never have to use this class. You can always implement the interfaces directly instead. The pattern is similar to the adapter classes in the AWT, such as `MouseAdapter` and `WindowAdapter`:

```
package org.xml.sax.helpers;

public class DefaultHandler
 implements EntityResolver, DTDHandler, ContentHandler, ErrorHandler {

  // Default implementation of the EntityResolver interface.
  public InputSource resolveEntity(String publicId, String systemId)
   throws SAXException {
    return null;
  }

  // Default implementation of the DTDHandler interface.
  public void notationDecl(String name, String publicId, String systemId)
   throws SAXException {}
  public void unparsedEntityDecl(String name, String publicId,
   String systemId, String notationName) throws SAXException{}

  // Default implementation of the ContentHandler interface.
  public void setDocumentLocator(Locator locator) {}
  public void startDocument() throws SAXException {}
  public void endDocument() throws SAXException {}
  public void startPrefixMapping(String prefix, String uri)
   throws SAXException {}
  public void endPrefixMapping(String prefix) throws SAXException {}
  public void startElement(String uri, String localName,
   String qualifiedName, Attributes attributes) throws SAXException {}
  public void endElement(String uri, String localName,
   String qualifiedName) throws SAXException {}
  public void characters(char[] text, int start, int length)
   throws SAXException {}
```

```
  public void ignorableWhitespace(char[] whitespace, int start,
   int length) throws SAXException {}
  public void processingInstruction(String target, String data)
   throws SAXException {}
  public void skippedEntity(String name) throws SAXException {}

  // Default implementation of the ErrorHandler interface.
  public void warning(SAXParseException ex) throws SAXException {}
  public void error(SAXParseException ex) throws SAXException {}
  public void fatalError(SAXParseException ex) throws SAXException {
    throw ex;
  }

}
```

## The LocatorImpl Class

LocatorImpl is a default implementation of the Locator interface for the convenience of parser writers. You probably won't need to use it directly. Besides the constructors, it adds setter methods to set the public ID, system ID, line number, and column number returned by the getter methods declared in Locator:

```
package org.xml.sax.helpers;

public class LocatorImpl implements Locator {

    public LocatorImpl();
    public LocatorImpl(Locator locator);

    public String getPublicId();
    public String getSystemId();
    public int    getLineNumber();
    public int    getColumnNumber();
    public void   setPublicId(String publicId);
    public void   setSystemId(String systemId);
    public void   setLineNumber(int lineNumber);
    public void   setColumnNumber(int columnNumber);

}
```

## The NamespaceSupport Class

NamespaceSupport is designed to help parser implementers handle namespaces correctly in their parsers. You probably won't need to use this class unless you're writing a parser:

```
package org.xml.sax.helpers;

public class NamespaceSupport {

 public final static String XMLNS="http://www.w3.org/XML/1998/namespace";

  public NamespaceSupport();

  public void        reset();
```

```
public void        pushContext();
public void        popContext();
public boolean     declarePrefix(String prefix, String uri);
public String[]    processName(String qualifiedName, String[] parts,
 boolean isAttribute);
public String      getURI(String prefix);
public Enumeration getPrefixes();
public String      getPrefix(String uri);
public Enumeration getPrefixes(String uri);
public Enumeration getDeclaredPrefixes();

}
```

## *The ParserAdapter Class*

The `ParserAdapter` class uses the Adapter design pattern to convert a SAX1 `org.xml.sax.Parser` object into a SAX2 `org.xml.sax.XMLReader` object. As more parsers support SAX2, this class becomes less necessary. Note that some SAX2 features are not available through an adapted SAX1 parser. For instance, a parser created with this adapter does not report skipped entities and does not support most features and properties, not even the core features and properties:

```
package org.xml.sax.helpers;

public class ParserAdapter implements XMLReader, DocumentHandler {

  public ParserAdapter() throws SAXException;
  public ParserAdapter(Parser parser);

  // Implementation of org.xml.sax.XMLReader.
  public void           setFeature(String name, boolean state)
   throws SAXNotRecognizedException, SAXNotSupportedException;
  public boolean        getFeature(String name)
   throws SAXNotRecognizedException, SAXNotSupportedException;
  public void           setProperty(String name, Object value)
   throws SAXNotRecognizedException, SAXNotSupportedException;
  public Object         getProperty(String name)
   throws SAXNotRecognizedException, SAXNotSupportedException;
  public void           setEntityResolver(EntityResolver resolver);
  public EntityResolver getEntityResolver();
  public void           setDTDHandler(DTDHandler handler);
  public DTDHandler     getDTDHandler();
  public void           setContentHandler(ContentHandler handler);
  public ContentHandler getContentHandler();
  public void           setErrorHandler(ErrorHandler handler);
  public ErrorHandler   getErrorHandler();
  public void parse(String systemId) throws IOException, SAXException;
  public void parse(InputSource input) throws IOException, SAXException;

  // Implementation of org.xml.sax.DocumentHandler.
  public void setDocumentLocator(Locator locator);
  public void startDocument() throws SAXException;
  public void endDocument() throws SAXException;
  public void startElement(String qualifiedName,
   AttributeList qualifiedAttributes) throws SAXException;
```

```
  public void endElement(String qualifiedName) throws SAXException;
  public void characters(char[] text, int start, int length)
   throws SAXException;
  public void ignorableWhitespace(char[] text, int start, int length)
   throws SAXException;
  public void processingInstruction(String target, String data)
   throws SAXException;

}
```

## The XMLFilterImpl Class

`XMLFilterImpl` is invaluable for implementing XML filters correctly. An instance of this class sits between an `XMLReader` and the client application's event handlers. It receives events from the reader and passes them to the application unchanged. However, by subclassing this class and overriding particular methods you can change the events that are sent before the application gets to see them. You chain a filter to an `XMLReader` by passing the reader as an argument to the filter's constructor. When parsing, you invoke the filter's `parse()` method, not the reader's `parse()` method.

```
package org.xml.sax.helpers;

public class XMLFilterImpl implements XMLFilter, EntityResolver,
 DTDHandler, ContentHandler, ErrorHandler {

  public XMLFilterImpl();
  public XMLFilterImpl(XMLReader parent);

  // Implementation of org.xml.sax.XMLFilter
  public void       setParent(XMLReader parent);
  public XMLReader getParent();

  // Implementation of org.xml.sax.XMLReader
  public void              setFeature(String name, boolean state)
   throws SAXNotRecognizedException, SAXNotSupportedException;
  public boolean           getFeature(String name)
   throws SAXNotRecognizedException, SAXNotSupportedException;
  public void              setProperty(String name, Object value)
   throws SAXNotRecognizedException, SAXNotSupportedException;
  public Object            getProperty(String name)
   throws SAXNotRecognizedException, SAXNotSupportedException;
  public void              setEntityResolver(EntityResolver resolver);
  public EntityResolver getEntityResolver();
  public void              setDTDHandler(DTDHandler handler);
  public DTDHandler        getDTDHandler();
  public void              setContentHandler(ContentHandler handler);
  public ContentHandler getContentHandler();
  public void              setErrorHandler(ErrorHandler handler);
  public ErrorHandler      getErrorHandler();
  public void parse(InputSource input) throws SAXException, IOException;
  public void parse(String systemId) throws SAXException, IOException
```

SAX Reference

```
    // Implementation of org.xml.sax.EntityResolver
    public InputSource resolveEntity(String publicId, String systemId)
     throws SAXException, IOException;

    // Implementation of org.xml.sax.DTDHandler
    public void notationDecl(String name, String publicId, String systemId)
     throws SAXException;
    public void unparsedEntityDecl(String name, String publicId,
     String systemId, String notationName) throws SAXException;

    // Implementation of org.xml.sax.ContentHandler
    public void setDocumentLocator(Locator locator);
    public void startDocument() throws SAXException;
    public void endDocument() throws SAXException;
    public void startPrefixMapping(String prefix, String uri)
     throws SAXException;
    public void endPrefixMapping(String prefix) throws SAXException;
    public void startElement(String namespaceURI, String localName,
     String qualifiedName, Attributes atts) throws SAXException;
    public void endElement(String namespaceURI, String localName,
     String qualifiedName) throws SAXException;
    public void characters(char[] text, int start, int length)
     throws SAXException;
    public void ignorableWhitespace(char[] text, int start, int length)
     throws SAXException;
    public void processingInstruction(String target, String data)
     throws SAXException;
    public void skippedEntity(String name) throws SAXException;

    // Implementation of org.xml.sax.ErrorHandler
    public void warning(SAXParseException ex) throws SAXException;
    public void error(SAXParseException ex) throws SAXException;
    public void fatalError(SAXParseException ex) throws SAXException;

  }
```

## *The XMLReaderAdapter Class*

`XMLReaderAdapter` is the reverse of `ParserAdapter`; it uses the Adapter design pattern to adapt a SAX2 `XMLReader` to a SAX1 `Parser`. This lets you use SAX2 parsers for legacy programs that were written to a SAX1 interface:

```
package org.xml.sax.helpers;

public class XMLReaderAdapter implements Parser, ContentHandler {

  public XMLReaderAdapter() throws SAXException;
  public XMLReaderAdapter(XMLReader reader);

  // Implementation of org.xml.sax.Parser.
  public void setLocale(Locale locale) throws SAXException;
  public void setEntityResolver(EntityResolver resolver);
  public void setDTDHandler(DTDHandler handler);
  public void setDocumentHandler(DocumentHandler handler);
  public void setErrorHandler(ErrorHandler handler);
```

```
    public void parse(String systemId) throws IOException, SAXException;
    public void parse(InputSource input) throws IOException, SAXException

    // Implementation of org.xml.sax.ContentHandler.
    public void setDocumentLocator(Locator locator);
    public void startDocument() throws SAXException;
    public void endDocument() throws SAXException;
    public void startPrefixMapping(String prefix, String uri)
     throws SAXException;
    public void endPrefixMapping(String prefix) throws SAXException;
    public void startElement(String namespaceURI, String localName,
     String qualifiedName, Attributes atts) throws SAXException;
    public void endElement(String namespaceURI, String localName,
     String qualifiedName) throws SAXException;
    public void characters(char[] text, int start, int length)
     throws SAXException;
    public void ignorableWhitespace(char[] text, int start, int length)
     throws SAXException;
    public void processingInstruction(String target, String data)
     throws SAXException;
    public void skippedEntity(String name) throws SAXException;

}
```

SAX Reference

## The XMLReaderFactory Class

XMLReaderFactory creates XMLReader instances in a parser-independent manner. The noargs createXMLReader() method instantiates the class named by the org.xml.sax.driver system property. The other createXMLReader() method instantiates the class named by its argument. This argument should be a fully packaged qualified name, such as org.apache.xerces.parsers.SAXParser:

```
package org.xml.sax.helpers;

public final class XMLReaderFactory {

  public static XMLReader createXMLReader() throws SAXException;
  public static XMLReader createXMLReader(String className)
   throws SAXException;

}
```

# SAX Features and Properties

Absolute URIs name a SAX parser's properties and features. Features have a boolean value; that is, for each parser, a recognized feature is either true or false. Properties have object values. SAX defines six core features and two core properties that parsers should recognize. In addition, parsers may add features and properties to this list, and most do.

## *SAX Core Features*

All SAX parsers should recognize six core features. Of these six, two, *http://xml.org/sax/features/namespaces* and *http://xml.org/sax/features/namespace-prefixes*, must be implemented by all conformant processors. The other four are optional and may not be implemented by all parsers.

### *http://xml.org/sax/features/namespaces*

When true, this feature indicates that the parser should perform namespace well-formedness checks and return namespace URIs, as requested. When false, the parser ignores namespaces and parses as required by the XML 1.0 specification, without the extra rules added by *Namespaces in XML*. This feature is true by default.

### *http://xml.org/sax/features/namespace-prefixes*

When true, this feature indicates that `xmlns` and `xmlns:prefix` attributes should be in the attributes list passed to `startElement()`. When false, these attributes are omitted. The default is false unless *http://xml.org/sax/features/namespaces* is false, in which case this feature defaults to true.

### *http://xml.org/sax/features/string-interning*

When this feature is true, all element names, prefixes, attribute names, namespace URIs, and local names are internalized using the `intern()` method of `java.lang.String`; that is, they compare equal when using ==.

### *http://xml.org/sax/features/validation*

When true, the parser validates. When false, it doesn't. The default is false for most parsers.

### *http://xml.org/sax/features/external-general-entities*

When true, the parser resolves external parsed general entities. When false, it doesn't. The default is true for most parsers that can resolve external entities. Turning on validation automatically activates this feature because validation requires resolving external entities.

### *http://xml.org/sax/features/external-parameter-entities*

When true, the parser resolves external parameter entities. When false, it doesn't. Turning on validation automatically activates this feature because validation requires resolving external entities.

## *SAX Core Properties*

SAX defines two required properties that parsers should recognize, though implementations are not required to support them.

### *http://xml.org/sax/properties/dom-node*

This property's value is an `org.w3c.dom.Node` object that represents the current node the parser visits.

### *http://xml.org/sax/properties/xml-string*

This property's value is a `java.lang.String` object containing the characters that were the source for the current event.

# The org.xml.sax.ext Package

The `org.xml.sax.ext` provides optional interfaces parsers may use to add basic SAX functionality.

## The DeclHandler Interface

`DeclHandler` is a callback interface a parser can use to provide information about the declarations it sees in the document's DTD. To configure an `XMLReader` with a `DeclHandler`, pass the name *http://xml.org/sax/handlers/DeclHandler* and an instance of your handler to the reader's `setProperty()` method:

```
try {
  parser.setProperty(
   "http://xml.org/sax/handlers/DeclHandler", new MyDeclHandlerClass());
}
catch(SAXException e) {
  System.out.println("This parser does not provide declarations.");
}
```

If the parser does not provide declaration events, it throws a `SAXNotRecognizedException` or a `SAXNotSupportedException`, which are both subclasses of `SAXException`. If it doesn't throw one of these exceptions, it parses the DTD and calls back to the methods in your `DeclHandler`:

```
package org.xml.sax.ext;

public interface DeclHandler {

  public void elementDecl(String name, String model) throws SAXException;
  public void attributeDecl(String elementName, String attributeName,
   String type, String valueDefault, String value) throws SAXException;
  public void internalEntityDecl(String name, String value)
   throws SAXException;
  public void externalEntityDecl(String name, String publicId,
   String systemId) throws SAXException;

}
```

SAX Reference

## *The LexicalHandler Interface*

`LexicalHandler` is a callback interface a parser can use to provide information about aspects of the document that are not normally relevant; specifically:

- CDATA sections
- Entity references
- Comments

Without a `LexicalHandler`, the parser simply ignores comments and expands text of entity references and CDATA sections. By using the `LexicalHandler` interface, however, you can save the comments and learn which text came from regular character data, which came from a CDATA section, and which came from an entity reference.

To configure an `XMLReader` with a `LexicalHandler`, pass an instance of your handler to the reader's `setProperty()` method with the name *http://xml.org/sax/handlers/LexicalHandler*:

```
try {
  parser.setProperty(
    "http://xml.org/sax/handlers/LexicalHandler",
    new MyLexicalHandlerClass()
  );
}
catch(SAXException e) {
  System.out.println("This parser does not provide lexical events.");
}
```

If the parser does not provide lexical events, it throws a `SAXNotRecognizedException` or a `SAXNotSupportedException`. If it doesn't throw one of these exceptions, it calls back to the methods in your `LexicalHandler`, as it encounters entity references, comments, and CDATA sections. The basic content of the resolved entities and CDATA sections are still reported through the `ContentHandler` interface, as normal:

```
package org.xml.sax.ext;

public interface LexicalHandler {

  public void startDTD(String name, String publicId, String systemId)
   throws SAXException;
  public void endDTD() throws SAXException;
  public void startEntity(String name) throws SAXException;
  public void endEntity(String name) throws SAXException;
  public void startCDATA() throws SAXException;
  public void endCDATA() throws SAXException;
  public void comment(char[] text, int start, int length)
   throws SAXException;

}
```

CHAPTER 23

# *Character Sets*



XML documents are written in the UTF-8 encoding of Unicode by default. However, they may be written in any character set the XML processor understands, provided you specify the character set in the encoding declaration. For example, a document written in the Latin-2 character set would need this XML declaration:

```
<?xml version="1.0" encoding="ISO-8859-9"?>
```

Most good XML processors understand a multitude of common character sets. The XML specification specifies 21 character set names, as shown in Table 23-1. When using any of these character sets, you should use these names. Of these character sets, only UTF-8 and UTF-16 must be supported by all XML processors, though many XML processors support all the character sets listed here.

*Table 23-1: Character Set Names Defined by the XML 1.0 Specification*

| *Name* | *Character Set* |
|---|---|
| UTF-8 | The default encoding used in XML documents, unless an encoding declaration specifies otherwise; a variable-width encoding of Unicode that uses one to four bytes per character. UTF-8 is designed such that all ASCII documents are legal UTF-8 documents, which is not true for other character sets, such as Cp1252 and Latin-1. This character set is the best encoding choice if your XML documents contain limited Chinese, Japanese, or Korean. |
| UTF-16 | A two-byte encoding of Unicode in which all Unicode characters defined in Unicode 3.0 and earlier (including the ASCII characters) occupy exactly two bytes. However, characters from planes 1 through 14, added in Unicode 3.1 and later, are encoded using surrogate pairs of four bytes each. This encoding is the best choice if your XML documents contain substantial amounts of Chinese, Japanese, or Korean. |
| ISO-10646-UCS-2 | The Basic Multilingual Plane of Unicode; i.e., plane 0. This character set is the same as UTF-16, except that it does not allow surrogate pairs to represent characters with code points beyond 65,535. The difference is significant only in Unicode 3.1 and later. Each Unicode character is represented as exactly one two-byte, unsigned integer. Determining endianness requires a byte-order mark at the beginning of the file. |

*Table 23-1: Character Set Names Defined by the XML 1.0 Specification (continued)*

| *Name* | *Character Set* |
|---|---|
| ISO-10646-UCS-4 | A four-byte encoding of Unicode in which each Unicode character is represented as exactly one four-byte, unsigned integer. Determining endianness requires a byte-order mark at the beginning of the file. |
| ISO-8859-1 | Latin-1, ASCII plus the characters needed for most Western European languages, including Danish, Dutch, English, Faroese, Finnish, Flemish, German, Icelandic, Italian, Norwegian, Portuguese, Spanish, and Swedish. Some non-European languages, such as Hawaiian, Indonesian, and Swahili are also written in this character set. |
| ISO-8859-2 | Latin-2, ASCII plus the characters needed for most Central European languages, including Croatian, Czech, Hungarian, Polish, Romanian, Slovak, and Slovenian. |
| ISO-8859-3 | Latin-3, ASCII plus the characters needed for Esperanto, Maltese, Turkish, and Galician. Latin-5, ISO-8859-9, however, is now preferred for Turkish. |
| ISO-8859-4 | Latin-4, ASCII plus the characters needed for the Baltic languages Latvian, Lithuanian, Greenlandic, and Lappish. Now largely replaced by Latin-6, ISO-8859-10. |
| ISO-8859-5 | ASCII plus the Cyrillic characters used for Byelorussian, Bulgarian, Macedonian, Russian, Serbian, and Ukrainian. |
| ISO-8859-6 | ASCII plus Arabic. |
| ISO-8859-7 | ASCII plus modern Greek. |
| ISO-8859-8 | ASCII plus Hebrew. |
| ISO-8859-9 | Latin-5, which is essentially the same as Latin-1 (ASCII plus Western Europe), except that some Turkish letters replace less commonly used Icelandic letters. |
| ISO-8859-10 | Latin-6, which covers the characters needed for the Northern European languages Estonian, Lithuanian, Greenlandic, Icelandic, Inuit, and Lappish. It's similar to Latin-4, but drops some symbols and the Latvian letter Ŗ, adds a few extra letters needed for Inuit and Lappish, and moves various characters around. ISO-8859-13 has superseded this character set. |
| ISO-8859-11 | This character set adds the Thai alphabet to basic ASCII. However, it is not well supported by current XML parsers; you're probably better off using Unicode instead. |
| ISO-8859-12 | There is currently no such character set, nor is there likely to be one in the foreseeable future. At one point, this was considered for Devanagari, so the number was reserved. However, this effort is not yet off the ground, and it now seems likely that the increasing acceptance of Unicode will make such a character set unnecessary. |
| ISO-8859-13 | Another character set designed to cover the Baltic languages. This set adds back in the Latvian letter Ŗ and other symbols dropped from Latin-6. |
| ISO-8859-14 | Latin-8, a variant of Latin-1 with extra letters needed for Gaelic and Welsh. These letters usually replace punctuation marks. |
| ISO-8859-15 | This character set, known officially as Latin-9 and unofficially as Latin-0, is a revision of Latin-1 that replaces the international currency symbol ¤ with the Euro symbol. It also replaces the seldom-used fraction characters ¼, ½, and ¾ with the uncommon French letters Œ, œ, Ÿ, and the ¦, ¨, and ´ symbols with Finnish letters. Otherwise, it's identical to ISO-8859-1. |
| ISO-2022-JP | A seven-bit encoding of the character set defined in the Japanese national standard JIS X-0208-1997 used on web pages and in email; see RFC 1468. |

*Table 23-1: Character Set Names Defined by the XML 1.0 Specification (continued)*

| *Name* | *Character Set* |
|---|---|
| Shift_JIS | The encoding of the Japanese national standard character set JIS X-0208-1997 used in Microsoft Windows. |
| EUC-JP | The encoding of the Japanese national standard character set JIS X-0208-1997 used by most Unixes. |

Some parsers do not understand all these encodings. Specifically, parsers based on James Clark's expat often support only UTF-8, UTF-16, ISO-8859-1, and US-ASCII. Xerces-C supports ASCII, UTF-8, UTF-16, UCS4, IBM037, IBM1140, ISO-8859-1, and Windows-1252. IBM's XML4C parser derived from the Xerces codebase adds about 17 more common encodings, including ISO-8859 character sets 1 through 9. However, for maximum cross-parser compatibility, you should convert your documents to either UTF-8 or UTF-16 before publishing them, even if you author them in another character set.

## Character Tables

The XML 1.0 specification divides Unicode into five overlapping sets:

*Name characters*
: Characters that can appear in an element, attribute, or entity name. These characters are letters, ideographs, digits, and the punctuation marks `-`, `.`, and `:`. In the tables that follow, the characters are shown in bold type.

*Name start characters*
: Characters that can be the first character of an element, attribute, or entity name. These characters are letters, ideographs, and the underscore `_`. In the tables that follow, these characters are shown with a gray background. Because name start characters are a subset of name characters, they are also shown in bold.

*Character data characters*
: This set includes all characters that can be used anywhere in an XML document, including element and attribute content, comments, and DTDs. This set includes almost all Unicode characters, except for surrogates and most C0 control characters. These characters are shown in a normal typeface. If they are name characters, then they will be bold. If they are also name start characters, they'll have a gray background.

*Illegal characters*
: This set includes characters that may not appear anywhere in an XML document, such as in part of a name, character data, or comment text. These characters are shown in italic, such as *NUL* or *BEL*. Most of these characters are either C0 control characters or half of a surrogate pair.

*Unassigned code points*
: These points are bytes or byte sequences that are not assigned to a character. A program might produce a file containing one of these byte sequences, but their meaning is undefined and they should be avoided. They are represented in the following tables as *N/A*.

Figure 23-1 shows the relationship between these sets. Note that all name start characters are name characters, and that all name characters are character data characters.

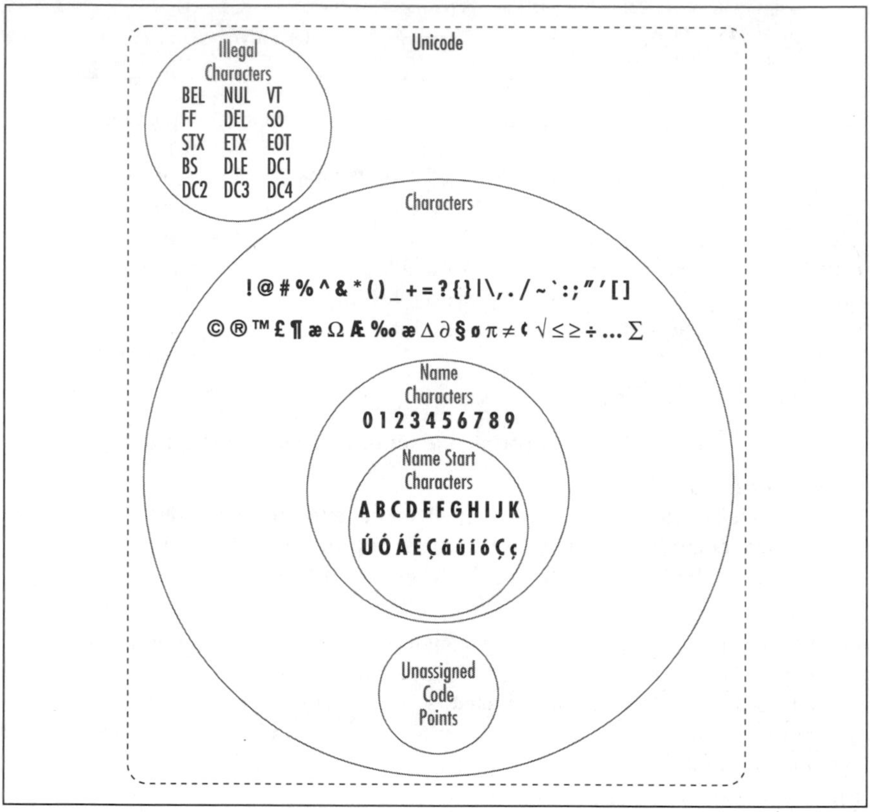


*Figure 23-1: XML's division of Unicode characters*

In all the tables that follow, the box's upper-lefthand corner contains the character's two-digit Unicode hexadecimal value and the upper-righthand corner contains the Unicode decimal value. You can include a decimal in an XML document by prefixing the decimal value with `&#` and suffixing it with a semicolon. Thus Unicode character 69, the capital letter E, can be written as `E`. Hexadecimal values work the same way, except that you prefix them with `&#x`. For example, in hexadecimal, the letter E is 45, so it can be written as `E`.

## ASCII

Most character sets in common use today are supersets of ASCII. That is, code points 0 through 127 are assigned to the same characters that they are assigned to in ASCII. Table 23-2 lists the ASCII character set. The only notable exceptions are the EBCDIC-derived character sets. Specifically, Unicode is a superset of ASCII and code points 1 through 127 identify the same characters in Unicode as they do in ASCII.

*Table 23-2: The First 128 Unicode Characters, (Known as the ASCII Character Set)*

| | | | | | | | |
|---|---|---|---|---|---|---|---|
| 00 0 *NUL* | 01 1 *SOH* | 02 2 *STX* | 03 3 *ETX* | 04 4 *EOT* | 05 5 *ENQ* | 06 6 *ACK* | 07 7 *BEL* |
| 08 8 *BS* | 09 9 TAB | 0A 10 LF | 0B 11 *VTB* | 0C 12 *FF* | 0D 13 CR | 0E 14 *SO* | 0F 15 *SI* |
| 10 16 *DLE* | 11 17 *DC1* | 11 18 *DC2* | 13 19 *DC3* | 14 20 *DC4* | 15 21 *NAK* | 16 22 *SYN* | 17 23 *ETB* |
| 18 24 *CAN* | 19 25 *EM* | 1A 26 *SUB* | 1B 27 *ESC* | 1C 28 *IS4* | 1D 29 *IS3* | 1E 30 *IS2* | 1F 31 *IS1* |
| 20 32 SP | 21 33 ! | 22 34 " | 23 35 # | 24 36 $ | 25 37 % | 26 38 & | 27 39 ' |
| 28 40 ( | 29 41 ) | 2A 42 * | 2B 43 + | 2C 44 , | 2D 45 - | 2E 46 . | 2F 47 / |
| 30 48 0 | 31 49 1 | 32 50 2 | 33 51 3 | 34 52 4 | 35 53 5 | 36 54 6 | 37 55 7 |
| 38 56 8 | 39 57 9 | 3A 58 : | 3B 59 ; | 3C 60 < | 3D 61 = | 3E 62 > | 3F 63 ? |
| 40 64 @ | 41 65 A | 42 66 B | 43 67 C | 44 68 D | 45 69 E | 46 70 F | 47 71 G |
| 48 72 H | 49 73 I | 4A 74 J | 4B 75 K | 4C 76 L | 4D 77 M | 4E 78 N | 4F 79 O |
| 50 80 P | 51 81 Q | 52 82 R | 53 83 S | 54 84 T | 55 85 U | 56 86 V | 57 87 W |
| 58 88 X | 59 89 Y | 5A 90 Z | 5B 91 [ | 5C 92 \ | 5D 93 ] | 5E 94 ^ | 5F 95 _ |
| 60 96 ` | 61 97 a | 62 98 b | 63 99 c | 64 100 d | 65 101 e | 66 102 f | 67 103 g |
| 68 104 h | 69 105 i | 6A 106 j | 6B 107 k | 6C 108 l | 6D 109 m | 6E 110 n | 6F 111 o |
| 70 112 p | 71 113 q | 72 114 r | 73 115 s | 74 116 t | 75 117 u | 76 118 v | 77 119 w |
| 78 120 x | 79 121 y | 7A 122 z | 7B 123 { | 7C 124 \| | 7D 125 } | 7E 126 ~ | 7F 127 *DEL* |

Characters 0 through 31 and character 127 are nonprinting control characters, sometimes called the C0 controls to distinguish them from the C1 controls used in the ISO-8859 character sets. Of these 33 characters, only the carriage return, line feed, and horizontal tab may appear in XML documents. The other 29 may not appear anywhere in an XML document, including in tags, comments, or parsed character data. They may not be inserted with character references, such as `&#31;`. For example, you may not use form feeds to insert page breaks.

## *ISO-8859-1, Latin-1*

The ISO-8859 standard defines several popular supersets of the ASCII character set. These character sets all provide the normal ASCII characters from code points 0 through 127, the C1 controls from 128 through 159, and change the characters from 160 through 255.

In particular, many Western European and American systems use a character set called Latin-1. This is the first code page defined in the ISO-8859 standard and is also called ISO-8859-1. Though all common encodings of Unicode encode code points 128 through 255 differently than Latin-1, code points 128 through 255 map to the same characters in both Latin-1 and Unicode. This situation does not occur in other character sets.

### *C1 Controls*

All ISO-8859 character sets begin with the same 32 extra nonprinting control characters in code points 128 through 159. These sets are used on terminals such as the DEC VT-320 to provide graphics functionality not included in ASCII, for example, erasing the screen and switching it into inverse video or graphics mode. These characters cause severe problems for anyone reading or editing an XML document on a terminal or terminal emulator.

Fortunately, these characters are not necessary in XML documents. Their inclusion in XML 1.0 was an oversight. They should have been banned like the C0 controls in ASCII. Unfortunately, many editors and documents incorrectly label documents written in the Cp1252 Windows character set as ISO-8859-1. Cp1252 does use the code points between 128 and 159 for noncontrol graphics characters. When documents written with this character set are displayed or edited on a dumb terminal, they can effectively disable or crash the user's session. Similar problems exist with most other single-byte Windows and Macintosh code pages.

In the spirit of being liberal in what you accept and conservative in what you generate, you should never use Cp1252, correctly labeled or otherwise. You should also avoid using other nonstandard code pages for documents that move beyond a single system. On the other hand, if you receive a document labeled as Cp1252 (or any other Windows and Macintosh code page), it can be displayed if you're careful not to throw it at a terminal unchanged. If you suspect that a document labeled as ISO-8859-1 that uses characters between 128 and 159 is in fact a Cp1252 document, you should probably reject it. This decision is difficult, however, given the prevalence of broken software that does not properly identify the documents it sends.

### *Latin-1*

Latin-1 covers most Western European languages that use some variant of the Latin alphabet. Characters 0 through 127 in this set are identical to the ASCII characters with the same code point. Characters 128 through 159 are the C1 control characters used only for dumb terminals. Character 160 is the nonbreaking space. Characters 161 through 255 are accented characters, such as è, á, and ö, non-U.S. punctuation marks and a few new letters, such as the German ß.

Table 23-3 shows the upper half of this character set. The lower half is identical to the ASCII character set shown in Table 23-2.

*Table 23-3: Unicode Characters Between 160 and 255 and the Second Half of the Latin-1, ISO-8859-1 Character Set*

| | | | | | | | |
|---|---|---|---|---|---|---|---|
| **80** 128 | **81** 129 | **82** 130 | **83** 131 | **84** 132 | **85** 133 | **86** 134 | **87** 135 |
| XXX | XXX | BPH | NBH | IND | NEL | SSA | ESA |
| **88** 136 | **89** 137 | **8A** 138 | **8B** 139 | **8C** 140 | **8D** 141 | **8E** 142 | **8F** 143 |
| HTS | HTJ | VTS | PLD | PLU | RI | SS2 | SS3 |
| **90** 144 | **91** 145 | **92** 146 | **93** 147 | **94** 148 | **95** 149 | **96** 150 | **97** 151 |
| DCS | PU1 | PU2 | STS | CCH | MW | SPA | EPA |
| **98** 152 | **99** 153 | **9A** 154 | **9B** 155 | **9C** 156 | **9D** 157 | **9E** 158 | **9F** 159 |
| SOS | XXX | SCI | CSI | ST | OSC | PM | APC |
| **A0** 160 | **A1** 161 | **A2** 162 | **A3** 163 | **A4** 164 | **A5** 165 | **A6** 166 | **A7** 167 |
| NBSP | ¡ | ¢ | £ | ¤ | ¥ | ¦ | § |
| **A8** 168 | **A9** 169 | **AA** 170 | **AB** 171 | **AC** 172 | **AD** 173 | **AE** 174 | **AF** 175 |
| ¨ | © | ª | « | ¬ | SHY | ® | ¯ |
| **B0** 176 | **B1** 177 | **B2** 178 | **B3** 179 | **B4** 180 | **B5** 181 | **B6** 182 | **B7** 183 |
| ° | ± | ² | ³ | ´ | µ | ¶ | · |
| **B8** 184 | **B9** 185 | **BA** 186 | **BB** 187 | **BC** 188 | **BD** 189 | **BE** 190 | **BF** 191 |
| ¸ | ¹ | º | » | ¼ | ½ | ¾ | ¿ |
| **C0** 192 | **C1** 193 | **C2** 194 | **C3** 195 | **C4** 196 | **C5** 197 | **C6** 198 | **C7** 199 |
| À | Á | Â | Ã | Ä | Å | Æ | Ç |
| **C8** 200 | **C9** 201 | **CA** 202 | **CB** 203 | **CC** 204 | **CD** 205 | **CE** 206 | **CF** 207 |
| È | É | Ê | Ë | Ì | Í | Î | Ï |
| **D0** 208 | **D1** 209 | **D2** 210 | **D3** 211 | **D4** 212 | **D5** 213 | **D6** 214 | **D7** 215 |
| Ð | Ñ | Ò | Ó | Ô | Õ | Ö | × |
| **D8** 216 | **D9** 217 | **DA** 218 | **DB** 219 | **DC** 220 | **DD** 221 | **DE** 222 | **DF** 223 |
| Ø | Ù | Ú | Û | Ü | Ý | Þ | ß |
| **E0** 224 | **E1** 225 | **E2** 226 | **E3** 227 | **E4** 228 | **E5** 229 | **E6** 230 | **E7** 231 |
| à | á | â | ã | ä | å | æ | ç |
| **E8** 232 | **E9** 233 | **EA** 234 | **EB** 235 | **EC** 236 | **ED** 237 | **EE** 238 | **EF** 239 |
| è | é | ê | ë | ì | í | î | ï |
| **F0** 240 | **F1** 241 | **F2** 242 | **F3** 243 | **F4** 244 | **F5** 245 | **F6** 246 | **F7** 247 |
| ð | ñ | ò | ó | ô | õ | ö | ÷ |
| **F8** 248 | **F9** 249 | **FA** 250 | **FB** 251 | **FC** 252 | **FD** 253 | **FE** 254 | **FF** 255 |
| ø | ù | ú | û | ü | ý | þ | ÿ |

Character Sets

## *HTML4 Entity Sets*

HTML 4.0 predefines several hundred named entities you can use in HTML documents, many of which are quite useful. For instance, the nonbreaking space is ` `. XML, however, defines only five named entities:

`&`
: The ampersand (&)

`<`
: The less-than sign (<)

`>`
: The greater-than sign (>)

`"`
: The straight double quote (")

`'`
: The apostrophe (')

Other characters you need can be inserted with character references in decimal or hexadecimal format. For instance, the nonbreaking space is Unicode character 160 (decimal). Therefore, you can insert it in your document as either ` ` or ` `. If you really want to type it as ` `, you can define this entity reference in your DTD. Doing so requires you to use a character reference:

```
<!ENTITY nbsp " ">
```

The XHTML 1.0 specification includes three DTD subsets that define the familiar HTML character references:

*Latin-1 characters, http://www.w3.org/TR/xhtml1/DTD/xhtml-lat1.ent*
: The non-ASCII, graphic characters included in ISO-8859-1 from code points 160 through 255, shown in Table 23-3

*Special characters, http://www.w3.org/TR/xhtml1/DTD/xhtml-special.ent*
: A few useful letters and punctuation marks not included in Latin-1

*Symbols, http://www.w3.org/TR/xhtml1/DTD/xhtml-symbol.ent*
: The Greek alphabet, plus various arrows, mathematical operators, and other symbols used in mathematics

Feel free to borrow these for your own use. They should be included in your document's DTD with these parameter entity references and PUBLIC identifiers:

```
<!ENTITY % HTMLlat1 PUBLIC
   "-//W3C//ENTITIES Latin 1 for XHTML//EN"
   "http://www.w3.org/TR/xhtml1/DTD/xhtml-lat1.ent">
%HTMLlat1;
<!ENTITY % HTMLspecial PUBLIC
    "-//W3C//ENTITIES Special for XHTML//EN"
    "http://www.w3.org/TR/xhtml1/DTD/xhtml-special.ent">
%HTMLspecial;
<!ENTITY % HTMLsymbol PUBLIC
    "-//W3C//ENTITIES Symbols for XHTML//EN"
    "http://www.w3.org/TR/xhtml1/DTD/xhtml-symbol.ent">
%HTMLsymbol;
```

However, we do recommend saving local copies and changing the system identifier to match the new location, rather than downloading them from *www.w3.org* every time you need to parse a file. You may import just one, two, or all three of them, depending on what you need. No interdependencies exist between these files.

Alternatively, just use the character references given in Table 23-4 through Table 23-6.

*Table 23-4: The HTML Latin-1 Entity Set*

| *Character* | *Meaning* | *XHTML Entity Reference* | *Hexadecimal Character Reference* | *Decimal Character Reference* |
|---|---|---|---|---|
| | Nonbreaking space |   |   |   |
| ¡ | Inverted exclamation mark | ¡ | ¡ | ¡ |
| ¢ | Cent sign | ¢ | ¢ | ¢ |
| £ | Pound sign | £ | £ | £ |
| ¤ | Currency sign | ¤ | ¤ | ¤ |
| ¥ | Yen sign, Yuan sign | ¥ | ¥ | ¥ |
| ¦ | Broken vertical bar | ¦ | ¦ | ¦ |
| § | Section sign | § | § | § |
| ¨ | Dieresis, spacing dieresis | ¨ | ¨ | ¨ |
| © | Copyright sign | © | © | © |
| ª | Feminine ordinal indicator | ª | ª | ª |
| « | Left-pointing double angle quotation mark, left-pointing guillemot | « | « | « |
| ¬ | Not sign | ¬ | ¬ | ¬ |
| - | Soft hyphen, discretionary hyphen |  |  |  |
| ® | Registered trademark sign | ® | ® | ® |
| | Macron, overline, APL overbar | ¯ | ¯ | ¯ |
| ° | Degree sign | ° | ° | ° |
| ± | Plus-or-minus sign | ± | ± | ± |
| ² | Superscript digit two, squared | ² | ² | ² |
| ³ | Superscript digit three, cubed | ³ | ³ | ³ |
| ´ | Acute accent, spacing acute | ´ | ´ | ´ |
| µ | Micro sign | µ | µ | µ |
| ¶ | Pilcrow sign, paragraph sign | ¶ | ¶ | ¶ |
| · | Middle dot, Georgian comma, Greek middle dot | · | · | · |
| ¸ | Cedilla, spacing cedilla | ¸ | ¸ | ¸ |
| ¹ | Superscript digit one | ¹ | ¹ | ¹ |
| º | Masculine ordinal indicator | º | º | º |
| » | Right-pointing double angle quotation mark, right-pointing guillemot | » | » | » |
| ¼ | Vulgar fraction one-quarter | ¼ | ¼ | ¼ |
| ½ | Vulgar fraction one-half | ½ | ½ | ½ |

*Table 23-4: The HTML Latin-1 Entity Set (continued)*

| *Character* | *Meaning* | *XHTML Entity Reference* | *Hexadecimal Character Reference* | *Decimal Character Reference* |
|---|---|---|---|---|
| ¾ | Vulgar fraction three-quarters | ¾ | ¾ | ¾ |
| ¿ | Inverted question mark | ¿ | ¿ | ¿ |
| À | Latin capital letter A with grave | À | À | À |
| Á | Latin capital letter A with acute | Á | Á | Á |
| Â | Latin capital letter A with circumflex | Â | Â | Â |
| Ã | Latin capital letter A with tilde | Ã | Ã | Ã |
| Ä | Latin capital letter A with dieresis | Ä | Ä | Ä |
| Å | Latin capital letter A with ring above, Latin capital letter A ring | Å | Å | Å |
| Æ | Latin capital letter AE, Latin capital ligature AE | Æ | Æ | Æ |
| Ç | Latin capital letter C with cedilla | Ç | Ç | Ç |
| È | Latin capital letter E with grave | È | È | È |
| É | Latin capital letter E with acute | É | É | É |
| Ê | Latin capital letter E with circumflex | Ê | Ê | Ê |
| Ë | Latin capital letter E with dieresis | Ë | Ë | Ë |
| Ì | Latin capital letter I with grave | Ì | Ì | Ì |
| Í | Latin capital letter I with acute | Í | Í | Í |
| Î | Latin capital letter I with circumflex | Î | Î | Î |
| Ï | Latin capital letter I with dieresis | Ï | Ï | Ï |
| Ð | Latin capital letter eth | Ð | Ð | Ð |
| Ñ | Latin capital letter N with tilde | Ñ | Ñ | Ñ |
| Ò | Latin capital letter O with grave | Ò | Ò | Ò |
| Ó | Latin capital letter O with acute | Ó | Ó | Ó |
| Ô | Latin capital letter O with circumflex | Ô | Ô | Ô |
| Õ | Latin capital letter O with tilde | Õ | Õ | Õ |
| Ö | Latin capital letter O with dieresis | Ö | Ö | Ö |
| × | Multiplication sign | × | × | × |
| Ø | Latin capital letter O with stroke | Ø | Ø | Ø |
| Ù | Latin capital letter U with grave | Ù | Ù | Ù |
| Ú | Latin capital letter U with acute | Ú | Ú | Ú |
| Û | Latin capital letter U with circumflex | Û | Û | Û |
| Ü | Latin capital letter U with dieresis | Ü | Ü | Ü |

*Table 23-4: The HTML Latin-1 Entity Set (continued)*

| *Character* | *Meaning* | *XHTML Entity Reference* | *Hexadecimal Character Reference* | *Decimal Character Reference* |
|---|---|---|---|---|
| Ý | Latin capital letter Y with acute | Ý | Ý | Ý |
| Þ | Latin capital letter thorn | Þ | Þ | Þ |
| ß | Latin small letter sharp s, ess-zett | ß | ß | ß |
| à | Latin small letter a with grave | à | à | à |
| á | Latin small letter a with acute | á | á | á |
| â | Latin small letter a with circumflex | â | â | â |
| ã | Latin small letter a with tilde | ã | ã | ã |
| ä | Latin small letter a with dieresis | ä | ä | ä |
| å | Latin small letter a with ring above | å | å | å |
| æ | Latin small letter ae, Latin small ligature ae | æ | æ | æ |
| ç | Latin small letter c with cedilla | ç | ç | ç |
| è | Latin small letter e with grave | è | è | è |
| é | Latin small letter e with acute | é | é | é |
| ê | Latin small letter e with circumflex | ê | ê | ê |
| ë | Latin small letter e with dieresis | ë | ë | ë |
| ì | Latin small letter i with grave | ì | ì | ì |
| í | Latin small letter i with acute | í | í | í |
| î | Latin small letter i with circumflex | î | î | î |
| ï | Latin small letter i with dieresis | ï | ï | ï |
| ð | Latin small letter eth | ð | ð | ð |
| ñ | Latin small letter n with tilde | ñ | ñ | ñ |
| ò | Latin small letter o with grave | ò | ò | ò |
| ó | Latin small letter o with acute | ó | ó | ó |
| ô | Latin small letter o with circumflex | ô | ô | ô |
| õ | Latin small letter o with tilde | õ | õ | õ |
| ö | Latin small letter o with dieresis | ö | ö | ö |
| ÷ | Division sign | ÷ | ÷ | ÷ |
| ø | Latin small letter o with stroke | ø | ø | ø |
| ù | Latin small letter u with grave | ù | ù | ù |
| ú | Latin small letter u with acute | ú | ú | ú |
| û | Latin small letter u with circumflex | û | û | û |
| ü | Latin small letter u with dieresis | ü | ü | ü |
| ý | Latin small letter y with acute | ý | ý | ý |
| þ | Latin small letter thorn | þ | þ | þ |

*Table 23-4: The HTML Latin-1 Entity Set (continued)*

| *Character* | *Meaning* | *XHTML Entity Reference* | *Hexadecimal Character Reference* | *Decimal Character Reference* |
|---|---|---|---|---|
| ÿ | Latin small letter y with dieresis | `ÿ` | `ÿ` | `ÿ` |

*Table 23-5: The HTML Special Characters Entity Set*

| *Character* | *Meaning* | *XHTML Entity Reference* | *Hexadecimal Character Reference* | *Decimal Character Reference* |
|---|---|---|---|---|
| " | Quotation mark, APL quote | `"` | `"` | `"` |
| & | Ampersand | `&` | `&` | `&` |
| ' | Apostrophe mark | `'` | `'` | `'` |
| < | Less-than sign | `<` | `<` | `<` |
| > | Greater-than sign | `>` | `>` | `>` |
| Œ | Latin capital ligature OE | `Œ` | `Œ` | `Œ` |
| œ | Latin small ligature oe | `œ` | `œ` | `œ` |
| Ŝ | Latin capital letter S with caron | `Š` | `Š` | `Š` |
| ŝ | Latin small letter s with caron | `š` | `š` | `š` |
| Ÿ | Latin capital letter Y with dieresis | `Ÿ` | `Ÿ` | `Ÿ` |
| ˆ | Modifier letter circumflex accent | `ˆ` | `ˆ` | `ˆ` |
| ~ | Small tilde | `˜` | `˜` | `˜` |
| | En space | ` ` | ` ` | ` ` |
| | Em space | ` ` | ` ` | ` ` |
| | Thin space | ` ` | ` ` | ` ` |
| Non-printing character | Zero width nonjoiner | `‌` | `‌` | `‌` |
| Non-printing character | Zero width joiner | `‍` | `‍` | `‍` |
| Non-printing character | Left-to-right mark | `‎` | `‎` | `‎` |
| Non-printing character | Right-to-left mark | `‏` | `‏` | `‏` |
| – | En dash | `–` | `–` | `–` |
| — | Em dash | `—` | `—` | `—` |
| ‘ | Left single quotation mark | `‘` | `‘` | `‘` |
| ’ | Right single quotation mark | `’` | `’` | `’` |
| ‚ | Single low-9 quotation mark | `‚` | `‚` | `‚` |
| “ | Left double quotation mark | `“` | `“` | `“` |
| ” | Right double quotation mark | `”` | `”` | `”` |
| „ | Double low-9 quotation mark | `„` | `„` | `„` |
| † | Dagger | `†` | `†` | `†` |
| ‡ | Double dagger | `‡` | `‡` | `‡` |

*Table 23-5: The HTML Special Characters Entity Set (continued)*

| *Character* | *Meaning* | *XHTML Entity Reference* | *Hexadecimal Character Reference* | *Decimal Character Reference* |
|---|---|---|---|---|
| ‰ | Per mille sign | `‰` | `‰` | `‰` |
| ‹ | Single left-pointing angle quotation mark | `‹` | `‹` | `‹` |
| › | Single right-pointing angle quotation mark | `›` | `›` | `›` |
| € | Euro sign | `€` | `€` | `€` |

*Table 23-6: The HTML Symbol Entity Set*

| *Character* | *Meaning* | *XHTML Entity Reference* | *Hexadecimal Character Reference* | *Decimal Character Reference* |
|---|---|---|---|---|
| *f* | Latin small f with hook, function, florin | `ƒ` | `ƒ` | `ƒ` |
| Α | Greek capital letter alpha | `Α` | `Α` | `Α` |
| Β | Greek capital letter beta | `Β` | `Β` | `Β` |
| Γ | Greek capital letter gamma | `Γ` | `Γ` | `Γ` |
| Δ | Greek capital letter delta | `Δ` | `Δ` | `Δ` |
| Ε | Greek capital letter epsilon | `Ε` | `Ε` | `Ε` |
| Ζ | Greek capital letter zeta | `Ζ` | `Ζ` | `Ζ` |
| Η | Greek capital letter eta | `Η` | `Η` | `Η` |
| Θ | Greek capital letter theta | `Θ` | `Θ` | `Θ` |
| Ι | Greek capital letter iota | `Ι` | `Ι` | `Ι` |
| Κ | Greek capital letter kappa | `Κ` | `Κ` | `Κ` |
| Λ | Greek capital letter lambda | `Λ` | `Λ` | `Λ` |
| Μ | Greek capital letter mu | `Μ` | `Μ` | `Μ` |
| Ν | Greek capital letter nu | `Ν` | `Ν` | `Ν` |
| Ξ | Greek capital letter xi | `Ξ` | `Ξ` | `Ξ` |
| Ο | Greek capital letter omicron | `Ο` | `Ο` | `Ο` |
| Π | Greek capital letter pi | `Π` | `Π` | `Π` |
| Ρ | Greek capital letter rho | `Ρ` | `Ρ` | `Ρ` |
| Σ | Greek capital letter sigma | `Σ` | `Σ` | `Σ` |
| Τ | Greek capital letter tau | `Τ` | `Τ` | `Τ` |
| Υ | Greek capital letter upsilon | `Υ` | `Υ` | `Υ` |
| Φ | Greek capital letter phi | `Φ` | `Φ` | `Φ` |
| Χ | Greek capital letter chi | `Χ` | `Χ` | `Χ` |
| Ψ | Greek capital letter psi | `Ψ` | `Ψ` | `Ψ` |
| Ω | Greek capital letter omega | `Ω` | `Ω` | `Ω` |
| α | Greek small letter alpha | `α` | `α` | `α` |
| β | Greek small letter beta | `β` | `β` | `β` |
| γ | Greek small letter gamma | `γ` | `γ` | `γ` |
| δ | Greek small letter delta | `δ` | `δ` | `δ` |
| ε | Greek small letter epsilon | `ε` | `ε` | `ε` |

*Table 23-6: The HTML Symbol Entity Set (continued)*

| *Character* | *Meaning* | *XHTML Entity Reference* | *Hexadecimal Character Reference* | *Decimal Character Reference* |
|---|---|---|---|---|
| ζ | Greek small letter zeta | ζ | ζ | ζ |
| η | Greek small letter eta | η | η | η |
| θ | Greek small letter theta | θ | θ | θ |
| ι | Greek small letter iota | ι | ι | ι |
| κ | Greek small letter kappa | κ | κ | κ |
| λ | Greek small letter lambda | λ | λ | λ |
| μ | Greek small letter mu | μ | μ | μ |
| ν | Greek small letter nu | ν | ν | ν |
| ξ | Greek small letter xi | ξ | ξ | ξ |
| ο | Greek small letter omicron | ο | ο | ο |
| π | Greek small letter pi | π | π | π |
| ρ | Greek small letter rho | ρ | ρ | ρ |
| ς | Greek small letter final sigma | ς | ς | ς |
| σ | Greek small letter sigma | σ | σ | σ |
| τ | Greek small letter tau | τ | τ | τ |
| υ | Greek small letter upsilon | υ | υ | υ |
| φ | Greek small letter phi | φ | φ | φ |
| χ | Greek small letter chi | χ | χ | χ |
| ψ | Greek small letter psi | ψ | ψ | ψ |
| ω | Greek small letter omega | ω | ω | ω |
| ϑ | Greek small letter theta symbol | ϑ | ϑ | ϑ |
| ϒ | Greek upsilon with hook symbol | ϒ | ϒ | ϒ |
| ϖ | Greek pi symbol | ϖ | ϖ | ϖ |
| • | Bullet, black small circle | • | • | • |
| … | Horizontal ellipsis, three-dot leader | … | … | … |
| ′ | Prime, minutes, feet | ′ | ′ | ′ |
| ″ | Double prime, seconds, inches | ″ | ″ | ″ |
| ‾ | Overline, spacing overscore | ‾ | ‾ | ‾ |
| ⁄ | Fraction slash | ⁄ | ⁄ | ⁄ |
| ℑ | Black letter capital I, imaginary part | ℑ | ℑ | ℑ |
| ℘ | Script capital P, power set, Weierstrass p | ℘ | ℘ | ℘ |
| ℜ | Black letter capital R, real part symbol | ℜ | ℜ | ℜ |
| ™ | Trademark sign | ™ | ™ | ™ |
| ℵ | Aleph symbol, first transfinite cardinal | ℵ | ℵ | ℵ |
| ← | Leftward arrow | ← | ← | ← |
| ↑ | Upward arrow | ↑ | ↑ | ↑ |

*Table 23-6: The HTML Symbol Entity Set (continued)*

| Character | Meaning | XHTML Entity Reference | Hexadecimal Character Reference | Decimal Character Reference |
|---|---|---|---|---|
| → | Rightward arrow | `→` | `→` | `→` |
| ↓ | Downward arrow | `↓` | `↓` | `↓` |
| ↔ | Left-right arrow | `↔` | `↔` | `↔` |
| ↵ | Downward arrow with corner leftward, carriage return | `↵` | `↵` | `↵` |
| ⇐ | Leftward double arrow | `⇐` | `⇐` | `⇐` |
| ⇑ | Upward double arrow | `⇑` | `⇑` | `⇑` |
| ⇒ | Rightward double arrow | `⇒` | `⇒` | `⇒` |
| ⇓ | Downward double arrow | `⇓` | `⇓` | `⇓` |
| ⇔ | Left-right double arrow | `⇔` | `⇔` | `⇔` |
| ∀ | For all | `∀` | `∀` | `∀` |
| ∂ | Partial differential | `∂` | `∂` | `∂` |
| ∃ | There exists | `∃` | `∃` | `∃` |
| ∅ | Empty set, null set, diameter | `∅` | `∅` | `∅` |
| ∇ | Nabla, backward difference | `∇` | `∇` | `∇` |
| ∈ | Element of | `∈` | `∈` | `∈` |
| ∉ | Not an element of | `∉` | `∉` | `∉` |
| ∋ | Contains as member | `∋` | `∋` | `∋` |
| ∏ | N-ary product, product sign | `∏` | `∏` | `∏` |
| ∑ | N-ary summation | `∑` | `∑` | `∑` |
| − | Minus sign | `−` | `−` | `−` |
| ∗ | Asterisk operator | `∗` | `∗` | `∗` |
| √ | Square root, radical sign | `√` | `√` | `√` |
| ∝ | Proportional to | `∝` | `∝` | `∝` |
| ∞ | Infinity | `∞` | `∞` | `∞` |
| ∠ | Angle | `∠` | `∠` | `∠` |
| ∧ | Logical and, wedge | `∧` | `∧` | `∧` |
| ∨ | Logical or, vee | `∨` | `∨` | `∨` |
| ∩ | Intersection, cap | `∩` | `∩` | `∩` |
| ∪ | Union, cup | `∪` | `∪` | `∪` |
| ∫ | Integral | `∫` | `∫` | `∫` |
| ∴ | Therefore | `∴` | `∴` | `∴` |
| ∼ | Tilde operator, varies with, similar to | `∼` | `∼` | `∼` |
| ≅ | Approximately equal to | `≅` | `≅` | `≅` |
| ≈ | Almost equal to, asymptotic to | `≈` | `≈` | `≈` |
| ≠ | Not equal to | `≠` | `≠` | `≠` |
| ≡ | Identical to | `≡` | `≡` | `≡` |
| ≤ | Less than or equal to | `≤` | `≤` | `≤` |
| ≥ | Greater than or equal to | `≥` | `≥` | `≥` |
| ⊂ | Subset of | `⊂` | `⊂` | `⊂` |

*Table 23-6: The HTML Symbol Entity Set (continued)*

| Character | Meaning | XHTML Entity Reference | Hexadecimal Character Reference | Decimal Character Reference |
|---|---|---|---|---|
| ⊃ | Superset of | `⊃` | `⊃` | `⊃` |
| ⊄ | Not a subset of | `⊄` | `⊄` | `⊄` |
| ⊆ | Subset of or equal to | `⊆` | `⊆` | `⊆` |
| ⊇ | Superset of or equal to | `⊇` | `⊇` | `⊇` |
| ⊕ | Circled plus, direct sum | `⊕` | `⊕` | `⊕` |
| ⊗ | Circled times, vector product | `⊗` | `⊗` | `⊗` |
| ⊥ | Up tack, orthogonal to, perpendicular | `⊥` | `⊥` | `⊥` |
| ⋅ | Dot operator | `⋅` | `⋅` | `⋅` |
| ⌈ | Left ceiling, APL upstile | `⌈` | `⌈` | `⌈` |
| ⌉ | Right ceiling | `⌉` | `⌉` | `⌉` |
| ⌊ | Left floor, APL downstile | `⌊` | `⌊` | `⌊` |
| ⌋ | Right floor | `⌋` | `⌋` | `⌋` |
| 〈 | Left-pointing angle bracket, bra | `⟨` | `〈` | `〈` |
| 〉 | Right-pointing angle bracket, ket | `⟩` | `〉` | `〉` |
| ◊ | Lozenge | `◊` | `◊` | `◊` |
| ♠ | Black spade suit | `♠` | `♠` | `♠` |
| ♣ | Black club suit, shamrock | `♣` | `♣` | `♣` |
| ♥ | Black heart suit, valentine | `♥` | `♥` | `♥` |
| ♦ | Black diamond suit | `♦` | `♦` | `♦` |

## Other Unicode Blocks

So far we've accounted for a little over 300 of the more than 50,000 Unicode characters. Many thousands are still unaccounted for. Outside the ranges defined in XHTML, standard entity names don't exist. You should either use an editor that can produce the characters you need in the appropriate character set or you should use character references. Most of the 50,000-plus Unicode characters are either Han ideographs, Hangul syllables, or rarely used characters. However, we do list a few of the most useful blocks in the following sections.

In the tables that follow, the upper-lefthand corner contains the character's hexadecimal Unicode value and the upper-righthand corner contains the character's decimal Unicode value. You can use either value to form a character reference so you can use these characters in element content and attribute values, even without an editor or fonts that support them.

### Latin Extended-A

The 128 characters in the Latin Extended-A block of Unicode, shown in Table 23-7, are used in conjunction with the normal ASCII and Latin-1 characters. They cover most European Latin letters missing from Latin-1. The block includes various characters you'll find in the upper halves of the other ISO-8859 Latin character sets, including ISO-8859-2, ISO-8859-3, ISO-8859-4, and ISO-8859-9. When combined with ASCII and Latin-1, this block lets you write Afrikaans, Basque, Breton, Catalan, Croatian, Czech, Esperanto, Estonian, French, Frisian, Greenlandic, Hungarian, Latvian, Lithuanian, Maltese, Polish, Provençal, Rhaeto-Romanic, Romanian, Romany, Sami, Slovak, Slovenian, Sorbian, Turkish, and Welsh.

*Table 23-7: Unicode's Latin Extended-A Block*

| | | | | | | | |
|---|---|---|---|---|---|---|---|
| **100** 256 | **101** 257 | **102** 258 | **103** 259 | **104** 260 | **105** 261 | **106** 262 | **107** 263 |
| Ā | ā | Ă | ă | Ą | Ą | Ć | ć |
| **108** 264 | **109** 265 | **10A** 266 | **10B** 267 | **10C** 268 | **10D** 269 | **10E** 270 | **10F** 271 |
| Ĉ | ĉ | Ċ | ċ | Č | Č | Ď | ď |
| **110** 272 | **111** 273 | **112** 274 | **113** 275 | **114** 276 | **115** 277 | **116** 278 | **117** 279 |
| Đ | đ | Ē | ē | Ĕ | Ĕ | Ė | ė |
| **118** 280 | **119** 281 | **11A** 282 | **11B** 283 | **11C** 284 | **11D** 285 | **11E** 286 | **11F** 287 |
| Ę | ę | Ě | ě | Ĝ | Ĝ | Ğ | ğ |
| **120** 288 | **121** 289 | **122** 290 | **123** 291 | **124** 292 | **125** 293 | **126** 294 | **127** 295 |
| Ġ | ġ | Ģ | ģ | Ĥ | Ĥ | Ħ | ħ |
| **128** 296 | **129** 297 | **12A** 298 | **12B** 299 | **12C** 300 | **12D** 301 | **12E** 302 | **12F** 303 |
| Ĩ | ĩ | Ī | ī | Ĭ | Ĭ | Į | į |
| **130** 304 | **131** 305 | **132** 306 | **133** 307 | **134** 308 | **135** 309 | **136** 310 | **137** 311 |
| İ | ı | Ĳ | ĳ | Ĵ | Ĵ | Ķ | ķ |
| **138** 312 | **139** 313 | **13A** 314 | **13B** 315 | **13C** 316 | **13D** 317 | **13E** 318 | **13F** 319 |
| ĸ | Ĺ | ĺ | Ļ | ļ | Ľ | ľ | Ŀ |
| **140** 320 | **141** 321 | **142** 322 | **143** 323 | **144** 324 | **145** 325 | **146** 326 | **147** 327 |
| ŀ | Ł | ł | Ń | ń | Ņ | ņ | Ň |
| **148** 328 | **149** 329 | **14A** 330 | **14B** 331 | **14C** 332 | **14D** 333 | **14E** 334 | **14F** 335 |
| ň | ŉ | Ŋ | ŋ | Ō | Ō | Ŏ | ŏ |
| **150** 336 | **151** 337 | **152** 338 | **153** 339 | **154** 340 | **155** 341 | **156** 342 | **157** 343 |
| Ő | ő | Œ | œ | Ŕ | R | Ŗ | ŗ |
| **158** 344 | **159** 345 | **15A** 346 | **15B** 347 | **15C** 348 | **15D** 349 | **15E** 350 | **15F** 351 |
| Ř | ř | Ś | ś | Ŝ | Ŝ | Ş | ş |
| **160** 352 | **161** 353 | **162** 354 | **163** 355 | **164** 356 | **165** 357 | **166** 358 | **167** 359 |
| Š | š | Ţ | ţ | Ť | Ť | Ŧ | ŧ |
| **168** 360 | **169** 361 | **16A** 362 | **16B** 363 | **16C** 364 | **16D** 365 | **16E** 366 | **16F** 367 |
| Ũ | ũ | Ū | ū | Ŭ | Ŭ | Ů | ů |
| **170** 368 | **171** 369 | **172** 370 | **173** 371 | **174** 372 | **175** 373 | **176** 374 | **177** 375 |
| Ű | ű | Ų | ų | Ŵ | Ŵ | Ŷ | ŷ |
| **178** 376 | **179** 377 | **17A** 378 | **17B** 379 | **17C** 380 | **17D** 381 | **17E** 382 | **17F** 383 |
| Ÿ | Ź | ź | Ż | ż | Ž | ž | ſ |

Character Sets

## *Latin Extended-B*

The Latin Extended-B block of Unicode, shown in Table 23-8, is used in conjunction with the normal ASCII and Latin-1 characters. It mostly contains characters used for transcription of non-European languages not traditionally written in a Roman script. For instance, it's used for the Pinyin transcription of Chinese and for many African languages.

*Table 23-8: The Latin Extended-B Block of Unicode*

| | | | | | | | |
|---|---|---|---|---|---|---|---|
| **180** 384 | **181** 385 | **182** 386 | **183** 387 | **184** 388 | **185** 389 | **186** 390 | **187** 391 |
| ƀ | Ɓ | Ƃ | ƃ | Ƅ | ƅ | Ɔ | Ƈ |
| **188** 392 | **189** 393 | **18A** 394 | **18B** 395 | **18C** 396 | **18D** 397 | **18E** 398 | **18F** 399 |
| ƈ | Ɖ | Ɗ | Ƌ | ƌ | ƍ | Ǝ | Ə |
| **190** 400 | **191** 401 | **192** 402 | **193** 403 | **194** 404 | **195** 405 | **196** 406 | **197** 407 |
| Ɛ | Ƒ | ƒ | Ɠ | Ɣ | ƕ | Ɩ | Ɨ |
| **198** 408 | **199** 409 | **19A** 410 | **19B** 411 | **19C** 412 | **19D** 413 | **19E** 414 | **19F** 415 |
| Ƙ | ƙ | ƚ | ƛ | Ɯ | Ɲ | ƞ | Ɵ |
| **1A0** 416 | **1A1** 417 | **1A2** 418 | **1A3** 419 | **1A4** 420 | **1A5** 421 | **1A6** 422 | **1A7** 423 |
| Ơ | ơ | Ƣ | ƣ | Ƥ | ƥ | Ʀ | Ƨ |
| **1A8** 424 | **1A9** 425 | **1AA** 426 | **1AB** 427 | **1AC** 428 | **1AD** 429 | **1AE** 430 | **1AF** 431 |
| ƨ | Ʃ | ƪ | ƫ | Ƭ | ƭ | Ʈ | Ư |
| **1B0** 432 | **1B1** 433 | **1B2** 434 | **1B3** 435 | **1B4** 436 | **1B5** 437 | **1B6** 438 | **1B7** 439 |
| ư | Ʊ | Ʋ | Ƴ | ƴ | Ƶ | ƶ | Ʒ |
| **1B8** 440 | **1B9** 441 | **1BA** 442 | **1BB** 443 | **1BC** 444 | **1BD** 445 | **1BE** 446 | **1BF** 447 |
| Ƹ | ƹ | ƺ | ƻ | Ƽ | ƽ | ƾ | ƿ |
| **1C0** 448 | **1C1** 449 | **1C2** 450 | **1C3** 451 | **1C4** 452 | **1C5** 453 | **1C6** 454 | **1C7** 455 |
| ǀ | ǁ | ǂ | ǃ | DŽ | Dž | dž | LJ |
| **1C8** 456 | **1C9** 457 | **1CA** 458 | **1CB** 459 | **1CC** 460 | **1CD** 461 | **1CE** 462 | **1CF** 463 |
| Lj | lj | NJ | Nj | nj | Ǎ | ǎ | Ǐ |
| **1D0** 464 | **1D1** 465 | **1D2** 466 | **1D3** 467 | **1D4** 468 | **1D5** 469 | **1D6** 470 | **1D7** 471 |
| ǐ | Ǒ | ǒ | Ǔ | ǔ | Ǖ | ǖ | Ǘ |
| **1D8** 472 | **1D9** 473 | **1DA** 474 | **1DB** 475 | **1DC** 476 | **1DD** 477 | **1DE** 478 | **1DF** 479 |
| ǘ | Ǚ | ǚ | Ǜ | ǜ | ǝ | Ǟ | ǟ |
| **1E0** 480 | **1E1** 481 | **1E2** 482 | **1E3** 483 | **1E4** 484 | **1E5** 485 | **1E6** 486 | **1E7** 487 |
| Ǡ | ǡ | Ǣ | ǣ | Ǥ | ǥ | Ǧ | ǧ |
| **1E8** 488 | **1E9** 489 | **1EA** 490 | **1EB** 491 | **1EC** 492 | **1ED** 493 | **1EE** 494 | **1EF** 495 |
| Ǩ | ǩ | Ǫ | ǫ | Ǭ | ǭ | Ǯ | ǯ |
| **1F0** 496 | **1F1** 497 | **1F2** 498 | **1F3** 499 | **1F4** 500 | **1F5** 501 | **1F6** 502 | **1F7** 503 |
| ǰ | DZ | Dz | dz | Ǵ | ǵ | *N/A* | *N/A* |
| **1F8** 504 | **1F9** 505 | **1FA** 506 | **1FB** 507 | **1FC** 508 | **1FD** 509 | **1FE** 510 | **1FF** 511 |
| *N/A* | *N/A* | Ǻ | ǻ | Ǽ | ǽ | Ǿ | ǿ |
| **200** 512 | **201** 513 | **202** 514 | **203** 515 | **204** 516 | **205** 517 | **206** 518 | **207** 519 |
| Ȁ | ȁ | Ȃ | ȃ | Ȅ | ȅ | Ȇ | ȇ |

*Table 23-8: The Latin Extended-B Block of Unicode (continued)*

| | | | | | | | |
|---|---|---|---|---|---|---|---|
| **208** 520 | **209** 521 | **20A** 522 | **20B** 523 | **20C** 524 | **20D** 525 | **20E** 526 | **20F** 527 |
| Ȉ | ȉ | Ȋ | ȋ | Ȍ | ȍ | Ȏ | ȏ |
| **210** 528 | **211** 529 | **212** 530 | **213** 531 | **214** 532 | **215** 533 | **216** 534 | **217** 535 |
| Ȑ | ȑ | Ȓ | ȓ | Ȕ | ȕ | Ȗ | ȗ |
| **218** 536 | **219** 537 | **21A** 538 | **21B** 539 | **21C** 540 | **21D** 541 | **21E** 542 | **21F** 543 |
| N/A | N/A | N/A | N/A | N/A | N/A | N/A | N/A |
| **220** 544 | **221** 545 | **222** 546 | **223** 547 | **224** 548 | **225** 549 | **226** 550 | **227** 551 |
| N/A | N/A | N/A | N/A | N/A | N/A | N/A | N/A |
| **228** 552 | **229** 553 | **22A** 554 | **22B** 555 | **22C** 556 | **22D** 557 | **22E** 558 | **22F** 559 |
| N/A | N/A | N/A | N/A | N/A | N/A | N/A | N/A |
| **230** 560 | **231** 561 | **232** 562 | **233** 563 | **234** 564 | **235** 565 | **236** 566 | **237** 567 |
| N/A | N/A | N/A | N/A | N/A | N/A | N/A | N/A |
| **238** 568 | **239** 569 | **23A** 570 | **23B** 571 | **23C** 572 | **23D** 573 | **23E** 574 | **23F** 575 |
| N/A | N/A | N/A | N/A | N/A | N/A | N/A | N/A |

## *IPA Extensions*

Linguists use the International Phonetic Alphabet to uniquely and unambiguously identify particular sounds of various spoken languages. Besides the symbols listed in this block, the IPA requires use of ASCII, various other extended Latin characters, the combining diacritical marks in Table 23-11, and a few Greek letters. Table 23-9 contains only the characters not found in more traditional alphabets.



*Table 23-9: The IPA Extensions Block of Unicode*

| | | | | | | | |
|---|---|---|---|---|---|---|---|
| **250** 592 | **251** 593 | **252** 594 | **253** 595 | **254** 596 | **255** 597 | **256** 598 | **257** 599 |
| ɐ | ɑ | ɒ | ɓ | ɔ | ɕ | ɖ | ɗ |
| **258** 600 | **259** 601 | **25A** 602 | **25B** 603 | **25C** 604 | **25D** 605 | **25E** 606 | **25F** 607 |
| ɘ | ə | ɚ | ɛ | ɜ | ɝ | ɞ | ɟ |
| **260** 608 | **261** 609 | **262** 610 | **263** 611 | **264** 612 | **265** 613 | **266** 614 | **267** 615 |
| ɠ | ɡ | ɢ | ɣ | ɤ | ɥ | ɦ | ɧ |
| **268** 616 | **269** 617 | **26A** 618 | **26B** 619 | **26C** 620 | **26D** 621 | **26E** 622 | **26F** 623 |
| ɨ | ɩ | ɪ | ɫ | ɬ | ɭ | ɮ | ɯ |
| **270** 624 | **271** 625 | **272** 626 | **273** 627 | **274** 628 | **275** 629 | **276** 630 | **277** 631 |
| ɰ | ɱ | ɲ | ɳ | ɴ | ɵ | ɶ | ɷ |
| **278** 632 | **279** 633 | **27A** 634 | **27B** 635 | **27C** 636 | **27D** 637 | **27E** 638 | **27F** 639 |
| ɸ | ɹ | ɺ | ɻ | ɼ | ɽ | ɾ | ɿ |
| **280** 640 | **281** 641 | **282** 642 | **283** 643 | **284** 644 | **285** 645 | **286** 646 | **287** 647 |
| ʀ | ʁ | ʂ | ʃ | ʄ | ʅ | ʆ | ʇ |
| **288** 648 | **289** 649 | **28A** 650 | **28B** 651 | **28C** 652 | **28D** 653 | **28E** 654 | **28F** 655 |
| ʈ | ʉ | ʊ | ʋ | ʌ | ʍ | ʎ | ʏ |
| **290** 656 | **291** 657 | **292** 658 | **293** 659 | **294** 660 | **295** 661 | **296** 662 | **297** 663 |
| ʐ | ʑ | ʒ | ʓ | ʔ | ʕ | ʖ | ʗ |

*Table 23-9: The IPA Extensions Block of Unicode (continued)*

| | | | | | | | |
|---|---|---|---|---|---|---|---|
| **298** 664 | **299** 665 | **29A** 666 | **29B** 667 | **29C** 668 | **29D** 669 | **29E** 670 | **29F** 671 |
| ʘ | ʙ | ʚ | ʛ | ʜ | ʝ | ʞ | ʟ |
| **2A0** 672 | **2A1** 673 | **2A2** 674 | **2A3** 675 | **2A4** 676 | **2A5** 677 | **2A6** 678 | **2A7** 679 |
| ʠ | ʡ | ʢ | ʣ | ʤ | ʥ | ʦ | ʧ |
| **2A8** 680 | **2A9** 681 | **2AA** 682 | **2AB** 683 | **2AC** 684 | **2AD** 685 | **2AE** 686 | **2AF** 687 |
| ʨ | N/A | N/A | N/A | N/A | N/A | N/A | N/A |

## Spacing Modifier Letters

The Spacing Modifier Letters block, shown in Table 23-10, includes characters from multiple languages and scripts that modify the preceding or following character, generally by changing its pronunciation.

*Table 23-10: The Spacing Modifier Letters Block of Unicode*

| | | | | | | | |
|---|---|---|---|---|---|---|---|
| **2B0** 688 | **2B1** 689 | **2B2** 690 | **2B3** 691 | **2B4** 692 | **2B5** 693 | **2B6** 694 | **2B7** 695 |
| ʰ | ʱ | ʲ | ʳ | ʴ | ʵ | ʶ | ʷ |
| **2B8** 696 | **2B9** 697 | **2BA** 698 | **2BB** 699 | **2BC** 700 | **2BD** 701 | **2BE** 702 | **2BF** 703 |
| ʸ | ʹ | ʺ | ʻ | ʼ | ʽ | ʾ | ʿ |
| **2C0** 704 | **2C1** 705 | **2C2** 706 | **2C3** 707 | **2C4** 708 | **2C5** 709 | **2C6** 710 | **2C7** 711 |
| ˀ | ˁ | ˂ | ˃ | ˄ | ˅ | ˆ | ˇ |
| **2C8** 712 | **2C9** 713 | **2CA** 714 | **2CB** 715 | **2CC** 716 | **2CD** 717 | **2CE** 718 | **2CF** 719 |
| ˈ | ˉ | ˊ | ˋ | ˌ | ˍ | ˎ | ˏ |
| **2D0** 720 | **2D1** 721 | **2D2** 722 | **2D3** 723 | **2D4** 724 | **2D5** 725 | **2D6** 726 | **2D7** 727 |
| ː | ˑ | ˒ | ˓ | ˔ | ˕ | ˖ | ˗ |
| **2D8** 728 | **2D9** 729 | **2DA** 730 | **2DB** 731 | **2DC** 732 | **2DD** 733 | **2DE** 734 | **2DF** 735 |
| ˘ | ˙ | ˚ | ˛ | ˜ | ˝ | ˞ | N/A |
| **2E0** 736 | **2E1** 737 | **2E2** 738 | **2E3** 739 | **2E4** 740 | **2E5** 741 | **2E6** 742 | **2E7** 743 |
| ˠ | ˡ | ˢ | ˣ | ˤ | ˥ | ˦ | ˧ |
| **2E8** 744 | **2E9** 745 | **2EA** 746 | **2EB** 747 | **2EC** 748 | **2ED** 749 | **2EE** 750 | **2EF** 751 |
| ˨ | ˩ | N/A | N/A | N/A | N/A | N/A | N/A |

## Greek and Coptic

The Greek block of Unicode is used primarily for the modern Greek language. Currently, it's the only option for the Greek-derived Coptic script, but it doesn't really serve that purpose very well, and a separate Coptic block is a likely addition in the future. Extending coverage to classical and Byzantine Greek requires many more accented characters, which are available in the Greek Extended Block, shown in Table 23-20, or by combining these characters with the Combining Diacritical Marks in Table 23-11. The Greek alphabet is also a fertile source of mathematical and scientific notation, though some common letters, such as Δ and Σ, are encoded separately in the Mathematical Operators block, shown in Table 23-26, for their use as mathematical symbols.

*Table 23-11: The Greek and Coptic Block of Unicode*

| | | | | | | | |
|---|---|---|---|---|---|---|---|
| **370** 880 | **371** 881 | **372** 882 | **373** 883 | **374** 884 | **375** 885 | **376** 886 | **377** 887 |
| N/A | N/A | N/A | N/A | ʹ | ͵ | N/A | N/A |
| **378** 888 | **379** 889 | **37A** 890 | **37B** 891 | **37C** 892 | **37D** 893 | **37E** 894 | **37F** 895 |
| N/A | N/A | ͺ | N/A | N/A | N/A | ; | N/A |
| **380** 896 | **381** 897 | **382** 898 | **383** 899 | **384** 900 | **385** 901 | **386** 902 | **387** 903 |
| N/A | N/A | N/A | N/A | ΄ | ΅ | Ά | · |
| **388** 904 | **389** 905 | **38A** 906 | **38B** 907 | **38C** 908 | **38D** 909 | **38E** 910 | **38F** 911 |
| Έ | Ή | Ί | N/A | Ό | N/A | Ύ | Ώ |
| **390** 912 | **391** 913 | **392** 914 | **393** 915 | **394** 916 | **395** 917 | **396** 918 | **397** 919 |
| ΐ | Α | Β | Γ | Δ | Ε | Ζ | Η |
| **398** 920 | **399** 921 | **39A** 922 | **39B** 923 | **39C** 924 | **39D** 925 | **39E** 926 | **39F** 927 |
| Θ | Ι | Κ | Λ | Μ | Ν | Ξ | Ο |
| **3A0** 928 | **3A1** 929 | **3A2** 930 | **3A3** 931 | **3A4** 932 | **3A5** 933 | **3A6** 934 | **3A7** 935 |
| Π | Ρ | N/A | Σ | Τ | Υ | Φ | Χ |
| **3A8** 936 | **3A9** 937 | **3AA** 938 | **3AB** 939 | **3AC** 940 | **3AD** 941 | **3AE** 942 | **3AF** 943 |
| Ψ | Ω | Ϊ | Ϋ | ά | έ | ή | ί |
| **3B0** 944 | **3B1** 945 | **3B2** 946 | **3B3** 947 | **3B4** 948 | **3B5** 949 | **3B6** 950 | **3B7** 951 |
| ΰ | α | β | γ | δ | ε | ζ | η |
| **3B8** 952 | **3B9** 953 | **3BA** 954 | **3BB** 955 | **3BC** 956 | **3BD** 957 | **3BE** 958 | **3BF** 959 |
| θ | ι | κ | λ | μ | ν | ξ | ο |
| **3C0** 960 | **3C1** 961 | **3C2** 962 | **3C3** 963 | **3C4** 964 | **3C5** 965 | **3C6** 966 | **3C7** 967 |
| π | ρ | ς | σ | τ | υ | φ | χ |
| **3C8** 968 | **3C9** 969 | **3CA** 970 | **3CB** 971 | **3CC** 972 | **3CD** 973 | **3CE** 974 | **3CF** 975 |
| ψ | ω | ϊ | ϋ | ό | ύ | ώ | N/A |
| **3D0** 976 | **3D1** 977 | **3D2** 978 | **3D3** 979 | **3D4** 980 | **3D5** 981 | **3D6** 982 | **3D7** 983 |
| ϐ | ϑ | ϒ | ϓ | ϔ | ϕ | ϖ | N/A |
| **3D8** 984 | **3D9** 985 | **3DA** 986 | **3DB** 987 | **3DC** 988 | **3DD** 989 | **3DE** 990 | **3DF** 991 |
| N/A | N/A | Ϛ | N/A | Ϝ | N/A | Ϟ | N/A |
| **3E0** 992 | **3E1** 993 | **3E2** 994 | **3E3** 995 | **3E4** 996 | **3E5** 997 | **3E6** 998 | **3E7** 999 |
| Ϡ | N/A | Ϣ | ϣ | Ϥ | ϥ | Ϧ | ϧ |
| **3E8** 1000 | **3E9** 1001 | **3EA** 1002 | **3EB** 1003 | **3EC** 1004 | **3ED** 1005 | **3EE** 1006 | **3EF** 1007 |
| Ϩ | ϩ | Ϫ | ϫ | Ϭ | ϭ | Ϯ | ϯ |
| **3F0** 1008 | **3F1** 1009 | **3F2** 1010 | **3F3** 1011 | **3F4** 1012 | **3F5** 1013 | **3F6** 1014 | **3F7** 1015 |
| ϰ | ϱ | ϲ | ϳ | N/A | N/A | N/A | N/A |
| **3F8** 1016 | **3F9** 1017 | **3FA** 1018 | **3FB** 1019 | **3FC** 1020 | **3FD** 1021 | **3FE** 1022 | **3FF** 1023 |
| N/A | N/A | N/A | N/A | N/A | N/A | N/A | N/A |

Character Sets

## *Cyrillic*

While Cyrillic is most familiar to Western readers from Russian, it's also used for other Slavic languages, including Serbian, Ukrainian, and Byelorussian, and for many non-Slavic languages of the former Soviet Union, such as Azerbaijani, Tuvan, and Ossetian. Indeed, many characters in the block displayed in Table 23-12 are not actually used in Russian, but only in other languages written in the Cyrillic script. Following the breakup of the Soviet Union, some non-Slavic languages, such as Moldavian and Azerbaijani, are now reverting to Latin-derived scripts.

*Table 23-12: The Cyrillic Block of Unicode*

| | | | | | | | |
|---|---|---|---|---|---|---|---|
| **400** 1024 | **401** 1025 | **402** 1026 | **403** 1027 | **404** 1028 | **405** 1029 | **406** 1030 | **407** 1031 |
| N/A | Ё | Ђ | Ѓ | Є | Ѕ | І | Ї |
| **408** 1032 | **409** 1033 | **40A** 1034 | **40B** 1035 | **40C** 1036 | **40D** 1037 | **40E** 1038 | **40F** 1039 |
| Ј | Љ | Њ | Ћ | Ќ | N/A | Ў | Џ |
| **410** 1040 | **411** 1041 | **412** 1042 | **413** 1043 | **414** 1044 | **415** 1045 | **416** 1046 | **417** 1047 |
| А | Б | В | Г | Д | Е | Ж | З |
| **418** 1048 | **419** 1049 | **41A** 1050 | **41B** 1051 | **41C** 1052 | **41D** 1053 | **41E** 1054 | **41F** 1055 |
| И | Й | К | Л | М | Н | О | П |
| **420** 1056 | **421** 1057 | **422** 1058 | **423** 1059 | **424** 1060 | **425** 1061 | **426** 1062 | **427** 1063 |
| Р | С | Т | У | Ф | Х | Ц | Ч |
| **428** 1064 | **429** 1065 | **42A** 1066 | **42B** 1067 | **42C** 1068 | **42D** 1069 | **42E** 1070 | **42F** 1071 |
| Ш | Щ | Ъ | Ы | Ь | Э | Ю | Я |
| **440** 1088 | **441** 1089 | **442** 1090 | **443** 1091 | **444** 1092 | **445** 1093 | **446** 1094 | **447** 1095 |
| р | с | т | у | ф | х | ц | ч |
| **448** 1096 | **449** 1097 | **44A** 1098 | **44B** 1099 | **44C** 1100 | **44D** 1101 | **44E** 1102 | **44F** 1103 |
| ш | щ | ъ | ы | ь | э | ю | я |
| **450** 1104 | **451** 1105 | **452** 1106 | **453** 1107 | **454** 1108 | **455** 1109 | **456** 1110 | **457** 1111 |
| N/A | ё | ђ | ѓ | є | ѕ | і | ї |
| **458** 1112 | **459** 1113 | **45A** 1114 | **45B** 1115 | **45C** 1116 | **45D** 1117 | **45E** 1118 | **45F** 1119 |
| ј | љ | њ | ћ | ќ | N/A | ў | џ |
| **460** 1120 | **461** 1121 | **462** 1122 | **463** 1123 | **464** 1124 | **465** 1125 | **466** 1126 | **467** 1127 |
| Ѡ | ѡ | Ѣ | ѣ | Ѥ | ѥ | Ѧ | ѧ |
| **468** 1128 | **469** 1129 | **46A** 1130 | **46B** 1131 | **46C** 1132 | **46D** 1133 | **46E** 1134 | **46F** 1135 |
| Ѩ | ѩ | Ѫ | ѫ | Ѭ | ѭ | Ѯ | ѯ |
| **470** 1136 | **471** 1137 | **472** 1138 | **473** 1139 | **474** 1140 | **475** 1141 | **476** 1142 | **477** 1143 |
| Ѱ | ѱ | Ѳ | ѳ | Ѵ | ѵ | Ѷ | ѷ |
| **478** 1144 | **479** 1145 | **47A** 1146 | **47B** 1147 | **47C** 1148 | **47D** 1149 | **47E** 1150 | **47F** 1151 |
| Ѹ | ѹ | Ѻ | ѻ | Ѽ | ѽ | Ѿ | ѿ |
| **480** 1152 | **481** 1153 | **482** 1154 | **483** 1155 | **484** 1156 | **485** 1157 | **486** 1158 | **487** 1159 |
| Ҁ | ҁ | ҂ | ҃ | ҄ | ҅ | ҆ | N/A |
| **488** 1160 | **489** 1161 | **48A** 1162 | **48B** 1163 | **48C** 1164 | **48D** 1165 | **48E** 1166 | **48F** 1167 |
| N/A | N/A | N/A | N/A | N/A | N/A | N/A | N/A |
| **490** 1168 | **491** 1169 | **492** 1170 | **493** 1171 | **494** 1172 | **495** 1173 | **496** 1174 | **497** 1175 |
| Ґ | ґ | Ғ | ғ | Ҕ | ҕ | Җ | җ |

*Table 23-12: The Cyrillic Block of Unicode (continued)*

| | | | | | | | |
|---|---|---|---|---|---|---|---|
| **498** 1176 | **499** 1177 | **49A** 1178 | **49B** 1179 | **49C** 1180 | **49D** 1181 | **49E** 1182 | **49F** 1183 |
| Ҙ | ҙ | Қ | қ | Ҝ | ҝ | Ҟ | ҟ |
| **4A0** 1184 | **4A1** 1185 | **4A2** 1186 | **4A3** 1187 | **4A4** 1188 | **4A5** 1189 | **4A6** 1190 | **4A7** 1191 |
| Ҡ | ҡ | Ң | ң | Ҥ | ҥ | Ҧ | ҧ |
| **4A8** 1192 | **4A9** 1193 | **4AA** 1194 | **4AB** 1195 | **4AC** 1196 | **4AD** 1197 | **4AE** 1198 | **4AF** 1199 |
| Ҩ | ҩ | Ҫ | ҫ | Ҭ | ҭ | Ү | ү |
| **4B0** 1200 | **4B1** 1201 | **4B2** 1202 | **4B3** 1203 | **4B4** 1204 | **4B5** 1205 | **4B6** 1206 | **4B7** 1207 |
| Ұ | ұ | Ҳ | ҳ | Ҵ | ҵ | Ҷ | ҷ |
| **4B8** 1208 | **4B9** 1209 | **4BA** 1210 | **4BB** 1211 | **4BC** 1212 | **4BD** 1213 | **4BE** 1214 | **4BF** 1215 |
| Ҹ | ҹ | Һ | һ | Ҽ | ҽ | Ҿ | ҿ |
| **4C0** 1216 | **4C1** 1217 | **4C2** 1218 | **4C3** 1219 | **4C4** 1220 | **4C5** 1221 | **4C6** 1222 | **4C7** 1223 |
| Ӏ | Ӂ | ӂ | Ӄ | ӄ | *N/A* | *N/A* | Ӈ |
| **4C8** 1224 | **4C9** 1225 | **4CA** 1226 | **4CB** 1227 | **4CC** 1228 | **4CD** 1229 | **4CE** 1230 | **4CF** 1231 |
| ӈ | *N/A* | *N/A* | Ӌ | ӌ | *N/A* | *N/A* | *N/A* |
| **4D0** 1232 | **4D1** 1233 | **4D2** 1234 | **4D3** 1235 | **4D4** 1236 | **4D5** 1237 | **4D6** 1238 | **4D7** 1239 |
| Ӑ | ӑ | Ӓ | ӓ | Ӕ | ӕ | Ӗ | ӗ |
| **4D8** 1240 | **4D9** 1241 | **4DA** 1242 | **4DB** 1243 | **4DC** 1244 | **4DD** 1245 | **4DE** 1246 | **4DF** 1247 |
| Ә | ә | Ӛ | ӛ | Ӝ | ӝ | Ӟ | ӟ |
| **4E0** 1248 | **4E1** 1249 | **4E2** 1250 | **4E3** 1251 | **4E4** 1252 | **4E5** 1253 | **4E6** 1254 | **4E7** 1255 |
| Ӡ | ӡ | Ӣ | ӣ | Ӥ | ӥ | Ӧ | ӧ |
| **4E8** 1256 | **4E9** 1257 | **4EA** 1258 | **4EB** 1259 | **4EC** 1260 | **4ED** 1261 | **4EE** 1262 | **4EF** 1263 |
| Ө | ө | Ӫ | ӫ | *N/A* | *N/A* | Ӯ | ӯ |
| **4F0** 1264 | **4F1** 1265 | **4F2** 1266 | **4F3** 1267 | **4F4** 1268 | **4F5** 1269 | **4F6** 1270 | **4F7** 1271 |
| Ӱ | ӱ | Ӳ | ӳ | Ӵ | ӵ | *N/A* | *N/A* |
| **4F8** 1272 | **4F9** 1273 | **4FA** 1274 | **4FB** 1275 | **4FC** 1276 | **4FD** 1277 | **4FE** 1278 | **4FF** 1279 |
| Ӹ | ӹ | *N/A* | *N/A* | *N/A* | *N/A* | *N/A* | *N/A* |

## Armenian

The Armenian script, shown in Table 23-13, is used for writing the Armenian language, currently spoken by about seven million people around the world.

*Table 23-13: The Armenian Block of Unicode*

| | | | | | | | |
|---|---|---|---|---|---|---|---|
| **530** 1328 | **531** 1329 | **532** 1330 | **533** 1331 | **534** 1332 | **535** 1333 | **536** 1334 | **537** 1335 |
| *N/A* | Ա | Բ | Գ | Դ | Ե | Զ | Է |
| **538** 1336 | **539** 1337 | **53A** 1338 | **53B** 1339 | **53C** 1340 | **53D** 1341 | **53E** 1342 | **53F** 1343 |
| Ը | Թ | Ժ | Ի | Լ | Խ | Ծ | Կ |
| **540** 1344 | **541** 1345 | **542** 1346 | **543** 1347 | **544** 1348 | **545** 1349 | **546** 1350 | **547** 1351 |
| Հ | Ձ | Ղ | Ճ | Մ | Յ | Ն | Շ |
| **548** 1352 | **549** 1353 | **54A** 1354 | **54B** 1355 | **54C** 1356 | **54D** 1357 | **54E** 1358 | **54F** 1359 |
| Ո | Չ | Պ | Ջ | Ռ | Ս | Վ | Տ |

*Table 23-13: The Armenian Block of Unicode (continued)*

| | | | | | | | |
|---|---|---|---|---|---|---|---|
| **550** 1360 | **551** 1361 | **552** 1362 | **553** 1363 | **554** 1364 | **555** 1365 | **556** 1366 | **557** 1367 |
| Ր | Ց | Ւ | Փ | Ք | Օ | Ֆ | N/A |
| **558** 1368 | **559** 1369 | **55A** 1370 | **55B** 1371 | **55C** 1372 | **55D** 1373 | **55E** 1374 | **55F** 1375 |
| N/A | ՙ | ՚ | ՛ | ՜ | ՝ | ՞ | ՟ |
| **560** 1376 | **561** 1377 | **562** 1378 | **563** 1379 | **564** 1380 | **565** 1381 | **566** 1382 | **567** 1383 |
| N/A | ա | բ | գ | դ | ե | զ | է |
| **568** 1384 | **569** 1385 | **56A** 1386 | **56B** 1387 | **56C** 1388 | **56D** 1389 | **56E** 1390 | **56F** 1391 |
| ը | թ | ժ | ի | լ | խ | ծ | կ |
| **570** 1392 | **571** 1393 | **572** 1394 | **573** 1395 | **574** 1396 | **575** 1397 | **576** 1398 | **577** 1399 |
| հ | ձ | ղ | ճ | մ | յ | ն | շ |
| **578** 1400 | **579** 1401 | **57A** 1402 | **57B** 1403 | **57C** 1404 | **57D** 1405 | **57E** 1406 | **57F** 1407 |
| ո | չ | պ | ջ | ռ | ս | վ | տ |
| **580** 1408 | **581** 1409 | **582** 1410 | **583** 1411 | **584** 1412 | **585** 1413 | **586** 1414 | **587** 1415 |
| ր | ց | ւ | փ | ք | օ | ֆ | և |
| **588** 1416 | **589** 1417 | **58A** 1418 | **58B** 1419 | **58C** 1420 | **58D** 1421 | **58E** 1422 | **58F** 1423 |
| N/A | ։ | N/A | N/A | N/A | N/A | N/A | N/A |

## *Hebrew*

The Hebrew alphabet, shown in Table 23-14, is used for Hebrew, Yiddish, and Judezmo. It's also occasionally used for mathematical notation.

*Table 23-14: The Hebrew Block of Unicode*

| | | | | | | | |
|---|---|---|---|---|---|---|---|
| **590** 1424 | **591** 1425 | **592** 1426 | **593** 1427 | **594** 1428 | **595** 1429 | **596** 1430 | **597** 1431 |
| N/A | ֑ | ֒ | ֓ | ֔ | ֕ | ֖ | ֗ |
| **598** 1432 | **599** 1433 | **59A** 1434 | **59B** 1435 | **59C** 1436 | **59D** 1437 | **59E** 1438 | **59F** 1439 |
| ֘ | ֙ | ֚ | ֛ | ֜ | ֝ | ֞ | ֟ |
| **5A0** 1440 | **5A1** 1441 | **5A2** 1442 | **5A3** 1443 | **5A4** 1444 | **5A5** 1445 | **5A6** 1446 | **5A7** 1447 |
| ֠ | ֡ | N/A | ֣ | ֤ | ֥ | ֦ | ֧ |
| **5A8** 1448 | **5A9** 1449 | **5AA** 1450 | **5AB** 1451 | **5AC** 1452 | **5AD** 1453 | **5AE** 1454 | **5AF** 1455 |
| ֨ | ֩ | ֪ | ֫ | ֬ | ֭ | ֮ | ֯ |
| **5B0** 1456 | **5B1** 1457 | **5B2** 1458 | **5B3** 1459 | **5B4** 1460 | **5B5** 1461 | **5B6** 1462 | **5B7** 1463 |
| ְ | ֱ | ֲ | ֳ | ִ | ֵ | ֶ | ַ |
| **5B8** 1464 | **5B9** 1465 | **5BA** 1466 | **5BB** 1467 | **5BC** 1468 | **5BD** 1469 | **5BE** 1470 | **5BF** 1471 |
| ָ | ֹ | N/A | ֻ | ּ | ֽ | ־ | ֿ |
| **5C0** 1472 | **5C1** 1473 | **5C2** 1474 | **5C3** 1475 | **5C4** 1476 | **5C5** 1477 | **5C6** 1478 | **5C7** 1479 |
| ׀ | ׁ | ׂ | ׃ | ׄ | N/A | N/A | N/A |
| **5C8** 1480 | **5C9** 1481 | **5CA** 1482 | **5CB** 1483 | **5CC** 1484 | **5CD** 1485 | **5CE** 1486 | **5CF** 1487 |
| N/A | N/A | N/A | N/A | N/A | N/A | N/A | N/A |
| **5D0** 1488 | **5D1** 1489 | **5D2** 1490 | **5D3** 1491 | **5D4** 1492 | **5D5** 1493 | **5D6** 1494 | **5D7** 1495 |
| א | ב | ג | ד | ה | ו | ז | ח |

*Table 23-14: The Hebrew Block of Unicode (continued)*

| | | | | | | | |
|---|---|---|---|---|---|---|---|
| **5D8** 1496 | **5D9** 1497 | **5DA** 1498 | **5DB** 1499 | **5DC** 1500 | **5DD** 1501 | **5DE** 1502 | **5DF** 1503 |
| ט | י | ך | כ | ל | ם | מ | ן |
| **5E0** 1504 | **5E1** 1505 | **5E2** 1506 | **5E3** 1507 | **5E4** 1508 | **5E5** 1509 | **5E6** 1510 | **5E7** 1511 |
| נ | ס | ע | ף | פ | ץ | צ | ק |
| **5E8** 1512 | **5E9** 1513 | **5EA** 1514 | **5EB** 1515 | **5EC** 1516 | **5ED** 1517 | **5EE** 1518 | **5EF** 1519 |
| ר | ש | ת | N/A | N/A | N/A | N/A | N/A |
| **5F0** 1520 | **5F1** 1521 | **5F2** 1522 | **5F3** 1523 | **5F4** 1524 | **5F5** 1525 | **5F6** 1526 | **5F7** 1527 |
| װ | ױ | ײ | ׳ | ״ | N/A | N/A | N/A |
| **5F8** 1528 | **5F9** 1529 | **5FA** 1530 | **5FB** 1531 | **5FC** 1532 | **5FD** 1533 | **5FE** 1534 | **5FF** 1535 |
| N/A | N/A | N/A | N/A | N/A | N/A | N/A | N/A |

## Arabic

The Arabic script, shown in Table 23-15, is used for many languages besides Arabic, including Kurdish, Pashto, Persian, Sindhi, and Urdu. Turkish was also written in the Arabic script until early in the twentieth century when Turkey converted to a modified Latin alphabet.

*Table 23-15: The Arabic Block of Unicode*

| | | | | | | | |
|---|---|---|---|---|---|---|---|
| **600** 1536 | **601** 1537 | **602** 1538 | **603** 1539 | **604** 1540 | **605** 1541 | **606** 1542 | **607** 1543 |
| N/A | N/A | N/A | N/A | N/A | N/A | N/A | N/A |
| **608** 1544 | **609** 1545 | **60A** 1546 | **60B** 1547 | **60C** 1548 | **60D** 1549 | **60E** 1550 | **60F** 1551 |
| N/A | N/A | N/A | N/A | ، | N/A | N/A | N/A |
| **610** 1552 | **611** 1553 | **612** 1554 | **613** 1555 | **614** 1556 | **615** 1557 | **616** 1558 | **617** 1559 |
| N/A | N/A | N/A | N/A | N/A | N/A | N/A | N/A |
| **618** 1560 | **619** 1561 | **61A** 1562 | **61B** 1563 | **61C** 1564 | **61D** 1565 | **61E** 1566 | **61F** 1567 |
| N/A | N/A | N/A | ؛ | N/A | N/A | N/A | ؟ |
| **620** 1568 | **621** 1569 | **622** 1570 | **623** 1571 | **624** 1572 | **625** 1573 | **626** 1574 | **627** 1575 |
| N/A | ء | آ | أ | ؤ | إ | ئ | ا |
| **628** 1576 | **629** 1577 | **62A** 1578 | **62B** 1579 | **62C** 1580 | **62D** 1581 | **62E** 1582 | **62F** 1583 |
| ب | ة | ت | ث | ج | ح | خ | د |
| **630** 1584 | **631** 1585 | **632** 1586 | **633** 1587 | **634** 1588 | **635** 1589 | **636** 1590 | **637** 1591 |
| ذ | ر | ز | س | ش | ص | ض | ط |
| **638** 1592 | **639** 1593 | **63A** 1594 | **63B** 1595 | **63C** 1596 | **63D** 1597 | **63E** 1598 | **63F** 1599 |
| ظ | ع | غ | N/A | N/A | N/A | N/A | N/A |
| **640** 1600 | **641** 1601 | **642** 1602 | **643** 1603 | **644** 1604 | **645** 1605 | **646** 1606 | **647** 1607 |
| ـ | ف | ق | ك | ل | م | ن | ه |
| **648** 1608 | **649** 1609 | **64A** 1610 | **64B** 1611 | **64C** 1612 | **64D** 1613 | **64E** 1614 | **64F** 1615 |
| و | ى | ي | ً | ٌ | ٍ | َ | ُ |
| **650** 1616 | **651** 1617 | **652** 1618 | **653** 1619 | **654** 1620 | **655** 1621 | **656** 1622 | **657** 1623 |
| ِ | ّ | ْ | N/A | N/A | N/A | N/A | N/A |

*Table 23-15: The Arabic Block of Unicode (continued)*

| | | | | | | | |
|---|---|---|---|---|---|---|---|
| **658** 1624 | **659** 1625 | **65A** 1626 | **65B** 1627 | **65C** 1628 | **65D** 1629 | **65E** 1630 | **65F** 1631 |
| N/A | N/A | N/A | N/A | N/A | N/A | N/A | N/A |
| **660** 1632 | **661** 1633 | **662** 1634 | **663** 1635 | **664** 1636 | **665** 1637 | **666** 1638 | **667** 1639 |
| ٠ | ١ | ٢ | ٣ | ٤ | ٥ | ٦ | ٧ |
| **668** 1640 | **669** 1641 | **66A** 1642 | **66B** 1643 | **66C** 1644 | **66D** 1645 | **66E** 1646 | **66F** 1647 |
| ٨ | ٩ | ٪ | ٫ | ٬ | ٭ | N/A | N/A |
| **670** 1648 | **671** 1649 | **672** 1650 | **673** 1651 | **674** 1652 | **675** 1653 | **676** 1654 | **677** 1655 |
| ٰ | ٱ | ٲ | ٳ | ٴ | ٵ | ٶ | ٷ |
| **678** 1656 | **679** 1657 | **67A** 1658 | **67B** 1659 | **67C** 1660 | **67D** 1661 | **67E** 1662 | **67F** 1663 |
| ٸ | ٹ | ٺ | ٻ | ټ | ٽ | پ | ٿ |
| **680** 1664 | **681** 1665 | **682** 1666 | **683** 1667 | **684** 1668 | **685** 1669 | **686** 1670 | **687** 1671 |
| ڀ | ځ | ڂ | ڃ | ڄ | څ | چ | ڇ |
| **688** 1672 | **689** 1673 | **68A** 1674 | **68B** 1675 | **68C** 1676 | **68D** 1677 | **68E** 1678 | **68F** 1679 |
| ڈ | ډ | ڊ | ڋ | ڌ | ڍ | ڎ | ڏ |
| **690** 1680 | **691** 1681 | **692** 1682 | **693** 1683 | **694** 1684 | **695** 1685 | **696** 1686 | **697** 1687 |
| ڐ | ڑ | ڒ | ړ | ڔ | ڕ | ږ | ڗ |
| **698** 1688 | **699** 1689 | **69A** 1690 | **69B** 1691 | **69C** 1692 | **69D** 1693 | **69E** 1694 | **69F** 1695 |
| ژ | ڙ | ښ | ڛ | ڜ | ڝ | ڞ | ڟ |
| **6A0** 1696 | **6A1** 1697 | **6A2** 1698 | **6A3** 1699 | **6A4** 1700 | **6A5** 1701 | **6A6** 1702 | **6A7** 1703 |
| ڠ | ڡ | ڢ | ڣ | ڤ | ڥ | ڦ | ڧ |
| **6A8** 1704 | **6A9** 1705 | **6AA** 1706 | **6AB** 1707 | **6AC** 1708 | **6AD** 1709 | **6AE** 1710 | **6AF** 1711 |
| ڨ | ک | ڪ | ګ | ڬ | ڭ | ڮ | گ |
| **6B0** 1712 | **6B1** 1713 | **6B2** 1714 | **6B3** 1715 | **6B4** 1716 | **6B5** 1717 | **6B6** 1718 | **6B7** 1719 |
| ڰ | ڱ | ڲ | ڳ | ڴ | ڵ | ڶ | ڷ |
| **6B8** 1720 | **6B9** 1721 | **6BA** 1722 | **6BB** 1723 | **6BC** 1724 | **6BD** 1725 | **6BE** 1726 | **6BF** 1727 |
| N/A | N/A | ں | ڻ | ڼ | ڽ | ھ | N/A |
| **6C0** 1728 | **6C1** 1729 | **6C2** 1730 | **6C3** 1731 | **6C4** 1732 | **6C5** 1733 | **6C6** 1734 | **6C7** 1735 |
| ۀ | ہ | ۂ | ۃ | ۄ | ۅ | ۆ | ۇ |
| **6C8** 1736 | **6C9** 1737 | **6CA** 1738 | **6CB** 1739 | **6CC** 1740 | **6CD** 1741 | **6CE** 1742 | **6CF** 1743 |
| ۈ | ۉ | ۊ | ۋ | ی | ۍ | ێ | N/A |
| **6D0** 1744 | **6D1** 1745 | **6D2** 1746 | **6D3** 1747 | **6D4** 1748 | **6D5** 1749 | **6D6** 1750 | **6D7** 1751 |
| ې | ۑ | ے | ۓ | ۔ | ە | ۖ | ۗ |
| **6D8** 1752 | **6D9** 1753 | **6DA** 1754 | **6DB** 1755 | **6DC** 1756 | **6DD** 1757 | **6DE** 1758 | **6DF** 1759 |
| ۘ | ۙ | ۚ | ۛ | ۜ | ۝ | ۞ | ۟ |
| **6E0** 1760 | **6E1** 1761 | **6E2** 1762 | **6E3** 1763 | **6E4** 1764 | **6E5** 1765 | **6E6** 1766 | **6E7** 1767 |
| ۠ | ۡ | ۢ | ۣ | ۤ | ۥ | ۦ | ۧ |
| **6E8** 1768 | **6E9** 1769 | **6EA** 1770 | **6EB** 1771 | **6EC** 1772 | **6ED** 1773 | **6EE** 1774 | **6EF** 1775 |
| ۨ | ۩ | ۪ | ۫ | ۬ | ۭ | N/A | N/A |
| **6F0** 1776 | **6F1** 1777 | **6F2** 1778 | **6F3** 1779 | **6F4** 1780 | **6F5** 1781 | **6F6** 1782 | **6F7** 1783 |
| ۰ | ۱ | ۲ | ۳ | ۴ | ۵ | ۶ | ۷ |
| **6F8** 1784 | **6F9** 1785 | **6FA** 1786 | **6FB** 1787 | **6FC** 1788 | **6FD** 1789 | **6FE** 1790 | **6FF** 1791 |
| ۸ | ۹ | N/A | N/A | N/A | N/A | N/A | N/A |

## *Devanagari*

The Devanagari script, shown in Table 23-16, is used for many languages of the Indian subcontinent, including Awadhi, Bagheli, Bhatneri, Bhili, Bihari, Braj Bhasa, Chhattisgarhi, Garhwali, Gondi, Harauti, Hindi, Ho, Jaipuri, Kachchhi, Kanauji, Konkani, Kului, Kumaoni, Kurku, Kurukh, Marwari, Mundari, Newari, Palpa, and Santali. It's also used for the classical language Sanskrit.

*Table 23-16: The Devanagari Block of Unicode*

| | | | | | | | |
|---|---|---|---|---|---|---|---|
| **900** 2304 | **901** 2305 | **902** 2306 | **903** 2307 | **904** 2308 | **905** 2309 | **906** 2310 | **907** 2311 |
| N/A | ँ | ं | ः | N/A | अ | आ | इ |
| **908** 2312 | **909** 2313 | **90A** 2314 | **90B** 2315 | **90C** 2316 | **90D** 2317 | **90E** 2318 | **90F** 2319 |
| ई | उ | ऊ | ऋ | ऌ | ऍ | ऎ | ए |
| **910** 2320 | **911** 2321 | **912** 2322 | **913** 2323 | **914** 2324 | **915** 2325 | **916** 2326 | **917** 2327 |
| ऐ | ऑ | ऒ | ओ | औ | क | ख | ग |
| **918** 2328 | **919** 2329 | **91A** 2330 | **91B** 2331 | **91C** 2332 | **91D** 2333 | **91E** 2334 | **91F** 2335 |
| घ | ङ | च | छ | ज | झ | ञ | ट |
| **920** 2336 | **921** 2337 | **922** 2338 | **923** 2339 | **924** 2340 | **925** 2341 | **926** 2342 | **927** 2343 |
| ठ | ड | ढ | ण | त | थ | द | ध |
| **928** 2344 | **929** 2345 | **92A** 2346 | **92B** 2347 | **92C** 2348 | **92D** 2349 | **92E** 2350 | **92F** 2351 |
| न | ऩ | प | फ | ब | भ | म | य |
| **930** 2352 | **931** 2353 | **932** 2354 | **933** 2355 | **934** 2356 | **935** 2357 | **936** 2358 | **937** 2359 |
| र | ऱ | ल | ळ | . | व | श | ष |
| **938** 2360 | **939** 2361 | **93A** 2362 | **93B** 2363 | **93C** 2364 | **93D** 2365 | **93E** 2366 | **93F** 2367 |
| स | ह | N/A | N/A | ़ | ऽ | ा | ि |
| **940** 2368 | **941** 2369 | **942** 2370 | **943** 2371 | **944** 2372 | **945** 2373 | **946** 2374 | **947** 2375 |
| ी | ु | ू | ृ | ॄ | ॅ | ॆ | े |
| **948** 2376 | **949** 2377 | **94A** 2378 | **94B** 2379 | **94C** 2380 | **94D** 2381 | **94E** 2382 | **94F** 2383 |
| ै | ॉ | ॊ | ो | ौ | ् | N/A | N/A |
| **950** 2384 | **951** 2385 | **952** 2386 | **953** 2387 | **954** 2388 | **955** 2389 | **956** 2390 | **957** 2391 |
| ॐ | ॑ | ॒ | ॓ | ॔ | N/A | N/A | N/A |
| **958** 2392 | **959** 2393 | **95A** 2394 | **95B** 2395 | **95C** 2396 | **95D** 2397 | **95E** 2398 | **95F** 2399 |
| क़ | ख़ | ग़ | ज़ | ड़ | ढ़ | फ़ | य़ |
| **960** 2400 | **961** 2401 | **962** 2402 | **963** 2403 | **964** 2404 | **965** 2405 | **966** 2406 | **967** 2407 |
| ॠ | ॡ | ॢ | ॣ | । | ॥ | ० | १ |
| **968** 2408 | **969** 2409 | **96A** 2410 | **96B** 2411 | **96C** 2412 | **96D** 2413 | **96E** 2414 | **96F** 2415 |
| २ | ३ | ४ | ५ | ६ | ७ | ८ | ९ |
| **970** 2416 | **971** 2417 | **972** 2418 | **973** 2419 | **974** 2420 | **975** 2421 | **976** 2422 | **977** 2423 |
| ॰ | N/A | N/A | N/A | N/A | N/A | N/A | N/A |
| **978** 2424 | **979** 2425 | **97A** 2426 | **97B** 2427 | **97C** 2428 | **97D** 2429 | **97E** 2430 | **97F** 2431 |
| N/A | N/A | N/A | N/A | N/A | N/A | N/A | N/A |

Character Sets

## *Thai*

The Thai script, shown in Table 23-17, is used for Thai and a few other Southeast Asian languages, including Kuy, Lavna, and Pali.

*Table 23-17: The Thai Block of Unicode*

| | | | | | | | |
|---|---|---|---|---|---|---|---|
| **E00** 3584 | **E01** 3585 | **E02** 3586 | **E03** 3587 | **E04** 3588 | **E05** 3589 | **E06** 3590 | **E07** 3591 |
| N/A | ก | ข | ฃ | ค | ฅ | ฆ | ง |
| **E08** 3592 | **E09** 3593 | **E0A** 3594 | **E0B** 3595 | **E0C** 3596 | **E0D** 3597 | **E0E** 3598 | **E0F** 3599 |
| จ | ฉ | ช | ซ | ฌ | ญ | ฎ | ฏ |
| **E10** 3600 | **E11** 3601 | **E12** 3602 | **E13** 3603 | **E14** 3604 | **E15** 3605 | **E16** 3606 | **E17** 3607 |
| ฐ | ฑ | ฒ | ณ | ด | ต | ถ | ท |
| **E18** 3608 | **E19** 3609 | **E1A** 3610 | **E1B** 3611 | **E1C** 3612 | **E1D** 3613 | **E1E** 3614 | **E1F** 3615 |
| ธ | น | บ | ป | ผ | ฝ | พ | ฟ |
| **E20** 3616 | **E21** 3617 | **E22** 3618 | **E23** 3619 | **E24** 3620 | **E25** 3621 | **E26** 3622 | **E27** 3623 |
| ภ | ม | ย | ร | ฤ | ล | ฦ | ว |
| **E28** 3624 | **E29** 3625 | **E2A** 3626 | **E2B** 3627 | **E2C** 3628 | **E2D** 3629 | **E2E** 3630 | **E2F** 3631 |
| ศ | ษ | ส | ห | ฬ | อ | ฮ | ฯ |
| **E30** 3632 | **E31** 3633 | **E32** 3634 | **E33** 3635 | **E34** 3636 | **E35** 3637 | **E36** 3638 | **E37** 3639 |
| ะ | ั | า | ำ | ิ | ี | ึ | ื |
| **E38** 3640 | **E39** 3641 | **E3A** 3642 | **E3B** 3643 | **E3C** 3644 | **E3D** 3645 | **E3E** 3646 | **E3F** 3647 |
| ุ | ู | ฺ | N/A | N/A | N/A | N/A | ฿ |
| **E40** 3648 | **E41** 3649 | **E42** 3650 | **E43** 3651 | **E44** 3652 | **E45** 3653 | **E46** 3654 | **E47** 3655 |
| เ | แ | โ | ใ | ไ | ๅ | ๆ | ็ |
| **E48** 3656 | **E49** 3657 | **E4A** 3658 | **E4B** 3659 | **E4C** 3660 | **E4D** 3661 | **E4E** 3662 | **E4F** 3663 |
| ่ | ้ | ๊ | ๋ | ์ | ํ | ๎ | ๏ |
| **E50** 3664 | **E51** 3665 | **E52** 3666 | **E53** 3667 | **E54** 3668 | **E55** 3669 | **E56** 3670 | **E57** 3671 |
| ๐ | ๑ | ๒ | ๓ | ๔ | ๕ | ๖ | ๗ |
| **E58** 3672 | **E59** 3673 | **E5A** 3674 | **E5B** 3675 | **E5C** 3676 | **E5D** 3677 | **E5E** 3678 | **E5F** 3679 |
| ๘ | ๙ | ๚ | ๛ | N/A | N/A | N/A | N/A |

## *Tibetan*

The Tibetan script, shown in Table 23-18, is used to write the various dialects of Tibetan and Dzongkha, Bhutan's main language. Like Chinese, Tibetan is divided into several mutually unintelligible spoken languages, though the written forms are identical.

*Table 23-18: The Tibetan Block of Unicode*

| | | | | | | | |
|---|---|---|---|---|---|---|---|
| **F00** 3840 | **F01** 3841 | **F02** 3842 | **F03** 3843 | **F04** 3844 | **F05** 3845 | **F06** 3846 | **F07** 3847 |
| ༀ | ༁ | ༂ | ༃ | ༄ | ༅ | ༆ | ༇ |
| **F08** 3848 | **F09** 3849 | **F0A** 3850 | **F0B** 3851 | **F0C** 3852 | **F0D** 3853 | **F0E** 3854 | **F0F** 3855 |
| ༈ | ༉ | ༊ | ་ | ༌ | ། | ༎ | ༏ |

*Table 23-18: The Tibetan Block of Unicode (continued)*

| | | | | | | | |
|---|---|---|---|---|---|---|---|
| **F10** 3856 | **F11** 3857 | **F12** 3858 | **F13** 3859 | **F14** 3860 | **F15** 3861 | **F16** 3862 | **F17** 3863 |
| ༐ | ༑ | ༒ | ༓ | ༔ | ༕ | ༖ | ༗ |
| **F18** 3864 | **F19** 3865 | **F1A** 3866 | **F1B** 3867 | **F1C** 3868 | **F1D** 3869 | **F1E** 3870 | **F1F** 3871 |
| ༘ | ༙ | ༚ | ༛ | ༜ | ༝ | ༞ | ༟ |
| **F20** 3872 | **F21** 3873 | **F22** 3874 | **F23** 3875 | **F24** 3876 | **F25** 3877 | **F26** 3878 | **F27** 3879 |
| ༠ | ༡ | ༢ | ༣ | ༤ | ༥ | ༦ | ༧ |
| **F28** 3880 | **F29** 3881 | **F2A** 3882 | **F2B** 3883 | **F2C** 3884 | **F2D** 3885 | **F2E** 3886 | **F2F** 3887 |
| ༨ | ༩ | ༪ | ༫ | ༬ | ༭ | ༮ | ༯ |
| **F30** 3888 | **F31** 3889 | **F32** 3890 | **F33** 3891 | **F34** 3892 | **F35** 3893 | **F36** 3894 | **F37** 3895 |
| ༰ | ༱ | ༲ | ༳ | ༴ | ༵ | ༶ | ༷ |
| **F38** 3896 | **F39** 3897 | **F3A** 3898 | **F3B** 3899 | **F3C** 3900 | **F3D** 3901 | **F3E** 3902 | **F3F** 3903 |
| ༸ | ༹ | ༺ | ༻ | ༼ | ༽ | ༾ | ༿ |
| **F40** 3904 | **F41** 3905 | **F42** 3906 | **F43** 3907 | **F44** 3908 | **F45** 3909 | **F46** 3910 | **F47** 3911 |
| ཀ | ཁ | ག | གྷ | ང | ཅ | ཆ | ཇ |
| **F48** 3912 | **F49** 3913 | **F4A** 3914 | **F4B** 3915 | **F4C** 3916 | **F4D** 3917 | **F4E** 3918 | **F4F** 3919 |
| N/A | ཉ | ཊ | ཋ | ཌ | ཌྷ | ཎ | ཏ |
| **F50** 3920 | **F51** 3921 | **F52** 3922 | **F53** 3923 | **F54** 3924 | **F55** 3925 | **F56** 3926 | **F57** 3927 |
| ཐ | ད | དྷ | ན | པ | ཕ | བ | བྷ |
| **F58** 3928 | **F59** 3929 | **F5A** 3930 | **F5B** 3931 | **F5C** 3932 | **F5D** 3933 | **F5E** 3934 | **F5F** 3935 |
| མ | ཙ | ཚ | ཛ | ཛྷ | ཝ | ཞ | ཟ |
| **F60** 3936 | **F61** 3937 | **F62** 3938 | **F63** 3939 | **F64** 3940 | **F65** 3941 | **F66** 3942 | **F67** 3943 |
| འ | ཡ | ར | ལ | ཤ | ཥ | ས | ཧ |
| **F68** 3944 | **F69** 3945 | **F6A** 3946 | **F6B** 3947 | **F6C** 3948 | **F6D** 3949 | **F6E** 3950 | **F6F** 3951 |
| ཨ | ཀྵ | N/A | N/A | N/A | N/A | N/A | N/A |
| **F70** 3952 | **F71** 3953 | **F72** 3954 | **F73** 3955 | **F74** 3956 | **F75** 3957 | **F76** 3958 | **F77** 3959 |
| N/A | ཱ | ི | ཱི | ུ | ཱུ | ྲྀ | ཷ |
| **F78** 3960 | **F79** 3961 | **F7A** 3962 | **F7B** 3963 | **F7C** 3964 | **F7D** 3965 | **F7E** 3966 | **F7F** 3967 |
| ླྀ | ཹ | ེ | ཻ | ོ | ཽ | ཾ | ཿ |
| **F80** 3968 | **F81** 3969 | **F82** 3970 | **F83** 3971 | **F84** 3972 | **F85** 3973 | **F86** 3974 | **F87** 3975 |
| ྀ | ཱྀ | ྂ | ྃ | ྄ | ྅ | ྆ | ྇ |
| **F88** 3976 | **F89** 3977 | **F8A** 3978 | **F8B** 3979 | **F8C** 3980 | **F8D** 3981 | **F8E** 3982 | **F8F** 3983 |
| ྈ | ྉ | ྊ | ྋ | N/A | N/A | N/A | N/A |
| **F90** 3984 | **F91** 3985 | **F92** 3986 | **F93** 3987 | **F94** 3988 | **F95** 3989 | **F96** 3990 | **F97** 3991 |
| ྐ | ྑ | ྒ | ྒྷ | ྔ | ྕ | N/A | ྗ |
| **F98** 3992 | **F99** 3993 | **F9A** 3994 | **F9B** 3995 | **F9C** 3996 | **F9D** 3997 | **F9E** 3998 | **F9F** 3999 |
| N/A | ྙ | ྚ | ྛ | ྜ | ྜྷ | ྞ | ྟ |
| **FA0** 4000 | **FA1** 4001 | **FA2** 4002 | **FA3** 4003 | **FA4** 4004 | **FA5** 4005 | **FA6** 4006 | **FA7** 4007 |
| ྠ | ྡ | ྡྷ | ྣ | ྤ | ྥ | ྦ | ྦྷ |
| **FA8** 4008 | **FA9** 4009 | **FAA** 4010 | **FAB** 4011 | **FAC** 4012 | **FAD** 4013 | **FAE** 4014 | **FAF** 4015 |
| ྨ | ྩ | ྪ | ྫ | ྫྷ | ྭ | N/A | N/A |
| **FB0** 4016 | **FB1** 4017 | **FB2** 4018 | **FB3** 4019 | **FB4** 4020 | **FB5** 4021 | **FB6** 4022 | **FB7** 4023 |
| N/A | ྱ | ྲ | ླ | ྴ | ྵ | ྶ | ྷ |

*Table 23-18: The Tibetan Block of Unicode (continued)*

| | | | | | | | |
|---|---|---|---|---|---|---|---|
| **FB8** 4024 | **FB9** 4025 | **FBA** 4026 | **FBB** 4027 | **FBC** 4028 | **FBD** 4029 | **FBE** 4030 | **FBF** 4031 |
| N/A | ྐྵ | N/A | N/A | N/A | N/A | N/A | N/A |
| **FC0** 4032 | **FC1** 4033 | **FC2** 4034 | **FC3** 4035 | **FC4** 4036 | **FC5** 4037 | **FC6** 4038 | **FC7** 4039 |
| N/A | N/A | N/A | N/A | N/A | N/A | N/A | N/A |
| **FC8** 4040 | **FC9** 4041 | **FCA** 4042 | **FCB** 4043 | **FCC** 4044 | **FCD** 4045 | **FCE** 4046 | **FCF** 4047 |
| N/A | N/A | N/A | N/A | N/A | N/A | N/A | N/A |

## Latin Extended Additional

The Latin Extended Additional characters, shown in Table 23-19, are single code point representations of letters combined with diacritical marks. This block is particularly useful for modern Vietnamese.

*Table 23-19: The Latin Extended Additional Block of Unicode*

| | | | | | | | |
|---|---|---|---|---|---|---|---|
| **1E00** 7680 | **1E01** 7681 | **1E02** 7682 | **1E03** 7683 | **1E04** 7684 | **1E05** 7685 | **1E06** 7686 | **1E07** 7687 |
| Ḁ | ḁ | Ḃ | ḃ | Ḅ | ḅ | Ḇ | ḇ |
| **1E08** 7688 | **1E09** 7689 | **1E0A** 7690 | **1E0B** 7691 | **1E0C** 7692 | **1E0D** 7693 | **1E0E** 7694 | **1E0F** 7695 |
| Ḉ | ḉ | Ḋ | ḋ | Ḍ | ḍ | Ḏ | ḏ |
| **1E10** 7696 | **1E11** 7697 | **1E12** 7698 | **1E13** 7699 | **1E14** 7700 | **1E15** 7701 | **1E16** 7702 | **1E17** 7703 |
| Ḑ | ḑ | Ḓ | ḓ | Ḕ | ḕ | Ḗ | ḗ |
| **1E18** 7704 | **1E19** 7705 | **1E1A** 7706 | **1E1B** 7707 | **1E1C** 7708 | **1E1D** 7709 | **1E1E** 7710 | **1E1F** 7711 |
| Ḙ | ḙ | Ḛ | ḛ | Ḝ | ḝ | Ḟ | ḟ |
| **1E20** 7712 | **1E21** 7713 | **1E22** 7714 | **1E23** 7715 | **1E24** 7716 | **1E25** 7717 | **1E26** 7718 | **1E27** 7719 |
| Ḡ | ḡ | Ḣ | ḣ | Ḥ | ḥ | Ḧ | ḧ |
| **1E28** 7720 | **1E29** 7721 | **1E2A** 7722 | **1E2B** 7723 | **1E2C** 7724 | **1E2D** 7725 | **1E2E** 7726 | **1E2F** 7727 |
| Ḩ | ḩ | Ḫ | ḫ | Ḭ | ḭ | Ḯ | ḯ |
| **1E30** 7728 | **1E31** 7729 | **1E32** 7730 | **1E33** 7731 | **1E34** 7732 | **1E35** 7733 | **1E36** 7734 | **1E37** 7735 |
| Ḱ | ḱ | Ḳ | ḳ | Ḵ | ḵ | Ḷ | ḷ |
| **1E38** 7736 | **1E39** 7737 | **1E3A** 7738 | **1E3B** 7739 | **1E3C** 7740 | **1E3D** 7741 | **1E3E** 7742 | **1E3F** 7743 |
| Ḹ | ḹ | Ḻ | ḻ | Ḽ | ḽ | Ḿ | ḿ |
| **1E40** 7744 | **1E41** 7745 | **1E42** 7746 | **1E43** 7747 | **1E44** 7748 | **1E45** 7749 | **1E46** 7750 | **1E47** 7751 |
| Ṁ | ṁ | Ṃ | ṃ | Ṅ | ṅ | Ṇ | ṇ |
| **1E48** 7752 | **1E49** 7753 | **1E4A** 7754 | **1E4B** 7755 | **1E4C** 7756 | **1E4D** 7757 | **1E4E** 7758 | **1E4F** 7759 |
| Ṉ | ṉ | Ṋ | ṋ | Ṍ | ṍ | Ṏ | ṏ |
| **1E50** 7760 | **1E51** 7761 | **1E52** 7762 | **1E53** 7763 | **1E54** 7764 | **1E55** 7765 | **1E56** 7766 | **1E57** 7767 |
| Ṑ | ṑ | Ṓ | ṓ | Ṕ | ṕ | Ṗ | ṗ |
| **1E58** 7768 | **1E59** 7769 | **1E5A** 7770 | **1E5B** 7771 | **1E5C** 7772 | **1E5D** 7773 | **1E5E** 7774 | **1E5F** 7775 |
| Ṙ | ṙ | Ṛ | ṛ | Ṝ | ṝ | Ṟ | ṟ |
| **1E60** 7776 | **1E61** 7777 | **1E62** 7778 | **1E63** 7779 | **1E64** 7780 | **1E65** 7781 | **1E66** 7782 | **1E67** 7783 |
| Ṡ | ṡ | Ṣ | ṣ | Ṥ | ṥ | Ṧ | ṧ |
| **1E68** 7784 | **1E69** 7785 | **1E6A** 7786 | **1E6B** 7787 | **1E6C** 7788 | **1E6D** 7789 | **1E6E** 7790 | **1E6F** 7791 |
| Ṩ | ṩ | Ṫ | ṫ | Ṭ | ṭ | Ṯ | ṯ |

*Table 23-19: The Latin Extended Additional Block of Unicode (continued)*

| | | | | | | | |
|---|---|---|---|---|---|---|---|
| **1E70** 7792 | **1E71** 7793 | **1E72** 7794 | **1E73** 7795 | **1E74** 7796 | **1E75** 7797 | **1E76** 7798 | **1E77** 7799 |
| Ṱ | ṱ | Ṳ | ṳ | Ṵ | ṵ | Ṷ | ṷ |
| **1E78** 7800 | **1E79** 7801 | **1E7A** 7802 | **1E7B** 7803 | **1E7C** 7804 | **1E7D** 7805 | **1E7E** 7806 | **1E7F** 7807 |
| Ṹ | ṹ | Ṻ | ṻ | Ṽ | ṽ | Ṿ | ṿ |
| **1E80** 7808 | **1E81** 7809 | **1E82** 7810 | **1E83** 7811 | **1E84** 7812 | **1E85** 7813 | **1E86** 7814 | **1E87** 7815 |
| Ẁ | ẁ | Ẃ | ẃ | Ẅ | ẅ | Ẇ | ẇ |
| **1E88** 7816 | **1E89** 7817 | **1E8A** 7818 | **1E8B** 7819 | **1E8C** 7820 | **1E8D** 7821 | **1E8E** 7822 | **1E8F** 7823 |
| Ẉ | ẉ | Ẋ | ẋ | Ẍ | ẍ | Ẏ | ẏ |
| **1E90** 7824 | **1E91** 7825 | **1E92** 7826 | **1E93** 7827 | **1E94** 7828 | **1E95** 7829 | **1E96** 7830 | **1E97** 7831 |
| Ẑ | ẑ | Ẓ | ẓ | Ẕ | ẕ | ẖ | ẗ |
| **1E98** 7832 | **1E99** 7833 | **1E9A** 7834 | **1E9B** 7835 | **1E9C** 7836 | **1E9D** 7837 | **1E9E** 7838 | **1E9F** 7839 |
| ẘ | ẙ | ẚ | ẛ | *N/A* | *N/A* | *N/A* | *N/A* |
| **1EA0** 7840 | **1EA1** 7841 | **1EA2** 7842 | **1EA3** 7843 | **1EA4** 7844 | **1EA5** 7845 | **1EA6** 7846 | **1EA7** 7847 |
| Ạ | ạ | Ả | ả | Ấ | ấ | Ầ | ầ |
| **1EA8** 7848 | **1EA9** 7849 | **1EAA** 7850 | **1EAB** 7851 | **1EAC** 7852 | **1EAD** 7853 | **1EAE** 7854 | **1EAF** 7855 |
| Ẩ | ẩ | Ẫ | ẫ | Ậ | ậ | Ắ | ắ |
| **1EB0** 7856 | **1EB1** 7857 | **1EB2** 7858 | **1EB3** 7859 | **1EB4** 7860 | **1EB5** 7861 | **1EB6** 7862 | **1EB7** 7863 |
| Ằ | ằ | Ẳ | ẳ | Ẵ | ẵ | Ặ | ặ |
| **1EB8** 7864 | **1EB9** 7865 | **1EBA** 7866 | **1EBB** 7867 | **1EBC** 7868 | **1EBD** 7869 | **1EBE** 7870 | **1EBF** 7871 |
| Ẹ | ẹ | Ẻ | ẻ | Ẽ | ẽ | Ế | ế |
| **1EC0** 7872 | **1EC1** 7873 | **1EC2** 7874 | **1EC3** 7875 | **1EC4** 7876 | **1EC5** 7877 | **1EC6** 7878 | **1EC7** 7879 |
| Ề | ề | Ể | ể | Ễ | ễ | Ệ | ệ |
| **1EC8** 7880 | **1EC9** 7881 | **1ECA** 7882 | **1ECB** 7883 | **1ECC** 7884 | **1ECD** 7885 | **1ECE** 7886 | **1ECF** 7887 |
| Ỉ | ỉ | Ị | ị | Ọ | ọ | Ỏ | ỏ |
| **1ED0** 7888 | **1ED1** 7889 | **1ED2** 7890 | **1ED3** 7891 | **1ED4** 7892 | **1ED5** 7893 | **1ED6** 7894 | **1ED7** 7895 |
| Ố | ố | Ồ | ồ | Ổ | ổ | Ỗ | ỗ |
| **1ED8** 7896 | **1ED9** 7897 | **1EDA** 7898 | **1EDB** 7899 | **1EDC** 7900 | **1EDD** 7901 | **1EDE** 7902 | **1EDF** 7903 |
| Ộ | ộ | Ớ | ớ | Ờ | ờ | Ở | ở |
| **1EE0** 7904 | **1EE1** 7905 | **1EE2** 7906 | **1EE3** 7907 | **1EE4** 7908 | **1EE5** 7909 | **1EE6** 7910 | **1EE7** 7911 |
| Ỡ | ỡ | Ợ | ợ | Ụ | ụ | Ủ | ủ |
| **1EE8** 7912 | **1EE9** 7913 | **1EEA** 7914 | **1EEB** 7915 | **1EEC** 7916 | **1EED** 7917 | **1EEE** 7918 | **1EEF** 7919 |
| Ứ | ứ | Ừ | ừ | Ử | ử | Ữ | ữ |
| **1EF0** 7920 | **1EF1** 7921 | **1EF2** 7922 | **1EF3** 7923 | **1EF4** 7924 | **1EF5** 7925 | **1EF6** 7926 | **1EF7** 7927 |
| Ự | ự | Ỳ | ỳ | Ỵ | ỵ | Ỷ | ỷ |
| **1EF8** 7928 | **1EF9** 7929 | **1EFA** 7930 | **1EFB** 7931 | **1EFC** 7932 | **1EFD** 7933 | **1EFE** 7934 | **1EFF** 7935 |
| Ỹ | ỹ | *N/A* | *N/A* | *N/A* | *N/A* | *N/A* | *N/A* |

Character Sets

## Greek Extended

The Greek Extended block, shown in Table 23-20, contains mostly archaic letters and accented letters that are used in classical and Byzantine Greek, but not in modern Greek.

*Table 23-20: The Greek Extended Block of Unicode*

| | | | | | | | |
|---|---|---|---|---|---|---|---|
| **1F00** 7936 | **1F01** 7937 | **1F02** 7938 | **1F03** 7939 | **1F04** 7940 | **1F05** 7941 | **1F06** 7942 | **1F07** 7943 |
| ἀ | ἁ | ἂ | ἃ | ἄ | ἅ | ἆ | ἇ |
| **1F08** 7944 | **1F09** 7945 | **1F0A** 7946 | **1F0B** 7947 | **1F0C** 7948 | **1F0D** 7949 | **1F0E** 7950 | **1F0F** 7951 |
| Ἀ | Ἁ | Ἂ | Ἃ | Ἄ | Ἅ | Ἆ | Ἇ |
| **1F10** 7952 | **1F11** 7953 | **1F12** 7954 | **1F13** 7955 | **1F14** 7956 | **1F15** 7957 | **1F16** 7958 | **1F17** 7959 |
| ἐ | ἑ | ἒ | ἓ | ἔ | ἕ | *N/A* | *N/A* |
| **1F18** 7960 | **1F19** 7961 | **1F1A** 7962 | **1F1B** 7963 | **1F1C** 7964 | **1F1D** 7965 | **1F1E** 7966 | **1F1F** 7967 |
| Ἐ | Ἑ | Ἒ | Ἓ | Ἔ | Ἕ | *N/A* | *N/A* |
| **1F20** 7968 | **1F21** 7969 | **1F22** 7970 | **1F23** 7971 | **1F24** 7972 | **1F25** 7973 | **1F26** 7974 | **1F27** 7975 |
| ἠ | ἡ | ἢ | ἣ | ἤ | ἥ | ἦ | ἧ |
| **1F28** 7976 | **1F29** 7977 | **1F2A** 7978 | **1F2B** 7979 | **1F2C** 7980 | **1F2D** 7981 | **1F2E** 7982 | **1F2F** 7983 |
| Ἠ | Ἡ | Ἢ | Ἣ | Ἤ | Ἥ | Ἦ | Ἧ |
| **1F30** 7984 | **1F31** 7985 | **1F32** 7986 | **1F33** 7987 | **1F34** 7988 | **1F35** 7989 | **1F36** 7990 | **1F37** 7991 |
| ἰ | ἱ | ἲ | ἳ | ἴ | ἵ | ἶ | ἷ |
| **1F38** 7992 | **1F39** 7993 | **1F3A** 7994 | **1F3B** 7995 | **1F3C** 7996 | **1F3D** 7997 | **1F3E** 7998 | **1F3F** 7999 |
| Ἰ | Ἱ | Ἲ | Ἳ | Ἴ | Ἵ | Ἶ | Ἷ |
| **1F40** 8000 | **1F41** 8001 | **1F42** 8002 | **1F43** 8003 | **1F44** 8004 | **1F45** 8005 | **1F46** 8006 | **1F47** 8007 |
| ὀ | ὁ | ὂ | ὃ | ὄ | ὅ | *N/A* | *N/A* |
| **1F48** 8008 | **1F49** 8009 | **1F4A** 8010 | **1F4B** 8011 | **1F4C** 8012 | **1F4D** 8013 | **1F4E** 8014 | **1F4F** 8015 |
| Ὀ | Ὁ | Ὂ | Ὃ | Ὄ | Ὅ | *N/A* | *N/A* |
| **1F50** 8016 | **1F51** 8017 | **1F52** 8018 | **1F53** 8019 | **1F54** 8020 | **1F55** 8021 | **1F56** 8022 | **1F57** 8023 |
| ὐ | ὑ | ὒ | ὓ | ὔ | ὕ | ὖ | ὗ |
| **1F58** 8024 | **1F59** 8025 | **1F5A** 8026 | **1F5B** 8027 | **1F5C** 8028 | **1F5D** 8029 | **1F5E** 8030 | **1F5F** 8031 |
| *N/A* | Ὑ | *N/A* | Ὓ | *N/A* | Ὕ | *N/A* | Ὗ |
| **1F60** 8032 | **1F61** 8033 | **1F62** 8034 | **1F63** 8035 | **1F64** 8036 | **1F65** 8037 | **1F66** 8038 | **1F67** 8039 |
| ὠ | ὡ | ὢ | ὣ | ὤ | ὥ | ὦ | ὧ |
| **1F68** 8040 | **1F69** 8041 | **1F6A** 8042 | **1F6B** 8043 | **1F6C** 8044 | **1F6D** 8045 | **1F6E** 8046 | **1F6F** 8047 |
| Ὠ | Ὡ | Ὢ | Ὣ | Ὤ | Ὥ | Ὦ | Ὧ |
| **1F70** 8048 | **1F71** 8049 | **1F72** 8050 | **1F73** 8051 | **1F74** 8052 | **1F75** 8053 | **1F76** 8054 | **1F77** 8055 |
| ὰ | ά | ὲ | έ | ὴ | ή | ὶ | ί |
| **1F78** 8056 | **1F79** 8057 | **1F7A** 8058 | **1F7B** 8059 | **1F7C** 8060 | **1F7D** 8061 | **1F7E** 8062 | **1F7F** 8063 |
| ὸ | ό | ὺ | ύ | ὼ | ώ | *N/A* | *N/A* |
| **1F80** 8064 | **1F81** 8065 | **1F82** 8066 | **1F83** 8067 | **1F84** 8068 | **1F85** 8069 | **1F86** 8070 | **1F87** 8071 |
| ᾀ | ᾁ | ᾂ | ᾃ | ᾄ | ᾅ | ᾆ | ᾇ |
| **1F88** 8072 | **1F89** 8073 | **1F8A** 8074 | **1F8B** 8075 | **1F8C** 8076 | **1F8D** 8077 | **1F8E** 8078 | **1F8F** 8079 |
| ᾈ | ᾉ | ᾊ | ᾋ | ᾌ | ᾍ | ᾎ | ᾏ |
| **1F90** 8080 | **1F91** 8081 | **1F92** 8082 | **1F93** 8083 | **1F94** 8084 | **1F95** 8085 | **1F96** 8086 | **1F97** 8087 |
| ᾐ | ᾑ | ᾒ | ᾓ | ᾔ | ᾕ | ᾖ | ᾗ |
| **1F98** 8088 | **1F99** 8089 | **1F9A** 8090 | **1F9B** 8091 | **1F9C** 8092 | **1F9D** 8093 | **1F9E** 8094 | **1F9F** 8095 |
| ᾘ | ᾙ | ᾚ | ᾛ | ᾜ | ᾝ | ᾞ | ᾟ |

*Table 23-20: The Greek Extended Block of Unicode (continued)*

| | | | | | | | |
|---|---|---|---|---|---|---|---|
| **1FA8** 8104 | **1FA9** 8105 | **1FAA** 8106 | **1FAB** 8107 | **1FAC** 8108 | **1FAD** 8109 | **1FAE** 8110 | **1FAF** 8111 |
| ᾨ | ᾩ | ᾪ | ᾫ | ᾬ | ᾭ | ᾮ | ᾯ |
| **1FB0** 8112 | **1FB1** 8113 | **1FB2** 8114 | **1FB3** 8115 | **1FB4** 8116 | **1FB5** 8117 | **1FB6** 8118 | **1FB7** 8119 |
| ᾰ | ᾱ | ᾲ | ᾳ | ᾴ | *N/A* | ᾶ | ᾷ |
| **1FB8** 8120 | **1FB9** 8121 | **1FBA** 8122 | **1FBB** 8123 | **1FBC** 8124 | **1FBD** 8125 | **1FBE** 8126 | **1FBF** 8127 |
| Ᾰ | Ᾱ | Ὰ | Ά | ᾼ | ᾽ | ι | ᾿ |
| **1FC0** 8128 | **1FC1** 8129 | **1FC2** 8130 | **1FC3** 8131 | **1FC4** 8132 | **1FC5** 8133 | **1FC6** 8134 | **1FC7** 8135 |
| ῀ | ῁ | ῂ | ῃ | ῄ | *N/A* | ῆ | ῇ |
| **1FC8** 8136 | **1FC9** 8137 | **1FCA** 8138 | **1FCB** 8139 | **1FCC** 8140 | **1FCD** 8141 | **1FCE** 8142 | **1FCF** 8143 |
| Ὲ | Έ | Ὴ | Ή | ῌ | ῍ | ῎ | ῏ |
| **1FD0** 8144 | **1FD1** 8145 | **1FD2** 8146 | **1FD3** 8147 | **1FD4** 8148 | **1FD5** 8149 | **1FD6** 8150 | **1FD7** 8151 |
| ῐ | ῑ | ῒ | ΐ | *N/A* | *N/A* | ῖ | ῗ |
| **1FD8** 8152 | **1FD9** 8153 | **1FDA** 8154 | **1FDB** 8155 | **1FDC** 8156 | **1FDD** 8157 | **1FDE** 8158 | **1FDF** 8159 |
| Ῐ | Ῑ | Ὶ | Ί | *N/A* | ῝ | ῞ | ῟ |
| **1FE0** 8160 | **1FE1** 8161 | **1FE2** 8162 | **1FE3** 8163 | **1FE4** 8164 | **1FE5** 8165 | **1FE6** 8166 | **1FE7** 8167 |
| ῠ | ῡ | ῢ | ΰ | ῤ | ῥ | ῦ | ῧ |
| **1FE8** 8168 | **1FE9** 8169 | **1FEA** 8170 | **1FEB** 8171 | **1FEC** 8172 | **1FED** 8173 | **1FEE** 8174 | **1FEF** 8175 |
| Ῠ | Ῡ | Ὺ | Ύ | Ῥ | ῭ | ΅ | ` |
| **1FF0** 8176 | **1FF1** 8177 | **1FF2** 8178 | **1FF3** 8179 | **1FF4** 8180 | **1FF5** 8181 | **1FF6** 8182 | **1FF7** 8183 |
| *N/A* | *N/A* | ῲ | ῳ | ῴ | *N/A* | ῶ | ῷ |
| **1FF8** 8184 | **1FF9** 8185 | **1FFA** 8186 | **1FFB** 8187 | **1FFC** 8188 | **1FFD** 8189 | **1FFE** 8190 | **1FFF** 8191 |
| Ὸ | Ό | Ὼ | Ώ | ῼ | ´ | ῾ | *N/A* |



## General Punctuation

The General Punctuation block, shown in Table 23-21, contains punctuation characters used across a variety of languages and scripts that are not already encoded in Latin-1. Several rows that appear below as letters are actually particular nonprinting characters (like the control characters in ASCII and Latin-1). For instance, character ` `, listed below as EMSP, is the em space, a space equal to the font size of the current font.

*Table 23-21: The General Punctuation Block of Unicode*

| | | | | | | | |
|---|---|---|---|---|---|---|---|
| **2000** 8192 | **2001** 8193 | **2002** 8194 | **2003** 8195 | **2004** 8196 | **2005** 8197 | **2006** 8198 | **2007** 8199 |
| NQSP | MQSP | ENSP | EMSP | 3/MSP | 4/MSP | 6/MSP | FSP |
| **2008** 8200 | **2009** 8201 | **200A** 8202 | **200B** 8203 | **200C** 8204 | **200D** 8205 | **200E** 8206 | **200F** 8207 |
| PSP | THSP | HSP | ZWSP | ZWNJ | ZWJ | LRM | RLM |
| **2010** 8208 | **2011** 8209 | **2012** 8210 | **2013** 8211 | **2014** 8212 | **2015** 8213 | **2016** 8214 | **2017** 8215 |
| ‐ | ‑ | ‒ | – | — | ― | ‖ | ‗ |
| **2018** 8216 | **2019** 8217 | **201A** 8218 | **201B** 8219 | **201C** 8220 | **201D** 8221 | **201E** 8222 | **201F** 8223 |
| ‘ | ’ | ‚ | ‛ | “ | ” | „ | ‟ |

*Table 23-21: The General Punctuation Block of Unicode (continued)*

| | | | | | | | |
|---|---|---|---|---|---|---|---|
| **2020** 8224 | **2021** 8225 | **2022** 8226 | **2023** 8227 | **2024** 8228 | **2025** 8229 | **2026** 8230 | **2027** 8231 |
| † | ‡ | • | ‣ | ․ | ‥ | … | ‧ |
| **2028** 8232 | **2029** 8233 | **202A** 8234 | **202B** 8235 | **202C** 8236 | **202D** 8237 | **202E** 8238 | **202F** 8239 |
| LSEP | PSEP | LRE | RLE | PDF | LRO | RLO | *N/A* |
| **2030** 8240 | **2031** 8241 | **2032** 8242 | **2033** 8243 | **2034** 8244 | **2035** 8245 | **2036** 8246 | **2037** 8247 |
| ‰ | ‱ | ′ | ″ | ‴ | ‵ | ‶ | ‷ |
| **2038** 8248 | **2039** 8249 | **203A** 8250 | **203B** 8251 | **203C** 8252 | **203D** 8253 | **203E** 8254 | **203F** 8255 |
| ‸ | ‹ | › | ※ | ‼ | ‽ | ‾ | ‿ |
| **2040** 8256 | **2041** 8257 | **2042** 8258 | **2043** 8259 | **2044** 8260 | **2045** 8261 | **2046** 8262 | **2047** 8263 |
| ⁀ | ⁁ | ⁂ | ⁃ | ⁄ | ⁅ | ⁆ | *N/A* |
| **2048** 8264 | **2049** 8265 | **204A** 8266 | **204B** 8267 | **204C** 8268 | **204D** 8269 | **204E** 8270 | **204F** 8271 |
| ?! | !? | ⁊ | ⁋ | ⁌ | ⁍ | *N/A* | *N/A* |

## Currency Symbols

The Currency Symbols block, shown in Table 23-22, includes a few monetary symbols not already included in other blocks, such as the Indian rupee sign, the Italian lira sign, and the Greek drachma sign.

*Table 23-22: The Currency Symbols Block of Unicode*

| | | | | | | | |
|---|---|---|---|---|---|---|---|
| **20A0** 8352 | **20A1** 8353 | **20A2** 8354 | **20A3** 8355 | **20A4** 8356 | **20A5** 8357 | **20A6** 8358 | **20A7** 8359 |
| ₠ | ₡ | ₢ | ₣ | ₤ | ₥ | ₦ | ₧ |
| **20A8** 8360 | **20A9** 8361 | **20AA** 8362 | **20AB** 8363 | **20AC** 8364 | **20AD** 8365 | **20AE** 8366 | **20AF** 8367 |
| ₨ | ₩ | ₪ | ₫ | € | *N/A* | *N/A* | *N/A* |

## Letter-like Symbols

The Letter-like Symbols block, shown in Table 23-23, covers characters that look like letters, but really aren't, such as the ℞ symbol used to represent a prescription.

*Table 23-23: The Letter-like Symbols Block of Unicode*

| | | | | | | | |
|---|---|---|---|---|---|---|---|
| **2100** 8448 | **2101** 8449 | **2102** 8450 | **2103** 8451 | **2104** 8452 | **2105** 8453 | **2106** 8454 | **2107** 8455 |
| ℀ | ℁ | ℂ | ℃ | ℄ | ℅ | ℆ | ℇ |
| **2108** 8456 | **2109** 8457 | **210A** 8458 | **210B** 8459 | **210C** 8460 | **210D** 8461 | **210E** 8462 | **210F** 8463 |
| ℈ | ℉ | ℊ | ℋ | ℌ | ℍ | ℎ | ℏ |
| **2110** 8464 | **2111** 8465 | **2112** 8466 | **2113** 8467 | **2114** 8468 | **2115** 8469 | **2116** 8470 | **2117** 8471 |
| ℐ | ℑ | ℒ | ℓ | ℔ | ℕ | № | ℗ |
| **2118** 8472 | **2119** 8473 | **211A** 8474 | **211B** 8475 | **211C** 8476 | **211D** 8477 | **211E** 8478 | **211F** 8479 |
| ℘ | ℙ | ℚ | ℛ | ℜ | ℝ | ℞ | ℟ |
| **2120** 8480 | **2121** 8481 | **2122** 8482 | **2123** 8483 | **2124** 8484 | **2125** 8485 | **2126** 8486 | **2127** 8487 |
| SM | TEL | TM | ℣ | ℤ | ℥ | Ω | ℧ |

*Table 23-23: The Letter-like Symbols Block of Unicode (continued)*

| **2128** 8488 | **2129** 8489 | **212A** 8490 | **212B** 8491 | **212C** 8492 | **212D** 8493 | **212E** 8494 | **212F** 8495 |
|---|---|---|---|---|---|---|---|
| ℨ | ℩ | K | Å | ℬ | ℭ | ℮ | ℯ |
| **2130** 8496 | **2131** 8497 | **2132** 8498 | **2133** 8499 | **2134** 8500 | **2135** 8501 | **2136** 8502 | **2137** 8503 |
| ℰ | ℱ | Ⅎ | ℳ | ℴ | ℵ | ℶ | ℷ |
| **2138** 8504 | **2139** 8505 | **213A** 8506 | **213B** 8507 | **213C** 8508 | **213D** 8509 | **213E** 8510 | **213F** 8511 |
| ℸ | N/A | N/A | N/A | N/A | N/A | N/A | N/A |

## Arrows

The Arrows block, shown in Table 23-24, contains commonly needed arrow characters.

*Table 23-24: The Arrows Block of Unicode*

| **2190** 8592 | **2191** 8593 | **2192** 8594 | **2193** 8595 | **2194** 8596 | **2195** 8597 | **2196** 8598 | **2197** 8599 |
|---|---|---|---|---|---|---|---|
| ← | ↑ | → | ↓ | ↔ | ↕ | ↖ | ↗ |
| **2198** 8600 | **2199** 8601 | **219A** 8602 | **219B** 8603 | **219C** 8604 | **219D** 8605 | **219E** 8606 | **219F** 8607 |
| ↘ | ↙ | ↚ | ↛ | ↜ | ↝ | ↞ | ↟ |
| **21A0** 8608 | **21A1** 8609 | **21A2** 8610 | **21A3** 8611 | **21A4** 8612 | **21A5** 8613 | **21A6** 8614 | **21A7** 8615 |
| ↠ | ↡ | ↢ | ↣ | ↤ | ↥ | ↦ | ↧ |
| **21A8** 8616 | **21A9** 8617 | **21AA** 8618 | **21AB** 8619 | **21AC** 8620 | **21AD** 8621 | **21AE** 8622 | **21AF** 8623 |
| ↨ | ↩ | ↪ | ↫ | ↬ | ↭ | ↮ | ↯ |
| **21B0** 8624 | **21B1** 8625 | **21B2** 8626 | **21B3** 8627 | **21B4** 8628 | **21B5** 8629 | **21B6** 8630 | **21B7** 8631 |
| ↰ | ↱ | ↲ | ↳ | ↴ | ↵ | ↶ | ↷ |
| **21B8** 8632 | **21B9** 8633 | **21BA** 8634 | **21BB** 8635 | **21BC** 8636 | **21BD** 8637 | **21BE** 8638 | **21BF** 8639 |
| ↸ | ↹ | ↺ | ↻ | ↼ | ↽ | ↾ | ↿ |
| **21C0** 8640 | **21C1** 8641 | **21C2** 8642 | **21C3** 8643 | **21C4** 8644 | **21C5** 8645 | **21C6** 8646 | **21C7** 8647 |
| ⇀ | ⇁ | ⇂ | ⇃ | ⇄ | ⇅ | ⇆ | ⇇ |
| **21C8** 8648 | **21C9** 8649 | **21CA** 8650 | **21CB** 8651 | **21CC** 8652 | **21CD** 8653 | **21CE** 8654 | **21CF** 8655 |
| ⇈ | ⇉ | ⇊ | ⇋ | ⇌ | ⇍ | ⇎ | ⇏ |
| **21D0** 8656 | **21D1** 8657 | **21D2** 8658 | **21D3** 8659 | **21D4** 8660 | **21D5** 8661 | **21D6** 8662 | **21D7** 8663 |
| ⇐ | ⇑ | ⇒ | ⇓ | ⇔ | ⇕ | ⇖ | ⇗ |
| **21D8** 8664 | **21D9** 8665 | **21DA** 8666 | **21DB** 8667 | **21DC** 8668 | **21DD** 8669 | **21DE** 8670 | **21DF** 8671 |
| ⇘ | ⇙ | ⇚ | ⇛ | ⇜ | ⇝ | ⇞ | ⇟ |
| **21E0** 8672 | **21E1** 8673 | **21E2** 8674 | **21E3** 8675 | **21E4** 8676 | **21E5** 8677 | **21E6** 8678 | **21E7** 8679 |
| ⇠ | ⇡ | ⇢ | ⇣ | ⇤ | ⇥ | ⇦ | ⇧ |
| **21E8** 8680 | **21E9** 8681 | **21EA** 8682 | **21EB** 8683 | **21EC** 8684 | **21ED** 8685 | **21EE** 8686 | **21EF** 8687 |
| ⇨ | ⇩ | ⇪ | N/A | N/A | N/A | N/A | N/A |
| **21F0** 8688 | **21F1** 8689 | **21F2** 8690 | **21F3** 8691 | **21F4** 8692 | **21F5** 8693 | **21F6** 8694 | **21F7** 8695 |
| N/A | N/A | N/A | N/A | N/A | N/A | N/A | N/A |
| **21F8** 8696 | **21F9** 8697 | **21FA** 8698 | **21FB** 8699 | **21FC** 8700 | **21FD** 8701 | **21FE** 8702 | **21FF** 8703 |
| N/A | N/A | N/A | N/A | N/A | N/A | N/A | N/A |

## *Mathematical Operators*

The Mathematical Operators block, shown in Table 23-25, contains a wide variety of symbols used in higher mathematics. A few of these symbols superficially resemble letters in other blocks. For instance, in most fonts, character 2206, ∆, is virtually identical to the Greek capital letter delta. However, using characters in this block is preferable for mathematical expressions, as it allows software to distinguish between the letters and mathematical symbols. Fonts may use the same glyph to represent different code points in cases like this.

*Table 23-25: The Mathematical Operators Block of Unicode*

| | | | | | | | |
|---|---|---|---|---|---|---|---|
| **2200** 8704 | **2201** 8705 | **2202** 8706 | **2203** 8707 | **2204** 8708 | **2205** 8709 | **2206** 8710 | **2207** 8711 |
| ∀ | ∁ | ∂ | ∃ | ∄ | ∅ | ∆ | ∇ |
| **2208** 8712 | **2209** 8713 | **220A** 8714 | **220B** 8715 | **220C** 8716 | **220D** 8717 | **220E** 8718 | **220F** 8719 |
| ∈ | ∉ | ∊ | ∋ | ∌ | ∍ | ∎ | ∏ |
| **2210** 8720 | **2211** 8721 | **2212** 8722 | **2213** 8723 | **2214** 8724 | **2215** 8725 | **2216** 8726 | **2217** 8727 |
| ∐ | ∑ | − | ∓ | ∔ | ∕ | ∖ | ∗ |
| **2218** 8728 | **2219** 8729 | **221A** 8730 | **221B** 8731 | **221C** 8732 | **221D** 8733 | **221E** 8734 | **221F** 8735 |
| ∘ | ∙ | √ | ∛ | ∜ | ∝ | ∞ | ∟ |
| **2220** 8736 | **2221** 8737 | **2222** 8738 | **2223** 8739 | **2224** 8740 | **2225** 8741 | **2226** 8742 | **2227** 8743 |
| ∠ | ∡ | ∢ | ∣ | ∤ | ∥ | ∦ | ∧ |
| **2228** 8744 | **2229** 8745 | **222A** 8746 | **222B** 8747 | **222C** 8748 | **222D** 8749 | **222E** 8750 | **222F** 8751 |
| ∨ | ∩ | ∪ | ∫ | ∬ | ∭ | ∮ | ∯ |
| **2230** 8752 | **2231** 8753 | **2232** 8754 | **2233** 8755 | **2234** 8756 | **2235** 8757 | **2236** 8758 | **2237** 8759 |
| ∰ | ∱ | ∲ | ∳ | ∴ | ∵ | ∶ | ∷ |
| **2238** 8760 | **2239** 8761 | **223A** 8762 | **223B** 8763 | **223C** 8764 | **223D** 8765 | **223E** 8766 | **223F** 8767 |
| ∸ | ∹ | ∺ | ∻ | ∼ | ∽ | ∾ | ∿ |
| **2240** 8768 | **2241** 8769 | **2242** 8770 | **2243** 8771 | **2244** 8772 | **2245** 8773 | **2246** 8774 | **2247** 8775 |
| ≀ | ≁ | ≂ | ≃ | ≄ | ≅ | ≆ | ≇ |
| **2248** 8776 | **2249** 8777 | **224A** 8778 | **224B** 8779 | **224C** 8780 | **224D** 8781 | **224E** 8782 | **224F** 8783 |
| ≈ | ≉ | ≊ | ≋ | ≌ | ≍ | ≎ | ≏ |
| **2250** 8784 | **2251** 8785 | **2252** 8786 | **2253** 8787 | **2254** 8788 | **2255** 8789 | **2256** 8790 | **2257** 8791 |
| ≐ | ≑ | ≒ | ≓ | ≔ | ≕ | ≖ | ≗ |
| **2258** 8792 | **2259** 8793 | **225A** 8794 | **225B** 8795 | **225C** 8796 | **225D** 8797 | **225E** 8798 | **225F** 8799 |
| ≘ | ≙ | ≚ | ≛ | ≜ | ≝ | ≞ | ≟ |
| **2260** 8800 | **2261** 8801 | **2262** 8802 | **2263** 8803 | **2264** 8804 | **2265** 8805 | **2266** 8806 | **2267** 8807 |
| ≠ | ≡ | ≢ | ≣ | ≤ | ≥ | ≦ | ≧ |
| **2268** 8808 | **2269** 8809 | **226A** 8810 | **226B** 8811 | **226C** 8812 | **226D** 8813 | **226E** 8814 | **226F** 8815 |
| ≨ | ≩ | ≪ | ≫ | ≬ | ≭ | ≮ | ≯ |
| **2270** 8816 | **2271** 8817 | **2272** 8818 | **2273** 8819 | **2274** 8820 | **2275** 8821 | **2276** 8822 | **2277** 8823 |
| ≰ | ≱ | ≲ | ≳ | ≴ | ≵ | ≶ | ≷ |
| **2278** 8824 | **2279** 8825 | **227A** 8826 | **227B** 8827 | **227C** 8828 | **227D** 8829 | **227E** 8830 | **227F** 8831 |
| ≸ | ≹ | ≺ | ≻ | ≼ | ≽ | ≾ | ≿ |

*Table 23-25: The Mathematical Operators Block of Unicode (continued)*

| | | | | | | | |
|---|---|---|---|---|---|---|---|
| **2280** 8832 | **2281** 8833 | **2282** 8834 | **2283** 8835 | **2284** 8836 | **2285** 8837 | **2286** 8838 | **2287** 8839 |
| ⊀ | ⊁ | ⊂ | ⊃ | ⊄ | ⊅ | ⊆ | ⊇ |
| **2288** 8840 | **2289** 8841 | **228A** 8842 | **228B** 8843 | **228C** 8844 | **228D** 8845 | **228E** 8846 | **228F** 8847 |
| ⊈ | ⊉ | ⊊ | ⊋ | ⊌ | ⊍ | ⊎ | ⊏ |
| **2290** 8848 | **2291** 8849 | **2292** 8850 | **2293** 8851 | **2294** 8852 | **2295** 8853 | **2296** 8854 | **2297** 8855 |
| ⊐ | ⊑ | ⊒ | ⊓ | ⊔ | ⊕ | ⊖ | ⊗ |
| **2298** 8856 | **2299** 8857 | **229A** 8858 | **229B** 8859 | **229C** 8860 | **229D** 8861 | **229E** 8862 | **229F** 8863 |
| ⊘ | ⊙ | ⊚ | ⊛ | ⊜ | ⊝ | ⊞ | ⊟ |
| **22A0** 8864 | **22A1** 8865 | **22A2** 8866 | **22A3** 8867 | **22A4** 8868 | **22A5** 8869 | **22A6** 8870 | **22A7** 8871 |
| ⊠ | ⊡ | ⊢ | ⊣ | ⊤ | ⊥ | ⊦ | ⊧ |
| **22A8** 8872 | **22A9** 8873 | **22AA** 8874 | **22AB** 8875 | **22AC** 8876 | **22AD** 8877 | **22AE** 8878 | **22AF** 8879 |
| ⊨ | ⊩ | ⊪ | ⊫ | ⊬ | ⊭ | ⊮ | ⊯ |
| **22B0** 8880 | **22B1** 8881 | **22B2** 8882 | **22B3** 8883 | **22B4** 8884 | **22B5** 8885 | **22B6** 8886 | **22B7** 8887 |
| ⊰ | ⊱ | ⊲ | ⊳ | ⊴ | ⊵ | ⊶ | ⊷ |
| **22B8** 8888 | **22B9** 8889 | **22BA** 8890 | **22BB** 8891 | **22BC** 8892 | **22BD** 8893 | **22BE** 8894 | **22BF** 8895 |
| ⊸ | ⊹ | ⊺ | ⊻ | ⊼ | ⊽ | ⊾ | ⊿ |
| **22C0** 8896 | **22C1** 8897 | **22C2** 8898 | **22C3** 8899 | **22C4** 8900 | **22C5** 8901 | **22C6** 8902 | **22C7** 8903 |
| ⋀ | ⋁ | ⋂ | ⋃ | ⋄ | ⋅ | ⋆ | ⋇ |
| **22C8** 8904 | **22C9** 8905 | **22CA** 8906 | **22CB** 8907 | **22CC** 8908 | **22CD** 8909 | **22CE** 8910 | **22CF** 8911 |
| ⋈ | ⋉ | ⋊ | ⋋ | ⋌ | ⋍ | ⋎ | ⋏ |
| **22D0** 8912 | **22D1** 8913 | **22D2** 8914 | **22D3** 8915 | **22D4** 8916 | **22D5** 8917 | **22D6** 8918 | **22D7** 8919 |
| ⋐ | ⋑ | ⋒ | ⋓ | ⋔ | ⋕ | ⋖ | ⋗ |
| **22D8** 8920 | **22D9** 8921 | **22DA** 8922 | **22DB** 8923 | **22DC** 8924 | **22DD** 8925 | **22DE** 8926 | **22DF** 8927 |
| ⋘ | ⋙ | ⋚ | ⋛ | ⋜ | ⋝ | ⋞ | ⋟ |
| **22E0** 8928 | **22E1** 8929 | **22E2** 8930 | **22E3** 8931 | **22E4** 8932 | **22E5** 8933 | **22E6** 8934 | **22E7** 8935 |
| ⋠ | ⋡ | ⋢ | ⋣ | ⋤ | ⋥ | ⋦ | ⋧ |
| **22E8** 8936 | **22E9** 8937 | **22EA** 8938 | **22EB** 8939 | **22EC** 8940 | **22ED** 8941 | **22EE** 8942 | **22EF** 8943 |
| ⋨ | ⋩ | ⋪ | ⋫ | ⋬ | ⋭ | ⋮ | ⋯ |
| **22F0** 8944 | **22F1** 8945 | **22F2** 8946 | **22F3** 8947 | **22F4** 8948 | **22F5** 8949 | **22F6** 8950 | **22F7** 8951 |
| ⋰ | ⋱ | N/A | N/A | N/A | N/A | N/A | N/A |
| **22F8** 8952 | **22F9** 8953 | **22FA** 8954 | **22FB** 8955 | **22FC** 8956 | **22FD** 8957 | **22FE** 8958 | **22FF** 8959 |
| N/A | N/A | N/A | N/A | N/A | N/A | N/A | N/A |

## Miscellaneous Technical

The Miscellaneous Technical block, shown in Table 23-26, contains assorted symbols taken from electronics, quantum mechanics, the APL programming language, the ISO-9995-7 standard for language-neutral keyboard pictograms, and other sources.

*Table 23-26: The Miscellaneous Technical Block of Unicode*

| | | | | | | | |
|---|---|---|---|---|---|---|---|
| **2300** 8960 | **2301** 8961 | **2302** 8962 | **2303** 8963 | **2304** 8964 | **2305** 8965 | **2306** 8966 | **2307** 8967 |
| ⌀ | N/A | ⌂ | ⌃ | ⌄ | ⌅ | ⌆ | ⌇ |
| **2308** 8968 | **2309** 8969 | **230A** 8970 | **230B** 8971 | **230C** 8972 | **230D** 8973 | **230E** 8974 | **230F** 8975 |
| ⌈ | ⌉ | ⌊ | ⌋ | ⌌ | ⌍ | ⌎ | ⌏ |
| **2310** 8976 | **2311** 8977 | **2312** 8978 | **2313** 8979 | **2314** 8980 | **2315** 8981 | **2316** 8982 | **2317** 8983 |
| ⌐ | ⌑ | ⌒ | ⌓ | ⌔ | ⌕ | ⌖ | ⌗ |
| **2318** 8984 | **2319** 8985 | **231A** 8986 | **231B** 8987 | **231C** 8988 | **231D** 8989 | **231E** 8990 | **231F** 8991 |
| ⌘ | ⌙ | ⌚ | ⌛ | ⌜ | ⌝ | ⌞ | ⌟ |
| **2320** 8992 | **2321** 8993 | **2322** 8994 | **2323** 8995 | **2324** 8996 | **2325** 8997 | **2326** 8998 | **2327** 8999 |
| ⌠ | ⌡ | ⌢ | ⌣ | ⌤ | ⌥ | ⌦ | ⌧ |
| **2328** 9000 | **2329** 9001 | **232A** 9002 | **232B** 9003 | **232C** 9004 | **232D** 9005 | **232E** 9006 | **232F** 9007 |
| ⌨ | 〈 | 〉 | ⌫ | ⌬ | ⌭ | ⌮ | ⌯ |
| **2330** 9008 | **2331** 9009 | **2332** 9010 | **2333** 9011 | **2334** 9012 | **2335** 9013 | **2336** 9014 | **2337** 9015 |
| ⌰ | ⌱ | ⌲ | ⌳ | ⌴ | ⌵ | ⌶ | ⌷ |
| **2338** 9016 | **2339** 9017 | **233A** 9018 | **233B** 9019 | **233C** 9020 | **233D** 9021 | **233E** 9022 | **233F** 9023 |
| ⌸ | ⌹ | ⌺ | ⌻ | ⌼ | ⌽ | ⌾ | ⌿ |
| **2340** 9024 | **2341** 9025 | **2342** 9026 | **2343** 9027 | **2344** 9028 | **2345** 9029 | **2346** 9030 | **2347** 9031 |
| ⍀ | ⍁ | ⍂ | ⍃ | ⍄ | ⍅ | ⍆ | ⍇ |
| **2348** 9032 | **2349** 9033 | **234A** 9034 | **234B** 9035 | **234C** 9036 | **234D** 9037 | **234E** 9038 | **234F** 9039 |
| ⍈ | ⍉ | ⍊ | ⍋ | ⍌ | ⍍ | ⍎ | ⍏ |
| **2350** 9040 | **2351** 9041 | **2352** 9042 | **2353** 9043 | **2354** 9044 | **2355** 9045 | **2356** 9046 | **2357** 9047 |
| ⍐ | ⍑ | ⍒ | ⍓ | ⍔ | ⍕ | ⍖ | ⍗ |
| **2358** 9048 | **2359** 9049 | **235A** 9050 | **235B** 9051 | **235C** 9052 | **235D** 9053 | **235E** 9054 | **235F** 9055 |
| ⍘ | ⍙ | ⍚ | ⍛ | ⍜ | ⍝ | ⍞ | ⍟ |
| **2360** 9056 | **2361** 9057 | **2362** 9058 | **2363** 9059 | **2364** 9060 | **2365** 9061 | **2366** 9062 | **2367** 9063 |
| ⍠ | ⍡ | ⍢ | ⍣ | ⍤ | ⍥ | ⍦ | ⍧ |
| **2368** 9064 | **2369** 9065 | **236A** 9066 | **236B** 9067 | **236C** 9068 | **236D** 9069 | **236E** 9070 | **236F** 9071 |
| ⍨ | ⍩ | ⍪ | ⍫ | ⍬ | ⍭ | ⍮ | ⍯ |
| **2370** 9072 | **2371** 9073 | **2372** 9074 | **2373** 9075 | **2374** 9076 | **2375** 9077 | **2376** 9078 | **2377** 9079 |
| ⍰ | ⍱ | ⍲ | ⍳ | ⍴ | ⍵ | ⍶ | ⍷ |
| **2378** 9080 | **2379** 9081 | **237A** 9082 | **237B** 9083 | **237C** 9084 | **237D** 9085 | **237E** 9086 | **237F** 9087 |
| ⍸ | ⍹ | ⍺ | N/A | N/A | N/A | N/A | N/A |
| **2380** 9088 | **2381** 9089 | **2382** 9090 | **2383** 9091 | **2384** 9092 | **2385** 9093 | **2386** 9094 | **2387** 9095 |
| N/A | N/A | N/A | N/A | N/A | N/A | N/A | N/A |
| **2388** 9096 | **2389** 9097 | **238A** 9098 | **238B** 9099 | **238C** 9100 | **238D** 9101 | **238E** 9102 | **238F** 9103 |
| N/A | N/A | N/A | N/A | N/A | N/A | N/A | N/A |
| **2390** 9104 | **2391** 9105 | **2392** 9106 | **2393** 9107 | **2394** 9108 | **2395** 9109 | **2396** 9110 | **2397** 9111 |
| N/A | N/A | N/A | N/A | N/A | N/A | N/A | N/A |
| **2398** 9112 | **2399** 9113 | **239A** 9114 | **239B** 9115 | **239C** 9116 | **239D** 9117 | **239E** 9118 | **239F** 9119 |
| N/A | N/A | N/A | N/A | N/A | N/A | N/A | N/A |

## *Optical Character Recognition*

The Optical Character Recognition block, shown in Table 23-27, includes the OCR-A characters that are not already encoded as ASCII and the magnetic ink character recognition symbols used on checks.

*Table 23-27: The Optical Character Recognition Block of Unicode*

| | | | | | | | |
|---|---|---|---|---|---|---|---|
| **2440** 9280 | **2441** 9281 | **2442** 9282 | **2443** 9283 | **2444** 9284 | **2445** 9285 | **2446** 9286 | **2447** 9287 |
| ⑀ | ⑁ | ⑂ | ⑃ | ⑄ | ⑅ | ⑆ | ⑇ |
| **2448** 9288 | **2449** 9289 | **244A** 9290 | **244B** 9291 | **244C** 9292 | **244D** 9293 | **244E** 9294 | **244F** 9295 |
| ⑈ | ⑉ | ⑊ | N/A | N/A | N/A | N/A | N/A |

## *Geometric Shapes*

The Geometric Shapes block, shown in Table 23-28, combines simple triangles, squares, circles, and other shapes found in character sets Unicode attempts to superset.

*Table 23-28: The Geometric Shapes Block of Unicode*

| | | | | | | | |
|---|---|---|---|---|---|---|---|
| **25A0** 9632 | **25A1** 9633 | **25A2** 9634 | **25A3** 9635 | **25A4** 9636 | **25A5** 9637 | **25A6** 9638 | **25A7** 9639 |
| ■ | □ | ▢ | ▣ | ▤ | ▥ | ▦ | ▧ |
| **25A8** 9640 | **25A9** 9641 | **25AA** 9642 | **25AB** 9643 | **25AC** 9644 | **25AD** 9645 | **25AE** 9646 | **25AF** 9647 |
| ▨ | ▩ | ▪ | ▫ | ▬ | ▭ | ▮ | ▯ |
| **25B0** 9648 | **25B1** 9649 | **25B2** 9650 | **25B3** 9651 | **25B4** 9652 | **25B5** 9653 | **25B6** 9654 | **25B7** 9655 |
| ▰ | ▱ | ▲ | △ | ▴ | ▵ | ▶ | ▷ |
| **25B8** 9656 | **25B9** 9657 | **25BA** 9658 | **25BB** 9659 | **25BC** 9660 | **25BD** 9661 | **25BE** 9662 | **25BF** 9663 |
| ▸ | ▹ | ► | ▻ | ▼ | ▽ | ▾ | ▿ |
| **25C0** 9664 | **25C1** 9665 | **25C2** 9666 | **25C3** 9667 | **25C4** 9668 | **25C5** 9669 | **25C6** 9670 | **25C7** 9671 |
| ◀ | ◁ | ◂ | ◃ | ◄ | ◅ | ◆ | ◇ |
| **25C8** 9672 | **25C9** 9673 | **25CA** 9674 | **25CB** 9675 | **25CC** 9676 | **25CD** 9677 | **25CE** 9678 | **25CF** 9679 |
| ◈ | ◉ | ◊ | ○ | ◌ | ◍ | ◎ | ● |
| **25D0** 9680 | **25D1** 9681 | **25D2** 9682 | **25D3** 9683 | **25D4** 9684 | **25D5** 9685 | **25D6** 9686 | **25D7** 9687 |
| ◐ | ◑ | ◒ | ◓ | ◔ | ◕ | ◖ | ◗ |
| **25D8** 9688 | **25D9** 9689 | **25DA** 9690 | **25DB** 9691 | **25DC** 9692 | **25DD** 9693 | **25DE** 9694 | **25DF** 9695 |
| ◘ | ◙ | ◚ | ◛ | ◜ | ◝ | ◞ | ◟ |
| **25E0** 9696 | **25E1** 9697 | **25E2** 9698 | **25E3** 9699 | **25E4** 9700 | **25E5** 9701 | **25E6** 9702 | **25E7** 9703 |
| ◠ | ◡ | ◢ | ◣ | ◤ | ◥ | ◦ | ◧ |
| **25E8** 9704 | **25E9** 9705 | **25EA** 9706 | **25EB** 9707 | **25EC** 9708 | **25ED** 9709 | **25EE** 9710 | **25EF** 9711 |
| ◨ | ◩ | ◪ | ◫ | ◬ | ◭ | ◮ | ◯ |
| **25F0** 9712 | **25F1** 9713 | **25F2** 9714 | **25F3** 9715 | **25F4** 9716 | **25F5** 9717 | **25F6** 9718 | **25F7** 9719 |
| N/A | N/A | N/A | N/A | N/A | N/A | N/A | N/A |
| **25F8** 9720 | **25F9** 9721 | **25FA** 9722 | **25FB** 9723 | **25FC** 9724 | **25FD** 9725 | **25FE** 9726 | **25FF** 9727 |
| N/A | N/A | N/A | N/A | N/A | N/A | N/A | N/A |

## Miscellaneous Symbols

The Miscellaneous Symbols block, shown in Table 23-29, contains mostly pictographic symbols found in vendor and national character sets that preceded Unicode.

*Table 23-29: The Miscellaneous Symbols Block of Unicode*

| | | | | | | | |
|---|---|---|---|---|---|---|---|
| **2600** 9728 | **2601** 9729 | **2602** 9730 | **2603** 9731 | **2604** 9732 | **2605** 9733 | **2606** 9734 | **2607** 9735 |
| ☀ | ☁ | ☂ | ☃ | ☄ | ★ | ☆ | ☇ |
| **2608** 9736 | **2609** 9737 | **260A** 9738 | **260B** 9739 | **260C** 9740 | **260D** 9741 | **260E** 9742 | **260F** 9743 |
| ☈ | ☉ | ☊ | ☋ | ☌ | ☍ | ☎ | ☏ |
| **2610** 9744 | **2611** 9745 | **2612** 9746 | **2613** 9747 | **2614** 9748 | **2615** 9749 | **2616** 9750 | **2617** 9751 |
| ☐ | ☑ | ☒ | ☓ | N/A | N/A | N/A | N/A |
| **2618** 9752 | **2619** 9753 | **261A** 9754 | **261B** 9755 | **261C** 9756 | **261D** 9757 | **261E** 9758 | **261F** 9759 |
| N/A | N/A | ☚ | ☛ | ☜ | ☝ | ☞ | ☟ |
| **2620** 9760 | **2621** 9761 | **2622** 9762 | **2623** 9763 | **2624** 9764 | **2625** 9765 | **2626** 9766 | **2627** 9767 |
| ☠ | ☡ | ☢ | ☣ | ☤ | ☥ | ☦ | ☧ |
| **2628** 9768 | **2629** 9769 | **262A** 9770 | **262B** 9771 | **262C** 9772 | **262D** 9773 | **262E** 9774 | **262F** 9775 |
| ☨ | ☩ | ☪ | ☫ | ☬ | ☭ | ☮ | ☯ |
| **2630** 9776 | **2631** 9777 | **2632** 9778 | **2633** 9779 | **2634** 9780 | **2635** 9781 | **2636** 9782 | **2637** 9783 |
| ☰ | ☱ | ☲ | ☳ | ☴ | ☵ | ☶ | ☷ |
| **2638** 9784 | **2639** 9785 | **263A** 9786 | **263B** 9787 | **263C** 9788 | **263D** 9789 | **263E** 9790 | **263F** 9791 |
| ☸ | ☹ | ☺ | ☻ | ☼ | ☽ | ☾ | ☿ |
| **2640** 9792 | **2641** 9793 | **2642** 9794 | **2643** 9795 | **2644** 9796 | **2645** 9797 | **2646** 9798 | **2647** 9799 |
| ♀ | ♁ | ♂ | ♃ | ♄ | ♅ | ♆ | ♇ |
| **2648** 9800 | **2649** 9801 | **264A** 9802 | **264B** 9803 | **264C** 9804 | **264D** 9805 | **264E** 9806 | **264F** 9807 |
| ♈ | ♉ | ♊ | ♋ | ♌ | ♍ | ♎ | ♏ |
| **2650** 9808 | **2651** 9809 | **2652** 9810 | **2653** 9811 | **2654** 9812 | **2655** 9813 | **2656** 9814 | **2657** 9815 |
| ♐ | ♑ | ♒ | ♓ | ♔ | ♕ | ♖ | ♗ |
| **2658** 9816 | **2659** 9817 | **265A** 9818 | **265B** 9819 | **265C** 9820 | **265D** 9821 | **265E** 9822 | **265F** 9823 |
| ♘ | ♙ | ♚ | ♛ | ♜ | ♝ | ♞ | ♟ |
| **2660** 9824 | **2661** 9825 | **2662** 9826 | **2663** 9827 | **2664** 9828 | **2665** 9829 | **2666** 9830 | **2667** 9831 |
| ♠ | ♡ | ♢ | ♣ | ♤ | ♥ | ♦ | ♧ |
| **2668** 9832 | **2669** 9833 | **266A** 9834 | **266B** 9835 | **266C** 9836 | **266D** 9837 | **266E** 9838 | **266F** 9839 |
| ♨ | ♩ | ♪ | ♫ | ♬ | ♭ | ♮ | ♯ |
| **2670** 9840 | **2671** 9841 | **2672** 9842 | **2673** 9843 | **2674** 9844 | **2675** 9845 | **2676** 9846 | **2677** 9847 |
| N/A | N/A | N/A | N/A | N/A | N/A | N/A | N/A |
| **2678** 9848 | **2679** 9849 | **267A** 9850 | **267B** 9851 | **267C** 9852 | **267D** 9853 | **267E** 9854 | **267F** 9855 |
| N/A | N/A | N/A | N/A | N/A | N/A | N/A | N/A |

## Dingbats

The Dingbats block, shown in Table 23-30, is based on characters in the popular Adobe Zapf Dingbats font.

*Table 23-30: The Dingbats Block of Unicode*

| | | | | | | | |
|---|---|---|---|---|---|---|---|
| **2700** 9984 | **2701** 9985 | **2702** 9986 | **2703** 9987 | **2704** 9988 | **2705** 9989 | **2706** 9990 | **2707** 9991 |
| N/A | ✁ | ✂ | ✃ | ✄ | N/A | ✆ | ✇ |
| **2708** 9992 | **2709** 9993 | **270A** 9994 | **270B** 9995 | **270C** 9996 | **270D** 9997 | **270E** 9998 | **270F** 9999 |
| ✈ | ✉ | N/A | N/A | ✌ | ✍ | ✎ | ✏ |
| **2710** 10000 | **2711** 10001 | **2712** 10002 | **2713** 10003 | **2714** 10004 | **2715** 10005 | **2716** 10006 | **2717** 10007 |
| ✐ | ✑ | ✒ | ✓ | ✔ | ✕ | ✖ | ✗ |
| **2718** 10008 | **2719** 10009 | **271A** 10010 | **271B** 10011 | **271C** 10012 | **271D** 10013 | **271E** 10014 | **271F** 10015 |
| ✘ | ✙ | ✚ | ✛ | ✜ | ✝ | ✞ | ✟ |
| **2720** 10016 | **2721** 10017 | **2722** 10018 | **2723** 10019 | **2724** 10020 | **2725** 10021 | **2726** 10022 | **2727** 10023 |
| ✠ | ✡ | ✢ | ✣ | ✤ | ✥ | ✦ | ✧ |
| **2728** 10024 | **2729** 10025 | **272A** 10026 | **272B** 10027 | **272C** 10028 | **272D** 10029 | **272E** 10030 | **272F** 10031 |
| N/A | ✩ | ✪ | ✫ | ✬ | ✭ | ✮ | ✯ |
| **2730** 10032 | **2731** 10033 | **2732** 10034 | **2733** 10035 | **2734** 10036 | **2735** 10037 | **2736** 10038 | **2737** 10039 |
| ✰ | ✱ | ✲ | ✳ | ✴ | ✵ | ✶ | ✷ |
| **2738** 10040 | **2739** 10041 | **273A** 10042 | **273B** 10043 | **273C** 10044 | **273D** 10045 | **273E** 10046 | **273F** 10047 |
| ✸ | ✹ | ✺ | ✻ | ✼ | ✽ | ✾ | ✿ |
| **2740** 10048 | **2741** 10049 | **2742** 10050 | **2743** 10051 | **2744** 10052 | **2745** 10053 | **2746** 10054 | **2747** 10055 |
| ❀ | ❁ | ❂ | ❃ | ❄ | ❅ | ❆ | ❇ |
| **2748** 10056 | **2749** 10057 | **274A** 10058 | **274B** 10059 | **274C** 10060 | **274D** 10061 | **274E** 10062 | **274F** 10063 |
| ❈ | ❉ | ❊ | ❋ | N/A | ❍ | N/A | ❏ |
| **2750** 10064 | **2751** 10065 | **2752** 10066 | **2753** 10067 | **2754** 10068 | **2755** 10069 | **2756** 10070 | **2757** 10071 |
| ❐ | ❑ | ❒ | N/A | N/A | N/A | ❖ | N/A |
| **2758** 10072 | **2759** 10073 | **275A** 10074 | **275B** 10075 | **275C** 10076 | **275D** 10077 | **275E** 10078 | **275F** 10079 |
| ❘ | ❙ | ❚ | ❛ | ❜ | ❝ | ❞ | N/A |
| **2760** 10080 | **2761** 10081 | **2762** 10082 | **2763** 10083 | **2764** 10084 | **2765** 10085 | **2766** 10086 | **2767** 10087 |
| N/A | ❡ | ❢ | ❣ | ❤ | ❥ | ❦ | ❧ |
| **2768** 10088 | **2769** 10089 | **276A** 10090 | **276B** 10091 | **276C** 10092 | **276D** 10093 | **276E** 10094 | **276F** 10095 |
| N/A | N/A | N/A | N/A | N/A | N/A | N/A | N/A |
| **2770** 10096 | **2771** 10097 | **2772** 10098 | **2773** 10099 | **2774** 10100 | **2775** 10101 | **2776** 10102 | **2777** 10103 |
| N/A | N/A | N/A | N/A | N/A | N/A | ❶ | ❷ |
| **2778** 10104 | **2779** 10105 | **277A** 10106 | **277B** 10107 | **277C** 10108 | **277D** 10109 | **277E** 10110 | **277F** 10111 |
| ❸ | ❹ | ❺ | ❻ | ❼ | ❽ | ❾ | ❿ |
| **2780** 10112 | **2781** 10113 | **2782** 10114 | **2783** 10115 | **2784** 10116 | **2785** 10117 | **2786** 10118 | **2787** 10119 |
| ➀ | ➁ | ➂ | ➃ | ➄ | ➅ | ➆ | ➇ |
| **2788** 10120 | **2789** 10121 | **278A** 10122 | **278B** 10123 | **278C** 10124 | **278D** 10125 | **278E** 10126 | **278F** 10127 |
| ➈ | ➉ | ➊ | ➋ | ➌ | ➍ | ➎ | ➏ |
| **2790** 10128 | **2791** 10129 | **2792** 10130 | **2793** 10131 | **2794** 10132 | **2795** 10133 | **2796** 10134 | **2797** 10135 |
| ➐ | ➑ | ➒ | ➓ | ➔ | N/A | N/A | N/A |
| **2798** 10136 | **2799** 10137 | **279A** 10138 | **279B** 10139 | **279C** 10140 | **279D** 10141 | **279E** 10142 | **279F** 10143 |
| ➘ | ➙ | ➚ | ➛ | ➜ | ➝ | ➞ | ➟ |

Character Sets

*Table 23-30: The Dingbats Block of Unicode (continued)*

| | | | | | | | |
|---|---|---|---|---|---|---|---|
| **27A0** 10144 | **27A1** 10145 | **27A2** 10146 | **27A3** 10147 | **27A4** 10148 | **27A5** 10149 | **27A6** 10150 | **27A7** 10151 |
| ➠ | ➡ | ➢ | ➣ | ➤ | ➥ | ➦ | ➧ |
| **27A8** 10152 | **27A9** 10153 | **27AA** 10154 | **27AB** 10155 | **27AC** 10156 | **27AD** 10157 | **27AE** 10158 | **27AF** 10159 |
| ➨ | ➩ | ➪ | ➫ | ➬ | ➭ | ➮ | ➯ |
| **27B0** 10160 | **27B1** 10161 | **27B2** 10162 | **27B3** 10163 | **27B4** 10164 | **27B5** 10165 | **27B6** 10166 | **27B7** 10167 |
| N/A | ➱ | ➲ | ➳ | ➴ | ➵ | ➶ | ➷ |
| **27B8** 10168 | **27B9** 10169 | **27BA** 10170 | **27BB** 10171 | **27BC** 10172 | **27BD** 10173 | **27BE** 10174 | **27BF** 10175 |
| ➸ | ➹ | ➺ | ➻ | ➼ | ➽ | ➾ | N/A |

# Index

## *D*

## *E*

## *F*



## *G*

## *H*



## *I*

## *J*



## *K*



## *L*

## *O*



## *P*

## *T*

## *U*



## *V*

## W



## X

## *Y*



## *Z*

# *About the Author*

**Elliotte Rusty Harold** is originally from New Orleans, to which he returns periodically in search of a decent bowl of gumbo. However, he currently resides in the Prospect Heights neighborhood of Brooklyn with his wife Beth and cats Charm (named after the quark) and Marjorie (named after his mother-in-law). He's an adjunct professor of computer science at Polytechnic University, where he teaches Java and object-oriented programming. His Cafe au Lait web site at *http://www.ibiblio.org/javafaq* has become one of the most popular independent Java sites on the Internet, and his spinoff site, Cafe con Leche, at *http://www.ibiblio.org/xml*, has become one of the Internet's most popular XML sites. Elliotte's previous books for O'Reilly include *Java I/O* and *Java Network Programming*.

**W. Scott Means** has been a professional software developer since 1988, when he joined Microsoft Corporation at the age of 17. He was one of the original developers of OS/2 1.1 and Windows NT, and did some of the early work on the Microsoft Network for the Advanced Technology and Business Development group. Most recently, he served as the CEO of Enterprise Web Machines, a South Carolina based Internet infrastructure venture. He is currently writing full-time and consulting on XML and Internet topics.

# *Colophon*

Our look is the result of reader comments, our own experimentation, and feedback from distribution channels. Distinctive covers complement our distinctive approach to technical topics, breathing personality and life into potentially dry subjects.

The bird on the cover of *XML in a Nutshell* is a peafowl, the largest bird in the Phasianinae family, which also includes pheasants and turkeys. People often incorrectly call peafowl peacocks. Peacocks are actually male peafowl; the females are called peahen. Two wild peafowl species exist today: the Indian Peafowl (*Pavo cristatus*) and the Green Peafowl of Southeast Asia (*Pavo muticus*), which may be endangered. These wild peafowl live in musters of eight to twelve birds in dense forest near water. Though they do not fly very well, and do so only for short distances, they do manage to escape most predators, and roost peacefully at night, high up in treetops.

The peafowl's most famous characteristic, of course, is its beautiful fan of feathers, known as a "train." Each blue-green train feather has a dark spot on its tip that looks much like an eye. Peacocks develop especially brilliant plumage, an indicator of sexual maturity, by age three. A healthy peacock has a full and vibrant train each year during the spring mating season. During this period, peacocks strut their stuff—display their "breeding plumage," as it is called—to attract peahen. Scientists theorize that the peacock's performance plays upon the peahen's instinctive drives to find healthy mates in the hope of producing hardy offspring. Each summer after the mating season, peafowl shed their train feathers, which are often collected by humans as eye-catching souvenirs.

Ann Schirmer was the production editor and copyeditor for *XML in a Nutshell*. Norma Emory was the proofreader. Claire Cloutier, Linley Dolby, and Mary Sheehan provided quality control. Matt Hutchinson, Darren Kelly, Erin Mark, Catherine Morris, Deborah Smith, Gabe Weiss, and Rachel Wheeler provided production assistance. Judy Hoer wrote the index.

Ellie Volckhausen designed the cover of this book, based on a series design by Edie Freedman. The cover image is an original illustration by Susan Hart. Emma Colby produced the cover layout with QuarkXPress 4.1, using Adobe's ITC Garamond font.

David Futato designed the interior layout based on a series design by Nancy Priest. Mike Sierra implemented the design in FrameMaker 5.5.6. The text and heading fonts are ITC Garamond Light and Garamond Book. Cliff Dyer, Erik Ray, and Robert Romano provided support for special Unicode characters used in this book. The tables of Unicode characters in Chapter 23 were produced in Microsoft Word 2000 by David Futato. The illustrations that appear in the book were produced by Robert Romano using Macromedia FreeHand 8 and Adobe Photoshop 5. This colophon was written by Sarah Jane Shangraw and Molly Shangraw.

Whenever possible, our books use a durable and flexible lay-flat binding. If the page count exceeds this binding's limit, perfect binding is used.

# XML

## *Learning WML & WMLScript*

*By Martin Frost*
*1st Edition October 2000*
*200 pages, ISBN 1-56592-947-0*

The next generation of mobile communicators is here, and delivering content will mean programming in WML and WMLScript. *Learning WML & WMLScript* gets developers up to speed quickly on these technologies, mapping out in detail the Wireless Application Environment (WAE), and its two major components: Wireless Markup Language (WML), and WMLScript. With these two technologies, developers can format information in almost all applications for display by mobile devices.

# How to stay in touch with O'Reilly

## 1. Visit Our Award-Winning Site

***http://www.oreilly.com/***

★ "Top 100 Sites on the Web" —*PC Magazine*
★ "Top 5% Web sites" —*Point Communications*
★ "3-Star site" —*The McKinley Group*

Our web site contains a library of comprehensive product information (including book excerpts and tables of contents), downloadable software, background articles, interviews with technology leaders, links to relevant sites, book cover art, and more. File us in your Bookmarks or Hotlist!

## 2. Join Our Email Mailing Lists

### *New Product Releases*

To receive automatic email with brief descriptions of all new O'Reilly products as they are released, send email to:
**ora-news-subscribe@lists.oreilly.com**
Put the following information in the first line of your message (*not* in the Subject field):
**subscribe ora-news**

### *O'Reilly Events*

If you'd also like us to send information about trade show events, special promotions, and other O'Reilly events, send email to:
**ora-news-subscribe@lists.oreilly.com**
Put the following information in the first line of your message (*not* in the Subject field):
**subscribe ora-events**

## 3. Get Examples from Our Books via FTP

There are two ways to access an archive of example files from our books:

### *Regular FTP*

- ftp to:
  **ftp.oreilly.com**
  (login: anonymous
  password: your email address)
- Point your web browser to:
  **ftp://ftp.oreilly.com/**

### *FTPMAIL*

- Send an email message to:
  **ftpmail@online.oreilly.com**
  (Write "help" in the message body)

## 4. Contact Us via Email

**order@oreilly.com**
To place a book or software order online. Good for North American and international customers.

**subscriptions@oreilly.com**
To place an order for any of our newsletters or periodicals.

**books@oreilly.com**
General questions about any of our books.

**software@oreilly.com**
For general questions and product information about our software. Check out O'Reilly Software Online at **http://software.oreilly.com/** for software and technical support information. Registered O'Reilly software users send your questions to:
**website-support@oreilly.com**

**cs@oreilly.com**
For answers to problems regarding your order or our products.

**booktech@oreilly.com**
For book content technical questions or corrections.

**proposals@oreilly.com**
To submit new book or software proposals to our editors and product managers.

**international@oreilly.com**
For information about our international distributors or translation queries. For a list of our distributors outside of North America check out:
**http://www.oreilly.com/distributors.html**

## 5. Work with Us

Check out our website for current employment opportunites:
**http://jobs.oreilly.com/**


O'Reilly & Associates, Inc.
101 Morris Street, Sebastopol, CA 95472 USA
TEL 707-829-0515 or 800-998-9938
(6am to 5pm PST)
FAX 707-829-0104

# International Distributors

*http://international.oreilly.com/distributors.html • international@oreilly.com*

### UK, Europe, Middle East and Africa (except France, Germany, Austria, Switzerland, Luxembourg, and Liechtenstein)

**INQUIRIES**
O'Reilly UK Limited
4 Castle Street
Farnham
Surrey, GU9 7HS
United Kingdom
Telephone: 44-1252-711776
Fax: 44-1252-734211
Email: information@oreilly.co.uk

**ORDERS**
Wiley Distribution Services Ltd.
1 Oldlands Way
Bognor Regis
West Sussex PO22 9SA
United Kingdom
Telephone: 44-1243-843294
UK Freephone: 0800-243207
Fax: 44-1243-843302 (Europe/EU orders)
or 44-1243-843274 (Middle East/Africa)
Email: cs-books@wiley.co.uk

### Germany, Switzerland, Austria, Luxembourg, and Liechtenstein

**INQUIRIES & ORDERS**
O'Reilly Verlag
Balthasarstr. 81
D-50670 Köln, Germany
Telephone: 49-221-973160-91
Fax: 49-221-973160-8
Email: anfragen@oreilly.de (inquiries)
Email: order@oreilly.de (orders)

### France

**INQUIRIES & ORDERS**
Éditions O'Reilly
18 rue Séguier
75006 Paris, France
Tel: 33-1-40-51-71-89
Fax: 33-1-40-51-72-26
Email: france@oreilly.fr

### Canada (French language books)

Les Éditions Flammarion ltée
375, Avenue Laurier Ouest
Montréal (Québec) H2V 2K3
Tel: 1-514-277-8807
Fax: 1-514-278-2085
Email: info@flammarion.qc.ca

### Hong Kong

City Discount Subscription Service, Ltd.
Unit A, 6th Floor, Yan's Tower
27 Wong Chuk Hang Road
Aberdeen, Hong Kong
Tel: 852-2580-3539
Fax: 852-2580-6463
Email: citydis@ppn.com.hk

### Korea

Hanbit Media, Inc.
Chungmu Bldg. 210
Yonnam-dong 568-33
Mapo-gu
Seoul, Korea
Tel: 822-325-0397
Fax: 822-325-9697
Email: hant93@chollian.dacom.co.kr

### Philippines

Global Publishing
G/F Benavides Garden
1186 Benavides St.
Manila, Philippines
Tel: 632-254-8949/632-252-2582
Fax: 632-734-5060/632-252-2733
Email: globalp@pacific.net.ph

### Taiwan

O'Reilly Taiwan
1st Floor, No. 21, Lane 295
Section 1, Fu-Shing South Road
Taipei, 106 Taiwan
Tel: 886-2-27099669
Fax: 886-2-27038802
Email: mori@oreilly.com

### China

O'Reilly Beijing
SIGMA Building, Suite B809
No. 49 Zhichun Road
Haidian District
Beijing 100031, P.R. China
Tel: 86-10-8809-7475
Fax: 86-10-8809-7463
Email: beijing@oreilly.com

### India

Shroff Publishers & Distributors Pvt. Ltd.
12, "Roseland", 2nd Floor
180, Waterfield Road, Bandra (West)
Mumbai 400 050
Tel: 91-22-641-1800/643-9910
Fax: 91-22-643-2422
Email: spd@vsnl.com

### Japan

O'Reilly Japan, Inc.
Yotsuya Y's Building
7 Banch 6, Honshio-cho
Shinjuku-ku
Tokyo 160-0003 Japan
Tel: 81-3-3356-5227
Fax: 81-3-3356-5261
Email: japan@oreilly.com

### Singapore, Indonesia, Malaysia and Thailand

TransQuest Publishers Pte Ltd
30 Old Toh Tuck Road #05-02
Sembawang Kimtrans Logistics Centre
Singapore 597654
Tel: 65-4623112
Fax: 65-4625761
Email: wendiw@transquest.com.sg

### All Other Countries

O'Reilly & Associates, Inc.
101 Morris Street
Sebastopol, CA 95472 USA
Tel: 707-829-0515
Fax: 707-829-0104
Email: order@oreilly.com

### Australia

Woodslane Pty., Ltd.
7/5 Vuko Place
Warriewood NSW 2102
Australia
Tel: 61-2-9970-5111
Fax: 61-2-9970-5002
Email: info@woodslane.com.au

### New Zealand

Woodslane New Zealand, Ltd.
21 Cooks Street (P.O. Box 575)
Waganui, New Zealand
Tel: 64-6-347-6543
Fax: 64-6-345-4840
Email: info@woodslane.com.au

### Argentina

Distribuidora Cuspide
Suipacha 764
1008 Buenos Aires
Argentina
Phone: 54-11-4322-8868
Fax: 54-11-4322-3456
Email: libros@cuspide.com